SANSKRIT GRAMMAR

Sanskrit Grammar

Including Both, the Classical Language and the Older Dialects of Veda and Brāhmaṇa

William Dwight Whitney

NATARAJ BOOKS
7073 Brookfield Plaza
Springfield, VA 22150

ISBN: 1-881338-54-1

First edition: 1879
This edition: 2004

Published by
NATARAJ BOOKS
7073 Brookfield Plaza
Springfield, VA 22150
U.S.A.

Printed and bound in India
by Nagri Printers, Delhi

PREFACE

TO THE FIRST EDITION.

It was in June, 1875, as I chanced to be for a day or two in Leipzig, that I was unexpectedly invited to prepare the Sanskrit grammar for the Indo-European series projected by Messrs. Breitkopf and Härtel. After some consideration, and consultation with friends, I accepted the task, and have since devoted to it what time could be spared from regular duties, after the satisfaction of engagements earlier formed. If the delay seems a long one, it was nevertheless unavoidable; and I would gladly, in the interest of the work itself, have made it still longer. In every such case, it is necessary to make a compromise between measurably satisfying a present pressing need, and doing the subject fuller justice at the cost of more time; and it seemed as if the call for a Sanskrit grammar on a somewhat different plan from those already in use — excellent as some of these in many respects are — was urgent enough to recommend a speedy completion of the work begun.

The objects had especially in view in the preparation of this grammar have been the following:

1. To make a presentation of the facts of the language primarily as they show themselves in use in the literature, and only secondarily as they are laid down by the native grammarians. The earliest European grammars were by the necessity of the case chiefly founded on their native prede-

cessors; and a traditional method was thus established which has been perhaps somewhat too closely adhered to, at the expense of clearness and of proportion, as well as of scientific truth. Accordingly, my attention has not been directed toward a profounder study of the grammatical science of the Hindu schools: their teachings I have been contented to take as already reported to Western learners in the existing Western grammars.

2. To include also in the presentation the forms and constructions of the older language, as exhibited in the Veda and the Brāhmana. Grassmann's excellent Index-Vocabulary to the Rig-Veda, and my own manuscript one to the Atharva-Veda (which I hope soon to be able to make public*), gave me in full detail the great mass of Vedic material; and this, with some assistance from pupils and friends, I have sought to complete, as far as the circumstances permitted, from the other Vedic texts and from the various works of the Brāhmana period, both printed and manuscript.

3. To treat the language throughout as an accented one, omitting nothing of what is known respecting the nature of the Sanskrit accent, its changes in combination and inflection, and the tone of individual words — being, in all this, necessarily dependent especially upon the material presented by the older accentuated texts.

4. To cast all statements, classifications, and so on, into a form consistent with the teachings of linguistic science. In doing this, it has been necessary to discard a few of the long-used and familiar divisions and terms of Sanskrit grammar — for example, the classification and nomenclature of „special tenses" and "general tenses" (which is so indefensible that one can only wonder at its having maintained itself so long), the order and terminology of the conjugation-classes, the separation in treatment of the facts of internal and ex-

* It was published, as vol. XII. of the Journal of the American Oriental Society, in 1881.

ternal euphonic combination, and the like. But care has been taken to facilitate the transition from the old to the new; and the changes, it is believed, will commend themselves to unqualified acceptance. It has been sought also to help an appreciation of the character of the language by putting its facts as far as possible into a statistical form. In this respect the native grammar is especially deficient and misleading.

Regard has been constantly had to the practical needs of the learner of the language, and it has been attempted, by due arrangement and by the use of different sizes of type, to make the work as usable by one whose object it is to acquire a knowledge of the classical Sanskrit alone as those are in which the earlier forms are not included. The custom of transliterating all Sanskrit words into European characters, which has become usual in European Sanskrit grammars, is, as a matter of course, retained throughout; and, because of the difficulty of setting even a small Sanskrit type with anything but a large European, it is practiced alone in the smaller sizes.

While the treatment of the facts of the language has thus been made a historical one, within the limits of the language itself, I have not ventured to make it comparative, by bringing in the analogous forms and processes of other related languages. To do this, in addition to all that was attempted beside, would have extended the work, both in content and in time of preparation, far beyond the limits assigned to it. And, having decided to leave out this element, I have done so consistently throughout. Explanations of the origin of forms have also been avoided, for the same reason and for others, which hardly call for statement.

A grammar is necessarily in great part founded on its predecessors, and it would be in vain to attempt an acknowledgment in detail of all the aid received from other scholars. I have had at hand always especially the very scholarly and reliable brief summary of Kielhorn, the full and excellent work of Monier Williams, the smaller grammar of Bopp (a wonder of learning and method for the time when it was prepared), and the volumes of Benfey and Müller. As regards the material of the language, no other aid, of course, has been at all comparable with the great Petersburg lexicon of Böhtlingk and Roth, the existence of which gives by itself a new character to all investigations of the Sanskrit language. What I have not found there or in the special collections made by myself or by others for me, I have called below "not quotable" — a provisional designation, necessarily liable to correction in detail by the results of further researches. For what concerns the verb, its forms and their classification and uses, I have had, as every one must have, by far the most aid from Delbrück, in his Altindisches Verbum and his various syntactical contributions. Former pupils of my own, Professors Avery and Edgren, have also helped me, in connection with this subject and with others, in a way and measure that calls for public acknowledgment. In respect to the important matter of the declension in the earliest language, I have made great use of the elaborate paper in the Journ. Am. Or. Soc. (printing contemporaneously with this work, and used by me almost, but not quite, to the end of the subject) by my former pupil Prof. Lanman; my treatment of it is founded on his. My manifold obligations to my own teacher, Prof. Weber of Berlin, also require to be mentioned: among other things, I owe to him the use of his copies of certain unpublished texts of the Brāhmana period, not otherwise accessible to me; and he was kind enough to look through with me my work in its inchoate condition, favoring me with valuable suggestions. For this last favor I have likewise to thank Prof. Delbrück — who, moreover, has taken the trouble to glance over for a like purpose the greater part of the proof-sheets of the grammar, as they came from the press. To Dr. L. von Schröder is due whatever use I have been able to make (unfortunately a very imperfect one) of the important Māitrāyaṇī-Sanhitā.*

Of the deficiencies of my work I am, I think, not less fully aware than any critic of it, even the severest, is likely to be. Should it be found to answer its intended purpose well enough to come to another edition, my endeavor will be to improve and complete it; and I shall be grateful for any corrections or suggestions which may aid me in making it a more efficient help to the study of the Sanskrit language and literature.

GOTHA, July 1879.

W. D. W.

PREFACE

TO THE SECOND EDITION.

In preparing a new edition of this grammar, I have made use of the new material gathered by myself during the intervening years,** and also of that gathered by others, so far as it was accessible to me and fitted into my plan; *** and I have had the benefit of kind suggestions from various quarters — for all of which I desire to return a grateful acknowledgment. By such help, I have been able not only to correct and repair certain errors and omissions of the first edition, but also to speak with more definiteness upon

* Since published in full by him, 1881—6.

** A part of this new material was published by myself in 1885, as a Supplement to the grammar, under the title "Roots, Verb-Forms, and Primary Derivatives of the Sanskrit Language".

*** Especially deserving of mention is Holtzmann's collection of material from the Mahābhārata, also published (1884) in the form of a Supplement to this work; also Böhtlingk's similar collection from the larger half of the Rāmāyaṇa.

very many points relating to the material and usages of the language.

In order not to impair the applicability of the references already made to the work by various authors, its paragraphing has been retained unchanged throughout; for increased convenience of further reference, the subdivisions of paragraphs have been more thoroughly marked, by letters (now and then changing a former lettering); and the paragraph-numbers have been set at the outer instead of the inner edge of the upper margin.

My remoteness from the place of publication has forbidden me the reading of more than one proof; but the kindness of Professor Lanman in adding his revision (accompanied by other timely suggestions) to mine, and the care of the printers, will be found, I trust, to have aided in securing a text disfigured by few errors of the press.

Circumstances beyond my control have delayed for a year or two the completion of this revision, and have made it in some parts less complete than I should have desired.

NEW-HAVEN, Sept. 1888.

W. D. W.

INTRODUCTION.

Brief Account of the Indian Literature.

It seems desirable to give here such a sketch of the history of Indian literature as shall show the relation to one another of the different periods and forms of the language treated in the following grammar, and the position of the works there quoted.

The name "Sanskrit" (saṁskṛta, 1087 d, *adorned*, *elaborated*, *perfected*), which is popularly applied to the whole ancient and sacred language of India, belongs more properly only to that dialect which, regulated and established by the labors of the native grammarians, has led for the last two thousand years or more an artificial life, like that of the Latin during most of the same period in Europe, as the written and spoken means of communication of the learned and priestly caste; and which even at the present day fills that office. It is thus distinguished, on the one hand, from the later and derived dialects — as the Prākrit, forms of language which have datable monuments from as early as the third century before Christ, and which are represented by inscriptions and coins, by the speech of the uneducated characters in the Sanskrit dramas (see below), and by a limited literature; the Pāli, a Prakritic dialect which became the sacred language of Buddhism in Farther India, and is still in service there as such; and yet later and more altered tongues forming the transition to the languages of modern India. And, on the other hand, it is distinguished, but very much less sharply and widely, from the older dialects or forms of speech presented in the canonical literature, the Veda and Brāhmaṇa.

This fact, of the fixation by learned treatment of an authorized mode of expression, which should thenceforth be used according to rule in the intercourse of the educated, is the cardinal one in Indian linguistic history; and as the native grammatical literature has determined the form of the language, so it has also to a large extent determined the grammatical treatment of the language by European scholars.

Much in the history of the learned movement is still obscure, and opinions are at variance even as to points of prime consequence. Only the concluding works in the development of the grammatical science have been preserved to us; and though they are evidently the perfected fruits of a long series of learned labors, the records of the latter are lost beyond recovery. The time and the place of the creation of Sanskrit are unknown; and as to its occasion, we have only our inferences and conjectures to rely upon. It seems, however, altogether likely that the grammatical sense of the ancient Hindus was awakened in great measure by their study of the traditional sacred texts, and by their comparison of its different language with that of contemporary use. It is certain that the grammatical study of those texts (**çākhās**, lit'ly *branches*), phonetic and other, was zealously and effectively followed in the Brahmanic schools; this is attested by our possession of a number of phonetico-grammatical treatises, **prātiçākhyas** (**prati çākhām** *belonging to each several text*), each having for subject one principal Vedic text, and noting all its peculiarities of form; these, both by the depth and exactness of their own researches and by the number of authorities which they quote, speak plainly of a lively scientific activity continued during a long time. What part, on the other hand, the notice of differences between the correct speech of the learned and the altered dialects of the vulgar may have borne in the same movement is not easy to determine; but it is not customary that a language has its proper usages fixed by rule until the danger is distinctly felt of its undergoing corruption.

The labors of the general school of Sanskrit grammar reached a climax in the grammarian Pāṇini, whose text-book, containing the facts of the language cast into the highly artful and difficult form of about four thousand algebraic-formula-like rules (in the statement and arrangement of which brevity alone is had in view, at the cost of distinctness and unambiguousness), became for all after time the authoritative, almost sacred, norm of correct speech. Respecting his period, nothing really definite and trustworthy is known; but he is with much probability held to have lived some time (two to four centuries) before the Christian era. He has had commentators in abundance, and has undergone at their hands some measure of amendment and completion; but he has not been overthrown or superseded. The chief and most authoritative commentary on his work is that called the **Mahābhāshya** *great comment*, by Patanjali.

A language, even if not a vernacular one, which is in tolerably wide and constant use for writing and speaking, is, of course, kept in life principally by direct tradition, by communication from teacher to scholar and the study and imitation of existing texts, and not by the learning of grammatical rules; yet the existence of grammatical authority, and especially of a single one, deemed infallible and of prescriptive value, could not fail to exert a strong regulative influence, leading to the avoidance more and more of what was, even if lingering in use, inconsistent with his teachings, and also, in the constant reproduction of texts, to the gradual effacement of whatever they might contain that was unapproved. Thus the whole more modern literature of India has been Paninized, so to speak, pressed into the mould prepared by him and his school. What are the limits of the artificiality of this process is not yet known.

The attention of special students of the Hindu grammar (and the subject is so intricate and difficult that the number is exceedingly small of those who have mastered it sufficiently to have a competent opinion on such general matters) has been hitherto mainly directed toward determining what the Sanskrit according to Pāṇini really is, toward explaining the language from the grammar. And, naturally enough, in India, or wherever else the leading object is to learn to speak and write the language correctly — that is, as authorized by the grammarians — that is the proper course to pursue. This, however, is not the way really to understand the language. The time must soon come, or it has come already, when the endeavor shall be instead to explain the grammar from the language: to test in all details, so far as shall be found possible, the reason of Pāṇini's rules (which contain not a little that seems problematical, or even sometimes perverse); to determine what and how much genuine usage he had everywhere as foundation, and what traces may be left in the literature of usages possessing an inherently authorized character, though unratified by him.

By the term "classical" or "later" language, then, as constantly used below in the grammar, is meant the language of those literary monuments which are written in conformity with the rules of the native grammar: virtually, the whole proper Sanskrit literature. For although parts of this are doubtless earlier than Pāṇini, it is impossible to tell just what parts, or how far they have escaped in their style the leveling influence of the grammar. The whole, too, may be called so far an artificial literature as it is written in a phonetic form (see grammar, **101 a**) which never can have been a truly vernacular and living one. Nearly all of it is metrical: not poetic works only, but narratives, histories (so far as anything deserving that name can be said to exist), and scientific treatises of every variety, are done into verse; a prose and a prose literature hardly has an existence (the principal exceptions, aside from the voluminous commentaries, are a few stories, as the **Daçakumāracarita** and the **Vāsavadattā**). Of linguistic history there is next to nothing in it all; but only a history of style, and this for the most part showing a gradual depravation, an increase of artificiality and an intensification of certain more undesirable features of the language — such as the use of passive constructions and of participles instead of verbs, and the substitution of compounds for sentences.

This being the condition of the later literature, it is of so much the higher consequence that there is an earlier literature, to which the suspicion of artificiality does not attach, or attaches at least only in a minimal degree, which has a truly vernacular character, and abounds in prose as well as verse.

The results of the very earliest literary productiveness of the Indian people are the hymns with which, when they had only crossed the threshold of the country, and when their geographical horizon was still limited to the river-basin of the Indus with its tributaries, they praised their gods, the deified powers of nature, and accompanied the rites of their comparatively simple worship. At what period these were made and sung cannot be determined with any approach to accuracy: it may have been as early as 2000 B. C. They were long handed down by oral tradition, preserved by the care, and increased by the additions and imitations, of succeeding generations; the mass was ever growing, and, with the change of habits and beliefs and religious practices, was becoming variously applied — sung in chosen extracts, mixed with other material into liturgies, adapted with more or less of distortion to help the needs of a ceremonial which was coming to be of immense elaboration and intricacy. And, at some time in the course of this history, there was made for preservation a great collection of the hymn-material, mainly its oldest and most genuine part, to the extent of over a thousand hymns and ten thousand verses, arranged according to traditional authorship and to subject and length and metre of hymn: this collection is the **Rig-Veda** *Veda of verses* (ṛc) or of *hymns*. Other collections were made also out of the same general mass of traditional material: doubtless later, although the interrelations of this period are as yet too unclear to allow of our speaking with entire confidence as to anything concerning them. Thus, the **Sāma-Veda** *Veda of chants* (**sāman**), containing only about a sixth as much, its verses nearly all found in the Rig-Veda also, but appearing here with numerous differences of reading: these were passages put together for chanting at the soma-sacrifices. Again, collections called by the comprehensive name of **Yajur-Veda** *Veda of sacrificial formulas* (**yajus**): these contained not verses alone, but also numerous prose utterances, mingled with the former, in the order in which they were practically employed in the ceremonies; they were strictly liturgical collections. Of these, there are in existence several texts, which have their mutual differences: the **Vājasaneyi-Saṁhitā** (in two slightly discordant versions, **Mādhyandina** and **Kāṇva**), sometimes also called the White Yajur-Veda; and the various and considerably differing texts of the Black Yajur-Veda, namely the **Tāittirīya-Saṁhitā**, the **Māitrāyaṇī-Saṁhitā**, the **Kapiṣṭhala-Saṁhitā**, and the **Kāṭhaka** (the two last not yet published). Finally, another historical collection, like the Rig-Veda, but made up mainly of later and less accepted material, and called (among other less current names) the **Atharva-Veda** *Veda of the Atharvans* (a legendary priestly family); it is somewhat more than half as bulky as the Rig-Veda, and contains a certain amount of material corresponding to that of the latter, and also a number of brief prose passages. To this last collection is very generally refused in the orthodox literature the name of Veda; but for us it is the most interesting of all, after the Rig-Veda, because it contains the largest amount of hymn-material (or **mantra**, as it is called, in distinction from the prose **brāhmaṇa**), and in a language which, though distinctly less antique than that of the other, is nevertheless truly Vedic. Two versions of it are extant, one of them in only a single known manuscript.

A not insignificant body of like material, and of various period (although doubtless in the main belonging to the latest time of Vedic productiveness, and in part perhaps the imitative work of a yet more modern time), is scattered through the texts to be later described, the **Brāhmaṇas** and the **Sūtras.** To assemble and sift and compare it is now one of the pressing needs of Vedic study.

The fundamental divisions of the Vedic literature here mentioned have all had their various schools of sectaries, each of these with a text of its own, showing some differences from those of the other schools: but those mentioned above are all that are now known to be in existence; and the chance of the discovery of others grows every year smaller.

The labor of the schools in the conservation of their sacred texts was extraordinary, and has been crowned with such success that the text of each school, whatever may be its differences from those of other schools, is virtually without various readings, preserved with all its peculiarities of dialect, and its smallest and most exceptional traits of phonetic form, pure and unobscured. It is not the place here to describe the means by which, in addition to the religious care of the sectaries, this accuracy was secured: forms of text, lists of peculiarities and treatises upon them, and so on. When this kind of care began in the case of each text, and what of original character may have been effaced before it, or lost in spite of it, cannot be told. But it is certain that the Vedic records furnish, on the whole, a wonderfully accurate and trustworthy picture of a form of ancient Indian language (as well as ancient Indian beliefs and institutions) which was a natural and undistorted one, and which goes back a good way behind the classical Sanskrit. Its differences from the latter the following treatise endeavors to show in detail.

Along with the verses and sacrificial formulas and phrases in the text of the Black Yajur-Veda are given long prose sections, in which the ceremonies are described, their meaning and the reason of the details and the accompanying utterances are discussed and explained, illustrative legends are reported or fabricated, and various speculations, etymological and other, are indulged in. Such matter comes to be called **brāhmaṇa** (apparently *relating to the brahman or worship*). In the White Yajur-Veda, it is separated into a work by itself, beside the **saṁhitā** or text of verses and formulas, and is called the **Çatapatha-Brāhmaṇa** *Brāhmana of a hundred ways.* Other similar collections are found, belonging to various other schools of Vedic study, and they bear the common name of **Brāhmaṇa**, with the name of the school, or some other distinctive title, prefixed. Thus, the **Aitareya** and **Kāuṣītaki-Brāhmaṇas**, belonging to the schools of the Rig-Veda, the **Pañcaviñça** and **Ṣaḍviñça-Brāhmaṇas** and other minor works, to the Sāma-Veda; the **Gopatha-Brāhmaṇa**, to the Atharva-Veda; and a **Jāiminīya-** or **Talavakāra-Brāhmaṇa**, to the Sāma-Veda, has recently (Burnell) been discovered in India; the **Tāittirīya-Brāhmaṇa** is a collection of mingled **mantra** and **brāhmaṇa**, like the **saṁhitā** of the same name, but supplementary and later. These works are likewise regarded as canonical by the schools, and are learned by their sectaries with the same extreme care which is devoted to the **saṁhitās**, and their condition of textual preservation is of a kindred excellence. To a certain extent, there is among them the possession of common material: a fact the bearings of which are not yet fully understood.

Notwithstanding the inanity of no small part of their contents, the Brāhmaṇas are of a high order of interest in their bearings on the history of Indian institutions; and philologically they are not less important, since they represent a form of language in most respects intermediate between the classical and that of the Vedas, and offer specimens on a large scale of a prose style, and of one which is in the main a natural and freely developed one — the oldest and most primitive Indo-European prose.

Beside the Brāhmaṇas are sometimes found later appendices, of a similar character, called **Āraṇyakas** (*forest-sections*): as the **Āitareya-Āraṇyaka**, **Tāittirīya-Āraṇyaka**, **Bṛhad-Āraṇyaka**, and so on. And from some of these, or even from the Brāhmaṇas, are extracted the earliest **Upaniṣads** (*sittings*, *lectures on sacred subjects*) — which, however, are continued and added to down to a comparatively modern time. The Upanishads are one of the lines by which the Brāhmaṇa literature passes over into the later theological literature.

Another line of transition is shown in the **Sūtras** (*lines, rules*). The works thus named are analogous with the Brāhmaṇas in that they belong to the schools of Vedic study and are named from them, and that they deal with the religious ceremonies: treating them, however, in the way of prescription, not of dogmatic explanation. They, too, contain some **mantra** or hymn-material, not found to occur elsewhere. In part (**çrāuta** or **kalpa-sūtras**), they take up the great sacrificial ceremonies, with which the Brāhmaṇas have to do; in part (**gṛhya-sūtras**), they teach the minor duties of a pious householder; in some cases (**sāmayācārika-sūtras**) they lay down the general obligations of one whose life is in accordance with prescribed duty. And out of the last two, or especially the last, come by natural development the law-books (**dharma-çāstras**), which make a conspicuous figure in the later literature: the oldest and most noted of them being that called by the name of **Manu** (an outgrowth, it is believed by many, of the Mānava Vedic school); to which are added that of Yājnavalkya, and many others.

Respecting the chronology of this development, or the date of any class of writings, still more of any individual work, the less that is said the better. All dates given in Indian literary history are pins set up to be bowled down again. Every important work has undergone so many more or less transforming changes before reaching the form in which it comes to us, that the question of original construction is complicated with that of final redaction. It is so with the law-book of Manu, just mentioned, which has well-founded claims to being regarded as one of the very oldest works of the proper Sanskrit literature, if not the oldest (it has been variously assigned, to periods from six centuries before Christ to four after Christ). It is so, again, in a still more striking degree, with the great legendary epic of the **Mahābhārata.** The ground-work of this is doubtless of very early date; but it has served as a text into which materials of various character and period have been inwoven, until it has become a heterogeneous mass, a kind of cyclopedia for the warrior-caste, hard to separate into its constituent parts. The story of **Nala**, and the philosophical poem **Bhagavad-Gītā,** are two of the most noted of its episodes. The **Rāmāyaṇa,** the other most famous epic, is a work of another kind: though also worked over and more or less altered in its transmission to our time, it is the production, in the main, of a single author (Vālmīki); and it is generally believed to be in part allegorical, representing the introduction of Aryan culture and dominion into Southern India. By its side stand a number of minor epics, of various authorship and period, as the **Raghuvança** (ascribed to the dramatist Kālidāsa), the **Māghakāvya,** the **Bhaṭṭikāvya** (the last, written chiefly with the grammatical intent of illustrating by use as many as possible of the numerous formations which, through taught by the grammarians, find no place in the literature).

The **Purāṇas,** a large class of works mostly of immense extent, are best mentioned in connection with the epics. They are pseudo-historical and prophetic in character, of modern date, and of inferior value. Real history finds no place in Sanskrit literature, nor is there any conscious historical element in any of the works composing it.

Lyric poetry is represented by many works, some of which, as the **Meghadūta** and **Gītagovinda,** are of no mean order of merit.

The drama is a still more noteworthy and important branch. The first indications of dramatical inclination and capacity on the part of the Hindus are seen in certain hymns of the Veda, where a mythological or legendary situation is conceived dramatically, and set forth in the form of a dialogue — well-known examples are the dialogue of Saramā and the Paṇis, that of Yama and his sister Yamī, that of Vasishtha and the rivers, that of Agni and the other gods — but there are no extant intermediaries between these and the standard drama. The beginnings of the latter date from a period when in actual life the higher and educated characters used Sanskrit, and the lower and uneducated used the popular dialects derived from it, the Prakrits; and their dialogue reflects this condition of things. Then, however, learning (not to call it pedantry) intervened, and sterotyped the new element; a Prakrit grammar grew up beside the Sanskrit grammar, according to the rules of which Prakrit could be made indefinitely on a substrate of Sanskrit; and none of the existing dramas need to date from the time of vernacular use of Prakrit, while most or all of them are undoubtedly much later. Among the dramatic authors, Kālidāsa is incomparably the chief, and his **Çakuntalā** as distinctly his masterpiece. His date has been a matter of much inquiry and controversy; it is doubtless some centuries later than our era. The only other work deserving to be mentioned along with Kālidāsa's is the **Mṛcchakaṭī** of Çūdraka, also of questionable period, but believed to be the oldest of the extant dramas.

A partly dramatic character belongs also to the fable, in which animals are represented as acting and speaking. The most noted works in this department are the **Pañcatantra**, which through Persian and Semitic versions has made its way all over the world, and contributes a considerable quota to the fable-literature of every European language, and, partly founded on it, the comparatively recent and popular **Hitopadeça** (*salutary instruction*).

Two of the leading departments of Sanskrit scientific literature, the legal and the grammatical, have been already sufficiently noticed; of those remaining, the most important by far is the philosophical. The beginnings of philosophical speculation are seen already in some of the later hymns of the Veda, more abundantly in the Brāhmaṇas and Āraṇyakas, and then especially in the Upanishads. The evolution and historic relation of the systems of philosophy, and the age of their text-books, are matters on which much obscurity still rests. There are six systems of primary rank, and reckoned as orthodox, although really standing in no accordance with approved religious doctrines. All of them seek the same end, the emancipation of the soul from the necessity of continuing its existence in a succession of bodies, and its unification with the All-soul; but they differ in regard to the means by which they seek to attain this end.

The astronomical science of the Hindus is a reflection of that of Greece, and its literature is of recent date; but as mathematicians, in arithmetic and geometry, they have shown more independence. Their medical science, although its beginnings go back even to the Veda, in the use of medicinal plants with accompanying incantations, is of little account, and its proper literature by no means ancient.

CONTENTS.

Chap.		Page.
	PREFACE	v
	INTRODUCTION	xi
I.	ALPHABET	1—9
II.	SYSTEM OF SOUNDS; PRONUNCIATION	10—34
	Vowels, 10; Consonants, 13; Quantity, 27; Accent, 28.	
III.	RULES OF EUPHONIC COMBINATION	34—87
	Introductory, 34; Principles, 37; Rules of Vowel Combination, 42; Permitted Finals, 49; Deaspiration, 53; Surd and Sonant Assimilation, 54; Combinations of Final s and r, 56; Conversion of s to ṣ, 61; Conversion of n to ṇ, 64; Conversion of Dental Mutes to Linguals and Palatals, 66; Combinations of Final n, 69; Combinations of Final m, 71; the Palatal Mutes and Sibilant, and h, 72; the Lingual Sibilant, 77; Extension and Abbreviation, 78; Strengthening and Weakening Processes, 81; Guṇa and Vṛddhi, 81; Vowel-lengthening, 84; Vowel-lightening, 85; Nasal Increment, 86; Reduplication, 87.	
IV.	DECLENSION	88—110
	Gender, Number, Case, 88; Uses of the Cases, 89; Endings of declension, 103; Variation of Stem, 107; Accent in Declension, 108.	
V.	NOUNS AND ADJECTIVES	111—176
	Classification etc., 111; Declension I., Stems in a, 112; Declension II., Stems in i and u, 116; Declension III., Stems in Long Vowels (ā, ī, ū): A. Root-words etc., 124; Stems in Diphthongs, 130; B. Derivative Stems etc., 131; Declension IV., Stems in ṛ or ar, 137; Declension V., Stems in Consonants, 141; A. Root-stems etc., 143; B. Derivative Stems in as, is, us, 153; C. Derivative Stems in an, 156; D. in in, 161; E. in ant or at, 163; F. Perfect Participles in vāṅs, 169; G. Comparatives in yāṅs or yas, 172; Comparison, 173.	

Chap.		Page.
VI.	NUMERALS . . . . Cardinals, 177; Ordinals etc., 183.	177—185
VII.	PRONOUNS . . . . Personal, 185; Demonstrative, 188; Interrogative, 194; Relative, 195; other Pronouns: Emphatic, Indefinite, 196; Nouns used pronominally, 197; Pronominal Derivatives, Possessives etc., 197; Adjectives declined pronominally, 199.	185—199
VIII.	CONJUGATION . . . . Voice, Tense, Mode, Number, Person, 200; Verbal Adjectives and Nouns, 203; Secondary Conjugations, 203; Personal Endings, 204; Subjunctive Mode, 209; Optative, 211; Imperative, 213; Uses of the Modes, 215; Participles, 220; Augment, 220; Reduplication, 222; Accent of the Verb, 223.	200—226
IX.	THE PRESENT-SYSTEM . . . . General, 227; Conjugations and Conjugation Classes, 228; Root-Class (second or **ad**-class), 231; Reduplicating Class (third or **hu**-class), 242; Nasal Class (seventh or **rudh**-class), 250; **nu** and **u**-Classes (fifth and eighth, or **su**- and **tan**-classes), 254; **nā**-Class (ninth or **krī**-class), 260; **a**-Class (first or **bhū**-class), 264; Accented **á**-Class (sixth or **tud**-class), 269; **ya**-Class (fourth or **div**-class), 271; Accented **yá**-Class or Passive Conjugation, 275; So-called tenth or **cur**-class, 277; Uses of the Present and Imperfect, 278.	227—278
X.	THE PERFECT-SYSTEM . . . . Perfect Tense, 279; Perfect Participle, 291; Modes of the Perfect, 292; Pluperfect, 295; Uses of the Perfect, 295.	279—296
XI.	THE AORIST-SYSTEMS . . . . Classification, 297; I. Simple Aorist: 1. Root-Aorist, 299; Passive Aorist 3d sing., 304; 2. the **a**-Aorist, 305; II. 3. Reduplicated Aorist, 308; III. Sibilant Aorist, 313; 4. the **s**-Aorist, 314; 5. the **iṣ**-Aorist, 320; 6. the **siṣ**-Aorist, 323; 7. the **sa**-Aorist, 325; Precative, 326; Uses of the Aorist, 328.	297—330
XII.	THE FUTURE-SYSTEMS . . . . I. The **s**-Future, 331; Preterit of the **s**-Future, Conditional, 334; II. The Periphrastic Future, 335; Uses of the Futures and Conditional, 337.	330—339

Chap. Page.

XIII. VERBAL ADJECTIVES AND NOUNS: PARTICIPLES, INFINITIVES, GERUNDS . . . . . . 340—360
Passive Participle in **tá** or **ná**, 340; Past Active Participle in **tavant**, 344; Future Passive Participles, Gerundives, 345; Infinitives, 347; Uses of the Infinitives, 351; Gerunds, 355; Adverbial Gerund in **am**, 359.

XIV. DERIVATIVE OR SECONDARY CONJUGATION . 360—391
I. Passive, 361; II. Intensive, 362; Present-System, 365; Perfect, Aorist, Future, etc., 370; III. Desiderative, 372; Present-System, 374; Perfect, Aorist, Future, etc., 376; IV. Causative, 378; Present-System, 380; Perfect, Aorist, Future, etc., 383; V. Denominative, 386.

XV. PERIPHRASTIC AND COMPOUND CONJUGATION 391—403
The Periphrastic Perfect, 392; Participial Periphrastic Phrases, 394; Composition with Prepositional Prefixes, 395; Other Verbal Compounds, 400.

XVI. INDECLINABLES . . . . 403—417
Adverbs, 403; Prepositions, 414; Conjunctions, 416; Interjections, 417.

XVII. DERIVATION OF DECLINABLE STEMS . . . . 418—480
A. Primary Derivatives, 420; **B.** Secondary Derivatives, 454.

XVIII. FORMATION OF COMPOUND STEMS . . . . 480—515
Classification, 480; I. Copulative Compounds, 485; II. Determinative Compounds, 489; **A.** Dependent Compounds, 489; **B.** Descriptive Compounds, 494; III. Secondary Adjective Compounds, 501; **A.** Possessive Compounds, 501; **B.** Compound with Governed Final Member, 511; Adjective Compounds as Nouns and as Adverbs, 512; Anomalous Compounds 514; Stem-finals altered in Composition, 514; Loose Construction with Compounds, 515.

APPENDIX . . . . 516—520
A. Examples of Various Sanskrit Type, 516; **B.** Example of Accentuated Text, 518; Synopsis of the conjugation of roots **bhū** and **kṛ**, 520.

SANSKRIT INDEX . . . . 521—539

GENERAL INDEX . . . . 540—551

ABBREVIATIONS.

AA. Āitareya-Āraṇyaka.
AB. Āitareya-Brāhmaṇa.
AÇS. Āçvalāyana-Çrāuta-Sūtra.
AGS. Āçvalāyana-Gṛhya-Sūtra.
Āpast. Āpastamba-Sūtra.
APr. Atharva-Prātiçākhya.
AV. Atharva-Veda.
B. or Br. Brāhmaṇas.
BAU. Bṛhad-Āraṇyaka-Upaniṣad.
BhG. Bhagavad-Gītā.
BhP. Bhāgavata-Purāṇa.
BR. Böhtlingk and Roth (Petersburg Lexicon).
C. Classical Sanskrit.
Ç. Çakuntalā.
Çatr. Çatruṁjaya-Māhātmyam.
ÇB. Çatapatha-Brāhmaṇa.
ÇÇS. Çāñkhayana-Çrāuta-Sūtra.
ÇGS. Çāñkhāyana-Gṛhya-Sūtra.
ChU. Chāndogya-Upaniṣad.
ÇvU. Çvetāçvatara-Upaniṣad.
DKC. Daça-Kumāra-Carita.
E. Epos (MBh. and R.).
GB. Gopatha-Brāhmaṇa.
GGS. Gobhilīya-Gṛhya-Sūtra.
H. Hitopadeça.
Har. Harivaṅça.
JB. Jāiminīya (or Talavakāra) Brāhmaṇa.
JUB. Jāiminīya-Upaniṣad-Brāhmaṇa.
K. Kāṭhaka.
Kap. Kapiṣṭhala-Saṁhitā.
KB. Kāuṣītaki- (or Çāñkhāyana-) Brāhmaṇa.
KBU. Kāuṣītaki-Brāhmaṇa-Upaniṣad.
KÇS. Kātyāyana-Çrāuta-Sūtra.
KS. Kāuçika-Sūtra.
KSS. Kathā-Sarit-Sāgara.
KṭhU. Kaṭha-Upaniṣad.
KU. Kena-Upaniṣad.
LÇS. Lāṭyāyana-Çrāuta-Sūtra.
M. Manu.
MāiU. Māitrī-Upaniṣad.
MBh. Mahābhārata.
MdU. Muṇḍaka-Upaniṣad.
Megh. Meghadūta.
MS. Māitrāyaṇī-Saṁhitā.
Nāiṣ. Nāiṣadhīya.
Nir. Nirukta.
Pañc. Pañcatantra.
PB. Pañcaviṅça- (or Tāṇḍya-) Brāhmaṇa.
PGS. Pāraskara-Gṛhya-Sūtra.
PU. Praçna Upaniṣad.
R. Rāmāyaṇa.
Ragh. Raghuvaṅça.
RPr. Rigveda-Prātiçākhya.
RT. Rāja-Taraṅgiṇī.
RV. Rig-Veda.
S. Sūtras.
ṢB. Ṣaḍviṅça-Brāhmaṇa.
Spr. Indische Sprüche (Böhtlingk).
SV. Sāma-Veda.
TA. Tāittirīya-Āraṇyaka.
TB. Tāittirīya-Brāhmaṇa.
TPr. Tāittirīya-Prātiçākhya.
Tribh. Tribhāṣyaratna (comm. to TPr.).
TS. Tāittirīya-Saṁhitā.
U. Upaniṣads.
V. Vedas (RV., AV., SV.).
Vas. Vasiṣṭha.
VBS. Varāha-Bṛhat-Saṁhitā.
Vet. Vetālapañcaviṅçati.
Vikr. Vikramorvaçī.
VPr. Vājasaneyi-Prātiçākhya.
VS. Vājasaneyi-Saṁhitā.
VS. Kāṇ. do. Kāṇva-text.
Y. Yājñavalkya.

CHAPTER I.

ALPHABET.

1. THE natives of India write their ancient and sacred language in a variety of alphabets — generally, in each part of the country, in the same alphabet which they use for their own vernacular. The mode of writing, however, which is employed throughout the heart of Aryan India, or in Hindustan proper, is alone adopted by European scholars: it is called the **devanāgarī**.

a. This name is of doubtful origin and value. A more comprehensive name is **nāgarī** (perhaps, *of the city*); and **deva-nāgarī** is **nāgarī** *of the gods*, or *of the Brahmans*.

2. Much that relates to the history of the Indian alphabets is still obscure. The earliest written monuments of known date in the country are the inscriptions containing the edicts of Açoka or Piyadasi, of about the middle of the third century B. C. They are in two different systems of characters, of which one shows distinct signs of derivation from a Semitic source, while the other is also probably, though much less evidently, of the same origin. From the latter, the Lath, or Southern Açoka character (of Girnar), come the later Indian alphabets, both those of the northern Aryan languages and those of the southern Dravidian languages. The **nāgarī**, **devanāgarī**, Bengālī, Guzerātī, and others, are varieties of its northern derivatives; and with them are related some of the alphabets of peoples outside of India — as in Tibet and Farther India — who have adopted Hindu culture or religion.

a. There is reason to believe that writing was first employed in India for practical purposes — for correspondence and business and the like — and only by degrees came to be applied also to literary use. The literature, to a great extent, and the more fully in proportion to its claimed sanctity and authority, ignores all written record, and assumes to be kept in existence by oral tradition alone.

3. Of the **devanāgarī** itself there are minor varieties, depending on differences of locality or of period, as also of individual hand (see examples in Weber's catalogue of the Berlin Sanskrit MSS., in Rājendralāla Mitra's notices of MSS. in Indian libraries, in the published fac-similes of inscriptions, and so on); and these are in some measure reflected in the type prepared for printing, both in India and in Europe. But a student who makes himself familiar with one style of printed characters will have little difficulty with the others, and will soon learn, by practice, to read the manuscripts. A few specimens of types other than those used in this work are given in Appendix **A**.

a. On account of the difficulty of combining them with the smaller sizes of our Roman and Italic type, the **devanāgarī** characters are used below only in connection with the first or largest size. And, in accordance with the laudable usage of recent grammars, they are, wherever given, also transliterated, in **Clarendon** letters; while the latter alone are used in the other sizes.

4. The student may be advised to try to familiarize himself from the start with the **devanāgarī** mode of writing. At the same time, it is not indispensable that he should do so until, having learned the principal paradigms, he comes to begin reading and analysing and parsing; and many will find the latter the more practical, and in the end equally or more effective, way.

5. The characters of the **devanāgarī** alphabet, and the European letters which will be used in transliterating them, are as follows:

		short		long	
Vowels: simple		1	अ **a**	2	आ **ā**
	palatal	3	इ **i**	4	ई **ī**
	labial	5	उ **u**	6	ऊ **ū**
	lingual	7	ऋ **ṛ**	8	ॠ **ṝ**
	dental	9	ऌ **ḷ**	[10	ॡ **ḹ**]
diphthongs	palatal	11	ए **e**	12	ऐ **āi**
	labial	13	ओ **o**	14	औ **āu**

Visarga 15 ः **ḥ**

Anusvāra 16 ं, ँ **ṅ** or **ṁ** (see **73c**).

		surd		surd asp.		sonant		son. asp.		nasal	
Mutes	guttural	17	क **k**	18	ख **kh**	19	ग **g**	20	घ **gh**	21	ङ **n̄**
	palatal	22	च **c**	23	छ **ch**	24	ज **j**	25	झ **jh**	26	ञ **ñ**
	lingual	27	ट **ṭ**	28	ठ **ṭh**	29	ड **ḍ**	30	ढ **ḍh**	31	ण **ṇ**
	dental	32	त **t**	33	थ **th**	34	द **d**	35	ध **dh**	36	न **n**
	labial	37	प **p**	38	फ **ph**	39	ब **b**	40	भ **bh**	41	म **m**

Semivowels	palatal	42	य	y
	lingual	43	र	r
	dental	44	ल	l
	labial	45	व	v
Sibilants	palatal	46	श	ç
	lingual	47	ष	ṣ
	dental	48	स	s
Aspiration		49	ह	h

a. To these may be added a lingual ḷ ळ, which in some of the Vedic texts takes the place of ड ḍ when occurring between two vowels (**54**).

6. A few other sounds, recognized by the theories of the Hindu grammarians, but either having no separate characters to represent them or only very rarely and exceptionally written, will be noticed below (**71 b, c, 230**). Such are the guttural and labial breathings, the nasal semivowels, and others.

7. The order of arrangement given above is that in which the sounds are catalogued and described by the native grammarians; and it has been adopted by European scholars as the alphabetic order, for indexes, dictionaries, etc.: to the Hindus, the idea of an alphabetic arrangement for such practical uses is wanting.

a. In some works (as the Petersburg lexicon), a **visarga** which is regarded as equivalent to and exchangeable with a sibilant (**172**) is, though written as **visarga**, given the alphabetic place of the sibilant.

8. The theory of the **devanāgarī**, as of the other Indian modes of writing, is syllabic and consonantal. That is to say, it regards as the written unit, not the simple sound, but the syllable (**akṣara**); and further, as the substantial part of the syllable, the consonant or the consonants which precede the vowel — this latter being merely implied, or, if written, being written by a subordinate sign attached to the consonant.

9. Hence follow these two principles:

A. The forms of the vowel-characters given in the alphabetical scheme above are used only when the vowel forms a syllable by itself, or is not combined with a preceding consonant: that is, when it is either initial or preceded by another vowel. In combination with a consonant, other modes of representation are used.

B. If more consonants than one precede the vowel, forming with it a single syllable, their characters must be combined into a single compound character.

a. Native Hindu usage, in manuscripts and inscriptions, treats the whole material of a sentence alike, not separating its words from one another, any more than the syllables of the same word: a final consonant is combined into one written syllable with the initial vowel or consonant or consonants of the following word. It never occurred to the Hindus to space their words in any way, even where the mode of writing admitted such treatment; nor to begin a paragraph on a new line; nor to write one line of verse under another: everything, without exception, is written solid by them, filling the whole page.

b. Thus, the sentence and verse-line **aham rudrebhir vasubhiç carāmy aham ādityāir uta viçvadevāiḥ** (Rig-Veda X. 125. 1: see Appendix B) *I wander with the Vasus, the Rudras, I with the Ādityas and the All-Gods* is thus syllabized: **a haṁ ru dre bhi rva su bhi ça rā mya ha mā di tyāi ru ta vi çva de vāiḥ**, each syllable ending with a vowel (or a vowel modified by the nasal-sign **anusvāra**, or having the sign of a final breathing, **visarga**, added: these being the only elements that can follow a vowel in the same syllable); and it is (together with the next line) written in the manuscripts after this fashion:

अहंरुद्रेभिर्वसुभिश्चराम्यहमादित्यै
रुतविश्वदेवैः । अहंमित्रावरुणोभा
बिभर्म्यहमिन्द्राग्नीअहमश्विनोभा ॥

Each syllable is written separately, and by many scribes the successive syllables are parted a little from one another: thus,

अ हं रु द्रे भि र्व सु भि श्च रा म्य ह मा दि त्यै

and so on.

c. In Western practice, however, it is almost universally customary to divide paragraphs, to make the lines of verse follow one another, and also to separate the words so far as this can be done without changing the mode of writing them. See Appendix B, where the verse here given is so treated.

d. Further, in works prepared for beginners in the language, it is not uncommon to make a more complete separation of words by a free use of the **virāma**-sign (**11**) under final consonants: thus, for example,

अहं रुद्रेभिर् वसुभिश् चराम्य् अहम् आदित्यैर् उत विश्वदेवैः ।

or even by indicating also the combinations of initial and final vowels (**126, 127**): for example,

अहं मित्रावरुणो ऽभा बिभर्म्य् अहम् इन्द्राग्नी अहम् अश्विनो ऽभा ॥

e. In transliterating, Western methods of separation of words are of course to be followed; to do otherwise would be simple pedantry.

10. Under **A**, it is to be noticed that the modes of indicating a vowel combined with a preceding consonant are as follows:

a. The short अ **a** has no written sign at all; the consonant-sign itself implies a following अ **a**, unless some other vowel-sign is attached to it (or else the **virāma**: **11**). Thus, the consonant-signs as given above in the alphabetic scheme are really the signs of the syllables **ka**, **kha**, etc. etc. (to **ha**).

b. The long आ **ā** is written by a perpendicular stroke after the consonant: thus, का **kā**, धा **dhā**, हा **ha**.

c. Short इ **i** and long ई **ī** are written by a similar stroke, which for short **i** is placed before the consonant and for long **ī** is placed after it, and in either case is connected with the consonant by a hook above the upper line: thus, कि **ki**, की **kī**; भि **bhi**, भी **bhī**; नि **ni**, नी **nī**.

The hook above, turning to the left or to the right, is historically the essential part of the character, having been originally the whole of it; the hooks were only later prolonged, so as to reach all the way down beside the consonant. In the MSS., they almost never have the horizontal stroke drawn across them above, though this is added in the printed characters: thus, originally कि **ki**, की **kī**; in the MSS., कि, की; in print, कि, की.

d. The **u**-sounds, short and long, are written by hooks attached to the lower end of the consonant-sign: thus, कु **ku**, कू **kū**; डु **ḍu**, डू **ḍū**. On account of the necessities of combination, **du** and **dū** are somewhat disguised: thus, दु, दू; and the forms with र **r** and ह **h** are still more irregular: thus, रु **ru**, रू **rū**; हु **hu**, हू **hū**.

e. The ṛ-vowels, short and long, are written by a subjoined hook, single or double, opening toward the right: thus, कृ **kṛ**, कॄ **kṝ**; दृ **dṛ**, दॄ **dṝ**. In the h-sign, the hooks are usually attached to the middle: thus, हृ **hṛ**, हॄ **hṝ**.

As to the combination of ṛ with preceding r, see below, **14d**.

f. The ḷ-vowel is written with a reduced form of its full initial character: thus, कॢ **kḷ**; the corresponding long has no real occurrence (**23a**), but would be written with a similar reduced sign.

g. The diphthongs are written by strokes, single or double, above the upper line, combined, for ओ **o** and औ **āu**, with the ā-sign after the consonant: thus, के **ke**, कै **kāi**; को **ko**, कौ **kāu**.

h. In some **devanāgarī** manuscripts (as in the Bengālī alphabet), the single stroke above, or one of the double ones, is replaced by a sign like the ā-sign before the consonant: thus, के **ke**, कै **kāi**; को **ko**, कौ **kāu**.

11. A consonant-sign, however, is capable of being made to signify the consonant-sound alone, without an added vowel, by having written beneath it a stroke called the **virāma** (*rest*, *stop*): thus, क् **k**, द् **d**, ह् **h**.

a. Since, as was pointed out above, the Hindus write the words of a sentence continuously like one word (**9a, b**), the **virāma** is in general called for only when a final consonant occurs before a pause. But it is also occasionally resorted to by scribes, or in print, in order to avoid an awkward or difficult combination of consonant-signs: thus,

लिड्भिः **liḍbhiḥ**, लिट्सु **liṭsu**, अङ्क्ष्व **aṅkṣva**;

and it is used to make a separation of words in texts prepared for beginners (**9d**).

12. Under B, it is to be noticed that the consonant combinations are for the most part not at all difficult to make or to recognise for one who is familiar with the simple signs. The characteristic part of a consonant-sign that is to be added to another is taken (to the exclusion of the horizontal or of the perpendicular framing-line, or of both), and they are put together according to convenience, either side by side, or one above the other; in a few combinations either arrangement is allowed. The consonant that is to be pronounced first is set before the other in the one order, and above it in the other order.

a. Examples of the side-by-side arrangement are: ग्ग **gga**, ज्ज **jja**, प्य **pya**, न्म **nma**, त्थ **ttha**, भ्य **bhya**, स्क **ska**, ष्ण **ṣṇa**, त्क **tka**.

b. Examples of the above-and-below arrangement are: क्क **kka**, क्व **kva**, च्च **cca**, ञ्ज **ñja**, द्द **dda**, प्त **pta**, त्न **tna**, त्व **tva**.

13. In some cases, however, there is more or less abbreviation or disguise of the independent form of a consonant-sign in combination. Thus,

a. Of क **k** in क्त **kta**, क्ल **kla**; and in क्ण **kṇa** etc.;

b. Of त **t** in त्त **tta**;

c. Of द **d** in द्ग **dga**, द्न **dna**, etc..

d. Of म **m** and य **y**, when following other consonants: thus, क्य **kya**, क्म **kma**, ङ्म **ṅma**, ञ्य **ñya**, द्म dma, द्य **dya**, ह्म **hma**, ह्य **hya**, छ्य **chya**, ढ्य **ḍhya**.

e. Of श ç, which generally becomes श्‍ when followed by a consonant: thus, श्च çca, श्न çna, श्व çva, श्य çya. The same change is usual when a vowel-sign is added below: thus, शु çu, शृ çṛ.

f. Other combinations, of not quite obvious value, are ण्ण ṇṇa, ल्ल lla, ड्ढ ḍḍha, द्भ dbha, ष्ट ṣṭa, ष्ठ ṣṭha; and the compounds of ह् h: as ह्ण hṇa, ह्न hna.

g. In a case or two, no trace of the constituent letters is recognizable: thus, क्ष **kṣa**, ज्ञ **jña**.

14. The semivowel र् r, in making combinations with other consonants, is treated in a wholly peculiar manner, analogous with that in which the vowels are treated.

a. If pronounced before another consonant or combination of consonants, it is written above the latter, with a hook opening to the right (much like the sign of the vowel ṛ, as written under a consonant: **10e**): thus, **र्क rka, र्ष rṣa, र्त्व rtva, र्म्य rmya, र्त्स्न rtsna.**

b. Then, if a consonant-group thus containing r as first member is followed by a vowel that has its sign, or a part of its sign, or its sign of nasality (**anusvāra: 70, 71**), written above the line, the r-sign is placed furthest to the right: thus, **र्के rke, र्कं rkaṅ, र्कि rki, र्की rkī, र्को rko, र्कीं rkīṅ, र्कों rkoṅ.**

c. If r is pronounced after another consonant, whether before a vowel or before yet another consonant, it is written with a straight stroke below, slanting to the left: thus, **प्र pra, ध्र dhra, ग्र gra, स्र sra, द्ध्र ddhra, न्त्र ntra, ग्र्य grya, स्र्व srva, न्त्र्य ntrya**; and, with modifications of a preceding consonant-sign like those noted above (13), **त्र tra, द्र dra, श्र çra, ह्र hra.**

d. When **र** r is to be combined with a following **ऋ** ṛ, it is the vowel which is written in full, with its initial character, and the consonant in subordination to it: thus, **ॠ rṛ.**

15. Further combinations, of three, or four, or even five consonant-signs, are made according to the same rules. Examples are:

of three consonants, **त्त्व ttva, द्ध्य ddhya, द्व्य dvya, द्र्य drya, ध्र्य dhrya, प्स्व psva, श्च्य çcya, ष्ठ्य ṣṭhya, ह्व्य hvya;**

of four consonants, **क्त्र्य ktrya, ङ्क्ष्य ṅkṣya, ष्ट्र्य ṣṭrya, त्स्म्य tsmya;**

of five consonants, **र्त्स्न्य rtsnya.**

a. The manuscripts, and the type-fonts as well, differ from one another more in their management of consonant combinations than in any other respect, often having peculiarities which one needs a little practice to understand. It is quite useless to give in a grammar the whole series of possible combinations (some of them excessively rare) which are provided for in any given type-font, or even in all. There is nothing which due familiarity with the simple signs and with the above rules of combination will not enable the student readily to analyse and explain.

16. a. A sign called the **avagraha** *(separator)* — namely ऽ — is occasionally used in the manuscripts, sometimes in the manner of a hyphen, sometimes as a mark of hiatus, sometimes to mark the elision of initial अ **a** after final ए **e** or ओ **o** (135). In printed texts, especially European, it is ordinarily applied to the use last mentioned, and to that alone: thus, ते ऽब्रुवन् **te 'bruvan,** सो ऽब्रवीत् **so 'bravīt,** for **te abruvan, so abravīt.**

b. If the elided initial-vowel is nasal, and has the **anusvāra**-sign (70, 71) written above, this is usually and more properly transferred to the eliding vowel; but sometimes it is written instead over the **avagraha**-sign: thus, for **so 'ṅçumān,** from **so aṅçumān,** either सों ऽशुमान् or सो ऽंशुमान्.

c. The sign ° is used in place of something that is omitted, and to be understood from the connection: thus, वीरसेनसुतस् °तम् °तेन **vīrasenasutas -tam -tena.**

d. Signs of punctuation are । and ॥.

At the end of a verse, a paragraph, or the like, the latter of them is ordinarily written twice, with the figure of enumeration between: thus, ॥ १० ॥.

17. The numeral figures are

१ 1, २ 2, ३ 3, ४ 4, ५ 5, ६ 6, ७ 7, ८ 8, ९ 9, ० 0.

In combination, to express larger numbers, they are used in precisely the same way as European digits: thus, २५ 25, ६३० 630, ७००० 7000, १८९४ 1894.

18. The Hindu grammarians call the different sounds, and the characters representing them, by a **kāra** *(maker)* added to the sound of the letter, if a vowel, or to the letter followed by **a**, if a consonant. Thus, the sound or character **a** is called **akāra; k** is **kakāra;** and so on. But the **kāra** is also omitted, and **a, ka,** etc. are used alone. The **r,** however, is not called **rakāra,** but only **ra,** or **repha** *snarl*: the sole example of a specific name for an alphabetic element of its class. The **anusvāra** and **visarga** are also known by these names alone.

CHAPTER II.

SYSTEM OF SOUNDS; PRONUNCIATION.

I. Vowels.

19. The a, i, and u-vowels. **The Sanskrit has these three earliest and most universal vowels of Indo-European language, in both short and long form — अ a and आ ā, इ i and ई ī, उ u and ऊ ū. They are to be pronounced in the "Continental" or "Italian" manner — as in *far* or *farther*, *pin* and *pique*, *pull* and *rule*.**

20. The a is the openest vowel, an utterance from the expanded throat, stands in no relation of kindred with any of the classes of consonantal sounds, and has no corresponding semivowel. Of the close vowels i and u, on the other hand, i is palatal, and shades through its semivowel y into the palatal and guttural consonant-classes; u is similarly related, through its semivowel v, to the labial class, as involving in its utterance a narrowing and rounding of the lips.

a. The Paninean scheme (commentary to Pāṇini's grammar i. 1. 9) classes a as guttural, but apparently only in order to give that series as well as the rest a vowel; no one of the Prātiçākhyas puts a into one class with k etc. All these authorities concur in calling the i- and u-vowels respectively palatal and labial.

21. The short a is not pronounced in India with the full openness of ā, as its corresponding short, but usually as the "neutral vowel" (English so-called "short *u*", of *but, son, blood*, etc.). This peculiarity appears very early, being acknowledged by Pāṇini and by two of the Prātiçākhyas (APr. i. 36; VPr. i. 72), which call the utterance saṁvṛta, *covered up, dimmed*. It is wont to be ignored by Western scholars, except those who have studied in India.

22. The a-vowels are the prevailing vowel-sounds of the language, being about twice as frequent as all the others (including diphthongs) taken together. The i-vowels, again, are about twice as numerous as the u-vowels. And, in each pair, the short vowel is more than twice ($2^1/_2$ to 3 times) as common as the long.

a. For more precise estimates of frequency, of these and of the other

alphabetic elements, and for the way in which they were obtained, see below, 75.

23. **The ṛ- and ḷ-vowels.** To the three simple vowels already mentioned the Sanskrit adds two others, the ṛ-vowel and the ḷ-vowel, plainly generated by the abbreviation of syllables containing respectively a र् r or ल् l along with another vowel: the ऋ ṛ coming almost always (see 237, 241-3) from अर् ar or र ra, the ऌ ḷ from अल् al.

a. Some of the Hindu grammarians add to the alphabet also a long ḹ: but this is only for the sake of an artificial symmetry, since the sound does not occur in a single genuine word in the language.

24. The vowel ऋ ṛ is simply a smooth or untrilled *r*-sound, assuming a vocalic office in syllable-making — as, by a like abbreviation, it has done also in certain Slavonic languages. The vowel ऌ ḷ is an *l*-sound similarly uttered — like the English *l*-vowel in such words as *able*, *angle*, *addle*.

a. The modern Hindus pronounce these vowels as *ri*, *rī*, *li* (or even *lri*), having long lost the habit and the facility of giving a vowel value to the pure *r*- and *l*-sounds. Their example is widely followed by European scholars; and hence also the (distorting and altogether objectionable) transliterations ṛi, ṛī, ḷi. There is no real difficulty in the way of acquiring and practising the true utterance.

b. Some of the grammarians (see APr. i. 37, note) attempt to define more nearly the way in which, in these vowels, a real *r*- or *l*-element is combined with something else.

25. Like their corresponding semivowels, r and l, these vowels belong respectively in the general lingual and dental classes; the euphonic influence of ṛ and ṝ (189) shows this clearly. They are so ranked in the Paninean scheme; but the Prātiçākhyas in general strangely class them with the **jihvāmūlīya** sounds, our "gutturals" (39).

26. The short ṛ is found in every variety of word and of position, and is not rare, being just about as frequent as long ū. Long ṝ is very much more unusual, occurring only in certain plural cases of noun-stems in ṛ (**371b, d, 375**). The ḷ is met with only in some of the forms and derivatives of a single not very common verbal root (**kḷp**).

27. **The diphthongs.** Of the four diphthongs, two, the ए e and ओ o, are in great part original Indo-European sounds. In the Sanskrit, they wear the aspect of being products of the increment or strengthening of इ i and उ u respectively; and they are called the corresponding **guna**-vowels to the latter (see below, **235** ff.). The other two, ऐ **āi** and औ **āu**, are held to be of peculiar Sanskrit growth; they are also in general results of another and higher increment of इ i and उ u, to which they are called the corresponding vṛddhi-vowels (below, **235** ff.). But all are likewise sometimes generated by euphonic combination (**127**); and ओ o, especially, is common as result of the alteration of a final अस् **as** (**175**).

28. The ए **e** and ओ **o** are, both in India and in Europe, usually pronounced as they are transliterated — that is, as long *e*- (English "long *a*", or *e* in *they*) and *o*-sounds, without diphthongal character.

a. Such they apparently already were to the authors of the Prātiçākhyas, which, while ranking them as diphthongs (**sandhyakṣara**), give rules respecting their pronunciation in a manner implying them to be virtually unitary sounds. But their euphonic treatment (**131-4**) clearly shows them to have been still at the period when the euphonic laws established themselves, as they of course were at their origin, real diphthongs, *ai* (*a* + *i*) and *au* (*a* + *u*). From them, on the same evidence, the heavier or **vṛddhi** diphthongs were distinguished by the length of their *a*-element, as *āi* (*ā* + *i*) and *āu* (*ā* + *u*).

b. The recognizable distinctness of the two elements in the **vṛddhi**-diphthongs is noticed by the Prātiçākhyas (see APr. i. 40, note); but the relation of those elements is either defined as equal, or the *a* is made of less quantity than the *i* and *u*.

29. The lighter or **guṇa**-diphthongs are much more frequent (6 or 7 times) than the heavier or **vṛddhi**-diphthongs, and the **e** and **āi** than the **o** and **āu** (a half more). Both pairs are somewhat more than half as common as the simple **i**- and **u**-vowels.

30. The general name given by the Hindu grammarians to the vowels is **svara** *tone;* the simple vowels are called **samānākṣara** *homogeneous syllable*, and the diphthongs are called **sandhyakṣara** *combination-syllable*. The position of the organs in their utterance is defined to be one of openness, or of non-closure.

a. As to quantity and accent, see below, **76** ff., **80** ff.

II. Consonants.

31. The Hindu name for 'consonant' is **vyañjana** *manifester*. The consonants are divided by the grammarians into **sparça** *contact* or mute, **antahsthā**, *intermediate* or semivowel, and **ūṣman** *spirant*. They will here be taken up and described in this order.

32. Mutes. The mutes, **sparça**, are so called as involving a complete closure or contact (**sparça**), and not an approximation only, of the mouth-organs by which they are produced. They are divided into five classes or series (**varga**), according to the organs and parts of organs by which the contact is made; and each series is composed of five members, differing according to the accompaniments of the contact.

33. The five mute-series are called respectively guttural, palatal, lingual (or cerebral), dental, and labial; and they are arranged in the order as just mentioned, beginning with the contact made furthest back in the mouth, coming forward from point to point, and ending with the frontmost contact.

34. In each series there are two surd members, two sonant, and one nasal (which is also sonant): for example, in the labial series, प् **p** and फ् **ph**, ब् **b** and भ् **bh**, and म् **m**.

a. The members are by the Hindu grammarians called respectively *first*, *second*, *third*, *fourth*, and *last* or *fifth*.

b. The surd consonants are known as **aghoṣa** *toneless*, and the sonants as **ghoṣavant** *having tone*; and the descriptions of the grammarians are in accordance with these terms. All alike recognise a difference of tone, and not in any manner a difference of force, whether of contact or of expulsion, as separating the two great classes in question. That the difference depends on **vivāra** *opening*, or **saṁvāra** *closure* (of the glottis), is also recognised by them.

35. The first and third members of each series are the ordinary corresponding surd and sonant mutes of European languages: thus, क् **k** and ग् **g**, त् **t** and द् **d**, प् **p** and ब् **b**.

36. Nor is the character of the nasal any more doubtful. What म् **m** is to प् **p** and ब् **b**, or न् **n** to त् **t** and द् **d**, that is also each other nasal to its own series of mutes: a sonant expulsion into and through the nose, while the mouth-organs are in the mute-contact.

a. The Hindu grammarians give distinctly this definition. The nasal (**anunāsika** *passing through the nose*) sounds are declared to be formed by mouth and nose together; or their nasality (**ānunāsikya**) to be given them by unclosure of the nose.

37. The second and fourth of each series are aspirates: thus, beside the surd mute क् **k** we have the corresponding surd aspirate ख् **kh**, and beside the sonant ग् **g**, the corresponding sonant aspirate घ् **gh**. Of these, the precise character is more obscure and difficult to determine.

a. That the aspirates, all of them, are real mutes or contact sounds, and not fricatives (like European *th* and *ph* and *ch*, etc.), is beyond question.

b. It is also not doubtful in what way the surd **th**, for example, differs from the unaspirated **t**: such aspirates are found in many Asiatic languages, and even in some European; they involve the slipping-out of an audible bit of *flatus* or aspiration between the breach of mute-closure and the following sound, whatever it may be. They are accurately enough represented by the **th** etc., with which, in imitation of the Latin treatment of the similar ancient Greek aspirates, we are accustomed to write them.

c. The sonant aspirates are generally understood and described as made in a similar way, with a perceptible *h*-sound after the breach of sonant mute-closure. But there are great theoretical difficulties in the way of accepting this explanation; and some of the best phonetic observers deny that the modern Hindu pronunciation is of such a character, and define the element following the mute as a "glottal buzz", rather, or as an emphasized utterance of the beginning of the succeeding sound. The question is one of great difficulty, and upon it the opinions of the highest authorities are much at variance. Sonant aspirates are still in use in India, in the pronunciation of the vernacular as well as of the learned languages.

d. By the Prātiçākhyas, the aspirates of both classes are called **soṣman**: which might mean either *accompanied by a rush of breath* (taking **ūṣman** in its more etymological sense), or *accompanied by a spirant* (below, **59**). And some native authorities define the surd aspirates as made by the combination of each surd non-aspirate with its own corresponding surd spirant; and the sonant aspirates, of each sonant non-aspirate with the sonant spirant, the **h**-sound (below, **65**). But this would make the two classes of aspirates of quite diverse character, and would also make **th** the same as **ts**, **ṭh** as **tṣ**, **ch** as **cç** — which is in any measure plausible only of the last. Pāṇini has no name for aspirates; the scheme given in his comment (to i. 1. 9) attributes to them **mahāprāṇa** *great expiration*, and to the non-aspirates **alpaprāṇa** *small expiration*.

e. It is usual among European scholars to pronounce both classes of aspirates as the corresponding non-aspirates with a following **h**: for example, थ् **th** nearly as in English *boathook*, फ् **ph** as in *haphazard*, ध् **dh** as in *madhouse*, भ् **bh** as in *abhor*, and so on. This is (as we have seen above) strictly accurate only as regards the surd aspirates.

38. The sonant aspirates are (in the opinion of most), or at leas represent, original Indo-European sounds, while the surd aspirates are a special Indian development. The former are more than twice as common as the latter. The unaspirated (non-nasal) mutes are very much more frequent (5 times) than the aspirates (for the special frequency of **bh** and original **gh**, see **50** and **66**); and among them the surds are more numerous ($2\frac{1}{2}$ times) than the sonants. The nasals (chiefly **n** and **m**) are nearly as frequent as the surd non-aspirates.

We take up now the several mute-series.

39. Guttural series: क् **k**, ख् **kh**, ग् **g**, घ् **gh**, ङ् **ṅ**. These are the ordinary European *k* and *g*-sounds, with their corresponding aspirates and nasal (the last, like English *ng* in *singing*).

a. The gutturals are defined by the Prātiçākhyas as made by contact of the base of the tongue with the base of the jaw, and they are called, from the former organ, **jihvāmūlīya** *tongue-root sounds*. The Paninean scheme describes them simply as made in the throat (**kaṇṭha**). From the euphonic influence of a **k** on a following **s** (below, **180**), we may perhaps infer that in their utterance the tongue was well drawn back in the mouth.

40. The **k** is by far the commonest of the guttural series, occurring considerably more often than all the other four taken together. The nasal, except as standing before one of the others of the same series, is found only as final (after the loss of a following **k**: **386**, **407**) in a very small number of words, and as product of the assimilation of final **k** to a following nasal (**161**).

41. The Sanskrit guttural series represents only a minority of Indo-European gutturals; these last have suffered more and more general corruption than any other class of consonants. By processes of alteration which began in the Indo-European period, the palatal mutes, the palatal sibilant **ç**, and the aspiration **h**, have come from gutturals. See these various sounds below.

42. Palatal series: च् **c**, छ् **ch**, ज् **j**, झ् **jh**, ञ् **ñ**.

The whole palatal series is derivative, being generated by the corruption of original gutturals. The **c** comes from an original **k** — as does also, by another degree of alteration, the palatal sibilant **ç** (see below, **64**). The **j**, in like manner, comes from a **g**; but the

Sanskrit **j** includes in itself two degrees of alteration, one corresponding to the alteration of **k** to **c**, the other to that of **k** to **ç** (see below, **219**). The **c** is somewhat more common than the **j** (about as four to three). The aspirate **ch** is very much less frequent (a tenth of **c**), and comes from the original group **sk**. The sonant aspirate **jh** is excessively rare (occurring but once in RV., not once in AV., and hardly half-a-dozen times in the whole older language); where found, it is either onomatopoetic or of anomalous or not Indo-European origin. The nasal, **ñ**, never occurs except immediately before — or, in a small number of words, also after (**201**) — one of the others of the same series.

43. Hence, in the euphonic processes of the language, the treatment of the palatals is in many respects peculiar. In some situations, the original unaltered guttural shows itself — or, as it appears from the point of view of the Sanskrit, the palatal reverts to its original guttural. No palatal ever occurs as a final. The **j** is differently treated, according as it represents the one or the other degree of alteration. And **c** and **j** (except artificially, in the algebraic rules of the grammarians) do not interchange, as corresponding surd and sonant.

44. The palatal mutes are by European scholars, as by the modern Hindus also, pronounced with the compound sounds of English *ch* and *j* (in *church* and *judge*).

a. Their description by the old Hindu grammarians, however, gives them a not less absolutely simple character than belongs to the other mutes. They are called **tālavya** *palatal*, and declared to be formed against the palate by the middle of the tongue. They seem to have been, then, brought forward in the mouth from the guttural point, and made against the hard palate at a point not far from the lingual one (below, **45**), but with the upper flat surface of the tongue instead of its point. Such sounds, in all languages, pass easily into the (English) *ch*- and *j*-sounds. The value of the **ch** as making the preceding vowel "long by position" (**227**), and its frequent origination from **t + ç** (**203**), lead to the suspicion that it, at least, may have had this character from the beginning: compare **37** d, above.

45. Lingual series: ट **ṭ**, ठ **ṭh**, ड **ḍ**, ढ **ḍh**, ण **ṇ**. The lingual mutes are by all the native authorities defined as uttered with the tip of the tongue turned up and drawn back into the dome of the palate (somewhat as the usual English smooth *r* is pronounced). They are called by the grammarians **mūrdhanya**, literally *head-sounds*, *capitals*, *cephalics;* which term is in many European grammars rendered by 'cerebrals'. In practice, among European Sanskritists, no attempt is made to distinguish them from the dentals: ट् ṭ is pronounced like त् t, ड् ḍ like द् d, and so with the rest.

46. The linguals are another non-original series of sounds, coming mainly from the phonetic alteration of the next series, the dentals, but also in part occurring in words that have no traceable Indo-European connection, and are perhaps derived from the aboriginal languages of India. The tendency to lingualization is a positive one in the history of the language: dentals easily pass into linguals under the influence of contiguous or neighboring lingual sounds, but not the contrary; and all the sounds of the class become markedly more frequent in the later literature. The conditions of their ordinary occurrence are briefly these: 1. **ṣ** comes from **s**, much more rarely from **ç, j, kṣ**, in euphonic circumstances stated below (**180, 218 ff.**); 2. a dental mute following **ṣ** is assimilated to it, becoming lingual (**ṭ, ṭh, ṇ: 197**); 3. **n** is often changed to **ṇ** after a lingual vowel or semivowel or sibilant in the same word (**189 ff.**); 4. **ḍh**, which is of very rare occurrence,, comes from assimilation of a dental after **ṣ** (**198 a**) or **h** (**222**); 5. **ṭ** and **ḍ** come occasionally by substitution for some other sound which is not allowed to stand as final (**142, 145—7**). When originated in these ways, the lingual letters may be regarded as normal; in any other cases of their occurrence, they are either products of abnormal corruption, or signs of the non-Indo-European character of the words in which they appear.

a. In a certain number of passages numerically examined (below, **75**), the abnormal occurrences of lingual mutes were less than half of the whole number (74 out of 159), and most of them (43) were of **ṇ**: all were found more frequent in the later passages. In the Rig-Veda, only 15 words have an abnormal **ṭ**; only 6, such a **ṭh**; only 1, such a **ḍh**; about 20 (including 9 roots, nearly all of which have derivatives) show an abnormal **ḍ**, besides 9 that have **ṇḍ**; and 30 (including 1 root) show a **ṇ**.

b. Taken all together, the linguals are by far the rarest class of mutes (about $1^1/_2$ per cent. of the alphabet) — hardly half as frequent even as the palatals.

47. Dental series: त् t, थ् th, द् d, ध् dh, न् n. These are called by the Hindus also **dantya** *dental*, and are described as formed at the teeth (or at the roots of the teeth), by the tip of the tongue. They are practically the equivalents of our European *t, d, n*.

a. But the modern Hindus are said to pronounce their dentals with the tip of the tongue thrust well forward against the upper teeth, so that these sounds get a slight tinge of the quality belonging to the English and Modern Greek *th*-sounds. The absence of that quality in the European (especially the English) dentals is doubtless the reason why to the ear of a Hindu the latter appear more analogous with his linguals, and he is apt to use the linguals in writing European words.

48. The dentals are one of the Indo-European original mute-classes. In their occurrence in Sanskrit they are just about as frequent as all the other four classes taken together.

49. Labial series: प् p, फ् ph, ब् b, भ् bh, म् m. These sounds are called **oṣṭhya** *labial* by the Hindu grammarians also. They are, of course, the equivalents of our *p, b, m.*

50. The numerical relations of the labials are a little peculiar. Owing to the absence (or almost entire absence) of *b* in Indo-European, the Sanskrit **b** also is greatly exceeded in frequency by **bh**, which is the most common of all the sonant aspirates, as **ph** is the least common of the surd. The nasal **m** (notwithstanding its frequent euphonic mutations when final: **212** ff.) occurs just about as often as all the other four members of the series together.

a. From an early period in the history of the language, but increasingly later, **b** and **v** exchange with one another, or fail to be distinguished in the manuscripts. Thus, the double root-forms **bṛh** and **vṛh**, **bādh** and **vadh**, and so on. In the Bengal manuscripts, **v** is widely written instead of more original **b.**

51. Semivowels: य् y, र् r, ल् l, व् v.

a. The name given to this class of sounds by the Hindu grammarians is **antaḥsthā** *standing between* — either from their character as utterances intermediate between vowel and consonant, or (more probably) from the circumstance of their being placed between the mutes and spirants in the arrangement of the consonants.

b. The semivowels are clearly akin with the several mute series in their physical character, and they are classified along with those series — though not without some discordances of view — by the Hindu grammarians. They are said to be produced with the organs slightly in contact (**īṣatspṛṣṭa**), or in imperfect contact (**duḥspṛṣṭa**).

52. The र् r is clearly shown by its influence in the euphonic processes of the language to be a lingual sound, or one made with the tip of the tongue turned up into the dome of the palate. It thus resembles the English smooth *r*, and, like this, seems to have been untrilled.

a. The Paninean scheme reckons **r** as a lingual. None of the Prātiçākhyas, however, does so; nor are they entirely consistent with one another in its description. For the most part, they define it as made at "the roots of the teeth". This would give it a position like that of the vibrated *r*; but no authority hints at a vibration as belonging to it.

b. In point of frequency, **r** stands very high on the list of consonants; it is nearly equal with **v, n, m,** and **y,** and only exceeded by **t.**

53. The ल् **l** is a sound of dental position, and is so defined and classed by all the native authorities.

a. The peculiar character of an *l*-sound, as involving expulsion at the side of the tongue along with contact at its tip, is not noticed by any Hindu phonetist.

b. The semivowels **r** and **l** are very widely interchangeable in Sanskrit, both in roots and in suffixes, and even in prefixes: there are few roots containing a **l** which do not show also forms with **r**; words written with the one letter are found in other texts, or in other parts of the same text, written with the other. In the later periods of the language they are more separated, and the **l** becomes decidedly more frequent, though always much rarer than the **r** (only as 1 to 7 or 8 or 10).

54. Some of the Vedic texts have another *l*-sound, written with a slightly different character (it is given at the end of the alphabet, 5), which is substituted for a lingual **ḍ** (as also the same followed by **h** for a **ḍh**) when occurring between two vowels. It is, then, doubtless a lingual *l*, one made by breach (at the side of the tongue) of the lingual instead of the dental mute-closure.

a. Examples are: ईळे **īḻe,** for ईडे **īḍe,** but ईड्य **īḍya;** मीळ्हुषे **mīlhuṣe,** for मीढुषे **mīḍhuṣe,** but मीढ्वान् **mīḍhvān.** It is especially in the Rig-Veda and its auxiliary literature that this substitution is usual.

55. The य् **y** in Sanskrit, as in other languages generally, stands in the closest relationship with the vowel इ **i** (short or long); the two exchange with one another in cases innumerable.

a. And in the Veda (as the metre shows) an **i** is very often to be read where, in conformity with the rules of the later Sanskrit euphony, a **y** is written. Thus, the final **i**-vowel of a word remains **i** before an initial vowel; that of a stem maintains itself unchanged before an ending; and an ending of derivation — as **ya, tya** — has **i** instead of **y.** Such cases will be noticed in more detail later. The constancy of the phenomenon in certain words and classes of words shows that this was no merely optional interchange. Very probably, the Sanskrit **y** had everywhere more of an **i**-character than belongs to the corresponding European sound.

56. The **y** is by its physical character a palatal utterance; and it is classed as a palatal semivowel by the Hindu phonetists. It is one of the most common of Sanskrit sounds.

57. The व् **v** is pronounced as English or French *v* (German *w*) by the modern Hindus — except when preceded by a consonant in the same syllable, in which case it has rather the sound of English *w;* and European scholars follow the same practice (with or without the same exception).

a. By its whole treatment in the euphony of the language, however, the **v** stands related to an *u*-vowel precisely as **y** to an *i*-vowel. It is, then, a *v* only according to the original Roman value of that letter — that is to say, a *w*-sound in the English sense; though (as was stated above for the **y**) it may well have been less markedly separated from *u* than English *w*, or more like French *ou* in *oui* etc. But, as the original *w* has in most European languages been changed to *v* (English), so also in India, and that from a very early time: the Paninean scheme and two of the Prātiçākhyas (VPr. and TPr.) distinctly define the sound as made between the upper teeth and the lower lip — which, of course, identifies it with the ordinary modern *v*-sound. As a matter of practice, the usual pronunciation need not be seriously objected to; yet the student should not fail to note that the rules of Sanskrit euphony and the name of "semivowel" have no application except to a *w*-sound in the English sense: a *v*-sound (German *w*) is no semivowel, but a spirant, standing on the same articulate stage with the English *th*-sounds and the *f*.

58. The **v** is classed as a labial semivowel by the Hindu phonetical authorities. It has a somewhat greater frequency than the **y**.

a. In the Veda, under the same circumstances as the **y** (above, **55 a**), **v** is to be read as a vowel, **u**.

b. As to the interchange of **v** and **b**, see above, **50 a**.

59. Spirants. Under the name **ūṣman** (literally *heat, steam, flatus*), which is usually and well represented by *spirant*, some of the Hindu authorities include all the remaining sounds of the alphabet; others apply the term only to the three sibilants and the aspiration — to which it will here also be restricted.

a. The term is not found in the Paninean scheme; by different treatises the guttural and labial breathings, these and the **visarga**, or all these and **anusvāra**, are also (in addition to the sibilants and **h**) called **ūṣman**

(see APr. i. 31 note). The organs of utterance are described as being in the position of the mute-series to which each spirant belongs respectively, but unclosed, or unclosed in the middle.

60. The स् s. Of the three sibilants, or surd spirants, this is the one of plainest and least questioned character: it is the ordinary European *s* — a hiss expelled between the tongue and the roof of the mouth directly behind the upper front teeth.

a. It is, then, dental, as it is classed by all the Hindu authorities. Notwithstanding the great losses which it suffers in Sanskrit euphony, by conversion to the other sibilants, to **r**, to **visarga**, etc., it is still very high among the consonants in the order of frequency, or considerably more common than both the other two sibilants together.

61. The ष् ṣ. As to the character of this sibilant, also, there is no ground for real question: it is the one produced in the lingual position, or with the tip of the tongue reverted into the dome of the palate. It is, then, a kind of *sh*-sound; and by European Sanskritists it is pronounced as an ordinary *sh* (French *ch*, German *sch*), no attempt being made (any more than in the case of the other lingual sounds: **45**) to give it its proper lingual quality.

a. Its lingual character is shown by its whole euphonic influence, and it is described and classed as lingual by all the Hindu authorities (the APr. adds, i. 23, that the tongue in its utterance is trough-shaped). In its audible quality, it is a *sh*-sound rather than a *s*-sound; and, in the considerable variety of sibilant-utterance, even in the same community, it may coincide with the *sh* of some among ourselves. Yet the general and normal *sh* is palatal (see below, **63**); and therefore the sign ṣ, marked in accordance with the other lingual letters, is the only unexceptionable transliteration for the Hindu character.

b. In modern pronunciation in India, ṣ is much confounded with **kh**; and the manuscripts are apt to exchange the characters. Some later grammatical treatises, too, take note of the relationship.

62. This sibilant (as was noticed above, **46**, and will be more particularly explained below, **180** ff.) is no original sound, but a product of the lingualization of s under certain euphonic conditions. The exceptions are extremely few (9 out of 145 noted occurrences: **75**), and of a purely sporadic character. The Rig-Veda has (apart from √ sah, **182 b**) only twelve words which show a ṣ under other conditions.

a. The final ṣ of a root has in some cases attained a more independent value, and does not revert to s when the euphonic conditions are removed, but shows anomalous forms (**225–6**).

63. The श ç. This sibilant is by all the native authorities classed and described as palatal, nor is there anything in its history or its euphonic treatment to cast doubt on its character as such. It is, then, made with the flat of the tongue against the forward part of the palatal arch — that is to say, it is the usual and normal *sh*-sound. By European scholars it is variously pronounced — more often, perhaps, as *s* than as *sh*.

a. The two *sh*-sounds, ṣ and ç, are made in the same part of the mouth (the ṣ probably rather further back), but with a different part of the tongue; and they are doubtless not more unlike than, for example, the two *t*-sounds, written ṭ and t; and it would be not less proper to pronounce them both as one *sh* than to pronounce the linguals and dentals alike. To neglect the difference of s and ç is much less to be approved. The very near relationship of ṣ and ç is attested by their euphonic treatment, which is to a considerable extent the same, and by their not infrequent confusion by the writers of manuscripts.

64. As was mentioned above (**41**), the ç, like c, comes from the corruption of an original *k*-sound, by loss of mute-contact as well as forward shift of the point of production. In virtue of this derivation, it sometimes (though less often than c) "reverts" to k — that is, the original k appears instead of it (**43**); while, on the other hand, as a *sh*-sound, it is to a certain extent convertible to ṣ. In point of frequency, it slightly exceeds the latter.

65. The remaining spirant, ह h, is ordinarily pronounced like the usual European surd aspiration *h*.

a. This is not, however, its real character. It is defined by all the native authorities as not a surd element, but a sonant (or else an utterance intermediate between the two); and its whole value in the euphony of the language is that of a sonant: but what is its precise value is very hard to say. The Paninean scheme ranks it as guttural, as it does also a: this means nothing. The Prātiçākhyas bring it into no relation with the guttural class; one of them quotes the opinion of some authorities that "it has the same position with the beginning of the following vowel" (TPr. ii. 47) — which so far identifies it with our h. There is nothing in its euphonic influence to mark it as retaining any trace of gutturally articulated character.

By some of the native phonetists it is identified with the aspiration of the sonant aspirates — with the element by which, for example, **gh** differs from **g**. This view is supported by the derivation of **h** from the aspirates (next paragraph), by that of **ḷ+h** from **ḍh** (**54**), and by the treatment of initial **h** after a final mute (**163**).

66. The **h**, as already noticed, is not an original sound, but comes in nearly all cases from an older **gh** (for the few instances of its derivation from **dh** and **bh**, see below, **223g**). It is a vastly more frequent sound than the unchanged **gh** (namely, as 7 to 1): more frequent, indeed, than any of the guttural mutes except **k**. It appears, like **j** (**219**), to include in itself two stages of corruption of **gh**: one corresponding with that of **k** to **c**, the other with that of **k** to **ç**; see below, **223**, for the roots belonging to the two classes respectively. Like the other sounds of guttural derivation, it sometimes exhibits "reversion" (**43**) to its original.

67. The **: ḥ**, or **visarga** (**visarjanīya**, as it is uniformly called by the Prātiçākhyas and by Pāṇini, probably as *belonging to the end* of a syllable), appears to be merely a surd breathing, a final *h*-sound (in the European sense of *h*), uttered in the articulating position of the preceding vowel.

a. One Prātiçākhya (TPr. ii. 48) gives just this last description of it. It is by various authorities classed with **h**, or with **h** and **a**: all of them are alike sounds in whose utterance the mouth-organs have no definite shaping action.

68. The **visarga** is not original, but always only a substitute for final **s** or **r**, neither of which is allowed to maintain itself unchanged (**170 ff.**). It is a comparatively recent member of the alphabetic system; the other euphonic changes of final **s** and **r** have not passed through **visarga** as an intermediate stage. And the Hindu authorities are considerably discordant with one another as to how far **ḥ** is a necessary substitute, and how far a permitted one, alternative with a sibilant, before a following initial surd.

69. Before a surd guttural or labial, respectively, some of the native authorities permit, while others require, conversion of final **s** or **r** into the so-called **jihvāmūlīya** and **upadhmānīya** spirants. It may be fairly questioned, perhaps, whether these two sounds are not pure grammatical abstractions, devised (like the long **ḷ**-vowel: **23a**) in order to round out the alphabet to greater symmetry. At any rate, both manuscripts and printed texts in general make no account of them. Whatever individual character they may have must be, it would seem, in the direction of the (German) *ch*- and *f*-sounds. When written at all, they are wont to be transliterated by χ and φ.

70. The ः **anusvāra**, **ṅ** or **ṁ**, is a nasal sound lacking that closure of the organs which is required to make a nasal mute or contact-sound (**36**); in its utterance there is nasal resonance along with some degree of openness of the mouth.

71. There is discordance of opinion among both the Hindu phonetists and their modern European successors respecting the real character of this element; hence a little detail is necessary here with regard to its occurrence and their views of it.

a. Certain nasals in Sanskrit are of servile character, always to be assimilated to a following consonant, of whatever character that may be. Such are final **m** in sentence-combination (**213**), the penultimate nasal of a root, and a nasal of increment (**255**) in general. If one of these nasals stands before a contact-letter or mute, it becomes a nasal mute corresponding to the latter — that is, a nasal utterance in the same position of the mouth-organs which gives the succeeding mute. If, on the other hand, the following consonant does not involve a contact (being a semivowel or spirant), the nasal element is also without contact: it is a nasal utterance with unclosed mouth-organs. The question is, now, whether this nasal utterance becomes merely a nasal infection of the preceding vowel, turning it into a nasal vowel (as in French *on*, *en*, *un*, etc., by reason of a similar loss of a nasal mute); or whether it is an element of more individual character, having place between the vowel and the consonant; or, once more, whether it is sometimes the one thing and sometimes the other. The opinions of the Prātiçākhyas and Pāṇini are briefly as follows:

b. The Atharva-Prātiçākhya holds that the result is everywhere a nasalized vowel, except when **n** or **m** is assimilated to a following **l**; in that case, the **n** or **m** becomes a nasal **l**: that is, the nasal utterance is made in the **l**-position, and has a perceptible **l**-character.

c. The other Prātiçākhyas teach a similar conversion into a nasal counterpart to the semivowel, or a nasal semivowel, before **y** and **l** and **v** (not before **r** also). In most of the other cases where the Atharva-Prātiçākhya acknowledges a nasal vowel — namely, before **r** and the spirants — the others teach the intervention after the vowel of a distinct nasal element, called the **anusvāra** *after-tone*.

d. Of the nature of this nasal afterpiece to the vowel no intelligibly clear account is given. It is said (RPr.) to be either vowel or consonant; it is declared (RPr., VPr.) to be made with the nose alone, or (TPr.) to be nasal like the nasal mutes; it is held by some (RPr.) to be the sonant tone of the nasal mutes; in its formation, as in that of vowel and spirant, there is (RPr.) no contact. As to its quantity, see further on.

e. There are, however, certain cases and classes of cases where these other authorities also acknowledge a nasal vowel. So, especially, wherever a final **n** is treated (**208—9**) as if it were **ns** (its historically older form); and also in a small number of specified words. They also mention the doctrine of nasal vowel instead of **anusvāra** as held by some (and TPr. is uncertain and inconsistent in its choice between the one and the other).

f. In Pāṇini, finally, the prevailing doctrine is that of **anusvāra** everywhere; and it is even allowed in many cases where the Prātiçākhyas prescribe only a nasal mute. But a nasal semivowel is also allowed instead before a semivowel, and a nasal vowel is allowed in the cases (mentioned above) where some of the Prātiçākhyas require it by exception.

g. It is evidently a fair question whether this discordance and uncertainty of the Hindu phonetists is owing to a real difference of utterance in different classes of cases and in different localities, or whether to a different scholastic analysis of what is really everywhere the same utterance. If **anusvāra** is a nasal element following the vowel, it cannot well be any thing but either a prolongation of the same vowel-sound with nasality added, or a nasalized bit of neutral-vowel sound (in the latter case, however, the altering influence of an **i** or **u**-vowel on a following **s** ought to be prevented, which is not the case: see **183**.

72. The assimilated nasal element, whether viewed as nasalized vowel, nasal semivowel, or independent **anusvāra**, has the value of something added, in making a heavy syllable, or length by position (**79**).

a. The Prātiçākhyas (VPr., RPr.) give determinations of the quantity of the **anusvāra** combining with a short and with a long vowel respectively to make a long syllable.

73. a. Two different signs, ं and ँ, are found in the manuscripts, indicating the nasal sound here treated of. Usually they are written above the syllable, and there they seem most naturally to imply a nasal affection of the vowel of the syllable, a nasal (**anunāsika**) vowel. Hence some texts (Sāma- and Yajur-Vedas), when they mean a real **anusvāra**, bring one of the signs down into the ordinary consonant-place; but the usage is not general. As between the two signs, some manuscripts employ, or tend to employ, the ँ where a nasalized (**anunāsika**) vowel is to be recognized, and elsewhere the ं; and this distinction is consistently observed in many European printed texts; and the former is called the **anunāsika** sign: but the two are doubtless originally and properly equivalent.

b. It is a very common custom of the manuscripts to write the **anusvāra**-sign for any nasal following the vowel of a syllable, either before another consonant or as final (not before a vowel), without any reference to whether it is to be pronounced as nasal mute, nasal semivowel, or **anusvāra**. Some printed texts follow this slovenly and undesirable habit; but most write a nasal mute whenever it is to be pronounced — excepting where it is an assimilated **m** (**213**)

c. It is convenient also in transliteration to distinguish the assimilated **m** by a special sign, **ṁ**, from the **anusvāra** of more independent origin, **ṅ**; and this method will be followed in the present work.

74. This is the whole system of sounds recognised by the written character; for certain other transitional sounds, more or less widely recognised in the theories of the Hindu phonetists, see below, **230**.

75. The whole spoken alphabet, then, may be arranged in the following manner, in order to show, so far as is possible in a single scheme, the relations and important classifications of its various members:

Son.		a, ā 19·78 8·19					Vowels
			āi, e ·51 2·84			o, āu 1·88 ·18	Vowels
			i, ī 4·85 1·19	ṛ, ṝ ·74 ·01	ḷ ·01	u, ū 2·61 ·73	Vowels
Son.			y 4·25	r 5·05	l ·69	v 4·99	Semivowels
Son.		n̄ ·22	ñ ·35	ṇ 1·03	n 4·81	m 4·34	Nasals
Son.	ṅ ·63						Anusvāra
Son.	h 1·07						Aspiration
Surd	ḥ 1·31						Visarga
Surd			ç 1·57	ṣ 1·45	s 3·56		Sibilants
Son.		gh ·15	jh ·01	ḍh ·03	dh ·83	bh 1·27	asp. — Mutes
Son.		g ·82	j ·94	ḍ ·21	d 2·85	b ·46	unasp. — Mutes
Surd		kh ·13	ch ·17	ṭh ·06	th ·58	ph ·03	asp. — Mutes
Surd		k 1·99	c 1·26	ṭ ·26	t 6·65	p 2·46	unasp. — Mutes
		Gutt.	Pal.	Ling.	Dent.	Lab.	

a. The figures set under the characters give the average percentage of frequency of each sound, found by counting the number of times which it occurred in an aggregate of 10,000 sounds of continuous text, in ten different passages, of 1,000 sounds each, selected from different epochs of the literature: namely, two from the Rig-Veda, one from the Atharva-Veda, two from different Brāhmaṇas, and one each from Manu, Bhagavad-Gītā, Çakuntalā, Hitopadeça, and Vāsavadattā (J.A.O.S., vol. X., p. cl).

III. Quantity of sounds and syllables.

76. The Hindu grammarians take the pains to define the quantity of a consonant (without distinction among consonants of different classes) as half that of a short vowel.

77. They also define the quantity of a long (**dīrgha**) vowel or diphthong as twice that of a short (**hrasva**) vowel — making no distinction in this respect between the **guṇa**- and the **vṛddhi**-diphthongs.

78. Besides these two vowel-quantities, the Hindus acknowledge a third, called **pluta** (literally *swimming*), or protracted, and having three *moras* or three times the quantity of a short vowel. A protracted vowel is marked by a following figure 3: thus, आ३ ā3.

a. The protracted vowels are practically of rare occurrence (in RV., three cases; in AV., fifteen; in the Brāhmaṇa literature, decidedly more frequent). They are used in cases of questioning, especially of a balancing between two alternatives, and also of calling to a distance or urgently. The protraction is of the last syllable in a word, or in a whole phrase; and the protracted syllable has usually the acute tone, in addition to any other accent the word may have; sometimes it takes also **anusvāra**, or is made nasal.

b. Examples are: **adháḥ svid āsī́3d upári svid āsī3t** (RV.) *was it, forsooth, below? was it, forsooth, above?* **idám bhū́yā́3 idā́3m íti** (AV.) *saying, is this more, or is that?* **ágnā́3i pátnīvā́3ḥ sómam piba** (TS.) *O Agni! thou with thy spouse! drink the soma.*

c. A diphthong is protracted by prolongation of its first or **a**-element: thus, **e** to **ā3i, o** to **ā3u.**

d. The sign of protraction is also sometimes written as the result of accentual combination, when so-called **kampa** occurs: see below, **90 c, d.**

79. For metrical purposes, syllables (not vowels) are distinguished by the grammarians as heavy (**guru**) or light (**laghu**). A syllable is heavy if its vowel is long, or short and followed by more than one consonant ("long by position"). **Anusvāra** and **visarga** count as full consonants in making a heavy syllable. The last syllable of a **pāda** (primary division of a verse) is reckoned as either heavy or light.

a. The distinction in terms between the difference of long and short in vowel-sound and that of heavy and light in syllable-construction is valuable, and should be observed.

IV. Accent.

80. The phenomena of accent are, by the Hindu grammarians of all ages alike, described and treated as depending on a variation of tone or pitch; of any difference of stress involved, they make no account.

81. The primary tones (**svara**) or accent-pitches are two: a higher (**udātta** *raised*), or acute; and a lower (**anudātta** *not raised*), or grave. A third (called **svarita**: a term of doubtful meaning) is always of secondary origin, being (when not enclitic: see below, **85**) the result of actual combination of an acute vowel and a following grave vowel into one syllable. It is also uniformly defined as compound in pitch, a union of higher and lower tone within the limits of a single syllable. It is thus identical in physical character with the Greek and Latin circumflex, and fully entitled to be called by the same name.

82. Strictly, therefore, there is but one distinction of tone in the Sanskrit accentual system, as described by the native grammarians and marked in the written texts: the accented syllable is raised in tone above the unaccented; while then further, in certain cases of the fusion of an accented and an unaccented element into one syllable, that syllable retains the compounded tone of both elements.

83. The **svarita** or circumflex is only rarely found on a pure long vowel or diphthong, but almost always on a syllable in which a vowel, short or long, is preceded by a **y** or **v** representing an originally acute **i**- or **u**-vowel.

a. In transliteration, in this work, the **udātta** or acute will be marked with the ordinary sign of acute, and the **svarita** or circumflex (as being a downward slide of the voice forward with what is usually called the grave accent: thus, **á**, acute. **yà** or **và**, circumflex.

84. The Prātiçākhyas distinguish and name separately the circumflexed tones arising by different processes of combination: thus, the circumflex is called

a. Kṣāipra *(quick)*, when an acute **i** or **u**-vowel (short or long) is converted into **y** or **v** before a dissimilar vowel of grave tone: thus, **vyàpta** from **ví-āpta, apsvàntár** from **apsú antár.**

b. Jātya *(native)* or **nitya** *(own)*, when the same combination lies further back, in the make-up of a stem or form, and so is constant, or belongs to the word in all circumstances of its occurrence: thus, **kvà** (from **kúa**), **svàr** (**súar**), **nyàk** (**niak**), **budhnyà** (**budhnía**), **kanyā̀** (**kaníā**), **nadyàs** (**nadī-as**), **tanvā̀** (**tanū-ā**).

c. The words of both the above classes are in the Veda, in the great majority of cases, to be read with restoration of the acute vowel as a separate syllable: thus, **apsú antár, súar, nadías,** etc. In some texts, part of them are written correspondingly: thus, **súvar, tanúvā, budhníya.**

d. Praçliṣṭa, when the acute and grave vowels are of such character that they are fused into a long vowel or diphthong (**128 c**): thus **divī̀ 'va** (RV. AV. etc.), from **diví iva; sū̀dgātā** (TS.), from **sú-udgātā; nāì 'vā̀ 'çnīyāt** (ÇB.), from **ná evá açnīyāt.**

e. Abhinihita, when an initial grave **a** is absorbed by a final acute **é** or **ó** (**135 a**): thus, **tè 'bruvan,** from **té abruvan; sò 'bravīt,** from **só abravīt.**

85. But further, the Hindu grammarians agree in declaring the (naturally grave) syllable following an acute, whether in the same or in another word, to be **svarita** or circumflex — unless, indeed, it be itself followed by an acute or circumflex; in which case it retains its grave tone. This is called by European scholars the enclitic or dependent circumflex.

a. Thus, in **téna** and **té ca**, the syllable **na** and word **ca** are regarded and marked as circumflex; but in **téna té** and **te ca svàr** they are grave.

b. This seems to mean that the voice, which is borne up at the higher pitch to the end of the acute syllable, does not ordinarily drop to grave pitch by an instantaneous movement, but descends by a more or less perceptible slide in the course of the following syllable. No Hindu authority suggests the theory of a middle or intermediate tone for the enclitic, any more than for the independent circumflex. For the most part, the two are identified with one another, in treatment and designation. The enclitic circumflex is likewise divided into a number of sub-varieties, with different names: they are of too little consequence to be worth reporting.

86. The essential difference of the two kinds of circumflex is shown clearly enough by these facts: 1. the independent circumflex takes the place of the acute as the proper accent of a word, while the enclitic is the mere shadow following an acute, and following it in another word precisely as in the same word; 2. the independent circumflex maintains its character in all situations, while the enclitic before a following circumflex or acute loses its circumflex character, and becomes grave; moreover, 3. in many of the systems of marking accent (below, **88**), the two are quite differently indicated.

87. The accentuation is marked in manuscripts only of the older literature: namely, in the primary Vedic texts, or **saṁhitās**, in two of the Brāhmaṇas (Tāittirīya and Çatapatha), in the Tāittirīya-Araṇyaka, in certain passages of the Āitareya-Āraṇyaka, and in the Suparṇādhyāya. There are a number of methods of writing accent, more or less different from one another; the one found in manuscripts of the Rig-Veda, which is most widely known, and of which most of the others are only slight modifications, is as follows.

a. The acute syllable is left unmarked; the circumflex, whether independent or enclitic, has a short perpendicular stroke above; and the grave next preceding an acute or (independent) circumflex has a short horizontal stroke below. Thus,

अ॒ग्निम् agním; जु॒होति॑ juhóti; त॒न्वा॑ tanva; क्व॑ kvà.

b. But the introductory grave stroke below cannot be given if an acute syllable is initial; hence an unmarked syllable at the beginning of a word is to be understood as acute; and hence also, if several grave syllables precede an acute at the beginning of a sentence, they must all alike have the grave sign. Thus,

इन्द्र॑ः índraḥ; ते té; क॒रि॒ष्यसि॑ kariṣyási; तु॒वि॒जा॒ता tuvijātá.

c. All the grave syllables, however, which follow a marked circumflex are left unmarked, until the occurrence of another accented syllable causes the one which precedes it to take the preparatory stroke below. Thus,

सु॒दृशी॑कसंदृक् sudṛ́çīkasaṁdṛk;

but सु॒दृशी॑कसंदृ॒ग्गवा॑म् sudṛ́çīkasaṁdṛg gávām.

d. If an independent circumflex be followed by an acute (or by another independent circumflex), a figure 1 is set after the former circumflexed vowel if it be short, or a figure 3 if it be long, and the signs of accent are applied as in the following examples:

अ॒प्स्व१॒न्तः apsv àntáḥ (from apsú antáḥ);

रा॒यो३॒ऽवनि॑ः rāyò 3 vániḥ (from rāyó ávániḥ).

The rationale of this mode of designation is not well understood; the Prātiçākhyas give no account of it. In the scholastic utterance of the syllable so designated is made a peculiar quaver or *roulade* of the voice, called **kampa** or **vikampana**.

e. The accent-marks are written with red ink in the manuscripts, being added after the text is written, and perhaps often by another hand.

88 a. Nearly accordant with this, the Rig-Veda method of designating accent, are the methods employed in the manuscripts of the Atharva-Veda, of the Vājasaneyi-Saṁhitā, and of the Tāittirīya-Saṁhitā, Brāhmaṇa. and Āraṇyaka. Their differences from it are of trifling importance, consisting mainly in peculiar ways of marking the circumflex that precedes an acute (**87 d**). In some manuscripts of the Atharva-Veda, the accent-marks are dots instead of strokes, and that for the circumflex is made within the syllable instead of above it.

b. In most manuscripts of the Māitrāyaṇī-Saṁhitā, the acute syllable itself, besides its surroundings, is marked — namely, by a perpendicular stroke above the syllable (like that of the ordinary circumflex in the RV. method). The independent circumflex has a hook beneath the syllable, and the circumflex before an acute (**87 d**) is denoted simply by a figure 3, standing before instead of after the circumflexed syllable.

c. The Çatapatha-Brāhmaṇa uses only a single accent-sign, the horizontal stroke beneath the syllable (like the mark for grave in RV.). This is put under an acute, or, if two or more acutes immediately follow one another, only under the last of them. To mark an independent circumflex, it is put under the preceding syllable. The method is an imperfect one, allowing many ambiguities.

d. The Sāma-Veda method is the most intricate of all. It has a dozen different signs, consisting of figures, or of figures and letters combined, all placed above the syllables, and varying according both to the accentual character of the syllable and to its surroundings. Its origin is obscure; if anything more is indicated by it than by the other simpler systems, the fact has not been demonstrated.

89. In this work, as everything given in the **devanāgarī** characters is also given in transliteration, it will in general be unnecessary to mark the accent except in the transliterated form; where, however, the case is otherwise, there will be adopted the method of marking only the really accented syllables, the acute and the independent circumflex: the latter by the usual **svarita**-sign, the former by a small **u** (for **udātta**) above the syllable: thus,

इन्द्र índra, अग्ने ágne, स्वर् svàr, नद्यस् nadyàs.

a. These being given, everything else which the Hindu theory recognizes as dependent on and accompanying them can readily be understood as implied.

90. The theory of the Sanskrit accent, as here given (a consistent and intelligible body of phenomena), has been overlaid by the Hindu theorists, especially of the Prātiçākhyas, with a number of added features, of a much more questionable character. Thus:

a. The unmarked grave syllables following a circumflex (either at the end of a sentence, or till the near approach of another acute) are declared to have the same high tone with the (also unmarked) acute. They are called **pracaya** or **pracita** (*accumulated:* because liable to occur in an indefinite series of successive syllables).

b. The circumflex, whether independent or enclitic, is declared to begin on a higher pitch than acute, and to descend to acute pitch in ordinary cases: the concluding instant of it being brought down to grave pitch, however, in the case of an independent circumflex which is immediately followed by another ascent of the voice to higher pitch, in acute or independent circumflex (a **kampa** syllable: **87 d**).

c. Pāṇini gives the ambiguous name of **ekaçruti** (*monotone*) to the **pracita** syllables, and says nothing of the uplifting of the circumflex to a higher plane; he teaches, however, a depression below the grave pitch for the marked grave syllable before acute or circumflex, calling it **sannatara** (otherwise **anudāttatara**).

91. The system of accentuation as marked in the Vedic texts appears to have assumed in the traditional recitation of the Brahmanic schools a peculiar and artificial form, in which the designated syllables, grave and circumflex (equally the enclitic and the independent circumflex), have acquired a conspicuous value, while the undesignated, the acute, has sunk into insignificance.

92. The Sanskrit accent taught in the native grammars and represented by the accentuated texts is essentially a system of word-accent only. No general attempt is made (any more than in the Greek system) to define or mark a sentence-accent, the effect of the emphasis and modulation of the sentence in modifying the independent accent of individual words. The only approach to it is seen in the treatment of vocatives and personal verb-forms.

a. A vocative is usually without accent except at the beginning of a sentence: for further details, see **314**.

b. A personal verb-form is usually accentless in an independent clause, except when standing at the beginning of the clause: for further details, see **591** ff.

93. Certain other words also are, usually or always, without accent.

a. The particles **ca, vā, u, sma, iva, cid, svid, ha,** and the Vedic **kam** (or **kám**), **gha, bhala, samaha, īm, sīm,** are always without accent; also **yathā** in RV. (sometimes also elsewhere) in the sense of **iva,** at the end of a **pāda** or verse-division.

b. The same is true of certain pronouns and pronominal stems: **mā, me, nāu, nas, tvā, te, vām, vas** (**491 b**), **ena** (**500**), **tva** (**503b**), **sama** (**513c**).

c. The cases of the pronominal stem **a** are sometimes accented and sometimes accentless (**502**).

d. An accentless word is not allowed to stand at the beginning of a sentence; also not of a **pāda** or primary division of a verse; a **pāda** is, in all matters relating to accentuation, treated like an independent sentence.

94. Some words have more than a single accented syllable. Such are:

a. Certain dual copulative compounds in the Veda (see **1255**), as **mitrā́váruṇā, dyā́vāpṛthivī́**. Also, a few other Vedic compounds (see **1267d**), as **bṛ́haspáti, tánūnápāt**.

b. In a few cases, the further compounds and derivatives of such compounds, as **dyā́vāpṛthivī́vant, bṛ́haspátipraṇutta**.

c. Infinitive datives in **tavāí** (see **972 a**), as **étavāí, ápabhartavāí**.

d. A word naturally barytone, but having its final syllable protracted (see **78a**).

e. The particle **vā́vá** (in the Brāhmanas).

95. On the place of the accented syllable in a Sanskrit word there is no restriction whatever depending upon either the number or the quantity of the preceding or following syllables. The accent rests where the rules of inflection or derivation or composition place it, without regard to any thing else.

a. Thus, **índre, agnāú, índreṇa, agnínā, agnīnā́m, bāhúcyuta, ánapacyuta, parjányajinvita, abhimātiṣāhá, ánabhimlātavarṇa, abhiçasticā́tana, híraṇyavāçīmattama, cátuçcatvāriṅçadakṣara.**

96. Since the accent is marked only in the older literature, and the statements of the grammarians, with the deduced rules of accentuation, are far from being sufficient to settle all cases, the place of the stress of voice for a considerable part of the vocabulary is undetermined. Hence it is a general habit with European scholars to pronounce Sanskrit words according to the rules of the Latin accent.

97. In this work, the accent of each word and form will in general be marked, so far as there is authority determining its place and character. Where specific words and forms are quoted, they will only be so far accentuated as they are found with accent in accentuated texts.

CHAPTER III.

RULES OF EUPHONIC COMBINATION.

Introductory.

98. The words in Sanskrit, as in the other languages related with it, are in great part analysable into roots, suffixes of derivation, and endings of inflection, these last being added mostly to stems containing suffixes, but also sometimes directly to roots.

a. There are, of course, a certain number of uninflected words — indeclinables, particles; and also not a few that are incapable of analysis.

99. The Sanskrit, indeed, possesses an exceptionally analysable character; its formative processes are more regular and transparent than those of any other Indo-European tongue. Hence the prevailing method of the Hindu native science of grammar, which sets up a certain body of roots, and prescribes the processes by which these may be made stems and words, giving the various added elements, and laying down the rules by which their combination is effected. And the same general method is, for like reason, followed also by European grammarians.

100. The euphonic laws, accordingly, which govern the combination of suffix or of ending with root or stem, possess a high practical importance, and require to be laid down in preparation for the topics of declension and conjugation.

101. Moreover, the formation of compounds, by joining two or more simple stems, is extremely frequent in Sanskrit; and this kind of combination has its own peculiar euphonic rules. And once more, in the form of the language as handed down to us by its literature, the words composing a sentence or paragraph are adapted to and combined with one another by nearly the same rules which govern the making of compounds; so that it is impossible to take apart and understand a Sanskrit sentence without knowing those rules. Hence

an increased degree of practical importance belonging to the subject of euphonic combination.

a. This euphonic interdependence of the words of a sentence is unknown to any other language in anything like the same degree; and it cannot but be suspected of being at least in part artificial, implying an erection into necessary and invariable rules of what in the living language were only optional practices. This is strongly indicated, indeed, by the evidence of the older dialect of the Vedas and of the derived Prakritic dialects, in both of which some of the rules (especially that as to the hiatus: see **113**) are often violated.

102. The roots which are authenticated by their occurrence in the literary monuments of the language, earlier and later, number between eight and nine hundred. About half of these belong fully to the language throughout its whole history; some (about a hundred and fifty) are limited to the earlier or pre-classical period; some, again (over a hundred and twenty), make their first appearance in the later language.

a. There are in this number roots of very diverse character. Those occurring only later are, at least in great part, presumably of secondary origin; and a certain number are even doubtless artificial, used once or twice because found in the root-lists of the Hindu grammarians (**103**). But also of the rest, some are plainly secondary, while others are questionable; and not a few are variations or differentiated forms of one another. Thus, there are roots showing respectively **r** and **l**, as **rabh** and **labh**, **mruc** and **mluc**, **kṣar** and **kṣal**; roots with and without a strengthening nasal, as **vand** and **vad**, **mand** and **mad**; roots in **ā** and in a nasal, as **khā** and **khan**, **gā** and **gam**, **jā** and **jan**; roots made by an added **ā**, as **trā** from **tṛ**, **mnā** from **man**, **psā** from **bhas**, **yā** from **i**; roots the product of reduplication, as **jakṣ** from **ghas**, **dudh** from **dhū**; roots with a final sibilant of formative origin, as **bhakṣ** and **bhikṣ** from **bhaj**, **nakṣ** from **naç**, **çruṣ** from **çru**, **hās** from **hā**; root-forms held apart by a well-established discordance of inflection and meaning, which yet are probably different sides of one root, as **kṛṣ** *drag* and **kṛṣ** *plough*, **vid** *know* and **vid** *find*, **vṛ** *enclose* and **vṛ** *choose*; and so on. In many such cases it is doubtful whether we ought to acknowledge two roots or only one; and no absolute rule of distinction can be laid down and maintained.

103. The list of roots given by the Hindu grammarians contains about two thousand roots, without including all those which students of the language are compelled to recognize. Considerably more than half of this number, then, are unauthenticated by use; and although some of these may yet come to light, or may have existed without finding their way into any of the preserved literary documents, it is certain that most are fictitious: made in part for the explanation of words falsely described as their derivatives, but in the main for unknown and perhaps undiscoverable reasons.

a. The roots unauthenticated by traceable use will be made no account of in this grammar — or, if noticed, will be specified as of that character.

104. The forms of the roots as here used will be found to differ in certain respects from those given by the native grammarians and adopted by some European works. Thus:

a. Those roots of which the initial **n** and **s** are regularly converted to **ṇ** and **ṣ** after certain prefixes are by the Hindu grammarians given as beginning with **ṇ** and **ṣ**; no western authority follows this example.

b. The Hindus classify as simple roots a number of derived stems: reduplicated ones, as **dīdhī, jāgṛ, daridrā**; present-stems, as **ūrṇu**; and denominative stems, as **avadhīr, kumār, sabhāg, mantr, sāntv, arth,** and the like. These are in European works generally reduced to their true value.

c. A number of roots ending in an **ā** which is irregularly treated in the present-system are written in the Hindu lists with diphthongs — **e** or **āi** or **o**; here they will be regarded as **ā**-roots (see **251**). The **o** of such root-forms, especially, is purely arbitrary; no forms or derivatives made from the roots justify it.

d. The roots showing interchangeably **ṛ** and **ir** and **īr** or **ur** and **ūr** (**242**) are written by the Hindus with **ṛ** or with **ṝ**, or with both. The **ṝ** here also is only formal, intended to mark the roots as liable to certain modifications, since it nowhere shows itself in any form or derivative. Such roots will in this work be written with **ṛ**.

e. The roots, on the other hand, showing a variation between **ṛ** and **ar** (rarely **ra**) as weak and strong forms will be here written with **ṛ**, as by the native grammarians, although many European authorities prefer the other or strong form. So long as we write the unstrengthened vowel in **vid** and **çī**, in **mud** and **bhū**, and their like, consistency seems to require that we write it in **sṛj** and **kṛ** also — in all cases alike, without reference to what may have been the more original Indo-European form.

105. In many cases of roots showing more than one form, the selection of a representative form is a matter of comparative indifference. To deal with such cases according to their historical character is the part rather of an Indo-European comparative grammar than of a Sanskrit grammar. We must be content to accept as roots what elements seem to have on the whole that value in the existing condition of the language.

106. Stems as well as roots have their variations of form (**311**). The Hindu grammarians usually give the weaker form as the normal one, and derive the other from it by a strengthening change; some European authorities do the same, while others prefer the contrary method; the choice is of unessential consequence, and may be determined in any case by motives of convenience.

107. We shall accordingly consider first of all, in the present chapter, the euphonic principles and laws which govern the combination of the elements of words and of words as elements of the sentence; then will be taken up the subject of inflection, under the two heads of declension and conjugation; and an account of the classes of uninflected words will follow.

a. The formation of conjugational stems (tense and mode-stems; also participles and infinitive) will be taught, as is usual, in connection with the processes of conjugational inflection; that of uninflected words, in connection with the various classes of those words. But the general subject of derivation, or the formation of declinable stems, will be taken up by itself later (chap. XVII.); and it will be followed by an account of the formation of compound stems (chap. XVIII.).

108. It is by no means to be expected of beginners in the language that they will attempt to master the rules of euphonic combination in a body, before going on to learn the paradigms of inflection. On the contrary, the leading paradigms of declension may best be learned outright, without attention, or with only a minimum of attention, to euphonic rule. In taking up conjugation, however, it is practically, as well as theoretically, better to learn the forms as combinations of stem and ending, with attention to such laws of combination as apply in the particular cases concerned. The rules of external combination, governing the make-up of the sentence out of words, should be grappled with only when the student is prepared to begin the reading or the formation of sentences.

Principles of Euphonic Combination.

109. The rules of combination (saṁdhi *putting together*) are in some respects different, according as they apply —

a. to the internal make-up of a word, by the addition of derivative and inflectional endings to roots and stems;

b. to the more external putting together of stems to make compound stems, and the yet looser and more accidental collocation of words in the sentence.

c. Hence they are usually divided into rules of internal combination, and rules of external combination.

110. **In both classes of cases, however, the general principles of combination are the same — and likewise, to a great extent, the specific rules. The differences depend in part on the occurrence or non-occurrence of certain combinations in the one class or the other; in part, on the difference of treatment of the same sound as final of a root or of an ending, the former being more persistent than the latter, in part, on the occurrence in external combination of certain changes which are apparently phonetic but really historical; and, most frequent and conspicuous of all, on the fact that (157) vowels and semivowels and nasals exercise a sonantizing influence in external combination, but not in internal. Hence, to avoid unnecessary repetition as well as the separation of what really belongs together, the rules for both kinds of combination are given below in connection with one another.**

111. a. Moreover, before case-endings beginning with bh and s (namely, bhyām, bhis, bhyas, su), the treatment of the finals of stems is in general the same as in the combinations of words (pada) with one another — whence those endings are sometimes called pada-endings, and the cases they form are known as pada-cases.

b. The importance of this distinction is somewhat exaggerated by the ordinary statement of it. In fact, **dh** is the only sonant mute initial of an ending occurring in conjugation, as **bh** in declension; and the difference of their treatment is in part owing to the one coming into collision usually with the final of a root and the other of an ending, and in part to the fact that **dh**, as a dental, is more assimilable to palatals and linguals than **bh**. A more marked and problematic distinction is made between **su** and the verbal endings **si**, **sva**, etc., especially after palatal sounds and **ṣ**.

c. Further, before certain of the suffixes of derivation the final of a stem is sometimes treated in the same manner as that of a word in composition.

d. This is especially the case before secondary suffixes having a markedly distinct office, like the possessive **mant** and **vant**, the abstract-making **tva**, the suffix of material **maya**, and so on; and it is much more frequent in the later language than in the earlier. The examples are sporadic in character, and no rule can be given to cover them: for details, see the various suffixes, in chap. XVII. In the RV. (as may be mentioned here) the only examples are **vidyúnmant** (beside **garútmant**, **kakúdmant**, etc.), **pṛ́ṣadvant** (beside **datvánt**, **marútvant**, etc.), **dhṛṣadvín** (beside **namasvín** etc.), **çagmá** (beside **ajmá**, **idhmá**, etc.), **mṛnmáya** (beside **manasmáya** etc.), and **ahaṁyú**, **kiṁyú**, **çaṁyú**, and **aṅhoyú**, **duvoyú**, **áskṛdhoyu** (beside **namasyú**, **vacasyú**, etc.); and the AV. adds only **sáhovan** (RV. **sahā́van**).

112. The leading rules of internal combination (as already stated: **108**) are those which are of most immediate importance to a beginner in the language, since his first task is to master the principal paradigms of inflection; the rules of external combination may better be left untouched until he comes to dealing with words in sentences, or to translating. Then, however, they are indispensable, since the proper form of the words that compose the sentence is not to be determined without them.

a. The general principles of combination underlying the euphonic rules, and determining their classification, may be stated as follows:

113. Hiatus. In general, hiatus is forbidden; every syllable except the initial one of a sentence, or of a word or phrase not forming part of a sentence, must begin with a consonant (or with more than one).

a. For details, and for exceptions, see **125** ff.

b. In the earlier language, however, hiatus in every position was abundantly admitted. This appears plainly from the *mantras*, or metrical parts of the Veda, where in innumerable instances **y** and **v** are to be read as **i** and **u**, and, less often, a long vowel is to be resolved into two vowels, in order to make good the metre: e. g., **vāryāṇām** has to be read as **vā-ri-ā-ṇa-ām**, **svaçvyam** as **su-aç-vi-am**, and so on. In the Brāhmaṇas, also, we find **tvac, svar, dyāus** described as dissyllables, **vyāna** and **satyam** as trisyllables, **rājanya** as of four syllables, and the like. See further **129e**.

114. Deaspiration. An aspirate mute is liable to lose its aspiration, being allowed to stand unchanged only before a vowel or semivowel or nasal.

115. Assimilation. The great body of euphonic changes in Sanskrit, as elsewhere, falls under the general head of assimilation — which takes place both between sounds which are so nearly alike that the difference between them is too insignificant to be worth preserving, and between those which are so diverse as to be practically incompatible.

116. In part, assimilation involves the conversion of one sound to another of the same series, without change of articulating position; in part, it involves a change of position, or transfer to another series.

117. Of changes within the series, the most frequent and important occur in the adaptation of surd and sonant sounds to one another; but the nasals and **l** have also in certain cases their special assimilative influence. Thus;

a. In the two classes of non-nasal mutes and spirants, surd and sonant are wholly incompatible; no surd of either class can either precede or follow a sonant of either.

b. A mute, surd or sonant, is assimilated by being changed to its correspondent of the other kind; of the spirants, the surd **s** is the only one having a sonant correspondent, namely **r**, to which it is convertible in external combination (**164** ff.).

c. The nasals are more freely combinable: a nasal may either precede or follow a mute of either kind, or the sonant spirant **h**; it may also follow a surd spirant (sibilant); no nasal, however, ever precedes a sibilant in the interior of a word (it is changed instead to **anusvāra**); and in external combination their concurrence is usually avoided by insertion of a surd mute.

d. A semivowel has still less sonantizing influence; and a vowel least of all: both are freely preceded and followed by sounds of every other class, in the interior of a word.

e. Before a sibilant, however, is found, of the semivowels, only **r** and very rarely **l**. Moreover, in external combination, **r** is often changed to its surd correspondent **s**.

But

f. In composition and sentence-collocation, initial vowels and semivowels and nasals also require the preceding final to be sonant. And

g. Before a nasal and **l**, the assimilative process is sometimes carried further, by the conversion of a final mute to a nasal or **l** respectively.

118. Of conversions involving a change of articulate position, the most important are those of dental sounds to lingual, and, less often, to palatal. Thus:

a. The dental **s** and **n** are very frequently converted to **ṣ** and **ṇ** by the assimilating influence of contiguous or neighboring lingual sounds: the **s**, even by sounds — namely, **i**- and **u**-vowels and **k** — which have themselves no lingual character.

b. A non-nasal dental mute is (with a few exceptions in external combination) made lingual when it comes into collision with a lingual sound.

c. The dental mutes and sibilant are made palatal by a contiguous palatal.

But also:

d. A **m** (not radical) is assimilated to a following consonant, of whatever kind.

e. For certain anomalous cases, see **151**.

119. The euphonic combinations of the palatal mutes, the palatal sibilant, and the aspiration, as being sounds derived by phonetic alteration from more original gutturals (**42** ff.), are made peculiar

and complicated by two circumstances: their reversion to a guttural form (or the appearance of the unaltered guttural instead of them: 43); and the different treatment of j and h according as they represent one or another degree of alteration — the one tending, like c, more to the guttural reversion, the other showing, like ç, a more sibilant and lingual character.

120. The lingual sibilant ṣ, also of derivative character (from dental s), shows as radical final peculiar and problematic phenomena of combination.

121. Extension and abbreviation of consonant-groups. The native grammarians allow or require certain extensions, by duplication or insertion, of groups of consonants. And, on the other hand, abbreviation of certain other groups is allowed, and found often practised in the manuscripts.

122. Permitted Finals. The permitted occurrence of consonants at the end of a word is quite narrowly restricted. In general, only one consonant is allowed after the last vowel; and that must be neither the aspiration, nor a sibilant, nor a semivowel (save rarely ल् l), nor an aspirate mute, nor a sonant mute if not nasal, nor a palatal.

123. Increment and Decrement. Besides these more or less regular changes accompanying the combination of the parts that make up words, there is another class of a different character, not consisting in the mutual adaptations of the parts, but in strengthening or weakening changes of the parts themselves.

124. It is impossible to carry through a perfectly systematic arrangement of the detailed rules of euphonic combination, because the different varieties of euphonic change more or less overlap and intersect one another. The order observed below will be as follows:

1. Rules of vowel combination, for the avoidance of hiatus.
2. Rules as to permitted finals (since these underlie the further treatment of final consonants in external combination).
3. Rules for loss of aspiration of an aspirate mute.
4. Rules of surd and sonant assimilation, including those for final s and r.

5. **Rules for the conversion of dental sounds to lingual and palatal.**

6. **Rules for the changes of final nasals, including those in which a former final following the nasal re-appears in combination.**

7. **Rules regarding the special changes of the derivative sounds — the palatal mutes and sibilant, the aspiration, and the lingual sibilant.**

8. **Rules as to extension and abbreviation of consonant groups.**

9. **Rules for strengthening and weakening processes.**

Everywhere, rules for more sporadic and less classifiable cases will be given in the most practically convenient connection; and the Index will render what help is needed toward finding them.

Rules of Vowel Combination.

125. The concurrence of two vowels, or of vowel and diphthong, without intervening consonant, is forbidden by the euphony of the later or classical language. It is avoided, according to the circumstances of the case, either by fusion of the two concurrent sounds into one, by the reduction of one of them to a semivowel, or by development of a semivowel between them.

a. For the not infrequent cases of composition and sentence-combination in which the recent loss of a **s** or **y** or **v** between vowels leaves a permanent hiatus, see below, **132** ff., **175—7**; for certain final vowels which are maintained unchanged in sentence-combination before an initial vowel, see **138**.

b. A very few words in their admitted written form show interior hiatus; such are **títaü** *sieve* (perhaps for **titasu**, BR.), **práüga** *wagon-pole* (for **prayuga**); and, in RV., **suūtí**.

c. The texts of the older dialect are written according to the euphonic rules of the later language, although in them (see **113b**) the hiatus is really of frequent occurrence. Hence they are not to be read as written, but with constantly recurring reversal of the processes of vowel-combination which they have been made artificially to undergo. See further **129e**.

d. Also in the later language, hiatus between the two **pādas** or primary divisions of a metrical line is tolerably frequent, and it is not unknown in sporadic cases even in the interior of a **pāda**.

e. The rules of vowel combination, as regards both the resulting sound and its accent, are nearly the same in internal and in external **saṁdhi**.

126. Two similar simple vowels, short or long, coalesce and form the corresponding long vowel: thus, two a-vowels (either or both of them short or long) form आ ā; two i-vowels, ई ī; two u-vowels, ऊ ū; and, theoretically, two ṛ-vowels form ॠ ṝ, but it is questionable whether the case ever practically occurs. Examples are:

स चाप्रजः sa cā 'prajaḥ (ca + aprajaḥ);

अतीव atī 'va (ati + iva);

सूक्तम् sūktam (su-uktam);

राजासीत् rājā "sīt (rājā + āsīt);

अधीश्वरः adhīçvaraḥ (adhi-īçvaraḥ);

जुहूपभृत् juhūpabhṛt (juhū — upabhṛt).

a. As the above examples indicate, it will be the practice everywhere in this work, in transliteration (not in the devanāgarī text), to separate independent words; and if an initial vowel of a following word has coalesced with a final of the preceding, this will be indicated by an apostrophe — single if the initial vowel be the shorter, double if it be the longer, of the two different initials which in every case of combination yield the same result.

127. An a-vowel combines with a following i-vowel to ए e; with an u-vowel, to ओ o; with ऋ ṛ, to अर् ar; with ऌ ḷ (theoretically), to अल् al; with ए e or ऐ āi, to ऐ āi; with ओ o or औ āu, to औ āu. Examples are:

राजेन्द्र rājendra (rāja-indra);

हितोपदेशः hitopadeçaḥ (hita-upadeçaḥ);

महर्षिः maharṣiḥ (mahā-ṛṣiḥ);

सैव sāi 'va (sā + eva);

राजैश्वर्यम् rājāiçvaryam (rāja-āiçvaryam);

दिवौकसः divāukasaḥ (divā-okasaḥ);

ज्वरौषधम् jvarāuṣadham (jvara-āuṣadham).

a. In the Vedic texts, the vowel ṛ is ordinarily written unchanged after the a-vowel, which, if long, is shortened: thus, maharṣiḥ instead of maharṣiḥ. The two vowels, however, are usually pronounced as one syllable.

b. When successive words like indra ā ihi are to be combined, the first combination, to indrā, is made first, and the result is indre " 'hi (not indrāi " 'hi, from indra e 'hi).

128. As regards the accent of these vowel combinations, it i to be noticed that, 1. as a matter of course, the union of acute witl acute yields acute, and that of grave with grave yields grave; that of circumflex with circumflex cannot occur; 2. a circumflex with following acute yields acute, the final grave element of the former being raised to acute pitch; a grave with following acute does the same, as no upward slide of the voice on a syllable is acknowledged in the language; but, 3. when the former of the fused elements is acute and the latter grave, we might expect the resulting syllable to be in general circumflex, to represent both the original tones. Pāṇini in fact allows this accent in every such case; and in a single accentuated Brāhmaṇa text (ÇB.), the circumflex is regularly written. But the language shows, on the whole, an indisposition to allow the circumflex to rest on either long vowel or diphthong as its sole basis, and the acute element is suffered to raise the other to its own level of pitch, making the whole syllable acute. The only exception to this, in most of the texts, is the combination of í and i, which becomes ì: thus, divì 'va, from diví iva; in the Tāittirīya texts alone such a case follows the general rule, while ú and u, instead, make ù: thus, sùdgātā from sú-udgātā.

129. The i-vowels, the u-vowels, and ऋ ṛ, before a dissimilar vowel or a diphthong, are regularly converted each into its own corresponding semivowel, य् y or व् v or र् r. Examples are:

इत्याह ity āha (iti + āha);

मध्विव madhv iva (madhu + iva);

दुहित्रर्थे duhitrarthe (duhitṛ-arthe);

स्त्र्यस्य stry asya (strī + asya);

वध्वै vadhvāi (vadhū-āi).

a. But in internal combination the i and u-vowels are not seldom changed instead to iy and uv — and this especially in monosyllables, or after two consonants, where otherwise a group of consonants difficult of pronunciation would be the result. The cases will be noticed below, in explaining inflected forms.

b. A radical i-vowel is converted into y even before i in perfect tense-inflection: so ninyima (ninī + ima).

c. In a few sporadic cases, i and u become iy and uv even in word-composition: e. g., triyavi (tri + avi), viyañga (vi + añga), suvita (su + ita): compare 1204b, c.

d. Not very seldom, the same word (especially as found in different texts of the older language) has more than one form, showing various treatment of an **i** or **u**-vowel: e. g. **svàr** or **súvar, tanvè** or **tanúve, budhnyà** or **budhníya, rā́tryāi** or **rā́triyāi.** For the most part, doubtless, these are only two ways of writing the same pronunciation, **sú-ar, budhní-a,** and so on; and the discordance has no other importance, historical or phonetic. There is more or less of this difference of treatment of an **i-** or **u**-element after a consonant in all periods of the language.

e. In the older language, there is a marked difference, in respect to the frequency of vowel-combination for avoiding hiatus as compared with that of non-combination and consequent hiatus, between the class of cases where two vowel-sounds, similar or dissimilar, would coalesce into one (**126, 127**) and that where an **i-** or **u**-vowel would be converted into a semivowel. Thus, in word-composition, the ratio of the cases of coalesced vowels to those of hiatus are in RV. as five to one, in AV. as nineteen to one, while the cases of semivowel-conversion are in RV. only one in twelve, in AV. only one in five; in sentence-combination, the cases of coalescence are in both RV. and AV. about as seven to one, while those of semivowel-conversion are in RV. only one in fifty, in AV. one in five.

f. For certain cases of the loss or assimilation of **i** and **u** before **y** and **v** respectively, see **233a.**

130. As regards the accent — here, as in the preceding case (**128**), the only combination requiring notice is that of an acute **i-** or **u**-vowel with a following grave: the result is circumflex; and such cases of circumflex are many times more frequent than any and all others. Examples are:

व्युंष्टि **vyùṣṭi** (ví-uṣṭi); अभ्यंर्चति **abhyàrcati;**

नद्यौं **nadyāù** (nadí-āu);

स्विंष्ट **sviṣṭa** (sú-iṣṭa); तन्वंस् **tanvàs** (tanū́-as).

a. Of a similar combination of acute **ṛ́** with following grave, only a single case has been noted in accented texts: namely, **vijñātr ètát** (i. e. **vijñātṛ́ etát**: CB. xiv. 6. 8[11]); the accentuation is in accordance with the rules for **i** and **u**.

131. Of a diphthong, the final **i-** or **u**-element is changed to its corresponding semivowel, य् **y** or व् **v**, before any vowel or diphthong: thus, ए **e** (really **ai**: **28a**) becomes अय् **ay**, and ओ **o** (that is, **au**: **28a**) becomes अव् **av**; ऐ **āi** becomes आय् **āy**, and औ **āu** becomes आव् **āv**.

a. No change of accent, of course, occurs here; each original syllable retains its syllabic identity, and hence also its own tone.

b. Examples can be given only for internal combination, since in external combination there are further changes: see the next paragraph. Thus,

नय **naya** (ne-a); नाय **nāya** (nāi-a);

भव **bhava** (bho-a); भाव **bhāva** (bhāu-a).

132. In external combination, we have the important additional rule that the semivowel resulting from the conversion of the final element of a diphthong is in general dropped; and the resulting hiatus is left without further change.

133. That is to say, a final ए **e** (the most frequent case) becomes simply अ **a** before an initial vowel (except अ **a**: see **135**, below), and both then remain unchanged; and a final ऐ **āi**, in like manner, becomes (everywhere) आ **ā**. Thus,

त आगताः **ta āgatāḥ** (te + āgatāḥ);
नगर इह **nagara iha** (nagare + iha);
तस्मा अददात् **tasmā adadāt** (tasmāi + adadāt);
स्त्रिया उक्तम् **striyā uktam** (striyāi + uktam).

a. The later grammarians allow the **y** in such combinations to be either retained or dropped; but the uniform practice of the manuscripts, of every age, in accordance with the strict requirement of the Vedic grammars (Prātiçākhyas), is to omit the semivowel and leave the hiatus.

b. The persistence of the hiatus caused by this omission is a plain indication of the comparatively recent loss of the intervening consonantal sound.

c. Instances, however, of the avoidance of hiatus by combination of the remaining final vowel with the following initial according to the usual rules are met with in every period of the language, from the RV. down; but they are rare and of sporadic character. Compare the similar treatment of the hiatus after a lost final **s**, **176—7**.

d. For the peculiar treatment of this combination in certain cases by the MS., see below, **176 d**.

134. a. The diphthong **o** (except as phonetic alteration of final **as**: see **175 a**) is an unusual final, appearing only in the stem **go** (**361 c**), in the voc. sing. of **u**-stems (**341**), in words of which the final **a** is combined with the particle u, as atho, and in a few interjections. In the last two classes it is uncombinable (below, **138 c, f**); the vocatives sometimes retain the **v** and sometimes lose it (the practices of different texts are too different to be briefly stated); go (in composition only) does not ordinarily lose its final element, but remains **gav** or **go**. A final **as** becomes **a**, with following hiatus, before any vowel save **a** (for which, see the next paragraph).

b. The व् v of आव् āv from औ āu is usually retained: thus,

तावेव tāv eva (tāu + eva);

उभाविन्द्राग्नी ubhāv indrāgnī (ubhāu + indrāgnī).

c. In the older language, however, it is in some texts dropped before an u-vowel: thus, **tā́ ubhāú**; in other texts it is treated like **āi**, or loses its **u**-element before every initial vowel: thus, **tā́ evá, ubhā́ indrāgnī́.**

135. After final ए e or ओ o, an initial अ a disappears.

a. The resulting accent is as if the a were not dropped, but rather absorbed into the preceding diphthong, having its tone duly represented in the combination. If, namely, the e or o is grave or circumflex and the a acute, the former becomes acute; if the e or o is acute and the a grave, the former becomes circumflex, as usually in the fusion of an acute and a grave element. If both are acute or both grave, no change, of course, is seen in the result. Examples are:

ते ऽब्रुवन् tè 'bruvan (té abruvan);

सो ऽब्रवीत् sò 'bravīt (sáḥ abravīt);

हिंसितव्यो ऽग्निः hiṅsitavyò 'gníḥ (hiṅsitavyàḥ agníḥ);

यदिन्द्रो ऽब्रवीत् yád indró 'bravīt (yád índraḥ ábravīt);

यद्राजन्यो ऽब्रवीत् yád rājanyó 'bravīt (yád rājanyàḥ ábravīt).

b. As to the use of the **avagraha** sign in the case of such an elision, see above, **16.** In transliteration, the reversed apostrophe, or rough breathing, will be used in this work to represent it.

c. This elision or absorption of initial **a** after final **e** or **o**, which in the later language is the invariable rule, is in the Veda only an occasional occurrence. Thus, in the RV., out of nearly 4500 instances of such an initial **a**, it is, as the metre shows, to be really omitted only about seventy times; in the AV., less than 300 times out of about 1600. In neither work is there any accordance in respect to the combination in question between the written and spoken form of the text: in RV., the **a** is (as written) elided in more than three quarters of the cases; in AV., in about two thirds; and in both texts it is written in a number of instances where the metre requires its omission.

d. In a few cases, an initial **ā** is thus elided, especially that of **ātman.**

e. To the rules of vowel combination, as above stated, there are certain exceptions. Some of the more isolated of these will be

noticed where they come up in the processes of inflection etc.; a few require mention here.

136. In internal combination:

a. The augment **a** makes with the initial vowel of a root the combinations **āi, āu, ār** (**vṛddhi**-vowels: **235**), instead of **e, o, ar** (**guṇa**-vowels), as required by **127**: thus, **āita** (**a + ita**), **āubhnāt** (**a + ubhnāt**), **ārdhnot** (**a + ṛdhnot**).

b. The final **o** of a stem (**1203a**) becomes **av** before the suffix **ya** (originally **ia**: **1210a**).

c. The final vowel of a stem is often dropped when a secondary suffix is added (**1203a**).

d. For the weakening and loss of radical vowels, and for certain insertions, see below, **249** ff., **257—8**.

137. In external combination:

a. The final **a** or **ā** of a preposition, with initial **ṛ** of a root, makes **ār** instead of **ar**: Thus, **ārchati** (**ā + ṛchati**), **avārchati** (**ava + ṛchati**), **upārṣati** (ÇB.: **upa + ṛṣati**; but AV. **uparṣanti**).

b. Instances are occasionally met with of a final **a** or **ā** being lost entirely before initial **e** or **o**: thus, in verb-forms, **av' eṣyāmas** AB., **up' eṣatu** etc. AV.; in derivatives, as **upetavya, upetṛ**; in compounds, as **daçoni, yathetam**, and (permissibly) compounds with **oṣṭha** (not rare), **otu** (not quotable), **odana**, as **adharoṣṭha** or **adharāuṣṭha, tilodana** or **tilāudana**; and even in sentence-combination, as **iv' etayas, açvin' eva, yath' ociṣe** (all RV.), **tv' eman** and **tv' odman** B.; and always with the exclamation **om** or **oṁkāra**.

c. The form **ūh** from √**vah** sometimes makes the heavier or **vṛddhi** (**235**) diphthongal combination with a preceding **a**-vowel: thus, **prāuḍhi, akṣāuhiṇī** (from **pra + ūḍhi**, etc.).

138. Certain final vowels, moreover, are uncombinable (**pragṛhya**), or maintain themselves unchanged before any following vowel. Thus,

a. The vowels **ī, ū**, and **e** as dual endings, both of declensional and of conjugational forms. Thus, **bandhū āsāte imāu; girī ārohatam**.

b. The pronoun **amī** (nom. pl.: **501**); and the Vedic pronominal forms **asmé, yuṣmé, tvé** (**492 a**).

c. A final **o** made by combination of a final **a**-vowel with the particle **u** (**1122b**): thus, **atho, mo, no**.

d. A final **ī** of a Vedic locative case from an **i**-stem (**336f**).

e. A protracted final vowel (**78**).

f. The final, or only, vowel of an interjection, as **aho, he, ā, i, u**.

g. The older language shows occasional exceptions to these rules: thus, a dual **ī** combined with a following **i**, as **nṛpátī 'va**; an **a** elided after **o**, as **átho 'si**; a locative **ī** turned into a semivowel, as **védy asyām**.

Permitted Finals.

139. The sounds allowed to occur as finals in Sanskrit words standing by themselves (not in euphonic combination with something following) are closely limited, and those which would etymologically come to occupy such a position are often variously altered, in general accordance with their treatment in other circumstances, or are sometimes omitted altogether.

a. The variety of consonants that would ever come at the end of either an inflected form or a derivative stem in the language is very small: namely, in forms, only **t** (or **d**), **n**, **m**, **s**; in derivative stems, only **t**, **d**, **n**, **r**, **s** (and, in a few rare words, **j**). But almost all consonants occur as finals of roots; and every root is liable to be found, alone or as last member of a compound, in the character of a declined stem.

140. All the vowel sounds, both simple and diphthongal, may be sounded at the end of a word.

a. But neither **ṝ** nor **ḹ** ever actually occurs; and **ṛ** is rare (only as neuter sing. of a stem in **ṛ** or **ar**, or as final of such a stem in composition).

Thus, **índra**, **çiváyā**, **ákāri**, **nadī́**, **dā́tu**, **camū́**, **janayitṛ́**, **ágne**, **çivā́yāi**, **vā́yo**, **agnāú**.

141. Of the non-nasal mutes, only the first in each series, the non-aspirate surd, is allowed; the others — surd aspirate, and both sonants — whenever they would etymologically occur, are converted into this.

Thus, **agnimát** for **agnimáth**, **suhṛ́t** for **suhṛ́d**, **vīrút** for **vīrúdh**, **triṣṭúp** for **triṣṭúbh**.

a. In a few roots, when their final (sonant aspirate) thus loses its aspiration, the original sonant aspiration of the initial reappears: compare ह **h**, below, **147**.

Thus, **dagh** becomes **dhak**, **budh** becomes **bhut**, and so on.

The roots exhibiting this change are stated below, **155**.

b. There was some question among the Hindu grammarians as to whether the final mute is to be estimated as of surd or of sonant quality; but the great weight of authority, and the invariable practice of the manuscripts, favor the surd.

142. The palatals, however, form here (as often elsewhere) an exception to the rules for the other mutes. No palatal is allowed as final. The च् c reverts (**43**) to its original क् k: thus, वाक् **vák**, अंहोमुक् **aṅhomúk**. The छ् **ch** (only quotable in the root प्रछ् **prach**) becomes ट् ṭ: thus, प्राट् **prāṭ**. The ज् j either reverts to its original guttural or becomes ट् ṭ, in accordance with its treatment in other combinations (**219**): thus, भिषक् **bhiṣák**, विराट् **virā́ṭ**. The झ् **jh** does not occur, but is by the native grammarians declared convertible to ट् ṭ.

143. Of the nasals, the म् m and न् n are extremely common, especially the former (म् m and स् s are of all final consonants the most frequent); the ण् ṇ is allowed, but is quite rare; ङ् ṅ is found (remaining after the loss of a following क् k) in a very small number of words (**386 b, c, 407 a**); ञ् ñ never occurs.

a. But the final m of a root is changed to n (compare **212 a**, below): thus, **akran** from **kram**, **ágan**, **ajagan**, **aganīgan** from **gam**, **ánān** from **nam**, **ayān** from **yam**, **praçān** from **çam**; no other cases are quotable.

144. Of the semivowels, the ल् l alone is an admitted final, and it is very rare. The र् r is (like its nearest surd correspondent, स् **s**: **145**) changed as final to **visarga**. Of य् **y** and व् v there is no occurrence.

145. Of the sibilants, none may stand unaltered at the end of a word. The स् s (which of all final consonants would otherwise be the commonest) is, like र् **r**, changed to a breathing, the **visarga**. The श् ç either reverts (**43**) to its original क् k, or, in some roots, is changed to ट् ṭ (in accordance with its changes in inflection and derivation: see below, **218**): thus, दिक् **dik**, but विट् **viṭ**. The ष् ṣ is likewise changed to ट् ṭ: thus, प्रावृट् **prāvṛṭ**.

a. The change of ṣ to ṭ is of rare occurrence: see below, **226 d**.

b. Final radical **s** is said by the grammarians to be changed to **t**; but no sure example of the conversion is quotable: see **168**; and compare **555a.**

146. The compound क्ष् **kṣ** is prescribed to be treated as simple ष् **ṣ** (not becoming क् **k** by **150**, below). But the case is a rare one, and its actual treatment in the older language irregular.

a. In the only RV. cases where the **kṣ** has a quasi-radical character — namely **anák** from **anákṣ**, and **ámyak** from √**myakṣ** — the conversion is to **k**. Also, of forms of the **s**-aorist (see **890**), we have **adhāk, asrāk, arāik**, etc. (for **adhākṣ-t** etc.); but also **aprāṭ, ayāṭ, avāṭ, asrāṭ** (for **aprākṣ-t** etc.). And RV. has twice **ayās** from √**yaj**, and AV. twice **srās** from √**sṛj** (wrongly referred by BR. to √**sraṅs**), both 2d sing., where the personal ending has perhaps crowded out the root-final and tense-sign.

b. The numeral **ṣaṣ** *six* is perhaps better to be regarded as **ṣakṣ**, with its **kṣ** treated as **ṣ**, according to the accepted rule.

147. The aspiration ह् **h** is not allowed to maintain itself, but (like ज् **j** and श् **ç**) either reverts to its original guttural form, appearing as क् **k**, or is changed to ट् **ṭ** — both in accordance with its treatment in inflection: see below, **222.** And, also as in inflection, the original sonant aspiration of a few roots (given at **155b**) reappears when their final thus becomes deaspirated. Where the ह् **h** is from original ध् **dh** (**223e**), it becomes त् **t**.

148. The **visarga** and **anusvāra** are nowhere etymological finals; the former is only the substitute for an original final स् **s** or र् **r**; the latter occurs as final only so far as it is a substitute for म् **m** (**213h**).

149. Apart from the vowels, then, the usual finals, nearly in the order of their frequency, are : **ḥ**, म् **m**, न् **n**, त् **t**, क् **k**, प् **p**, ट् **ṭ**; those of only sporadic occurrence are ङ् **ṅ**, ल् **l**, ण् **ṇ**; and, by substitution, ं **ṁ**.

150. In general, only one consonant, of whatever kind, is allowed to stand at the end of a word; if two or more would etymologically occur there, the last is dropped, and again the last, and so on, till only one remains.

a. Thus, **tudants** becomes **tudant**, and this **tudan**; **udañc-s** becomes **udañk** (142), and this **udañ**; and **achāntst** (s-aor., 3d sing., of √**chand** [890 b]) is in like manner reduced to **achān**.

b. But a non-nasal mute, if radical and not suffixal, is retained after **r**: thus, **ū́rk** from **ūrj**, **várk** from √**vṛj**, **avart** from √**vṛt**, **ámārṭ** from √**mṛj**, **suhā́rt** from **suhārd**. The case is not a common one.

c. For relics of former double finals, preserved by the later language under the disguise of apparent euphonic combinations, see below, **207** ff.

151. Anomalous conversions of a final mute to one of another class are occasionally met with. Examples are:

a. Of final **t** to **k**: thus, 1. in a few words that have assumed a special value as particles, as **jyók**, **tāják** (beside **tāját**), **ṛ́dhak** (beside **ṛ́dhat**), **pṛ́thak**, **drāk**; and of kindred character is **khādagdánt** (TA.); 2. in here and there a verbal form, as **sāviṣak** (AV. and VS. Kāṇ.), **dambhiṣak** (Āpast.), **aviṣyak** (Pārask.), **āhalak** (VS. MS.; = **āharat**); 3. in root-finals or the **t** added to root-stems (**383** e), as **-dhṛk** for **-dhṛt** (Sūtras and later) at the end of compounds, **suçrúk** (TB.), **pṛkṣú** (SV.); and 4. we may further note here the anomalous **eñkṣva** (AB.; for **intsva**, √**idh**) and **avāksam** (AB.), and the feminines in **knī** from masculines in **ta** (**1176** d).

b. Of final **d** or **t** to a lingual: thus, **pad** in Vedic **paḍbhís**, **páḍgṛbhi**, **páḍbīça**; **upānáḍbhyām** (ÇB.); **vy avāṭ** (MS. iii. 4. 9; √**vas** *shine*), and perhaps **ápā 'rāṭ** (MS.; or √**raj**?).

c. Of **k** or **j** to **t**, in an isolated example or two, as **samyát**, **ásṛt**, **viçvasṛ́t** (TS. K.), and **prayátsu** (VS. TS.; AV. **-kṣu**).

d. In Tāittirīya texts, of the final of **anuṣṭúbh** and **triṣṭúbh** to a guttural: as, **anuṣṭúk ca**, **triṣṭúgbhis**, **anuṣṭúgbhyas**.

e. Of a labial to a dental: in **kakúd** for and beside **kakúbh**; in **saṁsṛ́dbhis** (TS.) from √**sṛp**; and in **adbhís**, **adbhyás**, from **ap** or **āp** (**393**). Excepting the first, these look like cases of dissimilation; yet examples of the combination **bbh** are not very rare in the older language: thus, **kakúbbhyām**, **triṣṭúbbhis**, **kakubbhaṇḍá**, **anuṣṭúb bhí**.

f. The forms **pratidhúṣas**, **-ṣā** (Tāittirīya texts) from **pratidúh** are isolated anomalies.

152. For all the processes of external combination — that is to say, in composition and sentence-collocation — a stem-final or word-final is in general to be regarded as having, not its etymological form, but that given it by the rules as to permitted finals. From this, however, are to be excepted the **s** and **r**: the various transformations of these sounds have nothing to do with the visarga to which as finals before a pause they have — doubtless at a comparatively recent period of phonetic history — come to be reduced. Words will everywhere in this work be written with final **s** or **r** instead of **ḥ**; and the rules of combination will be stated as for the two more original sounds, and not for the **visarga.**

Deaspiration.

153. An aspirate mute is changed to a non-aspirate before another non-nasal mute or before a sibilant; it stands unaltered only before a vowel or semivowel or nasal.

a. Such a case can only arise in internal combination, since the processes of external combination presuppose the reduction of the aspirate to a non-aspirate surd (**152**).

b. Practically, also, the rules as to changes of aspirates concern almost only the sonant aspirates, since the surd, being of later development and rarer occurrence, are hardly ever found in situations that call for their application.

154. Hence, if such a mute is to be doubled, it is doubled by prefixing its own corresponding non-aspirate.

a. But in the manuscripts, both Vedic and later, an aspirate mute is not seldom found written double — especially, if it be one of rare occurrence: for example (RV.), **akhkhalī, jájhjhatī.**

155. In a few roots, when a final sonant aspirate (घ् **gh,** ध् **dh,** भ् **bh;** also ह् **h,** as representing an original घ् **gh**) thus loses its aspiration, the initial sonant consonant (ग् **g** or द् **d** or ब् **b**) becomes aspirate.

a. That is to say, the original initial aspirate of such roots is restored, when its presence does not interfere with the euphonic law, of comparatively recent origin, which (in Sanskrit as in Greek) forbids a root to both begin and end with an aspirate.

b. The roots which show this peculiar change are:

in **gh** — **dagh**;

in **h** (for original **gh**) -- **dah, dih, duh, druh, dṛṅh, guh**; and also **grah** (in the later desiderative **jighṛkṣa**);

in **dh** — **bandh, bādh, budh**;

in **bh** — **dabh** (but only in the later desiderative **dhipsa,** for which the older language has **dipsa**).

c. The same change appears when the law as to finals causes the loss of the aspiration at the end of the root: see above, **141**.

d. But from **dah, duh, druh,** and **guh** are found in the Veda also forms without the restored initial aspirate: thus, **dakṣat; adukṣat; dudukṣa** etc.; **jugukṣa; mitradrúk.**

e. The same analogy is followed by **dadh,** the abbreviated substitute of the present-stem **dadhā,** from √**dhā (667),** in some of the forms of conjugation: thus, **dhatthas** from **dadh+thas, adhatta** from **adadh+ta, adhaddhvam** from **adadh+dhvam,** etc.

f. No case is met with of the throwing back of an aspiration upon combination with the 2d sing. impv. act. ending **dhi:** thus, **dugdhi, daddhi** (RV.), but **ḍhugdhvam, dhaddhvam.**

Surd and Sonant Assimilation.

156. Under this head, there is especially one very marked and important difference between the internal combinations of a root or stem with suffixes and endings, and the external combinations of stem with stem in composition and of word with word in sentence-making: namely —

157. a. In internal combination, the initial vowel or semivowel or nasal of an ending of inflection or derivation exercises no altering influence upon a final consonant of the root or stem to which it is added.

b. To this rule there are some exceptions: thus, some of the derivatives noted at **111 d;** final **d** of a root before the participial suffix **na (957 d);** and the forms noted below, **161 b.**

c. In external combination, on the other hand, an initial sonant of whatever class, even a vowel or semivowel or nasal, requires the conversion of a final surd to sonant.

d. It has been pointed out above (**152**) that in the rules of external combination only admitted finals, along with **s** and **r,** need be taken account of, all others being regarded as reduced to these before combining with initials.

158. Final vowels, nasals, and ऌ l are nowhere liable to change in the processes of surd and sonant assimilation.

a. The **r,** however, has a corresponding surd in **s,** to which it is sometimes changed in external combination, under circumstances that favor a surd utterance (**178**).

159. With the exceptions above stated, the collision of surd and sonant sounds is avoided in combinations — and, regularly and usually, by assimilating the final to the following initial, or by regressive assimilation.

Thus, in internal combination: **átsi, átti, atthás, attá** (√**ad** + **si** etc.); **çagdhí, çagdhvám** (√**çak** + **dhi** etc.); — in external combination, **ábhūd ayám, jyóg jīva, ṣáḍ açītáyaḥ, triṣṭúb ápi, dig-gaja, ṣaḍ-ahá, arcád-dhūma, bṛhád-bhānu, ab-já.**

160. If, however, a final sonant aspirate of a root is followed by त् t or थ् th of an ending, the assimilation is in the other direction, or progressive: the combination is made sonant, and the aspiration of the final (lost according to **153**, above) is transferred to the initial of the ending.

Thus, **gh** with **t** or **th** becomes **gdh**; **dh** with the same becomes **ddh**, as **buddhá** (√**budh** + **ta**), **runddhás** (√**rundh** + **thas** or **tas**); **bh** with the same becomes **bdh**, as **labdhá** (√**labh** + **ta**), **labdhvā́** (√**labh** + **tvā**).

a. Moreover, **h**, as representing original **gh**, is treated in the same manner: thus, **dugdhá, dógdhum** from **duh** — and compare **rūḍhá** and **līḍhá** from **ruh** and **lih**, etc., **222 b**.

b. In this combination, as the sonant aspiration is not lost but transferred, the restoration of the initial aspiration (**155**) does not take place.

c. In **dadh** from √**dhā** (**155 e**), the more normal method is followed; the **dh** is made surd, and the initial aspirated: thus, **dhatthas, dhattas.** And RV. has **dhaktam** instead of **dagdham** from √**dagh**; and TA. has **inttām** instead of **inddhām** from √**idh**.

161. Before a nasal in external combination, a final mute may be simply made sonant, or it may be still further assimilated, being changed to the nasal of its own class.

Thus, either **tád námas** or **tán námas, vā́g me** or **vā́ñ me, báḍ mahā́n** or **báṇ mahā́n, triṣṭúb nūnám** or **triṣṭúm nūnám.**

a. In practice, the conversion into a nasal is almost invariably made in the manuscripts, as, indeed, it is by the Prātiçākhyas required and not permitted merely. Even by the general grammarians it is required in the compound **ṣáṇṇavati**, and before **mātrā**, and the suffix **maya** (**1225**): thus, **vāṅmáya, mṛnmáya.**

b. Even in internal combination, the same assimilation is made in some of the derivatives noted at **111 d**, and in the **na**-participles (**957 d**). And a few sporadic instances are met with even in verb-inflection: thus,

stinnoti, stinnuyāt (MS.; for **stighn-**), **mr̥nnīta** (LÇS.; for **mr̥dn-**), **jāñmayana** (KS.; for **jāgm-**); these, however (like the double aspirates, **154 a**), are doubtless to be rejected as false readings.

162. Before **l**, a final **t** is not merely made sonant, but fully assimilated, becoming **l**: thus, **tál labhate, úlluptam.**

163. Before ह् **h** (the case occurs only in external combination), a final mute is made sonant; and then the ह् **h** may either remain unchanged or be converted into the sonant aspirate corresponding with the former: thus, either तद्धि **tád hi** or तद्धि **tád dhí.**

a. In practice, the latter method is almost invariably followed; and the grammarians of the Prātiçākhya period are nearly unanimous in requiring it. The phonetic difference between the two is very slight.

Examples are: **vā́g ghutáḥ, ṣáḍḍhotā** (**ṣaṭ + hotā**), **taddhita** (**tat + hita**), **anuṣṭúb bhí.**

Combinations of final स् s and र् r.

164. The euphonic changes of स् **s** and र् **r** are best considered together, because of the practical relation of the two sounds, in composition and sentence-collocation, as corresponding surd and sonant: in a host of cases स् **s** becomes र् **r** in situations requiring or favoring the occurrence of a sonant; and, much less often, र् **r** becomes स् **s** where a surd is required.

a. In internal combination, the two are far less exchangeable with one another: and this class of cases may best be taken up first.

165. Final **r** radical or quasi-radical (that is, not belonging to an ending of derivation) remains unchanged before both surd and sonant sounds, and even before **su** in declension: thus, **píparṣi, caturthá, catúrṣu, pūrṣú.**

166. Final radical **s** remains before a surd in general, and usually before **s**, as in **çā́ssi, çāssva, āsse, āçī́ṣṣu** (the last is also written **āçī́ḥṣu: 172**): but it is lost in **ási** (√**as + si: 636**). Before a sonant (that is, **bh**) in declension, it is treated as in external combination: thus, **āçī́rbhis.** Before a sonant (that is, **dh**) in conjugation, it appears to be dropped, at least after long **ā**: thus, **çādhi, çaçādhi, cakādhi** (the only quotable cases); in **edhí** (√**as + dhi: 636**) the root syllable is irregularly altered; but in 2d perss. pl., made with **dhvam**, as **ādhvam, çādhvam, arādhvam (881 a), vadhvam** (√**vas**

clothe), it is, on account of the equivalence and interchangeability of **dhv** and **ddhv** (**232**), impossible to say whether the **s** is omitted or converted into **d**.

a. Final radical **s** is very rare; RV. (twice, both 2d pers. sing.) treats **ághas** from √**ghas** in the same manner as any ordinary word ending in **as**.

b. For certain cases of irregular loss of the **s** of a root or tense-stem, see **233 b—e**.

167. In a very few cases, final radical **s** before **s** is changed to **t** (perhaps by dissimilation): they are, from √**vas** *dwell* (also sporadically from **vas** *shine*, ÇB., and **vas** *clothe*, Har.), the future **vatsyā́mi** and aorist **ávātsam**; from √**ghas**, the desiderative stem **jíghatsa**.

a. For **t** as apparent ending of the 3d sing. in **s**-verbs, see **555 a**.

168. According to the grammarians, the final **s** of certain other roots, used as noun-stems, becomes **t** at the end of the word, and before **bh** and **su**: thus, **dhvat, dhvadbhis, sradbhyas, sratsu**. But genuine examples of such change are not quotable.

a. Sporadic cases of a like conversion are found in the Veda: namely, **mādbhís** and **mādbhyás** from **mā́s**; **uṣádbhis** from **uṣás**; **svátavadbhyas** from **svátavas**; **svávadbhis** etc. (not quotable) from **svávas**. But the actuality of the conversion here is open to grave doubt; it rather seems the substitution of a **t**-stem for a **s**-stem. The same is true of the change of **vāṅs** to **vat** in the declension of perfect participles (**458**). The stem **anaḍvah** (**404**), from **anas-vah**, is anomalous and isolated.

b. In the compounds **ducchúnā** (**dus-çunā**) and **párucchepa** (**parus-çepa**), the final **s** of the first member is treated as if a **t** (**203**).

169. As the final consonant of derivative stems and of inflected forms, both of declension and of conjugation, **s** is extremely frequent; and its changes form a subject of first-rate importance in Sanskrit euphony. The **r**, on the other hand, is quite rare.

a. The **r** is found as original final in certain case-forms of stems in **ṛ** or **ar** (**369** ff.); in root-stems in **ir** and **ur** from roots in **ṝ** (**383 b**); in a small number of other stems, as **svàr, áhar** and **ū́dhar** (beside **áhan** and **ū́dhan**: **430**), **dvā́r** or **dur**, and the Vedic **vádhar, uṣar-, vasar-, vanar-, çrutar-, sapar-, sabar-, athar-** (cf. **176 c**); in a few particles, as **antár, prātár, púnar**; and in the numeral **catúr** (**482 g**).

b. The euphonic treatment of **s** and **r** yielding precisely the same result after all vowels except **a** and **ā**, there are certain forms with regard to which it is uncertain whether they end in **s** or **r**, and opinions differ respecting them. Such are **ur** (or **us**) of the gen.-abl. sing. of **ṛ**-stems (**371 c**), and **us** (or **ur**) of the 3d plur. of verbs (**550 c**).

170. a. The स् **s**, as already noticed (**145**), becomes **visarga** before a pause.

b. It is retained unchanged only when followed by त् **t** or थ् **th**, the surd mutes of its own class.

c. Before the palatal and lingual surd mutes — च् **c** and छ् **ch**, ट् **ṭ** and ठ् **ṭh** — it is assimilated, becoming the sibilant of either class respectively, namely श् **ç** or ष् **ṣ**.

d. Before the guttural and labial surd mutes — क् **k** and ख् **kh**, प् **p** and फ् **ph** — it is also theoretically assimilated, becoming respectively the **jihvāmūlīya** and **upadhmānīya** spirants (**69**); but in practice these breathings are unknown, and the conversion is to **visarga**.

Examples are: to **b. tatas te, cakṣus te**; to **c. tataç ca, tasyāç chāyā**; **pādaṣ ṭalati**; to **d. nalaḥ kāmam, puruṣaḥ khanati**; **yaçaḥ prāpa, vṛkṣaḥ phalavān.**

171. The first three of these rules are almost universal; to the last one there are numerous exceptions, the sibilant being retained (or, by **180**, converted into **ṣ**), especially in compounds; but also, in the Veda, even in sentence combination.

a. In the Veda, the retention of the sibilant in compounds is the general rule, the exceptions to which are detailed in the Vedic grammars.

b. In the later language, the retention is mainly determined by the intimacy or the antiquity and frequency of the combination. Thus, the final sibilant of a preposition or a word filling the office of a preposition before a verbal root is wont to be preserved; and that of a stem before a derivative of √**kṛ**, before **pati**, before **kalpa** and **kāma**, and so on. Examples are **namaskāra, vācaspati, āyuṣkāma, payaskalpa.**

c. The Vedic retention of the sibilant in sentence-collocation is detailed in full in the Prātiçākhyas. The chief classes of cases are: 1. the final of a preposition or its like before a verbal form; 2. of a genitive before a governing noun: as **divás putráḥ, iḍás padé**; 3. of an ablative before **pári**: as **himávatas pári**; 4. of other less classifiable cases: as **dyāúṣ pitā́, tríṣ pūtvā́, yás pátiḥ, paridhíṣ pátāti**, etc.

172. Before an initial sibilant — श् **ç**, ष् **ṣ**, स् **s** — स् **s** is either assimilated, becoming the same sibilant, or it is changed into **visarga**.

a. The native grammarians are in some measure at variance (see APr. ii. 40, note) as to which of these changes should be made, and in part they allow either at pleasure. The usage of the manuscripts is also discordant; the conversion to **visarga** is the prevalent practice, though the sibilant is also not infrequently found written, especially in South-Indian manuscripts. European editors generally write **visarga**; but the later dictionaries and glossaries generally make the alphabetic place of a word the same as if the sibilant were read instead.

Examples are: **manuḥ svayam** or **manus svayam; indraḥ çūraḥ** or **indraç çūraḥ; tāḥ ṣaṭ** or **tāṣ ṣaṭ.**

173. There are one or two exceptions to these rules:

a. If the initial sibilant has a surd mute after it, the final **s** may be dropped altogether — and by some authorities is required to be so dropped. Thus. **vāyava stha** or **vāyavaḥ stha; catustanām** or **catuḥ-stanām.** With regard to this point the usage of the different manuscripts and editions is greatly at variance.

b. Before **ts,** the **s** is allowed to become **visarga,** instead of being retained.

174. Before a sonant, either vowel or consonant (except र् **r**: see **179**), स् **s** is changed to the sonant र् **r** — unless, indeed, it be preceded by अ **a** or आ **ā**.

Examples are: **devapatir iva, çrīr iva; manur gacchati, tanūr apsu; svasṝr ajanayat; tayor adṛṣṭakāmaḥ; sarvāir guṇāiḥ; agner manve.**

a. For a few cases like **dūḍāça, dūṇāça,** see below, **199d.**

b. The exclamation **bhos** (**456**) loses its **s** before vowels and sonant consonants: thus, **bho nāiṣadha** (and the **s** is sometimes found omitted also before surds).

c. The endings अस् **as** and आस् **ās** (both of which are extremely common) follow rules of their own, namely:

175. a. Final अस् **as**, before any sonant consonant and before short अ **a**, is changed to ओ **o** — and the अ **a** after it is lost.

b. The resulting accentuation, and the fact that the loss of **a** is only occasional in the older language of the Veda, have been pointed out above, **135 a, c.**

Examples are: **nalo nāma, brahmaṇyo vedavit; manobhava; hantavyo 'smi; anyonya (anyas + anya), yaçortham (yaças + artham).**

c. Final अस् **as** before any other vowel than अ **a** loses its स् **s**, becoming simple अ **a**; and the hiatus thus occasioned remains.

d. That is to say, the **o** from **as** is treated as an original **e** is treated in the same situation: see **132—3**.

Examples are: **bṛhadaçva uvāca, āditya iva, námaüktí, vásyaïṣṭi.**

176. Exceptions to the rules as to final **as** are:

a. The nominative masculine pronouns **sás** and **eṣás** and (Vedic) **syás** (**495 a, 499 a, b**) lose their **s** before any consonant: thus, **sa dadarça** *he saw*, **eṣa puruṣaḥ** *this man*; but **so 'bravīt** *he said*, **puruṣa eṣaḥ**.

b. Instances are met with, both in the earlier and in the later language, of effacement of the hiatus after alteration of **as**, by combination of the remaining final **a** with the following initial vowel: thus, **tato 'vāca** (**tatas + uvāca**), **payoṣṇī** (**payas + uṣṇī**), **adhāsana** (**adhas + āsana**): compare **133 c, 177 b**. In the Veda, such a combination is sometimes shown by the metre to be required, though the written text has the hiatus. But **sa** in RV. is in the great majority of cases combined with the following vowel: e. g., **sé 'd** for **sá íd, sā́ 'smāi** for **sá asmāi, sāú 'ṣadhīḥ** for **sá óṣadhīḥ**; and similar examples are found also in the other Vedic texts.

c. Other sporadic irregularities in the treatment of final **as** occur. Thus, it is changed to **ar** instead of **o** once in RV. in **avás**, once in SV. in **ávas** (RV. **ávo**), once in MS. in **dambhiṣas**; in **bhuvas** (second of the trio of sacred utterances **bhūs, bhuvas, svar**), except in its earliest occurrences; in a series of words in a Brāhmaṇa passage (TS. K.), viz. **jinvár, ugrár, bhīmár, tveṣár, çrutár, bhūtár,** and (K. only) **pūtár**; in **janar** and **mahar**; and some of the **ar**-stems noted at **169 a** are perhaps of kindred character. On the other hand, **as** is several times changed to **o** in RV. before a surd consonant; and **sás** twice, and **yás** once, retains its final sibilant in a like position.

d. In MS., the final **a** left before hiatus by alteration of either **as** (**o**) or **e** (**133**) is made long if itself unaccented and if the following initial vowel is accented: thus, **sū́rā éti** (from **sū́ras + éti**), **nirupyátā índrāya** (from **-yáte + índ-**), and also **kāryā̀ éka-** (from **kāryàs**, because virtually **kāríās**); but **ādityá índraḥ** (from **ādityás + índraḥ**), **etá ítare** (from **eté + ítare**).

177. Final आस् **ās** before any sonant, whether vowel or consonant, loses its स् **s**, becoming simple आ **ā**; and a hiatus thus occasioned remains.

a. The maintenance of the hiatus in these cases, as in that of **o** and **e** and **āi** (above, **133—4**), seems to indicate a recent loss of the intermediate sound. Opinions are divided as to what this should have been. Some of the native grammarians assimilate the case of **ās** to that of **āi**, assuming the conversion to **āy** in both alike — but probably only as a matter of formal convenience in rule-making.

b. Here, too (as in the similar cases of **e** and **āi** and **o**: 133 c, 176 b), there are examples to be found, both earlier and later, of effacement of the hiatus.

178. Final र् **r**, in general, shows the same form which स् **s** would show under the same conditions.

a. Thus, it becomes **visarga** when final, and a sibilant or visarga before an initial surd mute or sibilant (170): thus, rudatī́ punaḥ, dvās tat, svàc ca, catúçcatvāriṅçat; and (111 c, d) prātastána, antastya, catuṣṭaya, dhūstva; prātaḥ karoti, antaḥpāta.

b. But original final **r** preceded by **a** or **ā** maintains itself unchanged before a sonant: thus, punar eti, prātarjit, ákar jyótiḥ, áhār dā́mnā, vā́rdhi.

c. The **r** is preserved unchanged even before a surd in a number of Vedic compounds: thus, aharpáti; svàrcanas, svàrcakṣas, svàrpati, svarṣā́, svàrṣāti; dhūrṣád, dhūrṣah; pū́rpati, vārkāryá, āçī́rpada, punartta; and in some of these the **r** is optionally retained in the later language. The RV. also has āvar támaḥ once in sentence-combination.

d. On the other hand, final **ar** of the verb-form **āvar** is changed to **o** before a sonant in several cases in RV. And **r** is lost, like **s**, in one or two cases in the same text: thus, akṣā́ índuḥ, áha evá.

179. A double **r** is nowhere admitted: if such would occur, either by retention of an original **r** or by conversion of **s** to **r**, one **r** is omitted, and the preceding vowel, if short, is made long by compensation.

Thus, punā ramate, nṛpatī rājati, mātū́ rihán, jyotīratha, dūrohaṇá.

a. In some Vedic texts, however, there are instances of **ar** changed to **o** before initial **r**: thus, svò rohāva.

Conversion of स् s to ष् ṣ.

180. The dental sibilant स् **s** is changed to the lingual ष् **ṣ**, if immediately preceded by any vowel save अ **a** and आ **ā**, or by क् **k** or र् **r** — unless the स् **s** be final, or followed by र् **r**.

a. The assimilating influence of the preceding lingual vowels and semivowel is obvious enough; that of **k** and the other vowels appears to be due to a somewhat retracted position of the tongue in the mouth during their utterance, causing its tip to reach the roof of the mouth more easily at a point further back than the dental one.

b. The general Hindu grammar prescribes the same change after a l also; but the Prātiçākhyas give no such rule, and phonetic considerations, the l being a dental sound, are absolutely against it. Actual cases of the combination do not occur in the older language, nor have any been pointed out in the later.

c. The vowels that cause the alteration of **s** to **ṣ** may be called for brevity's sake "alterant" vowels.

181. Hence, in the interior of a Sanskrit word, the dental **s** is not usually found after any vowel save **a** and **ā**, but, instead of it, the lingual **ṣ**. But —

a. A following **r** prevents the conversion: thus, **usra, tisras, tamisra.** And it is but seldom made in the forms and derivatives of a root containing an *r*-element (whether **r** or **ṛ**), whatever the position of that element: thus, **sisarti, sisṛtam, sarīsṛpá, tistire, parisrút.** To this rule there are a few exceptions, as **viṣṭír, viṣṭārá, níṣṭṛta, víṣpardhas, gáviṣṭhira,** etc. In **ajuṣran** the final **ṣ** of a root is preserved even immediately before **r.**

b. This dissimilating influence of a following **r**, as compared with the invariable assimilating influence of a preceding **r**, is peculiar and problematical.

c. The recurrence of **ṣ** in successive syllables is sometimes avoided by leaving the former **s** unchanged: thus, **sisakṣi,** but **siṣakti; yāsisīṣṭhās,** but **yāsiṣīmahi.** Similarly, in certain desiderative formations: see below, **184 e.**

d. Other cases are sporadic: RV. has the forms **sisice** and **sisicus** (but **siṣicatus**), and the stems **ṛbīsa, kīstá, bísa, busá, bṛsaya;** a single root **pis,** with its derivative **pesuka,** is found once in ÇB.; MS. has **mṛsmṛṣā́; músala** begins to be found in AV.; and such cases grow more numerous; for **puṅs** and the roots **niṅs** and **hiṅs,** see below, **183 a.**

182. On the other hand (as was pointed out above, **62**), the occurrence of **ṣ** in Sanskrit words is nearly limited to cases falling under this rule: others are rather sporadic anomalies — except where **ṣ** is the product of **ç** or **kṣ** before a dental, as in **draṣṭum, caṣṭe, tvaṣṭar:** see **218, 221.** Thus, we find —

a. Four roots, **kaṣ, laṣ, bhaṣ, bhāṣ,** of which the last is common and is found as early as the Brāhmaṇas.

b. Further, in RV., **áṣa, kaváṣa, caṣā́la, cā́ṣa, jálāṣa, pāṣyà, baṣkáya, váṣaṭ** (for **vakṣat**?), **kā́ṣṭhā;** and, by anomalous alteration of original **s, -ṣāh** (**turāṣā́h** etc.), **áṣāḍha, upaṣṭút,** and probably **apāṣṭhá** and **aṣṭhīvánt.** Such cases grow more common later.

c. The numeral **ṣaṣ,** as already noted (**146 b**), is more probably **ṣakṣ.**

183. The nasalization of the alterant vowel — or, in other words, its being followed by **anusvāra** — does not prevent its altering effect upon the sibilant: thus, **haviṅṣi, parūṅṣi.** And the alteration takes place in the initial **s** of an ending after the final **s** of a stem, whether the latter be regarded as also changed to **ṣ** or as converted into **visarga**: thus, **haviṣṣu** or **haviḥṣu, paruṣṣu** or **paruḥṣu.**

a. But the **s** of **puṅs (394)** remains unchanged, apparently on account of the retained sense of its value as **puṅs;** also that of √**hiṅs,** because of its value as **hins (hinasti** etc.); √**niṅs** (RV. only) is more questionable.

184. The principal cases of alteration of **s** in internal combination are these:

a. In endings, inflectional or derivative, beginning with **s** — thus, **su; si, se, sva; s** of sibilant-aorist, future, and desiderative; suffixes **sna, snu, sya,** etc. — after a final alterant vowel or consonant of root or stem, or a union-vowel: thus, **juhoṣi, çeṣe, anāiṣam, bhaviṣyāmi, çuçrūṣe, deṣṇa, jiṣṇu, vikṣu, akārṣam.**

b. The final **s** of a stem before an ending or suffix: thus, **haviṣā, haviṣas,** etc., from **havis; çakṣuṣmant, çociṣka, mānuṣa, manuṣya, jyotiṣṭva.**

c. Roots having a final sibilant (except **ç**) after an alterant vowel are — with the exception of fictitious ones and **pis, niṅs, hiṅs** — regarded as ending in **ṣ,** not **s;** and concerning the treatment of this **ṣ** in combination, see below, **225—6.**

d. The initial **s** of a root after a reduplication: thus, **siṣyade, suṣvāpa, siṣāsati, coṣkūyate, saniṣvaṇat.**

e. Excepted is in general an initial radical **s** in a desiderative stem, when the desiderative-sign becomes **ṣ:** thus, **sisīrṣati** from √**sṛ, sisaṅkṣati** from √**sañj.** And there are other scattering cases, as **tresus** (perf. from √**tras**), etc.

185. But the same change occurs also, on a considerable scale, in external combination, especially in composition. Thus:

a. Both in verbal forms and in derivatives, the final **i** or **u** of a preposition or other like prefix ordinarily lingualizes the initial **s** of the root to which it is prefixed; since such combinations are both of great frequency and of peculiar intimacy, analogous with those of root or stem and affix: thus, **abhiṣā́c, pratiṣṭhā́, níṣikta, víṣita; anuṣvadhám, suṣéka;** the cases are numberless.

b. The principal exceptions are in accordance with the principles already laid down: namely, when the root contains an *r*-element, and when a recurrence of the sibilant would take place. But there are also others, of a more irregular character; and the complete account of the treatment of initial radical **s** after a prefix would be a matter of great detail, and not worth giving here.

c. Not infrequently, the initial **s**, usually altered after a certain prefix, retains the altered sibilant even after an interposed **a** of augment or reduplication: thus, **aty aṣṭhāt, abhy aṣṭhām, pary aṣasvajat, vy aṣahanta, ny aṣadāma, ṇir aṣṭhāpayan, abhy aṣiñcan, vy aṣṭabhnāt; vi taṣṭhe, vi taṣṭhire.**

d. Much more anomalous is the occasional alteration of initial radical **s** after an **a**-element of a prefix. Such cases are **ava ṣṭambh** (against **ni stambh** and **prati stambh**) and (according to the grammarians) **ava ṣvan.**

186. In other compounds, the final alterant vowel of the first member not infrequently (especially in the Veda) lingualizes the initial **s** of the second: for example, **yudhiṣṭhira, pitṛṣvasṛ, goṣṭhá, agniṣṭomá, anuṣṭúbh, tríṣaṁdhi, diviṣád, parameṣṭhín, abhiṣeṇá, pitṛṣád, puruṣṭutá.**

a. A very few cases occur of the same alteration after an **a**-element: thus, **saṣṭúbh, avaṣṭambha, savyaṣṭhá, apāṣṭhá, upaṣṭút;** also √**sah,** when its final, by **147,** becomes **ṭ**: thus, **satrāṣā́ṭ** (but **satrāsā́ham**).

187. The final **s** of the first member of a compound often becomes **ṣ** after an alterant vowel: thus, the **s** of a prepositional prefix, as **niṣṣídhvan, duṣṭára** (for **duṣṣṭára**), **āvíṣkṛta;** and, regularly, a **s** retained instead of being converted to visarga before a labial or guttural mute (**171 a**), as **haviṣpā́, jyotiṣkṛ́t; tapuṣpā́.**

188. Once more, in the Veda, the same alteration, both of an initial and of a final **s**, is not infrequent even between the words composing a sentence. The cases are detailed in the Prātiçākhya belonging to each text, and are of very various character. Thus:

a. The initial **s**, especially of particles: as **ū ṣú, hí ṣma, kám u ṣvít;** — also of pronouns: as **hí ṣáḥ;** — of verb-forms, especially from √**as**: as **hí ṣṭhá, diví ṣṭha;** — and in other scattering cases: as **u ṣṭuhi, nū́ ṣthirám, trī́ ṣadhásthā, ádhi ṣṇóḥ, nákiḥ ṣáḥ, yájuḥ ṣkannám, agníḥ ṣṭave.**

b. A final **s**, oftenest before pronouns (especially toneless ones): as **agniṣ ṭvā, niṣ ṭe, īyúṣ ṭé, çúciṣ ṭvám, sádhiṣ ṭáva;** — but also in other cases, and wherever a final **s** is preserved, instead of being turned into visarga, before a guttural or labial (**171**): as **tríṣ pūtvā́, ā́yuṣ kṛṇotu, vā́stoṣ pátiḥ, dyāuṣ pitā́, víbhiṣ pátat.**

Conversion of न् n to ण् ṇ.

189. The dental nasal न् n, when immediately followed by a vowel or by न् n or म् m or य् y or व् v, is turned into the lingual ण् ṇ if preceded in the same word by the lingual sibilant or semivowel or vowels — that is to say, by ष ṣ, र r, or ऋ ṛ or ॠ ṝ —: and this, not only if the altering letter stands immediately before the nasal, but at whatever distance from the latter it may be found: unless, indeed, there intervene (a consonant moving the front of the tongue: namely) a palatal (except य y), a lingual, or a dental.

a. We may thus figure to ourselves the *rationale* of the process: in the marked proclivity of the language toward lingual utterance, especially of the nasal, the tip of the tongue, when once reverted into the loose lingual position by the utterance of a non-contact lingual element, tends to hang there and make its next nasal contact in that position; and does so, unless the proclivity is satisfied by the utterance of a lingual mute, or the organ is thrown out of adjustment by the utterance of an element which causes it to assume a different posture. This is not the case with the gutturals or labials, which do not move the front part of the tongue (and, as the influence of **k** on following **s** shows, the guttural position favors the succession of a lingual): and the **y** is too weakly palatal to interfere with the alteration (as its next relative, the **i**-vowel, itself lingualizes a **s**).

b. This is a rule of constant application; and (as was pointed out above, **46**) the great majority of occurrences of ṇ in the language are the result of it.

190. The rule has force especially —

a. When suffixes, of inflection or derivation, are added to roots or stems containing one of the altering sounds: thus, **rudréṇa, rudrā́ṇām, vā́riṇe, vā́riṇī, vā́rīṇi, dātṝṇi, hárāṇi, dvéṣāṇi, krīṇā́mi, çṛṇóti, kṣubhāṇá, ghṛṇá, kárṇa, vṛkṇá, rugṇá, dráviṇa, iṣáṇi, purāṇá, réknas, cákṣaṇa, cíkīrṣamāṇa, kṛ́pamāṇa.**

b. When the final **n** of a root or stem comes to be followed, in inflection or derivation, by such sounds as allow it to feel the effect of a preceding altering cause: thus, from √**ran, ráṇanti, ráṇyati, rāraṇa, arāṇiṣus**; from **brahman, bráhmaṇā, bráhmāṇi, brāhmaṇá, brahmaṇyà, bráhmaṇvant.**

c. The form **piṇak** (RV.: 2d and 3d sing. impf.), from √**piṣ**, is wholly anomalous.

191. This rule (like that for the change of **s** to **ṣ**) applies strictly and especially when the nasal and the cause of its alteration both lie within the limits of the same integral word; but (also like the other) it is extended, within certain limits, to compound words — and even, in the Veda, to contiguous words in the sentence.

192. **Especially, a preposition or similar prefix to a root, if it contain r or end in euphonic r for s (174), very often lingualizes the n of a root or of its derived stems and forms. Thus:**

a. The initial **n** of a root is usually and regularly so altered, in all forms and derivatives, after **parā, pari, pra, nir** (for **nis**), **antar, dur** (for **dus**): thus, **párā ṇaya, pári ṇīyate, prá ṇudasva; parāṇutti, pariṇāma, praṇavá, nirṇíj, durṇáça.** Roots suffering this change are written with initial **ṇ** in the native root-lists. The only exceptions of importance are **nṛt, nabh, nand,** and **naç** when its **ç** becomes **ṣ** (as in **pránaṣṭa**).

b. The final **n** of a root is lingualized in some of the forms of **an** and **han**: thus, **prā́ 'ṇiti, prāṇá, prá haṇyate, praháṇana.**

c. The class-signs **nu** and **nā** are altered after the roots **hi** and **mi**: thus, **pári hiṇomi, prá miṇanti** (but the latter not in the Veda).

d. The 1st sing. impv. ending **āni** is sometimes altered: thus, **prá bhavāṇi.**

e. Derivatives by suffixes containing **n** sometimes have **ṇ** by influence of a preposition: thus, **prayā́ṇa.**

f. The **n** of the preposition **ni** is sometimes altered, like the initial of a root, after another preposition: thus, **praṇipāta, praṇidhi.**

193. In compound words, an altering cause in one member sometimes lingualizes a **n** of the next following member — either its initial or final **n**, or **n** in its inflectional or derivative ending. The exercise of the altering influence can be seen to depend in part upon the closeness or frequency of the compound, or its integration by being made the base of a derivative. Examples are: **grāmaṇí, triṇāman, urūṇasá; vṛtraháṇam** etc. (but **vṛtraghnā́** etc.: **195 a**), **nṛmáṇas, drughaṇá; pravā́haṇa, nṛpā́ṇa, pūryā́ṇa, pitṛyā́ṇa; svargéṇa, durgā́ṇi, usráyāmṇe, tryañgā́ṇām.**

194. Finally, in the Veda, a **n** (usually initial) is occasionally lingualized even by an altering sound in another word. The toneless pronouns **nas** and **ena-** are oftenest thus affected: thus, **pári ṇas, prā́i 'ṇān, índra eṇam;** but also the particle **ná** *like:* thus, **vā́r ṇá;** and a few other cases, as **vā́r ṇā́ma, púnar ṇayāmasi, agnér áveṇa.** More anomalous, and perhaps to be rejected as false readings, are such as **tríṇ imā́n** and **akṣā́n áva** and **suhā́rṇ ṇaḥ** (MS.), and **vyṛṣaṇ vā** (Āpast.).

195. a. The immediate combination of a **n** with a preceding guttural or labial seems in some cases to hinder the conversion to **ṇ**: thus, **vṛtraghnā́** etc., **kṣubhnāti, tṛpnoti** (but in Veda **tṛpṇu**), **kṣepnú, suṣumná.**

b. The RV. has the exceptions **úṣṭrānām** and **rāṣṭrā́nām.**

Conversion of dental mutes to linguals and palatals.

196. When a dental mute comes in contact with a lingual or palatal mute or sibilant, the dental is usually assimilated, becoming lingual or palatal respectively.

The cases are the following:

197. A dental surd mute or nasal, or the dental sibilant, when immediately preceded by a ṣ, is everywhere converted into the corresponding lingual.

a. Under this rule, the combinations **ṣṭ, ṣṭh,** and **ṣṇ** are very common; **ṣṣ** is rarely so written, the **visarga** being put instead of the former sibilant (**172**): thus, **jyótiḥṣu** instead of **jyótiṣṣu.**

b. Much less often, **dh** is changed to **ḍh** after final **ṣ** of a root or tense-stem, with loss of the **ṣ** or its conversion to **ḍ**: see **226 c.**

c. Those cases in which final **ṣ** becomes **ṭ** before **su** (e. g. **dviṭsú: 226 b**) do not, of course, fall under this rule.

198. In the other (comparatively infrequent) cases where a dental is preceded by a lingual in internal combination, the dental (except of **su** loc. pl.) becomes lingual. Thus:

a. A **n** following immediately a **ṇ** made such by the rule given at **189**, above — or, as it may be expressed, a double as well as a single **n** — is subject to the lingualization: thus, the participles **arṇṇá, kṣuṇṇa, kṣviṇṇa, chṛṇṇá, tṛṇṇá**; and, after prefixes (**185 a**), **niṣaṇṇa, pariviṇṇa, viṣaṇṇa, víṣyaṇṇa.** But TS. has **ádhiṣkanna,** and RV. **yájuḥ ṣkannám.**

b. Only a very few other instances occur: **íṭṭe** and **áiṭṭa** from **√īḍ; ṣaḍḍhā́** (also **ṣaḍdhā́** and **ṣoḍhā́**), and **ṣaṇṇā́m** (**ṣaṣ+nām**: anomalous gen. pl. of **ṣaṣ: 483**). A small number of words follow the same rule in external combination: see below, **199.**

c. But **tāḍhi** (Vedic: **√taḍ+dhi**) shows loss of the final lingual after assimilation of the dental, and compensatory lengthening.

d. Some of the cases of abnormal occurrence of **ḍ** are explained in a similar way, as results of a lingualized and afterward omitted sibilant before **d**: thus **nīḍá** from **nisda, √pīḍ** from **pisd, √mṛḍ** from **mṛsd.** For words exhibiting a like change in composition, see below, **199 c.**

199. In external combination —

a. A final **t** is directed to be assimilated to an initial lingual mute: thus, **taṭ-ṭīkā, taḍ ḍayate, taṭ-ṭhālinī, taḍ ḍhāukate**: but the case never occurs in the older language, and very rarely in the later. For final **n** before a lingual, see **205 b.**

b. An initial dental after a final lingual usually remains unchanged; and **su** of the loc. pl. follows the same rule: thus, **ṣáṭtriṅçat, ā́naḍ diváḥ, ekarā́ṭ tvám; ṣaṭsú, rāṭsú.**

c. Exceptions are: a few compounds with **ṣaṣ** *six* showing double **ṇ** (**198 b**): namely, **ṣáṇṇavati, ṣaṇṇābhi** (and one or two others not quotable); and IB. has **ṣaṇ ṇiramimīta.**

d. In a few compounds, moreover, there appears a lingualized dental, with compensatory lengthening, after a lost lingual sibilant or its representative: namely, in certain Vedic compounds with dus: dūḍábha, dūḍā́ç, dūḍhī́, dūṇáça, dūṇā́ça (compare the anomalous puroḍā́ç and -ḍā́ça: puras+√dāç); and, in the language of every period, certain compounds of ṣaṣ, with change of its vowel to an alterant quality (as in voḍhum and soḍhum: 224b): ṣóḍaça, ṣoḍhā́ (also ṣaḍḍhā́ and ṣaḍḍhā́), ṣoḍant.

e. Between final ṭ and initial s, the insertion of a t is permitted — or, according to some authorities, required: thus, ṣáṭ sahásrāḥ or ṣáṭt sahásrāḥ.

200. The cases of assimilation of a dental to a contiguous palatal occur almost only in external combination, and before an initial palatal. There is but one case of internal combination, namely:

201. A न् n coming to follow a palatal mute in internal combination is itself made palatal.

Thus, yācñā́ (the only instance after c), yajñá, jajñé, ajñata, rā́jñā, rā́jñī.

202. a. A final त् t before an initial palatal mute is assimilated to it, becoming च् c before च् c or छ् ch, and ज् j before ज् j (झ् jh does not occur).

Thus, uc carati, etac chattram, vidyuj jāyate; yātayájjana, vidyujjihva, bṛhácchandas, saccarita.

b. A final न् n is assimilated before ज् j, becoming ञ् ñ.

c. All the grammarians, of every period, require this assimilation of n to j; but it is more often neglected, or only occasionally made, in the manuscripts.

d. For n before a surd palatal, see below, **208.**

203. Before the palatal sibilant श् ç, both त् t and न् n are assimilated, becoming respectively च् c and ञ् ñ; and then the following श् ç may be, and in practice almost always is, converted to छ् ch.

Thus, vedavic chūraḥ (-vit çū-), tac chrutvā, hṛcchaya (hṛt + çaya); bṛhañ cheṣaḥ or çeṣaḥ, svapañ chete or çete.

a. Some authorities regard the conversion of ç to ch after t or n as everywhere obligatory, others as only optional; some except, peremptorily or optionally, a ç followed by a mute. And some require the same conversion after every mute save m, reading also vípaṭ chutudrī́, ā́naṭ chúci, anuṣṭup chāradī, çuk chuci. The manuscripts generally write ch, instead of cch, as result of the combination of t and ç.

b. In the MS., t und ç are anomalously combined into ñ ç: e. g. tañ çatám, etāvañçás.

Combinations of final न् n.

204. Final radical n is assimilated in internal combination to a following sibilant, becoming **anusvāra.**

Thus, **váṅsi, váṅsva, váṅsat, maṅsyáte, jíghāṅsati.**

a. According to the grammarians, it is treated before **bh** and **su** in declension as in external combination. But the cases are, at best, excessively rare, and RV. has **ráṅsu** and **váṅsu** (the only Vedic examples).

b. Final **n** of a derivative suffix is regularly and usually dropped before a consonant in inflection and composition — in composition, even before a vowel; and a radical **n** occasionally follows the same rule: see **421 a, 439, 1203 c, 637.**

c. For assimilation of **n** to a preceding palatal, see **201.**

The remaining cases are those of external combination.

205. a. The assimilation of n in external combination to a following sonant palatal and the palatal sibilant ç have been already treated (**202 b, 203**).

b. The n is also declared to be assimilated (becoming ṇ) before a sonant lingual (ḍ, ḍh, ṇ), but the case rarely if ever occurs.

206. A n is also assimilated to a following initial l, becoming (like **m: 213 d**) a nasal l.

a. The manuscripts to a great extent disregard this rule, leaving the **n** unchanged; but also they in part attempt to follow it — and that, either by writing the assimilated **n** (as the assimilated **m, 213 f,** and just as reasonably) with the **anusvāra**-sign, or else by doubling the l and putting a sign of nasality above; the latter, however, is inexact, and a better way would be to separate the two l's, writing the first with **virāma** and a nasal sign above. Thus (from **trīn lokān**):

manuscripts त्रींलोकान् or त्रीँल्लोकान्; better त्रीँल् लोकान्.

The second of these methods is the one oftenest followed in printed texts.

207. Before the lingual and dental sibilants, ṣ and s, final n remains unchanged; but a t may also be inserted between the nasal and the sibilant: thus, **tā́n ṣáṭ** or **tā́nt ṣáṭ; mahā́n sán** or **mahā́nt sán.**

a. According to most of the grammarians of the Prātiçākhyas (not RPr.), the insertion of the **t** in such cases is a necessary one. In the manuscripts it is very frequently made, but not uniformly. It is probably a purely phonetic phenomenon, a transition-sound to ease the double change of sonant to surd and nasal to non-nasal utterance — although the not infrequent cases in which final **n** stands for original **nt** (as **bháran, ábharan, agnimā́n**) may have aided to establish it as a rule. Its analogy with the conversion of **n ç** into **ñch (203)** is palpable.

208. Before the surd palatal, lingual, and dental mutes, there is inserted after final **n** a sibilant of each of those classes respectively, before which the **n** becomes **anusvāra**: thus, **devāṅç ca, bhavāṅç chidyate, kumārāṅs trīn, abharaṅs tataḥ, dadhaṅç** (425 c) **carum.**

a. This rule, which in the classical language has established itself in the form here given, as a phonetic rule of unvarying application, really involves a historic survival. The large majority of cases of final **n** in the language (not far from three quarters) are for original **ns**; and the retention of the sibilant in such cases, when once its historical ground had been forgotten, was extended by analogy to all others.

b. Practically, the rule applies only to **n** before **c** and **t**, since cases involving the other initials occur either not at all, or only with extreme rarity (the Veda does not present an example of any of them). In the Veda, the insertion is not always made, and the different texts have with regard to it different usages, which are fully explained in their Prātiçākhyas; in general, it is less frequent in the older texts. When the **ç** does not appear between **n** and **c**, the **n** is of course assimilated, becoming **ñ** (203).

209. The same retention of original final **s** after a nasal, and consequent treatment of (apparent) final **ān, īn, ūn, ṝn** as if they were **āṅs, īṅs, ūṅs, ṝṅs** (long nasalized vowel with final **s**), shows itself also in other Vedic forms of combination, which, for the sake of unity, may be briefly stated here together:

a. Final **ān** becomes **āṅ** (nasalized **ā**) before a following vowel: that is to say, **āṅs**, with nasal vowel, is treated like **ās**, with pure vowel (177): thus, **devā́ṅ é 'há, úpabaddhāṅ ihá, mahā́ṅ asi.** This is an extremely common case, especially in RV. Once or twice, the **s** appears as **ḥ** before **p**: thus, **svátavāṅḥ pāyúḥ.**

b. In like manner, **s** is treated after nasal **ī, ū, ṝ** as it would be after those vowels when pure, becoming **r** before a sonant sound (174), and (much more rarely) **ḥ** before a surd (170): thus, **raçmī́ṅr iva, sūnū́ṅr yuvanyū́ṅr út, nṝ́ṅr abhí; nṝ́ṅḥ pā́tram** (and **nṝ́ṅṣ p-**, MS.).

c. RV. has once **-īṅ** before **y**. MS. usually has **aṅ** instead of **āṅ**.

210. The nasals **n, ṇ, ṅ**, occurring as finals after a short vowel, are doubled before any initial vowel: thus, **pratyáṅṅ úd eṣi, udyánn ādityáḥ, āsánn-iṣu.**

a. This is also to be regarded as a historical survival, the second nasal being an assimilation of an original consonant following the first. It is always written in the manuscripts, although the Vedic metre seems to show that the duplication was sometimes omitted. The RV. has the compound **vṛṣaṇaçva.**

211. The nasals **ṅ** and **ṇ** before a sibilant are allowed to insert respectively **k** and **ṭ** — as **n** (207) inserts **t**: thus, **pratyáṅk sómaḥ.**

Combinations of final म् m.

212. Final radical म् **m**, in internal combination, is assimilated to a following mute or spirant — in the latter case, becoming **anusvāra**; in the former, becoming the nasal of the same class with the mute.

a. Before **m** or **v** (as when final: **143 a**), it is changed to **n**: thus, from **√gam** come **áganma, aganmahi, ganvahi, jaganvā́ṅs** (which appear to be the only quotable cases). According to the grammarians, the same change is made in the inflection of root-stems before **bh** and **su**: thus, **praçānbhis, praçānsu** (from **praçām: pra+√çam**). No derived noun-stem ends in **m**.

b. The ÇB. and KÇS. have **kámvant** and **çámvant**, and ChU. has **kamvara**.

213. Final म् **m** in external combination is a servile sound, being assimilated to any following consonant. Thus:

a. It remains unchanged only before a vowel or a labial mute.

b. But also, by an anomalous exception, before **r** of the root **rāj** in **samrā́j** and its derivatives **samrājñī** and **sāmrājya.**

c. Before a mute of any other class than labial, it becomes the nasal of that class.

d. Before the semivowels **y, l, v** it becomes, according to the Hindu gramarians, a nasal semivowel, the nasal counterpart of each respectively (see **71**).

e. Before **r**, a sibilant, or **h**, it becomes **anusvāra** (see **71**).

f. The manuscripts and the editions in general make no attempt to distinguish the nasal tones produced by the assimilation of **m** before a following semivowel from that before a spirant.

g. But if **h** be immediately followed by another consonant (which can only be a nasal or semivowel), the **m** is allowed to be assimilated to that following consonant. This is because the **h** has no position of the mouth-organs peculiar to itself, but is uttered in the position of the next sound. The Prātiçākhyas do not take any notice of the case.

h. Cases are met with in the Veda where a final **m** appears to be dropped before a vowel, the final and initial vowels being then combined into one. The **pada**-text then generally gives a wrong interpretation. Thus, **saṁvánano 'bhayaṁkarám** (RV. viii. 1. 2; **pada**-text **-nanā ubh-**; SV. **-nanam**).

i. It has been pointed out above (**73**) that the assimilated **m** is generally represented in texts by the **anusvāra**-sign, and that in this work it is transliterated by **ṁ** (instead of a nasal mute or **ṅ**).

The palatal mutes and sibilant, and ह् h.

214. These sounds show in some situations a reversion (**43**) to the original gutturals from which they are derived. The treatment of j and h, also, is different, according as they represent the one or the other of two different degrees of alteration from their originals.

215. The palatals and h are the least stable of alphabetic sounds, undergoing, in virtue of their derivative character, alteration in many cases where other similar sounds are retained.

216. Thus, in derivation, even before vowels, semivowels, and nasals, reversion to guttural form is by no means rare. The cases are the following:

a. Before **a** of suffix **a**, final **c** becomes **k** in **añká, çvañka, arká, pāká, vāká, çúka, parka, marká, vṛ́ka, prátīka** etc., **reka, séka, moka, roká, çóka, toká, mroká, vraská**; — final **j** becomes **g** in **tyāgá, bhága, bhāgá, yāga, añga, bhañgá, sañga, svañga, ṛñga, tuñga, yuñga, varga, mārga, mṛgá, varga, sarga, nega, vega, bhóga, yugá, yóga, loga, róga**; — final **h** becomes **gh** in **aghá, maghá, arghá, dīrghá** (and **drā́ghīyas, drā́ghiṣṭha**), **degha, meghá, ogha, dógha, drogha, mógha**; and in **dúghāna** and **méghamāna**. In **neka** (**√nij**) we have further an anomalous substitution of a surd for the final sonant of the root.

b. In another series of derivatives with **a**, the altered sound appears: examples are **ajá, yāja, çucá, çoca, vrajá, vevijá, yuja, ūrjá, dóha**.

c. Before the suffixes **as** and **ana**, the guttural only rarely appears: namely, in **áñkas, ókas, rókas, çókas, bhárgas**, and in **rogaṇa**; also in **ābhogáya**.

d. Before an **i**-vowel, the altered sound appears (except in **ābhogí, ógīyaṅs, tigitá, mokí, sphigí**): thus, **ājí, tují, rúci, çácī, vívici, rociṣṇú**.

e. Before **u**, the guttural reappears, as a rule (the cases are few): thus, **añku, vañkú, rekú, bhṛ́gu, mā́rguka, raghú** (and **rághīyaṅs**).

f. Before **n**, the examples of reversion are few, except of **j** (becoming **g**) before the participial ending **na** (**957 c**): thus, **rékṇas, vagnú** (with the final also made sonant); and participles **bhagná, rugṇá**, etc.; and apparently **pṛgṇa** from **√pṛc**.

g. Before **m** (of **ma, man, mant, min**), the guttural generally appears: thus, **rukmá, tigmá, yugma, ṛgma** (with sonant change); **takmán, vákman, sákman, yugmán; rúkmant; ṛgmín** and **vāgmín** (with sonant change): — but **ájman, ojmán, bhujmán**.

h. Before **y**, the altered sound is used: thus, **pacya, yajya, yajyu, yujya, bhujyu**. Such cases as **bhogya, yogya, negya, okya** are doubtless secondary derivatives from **bhoga** etc.

i. Before **r**, the cases are few, and the usage apparently divided. thus, **takra, sakra, vakrá, çukrá, vigrá, ugrá, túgra, mṛgrà, váñkri**; but **vájra** and **pajrá** (?).

j. Before **v** (of the suffixes **va, van, vin**, etc., and participial **vāṅs**) the guttural is regularly preserved: thus, **ṛkvá, pakvá, vákva; vákvan, ṛ́kvan, rikvan, çukvan, mṛgvan, túgvan, yugvan; ṛ́kvant, pṛ́kvant; vāgvín, vagvaná, vagvanú** [with further sonant change; **vivakvā́ṅs, ririkvā́ṅs, vivikvā́ṅs, rurukvā́ṅs, çuçukvā́ṅs; çuçukvaná, çuçukváni**: also before the union-vowel **i** in **okivā́ṅs** (RV., once). An exception is **yájvan.**

k. The reversion of **h** in derivation is comparatively rare. The final **j** which is analogous with **ç** (**219**) shows much less proclivity to reversion than that which corresponds with **c**.

l. A like reversion shows itself also to some extent in conjugational stem-formation and inflection. Thus, the initial radical becomes guttural after the reduplication in the present or perfect or desiderative or intensive stems, or in derivatives, of the roots **ci, cit, ji, hi, han**, and in **jáguri** (√**jṛ**); and **han** becomes **ghn** on the elision of **a** (**402, 637**). The RV. has **vivakmi** from √**vac** and **vāvakre** from √**vañc**; and SV. has **sasṛgmahe** (RV. **-sṛj-**). And before **ran** etc. of 3d pl. mid. we have **g** for radical **j** in **asṛgran, asṛgram, asasṛgram** (all in RV.).

217. Final च् **c** of a root or stem, if followed in internal combination by any other sound than a vowel or semivowel or nasal, reverts (**43**) to its original guttural value, and shows everywhere the same form which a क् **k** would show in the same situation.

Thus, **vákti, uváktha, vákṣi, vakṣyā́mi, vagdhi; vāgbhís, vākṣú; uktá, ukthá, vaktár.**

a. And, as final **c** becomes **k** (above **142**), the same rule applies also to **c** in external combination: thus, **vā́k ca, vā́g ápi, vā́ñ me.**

Examples of **c** remaining unchanged in inflection are: **ucyáte, riricré, vācí, mumucmáhe.**

218. Final श् **ç** reverts to its original क् **k**, in internal combination, only before the स् **s** of a verbal stem or ending (whence, by **180**, क्ष् **kṣ**); before त् **t** and थ् **th**, it everywhere becomes ष् **ṣ** (whence, by **197**, ष्ट **ṣṭ** and ष्ठ **ṣṭh**); before ध् **dh**, भ् **bh**, and सु **su** of the loc. pl., as when final (**145**), it regularly becomes the lingual mute (ट् **ṭ** or ड् **ḍ**).

Thus, **ávikṣata, vekṣyā́mi; vā́ṣṭi, viṣṭá, dídeṣṭu; didiḍḍhi, viḍbhís.**

a. But a few roots exhibit the reversion of final **ç** to **k** before **bh** and **su**, and also when final (**145**): they are **diç, dṛç, spṛç,** and optionally **naç**; and **viç** has in V. always **vikṣú,** loc. pl., but **víṭ, viḍbhís,** etc. Examples are **díksaṁçita, dṛgbhís, hṛdispṛ́k, nák** (or **naṭ**).

Examples of **ç** remaining unchanged before vowels etc. are: **viçí, viviçyās, aviçran, açnomi, vaçmi, uçmási.**

b. A **ç** remains irregularly unchanged before **p** in the compound **viçpáti.**

219. Final ज् **j** is in one set of words treated like च् **c,** and in another set like श् **ç.**

Thus, from **yuj**: **áyukthās, áyukta, yuñkté, yukti, yóktra, yokṣyā́mi, yukṣú**; **yuñgdhí, áyugdhvam, yugbhís.**

Again, from **mṛj** etc.: **ámṛkṣat, srakṣyā́mi**; **mā́rṣṭi, mṛṣṭá, sṛ́ṣṭi, rāṣṭrá**; **mṛḍḍhí, mṛḍḍhvám, rāḍbhís, rāṭsú, rā́ṭ.**

a. To the former or **yuj**-class belong (as shown by their quotable forms) about twenty roots and radical stems: namely, **bhaj, saj, tyaj** (not V.), **raj** *color*, **svaj, majj, nij, tij, vij, 1** and **2 bhuj, yuj, ruj, vṛj, añj, bhañj, çiñj**; **ū́rj, sráj, bhiṣáj, ásṛj**; — also, stems formed with the suffixes **aj** and **ij** (**383.IV**), as **tṛṣṇáj, vaṇíj**; and **ṛtvíj,** though containing the root **yaj.**

b. To the latter or **mṛj**-class belong only about one third as many: namely, **yaj, bhrajj, vraj, rāj, bhrāj, mṛj, sṛj.**

c. A considerable number of **j**-roots are not placed in circumstances to exhibit the distinction; but such roots are in part assignable to one or the other class on the evidence of the related languages. The distinction appears, namely, only when the **j** occurs as final, or is followed, either in inflection or in derivation, by a dental mute (**t, th, dh**), or, in noun-inflection, by **bh** or **su.** In derivation (above, **216**) we find a **g** sometimes from the **mṛj**-class: thus, **mārga, sárga,** etc.; and (**216l**) before Vedic mid. endings, **sasṛgmahe, asṛgran,** etc. (beside **sasṛjrire**) — while from the **yuj**-class occur only **yuyujre, ayujran, bubhujrire,** with **j.** And MS. has **viçvasṛ́k** from (√**sṛj**).

220. Final **ch** falls under the rules of combination almost only in the root **prach,** in which it is treated as if it were **ç** (**praç** being, indeed, its more original form): thus, **prakṣyā́mi, pṛṣṭá,** and also the derivative **praçná.** As final and in noun-inflection (before **bh** and **su**), it is changed to the lingual mute: thus, **prāḍvivāka.**

a. Mūrtá is called the participle of **mūrch,** and a gerund **mūrtvā́** is given to the same root. They (with **mū́rti**) must doubtless come from a simpler form of the root.

b. Of **jh** there is no occurrence: the grammarians require it to be treated like **c.**

221. The compound **kṣ** is not infrequent as final of a root (generally of demonstrably secondary origin), or of a tense-stem (**s-aorist**: see below, **878** ff.); and, in the not very frequent cases of its internal combination, it is treated as if a single sound, following the rules for **ç**: thus **çákṣe** (**cakṣ** + **se**), **cákṣva**; **cáṣṭe, ácaṣṭa, ásrāṣṭam, ásṛṣṭa, tváṣṭar.** As to its treatment when final, see **146.**

a. Thus, we are taught by the grammarians to make such forms as **goráṭ, goráḍbhis, goráṭsu** (from **gorákṣ**); and we actually have **ṣáṭ, ṣaḍbhís, ṣaṭsú** from **ṣakṣ** or **ṣaṣ** (**146b**). For **jagdha** etc. from √**jakṣ**, see **233** f.

b. In the single anomalous root **vraçc,** the compound **çc** is said to follow the rules for simple **ç.** From it are quotable the future **vrakṣyáti,** the gerunds **vṛṣṭvā́** (AV.) and **vṛktvī́** (RV.), and the participle (**957 c**) **vṛkṇá.** Its **c** reverts to **k** in the derivative **vraska.**

222. The roots in final ह् **h,** like those in ज् **j,** fall into two classes, exhibiting a similar diversity of treatment, appearing in the same kinds of combination.

a. In the one class, as **duh,** we have a reversion of **h** (as of **c**) to a guttural form, and its treatment as if it were still its original **gh**: thus, **ádhukṣam, dhokṣyā́mi; dugdhā́m, dugdhá; ádhok, dhúk, dhugbhís, dhukṣú.**

b. In the other class, as **ruh** and **sah,** we have a guttural reversion (as of **ç**) only before **s** in verb-formation and derivation: thus, **árukṣat, rokṣyā́mi, sākṣīyá, sakṣáṇi.** As final, in external combination, and in noun-inflection before **bh** and **su,** the **h** (like **ç**) becomes a lingual mute: thus, **turāṣā́ṭ, pṛtanāṣā́ḍ ayodhyáḥ, turāṣā́ḍbhis, turāṣā́ṭsu.** But before a dental mute (**t, th, dh**) in verb-inflection and in derivation, its euphonic effect is peculiarly complicated: it turns the dental into a lingual (as would **ç**); but it also makes it sonant and aspirate (as would **ḍh**: see **160**); and further, it disappears itself, and the preceding vowel, if short, is lengthened: thus, from **ruh** with **ta** comes **rūḍhá,** from **leh** with **ti** comes **léḍhi,** from **guh** with **tar** comes **gūḍhár,** from **meh** with **tum** comes **méḍhum,** from **lih** with **tas** or **thas** comes **līḍhás,** from **lih** with **dhvam** comes **līḍhvám,** etc.

c. This is as if we had to assume as transition sound a sonant aspirate lingual sibilant **ẓh,** with the euphonic effects of a lingual and of a sonant aspirate (**160**), itself disappearing under the law of the existing language which admits no sonant sibilant.

223. The roots of the two classes, as shown by their forms found in use, are:

a. of the first or **duh-class**: **dah, dih, duh, druh, muh, snih** (and the final of **uṣṇíh** is similarly treated);

b. of the second or ruh-class: **vah, sah, mih, rih** or **lih, guh, ruh, dṛṅh, tṛṅh, bṛh, baṅh, spṛh** (?).

c. But **muh** forms also (not in RV.) the participle **mūḍha** and agent-noun **mūḍhár,** as well as **mugdhá** and **mugdhár;** and **druh** and **snih** are allowed by the grammarians to do likewise: such forms as **drūḍha** and **snīḍha,** however, have not been met with in use.

d. From roots of the **ruh**-class we find also in the Veda the forms **gartārúk,** nom. sing., and **prāṇadhṛ́k** and **dadhṛ́k;** and hence **puruspṛ́k** (the only occurrence) does not certainly prove √**spṛh** to be of the **duh**-class.

e. A number of other **h**-roots are not proved by their occurring forms to belong to either class; they, too, are with more or less confidence assigned to the one or the other by comparison with the related languages.

f. In derivation, before certain suffixes (**216**), we have **gh** instead of **h** from verbs of either class.

g. The root **nah** comes from original **dh** instead of **gh,** and its reversion is accordingly to a dental mute: thus, **natsyā́mi, naddhá, upānádbhis, upānadyuga, anupānatka.** So also the root **grah** comes from (early Vedic) **grabh,** and shows labials in many forms and derivatives (though it is assimilated to other **h**-roots in the desiderative stem **jighṛkṣa**). In like manner, **h** is used for **dh** in some of the forms and derivatives of √**dhā** *put;* and further analogous facts are the stem **kakuhá** beside **kakubhá,** the double imperative ending **dhi** and **hi,** and the dative **máhyam** beside **túbhyam** (**491**).

224. Irregularities of combination are:

a. The vowel **ṛ** is not lengthened after the loss of the **h**-element: thus, **dṛḍhá, tṛḍhá, bṛḍhá** (the only cases; and in the Veda their first syllable has metrical value as heavy or long).

b. The roots **vah** and **sah** change their vowel to **o** instead of lengthening it: thus, **voḍhám, voḍhā́m, voḍhár, sóḍhum.** But from **sah** in the older language forms with **ā** are more frequent: thus, **sāḍhá, áṣāḍha** (also later), **sā́ḍhar.** The root **tṛṅh** changes the vowel of its class-sign **na** into **e** instead of lengthening it: thus, **tṛṇeḍhi, tṛṇéḍhu, atṛṇet** (the grammarians teach also **tṛṇehmi** and **tṛṇekṣi:** but no such forms are quotable, and, if ever actually in use, they must have been made by false analogy with the others).

c. These anomalous vowel-changes seem to stand in connection with the fact that the cases showing them are the only ones where other than an alterant vowel (**180**) comes before the lingualized sibilant representative of the **h.** Compare **ṣóḍaça** etc.

d. Apparently by dissimilation, the final of **vah** in the anomalous compound **anaḍvah** is changed to **d** instead of **ḍ:** see **404.**

The lingual sibilant ष ṣ.

225. Since the lingual sibilant, in its usual and normal occurrences, is (**182**) the product of lingualization of **s** after certain alterant sounds, we might expect final radical **ṣ**, when (in rare cases) it comes to stand where a **ṣ** cannot maintain itself, to revert to its original, and be treated as a **s** would be treated under the same circumstances. That, however, is true only in a very few instances.

a. Namely, in the prefix **dus** (evidently identical with √**duṣ**); in **sajū́s** (adverbially used case-form from √**juṣ**); in (RV.) **vivés** and **ávives**, from √**viṣ**; in **ā́íyes** (RV.), from √**īṣ**; and in **āçís**, from **çiṣ** as secondary form of √**çās**. All these, except the first two, are more or less open to question.

226. In general, final lingual ष **ṣ**, in internal combination, is treated in the same manner as palatal श **ç**. Thus:

a. Before **t** and **th** it remains unchanged, and the latter are assimilated: e. g. **dviṣṭas, dviṣṭhas, dvéṣṭum.**

This is a common and perfectly natural combination.

b. Before **dh, bh,** and **su**, as also in external combination (**145**), it becomes a lingual mute; and **dh** is made lingual after it: e. g. **piṇḍḍhi, viḍḍhi, viviḍḍhi, dviḍḍhvam, dviḍbhís, dviṭsú; bhinnaviṭka.**

c. So also the **dh** of **dhvam** as ending of 2d pl. mid. becomes **ḍh** after final **ṣ** of a tense-stem, whether the **ṣ** be regarded as lost or as converted to **ḍ** before it (the manuscripts write simply **ḍhv**, not **ḍḍhv**; but this is ambiguous: see **232**). Thus, after **ṣ** of **s**-aorist stems (**881 a**), **astoḍhvam, avṛḍhvam, cyoḍhvam** (the only quotable cases), from **astoṣ+dhvam** etc.; but **arādhvam** from **arās+dhvam.** Further, after the **ṣ** of **iṣ**-aorist stems (**901a**), **āindhiḍhvam, artiḍhvam, ajaniḍhvam, vepiḍhvam** (the only quotable cases), from **ajaniṣ+dhvam** etc. Yet again, in the precative (**924**), as **bhaviṣīḍhvam,** if, as is probable (unfortunately, no example of this person is quotable from any part of the literature), the precative-sign **s** (**ṣ**) is to be regarded as present in the form. According, however, to the Hindu grammarians, the use of **ḍh** or of **dh** in the **iṣ**-aorist and precative depends on whether the **i** of **iṣ** or of **iṣī** is or is not "preceded by a semivowel or **h**" — which both in itself appears senseless and is opposed to the evidence of all the quotable forms. Moreover, the same authorities prescribe the change of **dh** to **ḍh,** under the same restriction as to circumstances, in the perf. mid. ending **dhve** also: in this case, too, without any conceivable reason; and no example of **ḍhve** in the 2d pl. perf. has been pointed out in the literature.

d. The conversion of **ṣ** to **ṭ** (or **ḍ**) as final and before **bh** and **su** is parallel with the like conversion of **ç**, and of **j** and **h** in the **mṛj** and

ruh classes of roots, and perhaps with the occasional change of **s** to **ṭ** (**167—8**). It is a very infrequent case, occurring (save as it may be assumed in the case of **ṣaṣ**) only once in RV. and once in AV. (**-dviṭ** and **-pruṭ**), although those texts have more than 40 roots with final **ṣ**; in the Brāhmaṇas, moreover, have been noticed further only **-pruṭ** and **víṭ** (ÇB.), and **-çliṭ** (K.). From **piṅṣ**, RV. has the anomalous form **piṇak** (2d and 3d sing., for **pinaṣ-s** and **pinaṣ-t**).

e. Before **s** in internal combination (except **su** of loc. pl.) it becomes **k**: thus, **dvékṣi, dvekṣyā́mi, ádvikṣam.**

f. This change is of anomalous phonetic character, and difficult of explanation. It is also practically of very rare occurrence. The only RV. examples (apart from **piṇak**, above) are **vivekṣi**, from √**viṣ**, and the desid. stem **ririkṣa** from √**riṣ**; AV. has only **dvikṣat** and **dvikṣata**, and the desid. stem **çiçlikṣa** from √**çliṣ**. Other examples are quotable from √√**kṛṣ** and **piṣ** and **viṣ** (ÇB etc.), and **çiṣ** (ÇB.); and they are by the Hindu grammarians prescribed to be formed from about half-a-dozen other roots.

Extension and Abbreviation.

227. As a general rule, **ch** is not allowed by the grammarians to stand in that form after a vowel, but is to be doubled, becoming **cch** (which the manuscripts sometimes write **chch**).

a. The various authorities disagree with one another in detail as to this duplication. According to Pāṇini, **ch** is doubled within a word after either a long or a short vowel; and, as initial, necessarily after a short and after the particles **ā́** and **mā́**, and optionally everywhere after a long. In RV., initial **ch** is doubled after a long vowel of **ā́** only, and certain special cases after a short vowel are excepted. For the required usage in the other Vedic texts, see their several Prātiçākhyas. The Kāṭhaka writes for original **ch** (not **ch** from combination of **t** or **n** with **ç**: **203**) after a vowel everywhere **çch.** The manuscripts in general write simple **ch.**

b. Opinions are still at variance as to how far this duplication has an etymological ground, and how far it is only an acknowledgment of the fact that **ch** makes a heavy syllable even after a short vowel (makes "position": **79**). As the duplication is accepted and followed by most European scholars, it will be also adopted in this work in words and sentences (not in roots and stems).

228. After **r**, any consonant (save a spirant before a vowel) is by the grammarians either allowed or required to be doubled (an aspirate, by prefixing the corresponding non-aspirate: **154**).

Thus:

अर्क **arka,** or अर्क्क **arkka;** कार्य **kārya,** or कार्य्य **kāryya;**
अर्थ **artha,** or अर्त्थ **arttha;** दीर्घ **dīrgha,** or दीर्ग्घ **dīrggha.**

a. Some of the authorities include, along with **r**, also **h** or **l** or **v**, or more than one of them, in this rule.

b. A doubled consonant after **r** is very common in manuscripts and inscriptions, as also in native text-editions and in the earlier editions prepared by European scholars — in later ones, the duplication is universally omitted.

c. On the other hand, the manuscripts often write a single consonant after **r** where a double one is etymologically required: thus, **kārtikeya, vārtika,** for **kārttikeya, vārttika.**

229. The first consonant of a group — whether interior, or initial after a vowel of a preceding word — is by the grammarians either allowed or required to be doubled.

a. This duplication is allowed by Pāṇini and required by the Prātiçākhyas — in both, with mention of authorities who deny it altogether. For certain exceptions, see the Prātiçākhyas; the meaning of the whole matter is too obscure to justify the giving of details here.

230. Other cases of extension of consonant-groups, required by some of the grammatical authorities, are the following:

a. Between a non-nasal and a nasal mute, the insertion of so-called **yamas** (*twins*), or nasal counterparts, is taught by the Prātiçākhyas (and assumed in Pāṇini's commentary): see APr. i. 99, note.

b. Between **h** and a following nasal mute the Prātiçākhyas teach the insertion of a nasal sound called **nāsikya**: see APr. i. 100, note.

c. Between **r** and a following consonant the Prātiçākhyas teach the insertion of a **svarabhakti** or *vowel-fragment:* see APr. i. 101—2, note.

d. Some authorities assume this insertion only before a spirant; the others regard it as twice as long before a spirant as before any other consonant — namely, a half or a quarter *mora* before the former, a quarter or an eighth before the latter. One (VPr.) admits it after **l** as well as **r**. It is variously described as a fragment of the vowel **a** or of **ṛ** (or **ḷ**).

e. The RPr. puts a **svarabhakti** also between a sonant consonant and a following mute or spirant; and APr. introduces an element called **sphoṭana** (*distinguisher*) between a guttural and a preceding mute of another class.

f. For one or two other cases of yet more doubtful value, see the Prātiçākhyas.

231. After a nasal, the former of two non-nasal mutes may be dropped, whether homogeneous only with the nasal, or with both: thus, **yuñdhí** for **yuñgdhí, yuñdhvám** for **yuñgdhvám, āñtám** for **āñktám, pañtí** for **pañktí, chintā́m** for **chinttā́m, bhinthá** for **bhintthá, indhé** for **inddhé.**

a. This abbreviation, allowed by Pāṇini, is required by APr. (the other Prātiçākhyas take no notice of it). It is the more usual practice of the manuscripts, though the full group is also often written.

232. In general, a double mute (including an aspirate which is doubled by the prefixion of a non-aspirate) in combination with any other consonant is by the manuscripts written as simple.

a. That is to say, the ordinary usage of the manuscripts makes no difference between those groups in which a phonetic duplication is allowed by the rules given above (**228, 229**) and those in which the duplication is etymological. As every **tv** after a vowel may also be properly written **ttv**, so **daṭtvā́** and **tattvá** may be, and almost invariably are, written as **datvā́** and **tatvá**. As **kártana** is also properly **kárttana**, so **kārttika** (from **kṛtti**) is written as **kārtika**. So in inflection, we have always, for example, **majñā́** etc., not **majjñā́**, from **majján**. Even in composition and sentence-collocation the same abbreviations are made: thus, **hṛdyotá** for **hṛddyotá**; **chinráty asya** for **chinátty asya**. Hence it is impossible to determine by the evidence of written usage whether we should regard **ādhvam** or **āddhvam** (from √**ās**), **ádviḍhvam** or **ádviḍḍhvam** (from √**dviṣ**), as the true form of a second person plural.

233. a. Instances are sometimes met with of apparent loss (perhaps after conversion to a semivowel) of **i** or **u** before **y** or **v** respectively. Thus, in the Brāhmaṇas, **tú** and **nú** with following **vāí** etc. often make **tvāí, nvāí** (also **tvā́vá, ánvāí**); and other examples from the older language are **anvart-** (**anu**+√**vart**); **paryan, paryanti, paryāyāt, paryāṇa** (**pari**+**yan**, etc.); **abhyàrti** (**abhi**+**iyarti**); **antaryāt** (**antar**+**iyāt**); **cārvāc, cārvāka, cārvadana** (**cāru**+**vāc**, etc.); **kyànt** for **kíyant**; **dvyoga** (**dvi**+**yoga**); **anvā, anvāsana** (**anu**+**vā**, etc.); probably **vyùnoti** for **ví yunoti** (RV.), **urváçī** (**uru-vaçī**), **çíçvarī** for **çíçu-varī** (RV.); **vyāmá** (**vi**+**yāma**); and the late **svarṇa** for **suvarṇa**. More anomalous abbreviations are the common **tṛcá** (**tri**+**ṛca**); and **dvṛca** (**dvi**+**ṛca**: S.) and **treṇī** (**tri**+**eṇī**: Āpast.).

Further, certain cases of the loss of a sibilant require notice. Thus:

b. According to the Hindu grammarians, the **s** of **s**-aorist stems is lost after a short vowel in the 2d and 3d sing. middle: thus, **adithās** and **adita** (1st sing. **adiṣi**), **akṛthas** and **akṛta** (1st sing. **akṛṣi**). It is, however, probable that such cases are to be explained in a different manner: see **834a.**

c. The **s** between two mutes is lost in all combinations of the roots **sthā** and **stambh** with the prefix **ud**: thus, **út thus, útthita, út thāpaya, úttabdha**, etc.

d. The same omission is now and then made in other similar cases: thus **cit kámbhanena** (for **skámbh-**: RV.); **tasmāt tute** (for **stute**) and **puroruk tuta** (for **stuta**: K.); the compounds **ṛkthā** (**ṛk**+**sthā**: PB.) and **utphuliṅga**; the derivative **utphāla** (√**sphal**). On the other hand, we have **vidyút stanáyantī** (RV.), **utsthala, kakutstha**, etc.

e. So also the tense-sign of the **s**-aorist is lost after a final consonant of a root before the initial consonant of an ending: thus, **achāntta**

(and for this, by **231, achānta**) for **achāntsta, çāpta** for **çāpsta, tāptam** for **tāpstam, abhākta** for **abhāksta, amāuktam** for **amāukstam.** These are the only quotable cases: compare **883**.

f. A final **s** of root or tense-stem is in a few instances lost after a sonant aspirate, and the combination of mutes is then made as if no sibilant had ever intervened. Thus, from the root **ghas,** with omission of the vowel and then of the final sibilant, we have the form **gdha** (for **ghs-ta:** 3d sing. mid.), the participle **gdha** (in **agdhád**), and the derivative **gdhi** (for **ghs-ti**; in **sá-gdhi**); and further, from the reduplicated form of the same root, or **√jakṣ,** we have **jagdha, jagdhum, jagdhvā, jagdhi** (from **jaghs-ta** etc.); also, in like manner, from **baps,** reduplication of **bhas,** the form **babdhām** (for **babhs-tām**). According to the Hindu grammarians, the same utter loss of the aorist-sign **s** takes place after a final sonant aspirate of a root before an ending beginning with **t** or **th:** thus, from **√rudh, s**-aorist stem **arāuts** act. and **aruts** mid., come the active dual and plural persons **arāuddham** and **arāuddhām** and **arāuddha,** and the middle singular persons **aruddhās** and **aruddha.** None of the active forms, however, have been found quotable from the literature, ancient or modern; and the middle forms admit also of a different explanation: see **834, 883.**

Strengthening and Weakening Processes.

234. Under this head, we take up first the changes that affect vowels, and then those that affect consonants — adding, for convenience's sake, in each case, a brief notice of the vowel and consonant elements that have come to bear the apparent office of connectives.

Guṇa and Vṛddhi.

235. The so-called **guṇa** and **vṛddhi**-changes are the most regular and frequent of vowel-changes, being of constant occurrence both in inflection and in derivation.

a. A guṇa-vowel (**guṇa** *secondary quality*) differs from the corresponding simple vowel by a prefixed **a**-element, which is combined with the other according to the usual rules; a vṛddhi-vowel (**vrddhi** *growth, increment*), by the further prefixion of **a** to the guṇa-vowel. Thus, of इ **i** or ई **ī** the corresponding guṇa is (**a**+**i**=) ए **e**; the corresponding vṛddhi is (**a**+**e**=) ऐ **āi**. But in all gunating processes अ **a** remains unchanged — or, as it is sometimes expressed,

अ **a** is its own **guṇa**; आ **ā**, of course, remains unchanged for both **guṇa** and **vṛddhi**.

236. The series of corresponding degrees is then as follows:

simple vowel	a ā	i ī	u ū	ṛ	ḷ
guṇa	a ā	e	o	ar	al
vṛddhi	ā	āi	āu	ār	

a. There is nowhere any occurrence of ṝ in a situation to undergo either **guṇa** or **vṛddhi**-change; nor does ḷ (**26**) ever suffer change to **vṛddhi**. Theoretically, ṝ would have the same changes as ṛ; and the **vṛddhi** of ḷ would be **āl**.

b. In secondary derivatives requiring **vṛddhi** of the first syllable (**1204**), the **o** of **go** (**361 c**) is strengthened to **gāu**: thus, **gāumata**, **gāuṣṭhika**.

237. The historical relations of the members of each vowel-series are still matters of some difference of opinion. From the special point of view of the Sanskrit, the simple vowels wear the aspect of being in general the original or fundamental ones, and the others of being products of their increment or strengthening, in two several degrees — so that the rules of formation direct **a, i, u, ṛ, ḷ** to be raised to **guṇa** or **vṛddhi** respectively, under specified conditions. But **ṛ** has long been so clearly seen to come by abbreviation or weakening from an earlier **ar** (or **ra**) that many European grammarians have preferred to treat the **guṇa**-forms as the original and the other as the derivative. Thus, for example: instead of assuming certain roots to be **bhṛ** and **vṛdh**, and making from them **bharati** and **vardhati**, and **bhṛta** and **vṛddha**, by the same rules which from **bhū** and **nī** and from **budh** and **cit** form **bhavati** and **nayati**, **bodhati** and **cetati**, **bhūta** and **nīta**, **buddha** and **citta** — they assume **bhar** and **vardh** to be the roots, and give the rules of formation for them in reverse. In this work, as already stated (**104 e**), the **ṛ**-form is preferred.

238. The **guṇa**-increment is an Indo-European phenomenon, and is in many cases seen to occur in connection with an accent on the increased syllable. It is found —

a. In root-syllables: either in inflection, as **dvéṣṭi** from √**dviṣ**, **dóhmi** from √**duh**; or in derivation, as **dvéṣa**, **dóhas**, **dvéṣṭum**, **dógdhum**.

b. In formative elements: either conjugational class-signs, as **tanómi** from **tanu**; or suffixes of derivation, in inflection or in further derivation, as **matáye** from **matí**, **bhānávas** from **bhānú**, **pitáram** from **pitṛ́** (or **pitár**), **hantavyà** from **hántu**.

239. The **vṛddhi**-increment is specifically Indian, and its occurrence is less frequent and regular. It is found —

a. In root and suffix-syllables, instead of **guṇa**: thus, **stāúti** from √**stu**, **sákhāyam** from **sákhi**, **ánāiṣam** from √**nī**, **ákārṣam** and **kāráyati** and **kāryà** from √**kṛ** (or **kar**), **dātā́ram** from **dātṛ́** (or **dātár**).

b. Especially often, in initial syllables in secondary derivation: thus, **mānasá** from **mánas**, **vāidyutá** from **vidyút**, **bhāumá** from **bhū́mi**, **pā́rthiva** from **pṛthivī́** (1204).

But —

240. The **guṇa**-increment does not usually take place in a heavy syllable ending with a consonant: that is to say, the rules prescribing **guṇa** in processes of derivation and inflection do not apply to a short vowel which is "long by position", nor to a long vowel unless it be final: thus, **cétati** from √**cit**, but **níndati** from √**nind**; **náyati** from √**nī**, but **jī́vati** from √**jīv**.

a. The **vṛddhi**-increment is not liable to this restriction.

b. Exceptions to the rule are occasionally met with: thus, **ehá, ehas** from √**īh**; **heḍáyāmi, héḍas,** etc., from √**hīḍ**; **coṣa** etc. from √**cūṣ**; **óhate** etc. from √**ūh** *consider;* and especially, from roots in **īv**: **didéva deviṣyati, dévana,** etc., from √**dīv**; **tiṣṭheva** from √**ṣṭhīv**; **srevā́yāmi, srévuka,** from √**srīv** — on account of which it is, doubtless, that these roots are written with **iv** (**div** etc.) by the Hindu grammarians, although they nowhere show a short **i,** in either verb-forms or derivatives.

c. A few cases occur of prolongation instead of increment: thus, **dūṣáyati** from √**duṣ**, **gū́hati** from √**guh.**

The changes of **ṛ** (more original **ar** or **ra**) are so various as to call for further description.

241. The increments of **ṛ** are sometimes **ra** and **rā**, instead of **ar** and **ār**: namely, especially, where by such reversal a difficult combination of consonants is avoided: thus, from √**dṛç**, **drakṣyā́mi** and **ádrākṣam**; but also **pṛthú** and **prath**, **pṛch** and **prach**, **kṛpā́** and **ákrapiṣṭa**.

242. In a number of roots (about a dozen quotable ones) ending in **ṛ** (for more original **ar**), the **ṛ** exchanges both with **ar**, and more irregularly, in a part of the forms, with **ir** — or also with **ur** (especially after a labial, in **pṛ**, **mṛ**, **vṛ**, sporadically in others): which **ir** and **ur**, again, are liable to prolongation into **īr** and **ūr**. Thus, for example, from **tṛ** (or **tar**), we have **tarati, titarti, tatāra, atāriṣam,** by regular processes; but also **tirati, tīryati, tīrtvā, -tīrya, tīrṇa,** and even (V.) **turyāma, tuturyāt, tarturāṇa.** The treatment of such roots has to be described in speaking of each formation.

a. For the purpose of artificially indicating this peculiarity of treatment, such roots are by the Hindu grammarians written with long **ṝ**, or with both **ṛ** and **ṝ**: no **ṝ** actually appears anywhere among their forms.

b. The (quotable) r̥-roots are 2 kr̥ *strew*, 1 gr̥ *sing*, 2 gr̥ *swallow*, 1 jr̥ *wear out*, tr̥, 1 çr̥ *crush*.

c. The (quotable) r̥ and r̄-roots are r̥, 1 dr̥ *pierce*, 1 pr̥ *fill*, 1 mr̥ *die*, 2 vr̥ *choose*, str̥, hvr̥.

d. Forms analogous with these are sometimes made also from other roots: thus, cīrṇa, cīrtvā, carcūryá, from √car; spūrdhán and spūrdháse from √ spr̥dh.

243. In a few cases r̥ comes from the contraction of other syllables than **ar** and **ra**: thus, in tr̥ta and tr̥tīya, from **ri**; in çr̥ṇu, from **ru**; in bhr̥kūṭi, from **rū**.

Vowel-lengthening.

244. Vowel-lengthening concerns especially **i** and **u**, since the lengthening of **a** is in part (except where in evident analogy with that of **i** and **u**) indistinguishable from its increment, and r̥ is made long only in certain plural cases of stems in r̥ (or **ar: 369** ff.). Lengthening is a much more irregular and sporadic change than increment, and its cases will in general be left to be pointed out in connection with the processes of inflection and derivation: a few only will be mentioned here.

245. a. Final radical **i** and **u** are especially liable to prolongation before **y**: as in passive and gerund and so on.

b. Final radical **ir** and **ur** (from variable r̥-roots: **242**) are liable to prolongation before all consonants except those of personal endings: namely, before **y** and **tvā** and **na**: and in declension before **bh** and **s** (**392**). Radical **is** has the same prolongation in declension (**392**).

246. Compensatory lengthening, or absorption by a vowel of the time of a lost following consonant, is by no means common. Certain instances of it have been pointed out above (**179, 198 c, d, 199 d, 222 b**). Perhaps such cases as **pitā** for **pitars** (**371 a**) and **dhanī** for **dhanins** (**439**) are to be classed here.

247. The final vowel of a former member of a compound is often made long, especially in the Veda. Prolongations of final **a**, and before **v**, are most frequent; but cases are found of every variety. Examples are: devāvī́, vayunāvíd, prāvŕ̥ṣ, r̥tā́vasu, índrāvant, sadanāsád, çatā́magha, viçvā́nara, ékādaça; apījū́, pariṇáh, vīrúdh, tuvīmaghá, tvíṣīmant, çáktīvant; vasūjū́, anūrúdh, sūmā́ya, purūvásu.

248. In the Veda, the final vowel of a word — generally **a**, much less often **i** and **u** — is in a large number of cases prolonged. Usually the prolongation takes place where it is favored by the metre, but sometimes even where the metre opposes the change (for details, see the various Prātiçākhyas).

Words of which the finals are thus treated are:

a. Particles: namely, **áthā, ádhā, evā́, utā́, ghā́, hā, ihā́, ivā, cā, smā, nā́, aṅgā́, kílā, átrā, yátrā, tátrā, kútrā, anyátrā, ubhayátrā, adyā́, ácchā, ápā, prā́; átī, ní, yádī, nahí, abhí, ví; ū, tū́, nū́, sū́, makṣū́.**

b. Case-forms: especially instr. sing., as **enā́, ténā, yénā, svénā,** and others; rarely gen. sing., as **asyā, hariṇásyā.** Cases besides these are few: so **sī́mā, vṛṣabhā, hariyojanā** (voc.); **tanvī̀** (loc.); and **urū́** and (not rarely) **purū́.**

c. Verb-forms ending in **a,** in great number and variety: thus (nearly in the order of their comparative frequency), 2d sing. impv. act., as **pibā, syā, gamayā, dhāráyā;** — 2d pl. act. in **ta** and **tha,** as **sthā, attā, bibhṛtā, jayatā, çṛṇutā, anadatā, nayathā, jīvayathā** (and one or two in **tana: aviṣṭanā, hantanā**); — 1st pl. act. in **ma,** as **vidmā, riṣāmā, ṛdhyāmā, ruhemā, vanuyāmā, cakṛmā, marmṛjmā;** — 2d sing. impv. mid. in **sva,** as **yukṣvā, īḍiṣvā, dadhiṣvā, vahasvā;** — 1st and 3d sing. perf. act., as **vedā, viveçā, jagrabhā;** 2d sing. perf. act., **vetthā;** — 2d pl. perf. act., **anajā, cakrā.** Of verb-forms ending in **i,** only the 2d sing. impv. act.: thus, **kṛdhī, kṛṇuhī́, kṣidhī́, çrudhī, çṛṇudhī, çṛṇuhī, dīdihī, jahī.**

d. To these may be added the gerund in **ya** (**993 a**), as **abhigū́ryā, ā́cyā.**

Vowel-lightening.

249. The alteration of short **a** to an **i** or **u**-vowel in the formative processes of the language, except in **ṛ** or **ar** roots (as explained above), is a sporadic phenomenon only.

250. But the lightening of a long **ā** especially to an **i**-vowel (as also its loss), is a frequent process; no other vowel is so unstable.

a. Of the class-sign **nā** (of the **krī**-class of verbs: **717 ff.**), the **ā** is in weak forms changed to **ī,** and before vowel-endings dropped altogether. The final **ā** of certain roots is treated in the same manner: thus, **mā, hā,** etc. (**662—6**). And from some roots, **ā-** and **ī-** or **i**-forms so interchange that it is difficult to classify them or to determine the true character of the root.

b. Radical **ā** is weakened to the semblance of the union-vowel **i** in certain verbal forms: as perfect **dadima** from √**dā** etc. (**794k**); aorist **adhithās** from √**dhā** etc. (**834 a**); present **jahimas** from √**hā** etc. (**665**).

c. Radical **ā** is shortened to the semblance of stem-**a** in a number of reduplicated forms, as **tiṣṭha, piba, dada,** etc.: see **671—4**; also in a few aorists, as **áhvam, ákhyam,** etc.: see **847.**

d. Radical **ā** sometimes becomes **e,** especially before **y**: as **stheyāsam, deya.**

251. Certain **ā**-roots, because of their peculiar exchanges with **ī** and **i**-forms, especially in forming the present stem, are given by the Hindu grammarians as roots ending in **e** or **āi** or **o.** Thus, from 2 **dhā** *suck* (**dhe**) come the present **dháyati** and participle and gerund **dhītá, dhītvā́**; the other forms are made from **dhā**, as **dadhus, adhāt, dhāsyati, dhā́tave, dhāpayati.** From 2 **gā** *sing* (**gāi**) come the present **gā́yati,** the participle and gerund **gītá** and **gītvā́,** and passive **gīyáte,** and the other forms from **gā.** From 3 **dā** *cut* (**do**) come the present **dyáti** and participle **ditá** or **diná,** and the other forms from **dā.** The irregularities of these roots will be treated below, under the various formations (see especially **761 d** ff.).

252. By a process of abbreviation essentially akin with that of **ar** or **ra** to **ṛ**, the **va** (usually initial) of a number of roots becomes **u,** and the **ya** of a much smaller number becomes **i,** in certain verbal forms and derivatives. Thus, from **vac** come **uvā́ca, ucyā́sam, uktvā́, uktá, uktí, ukthá,** etc.; from **yaj** come **iyā́ja, ijyā́sam, iṣṭvā́, iṣṭá, íṣṭi,** etc. See below, under the various formations.

a. To this change is given by European grammarians the name of **samprasāraṇa,** by adaptation of a term used in the native grammar.

253. A short **a,** of root or ending, is not infrequently lost between consonants in a weakened syllable: thus, in verb-forms, **ghnánti, ápaptam, jagmús, jajñús, ájñata**; in noun-forms, **rā́jñe, rā́jñī.**

254. Union-vowels. All the simple vowels come to assume in certain cases the aspect of union-vowels, or insertions between root or stem and ending of inflection or of derivation.

a. That character belongs oftenest to **i,** which is very widely used: 1. before the **s** of aorist and future and desiderative stems, as in **ájīviṣam, jīviṣyā́mi, jíjīviṣāmi**; 2. in tense-inflection, especially perfect, as **jijīvimá**; occasionally also present, as **ániti, róditi**; 3. in derivation, as **jīvitá, khánitum, janitṛ́, rociṣṇú,** etc. etc.

b. Long **ī** is used sometimes instead of short: thus, **ágrahīṣam, grahīṣyā́mi; bravīti, vāvadīti; tarītṛ́, savītṛ́**; it is also often introduced before **s** and **t** of the 2d and 3d sing. of verbs: thus, **ā́sīs, ā́sīt.**

c. For details respecting these, and the more irregular and sporadic occurrences of **u**- and **a**-vowels in the same character, see below.

Nasal Increment.

255. Both in roots and in endings, a distinction of stronger and weaker forms is very often made by the presence or absence of a nasal element, a nasal mute or **anusvāra,** before a following consonant. In general, the stronger form is doubtless the more original; but, in the present condition of the language, the nasal has come in great measure to seem, and to some extent also to be used, as an actually strengthening element, introduced under certain conditions in formative and inflective processes.

a. Examples are, of roots: **ac** and **añc**, **grath** and **granth**, **vid** and **vind**, **daç** and **dañç**, **sras** and **sraṅs**, **dṛh** and **dṛṅh**: of endings, **bhárantam** and **bháratā**, **mánasī** and **mánāṅsi**.

256. A final **n**, whether of stem or of root, is less stable than any other consonant, where a weaker form is called for: thus, from **rā́jan** we have **rā́jā** and **rā́jabhis**, and in composition **rāja**; from **dhanín**, **dhanī́** and **dhaníbhis** and **dháni**; from √**han** we have **hathá** and **hatá**, etc. A final radical **m** is sometimes treated in the same way: thus, from √**gam**, **gahí**, **gatám**, **gatá**, **gáti**.

257. Inserted **n**. On the other hand, the nasal **n** has come to be used with great — and, in the later history of the language, with increasing — frequency as a union-consonant, inserted between vowels: thus, from **agní**, **agnínā** and **agnīnā́m**; from **mádhu**, **mádhunas**, **mádhunī**, **mádhūni**; from **çivá**, **çivéna**, **çivā́ni**, **çivā́nām**.

258. Inserted **y**. **a.** After final **ā** of a root, a **y** is often found as apparently a mere union-consonant before another vowel: thus, in inflection, **ádhāyi** etc. (**844**), **çāyáyati** etc. (1042), **çivā́yās** etc. (**363 c**), **gā́yati** etc. (**761 e**); further, in derivation, **-gāya**, **-yāyam**, **dāyaka** etc.; **-sthāyika**; **pāyána**, **-gāyana**; **dhā́yas**, **-hāyas**; **sthāyin** etc. (many cases); **-hitāyin**, **-tatāyin**; **sthāyuka**.

b. Other more sporadic cases of inserted **y** — such as that in the pronoun-forms **ayam**, **iyam**, **vayam**, **yūyam**, **svayam**; and in optative inflection before an ending beginning with a vowel (**565**) — will be pointed out below in their connection.

Reduplication.

259. Reduplication of a root (originating doubtless in its complete repetition) has come to be a method of radical increment or strengthening in various formative processes: namely,

a. in present-stem formation (**642** ff.): as **dádāmi**, **bibhármi**;

b. in perfect-stem formation, almost universally (**782** ff.): as **tatā́na**, **dadhāú**, **cakā́ra**, **riréca**, **lulópa**;

c. in aorist-stem formation (**856** ff.): as **ádīdharam**, **ácucyavam**;

d. in intensive and desiderative-stem formation, throughout (1000 ff., 1026 ff.): as **jáñghanti**, **jóhavīti**, **marmṛjyáte**; **pípāsati**, **jíghāṅsati**;

e. in the formation of derivative noun-stems (**1143 e**): as **pápri**, **cárcara**, **sāsahí**, **cikitú**, **malimlucá**.

f. Rules for the treatment of the reduplication in these several cases will be given in the proper connection below.

260. As, by reason of the strengthening and weakening changes indicated above, the same root or stem not seldom exhibits, in the processes of inflection and derivation, varieties of stronger and weaker form, the distinction and description of these varieties forms an important part of the subjects hereafter to be treated.

CHAPTER IV.

DECLENSION.

261. The general subject of declension includes nouns, adjectives, and pronouns, all of which are inflected in essentially the same manner. But while the correspondence of nouns and adjectives is so close that they cannot well be separated in treatment (chap. V.), the pronouns, which exhibit many peculiarities, will be best dealt with in a separate chapter (VII.); and the words designating number, or numerals, also form a class peculiar enough to require to be presented by themselves (chap. VI.).

262. Declensional forms show primarily case and number; but they also indicate gender — since, though the distinctions of gender are made partly in the stem itself, they also appear, to no inconsiderable extent, in the changes of inflection.

263. Gender. The genders are three, namely masculine, feminine, and neuter, as in the other older Indo-European languages; and they follow in general the same laws of distribution as, for example, in Greek and Latin.

a. The only words which show no sign of gender-distinction are the personal pronouns of the first and second person (**491**), and the numerals above *four* (**483**).

264. Number. The numbers are three — singular, dual, and plural.

a. A few words are used only in the plural: as **dārās** *wife*, **ā́pas** *water;* the numeral **dva** *two*, is dual only; and, as in other languages, many words are, by the nature of their use, found to occur only in the singular.

265. As to the uses of the numbers, it needs only to be remarked that the dual is (with only very rare and sporadic exceptions) used strictly in all cases where two objects are logically indicated, whether directly or by combination of two individuals: thus, **çivé te dyā́vāpṛthivī́ ubhé stām** *may heaven and earth both be propitious to thee!* **dāivaṁ ca mānuṣaṁ ca hotārāu vṛtvā** *having chosen both the divine and the human sacrificers;* **pathor devayānasya pitṛyāṇasya ca** *of the two paths leading respectively to the gods and to the Fathers.*

a. The dual is used alone (without **dva** *two*) properly when the duality of the objects indicated is well understood: thus, **açvínāu** *the two Açvins;* **índrasya hárī** *Indra's two bays;* but **tasya dvāv açvāu staḥ** *he has two horses.* But now and then the dual stands alone pregnantly: thus, **vedaṁ vedāu vedān vā** *one Veda or two or more than two;* **ekaṣaṣṭe çate** *two hundred and sixty-one.*

266. Case. The cases are (including the vocative) eight: nominative, accusative, instrumental, dative, ablative, genitive, locative, and vocative.

a. The order in which they are here mentioned is that established for them by the Hindu grammarians, and accepted from these by Western scholars. The Hindu names of the cases are founded on this order: the nominative is called **prathamā** *first,* the accusative **dvitīyā** *second,* the genitive **ṣaṣṭhī** *sixth* (sc. **vibhakti** *division,* i. e. *case*), etc. The object sought in the arrangement is simply to set next to one another those cases which are to a greater or less extent, in one or another number, identical in form; and, putting the nominative first, as leading case, there is no other order by which that object could be attained. The vocative is not considered and named by the native grammarians as a case like the rest; in this work, it will be given in the singular (where alone it is ever distinguished from the nominative otherwise than by accent) at the end of the series of cases.

A compendious statement of the uses of the cases is given in the following paragraphs:

267. Uses of the Nominative. The nominative is the case of the subject of the sentence, and of any word qualifying the subject, whether attributively, in apposition, or as predicate.

268. One or two peculiar constructions call for notice:

a. A predicate nominative, instead of an objective predicate in the accusative, is used with middle verb-forms that signify regarding or calling one's self: thus, **sómam manyate papivā́n** (RV.) *he thinks he has been drinking soma;* **sá manyeta purāṇavít** (AV.) *he may regard himself as wise in ancient things;* **durgā́d vā́ āhartā́ 'vocathāḥ** (MS.) *thou hast claimed to be a savior out of trouble;* **índro brāhmaṇó brúvāṇaḥ** (TS.) *Indra pretending to be a Brahman;* **katthase satyavādī** (R.) *thou boastest thyself truthful.* Similarly with the phrase **rūpaṁ kṛ**: thus, **kṛṣṇó rūpáṁ kṛtvā́** (TS.) *taking on a black form* (i. e. *making shape for himself as one that is black*).

b. A word made by **iti** (1102) logically predicate to an object is ordinarily nominative: thus, **svargó loká íti yáṁ vádanti** (AV.) *what they call the heavenly world;* **tam agniṣṭoma ity ācakṣate** (AB.) *it they style* **agniṣṭoma; vidarbharājatanayāṁ damayantī 'ti viddhi mām** (MBh.) *know me for the Vidarbha-king's daughter, Damayantī by* *name*. Both constructions are combined in **ajñaṁ hi bālam ity āhuḥ pite 'ty eva tu mantradam** (M.) *for to an ignorant man they give the name of 'child', but that of 'father' to one who imparts the sacred texts.*

c. A nominative, instead of a second vocative, is sometimes added to a vocative by **ca** *and:* thus, **índraç ca sómam pibatam bṛhaspate** (RV.) *together with Indra, do ye two drink the soma, O Bṛhaspati!* **víçve devā yájamānaç ca sīdatā** (TS.) *O ye All-Gods, and the sacrificer, take seats!*

269. Uses of the Accusative. The accusative is especially the case of the direct object of a transitive verb, and of any word qualifying that object, as attribute or appositive or objective predicate. The construction of the verb is shared, of course, by its participles and infinitives; but also, in Sanskrit, by a number of other derivatives, having a more or less participial or infinitival character, and even sometimes by nouns and adjectives. A few prepositions are accompanied by the accusative. As less direct object, or goal of motion or action, the accusative is construed especially with verbs of approach and address. It is found used more adverbially as adjunct of place or time or manner; and a host of adverbs are accusative cases in form. Two accusatives are often found as objects of the same verb.

270. The use of the accusative as direct object of a transitive verb and of its infinitives and participles hardly needs illustration; an example or two are: **agním īḍe** *I praise Agni;* **námo bhárantaḥ** *bringing homage;* **bhū́yo dā́tum arhasi** *thou shouldst give more.* Of predicate words qualifying the object, an example is **tám ugráṁ kṛṇomi tám bráhmāṇam** (RV.) *him I make formidable, him a priest.*

271. Of verbal derivatives having so far a participial character that they share the construction of the verb, the variety is considerable: thus —

a. Derivatives in **u** from desiderative stems (**1038**) have wholly the character of present participles: thus, **damayantīm abhīpsavaḥ** (MBh.) *desiring to win Damayantī;* **didṛkṣur janakātmajām** (R.) *desiring to see Janaka's daughter.* Rarely, also, the verbal noun in **ā** from such a root: thus, **svargam abhikāñkṣayā** (R.) *with desire of paradise.*

b. So-called primary derivatives in **in** have the same character: thus, **mā́m kāmínī** (AV.) *loving me;* **enam abhibhāṣiṇī** (MBh.) *addressing him.* Even the obviously secondary **garbhín** has in ÇB. the same construction: thus, **sárvāṇi bhūtā́ni garbhy àbhavat** *he became pregnant with all beings.*

c. Derivatives in **aka,** in the later language: as, **bhavantam abhivādakaḥ** (MBh.) *intending to salute you;* **mithilām avarodhakaḥ** (R.) *besieging Mithilā.*

d. Nouns in **tar,** very frequently in the older language, and as periphrastic future forms (**942** ff.) in the later: thus, **hántā yó vṛtráṁ**

sánito 'tá vā́jaṁ dā́tā maghā́ni (RV.) *who slayeth the dragon, winneth booty, bestoweth largesses;* **tāu hī 'daṁ sarvaṁ hartārāu** (JB.) *for they seize on this universe;* **tyaktāraḥ saṁyuge prāṇān** (MBh.) *risking life in battle.*

e. The root itself, in the older language, used with the value of a present participle at the end of a compound: thus, **yáṁ yajñám paribhū́r ási** (RV.) *what offering thou surroundest (protectest);* **áhim apáḥ pariṣṭhā́m** (RV.) *the dragon confining the waters.* Also a superlative of a root-stem (**468, 471**): thus, **tváṁ vásu devayaté vániṣṭhaḥ** (RV.) *thou art chief winner of wealth for the pious;* **tā́ sómaṁ somapā́tamā** (RV.) *they two are the greatest drinkers of soma.*

f. The derivative in **i** from the (especially the reduplicated) root, in the older language: thus, **babhrír vájram papíḥ sómaṁ dadír gā́ḥ** (RV.) *bearing the thunderbolt, drinking the soma, bestowing kine;* **yajñám ātániḥ** (RV.) *extending the sacrifice.*

g. Derivatives in **uka,** very frequently in the Brāhmaṇa language: thus, **vatsā́ñç ca ghā́tuko vṛ́kaḥ** (AV.) *and the wolf destroys his calves;* **véduko vā́so bhavati** (TS.) *he wins a garment;* **kā́mukā enaṁ stríyo bhavanti** (MS.) *the women fall in love with him.*

h. Other cases are more sporadic: thus, derivatives in **a,** as **índro dṛḍhā́ cid ārujáḥ** (RV.) *Indra breaks up even what is fast;* **nāi 'vā 'rhaḥ pāitṛkaṁ riktham** (M.) *by no means entitled to his father's estate;* — in **atnu,** as **vīḍú cid ārujatnúbhiḥ** (RV.) *with the breakers of whatever is strong;* — in **atha,** as **yajáthāya devā́n** (RV.) *to make offering to the gods;* — in **ana,** as **taṁ nivāraṇe** (MBh.) *in restraining him;* **svamāṅsam iva bhojane** (R.) *as if in eating one's own flesh;* — in **ani,** as **samátsu turváṇiḥ pṛtanyū́n** (RV.) *overcoming foes in combats;* — in **ti,** as **ná táṁ dhūrtíḥ** (RV.) *there is no injuring him;* — in **van,** as **ápaçcāddaghvā́ 'nnam bhavati** (MS.) *he does not come short of food;* — in **snu,** as **sthirā́ cin namayiṣṇavaḥ** (RV.) *bowing even firm things.*

272. Examples of an accusative with an ordinary noun or adjective are only occasional: such words as **ánuvrata** *faithful to,* **prátirūpa** *corresponding to,* **abhidhṛṣṇu** *daring to cope with,* **pratyáñc** *opposite to,* may be regarded as taking an accusative in virtue of the preposition they contain; also **ánuka,** as **ánukā devā́ váruṇam** (MS.) *the gods are inferior to Varuṇa.* RV. has **tám antárvatīḥ** *pregnant with him;* and AV. has **mā́ṁ kā́mena** *through loving me.*

273. The direct construction of cases with prepositions is comparatively restricted in Sanskrit (**1123** ff.). With the accusative are oftenest found **prati,** *opposite to, in reference to,* etc.; also **anu** *after, in the course of;* **antar** or **antarā** *between;* rarely **ati** *across;* **abhi** *against, to;* and others (**1129**). Case-forms which have assumed a prepositional value are also often used with the accusative: as **antareṇa, uttareṇa, dakṣiṇena, avareṇa, ūrdhvam, ṛte.**

274. The accusative is very often found also as object of verbs which in the related languages are not transitive.

a. It stands especially as the goal of motion, with verbs of going, bringing, sending, and the like: thus, **vidarbhān agaman** (MBh.) *they went to Vidarbha;* **divaṁ yayuḥ** (MBh.) *they went to heaven;* **vanagulmān dhāvantaḥ** (MBh.) *running to woods and bushes;* **apó dívam úd vahanti** (AV.) *they carry up waters to the sky;* **devā́n yaje** (AV.) *I make offering to the gods.*

b. With verbs meaning *go,* this is an extremely common construction; and the use of such a verb with an abstract noun makes peculiar phrases of *becoming:* thus, **samatām eti** *he goes to equality* (i. e. *becomes equal);* **sa gacched badhyatām mama** (MBh.) *he shall become liable to be slain by me;* **sa pañcatvam āgataḥ** (H.) *he was resolved into the five elements* (*underwent dissolution, died*).

c. Verbs of speaking follow the same rule: thus, **tam abravīt** *he said to him;* **prākroçad uccāir nāiṣadham** (MBh.) *she cried out loudly to the Nishadhan;* **yás tvo 'vā́ca** (AV.) *who spoke to thee.*

d. The assumption of an accusative object is exceptionally easy in Sanskrit, and such an object is often taken by a verb or phrase which is strictly of intransitive character: thus, **sáhasā prá 'sy anyā́n** (RV.) *in might thou excellest* (lit. *art ahead*) *others;* **devā́ vāí bráhma sám avadanta** (MS.) *the gods were discussing* (lit. *were talking together*) **brahman; antár vāí mā yajñād yanti** (MS.) *surely they are cutting me off* (lit. *are going between*) *from the offering;* **tā́ṁ sám babhūva** (ÇB.) *he had intercourse with her.*

275. Examples of the cognate accusative, or accusative of implied object, are not infrequent: thus, **tápas tapyāmahe** (AV.) *we do penance;* **té hāi 'tā́m edhatúm edhā́ṁ cakrire** (ÇB.) *they prospered with that prosperity;* **uṣitvā sukhavāsam** (R.) *abiding happily.*

276. The accusative is often used in more adverbial constructions. Thus:

a. Occasionally, to denote measure of space: thus, **yojanaçataṁ gantum** (MBh.) *to go a hundred leagues;* **ṣaḍ ucchrito yojanāni** (MBh.) *six leagues high.*

b. Much more often, to denote measure or duration of time: thus, **sá saṁvatsarám ūrdhvò 'tiṣṭhat** (AV.) *he stood a year upright;* **tisró rā́trīr dīkṣitáḥ syāt** (TS.) *let him be consecrated three nights;* **gatvā trīn ahorātrān** (MBh.) *having traveled three complete days.*

c. Sometimes, to denote the point of space, or, oftener, of time: thus, **yām asya díçaṁ dásyuḥ syā́t** (ÇB.) *whatever region his enemy may be in;* **ténāi 'tā́ṁ rā́triṁ sahā́" jagāma** (ÇB.) *he arrived that night with him;* **imāṁ rajanīṁ vyuṣṭām** (MBh.) *this current night.*

d. Very often, to denote manner or accompanying circumstance. Thus, the neuter accusative of innumerable adjectives, simple or compound

(1111), is used adverbially, while certain kinds of compounds are thus used to such an extent that the Hindu grammarians have made of them a special adverbial class (1313).

e. Special cases are occasionally met with: thus, **brahmacáryam uvāsa** (ÇB.) *he kept a term of studentship;* **phalám pacyánte** (MS.) *they ripen their fruit;* **gā́ṁ dīvyadhvam** (MS., S.) *gamble for a cow.*

277. The accusative is, of course, freely used with other cases to limit the same verb, as the sense requires. And whenever it is usable with a verb in two different constructions, the verb may take two accusatives, one in each construction: and such combinations are quite frequent in Sanskrit. Thus, with verbs of appealing, asking, having recourse: as, **apó yācāmi bheṣajám** (RV.) *I ask the waters for medicine;* **tvām ahaṁ satyam icchāmi** (R.) *I desire truth from thee;* **tvāṁ vayaṁ çaraṇaṁ gatāḥ** (MBh.) *we have resorted to thee for succor;* — with verbs of bringing, sending, following, imparting, saying: as, **gurutvaṁ naraṁ nayanti** (H.) *they bring a man to respectability;* **sītā cā 'nvetu māṁ vanam** (R.) *and let Sītā accompany me to the forest;* **supéçasam mā́ 'va sṛjanty ástam** (RV.) *they let me go home well adorned;* **tām idam abravīt** (MBh.) *this he said to her;* — and in other less common cases: as, **vṛkṣám pakvám phálaṁ dhūnuhi** (RV.) *shake ripe fruit from the tree;* **tā́ṁ viṣám evā́ 'dhok** (AV.) *poison he milked from her;* **jitvā rājyaṁ nalam** (MBh.) *having won the kingdom from Nala;* **ámuṣṇītam paṇíṁ gā́ḥ** (RV.) *ye robbed the Paṇi of the kine;* **draṣṭum icchāvaḥ putram paçcimadarçanam** (R.) *we wish to see our son for the last time.*

a. A causative form of a transitive verb regularly admits two accusative objects: thus, **devā́ṅ uçatáḥ pāyayā havíḥ** (RV.) *make the eager gods drink the oblation;* **óṣadhīr evá phálaṁ grāhayati** (MS.) *he makes the plants bear fruit;* **vaṇijo dāpayet karān** (M.) *he should cause the merchants to pay taxes.* But such a causative sometimes takes an instrumental instead of a second accusative: see **282 b.**

278. Uses of the Instrumental. The instrumental is originally the *with*-case: it denotes adjacency, accompaniment, association — passing over into the expression of means and instrument by the same transfer of meaning which appears in the English prepositions *with* and *by*.

a. Nearly all the uses of the case are readily deducible from this fundamental meaning, and show nothing anomalous or difficult.

279. The instrumental is often used to signify accompaniment: thus, **agnír devébhir ā́ gamat** (RV.) *may Agni come hither along with the gods;* **marúdbhī rudráṁ huvema** (RV.) *we would call Rudra with the Maruts;* **dvāpareṇa sahāyena kva yāsyasi** (MBh.) *whither wilt thou go, with Dvāpara for companion?* **kathayan nāiṣadhena** (MBh.) *talking with the Nishadhan.* But the relation of simple accompaniment is more often helped to plainer expression by prepositions (**saha** etc.: **284**).

280. The instrumental of means or instrument or agent is yet more frequent: thus, **bhadráṁ kárṇebhiḥ çṛṇuyāma** (RV.) *may we hear with our ears what is propitious;* **çastreṇa nidhanam** (MBh.) *death by the sword;* **kecit padbhyāṁ hatā gajāiḥ** (MBh.) *some were slain by the elephants with their feet;* **pṛthak pāṇibhyāṁ darbhataruṇakāir navanītenā 'ñguṣṭhopakaniṣṭhikābhyām akṣiṇī ājya** (AGS.) *anointing their eyes with fresh butter, by help of the bunches of* **darbha**-*grass, with the thumb and ring-finger, using the two hands successively.* And this passes easily over into the expression of occasion or reason (for which the ablative is more frequent): thus, **kṛpayā** *through pity;* **tena satyena** *in virtue of that truth.*

281. Of special applications, the following may be noticed:

a. Accordance, equality, likeness, and the like: thus, **samáṁ jyótiḥ sū́ryeṇa** (AV.) *a brightness equal with the sun;* **yeṣām ahaṁ na pādarajasā tulyaḥ** (MBh.) *to the dust of whose feet I am not equal.*

b. Price (by which obtained): thus, **daçábhiḥ krīṇāti dhenúbhiḥ** (RV.) *he buys with ten kine;* **gavāṁ çatasahasreṇa dīyatāṁ çabalā mama** (R.) *let Çabalā be given me for a hundred thousand cows;* **sa te 'kṣahṛdayaṁ dātā rājā, 'çvahṛdayena vāi** (MBh.) *the king will give thee the secret science of dice in return for that of horses.*

c. Medium, and hence also space or distance or road, traversed: thus, **udnā́ ná nā́vam anayanta** (RV.) *they brought [him] as it were a ship by water;* **é 'há yātam pathíbhir devayā́nāiḥ** (RV.) *come hither by god-traveled paths;* **jagmur vihāyasā** (MBh.) *they went off through the air.*

d. Time passed through, or by the lapse of which anything is brought about: thus, **vidarbhān yātum icchāmy ekāhnā** (MBh.) *I wish to go to Vidarbha in the course of one day;* **te ca kālena mahatā yāuvanam pratipedire** (R.) *and they in a long time attained adolescence;* **tatra kālena jāyante mānavā dīrghajīvinaḥ** (M.) *there in time are born men long-lived.* This use of the instrumental borders upon that of the locative and ablative.

e. The part of the body on (or by) which anything is borne is usually expressed by the instrumental: as, **kukkuraḥ skandheno 'hyate** (H.) *a dog is carried on the shoulder;* and this construction is extended to such cases as **tulayā kṛtam** (H.) *put on* (i. e. *so as to be carried by*) *a balance.*

f. Not infrequent are such phrases as **bahunā kim pralāpena** (R.) *what is the use of* (i. e. *is gained by*) *much talking?* **ko nu me jīvitenā 'rthaḥ** (MBh.) *what object is life to me?* **nīrujas tu kim āuṣadhāiḥ** (H.) *but what has a well man to do with medicines?*

g. An instrumental of accompaniment is occasionally used almost or quite with the value of an instrumental absolute: thus, **na tvayā 'tra mayā 'vasthitena kā 'pi cintā kāryā** (Pañc.) *with me at hand, thou need'st feel no anxiety whatever on this point.*

282. a. The construction of a passive verb (or participle) with an instrumental of the agent is common from the earliest period, and becomes decidedly more so later, the passive participle with instrumental taking to no small extent the place of an active verb with its subject. Thus, **yaména dattáḥ** (RV.) *given by Yama;* **ṛṣibhir ī́ḍyaḥ** (RV.) *to be praised by sages;* **vyādhena jālaṁ vistīrṇam** (H.) *by the hunter a net [was] spread;* **tac chrutvā jaradgaveno 'ktam** (H.) *Jaradgava, hearing this, said;* **mayā gantavyam** (H.) *I shall go.* A predicate to the instrumental subject of such a construction is, of course, also in the instrumental: thus, **adhunā tavā 'nucareṇa mayā sarvathā bhavitavyam** (H.) *henceforth I shall always be thy companion;* **avahitāir bhavitavyam bhavadbhiḥ** (Vikr.) *you must be attentive.*

b. A causative verb sometimes takes an instrumental instead of an accusative as second object: thus, **tāṁ çvabhiḥ khādayed rājā** (M.) *the king should have her devoured by dogs;* **tā́ váruṇenā 'grāhayat** (MS.) *he caused Varuṇa to seize them.*

283. Many instrumental constructions are such as call in translation for other prepositions than *with* or *by;* yet the true instrumental relation is usually to be traced, especially if the etymological sense of the words be carefully considered.

a. More anomalously, however, the instrumental is used interchangeably with the ablative with words signifying separation: thus, **vatsāír víyutāḥ** (RV.) *separated from their calves;* **mā́ 'hám ātmánā ví rādhiṣi** (AV.) *let me not be severed from the breath of life;* **sa tayā vyayujyata** (MBh.) *he was parted from her;* **pāpmánāi 'vāí 'naṁ ví punanti** (MS.) *they cleanse him from evil* (compare English *parted with*). The same meaning may be given to the case even when accompanied by **saha** *with:* thus, **bhartrā saha viyogaḥ** (MBh.) *separation from her husband.*

284. The prepositions taking the instrumental (1127) are those signifying *with* and the like: thus, **saha,** with the adverbial words containing **sa** as an element, as **sākam, sārdham, saratham;** — and, in general, a word compounded with **sa, sam, saha** takes an instrumental as its regular and natural complement. But also the preposition **vinā** *without* takes sometimes the instrumental (cf. **283 a**).

285. Uses of the Dative. The dative is the case of the indirect object — of that toward or in the direction of or in order to or for which anything is or is done (either intransitively or to a direct object).

a. In more physical connections, the uses of the dative approach those of the accusative (the more proper *to*-case), and the two are sometimes interchangeable; but the general value of the dative as the *toward-* or *for-*case is almost everywhere distinctly to be traced.

286. Thus, the dative is used with —

a. Words signifying *give, share out, assign,* and the like: thus, **yó ná dádāti sákhye** (RV.) *who gives not to a friend;* **yácchā 'smāi çárma** (RV.) *bestow upon him protection.*

b. Words signifying *show, announce, declare,* and the like: thus, **dhanur darçaya rāmāya** (R.) *show the bow to Rāma;* **āvír ebhyo abhavat sūryaḥ** (RV.) *the sun was manifested to them;* **ṛtuparṇam bhīmāya pratyavedayan** (MBh.) *they announced Rituparṇa to Bhīma;* **tebhyaḥ pratijñāya** (MBh.) *having promised to them.*

c. Words signifying *give attention, have a regard* or *feeling, aspire,* and the like: thus, **niveçāya mano dadhuḥ** (MBh.) *they set their minds upon encamping;* **māté 'va putrébhyo mṛḍa** (AV.) *be gracious as a mother to her sons;* **kím asmábhyaṁ hṛṇīṣe** (RV.) *why art thou angry at us?* **kāmāya spṛhayaty ātmā** (Spr.) *the soul longs for love.*

d. Words signifying *please, suit, conduce,* and the like: thus, **yad-yad rocate viprebhyaḥ** (M.) *whatever is pleasing to Brahmans;* **tad ānantyāya kalpate** (KU.) *that makes for immortality.*

e. Words signifying *inclination, obeisance,* and the like: thus, **máhyaṁ namantām pradíçaç cátasraḥ** (RV.) *let the four quarters bow themselves to me;* **devebhyo namaskṛtya** (MBh.) *having paid homage to the gods.*

f. Words signifying *hurling* or *casting:* as **yéna dūḍáçe ásyasi** (AV.) *with which thou hurlest at the impious.*

g. In some of these constructions the genitive and locative are also used: see below.

287. In its more distinctive sense, as signifying *for, for the benefit of, with reference to,* and the like, the dative is used freely, and in a great variety of constructions. And this use passes over into that of the dative of end or purpose, which is extremely common. Thus, **íṣuṁ kṛṇvānā́ ásanāya** (AV.) *making an arrow for hurling;* **gṛhṇāmi te sāubhagatvā́ya hástam** (RV.) *I take thy hand in order to happiness;* **rāṣṭrā́ya máhyam badhyatāṁ sapátnebhyaḥ parābhúve** (AV.) *be it bound on in order to royalty for me, in order to destruction for my enemies.*

a. Such a dative is much used predicatively (and oftenest with the copula omitted), in the sense of *makes for, tends toward;* also *is intended for,* and so *must;* or *is liable to,* and so *can.* Thus, **upadeço mūrkhāṇām prakopāya na çāntaye** (H.) *good counsel [tends] to the exasperation, not the conciliation, of fools;* **sa ca tasyāḥ saṁtoṣāya nā 'bhavat** (H.) *and he was not to her satisfaction;* **sugopā́ asi ná dábhāya** (RV.) *thou art a good herdsman, not one for cheating* (i. e. *not to be cheated*).

b. These uses of the dative are in the older language especially illustrated by the dative infinitives, for which see **982**.

288. The dative is not used with prepositions (**1124**).

289. Uses of the Ablative. The ablative is the *from*-case, in the various senses of that preposition; it is used to express removal, separation, distinction, issue, and the like.

290. The ablative is used where expulsion, removal, distinction, release, defense, and other kindred relations are expressed: thus, **té sedhanti pathó vṛ́kam** (AV.) *they drive away the wolf from the path;* **mā́ prá**

gā́ma patháḥ (RV.) *may we not go away from the path*; **éti vā́ eṣā́ yajñamukhā́t** (MS.) *he verily goes away from the face of the sacrifice*; **āré asmád astu hetíḥ** (AV.) *far from us be your missile*; **pátāṁ no vŕ̥kāt** (RV.) *save us from the wolf*; **ástabhnād dyā́m avasrásaḥ** (RV.) *he kept* (lit. *made firm*) *the sky from falling*.

291. The ablative is used where procedure or issue from something as from a source or starting-point is signified: thus, **çukrā́ kr̥ṣṇā́d ajaniṣṭa** (RV.) *the bright one has been born from the black one*; **lobhāt krodhaḥ prabhavati** (MBh.) *passion arises from greed*; **vā́tāt te prāṇám avidam** (AV.) *I have won thy life-breath from the wind*; **yé prā́cyā diçó abhidā́santy asmā́n** (AV.) *who attack us from the eastern quarter*; **tac chrutvā sakhigaṇāt** (MBh.) *having heard that from the troop of friends*; **vāyúr antarikṣād abhā́ṣata** (MBh.) *the wind spoke from the sky*.

a. Hence also, procedure as from a cause or occasion is signified by the ablative: this is especially frequent in the later language, and in technical phraseology is a standing construction; it borders on instrumental constructions. Thus, **vájrasya çúṣṇād dadāra** (RV.) *from (by reason of) the fury of the thunderbolt he burst asunder*; **yasya daṇḍabhayāt sarve dharmam anurudhyanti** (MBh.) *from fear of whose rod all are constant to duty*; **akāramiçritatvād ekārasya** (Tribh.) *because e contains an element of* a.

b. Very rarely, an ablative has the sense of *after*: thus, **agacchann ahorātrāt tīrtham** (MBh.) *they went to the shrine after a whole day*; **ṭakārāt sakāre takāreṇa** (APr.) *after* ṭ, *before* s, *is inserted* t.

292. One or two special applications of the ablative construction are to be noticed:

a. The ablative with words implying fear (terrified recoil from): thus, **tásyā jātā́yāḥ sárvam abibhet** (AV.) *everything was afraid of her at her birth*; **yásmād réjanta kr̥ṣṭáyaḥ** (RV.) *at whom mortals tremble*; **yuṣmád bhiyā́** (RV.) *through fear of you*; **yasmān no 'dvijate lokaḥ** (BhG.) *of whom the world is not afraid*.

b. The ablative of comparison (distinction from): thus, **prá ririce divá índraḥ pr̥thivyā́ḥ** (RV.) *Indra is greater than the heaven and the earth*. With a comparative, or other word used in a kindred way, the ablative is the regular and almost constant construction: thus, **svādóḥ svādī́yaḥ** (RV.) *sweeter than the sweet*; **kiṁ tasmād duḥkhataram** (MBh.) *what is more painful than that?* **ko mitrād anyaḥ** (H.) *who else than a friend*; **gā avr̥ṇīthā mat** (AB.) *thou hast chosen the kine rather than me*; **ajñebhyo granthinaḥ çreṣṭhā granthibhyo dhāriṇo varāḥ** (M.) *possessors of texts are better than ignorant men; rememberers are better than possessors*; **tád anyátra tván nī́ dadhmasi** (AV.) *we set this down elsewhere (away) from thee*; **pū́rvā víçvasmād bhúvanāt** (RV.) *earlier than all beings*.

c. Occasionally, a probably possessive genitive is used with the comparative; or an instrumental (as in a comparison of equality): thus,

nā 'sti dhanyataro mama (R.) *there is no one more fortunate than I* (i. e. *my superior in fortune*); **putram mama prāṇāir garīyasam** (MBh.) *a son dearer than my life.*

d. Occasionally, an ablative is used instead of a partitive genitive: thus, **mithunād ekaṁ jaghāna** (R.) *he slew one out of the pair;* **tebhya ekam** (KSS.) *one of them.*

293. The ablative is used with a variety of prepositions and words sharing a prepositional character (**1128**); but all these have rather an adverbial value, as strengthening or defining the *from*-relation, than any proper governing force. We may notice here:

a. In the Veda, **ádhi** and **pári** are much used as directing and strengthening adjuncts with the ablative: as, **jātó himávatas pári** (AV.) *born from the Himalaya (forth)*; **samudrā́d ádhi jajñiṣe** (AV.) *thou art born from the ocean;* **cárantam pári tasthúṣaḥ** (RV.) *moving forth from that which stands fast.*

b. Also **purā́** (and **purás**), in the sense of *forward from*, and hence *before:* as, **purā́ járasaḥ** (RV.) *before old age:* and hence also, with words of protection and the like, *from:* as **çaçamānáḥ purā́ nidáḥ** (RV.) *securing from ill-will.*

c. Also **ā́**, in the sense of *hither from, all the way from:* as, **ā́ mū́lād ánu çuṣyatu** (AV.) *let it dry completely up from the root;* **tásmād ā́ nadyò nā́ma stha** (AV.) *since that time ye are called rivers.* But usually, and especially in the later language, the measurement of interval implied in **ā́** is reversed in direction, and the construction means *all the way to, until:* as, **yatī́ giríbhya ā́ samudrā́t** (RV.) *going from the mountains to the ocean;* **ā́ 'syá yajñásyo 'dṛ́caḥ** (VS.) *until the end of this sacrifice;* **ā ṣoḍaçāt** (M.) *till the sixteenth year;* **ā pradānāt** (Ç.) *until her marriage.*

294. Uses of the Genitive. **a.** The proper value of the genitive is adjectival; it belongs to and qualifies a noun, designating something relating to the latter in a manner which the nature of the case, or the connection, defines more nearly. Other genitive constructions, with adjective or verb or preposition, appear to arise out of this, by a more or less distinctly traceable connection.

b. The use of the genitive has become much extended, especially in the later language, by attribution of a noun-character to the adjective, and by pregnant verbal construction, so that it often bears the aspect of being a substitute for other cases — as dative, instrumental, ablative, locative.

295. The genitive in its normal adjective construction with a noun or pronoun is classifiable into the usual varieties: as, genitive of possession or appurtenance, including the complement of implied relation — this is, as elsewhere, the commonest of all; the so-called partitive genitive; the subjective and objective genitives; and so on. Genitives of apposition or equivalence (*city of Rome*), and of characteristic (*man of honor*), do not occur, and hardly that of material (*house of wood*). Examples are: **índrasya vájraḥ** *Indra's thunderbolt;* **pitā putrāṇām** *father of sons;* **putraḥ pituḥ** *son of the father;* **pituḥ kāmaḥ putrasya,** *the father's love of the son;* **ke naḥ** *which of us;* **çataṁ dāsīnām** *a hundred female slaves.*

a. The expression of possession etc. on the part of pronouns is made almost entirely by the genitive case, and not by a derived possessive adjective (**516**).

b. Exceptional cases like **nagarasya mārgaḥ** *the road to the city* (cf. *le chemin de Paris*), **yasyā 'haṁ dūta īpsitaḥ** (MBh.) *as messenger to whom I am wanted,* are occasionally met with.

296. The genitive is dependent on an adjective:

a. A so-called partitive genitive with a superlative, or another word of similar substantival value: thus, **çreṣṭhaṁ vīrāṇām** *best of heroes;* **vīrúdhāṁ vīryàvatī** (AV.) *of plants the mighty (mightiest) one.*

b. Very often, by a transfer of the possessive genitive from noun to adjective, the adjective being treated as if it had noun-value: thus, **tasya samaḥ** or **anurūpaḥ** or **sádṛçaḥ** *resembling him* (i. e. *his like*); **tasya priyā** *dear to him* (*his dear one*); **tasyā 'viditam** *unknown to him* (*his unknown thing*); **hávyaç carṣaṇīnā́m** (RV.) *to be sacrificed to by mortals* (*their object of sacrifice*); **īpsito naranārīṇām** (MBh.) *desired of men and women* (*their object of desire*); **yasya kasya prasūtaḥ** (H.) *of whomsoever born* (*his son*); **hantavyo 'smi na te** (MBh.) *I am not to be slain of thee;* **kim arthināṁ vañcayitavyam asti** (H.) *why should there be a deceiving of suppliants?*

c. In part, by a construction similar to that of verbs which take a genitive object: thus, **abhijñā rājadharmāṇām** (R.) *understanding the duties of a king.*

297. The genitive as object of a verb is:

a. A possessive genitive of the recipient, by pregnant construction, with verbs signifying *give, impart, communicate,* and the like: thus, **varān pradāyā 'sya** (MBh.) *having bestowed gifts upon him* (*made them his by bestowal*); **rājño niveditam** (H.) *it was made known to the king* (*made his by knowledge*); **yad anyasya pratijñāya punar anyasya dīyate** (M.) *that after being promised to one she is given to another.* This construction, by which the genitive becomes substitute for a dative or locative, abounds in the later language, and is extended sometimes to problematic and difficult cases.

b. A (in most cases, probably) partitive genitive, as a less complete or less absolute object than an accusative: thus, with verbs meaning *partake* (*eat, drink,* etc.), as **píba sutásya** (AV.) *drink (of) the soma;* **mádhvaḥ pāyaya** (RV.) *cause to drink the sweet draught;* — with verbs meaning *impart* (of the thing imparted) etc., as **dádāta no amṛ́tasya** (RV.) *bestow upon us immortality;* — with verbs meaning *enjoy, be satisfied* or *filled* *with:* as, **mátsy ándhasaḥ** (RV.) *do thou enjoy the juice;* **ājyasya pūrayanti** (S.) *they fill with butter;* — with verbs meaning *perceive note, care for, regard* with feeling of various kinds: as, **vásiṣṭhasya stuvatá índro açrot** (RV.) *Indra listened to Vasishtha who was praising him;* **yáthā máma smárāt** (AV.) *that he may think of me;* **tasya cukopa** (MBh.) *he was angry at him.*

c. A genitive of more doubtful character, with verbs meaning *rule* or *have authority:* as, **tvám īçiṣe vásūnām** (RV.) *thou art lord of good things;* **yáthā 'hám eṣā́ṁ virā́jāni** (AV.) *that I may rule over them;* **katham mṛtyuḥ prabhavati vedaçāstravidām** (M.) *how has death power over those who know the Vedas and treatises?*

d. A genitive, instead of an ablative, is sometimes found used with a verb of receiving of any kind (hearing included), and with one of fearing: thus, **yo rājñaḥ pratigṛhṇāti lubdhasya** (M.) *whoever accepts a gift from a greedy king;* **çṛṇu me** (MBh.) *learn from me;* **bibhīmas tava** (MBh.) *we are afraid of thee.*

298. A genitive in its usual possessive sense is often found as predicate, and not seldom with the copula omitted: thus, **yáthā́ 'so máma kévalaḥ** (AV.) *that thou mayest be wholly mine;* **sarvāḥ sampattayas tasya saṁtuṣṭaṁ yasya mānasam** (H.) *all good fortunes are his who has a contented mind;* — as objective predicate, **bhartuḥ putraṁ vijānanti** (M.) *they recognise a son as the husband's.*

299. a. The prepositional constructions of the genitive (**1130**) are for the most part with such prepositions as are really noun-cases and have the government of such: thus, **agre, arthe, kṛte,** and the like; also with other prepositional words which, in the general looseness of use of the genitive, have become assimilated to these. A few more real prepositions take the genitive: either usually, like **upári** *above,* or occasionally, like **adhás, antár, áti.**

b. A genitive is occasionally used in the older language with an adverb, either of place or of time: thus, **yátra kvà ca kurukṣetrásya** (ÇB.) *in whatever part of Kurukshetra;* **yátra tú bhū́mer jā́yeta** (MS.) *on what spot of earth he may be born;* **idā́nīm áhnaḥ** (RV.) *at this time of the day;* **yásyā rā́tryāḥ prātáḥ** (MS.) *on the morn of what night;* **dviḥ saṁvatsarasya** (K.) *twice a year.* Such expressions as the last occur also later.

300. a. The genitive is very little used adverbially; a few genitives of time occur in the older language: as, **aktos** *by night,* **vastos** *by day;* and there are found later such cases as **kasya cit kālasya** (Ç.) *after a certain time;* **tataḥ kālasya mahataḥ prayayāu** (R.) *then after a long time he went forth.*

b. A genitive, originally of possession, passing over into one of general concernment, comes in the later language (the construction is unknown earlier) to be used absolutely, with an agreeing participle, or quite rarely an adjective. From such cases as the following — **paçyato bakamūrkhasya nakulāir bhakṣitāḥ sutāḥ** (H.) *of the foolish heron, while he looked on, the young were eaten by the ichneumons*, or **gato 'rdharātraḥ kathāḥ kathayato mama** (KSS.) *half my night was passed in telling stories*, or **kartavyasya karmaṇaḥ kṣipram akriyamāṇasya kālaḥ pibati tadrasam** (H.) *of a work needing to be done but left undone time quickly drinks up its essence* — come into currency, by increasing independence of the genitive, such other cases as: **divaṁ jagāma munīnām paçyatāṁ tadā** (R.) *he went then to heaven, the ascetics looking on*; **evaṁ lālapatas tasya devadūtas tadā 'bhyetya vākyam āha** (MBh.) *as he thus lamented, a divine messenger coming addressed him*; **iti vādina evā 'syā dhenur āvavṛte vanāt** (Ragh.) *while he thus spoke, the cow came from the forest*. The genitive always indicates a living actor, and the participle is usually one of seeing or hearing or uttering, especially the former. The construction is said by the Hindu grammarians to convey an implication of disregard or despite; and such is often to be recognized in it, though not prevailingly.

301. Uses of the Locative. **a.** The locative is properly the *in*-case, the case expressing situation or location; but its sphere of use has been somewhat extended, so as to touch and overlap the boundaries of other cases, for which it seems to be a substitute.

b. Unimportant variations of the sense of *in* are those of *amid* or *among*, *on*, and *at*. Of course, also, situation in time as well as place is indicated by the case; and it is applied to yet less physical relations, to sphere of action and feeling and knowledge, to state of things, to accompanying circumstance; and out of this last grows the frequent use of the locative as the case absolute.

c. Moreover, by a pregnant construction, the locative is used to denote the place of rest or cessation of action or motion (*into* or *on to* instead of *in* or *on*; German *in* with accusative instead of dative: compare English *there* for *thither*).

302. a. The locative of situation in space hardly needs illustration. An example or two are: **yé devā́ diví sthá** (AV.) *which of you gods are in heaven*; **na deveṣu na yakṣeṣu tādṛk** (MBh.) *not among gods or Yakshas is such a one*; **párvatasya pṛṣṭhé** (RV.) *on the ridge of the mountain*; **vidáthe santu devā́ḥ** (RV.) *may the gods be at the assembly*; **daçame pade** (MBh.) *at the tenth step*.

b. The locative of time indicates the point of time at which anything takes place: thus, **asyā́ uṣáso vyùṣṭāu** (RV.) *at the shining forth of this dawn*; **etasminn eva kāle** (MBh.) *at just that time*; **dvādaçe varṣe** (MBh.) *in the twelfth year*. That the accusative is occasionally used in this sense, instead of the locative, was pointed out above (**276 c**).

c. The person with whom, instead of the place at which, one is or remains is put in the locative: thus, **tíṣṭhanty asmin paçávaḥ** (MS.) *animals abide with him*; **gurāu vasan** (M.) *living at a teacher's*; and, pregnantly, **tāvat tvayi bhaviṣyāmi** (MBh.) *so long will I cleave to thee*.

303. The locative of sphere or condition or circumstance is of very frequent use: thus, **máde áhim índro jaghāna** (RV.) *in fury Indra slew the dragon;* **mitrásya sumatāú syāma** (RV.) *may we be in the favor of Mitra;* **te vacane ratam** (MBh.) *delighted in thy words.*

a. This construction is, on the one hand, generalized into an expression for *in the matter* or *case of*, or *with reference to*, *respecting*, and takes in the later language a very wide range, touching upon genitive and dative constructions: thus, **é 'mám bhaja grā́me áçveṣu góṣu** (AV.) *be gennerous to him in retainers, in horses, in cattle;* **tám ít sakhitvá īmahe** (RV.) *him we beg for friendship;* **upāyo 'yam mayā dṛṣṭa ānayane tava** (MBh.) *this means was devised by me for (with reference to) bringing thee hither;* **satītve kāraṇaṁ striyāḥ** (H.) *the cause of (in the case of) a woman's chastity;* **na çakto 'bhavan nivāraṇe** (MBh.) *he was no capable of preventing.*

b. On the other hand, the expression by the locative of a condition of things in which anything takes place, or of a conditioning or accompanying circumstance, passes over into a well-marked absolute construction, which is known even in the earliest stage of the language, but becomes more frequent later. Transitional examples are: **háve tvā sū́ra údite háve madhyáṁdine diváḥ** (RV.) *I call to thee at the arisen sun (when the sun has risen), I call at midtime of the day;* **aparādhe kṛte 'pi ca na me kopaḥ** (MBh.) *and even in case of an offense committed, there is no anger on my part.*

c. The normal condition of the absolute construction is with a participle accompanying the noun: thus, **stīrṇé barhíṣi samidhāné agnāú** (RV.) *when the* **barhis** *is strewn and the fire kindled;* **kāle çubhe prāpte** (MBh.) *a propitious time having arrived;* **avasannāyāṁ rātrāv astācala-cūḍāvalambini candramasi** (H.) *the night having drawn to a close, and the moon resting on the summit of the western mountain.*

d. But the noun may be wanting, or may be replaced by an adverbial substitute (as **evam, tathā, iti**): thus, **varṣati** *when it rains;* [**sūrye**] **astamite** *after sunset;* **ādityasya dṛçyamāne** (S.) *while there is seen [some part] of the sun;* **ity ardhokte** (Ç.) *with these words half uttered;* **asmābhiḥ samanujñāte** (MBh.) *it being fully assented to by us;* **evam ukte kalinā** (MBh.) *it being thus spoken by Kali;* **tathā 'nuṣṭhite** (H.) *it being thus accomplished.* So likewise the participle may be wanting (a copula **sati** or the like having to be supplied): thus, **dūre bhaye** *the cause of fear being remote;* while, on the other hand, the participle **sati** etc. is sometimes redundantly added to the other participle: thus, **tathā kṛte sati** *it being thus done.*

e. The locative is frequently used adverbially or prepositionally (**1116**): thus, **-arthe** or **-kṛte** *in the matter of, for the sake of;* **agre** *in front of;* **ṛte** *without;* **samīpe** *near.*

304. The pregnant construction by which the locative comes to express the goal or object of motion or action or feeling exercised is not uncommon from the earliest time. It is by no means to be sharply distinguished from the ordinary construction; the two pass into one another, with a doubtful territory between. It occurs:

a. Especially with verbs, as of arriving, sending, placing, communicating, bestowing, and many others, in situations where an accusative or a dative (or a genitive, **297 a**) might be looked for, and exchangeable with them: thus, **sá íd devéṣu gacchati** (RV.) *that, truly, goes to (to be among) the gods;* **imáṁ no yajñám amŕteṣu dhehi** (RV.) *set this offering of ours among the immortals;* **yá āsiñcánti rásam óṣadhīṣu** (AV.) *who pour in the juice into the plants* (or, *the juice that is in the plants*); **mā prayacche 'çvare dhanam** (H.) *do not offer wealth to a lord;* **papāta medinyām** (MBh.) *he fell to (so as to be upon) the earth;* **skandhe kṛtvā** (H.) *putting on the shoulder;* **saṁçrutya pūrvam asmāsu** (MBh.) *having before promised us.*

b. Often also with nouns and adjectives in similar constructions (the instances not always easy to separate from those of the locative meaning *with reference to:* above, **303 a**): thus, **dayā sarvabhūteṣu** *compassion toward all creatures;* **anurāgaṁ nāiṣadhe** (MBh.) *affection for the Nishadhan;* **rājā samyag vṛttaḥ sadā tvayi** (MBh.) *the king has always behaved properly toward thee.*

305. The prepositions construed with the locative (**1126**) stand to it only in the relation of adverbial elements strengthening and directing its meaning.

306. Declensional forms are made by the addition of endings to the stem, or base of inflection.

a. The stem itself, however, in many words and classes of words, is liable to variation, especially as assuming a stronger form in some cases and a weaker in others.

b. And between stem and ending are sometimes inserted connecting elements (or what, in the recorded condition of the language, have the aspect of being such).

c. Respecting all these points, the details of treatment, as exhibited by each class of words or by single words, will be given in the following chapters. Here, however, it is desirable also to present a brief general view of them.

307. Endings: Singular. a. In the nominative, the usual masc. and fem. ending is **s** — which, however, is wanting in derivative **ā** and **ī**-stems; it is also euphonically lost (**150**) by consonant-stems. Neuters in general have no ending, but show in this case the bare stem; **a**-stems alone add **m** (as in the accus. masc.). Among the pronouns, **am** is a frequent masc. and fem. nom. ending (and is found even in du. and pl.); and neuters show a form in **d**.

b. In the accusative, m or am is the masc. and fem. ending — am being added after a consonant and ṛ, and after ī and ū in the radical division, and m elsewhere after vowels. The neuter accusative is like the nominative.

c. The instrumental ending for all genders alike is ā. With final i- and u-vowels, the ā is variously combined, and in the older language it is sometimes lost by contraction with them. Stems in a make the case end in ena (sometimes enā in V.), and those in ā make it end in ayā; but instances occur, in the early language, of immediate addition of ā to both a and ā.

d. The dative ending is in general e; and with it likewise the modes of combination of i and u final are various (and disappearance by contraction not unknown in the oldest language). The a-stems are quite irregular in this case, making it end in āya — excepted is the pronominal element -sma, which combines (apparently) with e to -smāi. In the personal pronouns is found bhyam (or hyam).

e. A fuller ending āi (like gen.-abl. ās and loc. ām: see below) belongs to feminine stems only. It is taken (with interposed y) by the great class of those in derivative ā; also by those in derivative ī, and (as reckoned in the later language) in derivative ū. And later it is allowed to be taken by feminine stems in radical ī and ū, and even by those in i and u: these last have it in the earliest language in only exceptional instances. For the substitution of āi for abl.-gen. ās, see below, h.

f. The ablative has a special ending, d (or t), only in a-stems, masc. and neut., the a being lengthened before it (except in the personal pronouns of 1st and 2d person, which have the same ending at in the pl., and even, in the old language, in the dual). Everywhere else, the ablative is identical with the genitive.

g. The genitive of a-stems (and of one pronominal u-stem, amu) adds sya. Elsewhere, the usual abl.-gen. ending is as; but its irregularities of treatment in combination with a stem-final are considerable. With i and u, it is either directly added (only in the old language), added with interposed n, or fused to es and os respectively. With ṛ (or ar) it yields ur (or us: 169 b).

h. The fuller ās is taken by feminine stems precisely as āi is taken in the dative: see above. But in the language of the Brāhmaṇas and Sūtras, the dative-ending āi is regularly and commonly used instead of ās, both of ablative and of genitive. See 365 d.

i. The locative ending is i in consonant- and ṛ- and a-stems (fusing with a to e in the latter). The i- and u-stems (unless the final vowel is saved by an interposed n) make the case end in āu; but the Veda has some relics or traces of the older forms (ay-i [?] and av-i) out of which this appears to have sprung. Vedic locatives from **i**-stems end also in **ā** and **ī**. The pronominal element **-sma** makes the locative **-smin**. Stems in **an** in the older language often lose the **i**, and use the bare stem as locative.

j. The ending **ām** is the locative correspondent to dat. **āi** and abl.-gen. **ās**, and is taken under the same circumstances: see above.

k. The vocative (unless by accent: **314**) is distinguished from the nominative only in the singular, and not quite always there. In **a**-stems, it is the unaltered stem, and so also in most consonant-stems; but neuters in **an** and **in** may drop the **n**; and the oldest language has sometimes a vocative in **s** from stems in **nt** and **ṅs**. Stems in **ṛ** change this to **ar**. In masc. and fem. **i**- and **u**-stems, the case ends respectively in **e** and **o**; in neuters, in the same or in **i** and **u**. Stems in **ā** change **ā** to **e**; derivative **ī** and **ū** are shortened; radical stems in long vowels use the nominative form.

308. Dual. **a.** The dual has — except so far as the vocative is sometimes distinguished from nominative and accusative by a difference of accent: **314** — only three case-forms: one for nom., accus., and voc.; one for instr., dat., and abl.; and one for gen. and loc.

b. But the pronouns of 1st and 2d person in the older language distinguish five dual cases: see **492b**.

c. The masc. and fem. ending for nom.-accus.-voc. is in the later language usually **āu**; but instead of this the Veda has prevailingly **ā**. Stems in **ā** make the case end in **e**. Stems in **i** and **u**, masc. and fem., lengthen those vowels; and derivative **ī** in the Veda remains regularly unchanged, though later it adds **āu**. The neuter ending is only **ī**; with final **a** this combines to **e**.

d. The universal ending for the instr.-dat.-abl. is **bhyām**, before which final **a** is made long. In the Veda, it is often to be read as two syllables, **bhiām**.

e. The universal ending of gen.-loc. is **os**; before this, **a** and **ā** alike become **e** (**ai**).

309. Plural. **a.** In the nominative, the general masculine and feminine ending is **as**. The old language, however, often makes the case in **āsas** instead of **ās** from **a**-stems, and in a few examples also from **ā**-stems. From derivative **ī**-stems, **īs** instead of **yas** is the regular and usual Vedic form. Pronominal **a**-stems make the masc. nom. in **e**.

b. The neuter ending (which is accusative also) is in general **i**; and before this the final of a stem is apt to be strengthened, by prolongation of a vowel, or by insertion of a nasal, or by both. But in the Veda the hence resulting forms in **āni**, **īni**, **ūni** are frequently abbreviated by loss of the **ni**, and sometimes by further shortening of the preceding vowel.

c. The **accusative** ending is also as in consonant-stems and in the radical division of ī- and ū-stems (and in the old language even elsewhere). Stems in short vowels lengthen those vowels and add in the masculine n (for ns, of which abundant traces remain), and in the feminine s. In the neuter, this case is like the nominative.

d. In the **instrumental**, the case-ending is everywhere bhis except in a-stems, where in the later language the case always ends in āis, but in the earlier either in āis or the more regular ebhis (ābhis in the two personal pronouns; and the pronominal stem a [501] makes ebhis only).

e. The **dative** and **ablative** have in the plural the same form, with the ending bhyas (in Veda often bhias), before which only a is altered, becoming e. But the two personal pronouns distinguish the two cases, having for the ablative the singular ending (as above pointed out), and for the dative the peculiar bhyam (almost never in Veda bhiam), which they extend also into the singular.

f. Of the **genitive**, the universal ending is ām; which (except optionally after radical ī and ū, and in a few scattering Vedic instances) takes after final vowels an inserted consonant, s in the pronominal declension, n elsewhere; before n, a short vowel is lengthened; before s, a becomes e. In the Veda, it is frequently to be pronounced in two syllables, as a-am.

g. The **locative** ending is su, without any exceptions, and the only change before it is that of a to e.

h. The **vocative**, as in the dual, differs from the nominative only by its accent.

310. The normal scheme of endings, as recognized by the native grammarians (and conveniently to be assumed as the basis of special descriptions), is this:

	Singular.		Dual.		Plural.	
	m. f.	n.	m. f.	n.	m. f.	n.
N.	s	—	āu	ī	as	i
A.	am	—	āu	ī	as	i
I.	ā		bhyām		bhis	
D.	e		bhyām		bhyas	
Ab.	as		bhyām		bhyas	
G.	as		os		ām	
L.	i		os		su	

a. It is taken in bulk by the consonantal stems and by the radical division of ī- and ū-stems; by other vowel-stems, with more or less considerable variations and modifications. The endings which have almost or quite unbroken range, through stems of all classes, are bhyām and os of the dual, and bhis, bhyas, ām, and su of the plural.

311. Variation of Stem. **a.** By far the most important matter under this head is the distinction made in large classes of words (chiefly those ending in consonants) between strong and weak stem-forms — a distinction standing in evident connection with the phenomena of accent. In the nom. and accus. sing. and du. and the nom. pl. (the five cases whose endings are never accented: **316 a**), the stem often has a stronger or fuller form than in the rest: thus, for example (**424**), राजानम् **rājān-am**, राजानौ **rājān-āu**, राजानस् **rājān-as**, against राज्ञा **rājñ-ā** and राजभिस् **rāja-bhis**; or (**450 b**) महान्तम् **mahānt-am** and (**447**) अदन्तम् **adánt-am** against महता **mahat-ā́** and अदता **adat-ā́**. These five, therefore, are called the cases with strong stem, or, briefly, the strong cases; and the rest are called the cases with weak stem, or the weak cases. And the weak cases, again, are in some classes of words to be distinguished into cases of weakest stem, or weakest cases, and cases of middle stem, or middle cases: the former having endings beginning with a vowel (instr., dat., abl.-gen., and loc. sing.; gen.-loc. du.; gen. pl.); the latter, with a consonant (inst.-dat.-abl. du.; instr., dat.-abl., and loc. pl.).

b. The class of strong cases, as above defined, belongs only to masculine and feminine stems. In neuter inflection, the only strong cases are the nom.-acc. pl.; while, in those stems that make a distinction of weakest and middle form, the nom.-acc. du. belongs to the weakest class, and the nom.-acc. sing. to the middle: thus, for example, compare (**408**) प्रत्यञ्चि **pratyáñc-i**, nom.-acc. pl. neut., and प्रत्यञ्चस् **pratyáñc-as**, nom. pl. masc.; प्रतीची **pratīc-ī́**, nom.-acc. du. neut., and प्रतीचोस् **pratīc-ós**, gen.-loc. du.; प्रत्यक् **pratyák**, nom.-acc. sing. neut., and प्रत्यग्भिस् **pratyág-bhis**, instr. pl.

312. Other variations concern chiefly the final vowel of a stem, and may be mainly left to be pointed out in detail below. Of consequence enough to mention here is only the **guṇa**-strengthening of a final **i** or **u**, which in the later language is always made before **as** of nom. pl. and **e** of dat. sing. in masc. and fem.; in the Veda, it does not always take place; nor is it forbidden in dat. sing. neut. also; and it is seen sometimes in loc. sing. Final **ṛ** has **guṇa**-strengthening in loc. sing.

313. Insertions between Stem and Ending. After vowel-stems, an added **n** often makes its appearance before an ending. This appendage is of least questionable origin in nom.-acc. pl. neut., where the interchange in the old language of the forms of **a-** and **i**-stems with those of **an-** and **in**-stems is pretty complete; and the **u**-stems follow their analogy. Elsewhere, it is most widely and firmly established in the gen. pl., where in the great mass of cases, and from the earliest period, the ending is virtually **nām** after a vowel. In the **i-** and **u**-stems of the later language, the instr. sing. of masc. and neut. is separated by its presence from the fem., and it is in the other weakest cases made a usual distinction of neuter forms from masculine; but the aspect of the matter in the Veda is very different: there the appearance of the **n** is everywhere sporadic; the neuter shows no special inclination to take it, and it is not excluded even from the feminine. In the ending **ena** from **a**-stems (later invariable, earlier predominating) its presence appears to have worked the most considerable transformation of original shape.

a. The place of **n** before gen. pl. **ām** is taken by **s** in pronominal **a-** and **ā**-stems.

b. The **y** after **ā** before the endings **āi, ās**, and **ām** is most probably an insertion, such as is made elsewhere (**258**).

Accent in Declension.

314. a. As a rule without exception, the vocative, if accented at all, is accented on the first syllable.

b. And in the Veda (the case is a rare one), whenever a syllable written as one is to be pronounced as two by restoration of a semivowel to vowel form, the first element only has the vocative accent, and the syllable as written is circumflex (**83—4**): thus, **dyāùs** (i. e. **díāus**) when dissyllabic, but **dyāús** when monosyllabic; **jyàke** when for **jíāke**.

c. But the vocative is accented only when it stands at the beginning of a sentence — or, in verse, at the beginning also of a metrical division or **pāda**; elsewhere it is accentless or enclitic: thus, **ágne yám yajñám paribhū́r ási** (RV.) *O Agni! whatever offering thou protectest;* but **úpa tvā 'gna é 'masi** (RV.) *unto thee, Agni, we come.*

d. A word, or more than one word, qualifying a vocative — usually an adjective or appositive noun, but sometimes a dependent noun in the genitive (very rarely in any other case) — constitutes, so far as accent is concerned, a unity with the vocative: thus (all the examples from RV.), at the beginning of a **pāda,** with first syllable of the combination accented, **índra bhrātaḥ** *O brother Indra!* **rā́jan soma** *O king Soma!* **yáviṣṭha dūta** *most youthful messenger!* **hótar yaviṣṭha sukrato** *most youthful skilled offerer!* **ū́rjo napāt sahasvan** *mighty son of strength!* — in the interior of a **pāda,** without accent, **sómāsa indra girvaṇaḥ** *the somas, O song-loving Indra!* **tā́v açvinā bhadrahastā supāṇī** *ye, O Açvins of propitious and beautiful hands!* **ā́ rājānā maha ṛtasya gopā** *hither, ye two kingly guardians of great order!*

e. On the other hand, two or more independent or coördinate vocatives at the beginning of a **pāda** are regularly and usually both accented: thus, **pítar mā́taḥ** *O father! O mother!* **ágna índra váruṇa mítra dévāḥ** *Agni! Indra! Varuṇa! Mitra! gods!* **çátamūte çátakrato** *thou of a hundred aids! of a hundred arts!* **vásiṣṭha çúkra dī́divaḥ pā́vaka** *best, bright, shining, cleansing one!* **ū́rjo napād bhádraçoce** *son of strength, propitiously bright one!* But the texts offer occasional irregular exceptions both to this and to the preceding rule.

f. For brevity, the vocative dual and plural will be given in the paradigms below along with the nominative, without taking the trouble to specify in each instance that, if the latter be accented elsewhere than on the first syllable, the accent of the vocative is different.

315. As regards the other cases, rules for change of accent in declension have to do only with monosyllables and with stems of more than one syllable which are accented on the final; for, if a stem be accented on the penult, or any other syllable further back — as in **sárpant, vā́ri, bhágavant, sumánas, sahásravāja** — the accent remains upon that syllable through the whole inflection (except in the vocative, as explained in the preceding paragraph).

a. The only exceptions are a few numeral stems: see **483.**

316. Stems accented on the final (including monosyllables) are subject to variation of accent in declension chiefly in virtue of the fact that some of the endings have, while others have not, or have in less degree, a tendency themselves to take the accent. Thus:

a. The endings of the nominative and accusative singular and dual and of the nominative plural (that is to say, of the strong cases: **311**) have no tendency to take the accent away from the stem, and are therefore only accented when a final vowel of the stem and the vowel of the ending are blended together into a single vowel or diphthong. Thus, from **dattá** come **dattāú** (= **dattá+āu**) and **dattā́s** (= **dattá+as**); but from **nadī́** come **nadyāù** (= **nadī́+āu**) and **nadyàs** (= **nadī́+as**).

b. All the other endings sometimes take the accent; but those beginning with a vowel (i. e. of the weakest cases: **311**) do so more readily than those beginning with a consonant (i. e. of the middle cases: **311**). Thus, from **nāús** come **nāvā́** and **nāubhís;** from **mahánt,** however, come **mahatā́** but **mahádbhis.**

The general rules of accent, then, may be thus stated:

317. In the declension of monosyllabic stems, the accent falls upon the ending in all the weak cases (without distinction of middle and weakest): thus, nāvā́, nāubhyā́m, nāvā́m, nāuṣú; vācí, vāgbhís, vācā́m, vākṣú.

a. But some monosyllabic stems retain the accent throughout: thus, **góbhis, gávām, góṣu.** For such cases, see below, **350, 361 c, d, 372, 390, 427.** And in the acc. pl. the stem is even oftener accented than the ending, some words also admitting either accentuation.

318. Of polysyllabic stems ending in consonants, only a few shift the accent to the ending, and that in the weakest (not the middle) cases. Such are:

a. Present participles in **ánt** or **át**: thus, from **tudánt, tudatā́** and **tudatós** and **tudatā́m**; but **tudádbhyām** and **tudátsu.**

b. A few adjectives having the form of such participles, as **mahatā́, bṛhatás.**

c. Stems of which the accented final loses its syllabic character by syncopation of the vowel: thus, **majjñā́, mūrdhné, dāmnás** (from **majján** etc.: **423**).

d. Other sporadic cases will be noticed under the different declensions.

e. Case-forms used adverbially sometimes show a changed accent: see **1110** ff.

319. Of polysyllabic stems ending in accented short vowels, the final of the stem retains the accent if it retains its syllabic identity: thus, **datténa** and **dattā́ya** from **dattá**; **agnínā** and **agnáye** from **agní**; and also **dattébhyas, agníbhis,** and so on. Otherwise, the accent is on the ending: and that, whether the final and the ending are combined into one, as in **dattāís, dhenāú, agnī́n, dhenū́s,** and so on; or whether the final is changed into a semivowel before the ending: thus, **dhenvā́, pitrā́, jāmyós, bāhvós,** etc.

a. But **ām** of the gen. pl. from stems in **í** and **ú** and **ṛ́** may, and in the older language always does, take the accent, though separated by **n** from the stem: thus, **agnīnā́m, dhenūnā́m, pitṝṇā́m.** In RV., even derivative **ī**-stems show usually the same shift: thus, **bahvīnā́m.** Of stems in **á**, only numerals (**483 a**) follow this rule: thus, **saptānā́m, daçānā́m.**

320. Root-words in **ī** and **ū** as final members of compounds retain the accent throughout, not shifting it to any of the endings. And in the older language there are polysyllabic words in long final vowels which follow in this respect as in others the analogy of the root-declension (below, **355** ff.). Apart from these, the treatment of stems in derivative long vowels is, as regards accent, the same as of those in short vowels — save that the tone is not thrown forward upon the ending in gen. plural.

CHAPTER V.

NOUNS AND ADJECTIVES.

321. a. THE accordance in inflection of substantive and adjective stems is so complete that the two cannot be separated in treatment from one another.

b. They may be classified, for convenience of description, as follows:

I. Stems in अ **a**;

II. Stems in इ **i** and उ **u**;

III. Stems in आ **ā**, ई **ī**, and ऊ **ū**: namely, **A.** radical-stems (and a few others inflected like them); **B.** derivative stems;

IV. Stems in ऋ **ṛ** (or अर् **ar**);

V. Stems in consonants.

c. There is nothing absolute in this classification and arrangement; it is merely believed to be open to as few objections as any other. No general agreement has been reached among scholars as to the number and order of Sanskrit declensions. The stems in **a** are here treated first because of the great predominance of the class.

322. The division-line between substantive and adjective, always an uncertain one in early Indo-European language, is even more wavering in Sanskrit than elsewhere. There are, however, in all the declensions as divided above — unless we except the stems in **ṛ** or **ar** — words which are distinctly adjectives; and, in general, they are inflected precisely like noun-stems of the same final: only, among consonant-stems, there are certain sub-classes of adjective stems with peculiarities of inflection to which there is among nouns nothing corresponding. But there are also two considerable classes of adjective-compounds, requiring special notice: namely —

323. Compound adjectives having as final member a bare verbal root, with the value of a present participle (**383** a ff.): thus, **su-dṛ́ç** *well-looking;* **pra-búdh** *foreknowing;* **a-drúh** *not hating;* **veda-víd** *Veda-knowing;* **vṛtra-hán**, *Vritra-slaying;* **upastha-sád** *sitting in the lap.* Every root is liable to be used in this way, and such compounds are not infrequent in all ages of the language: see chapter on Compounds, below (**1269**).

a. This class is essentially only a special class of compound adjectives, since in the earliest Veda the simple as well as the compounded root was sometimes used adjectively. But the compounded root was from the beginning much more often so used, and the later the more exclusively, so that practically the class is a separate and important one.

324. Compound adjectives having a noun as final member, but obtaining an adjective sense secondarily, by having the idea of *possession* added, and being inflected as adjectives in the three genders (**1293** ff.). Thus, **prajā́kāmá** *desire of progeny*, whence the adjective **prajā́kāma,** meaning *desirous* (i. e. *having desire*) *of progeny;* **sabhārya** (**sa**+**bhāryā**) *having one's wife along;* and so on.

a. In a few cases, also, the final noun is syntactically object of the preceding member (**1309-10**): thus, **atimātra** *immoderate* (**ati mātram** *beyond measure*); **yāvayáddveṣas** *driving away enemies.*

325. Hence, under each declension, we have to notice how a root or a noun-stem of that declension is inflected when final member of an adjective compound.

a. As to accent, it needs only to be remarked here that a root-word ending a compound has the accent, but (**320**) loses the peculiarity of monosyllabic accentuation, and does not throw the tone forward upon the ending (except **añc** in certain old forms: **410**).

Declension I.

Stems (masculine and neuter) in अ a.

326. a. This declension contains the majority of all the declined stems of the language.

b. Its endings deviate more widely than any others from the normal.

327. Endings: Singular. **a.** The nom. masc. has the normal ending **s.**

b. The acc. (masc. and neut.) adds **m** (not **am**); and this form has the office also of nom. neuter.

c. The instr. changes **a** to **ena** uniformly in the later language; and even in the oldest Vedic this is the predominant ending (in RV., eight ninths of all cases). Its final is in Vedic verse frequently made long (**enā**). But the normal ending **ā** — thus, **yajñā́, suhávā, mahitvā́** (for **yajñéna** etc.) — is also not rare in the Veda.

d. The dat. has **āya** (as if by adding **aya** to **a**), alike in all ages of the language.

e. The abl. has **t** (or doubtless **d**: it is impossible from the evidence of the Sanskrit to tell which is the original form of the ending), before which ā is made long: this ending is found in no other noun-declension, and elsewhere only in the personal pronouns (of all numbers).

f. The gen. has **sya** added to the final **a**; and this ending is also limited to **a**-stems (with the single exception of the pronoun **amúṣya**: **501**). Its final **a** is in only three cases made long in the Veda; and its **y** is vocalized (**asia**) almost as rarely.

g. The loc. ends in **e** (as if by combining the normal ending **i** with the final of the stem), without exception.

h. The voc. is the bare stem.

328. Dual. **a.** The dual endings in general are the normal ones.

b. The nom., acc., and voc. masc. end in the later language always in **āu**. In the Veda, however, the usual ending is simple **ā** (in RV., in seven eighths of the occurrences). The same cases in the neut. end in **e**, which appears to be the result of fusion of the stem-final with the normal ending **ī**.

c. The instr., dat., and abl. have **bhyām** (in only one or two Vedic instances resolved into **bhiām**), with the stem-final lengthened to **ā** before it.

d. The gen. and loc. have a **y** inserted after the stem-final before **os** (or as if the **a** had been changed to **e**). In one or two (doubtful) Vedic instances (as also in the pronominal forms **enos** and **yos**), **os** is substituted for the final **a**.

329. Plural. **a.** The nom. masc. has in the later language the normal ending **as** combined with the final **a** to **ās**. But in the Veda the ending **āsas** instead is frequent (one third of the occurrences in RV., but only one twenty-fifth in the peculiar parts of AV.).

b. The acc. masc. ends in **ān** (for earlier **āns**, of which abundant traces are left in the Veda, and, under the disguise of apparent euphonic combination, even in the later language: see above, **208** ff.).

c. The nom. and acc. neut. have in the later language always the ending **āni** (like the **an**-stems: see **421**; or else with **n**, as in the gen. pl., before normal **i**). But in the Veda this ending alternates with simple **ā** (which in RV. is to **āni** as three to two, in point of frequency; in AV., as three to four).

d. The instr. ends later always in **āis**; but in the Veda is found abundantly the more normal form **ebhis** (in RV., nearly as frequent as **āis**; in AV., only one fifth as frequent).

e. The dat. and abl. have **bhyas** as ending, with **e** instead of the final **a** before it (as in the Vedic instr. **ebhis**, the loc. pl., the gen. loc. du. [?], and the instr. sing.). The resolution into **ebhias** is not infrequent in the Veda.

f. The gen. ends in **ānām**, the final **a** being lengthened and having **n** inserted before the normal ending. The **ā** of the ending is not seldom (in less than half the instances) to be read as two syllables, **aam**: opinions are divided as to whether the resolution is historical or metrical only. A very small number (half-a-dozen) of examples of simple **ām** as ending instead of **ānām** occur in RV.

g. The loc. ends in **eṣu** — that is to say, with the normal ending, before which the stem-final is changed to **e** (with consequent change of **s** to **ṣ**: 180).

h. Of accent, in this declension, nothing requires to be said; the syllable accented in the stem retains its own accent throughout.

330. Examples of declension. As examples of the inflection of a-stems may be taken काम **kā́ma** m. *love;* देव **devá** m. *god;* आस्य **āsyà** n. *mouth.*

Singular:			
N.	कामस् **kā́mas**	देवस् **devás**	आस्यम् **āsyàm**
A.	कामम् **kā́mam**	देवम् **devám**	आस्यम् **āsyàm**
I.	कामेन **kā́mena**	देवेन **devéna**	आस्येन **āsyèna**
D.	कामाय **kā́māya**	देवाय **devā́ya**	आस्याय **āsyā̀ya**
Ab.	कामात् **kā́māt**	देवात् **devā́t**	आस्यात् **āsyā̀t**
G.	कामस्य **kā́masya**	देवस्य **devásya**	आस्यस्य **āsyàsya**
L.	कामे **kā́me**	देवे **devé**	आस्ये **āsyè**
V.	काम **kā́ma**	देव **déva**	आस्य **ā́sya**
Dual:			
N. A. V.	कामौ **kā́māu**	देवौ **devā́u**	आस्ये **āsyè**
I. D. Ab.	कामाभ्याम् **kā́mābhyām**	देवाभ्याम् **devā́bhyām**	आस्याभ्याम् **āsyā̀bhyām**
G. L.	कामयोस् **kā́mayos**	देवयोस् **deváyos**	आस्ययोस् **āsyàyos**
Plural:			
N. V.	कामास् **kā́mās**	देवास् **devā́s**	आस्यानि **āsyā̀ni**

A.	कामान् **kā́mān**	देवान् **devā́n**	आस्यानि **āsyàni**
I.	कामैस् **kā́māis**	देवैस् **devā́is**	आस्यैस् **āsyāis**
D. Ab.	कामेभ्यस् **kā́mebhyas**	देवेभ्यस् **devébhyas**	आस्येभ्यस् **āsyèbhyas**
G.	कामानाम् **kā́mānām**	देवानाम् **devā́nām**	आस्यानाम् **āsyànām**
L.	कामेषु **kā́meṣu**	देवेषु **devéṣu**	आस्येषु **āsyèṣu**

Examples of the peculiar Vedic forms are:

a. Sing.: instr. **ravátheṇā, yajñā́** (such genitive forms as **áçvasiā** are purely sporadic).

b. Du.: nom. etc. masc. **devā́**; gen.-loc. **pastyòs** (stem **pastyà**).

c. Pl.: nom.-voc. masc. **devā́sas**; neut. **yugā́**; instr. **devébhis**; gen. **caráthām, devā́naam.**

331. Among nouns, there are no irregularities in this declension. For irregular numeral bases in **a** (or **an**), see **483-4.** For the irregularities of pronominal stems in **a**, which are more or less fully shared also by a few adjectives of pronominal kindred, see the chapter on Pronouns (**495** ff.).

Adjectives.

332. Original adjectives in **a** are an exceedingly large class, the great majority of all adjectives. There is, however, no such thing as a feminine stem in **a**; for the feminine, the **a** is changed to **ā** — or often, though far less often, to **ī**; and its declension is then like that of **senā** or **devī** (**364**). An example of the complete declension of an adjective **a**-stem in the three genders will be given below (**368**)

a. Whether a masc.-neut. stem in **a** shall form its feminine in **ā** or in **ī** is a question to be determined in great part only by actual usage, and not by grammatical rule. Certain important classes of words, however, can be pointed out which take the less common ending **ī** for the feminine: thus, 1. the (very numerous) secondary derivatives in **a** with **vṛddhi** of the first syllable (**1204**): e. g. **āmitrá -trī́, mā́nuṣa -ṣī, pāvamānā́ -nī́, pāurṇamāsá -sī́**; 2. primary derivatives in **ana** with accent on the radical syllable (**1150**): e. g. **códana -nī, saṁgráhaṇa -ṇī, subhāgaṁkáraṇa -ṇī**; 3. primary derivatives in **a**, with strengthening of the radical syllable, having a quasi-participial meaning: e. g. **divākará -rī, avakrāmá -mī́,**

rathavāhá -hí (but there are many exceptions); 4. secondary derivatives in **maya** (**1225**) and **tana** (**1245 e**): e. g. **ayasmáya -yī**; **adyatana -nī**; 5. most ordinal numerals (**487 h**): e. g. **pañcamá -mí**, **navadaçá -çí**, **triñçattamá -mí**. Not a few words make the feminine in either **ā** or **ī**: e. g. **kévalā** or **-lī**, **ugrá** or **-rí**, **pāpá** or **-pí**, **rāmá** or **-mí**; but ordinarily only one of these is accepted as regular.

333. There are no verbal roots ending in **a**. But **a** is sometimes substituted for the final **ā** of a root (and, rarely, for final **an**), and it is then inflected like an ordinary adjective in **a** (see below, **354**).

334. a. A noun ending in **a**, when occurring as final member of an adjective compound, is inflected like an original adjective in **a**, making its feminine likewise in **ā** or **ī** (**367**).

b. For the most part, an adjective compound having a noun in **a** as final member makes its feminine in **ā**. But there are numerous exceptions, certain nouns taking, usually or always, **ī** instead. Some of the commonest of these are as follows: **akṣa** *eye* (e. g. **lohitākṣī**, **dvyakṣī**, **gavākṣī**), **parṇa** *leaf* (e. g. **tilaparṇī**, **saptaparṇī**; but **ekaparṇā**), **mukha** *face* (e. g. **kṛṣṇamukhī**, **durmukhī**; but **trimukhā** etc.), **añga** *limb*, *body* (e. g. **anavadyāñgī**, **sarvāñgī**; but **caturañgā** etc.), **keça** *hair* (e. g. **sukeçī**, **muktakeçī** or **-çā**, etc.), **karṇa**, *ear* (e. g. **mahākarṇī**; but **gokarṇā** etc.), **udara** *belly* (e. g. **lambodarī**), **mūla** *root* (e. g. **pañcamūlī**; but oftener **çatámūlā** etc.). The very great majority of such nouns (as the examples indicate) signify parts of the body.

c. On the other hand, a feminine noun ending in derivative **ā** shortens its final to **a** to form a masculine and neuter base: see **367 c**.

d. In frequent cases, nouns of consonant ending are, as finals of compounds, transferred to the **a**-declension by an added suffix **a** (**1209 a**) or **ka** (**1222**).

Declension II.

Stems (of all genders) in इ i and उ u.

335. The stems in इ i and उ u are inflected in so close accordance with one another that they cannot be divided into two separate declensions. They are of all the three genders, and tolerably numerous — those in इ i more numerous than those in उ u, especially in the feminine (there are more neuters in उ u than in इ i).

a. The endings of this declension also differ frequently and widely from the normal, and the irregularities in the older language are numerous.

336. Endings: Singular. a. The nom. masc. and fem. adds to the stem the normal ending **s**. The nom. and acc. neut. is the bare stem, without ending. In the Veda, the final **u** of a few neuters is lengthened (**248 b**): thus, **urū́, purū́.**

b. The acc. masc. and fem. adds **m** to the stem. Vedic forms in **iam** and **uam**, and, with **n**, **inam** and **unam**, are excessively rare, and doubtful.

c. The instr. fem. in the later language takes the normal ending **ā** simply, while the masc. and neut. insert **n** before it, making **inā** and **unā**. But in the Veda, forms in **yā** and **vā** (or **iā** and **uā**) are not infrequent in masc. and neut. also; while **inā** is found, very rarely, as a fem. ending. Moreover, fem. **yā** is often (in two thirds of the occurrences) contracted to **ī**; and this is even sometimes shortened to **i**. An adverbial instr. in **uyā́** from half-a-dozen stems in **u** occurs.

d. The dat. masc. and fem. gunates the final of the stem before the ending **e**, making **aye** and **ave**. These are the prevailing endings in the Veda likewise; but the more normal **ye** and **ve** (or **ue**) also occur; and the fem. has in this case, as in the instr., sometimes the form **ī** for **ie**. In the later language, the neuter is required in this, as in all the other weakest cases, to insert **n** before the normal ending: but in the Veda such forms are only sporadic; and the neut. dat. has also the forms **aye, ve, ave,** like the other genders.

e. The abl. and gen. masc. and fem. have regularly, both earlier and later, the ending **s** with gunated vowel before it: thus, **es, os**; and in the Veda, the neut. forms the cases in the same way; although **unas**, required later, is also not infrequent (**inas** does not occur). But the normal forms **yas** (or **ias**) and **vas** (or **uas**) are also frequent in both masc. and neuter. As masc. ending, **unas** occurs twice in RV. The anomalous **didyót** (so TS.; in the corresponding passages, **vidyót** VS., **didyāut** K., **didivás** MS.) is of doubtful character.

f. The loc. masc. and fem. has for regular ending in the later language **āu**, replacing both finals, **i** and **u**. And this is in the Veda also the most frequent ending; but, beside it, the **i**-stems form (about half as often in RV.) their loc. in **ā**: thus, **agnā́**; and this is found once even in the neuter. The RV. has a number of examples of masc. and neut. locatives in **avi** (the normal ending and the **u** gunated before it) from **u**-stems; and certain doubtful traces of a corresponding **ayi** from **i**-stems. Half-a-dozen locatives in **ī** (regarded by the Vedic grammarians as **pragṛhya** or uncombinable: **138 d**) are made from **i**-stems. The later language makes the neuter locatives in **ini** and **uni**; but the former never occurs in the oldest texts, and the latter only very rarely.

g. The later grammar allows the dat., abl.-gen., and loc. fem. to be formed at will with the fuller fem. terminations of long-vowel stems, namely **āi, ās** (for which, in Brāhmaṇa etc., **āi** is substituted: **307 h**), **ām.** Such forms are quite rare in the oldest language even from **i**-stems (less than 40 occurrences altogether in RV.; three times as many in AV.); and from **u**-stems they are almost unknown (five in RV. and AV.).

h. The voc. gunates the final of the stem, in masc. and fem., alike in the earlier and in the later language. In the neut., it is later allowed to be either of the same form or the unaltered stem; and this was probably the usage in the older time also; not instances enough are quotable to determine the question (AV. has **u** once, and VS. **o** once).

337. Dual. **a.** The later and earlier language agree in making the nom.- acc.-voc. masc. and fem. by lengthening the final of the stem. The same cases in the neuter (according to the rule given above) end later in **inī** and **unī**; but these endings are nearly unknown in the Veda (as, indeed, the cases are of only rare occurrence): AV. has **inī** twice (RV. perhaps once); VS. has **unī** once; RV. has **uī** from one **u**-stem, and **ī**, once shortened to **i**, from one or two **i**-stems.

b. The unvarying ending of instr.-dat.-abl., in all genders, is **bhyām** added to the unchanged stem.

c. The gen.-loc. of all ages adds **os** to the stem in masc. and fem.; in neut., the later language interposes, as elsewhere in the weakest cases, a **n**; probably in the earlier Vedic the form would be like that of the other genders; but the only occurrence noted is one **unos** in AV.

338. Plural. **a.** The nom.-voc. masc. and fem. adds the normal ending **as** to the gunated stem-final, making **ayas** and **avas.** The exceptions in the Veda are very few: one word (**ari**) has **ias** in both genders, and a few feminines have **īs** (like **ī**-stems); a very few **u**-stems have **uas**. The neut. nom.-acc. ends later in **īni** and **ūni** (like **āni** from **a: 329 c**); but the Veda has **ī** and **i** (about equally frequent) much oftener than **īni**; and **ū** and (more usually) **u,** more than half as often as **ūni.**

b. The accus. masc. ends in **īn** and **ūn,** for older **īns** and **ūns,** of which plain traces remain in the Veda in nearly half the instances of occurrence, and even not infrequently in the later language, in the guise of phonetic combination (**208** ff.). The accus. fem. ends in **īs** and **ūs.** But both masc. and fem. forms in **ias** and **uas** are found sparingly in the Veda.

c. The inst. of all genders adds **bhis** to the stem.

d. The dat.-abl. of all genders adds **bhyas** (in V., almost never **bhias**) to the stem.

e. The gen. of all genders is made alike in **īnām** and **ūnām** (of which the **ā** is not seldom, in the Veda, to be resolved into **aam**). Stems with accented final in the later language may, and in the earlier always do, throw forward the accent upon the ending.

f. The loc. of all genders adds **su** (as **ṣu: 180**) to the stem-final.

g. The accent is in accordance with the general rules already laid down, and there are no irregularities calling for special notice.

339. Examples of declension. As models of **i**-stems may be taken अग्नि **agní** m. *fire;* गति **gáti** f. *gait;* वारि **vā́ri** n. *water.*

Singular:			
N.	अग्निस् **agnís**	गतिस् **gátis**	वारि **vā́ri**
A.	अग्निम् **agním**	गतिम् **gátim**	वारि **vā́ri**
I.	अग्निना **agnínā**	गत्या **gátyā**	वारिणा **vā́riṇā**
D	अग्नये **agnáye**	गतये, गत्यै **gátaye, gátyāi**	वारिणे **vā́riṇe**
Ab. G.	अग्नेस् **agnés**	गतेस्, गत्यास् **gátes, gátyās**	वारिणस् **vā́riṇas**
L.	अग्नौ **agnāú**	गतौ, गत्याम् **gátāu, gátyām**	वारिणि **vā́riṇi**
V	अग्ने **ágne**	गते **gáte**	वारि, वारे **vā́ri, vā́re**
Dual:			
N. A. V.	अग्नी **agnī́**	गती **gátī**	वारिणी **vā́riṇī**
I. D. Ab.	अग्निभ्याम् **agníbhyām**	गतिभ्याम् **gátibhyām**	वारिभ्याम् **vā́ribhyām**
G. L.	अग्न्योस् **agnyós**	गत्योस् **gátyos**	वारिणोस् **vā́riṇos**
Plural:			
N. V.	अग्नयस् **agnáyas**	गतयस् **gátayas**	वारीणि **vā́rīṇi**
A.	अग्नीन् **agnī́n**	गतीस् **gátīs**	वारीणि **vā́rīṇi**
I.	अग्निभिस् **agníbhis**	गतिभिस् **gátibhis**	वारिभिस् **vā́ribhis**
D. Ab.	अग्निभ्यस् **agníbhyas**	गतिभ्यस् **gátibhyas**	वारिभ्यस् **vā́ribhyas**
G.	अग्नीनाम् **agnīnā́m**	गतीनाम् **gátīnām**	वारीणाम् **vā́rīṇām**
L.	अग्निषु **agníṣu**	गतिषु **gátiṣu**	वारिषु **vā́riṣu**

340. In order to mark more plainly the absence in Vedic language of some of the forms which are common later, all the forms of Vedic occurrence are added below, and in the order of their frequency.

a. Singular. Nom. **agnís** etc., as above.

b. Acc.: masc. **agním, yayíam, ūrmíṇam**(?); fem. and neut. as above.

c. Instr.: masc. **agnínā, rayyā́** and **ūrmiā́**; fem. **ácittī, ūtiā́, matyā́, suvṛktí, dhāsínā**; neut. wanting.

d. Dat.: masc. **agnáye**; fem. **tujáye, ūtí, turyāí**; neut. **çúcaye.**

e. Gen.-abl.: masc. **agnés, ávyas, ariás**; fem. **ádites, hetyā́s** and **bhū́miās**; neut. **bhū́res.**

f. Loc.: masc. **agnāú, agnā́, ājáyi**(?); fem. **ā́gatāu, úditā, dhánasātayi**(?), **védī, bhū́myām**; neut. **apratā́, saptáraçmāu.**

g. Voc.: as above (neut. wanting).

h. Dual. Nom.-acc.-voc.: masc. **hárī**; fem. **yuvatī́**; neut. **çúcī, máhi, háriṇī**(?).

i. Instr.-dat.-abl.: as above.

j. Gen.-loc.: masc. **hários**; fem. **yuvatyós** and **jāmiós**; neut. wanting.

k. Plural. Nom.: masc. **agnáyas**; fem. **matáyas, bhū́mīs**; neut. **çúcī, bhū́ri, bhū́rīṇi.**

l. Accus.: masc. **agnī́n**; fem. **kṣitī́s, çúcayas**(?).

m. Instr., dat.-abl., and loc., as above.

n. Gen.: masc. fem. **kavīnā́m, ṛ́ṣīṇaam** etc. (neut. wanting).

341. As models of u-stems may be taken शत्रु **çátru** m. *enemy;* धेनु **dhenú** f. *cow;* मधु **mádhu** n. *honey.*

Singular:

N.	शत्रुस् **çátrus**	धेनुस् **dhenús**	मधु **mádhu**
A.	शत्रुम् **çátrum**	धेनुम् **dhenúm**	मधु **mádhu**
I.	शत्रुणा **çátruṇā**	धेन्वा **dhenvā́**	मधुना **mádhunā**
D.	शत्रवे **çátrave**	धेनवे, धेन्वै **dhenáve, dhenvāí**	मधुने **mádhune**
Ab. G.	शत्रोस् **çátros**	धेनोस्, धेन्वास् **dhenós, dhenvā́s**	मधुनस् **mádhunas**
L.	शत्रौ **çátrāu**	धेनौ, धेन्वाम् **dhenāú, dhenvā́m**	मधुनि **mádhuni**
V.	शत्रो **çátro**	धेनो **dhéno**	मधु, मधो **mádhu, mádho**

Dual:			
N. A. V.	शत्रू **çátrū**	धेनू **dhenū́**	मधुनी **mádhunī**
I. D. Ab.	शत्रुभ्याम् **çátrubhyām**	धेनुभ्याम् **dhenúbhyām**	मधुभ्याम् **mádhubhyām**
G. L.	शत्र्वोस् **çátrvos**	धेन्वोस् **dhenvós**	मधुनोस् **mádhunos**
Plural:			
N. V.	शत्रवस् **çátravas**	धेनवस् **dhenávas**	मधूनि **mádhūni**
A.	शत्रून् **çátrūn**	धेनूस् **dhenū́s**	मधूनि **mádhūni**
I.	शत्रुभिस् **çátrubhis**	धेनुभिस् **dhenúbhis**	मधुभिस् **mádhubhis**
D. Ab.	शत्रुभ्यस् **çátrubhyas**	धेनुभ्यस् **dhenúbhyas**	मधुभ्यस् **mádhubhyas**
G.	शत्रूणाम् **çátrūṇām**	धेनूनाम् **dhenūnā́m**	मधूनाम् **mádhūnām**
L.	शत्रुषु **çátruṣu**	धेनुषु **dhenúṣu**	मधुषु **mádhuṣu**

342. The forms of Vedic occurrence are given here for the **u**-stems in the same manner as for the **i**-stems above.

a. Singular. Nom.: masc. and fem. as above; neut. **urú, urū́.**

b. Accus.: masc. **ketúm, ábhīruam, sucetúnam**(?); fem. **dhenúm.**

c. Instr.: masc. **ketúnā, paçvā́** and **krátuā**; fem. **ádhenuā** and **panvā́, āçuyā́**; neut. **mádhunā, mádhvā.**

d. Dat.: masc. **ketáve, çíçve**; fem. **çárave, íṣvāi**; neut. **páçve**(?), **uráve, mádhune.**

e. Abl.-gen.: masc. **manyós, pitvás, cā́ruṇas**; fem. **síndhos, íṣvās**; neut. **mádhvas** and **mádhuas, mádhos, mádhunas.**

f. Loc.: masc. **pūrāú, sūnávi**; fem. **síndhāu, rájjvām**; neut. **sā́nāu, sā́navi, sā́no, sā́nuni.**

g. Voc.: as above.

h. Dual. Nom.-acc.-voc.: masc. and fem. as above; neut. **urvī́, jā́nunī.**

i. Instr.-dat.-abl.: as above.

j. Gen.-loc.: as above (but **vos** or **uos**).

k. Plural. Nom.: masc. **ṛbhávas, mádhuas** and **mádhvas**; fem. **dhenávas, çatakratvas**; neut. **purū́ṇi, purú, purū́.**

l. Accus.: masc. **ṛtū́n, paçvás**; fem. **íṣūs, mádhvas.**

m. Instr., dat.-abl., and loc., as above; also gen. (but with the resolution **ūnaam** in part).

343. Irregular declension. There are no irregular u-stems, and only a very few i-stems.

a. Sákhi m. *friend* has for the five strong cases a peculiarly strengthened base (vriddhied), namely **sákhāy**, which in the nom. sing. is reduced to **sákhā** (without ending), and in the other cases takes the normal endings. The instr. and dat. sing. have the normal endings simply, without inserted **n** or **guṇa**; the abl.-gen. sing. adds **us**; and the loc. sing. adds **āu**: the rest is like **agní**. Thus:

Sing. **sákhā, sákhāyam, sákhyā, sákhye, sákhyus, sákhyāu, sákhe**; Du. **sákhāyāu, sákhibhyām, sákhyos**; Pl. **sákhāyas, sákhīn,** etc. etc.

b. The Veda has usually **sákhāyā** du., and often resolves the **y** to **i**, in **sákhiā, sákhius,** etc. The compounds are usually declined like the simple word, unless (1315 b) **sakha** be substituted.

c. There is a corresponding fem., **sakhī** (declined like **devī**: **364**); but the forms of **sakhi** are also sometimes found used with feminine value.

d. Páti m. is declined regularly in composition, and when it has the meaning *lord, master;* when uncompounded and when meaning *husband,* it is inflected like **sákhi** in the instr., dat., abl.-gen., and loc. sing., forming **pátyā, pátye, pátyus, pátyāu.** There are occasional instances of confusion of the two classes of forms.

e. For **pati** as final member of a possessive compound is regularly and usually substituted **patnī** in the fem.: thus, **jīvapatnī** *having a living husband;* **dāsapatnī** *having a barbarian for master.*

f. Jáni f. *wife* has the gen. sing. **jányus** in the Veda.

g. Arí *eager, greedy, hostile* has in the Veda **aryás** in pl. nom. and accus., masc. and fem. Its accus. sing. is **arím** or **aryám.**

h. Ví *bird* has in RV. the nom. **vés** (beside **vís**). In the plural it accents **víbhis, víbhyas,** but **vīnā́m.**

i. The stems **ákṣi** *eye*, **ásthi** *bone*, **dádhi** *curds*, and **sákthi** *thigh*, are defective, their forms exchanging with and complementing forms from stems in **án** (**akṣán** etc.): see the stems in **an,** below (**431**).

j. The stem **pathí** *road* is used to make up part of the inflection of **pánthan**: see below, **433.**

k. Króṣṭu m. *jackal* lacks the strong cases, for which the corresponding forms of **kroṣṭṛ́** are substituted.

Adjectives.

344. Original adjective stems in **i** are few; those in **u** are much more numerous (many derivative verb-stems forming a participial adjective in u). Their inflection is like that of nouns, and has been included in the rules given above. In those weak cases, however — namely, the dat., abl.-gen., and loc. sing., and the gen.-loc. dual — in which neuter nouns differ from masculines in the later language by an inserted n (we have seen above that this difference does not exist in the Veda), the neuter adjective is allowed to take either form. The stem is the same for masculine and neuter, and generally (and allowably always) for feminine also.

a. There are a few instances of a feminine noun in ī standing (sometimes with changed accent) beside a masculine in i: thus, **krími** m., **krimí** f.; **sákhi (343 a)** m., **sakhī́** f.; **dundubhí** m., **dundubhī** f.; **dhúni** m., **dhunī** f.; **çakúni** m., **çakunī** or **-ni** f. In the later language, especially, there is a very frequent interchange of i and ī as finals of the same stem. No adjective in i makes a regular feminine in ī.

b. With stems in u the case is quite different. While the feminine may, and in part does, end in u, like the masculine and neuter, a special feminine-stem is often made by lengthening the u to ū, or also by adding ī; and for some stems a feminine is formed in two of these three ways, or even in all the three: thus, **kārū, -dipsū́, çundhyū́, cariṣṇū́, vacasyū́; -aṇvī, urvī́, gurvī, pūrvī́** (with prolongation of u before r: compare **245 b**), **bahvī́, prabhvī́, raghvī́, sādhvī́, svādvī́**; — **pṛthú** and **pṛthvī́, vibhū́** and **vibhvī́, mṛdú** and **mṛdvī́, laghu** and **laghvī, vásu** and **vásvī; babhrú** and **babhrū́, bībhatsú** and **bībhatsū́, bhīrú** and **bhīrū**; — **tanú** and **tanū́** and **tanvī́, phalgú** and **phalgū́** and **phalgvī, mádhu** and **madhū́** and **mádhvī**. There are also some feminine noun-stems in ū standing (usually with changed accent) beside masculines in u: thus, **ágru** m., **agrū́** f.; **kádru** m., **kadrū́** f.; **gúggulu** m., **guggulū́** f.; **jatu** m., **jatū́** f.; **pṛ́dāku** m., **pṛdākū́** f.

345. Roots ending in i or u (or ṛ: **376 b**) regularly add a t when used as root-words or as root-finals of compounds; and hence there are no adjectives of the root-class in this declension.

a. Yet, in the Veda, a few words ending in a short radical u are declined as if this were suffixal: thus, **ásmṛtadhru, suṣṭú**; and the AV. has **pṛtanājí** (once). Roots in ū sometimes also shorten ū to u: thus, **prabhú, vibhú,** etc. (**354**); **go (361 e)** becomes **gu** in composition; and **re** perhaps becomes **ri (361 e)**; while roots in ā sometimes apparently weaken ā to i (in **-dhi** from √**dhā** etc.: **1155**).

346. Compound adjectives having nouns of this declension as final member are inflected in general like original adjectives of the same endings.

a. But in such compounds a final i or u is sometimes lengthened to form a feminine stem: thus, **suçronī, svayonī** or **-ni, -gātrayaṣṭī** or **-ṭi; vāmorū** or **-ru, durhaṇū** or **-ṇu, varatanū, mātṛbandhū**; and RV. has **áçiçvī** from **çíçu**.

Declension III.

Stems in long vowels: आ ā, ई ī, ऊ ū.

347. The stems ending in long vowels fall into two well-marked classes or divisions: A. monosyllabic stems — mostly bare roots — and their compounds, with a comparatively small number of others inflected like them; B. derivative feminine stems in आ ā and ई ī, with a small number in ऊ ū which in the later language have come to be inflected like them. The latter division is by far the larger and more important, since most feminine adjectives, and considerable classes of feminine nouns, ending in आ ā or ई ī, belong to it.

A. Root-words, and those inflected like them.

348. The inflection of these stems is by the normal endings throughout, or in the manner of consonant-stems (with अम् am, not म् m, in the accus. sing.); peculiarities like those of the other vowel-declensions are wanting. The simple words are, as nouns, with few exceptions feminine; as adjectives (rarely), and in adjective compounds, they are alike in masculine and feminine forms. They may, for convenience of description, be divided into the following sub-classes:

1. Root-words, or monosyllables having the aspect of such. Those in ā are so rare that it is hardly possible to make up a whole scheme of forms in actual use; those in ī and ū are more numerous, but still very few.

2. Compounds having such words, or other roots with long final vowels, as last member.

3. Polysyllabic words, of various origin and character, including in the Veda many which later are transferred to other declensions.

4. As an appendix to this class we may most conveniently describe the half-dozen stems, mostly of regular inflection, ending in diphthongs.

349. Monosyllabic stems. Before the endings beginning with vowels, final ī is changed to iy and ū to uv; while final ā is dropped altogether, except in the strong cases, and in the acc. pl., which is like the nominative (according to the grammarians, ā is lost here also: no instances of the occurrence of such a form appear to be quotable). Stems in ī and ū are in the later language allowed to take optionally the fuller endings **āi, ās, ām** in the singular (dat., abl.-gen., loc.); but no such forms are ever met with in the Veda (except **bhiyā́i** [?], RV., once). Before **ām** of gen. pl., **n** may or may not be inserted; in the Veda it is regularly inserted, with a single exception (**dhiyā́m,** once). The vocative is like the nominative in the singular as well as the other numbers; but instances of its occurrence in uncompounded stems are not found in the Veda, and must be extremely rare everywhere. The earlier Vedic dual ending is **ā** instead of **āu.**

350. To the ī- and ū-stems the rules for monosyllabic accent apply: the accent is thrown forward upon the endings in all the weak cases except the accus. pl., which is like the nom. But the ā-stems appear (the instances are extremely few) to keep the accent upon the stem throughout.

351. Examples of declension. As models of monosyllabic inflection we may take जा **jā́** f. *progeny;* धी **dhī́** f. *thought;* and भू **bhū́** f. *earth.*

a. The first of these is rather arbitrarily extended from the four cases which actually occur; of the loc. sing. and gen.-loc. du., no Vedic examples from ā-stems are found.

Singular:

N.	जास् **jā́s**	धीस् **dhī́s**	भूस् **bhū́s**
A.	जाम् **jā́m**	धियम् **dhíyam**	भुवम् **bhúvam**
I.	जा **jā́**	धिया **dhiyā́**	भुवा **bhuvā́**
D.	जे **jé**	धिये, धियै **dhiyé, dhiyā́i**	भुवे, भुवै **bhuvé, bhuvā́i**
Ab. G.	जस् **jás**	धियस्, धियास् **dhiyás, dhiyā́s**	भुवस्, भुवास् **bhuvás, bhuvā́s**
L.	जि **jí**	धियि, धियाम् **dhiyí, dhiyā́m**	भुवि, भुवाम् **bhuví, bhuvā́m**
V.	जास् **jā́s**	धीस् **dhī́s**	भूस् **bhū́s**

Dual:

N. A. V.	ज्ञौ jāú	धियौ dhíyāu	भुवौ bhúvāu
I. D. Ab.	ज्ञाभ्याम् jā́bhyām	धीभ्याम् dhībhyā́m	भूभ्याम् bhūbhyā́m
G. L.	ज्ञोस् jós	धियोस् dhiyós	भुवोस् bhuvós

Plural:

N.	ज्ञास् jā́s	धियस् dhíyas	भुवस् bhúvas
A.	ज्ञास् (ज्ञस् ?) jā́s, jás	धियस् dhíyas	भुवस् bhúvas
I.	ज्ञाभिस् jā́bhis	धीभिस् dhībhís	भूभिस् bhūbhís
D. Ab.	ज्ञाभ्यस् jā́bhyas	धीभ्यस् dhībhyás	भूभ्यस् bhūbhyás
G.	ज्ञानाम् (ज्ञाम् ?) jā́nām, jā́m	धियाम्, धीनाम् dhiyā́m, dhīnā́m	भुवाम्, भूनाम् bhuvā́m, bhūnā́m
L.	ज्ञासु jā́su	धीषु dhīṣú	भूषु bhūṣú

352. **Monosyllabic stems in composition.** When the nouns above described occur as final member of a compound, or when any root in **ā** or **ī** or **ū** is found in a like position, the inflection of an **ā**-stem is as above. But **ī** and **ū**-stems follow a divided usage: the final vowel before a vowel-ending is either converted into a short vowel and semivowel (**iy** or **uv**, as above) or into a semivowel simply (**y** or **v**). The accent is nowhere thrown forward upon the endings; and therefore, when **ī** and **ū** become **y** and **v**, the resulting syllable is circumflex (83—4). Thus:

Masc. and fem. Singular:

N. V.	-dhī́s		-bhū́s	
A.	-dhíyam	-dhyàm	-bhúvam	-bhvàm
I.	-dhíyā	-dhyā̀	-bhúvā	-bhvā̀
D.	-dhíye	-dhyè	-bhúve	-bhvè
Ab. G.	-dhíyas	-dhyàs	-bhúvas	-bhvàs
L.	-dhíyi	-dhyì	-bhúvi	-bhvì

Dual:				
N. A. V.	**-dhíyāu**	**-dhyāù**	**-bhúvāu**	**-bhvāù**
I. D. Ab.	**-dhī́bhyām**		**-bhū́bhyām**	
G. L.	**-dhíyos**	**-dhyòs**	**-bhúvos**	**-bhvòs**
Plural:				
N. A. V.	**-dhíyas**	**-dhyàs**	**-bhúvas**	**-bhvàs**
I.	**-dhī́bhis**		**-bhū́bhis**	
D. Ab.	**-dhī́bhyas**		**-bhū́bhyas**	
G.	**-dhíyām** / **-dhīnām**	**-dhyām̀**	**-bhúvām** / **-bhūnām**	**-bhvām̀**
L.	**-dhīṣu**		**-bhū́ṣu**	

a. As to the admissibility of the fuller endings **āi, ās,** and **ām** in the singular (feminine), grammatical authorities are somewhat at variance; but they are never found in the Veda, and have been omitted from the above scheme as probably unreal.

b. If two consonants precede the final **ī** or **ū**, the dissyllabic forms, with **iy** and **uv,** are regularly written; after one consonant, the usage is varying. The grammarians prescribe **iy** and **uv** when the monosyllabic stem has more the character of a noun, and **y** and **v** when it is more purely a verbal root with participial value. No such distinction, however, is to be seen in the Veda — where, moreover, the difference of the two forms is only graphic, since the **yā-** and **vā-**forms and the rest are always to be read as dissyllabic: **iā** or **īā** and **uā** or **ūā,** and so on.

c. As to neuter stems for such adjectives, see **367.**

353. A few further Vedic irregularities or peculiarities may be briefly noticed.

a. Of the **ā**-stems, the forms in **ās, ām, ā** (du.) are sometimes to be read as dissyllables, **aas, aam, aa.** The dative of the stem used as infinitive is **āí** (as if **ā́ + e**): thus, **prakhyāí, pratimāí, paradāí.**

b. Irregular transfer of the accent to the ending in compounds is seen in a case or two: thus, **avadyabhiyā́** (RV.), **ādhiā́** (AV.).

354. But compounds of the class above described are not infrequently transferred to other modes of inflection: the **ā** shortened to **a** for a masculine (and neuter) stem, or declined like a stem of the derivative **ā**-class (below, **364**) as feminine; the **ī** and **ū** shortened to **i** and **u,** and inflected as of the second declension.

a. Thus, compound stems in **-ga, -ja, -da, -stha, -bhu,** and others, are found even in the Veda, and become frequent later (being made from all, or nearly all, the roots in **ā**); and sporadic cases from yet others occur: for example, **çṛtapā́n, vayodhāís** and **ratnadhébhis, dhanasāís** (all RV.); and, from **ī** and **ū** compounds, **veṣaçrís** (TS.), **áhrayas** (RV.), **gaṇaçríbhis** (RV.), **karmaṇís** (ÇB.) and **ṛtaníbhyas** (RV.) and **senaníbhyas** (VS.) and **grāmaṇíbhis** (TB.), **supúnā** (AV.), **çitibhráve** (TS.).

b. Still more numerous are the feminines in **ā** which have lost their root-declension: examples are **prajā́** (of which the further compounds in part have root-forms), **svadhā́, çraddhā́, pratimā́,** and others.

c. Then, in the later language, a few feminines in **ī** are made from the stems in **a** shortened from **ā**: thus, **gopī, goṣṭhī, pannagī, pañkajī, bhujagī, bhujaṁgī, surāpī.**

355. Polysyllabic Stems. Stems of this division (**A**) of more than one syllable are very rare indeed in the later language, and by no means common in the earlier. The Rig-Veda, however, presents a not inconsiderable body of them; and as the class nearly dies out later, by the disuse of its stems or their transfer to other modes of declension, it may be best described on a Vedic basis.

a. Of stems in **ā**, masculines, half-a-dozen occur in the Veda: **pánthā, mánthā,** and **ṛbhukṣā́** are otherwise viewed by the later grammar: see below, **433—4**; **uçánā** (nom. pr.) has the anomalous nom. sing. **uçánā** (and loc. as well as dat. **uçáne**); **mahā́** *great* is found only in accus. sing. and abundantly in composition; **ā́tā** *frame* has only **ā́tāsu** not derivable from **ā́ta.**

b. Of stems in **ī**, over seventy are found in the Veda, nearly all feminines, and all accented on the final. Half of the feminines are formed from masculines with change of accent: thus, **kalyāṇī́** (m. **kalyā́ṇa**), **puruṣī́** (m. **púruṣa**); others show no change of accent: thus, **yamī́** (m. **yamá**); others still have no corresponding masculines: thus, **nadī́, lakṣmī́, sūrmī́.** The masculines are about ten in number: for example, **rathī́, prāvī́, starī́, ahī́, āpathī́.**

c. Of stems in **ū**, the number is smaller: these, too, are nearly all feminines, and all accented on the final. The majority of them are the feminine adjectives in **ū́** to masculines in **ú** or **u** (above, **344b**): thus, **caraṇyū́, cariṣṇū́, jighatsū́, madhū́.** A few are nouns in **ū́**, with change of accent: thus, **agrū́** (**ágru**), **pṛdākū́** (**pṛ́dāku**), **çvaçrū́** (**çváçura**); or without change, as **nṛtū́.** And a few have no corresponding masculines: thus, **tanū́, vadhū́, camū́.** The masculines are only two or three: namely, **prāçū́, kṛkadāçū́, makṣū́** (?); and their forms are of the utmost rarity.

356. The mode of declension of these words may be illustrated by the following examples: **rathī́** m. *charioteer;* **nadī́** f. *stream;* **tanū́** f. *body.*

a. No one of the selected examples occurs in all the forms; forms for which no example at all is quotable are put in brackets. No loc. sing. from any **ī**-stem occurs, to determine what the form would be. The stem **nadī́** is selected as example partly in order to emphasize the difference between the earlier language and the later in regard to the words of this division: **nadī́** is later the model of derivative inflection.

Singular:			
N.	**rathís**	**nadī́s**	**tanū́s**
A.	**rathíam**	**nadíam**	**tanúam**
I.	**rathíā**	**nadíā**	**tanúā**
D.	**rathíe**	**nadíe**	**tanúe**
Ab. G.	**rathías**	**nadías**	**tanúas**
L.	. . . .	. . . .	**tanúi**
V.	**ráthi** (?)	**nádi**	**tánu**
Dual:			
N. A. V.	**rathíā**	**nadíā**	**tanúā**
I. D. Ab.	[**rathī́bhyām**]	**nadī́bhyām**	[**tanū́bhyām**]
G. L.	[**rathíos**]	**nadíos**	**tanúos**
Plural:			
N. A.	**rathías**	**nadías**	**tanúas**
I.	[**rathī́bhis**]	**nadī́bhis**	**tanū́bhis**
D. Ab.	[**rathī́bhyas**]	**nadī́bhyas**	**tanū́bhyas**
G.	**rathī́nām**	**nadī́nām**	**tanū́nām**
L.	[**rathī́ṣu**]	**nadī́ṣu**	**tanū́ṣu**

b. The cases — **nadíam, tanúam,** etc. — are written above according to their true phonetic form, almost invariably belonging to them in the Veda; in the written text, of course, the stem-final is made a semivowel, and the resulting syllable is circumflexed: thus, **nadyàm, tanvàm,** etc.; only, as usual, after two consonants the resolved forms **iy** and **uv** are written instead; and also where the combination **yv** would otherwise result: thus, **cakríyā,** [**agrúvāi,**] and **mitrāyúvas.** The RV. really reads **staryàm** etc. twice, and **tanvàs** etc. four times; and such contractions are more often made in the AV. The ending **ā** of the nom.-acc.-voc. du. is the equivalent of the later **āu.** The nom. sing. in **s** from **ī**-stems is found in the older language about sixty times, from over thirty stems.

357. Irregularities of form, properly so called, are very few in this division: **camū́** as loc. sing. (instead of **camvì**) occurs a few times; and there is another doubtful case or two of the same kind; the final **ū́** is regarded as **pragṛhya** or uncombinable (**138**); **tanúi** is lengthened to **tanvī̀** in a passage or two; **-yúvas** is once or twice abbreviated to **-yū́s.**

358. The process of transfer to the other form of **ī-** and **ū**-declension (below, **362** ff.), which has nearly extinguished this category of words in the later language, has its beginnings in the Veda; but in RV. they are excessively scanty: namely, **dūtiā́m,** loc. sing., once, and **çvaçruā́m,** do., once, and **dravitnuā́,** instr. sing., with two or three other doubtful cases. In the Atharvan, we find the acc. sing. **kuhū́m, tanū́m, vadhū́m;** the instr. sing. **palāliā́** and one or two others; the dat. sing. **vadhvāí, çvaçruāí, agrúvāi;** the abl.-gen. sing. **punarbhúvās, pṛdākuā́s, çvaçruā́s;** and the loc. sing. **tanúām** (with anomalous accent). Accusatives plural in **īs** and **ūs** are nowhere met with.

359. Adjective compounds from these words are very few; those which occur are declined like the simple stems: thus, **híraṇyavāçīs** and **sahásrastarīs, átaptatanūs** and **sárvatanūs,** all nom. sing. masculine.

Stems ending in diphthongs.

360. There are certain monosyllabic stems ending in diphthongs, which are too few and too diverse in inflection to make a declension of, and which may be most appropriately disposed of here, in connection with the stems in **ī** and **ū,** with which they have most affinity. They are:

a. stems in **āu: nāú** and **glāú;**

b. stems in **āi: rāí;**

c. stems in **o: gó** and **dyó** (or **dyú, dív**).

361. a. The stem **nāú** f. *ship* is entirely regular, taking the normal endings throughout, and following the rules for monosyllabic accentuation (**317**) — except that the accus. pl. is said (it does not appear to occur in accented texts) to be like the nom. Thus: **nāús, nā́vam, nāvā́, nāvé, nāvás, nāví; nā́vāu, nāubhyā́m, nāvós; nā́vas, nā́vas, nāubhís, nāubhyás, nāvā́m, nāuṣú.** The stem **glāú** m. *ball* is apparently inflected in the same way; but few of its forms have been met with in use.

b. The stem **rāí** f. (or m.) *wealth,* might be better described as **rā** with a union-consonant **y** (**258**) interposed before vowel endings, and is regularly inflected as such, with normal endings and monosyllabic accent. Thus: **rā́s, rā́yam, rāyā́, rāyé, rāyás, rāyí; rā́yāu, rābhyā́m, rāyós; rā́yas, rāyás, rābhís, rābhyás, rāyā́m, rāsú.** But in the Veda the accus. pl. is either **rāyás** or **rā́yas;** for accus. sing. and pl. are also used the briefer forms **rā́m** (RV. once: **rā́yam** does not occur in V.) and **rā́s** (SV., once); and the gen.-sing. is sometimes anomalously accented **rā́yas.**

c. The stem **gó** m. or f. *bull* or *cow* is much more irregular. In the strong cases, except accus. sing., it is strengthened to **gāú,** forming (like **nāú**) **gāús, gā́vāu, gā́vas.** In accus. sing. and pl. it has (like **rāí**) the brief forms **gā́m** and **gā́s.** The abl.-gen. sing. is **gós** (as if from **gu**). The rest is regularly made from **go,** with the normal endings, but with accent always remaining irregularly upon the stem: thus, **gávā, gáve, gávi, gávos, gávām; góbhyām, góbhis, góbhyas, góṣu.** In the Veda, another form of the gen. pl. is **gónām;** the nom. etc. du. is (as in all other such cases) also **gā́vā;** and **gā́m, gós,** and **gā́s** are not infrequently to be pronounced as dissyllables. As acc. pl. is found a few times **gāvas.**

d. The stem **dyó** f. (but in V. usually m.) *sky, day* is yet more anomalous, having beside it a simpler stem **dyu,** which becomes **div** before a vowel-ending. The native grammarians treat the two as

independent words, but it is more convenient to put them together. The stem dyó is inflected precisely like gó, as above described. The complete declension is as follows (with forms not actually met with in use bracketed):

	Singular.		Dual.		Plural.	
N.		**dyāús**	**[dívāu]**	**dyā́vāu**	**dívas**	**dyā́vas**
A.	**dívam**	**dyā́m**			**divás, dyū́n**	**[dyā́s]**
I.	**divā́**	**[dyávā]**	**[dyúbhyām**	**dyóbhyām]**	**dyúbhis**	**[dyóbhis]**
D.	**divé**	**dyáve**			**[dyúbhyas**	**dyóbhyas]**
Ab.	**divás**	**dyós**				
G.	**divás**	**dyós**	**[divós**	**dyávos]**	**[divā́m**	**dyávām]**
L.	**diví**	**dyávi**			**dyúṣu**	**[dyóṣu]**

e. The dat. sing. **dyáve** is not found in the early language. Both **dívas** and **divás** occur as accus. pl. in V. As nom. etc. du., **dyā́vā** is, as usual, the regular Vedic form: once occurs **dyávī** (du.), as if a neuter form; and **dyāús** is found once used as ablative. The cases **dyāus, dyām,** and **dyūn** (once) are read in V. sometimes as dissyllables; and the first as accented vocative then becomes **dyāùs** (i. e. **díāus**: see **314**).

f. Adjective compounds having a diphthongal stem as final member are not numerous, and tend to shorten the diphthong to a vowel. Thus, from **nāu** we have **bhinnanu**; from **go**, several words like **águ, saptágu, sugu, bor hugú** (f. **-gū́** JB.); and, correspondingly, **rāi** seems to be reduced to **ri** in **bṛhádraye** and **ṛdhádrayas** (RV.). In derivation, **go** maintains its full form in **gotra, agótā, -gava** (f. **-gavī**), etc.; as first member of a compound, it is variously treated: thus, **gávāçir, gáviṣṭi** (but **gaāçir, gaïṣṭi** K.), etc.; **goaçvá** or **go'çva, góṛjīka, góopaça,** etc. In certain compounds, also, **dyu** or **dyo** takes an anomalous form: thus, **dyāurdā** (K.), **dyāurloká** (ÇB.), **dyāúsaṁçita** (AV.). In **revánt** (unless this is for **rayivant**) **rāi** becomes **re**. RV. has **ádhrigāvas** from **ádhrigu** (of questionable import); and AV. has **ghṛtastā́vas**, apparently accus. pl. of **ghṛtastú** or **-stó**.

B. Derivative stems in ā, ī, ū.

362. To this division belong all the ā and ī-stems which have not been specified above as belonging to the other or root-word division; and also, in the later language, most of the ī and ū-stems of the other division, by transfer to a more predominant mode of inflection. Thus:

1. **a.** The great mass of derivative feminine ā-stems, substantive and adjective.

b. The inflection of these stems has maintained itself with little change through the whole history of the language, being almost precisely the same in the Vedas as later.

2. c. The great mass of derivative feminine ī-stems.

d. This class is without exception in the later language. In the earlier, it suffers the exception pointed out above (355 b): that feminines made with change of accent follow this mode of declension only when the accent is not on the í: thus, táviṣī, páruṣṇī, páliknī, róhiṇī.

e. The ī-stems of this division in general are regarded as made by contraction of an earlier ending in yā. Their inflection has become in the later language somewhat mixed with that of the other division, and so far different from the Vedic inflection: see below, 363 g.

f. Very few derivative stems in ī are recognized by the grammarians as declined like the root-division; the Vedic words of that class are, if retained in use, transferred to this mode of inflection.

g. A very small number of masculine ī-stems (half-a-dozen) are in the Veda declined as of the derivative division: they are a few rare proper names, mā́talī etc.; and rā́ṣṭrī and sirī́ (only one case each).

3. h. The ū-stems are few in number, and are transfers from the other division, assimilated in inflection to the great class of derivative ī-stems (except that they retain the ending s of the nom. sing.).

363. Endings. The points of distinction between this and the other division are as follows:

a. In nom. sing. the usual s-ending is wanting: except in the ū-stems and a very few ī-stems — namely, lakṣmī, tarī, tantrī, tandrī — which have preserved the ending of the other division.

b. The accus. sing. and pl. add simply m and s respectively.

c. The dat., abl.-gen., and loc. sing. take always the fuller endings āi, ās, ām; and these are separated from the final of the ā-stems by an interposed y. In Brāhmaṇa etc., āi is generally substituted for ās (307 h).

d. Before the endings ā of instr. sing. and os of gen.-loc. du., the final of ā-stems is treated as if changed to e; but in the Veda, the instr. ending ā very often (in nearly half the occurrences) blends with the final to ā. The yā of ī-stems is in a few Vedic examples contracted to ī, and even to i. A loc. sing. in ī occurs a few times.

e. In all the weakest cases above mentioned, the accent of an ī- or ū-stem having acute final is thrown forward upon the ending. In the remaining case of the same class, the gen. pl., a n is always interposed between stem and ending, and the accent remains upon the former (in RV., however, it is usually thrown forward upon the ending, as in i and u-stems).

f. In voc. sing., final ā becomes e; final ī and ū are shortened.

g. In nom.-acc.-voc. du. and nom. pl. appears in ī (and ū)-stems a marked difference between the earlier and later language, the latter borrowing the forms of the other division. The du. ending āu is unknown in RV., and very rare in AV.; the Vedic ending is ī (a corresponding dual of ū-stems does not occur). The regular later pl. ending as has only a doubtful example or two in RV., and a very small number in AV.; the case there (and it is one of very frequent occurrence) adds **s** simply; and though **yas**-forms occur in the Brāhmaṇas, along with **īs**-forms, both are used rather indifferently as nom. and accus. (as, indeed, they sometimes interchange also in the epics). Of **ā**-stems, the du. nom. etc. ends in **e**, both earlier and later; in pl., of course, **s**-forms are indistinguishable from **as**-forms. The RV. has a few examples of **āsas** for **ās**.

h. The remaining cases call for no remark.

364. Examples of declension. As models of the inflection of derivative stems ending in long vowels, we may take सेना **sénā** f. *army;* कन्या **kanyā̀** f. *girl;* देवी **devī́** f. *goddess;* वधू **vadhū́** f. *woman.*

	Singular:			
N.	सेना **sénā**	कन्या **kanyā̀**	देवी **devī́**	वधूस् **vadhū́s**
A.	सेनाम् **sénām**	कन्याम् **kanyā̀m**	देवीम् **devī́m**	वधूम् **vadhū́m**
I.	सेनया **sénayā**	कन्यया **kanyàyā**	देव्या **devyā́**	वध्वा **vadhvā́**
D.	सेनायै **sénāyāi**	कन्यायै **kanyā̀yāi**	देव्यै **devyā́i**	वध्वै **vadhvā́i**
Ab. G.	सेनायास् **sénāyās**	कन्यायास् **kanyā̀yās**	देव्यास् **devyā́s**	वध्वास् **vadhvā́s**
L.	सेनायाम् **sénāyām**	कन्यायाम् **kanyā̀yām**	देव्याम् **devyā́m**	वध्वाम् **vadhvā́m**
V.	सेने **séne**	कन्ये **kánye**	देवि **dévi**	वधु **vádhu**
	Dual:			
N. A. V.	सेने **sene**	कन्ये **kanyè**	देव्यौ **devyā̀u**	वध्वौ **vadhvā̀u**
I. D. Ab.	सेनाभ्याम् **sénābhyām**	कन्याभ्याम् **kanyā̀bhyām**	देवीभ्याम् **devī́bhyām**	वधूभ्याम् **vadhū́bhyām**
G. L.	सेनयोस् **sénayos**	कन्ययोस् **kanyàyos**	देव्योस् **devyós**	वध्वोस् **vadhvós**

Plural:

N. V.	सेनास् **sénās**	कन्यास् **kanyā̀s**	देव्यस् **devyā̀s**	वध्वस् **vadhvā̀s**
A.	सेनास् **sénās**	कन्यास् **kanyā̀s**	देवीस् **devī́s**	वधूस् **vadhū́s**
I.	सेनाभिस् **sénābhis**	कन्याभिस् **kanyā̀bhis**	देवीभिस् **devī́bhis**	वधूभिस् **vadhū́bhis**
D. Ab.	सेनाभ्यस् **sénābhyas**	कन्याभ्यस् **kanyā̀bhyas**	देवीभ्यस् **devī́bhyas**	वधूभ्यस् **vadhū́bhyas**
G.	सेनानाम् **sénānām**	कन्यानाम् **kanyā̀nām**	देवीनाम् **devī́nām**	वधूनाम् **vadhū́nām**
L.	सेनासु **sénāsu**	कन्यासु **kanyā̀su**	देवीषु **devī́ṣu**	वधूषु **vadhū́ṣu**

a. In the Veda **vadhū́** is a stem belonging to the other division (like **tanū́,** above, **356**).

365. Examples of Vedic forms are:

a. ā-stems: instr. sing. **manīṣā́** (this simpler form is especially common from stems in **tā** and **iā**); nom. pl. **vaçā́sas** (about twenty examples); accus. pl. **araṁgamā́sas** (a case or two). Half the **bhyas-**cases are to be read as **bhias**; the **ām** of gen. pl. is a few times to be resolved into **aam**; and the **ā** and **ām** of nom. and accus. sing. are, very rarely, to be treated in the same manner.

b. ī-stems: instr. sing. **çámī, çámi**; loc. **gaurī́**; nom. etc. du. **devī́**; nom. pl. **devī́s**; gen. pl. **bahvīnā́m.** The final of the stem is to be read as a vowel (not **y**) frequently, but not in the majority of instances: thus, **deviā́, deviā́s, deviā́m, ródasios.**

c. The sporadic instances of transfer between this division and the preceding have been already sufficiently noticed.

d. Of the regular substitution made in the Brāhmaṇa language (**307 g, 336 g, 363 c**) of the dat. sing. ending **āi** for the gen.-abl. ending **ās,** in all classes of words admitting the latter ending, a few examples may be given here: **abhibhūtyāi rūpam** (AB.) *a sign of overpowering;* **triṣṭubhaç ca jagatyāi ca** (AB.) *of the metres triṣṭubh and jagatī;* **vāco dāivyāi ca mānuṣyāi ca** (AA.) *of speech, both divine and human;* **striyāi payaḥ** (AB.) *woman's milk;* **dhenvāí vā́ etád rétaḥ** (TB.) *that, forsooth, is the seed of the cow;* **jīrṇāyāi tvacaḥ** (KB.) *of dead skin;* **jyāyasī yājyāyāi** (AB.) *superior to the* **yājyā**; **asyāi divo 'smād antarikṣāt** (ÇÇS.) *from this heaven, from this atmosphere.* The same substitution is made once in the AV.: thus, **svápantv asyāi jñātáyaḥ** *let her relatives sleep.*

366. The noun **strī́** f. *woman* (probably contracted from **sūtrī́** *genetrix*), follows a mixed declension: thus, **strī́, stríyam** or **strī́m, striyā́, striyāí, striyā́s, striyā́m, strí; stríyāu, strībhyā́m, striyós; stríyas, stríyas** or **strī́s, strībhís, strībhyás, strīṇā́m, strīṣú** (but the accusatives **strī́m** and **strī́s** are not found in the older language, and the voc. **stri** is not quotable). The accentuation is that of a root-word; the forms (conspicuously the nom. sing.) are those of the other or derivative division.

Adjectives.

367. a. The occurrence of original adjectives in long final vowels, and of compounds having as final member a stem of the first division, has been sufficiently treated above, so far as masculine and feminine forms are concerned. To form a neuter stem in composition, the rule of the later language is that the final long vowel be shortened; and the stem so made is to be inflected like an adjective in **i** or **u** (**339, 341, 344**).

b. Such neuter forms are very rare, and in the older language almost unknown. Of neuters from **ī**-stems have been noted in the Veda only **hariçríyam,** acc. sing. (a masc. form), and **suādhías,** gen. sing. (same as masc. and fem.); from **ū**-stems, only a few examples, and from stem-forms which might be masc. and fem. also: thus, **vibhú, subhú,** etc. (nom.-acc. sing.: compare **354**); **supúā** and **mayobhúvā,** instr. sing.; and **mayobhú,** acc. pl. (compare **purú**: **342 k**); from **ā**-stems occur only half-a-dozen examples of a nom. sing. in **ās,** like the masc. and fem. form.

c. Compounds having nouns of the second division as final member are common only from derivatives in **ā**; and these shorten the final to **a** in both masculine and neuter: thus, from **a** *not* and **prajā** *progeny* come the masc. and neut. stem **apraja,** fem. **aprajā** *childless.* Such compounds with nouns in **ī** and **ū** are said to be inflected in masc. and fem. like the simple words (only with **īn** and **ūn** in acc. pl. masc.); but the examples given by the grammarians are fictitious.

d. Stems with shortened final are occasionally met with: thus, **ekapatni, āttalakṣmi;** and such adverbs (neut. sing. accus.) as **upabhāimi, abhyujjayini.** The stem **strī** is directed to be shortened to **stri** for all genders.

368. It is convenient to give a complete paradigm, for all genders, of an adjective-stem in अ **a.** We take for the purpose पाप **pāpá** *evil,* of which the feminine is usually made in आ **ā** in the later language, but in ई **ī** in the older.

	m.	n.	f.	f.
Singular:				
N.	पापस् pāpás	पापम् pāpám	पापा pāpā́	पापी pāpī́
A.	पापम् pāpám		पापाम् pāpā́m	पापीम् pāpī́m
I.	पापेन pāpéna		पापया pāpáyā	पाप्या pāpyā́
D.	पापाय pāpā́ya		पापायै pāpā́yāi	पाप्यै pāpyā́i
Ab.	पापात् pāpā́t		पापायास् pāpā́yās	पाप्यास् pāpyā́s
G.	पापस्य pāpásya		पापायास् pāpā́yās	पाप्यास् pāpyā́s
L.	पापे pāpé		पापायाम् pāpā́yām	पाप्याम् pāpyā́m
V.	पाप pā́pa		पापे pā́pe	पापि pā́pi
Dual:				
N. A. V.	पापौ pāpāú	पापे pāpé	पापे pāpé	पाप्यौ pāpyāù
I. D. Ab.	पापाभ्याम् pāpā́bhyām		पापाभ्याम् pāpā́bhyām	पापीभ्याम् pāpī́bhyām
G. L.	पापयोस् pāpáyos		पापयोस् pāpáyos	पाप्योस् pāpyós
Plural:				
N.	पापास् pāpā́s	पापानि pāpā́ni	पापास् pāpā́s	पाप्यस् pāpyàs
A.	पापान् pāpā́n	पापानि pāpā́ni	पापास् pāpā́s	पापीस् pāpī́s
I.	पापैस् pāpāís		पापाभिस् pāpā́bhis	पापीभिस् pāpī́bhis
D. Ab.	पापेभ्यस् pāpébhyas		पापाभ्यस् pāpā́bhyas	पापीभ्यस् pāpī́bhyas

G.	पापानाम् pāpā́nām	पापानाम् pāpā́nām	पापीनाम् pāpī́nām
L.	पापेषु pāpéṣu	पापासु pāpā́su	पापीषु pāpī́ṣu

Declension IV.

Stems in ऋ ṛ (or अर् ar).

369. This declension is a comparatively limited one, being almost entirely composed of derivative nouns formed with the suffix तृ tṛ (or तर् tar), which makes masculine *nomina agentis* (used also participially), and a few nouns of relationship.

a. But it includes also a few nouns of relationship not made with that suffix: namely **devṛ́** m., **svásṛ** and **nánāndṛ** f.; and, besides these, **nṛ́** m., **stṛ́** (in V.) m., **usṛ́** (in V.) f., **savyaṣṭhṛ** m., and the feminine numerals **tisṛ** and **catasṛ** (for which, see **482 e, g**). The feminines in tṛ are only **mātṛ́**, **duhitṛ́**, and **yā́tṛ**.

b. The inflection of these stems is quite closely analogous with that of stems in i and u (second declension); its peculiarity, as compared with them, consists mainly in the treatment of the stem itself, which has a double form, fuller in the strong cases, briefer in the weak ones.

370. Forms of the Stem. In the weak cases (excepting the loc. sing.) the stem-final is **ṛ**, which in the weakest cases, or before a vowel-ending, is changed regularly to **r** (**129**). But as regards the strong cases, the stems of this declension fall into two classes: in one of them — which is very much the larger, containing all the *nomina agentis*, and also the nouns of relationship **náptṛ** and **svásṛ**, and the irregular words **stṛ́** and **savyaṣṭhṛ** — the **ṛ** is vriddhied, or becomes **ār**; in the other, containing most of the nouns of relationship, with **nṛ́** and **usṛ́**, the **ṛ** is gunated, or changed to **ar**. In both classes, the loc. sing. has **ar** as stem-final.

371. Endings. These are in general the normal, but with the following exceptions:

a. The nom. sing. (masc. and fem.) ends always in **ā** (for original **ars** or **ārs**). The voc. sing. ends in **ar**.

b. The accus. sing. adds **am** to the (strengthened) stem; the accus. pl. has (like **i** and **u**-stems) **n** as masc. ending and **s** as fem. ending, with the **ṛ** lengthened before them.

c. The abl.-gen. sing. changes **ṛ** to **ur** (or **us**: **169 b**).

d. The gen. pl. (as in **i** and **u**-stems) inserts **n** before **ām**, and lengthens the stem-final before it. But the **ṛ** of **nṛ́** may also remain short.

e. The above are the rules of the later language. The older presents certain deviations from them. Thus:

f. The ending in nom.-acc.-voc. du. is (as universally in the Veda) regularly **ā** instead of **āu** (only ten **āu**-forms in RV.).

g. The **i** of loc. sing. is lengthened to **ī** in a few words: thus, **kartárī**.

h. In the gen. pl., the RV. has once **svásrām**, without inserted **n**; and **narā́m** instead of **nṛṇā́m** is frequent.

i. Other irregularities of **nṛ́** are the sing. dat. **náre**, gen. **náras**, and loc. **nári**. The Veda writes always **nṛṇā́m** in gen. pl., but its **ṛ** is in a majority of cases metrically long.

j. The stem **usṛ́** f. *dawn* has the voc. sing. **uṣar**, the gen. sing. **usrás**; and the accus. pl. also **usrás**, and loc. sing. **usrā́m** (which is metrically trisyllabic: **usṛ́ām**), as if in analogy with **ī** and **ū**-stems. Once occurs **usrí** in loc. sing., but it is to be read as if the regular trisyllabic form, **uṣári** (for the exchange of **s** and **ṣ**, see **181 a**).

k. From **stṛ́** come only **tā́ras** (apparently) and **stṛ́bhis**.

l. In the gen.-loc. du., the **r** is almost always to be read as a separate syllable, **ṛ**, before the ending **os**: thus, **pitṛós**, etc. On the contrary, **nánāndari** is once to be read **nánāndri**.

m. For neuter forms, see below, **375**.

372. Accent. The accentuation follows closely the rules for **i**- and **u**-stems: if on the final of the stem, it continues, as acute, on the corresponding syllable throughout, except in the gen. pl., where it may be (and in the Veda always is) thrown forward upon the ending; where, in the weakest cases, **ṛ** becomes **r**, the ending has the accent. The two monosyllabic stems, **nṛ́** and **stṛ́**, do not show the monosyllabic accent: thus (besides the forms already given above), **nṛ́bhis, nṛ́ṣu**.

373. Examples of declension. As models of this mode of inflection, we may take from the first class (with आर् **ār** in the strong forms) the stems दातृ **dātṛ́** m. *giver* and स्वसृ **svásṛ** f. *sister;* from the second class (with अर् **ar** in the strong forms), the stem पितृ **pitṛ́** m. *father*.

Singular:

N.	दाता **dātā́**	स्वसा **svásā**	पिता **pitā́**
A.	दातारम् **dātā́ram**	स्वसारम् **svásāram**	पितरम् **pitáram**

I.	दात्रा dātrā́	स्वस्रा svásrā	पित्रा pitrā́
D.	दात्रे dātré	स्वस्रे svásre	पित्रे pitré
Ab. G.	दातुर् dātúr	स्वसुर् svásur	पितुर् pitúr
L.	दातरि dātári	स्वसरि svásari	पितरि pitári
V.	दातर् dā́tar	स्वसर् svásar	पितर् pítar
Dual:			
N. A. V.	दातारौ dātā́rāu	स्वसारौ svásārāu	पितरौ pitárāu
I. D. Ab.	दातृभ्याम् dātṛ́bhyām	स्वसृभ्याम् svásṛbhyām	पितृभ्याम् pitṛ́bhyām
G. L.	दात्रोस् dātrós	स्वस्रोस् svásros	पित्रोस् pitrós
Plural:			
N. V.	दातारस् dātā́ras	स्वसारस् svásāras	पितरस् pitáras
A.	दातॄन् dātṝ́n	स्वसॄस् svásṝs	पितॄन् pitṝ́n
I.	दातृभिस् dātṛ́bhis	स्वसृभिस् svásṛbhis	पितृभिस् pitṛ́bhis
D. Ab.	दातृभ्यस् dātṛ́bhyas	स्वसृभ्यस् svásṛbhyas	पितृभ्यस् pitṛ́bhyas
G.	दातॄणाम् dātṝṇā́m	स्वसॄणाम् svásṝṇām	पितॄणाम् pitṝṇā́m
L.	दातृषु dātṛ́ṣu	स्वसृषु svásṛṣu	पितृषु pitṛ́ṣu

a. The feminine stem मातृ mātṛ́, *mother*, is inflected precisely like पितृ **pitṛ́**, excepting that its accusative plural is **मातॄस् mātṝ́s.**

b. The peculiar Vedic forms have been sufficiently instanced above; the only ones of other than sporadic occurrence being the nom. etc. du. dātā́rā, svásārā, pitárā, and the gen. pl. of nṛ́, narā́m.

c. The nom. pl. forms **pitaras** and **mātaras** etc. are found used also as accus. in the epics.

374. The stem **kroṣṭṹ** m. *jackal* (lit'ly *howler*) substitutes in the middle cases the corresponding forms of **króṣṭu**.

375. Neuter forms. The grammarians prescribe a complete neuter declension also for bases in tṛ, precisely accordant with that of vā́ri or mádhu (above, 339, 341). Thus, for example:

	Sing.	Du.	Plur.
N. A.	dhātṛ́	dhātṛ́ṇī	dhātṝ́ṇi
I.	dhātṛ́ṇā	dhātṛ́bhyām	dhātṛ́bhis
G.	dhātṛ́ṇas	dhātṛ́ṇos	dhātṝṇā́m
V.	dhā́tṛ, dhā́tar	dhā́tṛṇī	dhā́tṝṇi

a. The weakest cases, however (as of i- and u-stems used adjectively: **344**), are allowed also to be formed like the corresponding masculine cases: thus, **dhātrā́** etc.

b. No such neuter forms chance to occur in the Veda, but they begin to appear in the Brāhmaṇas, under influence of the common tendency (compare Germ. *Retter, Retterin;* Fr. *menteur, menteuse*) to give this *nomen agentis* a more adjective character, making it correspond in gender with the noun which it (appositively) qualifies. Thus, we have in TB. **bhartṛ́** and **janayitṛ́**, qualifying **antárikṣam**; and **bhartṝ́ṇi** and **janayitṝ́ṇi**, qualifying **nákṣatrāṇi**; as, in M., **grahītṝ́ṇi**, qualifying **indriyāṇi**.

c. When a feminine noun is to be qualified in like manner, the usual feminine derivative in ī is employed: thus, in TB., **bhartryàs** and **bhartryā̀ù, janayitryàs** and **janayitryā̀ù**, qualifying **ā́pas** and **ahorātré**; and such instances are not uncommon.

d. The RV. shows the same tendency very curiously once in the accus. pl. **mātṝ́n**, instead of **mātṝ́s**, in apposition with masculine nouns (RV. x. 35.2).

e. Other neuter forms in RV. are **sthātúr** gen. sing., **dhmātárī** loc. sing.; and for the nom. sing., instead of -tṛ, a few more or less doubtful cases, **sthātar, sthātúr, dhartári**.

Adjectives.

376. a. There are no original adjectives of this declension: for the quasi-adjectival character of the nouns composing it, see above (375 b). The feminine stem is made by the suffix ī: thus, **dātrī́, dhātrī́**.

b. Roots ending in ṛ (like those in i and u: **345**) add a t to make a declinable stem, when occurring as final member of a compound: thus, **karmakṛ́t** (√**kṛ**), **vajrabhṛ́t** (√**bhṛ**), **balihṛ́t** (√**hṛ**). From some **ṛ**-roots, also, are made stems in **ir** and **ur**: see below, **383 a, b.**

c. Nouns in **ṛ** as finals of adjective compounds are inflected in the same manner as when simple, in the masculine and feminine; in the neuter, they would doubtless have the peculiar neuter endings in nom.-acc.-voc. of all numbers.

d. But TS. has once **tvátpitāras**, nom. pl., *having thee for father.*

Declension V.

Stems ending in Consonants.

377. All stems ending in consonants may properly be classed together, as forming a single comprehensive declension; since, though some of them exhibit peculiarities of inflection, these have to do almost exclusively with the stem itself, and not with the declensional endings.

378. In this declension, masculines and feminines of the same final are inflected alike; and neuters are peculiar (as usually in the other declensions) only in the nom.-acc.-voc. of all numbers.

a. The majority of consonantal stems, however, are not inflected in the feminine, but form a special feminine derivative stem in ई **ī** (never in आ **ā**), by adding that ending to the weak form of the masculine.

b. Exceptions are in general the stems of divisions **A** and **B** — namely, the radical stems etc., and those in **as** and **is** and **us.** For special cases, see below.

379. Variations, as between stronger and weaker forms, are very general among consonantal stems: either of two degrees (strong and weak), or of three (strong, middle, and weakest): see above, **311.**

a. The peculiar neuter forms, according to the usual rule (**311 b**), are made in the plural from the strong stem, in singular and dual from the weak — or, when the gradation is threefold, in singular from the middle stem, in dual from the weakest.

b. As in the case of stems ending in short vowels (**ā́syāni, vā́rīṇi, mádhūni, dātṝ́ṇi,** etc.), a nasal sometimes appears in the special neuter plural cases which is found nowhere else in inflection. Thus, from the stems in **as, is, us,** the nom.-acc.-voc. pl. in **-āṅsi, -īṅṣi, -ūṅṣi** are very common at every period. According to the grammarians, the radical stems etc. (division **A**) are treated in the same way; but examples of such neuters are of extreme rarity in the language; no Vedic text offers one, and in the Brāhmaṇas and Sūtras have been noted only **-hunti** (AB. vii. 2. 3), **-vṛnti** (PB. xvi. 2. 7 et al.), **-bhāñji** (KB. xxvii. 7), **-bhṛ́nti** (ÇB. viii. 1. 3[1]), and **-yuñji** (LÇS. ii. 1. 8); while in the later language is found here and there a case, like **-çrunti** (Ragh.), **-pūṅṣi** (Çiç.); it may be questioned whether they are not later analogical formations.

380. The endings are throughout those given above (**310**) as the "normal"

a. By the general law as to finals (**150**), the **s** of the **nom. sing.** masc. and fem. is always lost; and irregularities of treatment of the final of the stem in this case are not infrequent.

b. The gen. and abl. sing. are never distinguished in form from one another — nor are, by ending, the nom. and accus. pl.: but these sometimes differ in stem-form, or in accent, or in both.

381. Change in the place of the accent is limited to monosyllabic stems and the participles in **ánt** (accented on the final). For details, see below, under divisions **A** and **E**.

a. But a few of the compounds of the root **añc** or **ac** show an irregular shift of accent in the oldest language: see below, **410**.

382. a. For convenience and clearness of presentation, it will be well to separate from the general mass of consonantal stems certain special classes which show kindred peculiarities of inflection, and may be best described together. Thus:

B. Derivative stems in **as, is, us**;

C. Derivative stems in **an** (**an, man, van**);

D. Derivative stems in **in** (**in, min, vin**);

E. Derivative stems in **ant** (**ant, mant, vant**);

F. Perfect active participles in **vāṅs**;

G. Comparatives in **yāṅs** or **yas.**

b. There remain, then, to constitute division **A**, especially radical stems, or those identical in form with roots, together with a comparatively small number of others which are inflected like these.

They will be taken up in the order thus indicated.

A. Root-stems, and those inflected like them.

383. The stems of this division may be classified as follows:

I. **a.** Root-stems, having in them no demonstrable element added to a root: thus, **ṛ́c** *verse*, **gír** *song*, **pád** *foot*, **díç** *direction*, **máh** (V.) *great*.

b. Such stems, however, are not always precisely identical in form with the root: thus, **vā́c** from √**vac**, **srā́j** from √**sṛj**, **mū́ṣ** from √**muṣ**, **vríç** from √**vraçc** (?), **úṣ** from √**vas** *shine;* — from roots in final **ṛ** come stems in **ir** and **ur**: thus, **gír**, **ā-çír**, **stír**; **júr**, **túr**, **dhúr**, **púr**, **múr**, **stúr**, **sphúr**; and **psúr** from √**psar**.

c. With these may be ranked the stems with reduplicated root, as **cikít**, **yavīyúdh**, **vánīvan**, **sasyád**.

d. Words of this division in uncompounded use are tolerably frequent in the older language: thus, in RV. are found more than a hundred of them; in AV., about sixty; but in the classical Sanskrit the power of using any root at will in this way is lost, and the examples are comparatively few. In all periods, however, the adjective use as final of a compound is very common (see below, **401**).

e. As to the infinitive use of various cases of the root-noun, see **971**.

II. **f.** Stems made by the addition of **t** to a final short vowel of a root.

g. No proper root-stem ends in a short vowel, although there are (**354**) examples of transfer of such to short-vowel-declensions; but **i** or **u** or **ṛ** adds a **t** to make a declinable form: thus, **-jít**, **-çrút**, **-kṛ́t**. Roots in **ṛ**, however, as has just been seen (**b**), also make stems in **ir** or **ur**.

h. As regards the frequency and use of these words, the same is true as was stated above respecting root-stems. The Veda offers examples of nearly thirty such formations, a few of them (**mít**, **rít**, **stút**, **hrút**, **vṛ́t**, and **dyút** if this is taken from **dyu**) in independent use. Of roots in **ṛ**, **t** is added by **kṛ**, **dhṛ**, **dhvṛ**, **bhṛ**, **vṛ**, **sṛ**, **spṛ**, **hṛ**, and **hvṛ**. The roots **gā** (or **gam**) and **han** also make **-gát** and **-hát** by addition of the **t** to an abbreviated form in **a** (thus, **adhvagát**, **dyugát**, **dvigat**, **navagát**, and **saṁhát**).

III. **i.** Monosyllabic (also a few apparently reduplicated) stems not certainly connectible with any verbal root in the language, but having the aspect of root-stems, as containing no traceable suffix:

thus, **tvác** *skin*, **páth** *road*, **hṛ́d** *heart*, **áp** and **vā́r** *water*, **dvā́r** *door*, **ā́s** *mouth*, **kakúbh** and **kakúd** *summit*.

j. Thirty or forty such words are found in the older language, and some of them continue in later use, while others have been transferred to other modes of declension or have become extinct.

k. Stems more or less clearly derivative, but made with suffixes of rare or even isolated occurrence. Thus:

1. derivatives (V.) from prepositions with the suffix **vat**: **arvāvát, āvát, udvát, nivát, parāvát, pravát, saṁvát**; — 2. derivatives (V.) n **tāt** (perhaps abbreviated from **tāti**), in a few isolated forms: thus, **uparátāt, devátāt, vṛkátāt, satyátāt, sarvátāt**; — 3. other derivatives in **t** preceded by various vowels: thus, **daçát, vehát, vahát, sravát, saçcát, vāghát; nápāt; taḍít, divít, yoṣít, rohít, sarít, harít; marút; yákṛt, çákṛt**; and the numerals for 30, 40, 50, **triṅçát** etc. (**475**); — 4. stems in **ad**: thus, **dṛṣád, dhṛṣád, bhasád, vanád, çarád, samád**; — 5. stems in **j** preceded by various vowels: thus, **tṛṣṇáj, dhṛṣáj, sanáj, bhiṣáj; uçíj, vaṇíj, bhuríj, niṇíj** (?); **ásṛj**; — 6. a few stems ending in a sibilant apparently formative: thus, **jñā́s, -dās, bhā́s, mā́s, bhī́ṣ**; — 7. a remnant of unclassifiable cases, such as **viṣṭáp, vípāç, kápṛth, çurúdh, iṣídh, pṛkṣúdh, raghá**ṭ (?), **sarágh, visrúh, uṣṇíh, kavā́ṣ**.

384. Gender. The root-stems are regularly feminine as *nomen actionis*, and masculine as *nomen agentis* (which is probably only a substantive use of their adjective value: below, **400**). But the feminine noun, without changing its gender, is often also used concretely: e. g., **druh** f. (√**druh** *be inimical*) means *harming, enmity*, and also *harmer, hater, enemy* — thus bordering on the masculine value. And some of the feminines have a completely concrete meaning. Through the whole division, the masculines are much less numerous than the feminines, and the neuters rarest of all.

a. The independent neuter stems are **hṛ́d** (also **-hārd**), **dám, vā́r, svàr, mā́s** *flesh*, **ā́s** *mouth*, **bhā́s, dós** (with which may be mentioned the indeclinables **çám** and **yós**); also the apparent derivatives **yákṛt, çákṛt, kápṛth, ásṛj**.

385. Strong and weak stem-forms. The distinction of these two classes of forms is usually made either by the presence or absence of a nasal, or by a difference in the quantity of the stem-vowel, as long or short; less often, by other methods.

386. A nasal appears in the strong cases of the following words:

1. Compounds having as final member the root **ac** or **añc**: see below, **407** ff.; and RV. has once **uruvyáñcam** from root **vyac**; — 2. The

stem **yuj**, sometimes, in the older language: thus, nom. sing. **yúñ** (for **yúñk**), accus. **yúñjam**, du. **yúñjā** (but also **yújam** and **yújā**); — 3. The stem **-dṛç**, as final of a compound in the older language; but only in the nom. sing. masc., and not always: thus, **anyādṛ́ñ**, **īdṛ́ñ**, **kīdṛ́ñ**, **tādṛ́ñ**, **etādṛñ**, **sadṛ́ñ** and **pratisadṛ́ñ**: but also **īdṛ́k**, **tādṛ́k**, **svardṛ́k**, etc.; — 4. For **path** and **puṁs**, which substitute more extended stems, and for **dant**, see below, **394—6**.

387. The vowel **a** is lengthened in strong cases as follows:

1. Of the roots **vac**, **sac**, **sap**, **nabh**, **ças**, in a few instances (V.), at the end of compounds; — 2. Of the roots **vah** and **sah**, but irregularly: see below, **403—5**; — 3. Of **ap** *water* (see **393**); also in its compound **rītyàp**; — 4. Of **pad** *foot*: in the compounds of this word, in the later language, the same lengthening is made in the middle cases also; and in RV. and AV. the nom. sing. neut. is both **-pat** and **-pāt**, while RV. has once **-pāde**, and **-pādbhis** and **-pātsu** occur in the Brāhmaṇas; — 5. Of **nas** *nose* (? **nā́sā** nom. du. fem., RV., once); — 6. Sporadic cases (V.) are: **yāj** (?), voc. sing.; **pāthás** and **-rāpas**, accus. pl.; **vánīvānas**, nom. pl. The strengthened forms **bhāj** and **rāj** are constant, through all classes of cases.

388. Other modes of differentiation, by elision of **a** or contraction of the syllable containing it, appear in a few stems:

1. In **-han**: see below, **402**; — 2. In **kṣam** (V.), along with prolongation of **a**: thus, **kṣā́mā** du., **kṣā́mas** pl.; **kṣamā́** instr. sing., **kṣámi** loc. sing., **kṣmás** abl. sing.; — 3. In **dvā́r**, contracted (V.) to **dur** in weak cases (but with some confusion of the two classes); — 4. In **svàr**, which becomes, in RV., **sūr** in weak cases; later it is indeclinable.

389. The endings are as stated above (**380**).

a. Respecting their combination with the final of the stem, as well as the treatment of the latter when it occurs at the end of the word, the rules of euphonic combination (chap. III.) are to be consulted; they require much more constant and various application here than anywhere else in declension.

b. Attention may be called to a few exceptional cases of combination (V.): **mādbhís** and **mādbhyás** from **mā́s** *month;* the wholly anomalous **paḍbhís** (RV. and VS.: AV. has always **padbhís**) from **pád**; and **saráṭ** and **saráḍbhyas** corresponding to a nom. pl. **sarághas** (instead of **saráhas**: **222**). **Dán** is apparently for **dám**, by **143 a**.

c. According to the grammarians, neuter stems, unless they end in a nasal or a semivowel, take in nom.-acc.-voc. pl. a strengthening nasal before the final consonant. But no such cases from neuter noun-stems appear ever to have been met with in use; and as regards adjective stems ending in a root, see above, **379 b**.

390. Monosyllabic stems have the regular accent of such, throwing the tone forward upon the endings in the weak cases.

a. But the accusative plural has its normal accentuation as a weak case, upon the ending, in only a minority (hardly more than a third) of the stems: namely in **datás, pathás, padás, nidás, apás, uṣás, jñāsás, puṁsás, māsás, mahás;** and sometimes in **vācás, srucás, hrutás, sridhás, kṣapás, vipás, durás, iṣás, dviṣás, druhás** (beside **vā́cas** etc.).

b. Exceptional instances, in which a weak case has the tone on the stem, occur as follows: **sádā, nádbhyas, tánā** (also **tanā́**) and **táne, bā́dhe** (infin.), **ráṇe** and **ráṅsu, váṅsu, sváni, vípas, kṣámi, sū́rā** and **sū́ras** (but **sūré**), **áṅhas,** and **vánas** and **bṛ́has** (in **vánaspáti, bṛ́haspáti**). On the other hand, a strong case is accented on the ending in **mahás,** nom. pl., and **kāsám** (AV.: perhaps a false reading). And **preṣā́,** instr. sing., is accented as if **préṣ** were a simple stem, instead of **pra-íṣ. Vimṛdháḥ** is of doubtful character. For the sometimes anomalous accentuation of stems in **ac** or **añc,** see **410.**

391. Examples of inflection. As an example of normal monosyllabic inflection, we may take the stem वाच् **vā́c** f *voice* (from √वच् **vac,** with constant prolongation): of inflection with strong and weak stem, पद् **pád** m. *foot:* of polysyllabic inflection, मरुत् **marút** m. *wind* or *wind-god:* of a monosyllabic root-stem in composition, त्रिवृत् **trivṛ́t** *three-fold,* in the neuter. Thus:

Singular:

N. V.	वाक् **vā́k**	पात् **pā́t**	मरुत् **marút**	त्रिवृत् **trivṛ́t**
A.	वाचम् **vā́cam**	पादम् **pā́dam**	मरुतम् **marútam**	त्रिवृत् **trivṛ́t**
I.	वाचा **vācā́**	पदा **padā́**	मरुता **marútā**	त्रिवृता **trivṛ́tā**
D.	वाचे **vācé**	पदे **padé**	मरुते **marúte**	त्रिवृते **trivṛ́te**
Ab. G.	वाचस् **vācás**	पदस् **padás**	मरुतस् **marútas**	त्रिवृतस् **trivṛ́tas**
L.	वाचि **vācí**	पदि **padí**	मरुति **marúti**	त्रिवृति **trivṛ́ti**

Dual:				
N. A. V.	वाचौ	पादौ	मरुतौ	त्रिवृती
	vácāu	**pádāu**	**marútāu**	**trivŕ̥tī**
I. D. Ab.	वाग्भ्याम्	पद्भ्याम्	मरुद्भ्याम्	त्रिवृद्भ्याम्
	vāgbhyā́m	**padbhyā́m**	**marúdbhyām**	**trivŕ̥dbhyām**
G. L.	वाचोस्	पदोस्	मरुतोस्	त्रिवृतोस्
	vācós	**padós**	**marútos**	**trivŕ̥tos**
Plural:				
N. V.	वाचस्	पादस्	मरुतस्	त्रिवृन्ति
	vā́cas	**pā́das**	**marútas**	**trivŕ̥nti**
A.	वाचस्	पदस्	मरुतस्	त्रिवृन्ति
	vācás, vā́cas	**padás**	**marútas**	**trivŕ̥nti**
I.	वाग्भिस्	पद्भिस्	मरुद्भिस्	त्रिवृद्भिस्
	vāgbhís	**padbhís**	**marúdbhis**	**trivŕ̥dbhis**
D. Ab.	वाग्भ्यस्	पद्भ्यस्	मरुद्भ्यस्	त्रिवृद्भ्यस्
	vāgbhyás	**padbhyás**	**marúdbhyas**	**trivŕ̥dbhyas**
G.	वाचाम्	पदाम्	मरुताम्	त्रिवृताम्
	vācā́m	**padā́m**	**marútām**	**trivŕ̥tām**
L.	वाक्षु	पत्सु	मरुत्सु	त्रिवृत्सु
	vākṣú	**patsú**	**marútsu**	**trivŕ̥tsu**

By way of illustration of the leading methods of treatment of a stem-final, at the end of the word and in combination with case-endings, characteristic case-forms of a few more stems are here added. Thus:

a. Stems in j: yuj-class (219 a, 142), **bhiṣáj** *physician:* **bhiṣák, bhiṣájam, bhiṣágbhis, bhiṣákṣu**; — **mr̥j**-class (219 b, 142), **samrā́j** *universal ruler:* **samrā́ṭ, samrā́jam, samrā́ḍbhis, samrā́ṭsu.**

b. Stems in dh: **-vŕ̥dh** *increasing:* **-vŕ̥t, -vŕ̥dham, -vŕ̥dbhis, vŕ̥tsu; -búdh** (155) *waking:* **-bhút, -búdham, -bhúdbhis, -bhútsu.**

c. Stems in bh: **-stúbh** *praising:* **-stúp, -stúbham, -stúbbhis, -stúpsu.**

d. Stems in ç: **díç** (218 a, 145) *direction:* **dík, díçam, digbhís, dikṣú**; — **víç** (218, 145) *the people:* **víṭ, víçam, viḍbhís, viṭsú** (V. **vikṣú**: 218 a).

e. Stems in ṣ (226 b, 145): **dvíṣ** *enemy:* **dvíṭ, dvíṣam, dviḍbhís, dviṭsú.**

f. Stems in h: duh-class (232—3 a, 155 b, 147), **-dúh** *milki* *yielding:* **-dhúk, -dúham, -dhúgbhis, -dhúkṣu;** — **ruh-class** (**223 b, 147**), **-lih** *licking:* **-liṭ, -liham, -liḍbhis, -liṭsu.**

g. Stems in **m** (**143 a, 212 a:** only **praçā́n**, nom. sing., quotable): **-çām** *quieting:* **-çā́n, çā́mam, -çā́nbhis, -çā́nsu.**

392. The root-stems in **ir** and **ur** (**383 b**) lengthen their vowel when the final **r** is followed by another consonant (**245 b**), and also in the nom. sing. (where the case-ending **s** is lost).

a. Thus, from **gír** f. *song* come **gī́r** (**gī́ḥ**), **gíram, girā́,** etc.; **gírāu, gīrbhyā́m, girós; gíras, gīrbhís, gīrbhyás, girā́m, gīrṣú** (**165**); and, in like manner, from **púr** f. *stronghold* come **pū́r** (**pū́ḥ**), **púram, purā́,** etc.; **púrāu, pūrbhyā́m, purós; púras, pūrbhís, pūrbhyás, purā́m, pūrṣú.**

b. There are no roots in **is** (except the excessively rare **pis**) or in **us**; but from the root **çās** with its **ā** weakened to **i** (**250**) comes the noun **āçís** f. *blessing,* which is inflected like **gír:** thus, **āçī́s** (**āçī́ḥ**), **āçíṣam, āçíṣā,** etc.; **āçíṣāu, āçīrbhyām, āçíṣos; āçíṣas, āçī́rbhis, āçī́rbhyas, āçíṣām, āçī́ḥṣu.** And **sajū́s** *together* is apparently a stereotyped nominative of like formation from the root **juṣ.** The form **aṣṭā́prūṭ** (TS.), from the root-stem **pruṣ,** is isolated and anomalous.

c. These stems in **ir, ur, is** show a like prolongation of vowel also in composition and derivation: thus, **gīrvāṇa, pūrbhíd, dhūrgata, dhūstva, āçīrdā́, āçī́rvant,** etc. (but also **gírvan, gírvaṇas**).

d. The native grammar sets up a class of quasi-radical stems like **jigamis** *desiring to go,* made from the desiderative conjugation-stem (**1027**), and prescribes for it a declension like that of **āçís:** thus, **jigamīs, jigamiṣā, jigamīrbhis, jigamīḥṣu,** etc. Such a class appears to be a mere figment of the grammarians, since no example of it has been found quotable from the literature, either earlier or later, and since there is, in fact, no more a desiderative stem **jigamis** than a causative stem **gamay.**

393. The stem **áp** f. *water* is inflected only in the plural, and with dissimilation of its final before **bh** to **d** (**151 e**): thus, **ā́pas, apás, adbhís, adbhyás, apā́m, apsú.**

a. But RV. has the sing. instr. **apā́** and gen. **apás.** In the earlier language (especially AV.), and even in the epics, the nom. and accus. pl. forms are occasionally confused in use, **ā́pas** being employed as accus., and **apás** as nominative.

b. Besides the stem **ap,** case-forms of this word are sometimes used in composition and derivation: thus, for example, **abjā́, āpodevata, āpomáya, apsumant.**

394. The stem **púṅs** m. *man* is very irregular, substituting **púmāṅs** in the strong cases, and losing its **s** (necessarily) before initial **bh** of a case-ending, and likewise (by analogy with this, or by an abbreviation akin with that noticed at **231**) in the loc. plural. The vocative is (in accordance with that of the somewhat similarly inflected perfect participles: see **462 a**) **púman** in the later language, but **púmas** in the earlier. Thus: **púmān, púmāṅsam, puṁsā́, puṁsé, puṁsás, puṁsí, púman; púmāṅsāu, pumbhyā́m, puṁsós; púmāṅsas, puṁsás, pumbhís, pumbhyás, puṁsā́m, puṁsú.**

a. The accentuation of the weak forms, it will be noticed, is that of a true monosyllabic stem. The forms with **bh**-endings nowhere occur in the older language, nor do they appear to have been cited from the later. Instances of the confusion of strong and weak forms are occasionally met with. As to the retention of **s** unlingualized in the weakest cases (whence necessarily follows that in the loc. pl.), see **183 a.**

b. This stem appears under a considerable variety of forms in composition and derivation: thus, as **puṁs** in **puṁçcalī́, puṁstva, púṁsvant, -puṁska,** etc.; as **pum** in **púṁvatsa, púṁrūpa, puṁvat, pumartha,** etc.; as **puṁsa** in **puṁsavant**; — at the end of a compound, either with its full inflection, as in **strīpúṁs** etc.; or as **puṁsa,** in **strīpuṁsa, mahāpuṁsa**; or as **puma** in **strīpuma** (TS. TA.).

395. The stem **path** m. *road* is defective in declension, forming only the weakest cases, while the strong are made from **pánthā** or **pánthan,** and the middle from **pathí**: see under **an**-stems, below, **433.**

396. The stem **dánt** m. *tooth* is perhaps of participial origin, and has, like a participle, the forms **dánt** and **dát,** strong and weak: thus (V.), **dán, dántam, datā́,** etc.; **datás** acc. pl. etc. But in the middle cases it has the monosyllabic and not the participial accent: thus, **dadbhís, dadbhyás.** In nom. pl. occurs also **-datas** instead of **-dantas.** By the grammarians, the strong cases of this word are required to be made from **dánta.**

397. A number of other words of this division are defective, making part of their inflection from stems of a different form.

a. Thus, **hṛ́d** n. *heart,* **mā́ṅs** or **mā́s** n. *meat,* **mā́s** m. *month,* **nā́s** f. *nose,* **niç** f. *night* (not found in the older language), **pṛ́t** f. *army,* are said by the grammarians to lack the nom. of all numbers and the accus. sing. and du. (the neuters, of course, the acc. pl. also), making them respectively from **hṛ́daya, māṅsá, mā́sa, nā́sikā, niçā, pṛtanā.** But the usage in the older language is not entirely in accordance with this requirement: thus, we find **mā́s** *flesh* accus. sing.; **mā́s** *month* nom. sing.; and **nā́sā** *nostrils* du. From **pṛ́t** occurs only the loc. pl. **pṛtsú** and (RV., once) the same case with double ending, **pṛtsúṣu.**

398. On the other hand, certain stems of this division, allowed by the grammarians a full inflection, are used to fill up the deficiencies of those of another form.

a. Thus, **ásṛj** n. *blood,* **çákṛt** n. *ordure,* **yákṛt** n. *liver,* **dós** n. (also m.) *fore-arm,* have beside them defective stems in **án**: see below, **432.** Of none of them, however, is anything but the nom.-acc. sing. found in the older language, and other cases later are but very scantily represented.

b. Of **ā́s** n. *mouth*, and **úd** *water*, only a case or two are found, in the older language, beside **āsán** and **āsyà**, and **udán** and **údaka** (432).

399. Some of the alternative stems mentioned above are instances of transition from the consonant to a vowel declension: thus, **dánta, mā́sa.** A number of other similar cases occur, sporadically in the older language, more commonly in the later. Such are **pā́da, -māda, -dāça, bhrājá, viṣṭápa, dvāra** and **dura, pura, dhura, -dṛça, nā́sā, nidā, kṣípā, kṣapā́, āçā́,** and perhaps a few others.

a. A few irregular stems will find a more proper place under the head of Adjectives.

Adjectives.

400. Original adjectives having the root-form are comparatively rare even in the oldest language.

a. About a dozen are quotable from the RV., for the most part only in a few scattering cases. But **mah** *great* is common in RV., though it dies out rapidly later. It makes a derivative feminine stem, **mahī́**, which continues in use, as meaning *earth* etc.

401. But compound adjectives, having a root as final member, with the value of a present participle, are abundant in every period of the language.

a. Possessive adjective compounds, also, of the same form, are not very rare: examples are **yatásruc** *with offered bowl;* **sū́ryatvac** *sun-skinned;* **cátuṣpad** *four-footed;* **suhā́rd** *kind-hearted, friendly;* **rītyàp** (i. e. **rītí-ap**) *having streaming waters;* **sahásradvār** *furnished with a thousand doors.*

b. The inflection of such compounds is like that of the simple root-stems, masculine and feminine being throughout the same, and the neuter varying only in the nom.-acc.-voc. of all numbers. But special neuter forms are of rare occurrence, and masc.-fem. are sometimes used instead.

c. Only rarely is a derivative feminine stem in **ī** formed: in the older language, only from the compounds with **ac** or **añc** (407 ff.), those with **han** (402), those with **pad**, as **ékapadī, dvipádī,** and with **dant**, as **vṛ́ṣadatī**, and **mahī́, ámucī** (AV.), **úpasadī** (? ÇB.).

Irregularities of inflection appear in the following:

402. The root **han** *slay*, as final of a compound, is inflected somewhat like a derivative noun in **an** (below, 420 ff.), becoming **hā** in the nom. sing., and losing its **n** in the middle cases and its **a** in the weakest cases (but only optionally in the loc. sing.). Further, when the vowel is lost, **h** in contact with following **n** reverts to its original **gh**. Thus:

	Singular.	Dual.	Plural.
N.	**vṛtrahā́**	**vṛtrahā́ṇāu** (N. A.)	**vṛtrahā́ṇas**
A.	**vṛtrahā́ṇam**		**vṛtraghnás**
I.	**vṛtraghnā́**	**vṛtrahábhyām** (I. D. Ab.)	**vṛtrahábhis**
D.	**vṛtraghné**		**vṛtrahábhyas** (D. Ab.)
Ab.	**vṛtraghnás** (Ab. G.)		
G.		**vṛtraghnós** (G. L.)	**vṛtraghnā́m**
L.	**vṛtraghní, -hā́ṇi**		**vṛtrahásu**
V.	**vṛ́trahan**	**vṛ́trahaṇāu**	**vṛ́trahaṇas.**

a. As to the change of **n** to **ṇ**, see **193, 195.**

b. A feminine is made by adding **ī** to, as usual, the stem-form shown in the weakest cases: thus, **vṛtraghnī́**.

c. An accus. pl. **-hánas** (like the nom.) also occurs. **Vṛtrahábhis** (RV., once) is the only middle case-form quotable from the older language. Transitions to the **a**-declension begin already in the Veda: thus, to **-há** (RV. AV.), **-ghná** (RV.), **-hana.**

403. The root **vah** *carry* at the end of a compound is said by the grammarians to be lengthened to **vāh** in both the strong and middle cases, and contracted in the weakest cases to **ūh**, which with a preceding **a**-vowel becomes **āu** (**137c**): thus, from **havyavā́h** *sacrifice-bearing* (epithet of Agni), **havyavā́ṭ, havyavā́ham, havyāúhā,** etc.; **havyavā́hāu, havyavā́ḍbhyām, havyāúhos; havyavā́has, havyāúhas, havyavā́ḍbhis,** etc. And **çvetavā́h** (not quotable) is said to be further irregular in making the nom. sing. in **vās** and the vocative in **vas** or **vās.**

a. In the earlier language, only strong forms of compounds with **vah** have been found to occur: namely, **-vā́ṭ, -vā́ham, -vā́hāu** or **-vā́hā,** and **-vā́has.** But feminines in **ī**, from the weakest stem — as **turyāuhī́, dityāuhī́, paṣṭhāuhī́** — are met with in the Brāhmaṇas. TS. has the irregular nom. sing. **paṣṭhavā́t.**

404. Of very irregular formation and inflection is one common compound of **vah**, namely **anaḍvā́h** (**anas + vah** *burden-bearing* or *cart-drawing*, i. e. *ox*). Its stem-form in the strong cases is **anaḍvā́h**, in the weakest **anaḍúh**, and in the middle **anaḍúd** (perhaps by dissimilation from **anaḍúḍ**). Moreover, its nom. and voc. sing. are made in **vān** and **van** (as if from a **vant**-stem). Thus:

	Singular.	Dual.	Plural.
N.	**anaḍvā́n**	**anaḍvā́hāu** (N. A.)	**anaḍvā́has**
A.	**anaḍvā́ham**		**anaḍúhas**
I.	**anaḍúhā**	**anaḍúdbhyām** (I. D. Ab.)	**anaḍúdbhis**
D.	**anaḍúhe**		**anaḍúdbhyas** (D. Ab.)
Ab.	**anaḍúhas** (Ab. G.)		
G.		**anaḍúhos** (G. L.)	**anaḍúhām**
L.	**anaḍúhi**		**anaḍútsu**
V.	**ánaḍvan**	**ánaḍvāhāu**	**ánaḍvāhas**

a. **Anaḍúdbhyas** (AV., once) is the only middle case-form quotable from the older language. But compounds showing the middle stem — as **anaḍucchata, anaḍudarha** — are met with in Brāhmaṇas etc.

b. The corresponding feminine stem (of very infrequent occurrence) is either **anaḍuhī́** (ÇB.) or **anaḍvāhī́** (K. MS.).

405. The root **sah** *overcome* has in the Veda a double irregularity: its **s** is changeable to **ṣ** even after an **a**-vowel — as also in its single occurrence as an independent adjective (RV., **tváṁ ṣā́ṭ**) — while it sometimes remains unchanged after an **i** or **u**-vowel; and its **a** is either prolonged or remains unchanged, in both strong and weak cases. The quotable forms are: **-ṣā́ṭ, -ṣā́ham** or **-sā́ham** or **-sáham, -sáhā, -sā́he** or **-sáhe, -ṣā́has** or **-ṣáhas** or **-sáhas; -sáhā** (du.); **-ṣā́has** or **-sáhas.**

406. The compound **avayā́j** (√**yaj** *make offering*) *a certain priest* or (BR.) *a certain sacrifice* is said to form the nom. and voc. sing. **avayā́s,** and to make its middle cases from **avayás.**

a. Its only quotable form is **avayā́s,** f. (RV. and AV., each once). If the stem is a derivative from **ava+√yaj** *conciliate,* **avayā́s** is very probably from **ava+√yā,** which has the same meaning. But **sadhamā́s** (RV., once) and **puroḍā́s** (RV. twice) show a similar apparent substitution in nom. sing. of the case-ending **s** after long **ā** for a final root-consonant (**d** and **ç** respectively). Compare also the alleged **çvetavā́s** (above, **403**).

407. Compounds with **añc** or **ac.** The root **ac** or **añc** makes, in combination with prepositions and other words, a considerable class of familiarly used adjectives, of quite irregular formation and inflection, in some of which it almost loses its character of root, and becomes an ending of derivation.

a. A part of these adjectives have only two stem-forms: a strong in **añc** (yielding **aṅ,** from **aṅks,** in nom. sing. masc.), and a weak in **ac;** others distinguish from the middle in **ac** a weakest stem in **c,** before which the **a** is contracted with a preceding **i** or **u** into **ī** or **ū.**

b. The feminine is made by adding **ī** to the stem-form used in the weakest cases, and is accented like them.

408. As examples of inflection we may take **prā́ñc** *forward, east,* **pratyáñc** *opposite, west,* **víṣvañc** *going apart.*

Singular:						
N. V.	**prā́ṅ**	**prā́k**	**pratyáṅ**	**pratyák**	**víṣvaṅ**	**víṣvak**
A.	**prā́ñcam**	**prā́k**	**pratyáñcam**	**pratyák**	**víṣvañcam**	**víṣvak**
I.	**prā́cā**		**pratīcā́**		**víṣūcā**	
D.	**prā́ce**		**pratīcé**		**víṣūce**	
Ab. G.	**prā́cas**		**pratīcás**		**víṣūcas**	
L.	**prā́ci**		**pratīcí**		**víṣūci**	
Dual:						
N. A. V.	**prā́ñcāu**	**prā́cī**	**pratyáñcāu**	**pratīcī́**	**víṣvañcāu**	**víṣūcī**
I. D. Ab.	**prā́gbhyām**		**pratyágbhyām**		**víṣvagbhyām**	
G. L.	**prā́cos**		**pratīcós**		**víṣūcos**	

	Plural:					
N. V.	**prā́ñcas**	**prā́ñci**	**pratyáñcas**	**pratyáñci**	**víṣvañcas**	**víṣvañci**
A.	**prā́cas**	**prā́ñci**	**pratīcás**	**pratyáñci**	**víṣūcas**	**víṣvañci**
I.	**prā́gbhis**		**pratyágbhis**		**víṣvagbhis**	
D. Ab.	**prā́gbhyas**		**pratyágbhyas**		**víṣvagbhyas**	
G.	**prā́cām**		**pratīcā́m**		**víṣūcām**	
L.	**prā́kṣu**		**pratyákṣu**		**víṣvakṣu**	

a. The feminine stems are **prā́cī, pratīcī́, víṣūcī,** respectively.

b. No example of the middle forms excepting the nom. etc. sing. neut. (and this generally used as adverb) is found either in RV. or AV. In the same texts is lacking the nom. etc. pl. neut. in **ñci**; but of this a number of examples occur in the Brāhmaṇas: thus, **prā́ñci, pratyáñci, arvā́ñci, samyáñci, sadhryañci, anvañci.**

409. a. Like **prā́ñc** are inflected **ápāñc, ávāñc, párāñc, arvā́ñc, adharā́ñc,** and others of rare occurrence.

b. Like **pratyáñc** are inflected **nyàñc** (i. e. **níañc**), **samyáñc** (**sam + añc,** with irregularly inserted **i**), and **údañc** (weakest stem **údīc: ud + añc,** with **i** inserted in weakest cases only), with a few other rare stems.

c. Like **víṣvañc** is inflected **anváñc,** also three or four others of which only isolated forms occur.

d. Still more irregular **is tiryáñc,** of which the weakest stem is **tiráçc** (**tirás + ac**: the other stems are made from **tir+añc** or **ac,** with the inserted **i**).

410. The accentuation of these words is irregular, as regards both the stems themselves and their inflected forms. Sometimes the one element has the tone and sometimes the other, without any apparent reason for the difference. If the compound is accented on the final syllable, the accent is shifted in RV. to the ending in the weakest cases provided their stem shows the contraction to **ī** or **ū**: thus, **prā́cā, arvā́cā, adharā́cas,** but **pratīcā́, anūcás, samīcī́.** But AV. and later texts usually keep the accent upon the stem: thus, **pratī́cī, samī́cī, anū́cī** (RV. has **pratī́cīm** once). The shift of accent to the endings, and even in polysyllabic stems, is against all usual analogy.

B. Derivative stems in as, is, us.

411. The stems of this division are prevailingly neuter; but there are also a few masculines, and one or two feminines.

412. The stems in अस् **as** are quite numerous, and mostly made with the suffix अस् **as** (a small number also with तस् tas and नस् nas, and some are obscure); the others are few, and almost all made with the suffixes इस् is and उस् us.

413. Their inflection is almost entirely regular But masculine and feminine stems in अस् as lengthen the vowel of the ending in nom. sing.; and the nom.-acc.-voc. pl. neut. make the same prolongation (of अ a or इ i or उ u) before the inserted nasal (anusvāra).

414. Examples of declension. As examples we may take मनस् mánas n. *mind;* अङ्गिरस् áṅgiras m. *Angiras;* हविस् havís n. *oblation.*

Singular:

N.	मनस् mánas	अङ्गिरास् áṅgirās	हविस् havís
A.	मनस् mánas	अङ्गिरसम् áṅgirasam	हविस् havís
I.	मनसा mánasā	अङ्गिरसा áṅgirasā	हविषा havíṣā
D.	मनसे mánase	अङ्गिरसे áṅgirase	हविषे havíṣe
Ab. G.	मनसस् mánasas	अङ्गिरसस् áṅgirasas	हविषस् havíṣas
L.	मनसि mánasi	अङ्गिरसि áṅgirasi	हविषि havíṣi
V.	मनस् mánas	अङ्गिरस् áṅgiras	हविस् havís

Dual:

N. A. V.	मनसी mánasī	अङ्गिरसौ áṅgirasāu	हविषी havíṣī
I. D. Ab.	मनोभ्याम् mánobhyām	अङ्गिरोभ्याम् áṅgirobhyām	हविर्भ्याम् havírbhyām
G. L.	मनसोस् mánasos	अङ्गिरसोस् áṅgirasos	हविषोस् havíṣos

Plural:

N. A. V.	मनांसि **mánāṅsi**	अङ्गिरसस् **áñgirasas**	हवींषि **havíṅṣi**
I.	मनोभिस् **mánobhis**	अङ्गिरोभिस् **áñgirobhis**	हविर्भिस् **havírbhis**
D. Ab.	मनोभ्यस् **mánobhyas**	अङ्गिरोभ्यस् **áñgirobhyas**	हविर्भ्यस् **havírbhyas**
G.	मनसाम् **mánasām**	अङ्गिरसाम् **áñgirasām**	हविषाम् **havíṣām**
L.	मनःसु **mánaḥsu**	अङ्गिरःसु **áñgiraḥsu**	हविःषु **havíḥṣu**

In like manner, चक्षुस् **cákṣus** n. *eye* forms चक्षुषा **cákṣuṣā**, चक्षुर्भ्याम् **cákṣurbhyām**, चक्षूंषि **cákṣūṅṣi**, and so on.

415. Vedic etc. Irregularities. **a.** In the older language, the endings **-asam** (acc. sing.) and **-asas** (generally nom.-acc. pl.; once or twice gen.-abl. sing.) of stems in **as** are not infrequently contracted to **-ām**, **-ās** — e. g. **āçā́m, vedhā́m; surā́dhās, ánāgās** — and out of such forms grow, both earlier and later, substitute-stems in **ā**, as **āçā́, jarā́, medhā́.** So from other forms grow stems in **a** and in **asa,** which exchange more or less with those in **as** through the whole history of the language.

b. More scattering irregularities may be mentioned, as follows: 1. The usual masc. and fem. du. ending in **ā** instead of **āu**; — 2. **uṣás** f. *dawn* often prolongs its **a** in the other strong cases, as in the nom. sing.: thus, **uṣā́sam, uṣā́sā, uṣā́sas** (and once in a weak case, **uṣā́sas**); and in its instr. pl. occurs once (RV.) **uṣádbhis** instead of **uṣóbhis**; — 3. from **toçás** is once (RV.) found a similar dual, **toçā́sā**; — 4. from **svávas** and **svátavas** occur in RV. a nom. sing. masc. in **vān,** as if from a stem in **vant**; and in the Brāhmaṇas is found the dat.-abl. pl. of like formation **svátavadbhyas.**

c. The stems in **is** and **us** also show transitions to stems in **i** and **u,** and in **iṣa** and **uṣa.** From **janús** is once (RV.) made the nom. sing. **janū́s,** after the manner of an **as**-stem (cf. also **janū́rvāsas** ÇB.).

416. The grammarians regard **uçánas** m. as regular stem-form of the proper name noticed above (**355 a**), but give it the irregular nom. **uçánā** and the voc. **uçanas** or **uçana** or **uçanan.** Forms from the **as**-stem, even nom., are sometimes met with in the later literature.

a. As to forms from **as**-stems to **áhan** or **áhar** and **ū́dhan** or **ū́dhar,** see below, **430.**

Adjectives.

417. a. A few neuter nouns in **as** with accent on the radical syllable have corresponding adjectives or appellatives in **ás**, with accent on the ending: thus, for example, **ápas** *work*, **apás** *active;* **táras** *quickness*, **tarás** *quick;* **yáças** *glory*, **yaçás** *glorious*. A few other similar adjectives — as **tavás** *mighty*, **vedhás** *pious* — are without corresponding nouns.

b. Original adjectives in **is** do not occur (as to alleged desiderative adjectives in **is**, see **392 d**). But in **us** are found as many adjectives as nouns (about ten of each class); and in several instances adjective and noun stand side by side, without difference of accent such as appears in the stems in **as**: e. g. **tápus** *heat* and *hot;* **vápus** *wonder* and *wonderful*.

418. Adjective compounds having nouns of this division as final member are very common: thus, **sumánas** *favorably minded;* **dīrgháyus** *long-lived;* **çukráçocis** *having brilliant brightness*. The stem-form is the same for all genders, and each gender is inflected in the usual manner, the stems in **as** making their nom. sing. masc. and fem. in **ās** (like **áñgiras**, above). Thus, from **sumánas**, the nom. and accus. are as follows:

	Singular. m. f.	n.	Dual. m. f.	n.	Plural. m. f.	n.
N.	**sumánās**	**-nas**	**sumánasāu**	**-nasī**	**sumánasas**	**-nāṅsi**
A.	**sumánasam**	**-nas**				

and the other cases (save the vocative) are alike in all genders.

a. In Veda and Brāhmaṇa, the neut. nom. sing. is in a considerable number of instances made in **ās**, like the other genders.

b. From **dīrghā́yus**, in like manner:

	Singular. m. f.	n.	Dual. m. f.	n.	Plural. m. f.	n.
N.	**dīrghā́yus**		**dīrghā́yuṣāu**	**-yuṣī**	**dīrghā́yuṣas**	**-yūṅṣi**
A.	**dīrghā́yuṣam**	**-yus**				
I.	**dīrghā́yuṣā**		**dīrghā́yurbhyām**		**dīrghā́yurbhis**	
	etc.		etc.		etc.	

419. The stem **anehás** *unrivalled* (defined as meaning *time* in the later language) forms the nom. sing. masc. and fem. **anehā́**.

C. Derivative stems in an.

420. The stems of this division are those made by the three suffixes अन् **an**, मन् **man**, and वन् **van**, together with a few of more questionable etymology which are inflected like them. They are almost exclusively masculine and neuter.

421. The stem has a triple form. In the strong cases

of the masculine, the vowel of the ending is prolonged to आ ā; in the weakest cases it is in general struck out altogether; in the middle cases, or before a case-ending beginning with a consonant, the final न् n is dropped. The न् n is also lost in the nom. sing. of both genders (leaving आ ā as final in the masculine, अ a in the neuter).

a. The peculiar cases of the neuter follow the usual analogy (**311 b**): the nom.-acc.-voc. pl. have the lengthening to आ ā, as strong cases; the nom.-acc.-voc. du., as weakest cases, have the loss of अ a — but this only optionally, not necessarily.

b. In the loc. sing., also, the **a** may be either rejected or retained (compare the corresponding usage with ṛ-stems: **373**). And after the **m** or **v** of **man** or **van**, when these are preceded by another consonant, the **a** is always retained, to avoid a too great accumulation of consonants.

422. The vocative sing. is in masculines the pure stem; in neuters, either this or like the nominative. The rest of the inflection requires no description.

423. As to accent, it needs only to be remarked that when, in the weakest cases, an acute **á** of the suffix is lost, the tone is thrown forward upon the ending.

424. Examples of declension. As such may be taken राजन् **rā́jan** m. *king;* आत्मन् **ātmán** m. *soul, self;* नामन् **nā́man** n. *name*. Thus:

	Singular:		
N.	राजा **rā́jā**	आत्मा **ātmā́**	नाम **nā́ma**
A.	राजानम् **rā́jānam**	आत्मानम् **ātmā́nam**	नाम **nā́ma**
I.	राज्ञा **rā́jñā**	आत्मना **ātmánā**	नाम्ना **nā́mnā**
D.	राज्ञे **rā́jñe**	आत्मने **ātmáne**	नाम्ने **nā́mne**

Ab. G.	राज्ञस् **rā́jñas**	आत्मनस् **ātmánas**	नाम्नस् **nā́mnas**
L.	राज्ञि, राजनि **rā́jñi, rā́jani**	आत्मनि **ātmáni**	नाम्नि, नामनि **nā́mni, nā́mani**
V.	राजन् **rā́jan**	आत्मन् **ā́tman**	नामन्, नाम **nā́man, nā́ma**
	Dual:		
N. A. V.	राजानौ **rā́jānāu**	आत्मानौ **ātmā́nāu**	नाम्नी, नामनी **nā́mnī, nā́manī**
I. D. Ab.	राजभ्याम् **rā́jabhyām**	आत्मभ्याम् **ātmábhyām**	नामभ्याम् **nā́mabhyām**
G. L.	राज्ञोस् **rā́jños**	आत्मनोस् **ātmános**	नाम्नोस् **nā́mnos**
	Plural:		
N.	राजानस् **rā́jānas**	आत्मानस् **ātmā́nas**	नामानि **nā́māni**
A.	राज्ञस् **rā́jñas**	आत्मनस् **ātmánas**	नामानि **nā́māni**
I.	राजभिस् **rā́jabhis**	आत्मभिस् **ātmábhis**	नामभिस् **nā́mabhis**
D. Ab.	राजभ्यस् **rā́jabhyas**	आत्मभ्यस् **ātmábhyas**	नामभ्यस् **nā́mabhyas**
G.	राज्ञाम् **rā́jñām**	आत्मनाम् **ātmánām**	नाम्नाम् **nā́mnām**
L.	राजसु **rā́jasu**	आत्मसु **ātmásu**	नामसु **nā́masu**

a. The weakest cases of **mūrdhán** m. *head*, would be accented **mūrdhnā́, mūrdhné, mūrdhnós, mūrdhnás** (acc. pl.), **mūrdhnā́m**, etc.; and so in all similar cases (loc. sing., **mūrdhní** or **mūrdháni**).

425. Vedic Irregularities. **a.** Here, as elsewhere, the ending of the nom.-acc.-voc. du. masc. is usually **ā** instead of **āu**.

b. The briefer form (with ejected **a**) of the loc. sing., and of the neut. nom.-acc.-voc. du., is quite unusual in the older language. RV. writes once **çatadā́vni**, but it is to be read **çatadā́vani**; and similar cases occur in AV. (but also several times **-mni**). In the Brāhmaṇas, too, such forms as **dhāmani** and **sāmanī** are very much more common than such as **ahni** and **lomnī**.

c. But throughout both Veda and Brahmaṇa, an abbreviated form of the loc. sing., with the ending **i** omitted, or identical with the stem, is of considerably more frequent occurrence than the regular form: thus, **mūrdhán, kárman, ádhvan,** beside **mūrdháni** etc. The **n** has all the usual combinations of a final **n**: e. g. **mūrdhann asya, mūrdhant sa, mūrdhaṅs tvā.**

d. In the nom.-acc. pl. neut., also, an abbreviated form is common, ending in **ā** or (twice as often) **a,** instead of **āni**: thus, **bráhma** and **bráhmā,** beside **bráhmāṇi**: compare the similar series of endings from a-stems, **329 c.**

e. From a few stems in **man** is made an abbreviated inst. sing., with loss of **m** as well as of **a**: thus, **mahinā́, prathinā́, variṇā́, dānā́, preṇā́, bhūnā́,** for **mahimnā́** etc. And **drāghmā́** and **raçmā́** (RV., each once) are perhaps for **drāghmáṇā, raçmánā.**

f. Other of the weakest cases than the loc. sing. are sometimes found with the **a** of the suffix retained: thus, for example, **bhū́manā, dā́mane, yā́manas, ukṣáṇas** (accus. pl.), etc. In the infinitive datives (**970 d**) — **trā́maṇe, vidmáne, dāváne,** etc. — the **a** always remains. About as numerous are the instances in which the **a,** omitted in the written form of the text, is, as the metre shows, to be restored in reading.

g. The voc. sing. in **vas,** which is the usual Vedic form from stems in **vant** (below, **454 b**), is found also from a few in **van,** perhaps by a transfer to the **vant**-declension: thus, **ṛtāvas, evayāvas, khidvas** (?), **prātaritvas, mātariçvas, vibhāvas.**

h. For words of which the **a** is not made long in the strong cases, see the next paragraph.

426. A few stems do not make the regular lengthening of **a** in the strong cases (except the nom. sing.). Thus:

a. The names of divinities, **pūṣán, aryamán**: thus, **pūṣā́, pūṣáṇam, pūṣṇā́,** etc.

b. In the Veda, **ukṣán** *bull* (but also **ukṣā́ṇam**); **yóṣan** *maiden*; **vṛ́ṣan** *virile, bull* (but **vṛ́ṣāṇam** and **vṛ́ṣāṇas** are also met with); **tmán,** abbreviation of **ātmán**; and two or three other scattering forms: **anarváṇam, jémanā.** And in a number of additional instances, the Vedic metre seems to demand **a** where **ā** is written.

427. The stems **çván** m. *dog* and **yúvan** *young* have in the weakest cases the contracted form **çún** and **yūn** (with retention of the accent); in the strong and middle cases they are regular. Thus, **çvā́, çvā́nam, çúnā, çúne,** etc., **çvábhyām, çvábhis,** etc.; **yúvā, yúvānam, yū́nā, yúvabhis,** etc.

a. In dual, RV. has once **yū́nā** for **yúvānā.**

428. The stem **maghávan** *generous* (later, almost exclusively a name of Indra) is contracted in the weakest cases to **maghón**: thus, **maghávā, maghávānam, maghónā, maghóne,** etc.

a. The RV. has once the weak form **maghónas** in nom. pl.

b. Parallel with this is found the stem **maghávant** (division E); and from the latter alone in the older language are made the middle cases: thus, **maghavadbhis, maghavatsu,** etc. (not **maghavabhis** etc.).

429 a. Stems in **a, ma, va,** parallel with those in **an, man, van,** and doubtless in many cases derived from them through transitional forms, are frequent in both the earlier and the later language, particularly as final members of compounds.

b. A number of **an**-stems are more or less defective, making a part of their forms from other stems. Thus:

430. a. The stem **áhan** n. *day* is in the later language used only in the strong and weakest cases, the middle (with the nom. sing., which usually follows their analogy) coming from **áhar** or **áhas**: namely, **áhar** nom.-acc. sing., **áhobhyām, áhobhis,** etc. (PB. has **aharbhis**); but **áhnā** etc., **áhni** or **áhani** (or **áhan**), **áhnī** or **áhanī, áhāni** (and, in V., **áhā**).

b. In the oldest language, the middle cases **áhabhis, áhabhyas, áhasu** also occur.

c. In composition, only **ahar** or **ahas** is used as preceding member; as final member, **ahar, ahas, ahan,** or the derivatives **aha, ahna.**

d. The stem **ū́dhan** n. *udder* exchanges in like manner, in the old language, with **ū́dhar** and **ū́dhas,** but has become later an **as**-stem only (except in the fem. **ūdhnī** of adjective compounds): thus, **ū́dhar** or **ū́dhas, ū́dhnas, ū́dhan** or **ū́dhani, ū́dhabhis, ū́dhaḥsu.** As derivatives from it are made both **ūdhanyà** and **ūdhasya.**

431. The neuter stems **akṣán** *eye,* **asthán** *bone,* **dadhán** *curds,* **sakthán** *thigh,* form in the later language only the weakest cases, **akṣṇā́, asthné, dadhnás, sakthní** or **saktháni,** and so on; the rest of the inflection is made from stems in **i, ákṣi** etc.: see above, **343 i.**

a. In the older language, other cases from the **an**-stems occur: thus, **akṣā́ṇi, akṣábhis,** and **akṣasu; asthā́ni, asthábhis,** and **asthábhyas; sakthā́ni.**

432. The neuter stems **asán** *blood,* **yakán** *liver,* **çakán** *ordure,* **āsán** *mouth,* **udán** *water,* **doṣán** *fore-arm,* **yūṣán** *broth,* are required to make their nom.-acc.-voc. in all numbers from the parallel stems **ásṛj, yákṛt, çákṛt, āsyà, údaka** (in older language **udaká**), **dós, yūṣá,** which are fully inflected.

a. Earlier occurs also the dual **doṣáṇī.**

433. The stem **pánthan** m. *road* is reckoned in the later language as making the complete set of strong cases, with the irregularity that the nom.-voc. sing. adds a **s.** The corresponding middle cases are made from **pathí,** and the weakest from **path.** Thus:

from **pánthan** — **pánthās, pánthānam; pánthānāu; pánthānas;**

from **pathí** — **pathíbhyām; pathíbhis, pathíbhyas, pathíṣu;**

from **path** — **pathā́, pathé, pathás, pathí; pathós; pathás** or **páthas** (accus.), **pathā́m.**

a. In the oldest language (RV.), however, the strong stem is only **pánthā**: thus, **pánthās,** nom. sing.; **pánthām,** acc. sing.; **pánthās,** nom. pl.; and even in AV., **pánthānam** and **pánthānas** are rare compared with the others. From **pathí** occur also the nom. pl. **patháyas** and gen. pl. **pathīnā́m.** RV. has once **pāthás,** acc. pl., with long **ā.**

434. The stems **mánthan** m. *stirring-stick*, and **ṛbhukṣán** m., an epithet of Indra, are given by the grammarians the same inflection with **pánthan**; but only a few cases have been found in use. In V. occur from the former the acc. sing. **mánthām,** and gen. pl. **mathīnā́m** (like the corresponding cases from **pánthan**); from the latter, the nom. sing. **ṛbhukṣā́s** and voc. pl. **ṛbhukṣās,** like the corresponding Vedic forms of **pánthan**; but also the acc. sing. **ṛbhukṣáṇam** and nom. pl. **ṛbhukṣáṇas,** which are after quite another model.

Adjectives.

435. Original adjective stems in **an** are almost exclusively those made with the suffix **van,** as **yájvan** *sacrificing,* **sútvan** *pressing the soma,* **jítvan** *conquering.* The stem is masc. and neut. only (but sporadic cases of its use as fem. occur in RV.); the corresponding fem. stem is made in **varī**: thus, **yájvarī, jítvarī.**

436. Adjective compounds having a noun in **an** as final member are inflected after the model of noun-stems; and the masculine forms are sometimes used also as feminine; but usually a special feminine is made by adding **ī** to the weakest form of the masculine stem: thus, **sómarājñī, kīlā́lodhnī, ékamūrdhnī, durṇā́mnī.**

437. But (as was pointed out above: **429 a**) nouns in **an** occurring as final members of compounds often substitute a stem in **a** for that in **an**: thus, **-rāja, -janma, -adhva, -aha**; their feminine is in **ā.** Occasional exchanges of stems in **van** and in **vant** also occur: thus, **vivásvan** and **vivásvant.**

a. The remaining divisions of the consonantal declension are made up of adjective stems only.

D. Derivative stems (adjective) in in.

438. The stems of this division are those formed with the suffixes इन् **in,** मिन् **min,** and विन् **vin.** They are masculine and neuter only; the corresponding feminine is made by adding ई ī.

a. The stems in **in** are very numerous, since almost any noun in **a** in the language may form a possessive derivative adjective with this suffix: thus, **bála** *strength*, **balín** m. n. **balínī** f. *possessing strength, strong*. Stems in **vin** (1232), however, are very few, and those in **min** (1231) still fewer.

439. Their inflection is quite regular, except that they lose their final न् n in the middle cases (before an initial consonant of the ending), and also in the nom. sing., where the masculine lengthens the इ i by way of compensation. The voc. sing. is in the masculine the bare stem; in the neuter, either this or like the nominative.

a. In all these respects, it will be noticed, the in-declension agrees with the an-declension; but it differs from the latter in never losing the vowel of the ending.

440. Example of inflection. As such may be taken बलिन् **balín** *strong*. Thus:

	Singular. m.	Singular. n.	Dual. m.	Dual. n.	Plural. m.	Plural. n.
N.	बली balī́	बलि balí	बलिनौ balínāu	बलिनी balínī	बलिनस् balínas	बलीनि balī́ni
A.	बलिनम् balínam	बलि balí				
I.	बलिना balínā		बलिभ्याम् balíbhyām		बलिभिस् balíbhis	
D.	बलिने balíne				बलिभ्यस् balíbhyas	
Ab.	बलिनस् balínas					
G.			बलिनोस् balínos		बलिनाम् balínām	
L.	बलिनि balíni				बलिषु balíṣu	
V.	बलिन् bálin	बलिन्, बलि bálin, báli	बलिनौ bálināu	बलिनी bálinī	बलिनस् bálinas	बलीनि bálīni

a. The derived feminine stem in inī is inflected, of course, like any other feminine in derivative ī (364).

441. a. There are no irregularities in the inflection of in-stems, in either the earlier language or the later — except the usual Vedic dual ending in ā instead of āu.

b. Stems in in exchange with stems in i throughout the whole history of the language, those of the one class being developed out of those of the other often through transitional forms. In a much smaller number of cases, stems in in are expanded to stems in ina: e. g. çākiná (RV.), çuṣmiṇa (B.), barhiṇa, bhajina.

E. Derivative stems (adjective) in ant (or at).

442. These stems fall into two sub-divisions: 1. those made by the suffix अन्त् ant (or अत् at), being, with a very few exceptions, active participles, present and future; 2. those made by the possessive suffixes मन्त् mant and वन्त् vant (or मत् mat and वत् vat). They are masculine and neuter only; the corresponding feminine is made by adding ई ī.

1. Participles in ant or at.

443. The stem has in general a double form, a stronger and a weaker, ending respectively in अन्त् ant and अत् at. The former is taken in the strong cases of the masculine, with, as usual, the nom.-acc.-voc. pl. neuter; the latter is taken by all the remaining cases.

a. But, in accordance with the rule for the formation of the feminine stem (below, 449), the future participles, and the present participles of verbs of the tud-class or accented á-class (752), and of verbs of the ad-class or root-class ending in ā, are by the grammarians allowed to make the nom.-acc.-voc. du. neut. from either the stronger or the weaker stem; and the present participles from all other present-stems ending in a are required to make the same from the strong stem.

444. Those verbs, however, which in the 3d pl. pres. active lose न् n of the usual ending न्ति nti (550 b), lose it also in the present participle, and have no distinction of strong and weak stem.

a. Such are the verbs forming their present-stem by reduplication without added **a**: namely, those of the reduplicating or **hu**-class (**655**) and the intensives (**1012**): thus, from √**hu**, present-stem **juhu**, participle-stem **júhvat**; intensive-stem **johu**, intensive participle-stem **jóhvat**. Further, the participles of roots apparently containing a contracted reduplication: namely, **cákṣat, dā́çat, dā́sat, çā́sat, sáçcat**; the aorist participle **dhákṣat**, and **vāghát**(?). **Vavṛdhánt** (RV., once), which has the **n** notwithstanding its reduplication, comes, like the desiderative participles (**1032**), from a stem in **a**: compare **vāvṛdhánta, vāvṛdhásva.**

b. Even these verbs are allowed by the grammarians to make the nom.-acc.-voc. pl. neut. in **anti**.

445. The inflection of these stems is quite regular. The nom. sing. masc. comes to end in अन् an by the regular (**150**) loss of the two final consonants from the etymological form अन्त्स् ants. The vocative of each gender is like the nominative.

446. Stems accented on the final syllable throw the accent forward upon the case-ending in the weakest cases (not in the middle also).

a. In the dual neut. (as in the feminine stem) from such participles, the accent is **ántī** if the **n** is retained, **atī́** if it is lost.

447. Examples of declension. As such may serve भवन्त् **bhávant** *being*, अदन्त् **adánt** *eating*, जुह्वत् **júhvat** *sacrificing*. Thus:

Singular:

N.	भवन् **bhávan**	भवत् **bhávat**	अदन् **adán**	अदत् **adát**	जुह्वत् **júhvat**	जुह्वत् **júhvat**
A.	भवन्तम् **bhávantam**	भवत् **bhávat**	अदन्तम् **adántam**	अदत् **adát**	जुह्वतम् **júhvatam**	जुह्वत् **júhvat**
I.	भवता **bhávatā**		अदता **adatā́**		जुह्वता **júhvatā**	
D.	भवते **bhávate**		अदते **adaté**		जुह्वते **júhvate**	
Ab. G.	भवतस् **bhávatas**		अदतस् **adatás**		जुह्वतस् **júhvatas**	
L.	भवति **bhávati**		अदति **adatí**		जुह्वति **júhvati**	

V.	भवन् bhávan	भवत् bhávat	अदन् ádan	अदत् ádat	जुह्वत् júhvat	
Dual:						
N. A. V.	भवन्तौ bhávantāu	भवन्ती bhávantī	अदन्तौ adántāu	अदती adatī́	जुह्वतौ júhvatāu	जुह्वती júhvatī
I. D. Ab.	भवद्भ्याम् bhávadbhyām		अदद्भ्याम् adádbhyām		जुह्वद्भ्याम् júhvadbhyām	
G. L.	भवतोस् bhávatos		अदतोस् adatós		जुह्वतोस् júhvatos	
Plural:						
N. V.	भवन्तस् bhávantas	भवन्ति bhávanti	अदन्तस् adántas	अदन्ति adánti	जुह्वतस् júhvatas	जुह्वति júhvati
A.	भवतस् bhávatas	भवन्ति bhávanti	अदतस् adatás	अदन्ति adánti	जुह्वतस् júhvatas	जुह्वति júhvati
I.	भवद्भिस् bhávadbhis		अदद्भिस् adádbhis		जुह्वद्भिस् júhvadbhis	
D. Ab.	भवद्भ्यस् bhávadbhyas		अदद्भ्यस् adádbhyas		जुह्वद्भ्यस् júhvadbhyas	
G.	भवताम् bhávatām		अदताम् adatā́m		जुह्वताम् júhvatām	
L.	भवत्सु bhávatsu		अदत्सु adátsu		जुह्वत्सु júhvatsu	

a. The future participle **bhaviṣyánt** may form in nom. etc. dual neuter either **bhaviṣyántī** or **bhaviṣyatī́**; **tudánt**, either **tudántī** or **tudatī́**; **yā́nt** (√yā), either **yā́ntī** or **yātī́**. And **júhvat,** in nom. etc. plural neuter, may make also **júhvanti** (beside **júhvati,** as given in the paradigm above).

b. But these strong forms (as well as **bhávantī,** du., and its like from present-stems in unaccented **a**) are quite contrary to general analogy, and of somewhat doubtful character. No example of them is quotable, either from the older or from the later language. The cases concerned, indeed, would be everywhere of rare occurrence.

448. The Vedic deviations from the model as above given are few. The dual ending **āu** is only one sixth as common as **ā.** Anomalous accent is seen in a case or two: **acodáte, rathirāyátām,** and **vāghádbhis** (if this is a participle). The only instance in V. of nom. etc. pl. neut. is **sā́nti,** with lengthened **ā** (compare the forms in **ānti,** below, **451 a, 454 c**); one or two examples in **anti** are quotable from B.

449. The feminine participle-stem, as already stated, is made by adding ई **ī** to either the strong or the weak stem-form of the masc.-neut. The rules as to which of the two forms shall be taken are the same with those given above respecting the nom. etc. dual neuter; namely:

a. Participles from tense-stems ending in unaccented **a** add **ī** to the strong stem-form, or make their feminine in **antī**.

b. Such are the **bhū** or unaccented **a**-class and the **dīv** or **ya**-class of present-stems (chap. IX.), and the desideratives and causatives (chap. XIV.): thus, from √**bhū** (stem **bháva**), **bhávantī**; from √**dīv** (stem **dī́vya**), **dī́vyantī**; from **búbhūṣa** and **bhāváya** (desid. and caus. of √**bhū**), **búbhūṣantī** and **bhāváyantī**.

c. Exceptions to this rule are now and then met with, even from the earliest period. Thus, RV. has **járatī**, and AV. the desiderative **síṣāsatī**; in B. occur **vadatī**, **çocatī**, **tṛpyatī**, and in S. further **tiṣṭhatī**, and the causative **namayatī**; while in the epics and later such cases (including desideratives and causatives) are more numerous (about fifty are quotable), though still only sporadic.

d. Participles from tense-stems in accented **á** may add the feminine-sign either to the strong or to the weak stem-form, or may make their feminines in **ántī** or in **atī́** (with accent as here noted).

e. Such are the present-stems of the **tud** or accented **á**-class (**751** ff.), the **s**-futures (**932** ff.), and the denominatives (**1053** ff.): thus, from √**tud** (stem **tudá**), **tudántī** or **tudatī́**; from **bhaviṣyá** (fut. of √**bhū**), **bhaviṣyántī** or **bhaviṣyatī́**; from **devayá** (denom. of **devá**), **devayántī** or **devayatī́**.

f. The forms in **ántī** from this class are the prevailing ones. No future fem. participle in **atī́** is quotable from the older language. From pres.-stems in **á** are found there **ṛñjatī́** and **siñcatī́** (RV.), **tudatī́** and **pinvatī** (AV.). From denominatives, **devayatī́** (RV.), **durasyatī́** and **çatrūyatī́** (AV.). In BhP. occurs **dhakṣyatī**.

g. Verbs of the **ad** or root-class (**611** ff.) ending in **ā** are given by the grammarians the same option as regards the feminine of the present participle: thus, from √**yā**, **yā́ntī** or **yātī́**. The older language affords no example of the former, so far as noted.

h. From other tense-stems than those already specified — that is to say, from the remaining classes of present-stems and from the intensives — the feminine is formed in **atī́** (or, if the stem be otherwise accented than on the final, in **atī**) only.

i. Thus, **adatī́** from √**ad**; **júhvatī** from √**hu**; **yuñjatī́** from √**yuj**; **sunvatī́** from √**su**; **kurvatī́** from √**kṛ**; **krīṇatī́** from √**krī**; **dédiçatī** from **dédiç** (intens. of √**diç**).

j. Feminine stems of this class are occasionally (but the case is much less frequent than its opposite: above, **c**) found with the nasal: thus, **yántī** (AV., once), **undántī** (ÇB.; but probably from the secondary **á**-stem), **gṛhṇantī** (S.), and, in the epics and later, such forms as **bruvantī**, **rudantī**, **cinvantī**, **kurvantī**, **jānantī**, **muṣṇantī**.

450. A few words are participial in form and inflection, though not in meaning. Thus:

a. bṛhánt (often written **vṛhánt**) *great;* it is inflected like a participle (with **bṛhatī́** and **bṛhánti** in du. and pl. neut.).

b. mahánt *great;* inflected like a participle, but with the irregularity that the **a** of the ending is lengthened in the strong forms: thus, **mahā́n**, **mahā́ntam**; **mahā́ntāu** (neut. **mahatī́**); **mahā́ntas**, **mahā́nti**: instr. **mahatā́** etc.

c. pṛ́ṣant *speckled*, and (in Veda only) **rúçant** *shining*.

d. jágat *movable*, *lively* (in the later language, as neuter noun, *world*), a reduplicated formation from √**gam** *go;* its nom. etc. neut. pl. is allowed by the grammarians to be only **jáganti**.

e. ṛhánt *small* (only once, in RV., **ṛhaté**).

f. All these form their feminine in **atī** only: thus, **bṛhatī́**, **mahatī́**, **pṛ́ṣatī** and **rúçatī** (contrary to the rule for participles), **jágatī**.

g. For **dánt** *tooth*, which is perhaps of participial origin, see above, **396**.

451. The pronominal adjectives **íyant** and **kíyant** are inflected like adjectives in **mant** and **vant**, having (**452**) **íyān** and **kíyān** as nom. masc. sing., **íyatī** and **kíyatī** as nom. etc. du. neut. and as feminine stems, and **íyanti** and **kíyanti** as nom. etc. plur. neut.

a. But the neut. pl. **íyānti** and the loc. sing. (?) **kíyāti** are found in RV.

2. Possessives in mant and vant.

452. The adjectives formed by these two suffixes are inflected precisely alike, and very nearly like the participles in अन्त् **ant**. From the latter they differ only by lengthening the अ **a** in the nom. sing. masc.

a. The voc. sing. is in **an**, like that of the participle (in the later language, namely: for that of the oldest, see below, **454 b**). The neut. nom. etc. are in the dual only **atī** (or **átī**), and in the plural **anti** (or **ánti**).

b. The feminine is always made from the weak stem: thus, **matī**, **vatī** (or **mátī**, **vátī**). One or two cases of **nī** instead of **ī** are met with: thus, **antárvatnī** (B. and later), **pativatnī** (C.).

c. The accent, however, is never thrown forward (as in the participle) upon the case-ending or the feminine ending.

453. To illustrate the inflection of such stems, it will be sufficient to give a part of the forms of पशुमन्त् **paçumánt** *possessing cattle*, and भगवन्त् **bhágavant** *fortunate, blessed*. Thus:

	m.	n.	m.	n.
Singular:				
N.	पशुमान् **paçumā́n**	पशुमत् **paçumát**	भगवान् **bhágavān**	भगवत् **bhágavat**
A.	पशुमन्तम् **paçumántam**	पशुमत् **paçumát**	भगवन्तम् **bhágavantam**	भगवत् **bhágavat**
I.	पशुमता **paçumátā** etc.		भगवता **bhágavatā** etc.	
V.	पशुमन् **páçuman**	पशुमत् **páçumat**	भगवन् **bhágavan**	भगवत् **bhágavat**
Dual:				
N. A. V.	पशुमन्तौ **paçumántāu**	पशुमती **paçumátī**	भगवन्तौ **bhágavantāu**	भगवती **bhágavatī**
	etc.		etc.	
Plural:				
N. V.	पशुमन्तस् **paçumántas**	पशुमन्ति **paçumánti**	भगवन्तस् **bhágavantas**	भगवन्ति **bhágavanti**
A.	पशुमतस् **paçumátas**	पशुमन्ति **paçumánti**	भगवतस् **bhágavatas**	भगवन्ति **bhágavanti**
I.	पशुमद्भिस् **paçumádbhis** etc.		भगवद्भिस् **bhágavadbhis** etc.	

454. Vedic Irregularities. **a.** In dual masc. nom. etc., **ā** (for **āu**) is the greatly prevailing ending.

b. In voc. sing. masc., the ending in the oldest language (RV.) is almost always in **as** instead of **an** (as in the perfect participle: below, **462 a**): thus, **adrivas, harivas, bhānumas, haviṣmas.** Such vocatives in RV. occur more than a hundred times, while not a single unquestionable instance of one in **an** is to be found. In the other Vedic texts, vocatives in **as** are extremely rare (but **bhagavas** and its contraction **bhagos** are met with, even in the later language); and in their reproduction of RV passages the **as** is usually changed to **an.** It was pointed out above (**425 g**) that the RV. makes the voc. in **as** also apparently from a few **an**-stems.

c. In RV., the nom. etc. pl. neut., in the only two instances that occur, ends in **ānti** instead of **anti**: thus, **ghṛtávānti, paçumánti.** No such forms have been noted elsewhere in the older language: the SV. reads **anti** in its version of the corresponding passages, and a few examples of the same ending are quotable from the Brāhmaṇas: thus, **tāvanti, etā́vanti, yā́vanti, ghṛtávanti, pravanti, ṛtumanti, yugmanti.** Compare **448, 451.**

d. In a few (eight or ten) more or less doubtful cases, a confusion of strong and weak forms of stem is made; they are too purely sporadic to require reporting. The same is true of a case or two where a masculine form appears to be used with a feminine noun.

455. The stem **árvant** *running, steed,* has the nom. sing. **árvā,** from **árvan**; and in the older language also the voc. **arvan** and accus. **árvāṇam.**

456. Besides the participle **bhávant**, there is another stem **bhávant,** frequently used in respectful address as substitute for the pronoun of the second person (but construed, of course, with a verb in the third person), which is formed with the suffix **vant,** and so declined, having in the nom. sing. **bhávān**; and the contracted form **bhos** of its old-style vocative **bhavas** is a common exclamation of address: *you, sir!* Its origin has been variously explained; but it is doubtless a contraction of **bhágavant.**

457. The pronominal adjectives **tā́vant, etā́vant, yā́vant,** and the Vedic **ī́vant, mā́vant, tvā́vant,** etc., are inflected like ordinary derivatives from nouns.

F. Perfect Participles in vāṅs.

458. The active participles of the perfect tense-system are quite peculiar as regards the modifications of their stem. In the strong cases, including the nom.-acc.-voc. pl. neut., the form of their suffix is वांस् **vāṅs,** which becomes, by regular process (**150**), **vān** in the nom. sing., and which is shortened to वन् **van** in the voc. sing. In the weakest cases, the suffix is contracted into उष् **uṣ.** In the middle cases, including the nom.-acc.-voc. neut. sing., it is changed to वत् **vat.**

a. A union-vowel **i**, if present in the strong and middle cases, disappears in the weakest, before **uṣ.**

459. The forms as thus described are masculine and neuter only; the corresponding feminine is made by adding ई ī to the weakest form of stem, ending thus in उषी úṣī.

460. The accent is always upon the suffix, whatever be its form.

461. Examples of inflection. To show the inflection of these participles, we may take the stems विद्वांस् vidvāṅs *knowing* (which has irregular loss of the usual reduplication and of the perfect meaning) from √विद् vid, and तस्थिवांस् tasthivāṅs *having stood* from √स्था sthā.

Singular:

	m.	n.	m.	n.
N.	विद्वान् vidvā́n	विद्वत् vidvát	तस्थिवान् tasthivā́n	तस्थिवत् tasthivát
A.	विद्वांसम् vidvā́ṅsam	विद्वत् vidvát	तस्थिवांसम् tasthivā́ṅsam	तस्थिवत् tasthivát
I.	विदुषा vidúṣā		तस्थुषा tasthúṣā	
D.	विदुषे vidúṣe		तस्थुषे tasthúṣe	
Ab. G.	विदुषस् vidúṣas		तस्थुषस् tasthúṣas	
L.	विदुषि vidúṣi		तस्थुषि tasthúṣi	
V.	विद्वन् vídvan	विद्वत् vídvat	तस्थिवन् tásthivan	तस्थिवत् tásthivat

Dual:

	m.	n.	m.	n.
N. A. V.	विद्वांसौ vidvā́ṅsāu	विदुषी vidúṣī	तस्थिवांसौ tasthivā́ṅsāu	तस्थुषी tasthúṣī
I. D. Ab.	विद्वद्भ्याम् vidvádbhyām		तस्थिवद्भ्याम् tasthivádbhyām	
G. L.	विदुषोस् vidúṣos		तस्थुषोस् tasthúṣos	

Plural:

N. V.	विद्वांसस् vidvā́ṅsas	विद्वांसि vidvā́ṅsi	तस्थिवांसस् tasthivā́ṅsas	तस्थिवांसि tasthivā́ṅsi
A.	विदुषस् vidúṣas	विद्वांसि vidvā́ṅsi	तस्थुषस् tasthúṣas	तस्थिवांसि tasthivā́ṅsi
I.	विद्वद्भिस् vidvádbhis		तस्थिवद्भिस् tasthivádbhis	
D. Ab.	विद्वद्भ्यस् vidvádbhyas		तस्थिवद्भ्यस् tasthivádbhyas	
G.	विदुषाम् vidúṣām		तस्थुषाम् tasthúṣām	
L.	विद्वत्सु vidvátsu		तस्थिवत्सु tasthivátsu	

a. The feminine stems of these two participles are विदुषी **vidúṣī** and तस्थुषी **tasthúṣī.**

b. Other examples of the different stems are:
from √kṛ — **cakṛvā́ṅs, cakṛvát, cakrúṣ, cakrúṣī;**
from √nī — **ninīvā́ṅs, ninīvát, ninyúṣ, ninyúṣī;**
from √bhū — **babhūvā́ṅs, babhūvát, babhūvúṣ, babhūvúṣī;**
from √tan — **tenivā́ṅs, tenivát, tenúṣ, tenúṣī.**

462. a. In the oldest language (RV.), the vocative sing. masc. (like that of **vant** and **mant**-stems: above, **454** b) has the ending **vas** instead of **van:** thus, **cikitvas** (changed to **-van** in a parallel passage of AV.), **titirvas, dīdivas, mīḍhvas.**

b. Forms from the middle stem, in **vat,** are extremely rare earlier: only three (**tatanvát** and **vavṛtvát,** neut. sing., and **jāgṛvádbhis,** instr. pl.), are found in RV., and not one in AV. And in the Veda the weakest stem (not, as later, the middle one) is made the basis of comparison and derivation: thus, **vidúṣṭara, ádāçuṣṭara, mīḍhúṣṭama, mīḍhúṣmant.**

c. An example or two of the use of the weak stem-form for cases regularly made from the strong are found in RV.: they are **cakrúṣam,** acc. sing., and **ábibhyuṣas,** nom. pl.; **emuṣám,** by its accent (unless an error), is rather from a derivative stem **emuṣá;** and ÇB. has **proṣúṣam.** Similar instances, especially from **vidvā́ṅs,** are now and then met with later (see BR., under **vidvā́ṅs**).

d. The AV. has once **bhaktivā́ṅsas,** as if a participial form from a noun; but K. and TB. give in the corresponding passage **bhaktivā́nas; cakhvā́ṅsam** (RV., once) is of doubtful character; **okivā́ṅsā** (RV., once) shows a reversion to guttural form of the final of √**uc,** elsewhere unknown.

G. Comparatives in yāṅs or yas.

463. The comparative adjectives of primary formation (below, **467**) have a double form of stem for masculine and neuter: a stronger, ending in यांस् **yāṅs** (usually ईयांस् **īyāṅs**), in the strong cases, and a weaker, in यस् **yas** (or ईयस् **īyas**), in the weak cases (there being no distinction of middle and weakest). The voc. sing. masc. ends in यन् **yan** (but for the older language see below, **465a**).

a. The feminine is made by adding ई **ī** to the weak masc.-neut. stem.

464. As models of inflection, it will be sufficient to give a part of the forms of श्रेयस् **çréyas** *better*, and of गरीयस् **gárīyas** *heavier*. Thus:

	Singular:			
N.	श्रेयान् çréyān	श्रेयस् çréyas	गरीयान् gárīyān	गरीयस् gárīyas
A.	श्रेयांसम् çréyāṅsam	श्रेयस् çréyas	गरीयांसम् gárīyāṅsam	गरीयस् gárīyas
I.	श्रेयसा çréyasā etc.		गरीयसा gárīyasā etc.	
V.	श्रेयन् çréyan	श्रेयस् çréyas	गरीयन् gárīyan	गरीयस् gárīyas
	Dual:			
N. A. V.	श्रेयांसौ çréyāṅsāu etc.	श्रेयसी çréyasī etc.	गरीयांसौ gárīyāṅsāu etc.	गरीयसी gárīyasī etc.
	Plural:			
N. V.	श्रेयांसस् çréyāṅsas	श्रेयांसि çréyāṅsi	गरीयांसस् gárīyāṅsas	गरीयांसि gárīyāṅsi
A.	श्रेयसस् çréyasas	श्रेयांसि çréyāṅsi	गरीयसस् gárīyasas	गरीयांसि gárīyāṅsi
I.	श्रेयोभिस् çréyobhis etc.		गरीयोभिस् gárīyobhis etc.	

a. The feminine stems of these adjectives are श्रेयसी **çréyasī** and गरीयसी **gárīyasī.**

465. a. The Vedic voc. masc. (as in the two preceding divisions: **454 b, 462 a**) is in **yas** instead of **yan:** thus, **ojīyas, jyāyas** (RV.: no examples elsewhere have been noted).

b. No example of a middle case occurs in RV. or AV.

c. In the later language are found a very few apparent examples of strong cases made from the weaker stem-form: thus, **kanīyasam** and **yavīyasam** acc. masc., **kanīyasāu** du., **yavīyasas** nom. pl.

Comparison.

466. Derivative adjective stems having a comparative and superlative meaning — or often also (and more originally) a merely intensive value — are made either directly from roots (by primary derivation), or from other derivative or compound stems (by secondary derivation).

a. The subject of comparison belongs more properly to the chapter of derivation; but it stands in such near relation to inflection that it is, in accordance with the usual custom in grammars, conveniently and suitably enough treated briefly here.

467. The suffixes of primary derivation are ईयस् **īyas** (or ईयांस् **īyāṅs**) for the comparative and इष्ठ **iṣṭha** for the superlative. The root before them is accented, and usually strengthened by gunating, if capable of it — or, in some cases, by nasalization or prolongation. They are much more frequently and freely used in the oldest language than later; in the classical Sanskrit, only a limited number of such comparatives and superlatives are accepted in use; and these attach themselves in meaning for the most part to other adjectives from the same root, which seem to be their corresponding positives; but in part also they are artificially connected with other words, unrelated with them in derivation.

a. Thus, from √**kṣip** *hurl* come **kṣépīyas** and **kṣépiṣṭha,** which belong in meaning to **kṣiprá** *quick;* from √**vṛ** *encompass* come **várīyas** and **váriṣṭha,** which belong to **urú** *broad;* while, for example,

kánīyas and **kániṣṭha** are attached by the grammarians to **yúvan** *young*, or **álpa** *small;* and **várṣīyas** and **várṣiṣṭha** to **vṛddhá** *old.*

468. From Veda and Brāhmaṇa together, considerably more than a hundred instances of this primary formation in **īyas** and **iṣṭha** (in many cases only one of the pair actually occurring) are to be quoted.

a. About half of these (in RV., the decided majority) belong, in meaning as in form, to the bare root in its adjective value, as used especially at the end of compounds, but sometimes also independently: thus, from √**tap** *burn* comes **tápiṣṭha** *excessively burning;* from √**yaj** *offer* come **yájīyas** and **yájiṣṭha** *better* and *best* (or *very well*) *sacrificing;* from √**yudh** *fight* comes **yódhīyas** *fighting better;* — in a few instances, the simple root is also found used as corresponding positive: thus, **jū́** *hasty, rapid* with **jávīyas** and **jáviṣṭha.**

b. In a little class of instances (eight), the root has a preposition prefixed, which then takes the accent: thus, **ā́gamiṣṭha** *especially coming hither;* **vícayiṣṭha** *best clearing away;* — in a couple of cases (**áçramiṣṭha, áparāvapiṣṭha, ástheyas**), the negative particle is prefixed; — in a single word (**çámbhaviṣṭha**), an element of another kind.

c. The words of this formation sometimes take an accusative object (see **271 e**).

d. But even in the oldest language appears not infrequently the same attachment in meaning to a derivative adjective which (as pointed out above) is usual in the later speech.

e. Besides the examples that occur also later, others are met with like **váriṣṭha** *choicest* (**vára** *choice*), **bárhiṣṭha** *greatest* (**bṛhánt** *great*), **óṣiṣṭha** *quickest* (**óṣam** *quickly*), and so on. Probably by analogy with these, like formations are in a few cases made from the apparently radical syllables of words which have no otherwise traceable root in the language: thus, **kradhīyas** and **kradhiṣṭha** (K.) from **kṛdhú, sthávīyas** and **sthávíṣṭha** from **sthūrá, çáçīyas** (RV.) from **çáçvant, áṇīyas** (AV.) and **áṇiṣṭha** (TS.) from **aṇú;** and so on. And yet again, in a few exceptional cases, the suffixes **īyas** and **iṣṭha** are applied to stems which are themselves palpably derivative: thus, **ā́çiṣṭha** from **āçú** (RV.: only case), **tī́kṣṇīyas** (AV.) from **tīkṣṇá, bráhmīyas** and **bráhmiṣṭha** (TS. etc.) from **bráhman, dhármiṣṭha** (TA.) from **dhárman, dráḍhiṣṭha** (TA.: instead of **dárhiṣṭha**) from **dṛḍhá, rághīyas** (TS.) from **raghu.** These are beginnings, not followed up later, of the extension of the formation to unlimited use.

f. In **návīyas** or **návyas** and **náviṣṭha,** from **náva** *new*, and in **sányas** from **sána** *old* (all RV.), we have also formations unconnected with verbal roots.

469. The stems in **iṣṭha** are inflected like ordinary adjectives in **a,** and make their feminines in **ā;** those in **īyas** have a peculiar declension, which has been described above (**463** ff.).

470. Of peculiarities and irregularities of formation, the following may be noticed:

a. The suffix **īyas** has in a few instances the briefer form **yas**, generally as alternative with the other: thus, **távīyas** and **távyas**, **návīyas** and **návyas**, **vásīyas** and **vásyas**, **pánīyas** and **pányas**; and so from **rabh** and **sah**; **sányas** occurs alone. From **bhū** come **bhū́yas** and **bhū́yiṣṭha**, beside which RV. has also **bhávīyas**.

b. Of roots in **ā**, the final blends with the initial of the suffix to **e**: thus, **sthéyas**, **dhéṣṭha**, **yéṣṭha**; but such forms are in the Veda generally to be resolved, as **dhā́iṣṭha**, **yā́iṣṭha**. The root **jyā** forms **jyéṣṭha**, but **jyā́yas** (like **bhū́yas**).

c. The two roots in **ī**, **prī** and **çrī**, form **préyas** and **préṣṭha** and **çréyas** and **çréṣṭha**.

d. From the root of **ṛjú** come, without strengthening, **ṛ́jīyas** and **ṛ́jiṣṭha**; but in the older language also, more regularly, **rájīyas** and **rájiṣṭha**.

471. The suffixes of secondary derivation are तर **tara** and तम **tama**. They are of almost unrestricted application, being added to adjectives of every form, simple and compound, ending in vowels or in consonants — and this from the earliest period of the language until the latest. The accent of the primitive remains (with rare exceptions) unchanged; and that form of stem is generally taken which appears before an initial consonant of a case-ending (weak or middle form).

a. Examples (of older as well as later occurrence) are: from vowel-stems, **priyátara**, **váhnitama**, **rathī́tara** and **rathī́tama** (RV.), **cā́rutara**, **potṛ́tama**, **saṁraktatara**; — from consonant-stems, **çáṁtama**, **çáçvattama**, **mṛḍayáttama**, **tavástara** and **tavástama**, **tuvíṣṭama**, **vápuṣṭara**, **tapasvítara**, **yaçasvítama**, **bhágavattara**, **hiraṇyavāçīmattama**; — from compounds, **ratnadhā́tama**, **abhibhū́tara**, **sukṛ́ttara**, **pūrbhíttama**, **bhūyiṣṭhabhā́ktama**, **bhūridā́vattara**, **çúcivratatama**, **strīkāmatama**.

b. But in the Veda the final **n** of a stem is regularly retained: thus, **madíntara** and **madíntama**, **vṛṣántama**; and a few stems even add a nasal: thus, **surabhíntara**, **rayíntama**, **madhúntama**. In a case or two, the strong stem of a present participle is taken: thus, **vrā́dhanttama**, **sáhanttama**; and, of a perfect participle, the weakest stem: thus, **vidúṣṭara**, **mīḍhúṣṭama**. A feminine final **ī** is shortened: thus, **devitamā** (RV.), **tejasvinitamā** (K.).

c. In the older language, the words of this formation are not much more frequent than those of the other: thus, in RV. the stems in **tara** and **tama** are to those in **īyas** and **iṣṭha** as three to two; in AV., only as six to five: but later the former win a great preponderance.

472. These comparatives and superlatives are inflected like ordinary adjectives in **a**, forming their feminine in **ā**.

473. a. That (especially in the Veda) some stems which are nouns rather than adjectives form derivatives of comparison is natural enough, considering the uncertain nature of the division-line between substantive and adjective value. Thus, we have **vīrátara, vīrátama, váhnitama, mātṛ́tama, nṛ́tama, marúttama,** and so on.

b. The suffixes **tara** and **tama** also make forms of comparison from some of the pronominal roots, as **ka, ya, i** (see below, **520**); and from certain of the prepositions, as **ud**; and the adverbially used accusative (older, neuter, **-taram**; later, feminine, **-tarām**) of a comparative in **tara** from a preposition is employed to make a corresponding comparative to the preposition itself (below, **1119**); while **-tarām** and **-tamām** make degrees of comparison from a few adverbs: thus, **natarā́m, natamā́m, kathaṁtarām, kutastarām, addhātamā́m, nīcāistarām,** etc.

c. By a wholly barbarous combination, finding no warrant in the earlier and more genuine usages of the language, the suffixes of comparison in their adverbial feminine form, **-tarām** and **-tamām,** are later allowed to be added to personal forms of verbs: thus, **sīdatetarām** (R.: the only case noted in the epics) *is more despondent,* **vyathayatitarām** *disturbs more,* **alabhatatarām** *obtained in a higher degree,* **hasiṣyatitarām** *will laugh more.* No examples of this use of **-tamām** are quotable.

d. The suffixes of secondary comparison are not infrequently added to those of primary, forming double comparatives and superlatives: thus, **garīyastara, çreṣṭhatara** and **çréṣṭhatama, pāpīyastara, pāpiṣṭhatara** and **-tama, bhūyastaram,** etc.

e. The use of **tama** as ordinal suffix is noted below (**487**); with this value, it is accented on the final, and makes its feminine in **ī**: thus, **çatatamá** m. n., **çatatamī́** f., *hundredth.*

474. From a few words, mostly prepositions, degrees of comparison are made by the briefer suffixes **ra** and **ma**: thus, **ádhara** and **adhamá, ápara** and **apamá, ávara** and **avamá, úpara** and **upamá, ántara, ántama, paramá, madhyamá, caramá, antima, ādima, paçcima.** And **ma** is also used to make ordinals (below, **487**).

CHAPTER VI.

NUMERALS.

475. The simple cardinal numerals for the first ten numbers (which are the foundation of the whole class), with their derivatives, the tens, and with some of the higher members of the decimal series, are as follows:

1	एक	**éka**	10	दश	**dáça**	100	शत	**çatá**
2	द्व	**dvá**	20	विंशति	**viṅçatí**	1000	सहस्र	**sahásra**
3	त्रि	**trí**	30	त्रिंशत्	**triṅçát**	10,000	अयुत	**ayúta**
4	चतुर्	**catúr**	40	चत्वारिंशत्	**catvāriṅçát**	100,000	लक्ष	**lakṣá**
5	पञ्च	**páñca**	50	पञ्चाशत्	**pañcāçát**	1,000,000	प्रयुत	**prayúta**
6	षष्	**ṣáṣ**	60	षष्टि	**ṣaṣṭí**	10,000,000	कोटि	**kóṭi**
7	सप्त	**saptá**	70	सप्तति	**saptatí**	10^8	अर्बुद	**arbudá**
8	अष्ट	**aṣṭá**	80	अशीति	**açītí**	10^9	महार्बुद	**mahārbuda**
9	नव	**náva**	90	नवति	**navatí**	10^{10}	खर्व	**kharvá**
10	दश	**dáça**	100	शत	**çatá**	10^{11}	निखर्व	**nikharva**

a. The accent **saptá** and **aṣṭá** is that belonging to these words in all accentuated texts; according to the grammarians, they are **sápta** and **áṣṭa** in the later language. See below, **483**.

b. The series of decimal numbers may be carried still further; but there are great differences among the different authorities with regard to their names; and there is more or less of discordance even from **ayúta** on.

c. Thus, in the TS. and MS. we find **ayúta, niyúta, prayúta, árbuda, nyàrbuda, samudrá, mádhya, ánta, parārdhá**; K. reverses the order of **niyúta** and **prayúta**, and inserts **badva** after **nyarbuda** (reading **nyarbudha**): these are probably the oldest recorded series.

d. In modern time, the only numbers in practical use above *thousand* are **lakṣa** (*lac* or *lakh*) and **koṭi** (*crore*); and an Indian sum is wont to be pointed thus: 123,45,67,890, to signify *123 crores, 45 lakhs, 67 thousand, eight hundred and ninety*.

e. As to the alleged stem-forms **pañcan** etc., see below, **484**. As to the form **ṣakṣ** instead of **ṣaṣ**, see above, **146 b**. The stem **dva** appears in composition and derivation also as **dvā** and **dvi**; **catúr** in composition is accented **cátur**. The older form of **aṣṭa** is **aṣṭā**: see below, **483**. Forms in **-çat** and **-çati** for the tens are occasionally interchanged: e. g. **viṅçat** (MBh. R.), **triṅçati** (AB.), **pañcāçati** (RT.).

f. The other numbers are expressed by the various composition and syntactical combination of those given above. Thus:

476. The odd numbers between the even tens are made by prefixing the (accented) unit to the ten to which its value is to be added: but with various irregularities. Thus:

a. **eka** in *11* becomes **ekā**, but is elsewhere unchanged;

b. **dva** becomes everywhere **dvā**; but in *42—72* and in *92* it is interchangeable with **dvi**, and in *82* **dvi** alone is used;

c. for **tri** is substituted its nom. pl. masc. **tráyas**; but **tri** itself is also allowed in *43—73* and in *93*, and in *83* **tri** alone is used;

d. **ṣaṣ** becomes **ṣo** in *16*, and makes the initial **d** of **daça** lingual (**199 d**); elsewhere its final undergoes the regular conversion (**226 b, 198 b**) to **ṭ** or **ḍ** or **ṇ**; and in *96* the **n** of **navati** is assimilated to it (**199 c**);

e. **aṣṭa** becomes **aṣṭā** (**483**) in *18—38*, and has either form in the succeeding combinations.

f. Thus:

11 **ékādaça**	31 **ékatriṅçat**	61 **ékaṣaṣṭi**	81 **ékāçīti**
12 **dvā́daça**	32 **dvā́triṅçat**	62 {**dvā́ṣaṣṭi** / **dvíṣaṣṭi**}	82 **dvyàçīti**
13 **tráyodaça**	33 **tráyastriṅçat**	63 {**tráyaḥṣaṣṭi** / **tríṣaṣṭi**}	83 **tryàçīti**
14 **cáturdaça**	34 **cátustriṅçat**	64 **cátuḥṣaṣṭi**	84 **cáturaçīti**
15 **páñcadaça**	35 **páñcatriṅçat**	65 **páñcaṣaṣṭi**	85 **páñcāçīti**
16 **ṣóḍaça**	36 **ṣáṭtriṅçat**	66 **ṣáṭṣaṣṭi**	86 **ṣáḍaçīti**
17 **saptádaça**	37 **saptátriṅçat**	67 **saptáṣaṣṭi**	87 **saptā́çīti**
18 **aṣṭā́daça**	38 **aṣṭā́triṅçat**	68 {**aṣṭáṣaṣṭi** / **aṣṭā́ṣaṣṭi**}	88 **aṣṭā́çīti**
19 **návadaça**	39 **návatriṅçat**	69 **návaṣaṣṭi**	89 **návāçīti**

g. The numbers *21—29* are made like those for *31—39;* the numbers *41—49*, *51—59*, *71—79*, and *91—99* are made like those for *61—69*.

h. The forms made with **dvā** and **trayas** are more usual than those with **dvi** and **tri,** which are hardly to be quoted from the older literature (V. and Br.). The forms made with **aṣṭā** (instead of **aṣṭa**) are alone found in the older literature (**483**), and are usual in the later.

477. The above are the normal expressions for the odd numbers. But equivalent substitutes for them are also variously made. Thus:

a. By use of the adjectives **ūna** *deficient* and **adhika** *redundant,* in composition with lesser numbers which are to be subtracted or added, and either independently qualifying or (more usually) in composition with larger numbers which are to be increased or diminished by the others: thus, **tryūnaṣaṣṭiḥ** *sixty deficient by three* (i. e. *57*); **aṣṭādhikanavatiḥ** *ninety increased by eight* (i. e. *98*); **ekādhikaṁ çatam** *a hundred increased by one* (i. e. *101*); **pañconaṁ çatam** *100 less 5* (i. e. *95*). For the nines, especially, such substitutes as **ekonaviṅçatiḥ** *20 less 1*, or *19*, are not uncommon; and later the **eka** *1* is left off, and **ūnaviṅçati** etc. have the same value.

b. A case-form of a smaller number, generally **éka** *one* is connected by **ná** *not* with a larger number from which it is to be deducted: thus, **ékayā ná triṅçát** (ÇB. PB. KB.) *not thirty by one* (*29*); **dvā́bhyāṁ nā́ 'çītím** (ÇB.) *not eighty by two* (*78*); **pañcábhir ná catvā́ri çatā́ni** (ÇB.) *not four hundred by five* (*395*); **ékasmān ná pañcāçát** (in ordinal) *49* (TS.); **ékasyāi** (abl. fem.: **307 h**) **ná pañcāçát** *49* (TS.); most often, **ékān** (i. e. **ékāt,** irregular abl. for **ékasmāt**) **ná viṅçatíḥ** *19;* **ékān ná çatám** *99*. This last form is admitted also in the later language; the others are found in the Brāhmaṇas.

c. Instances of multiplication by a prefixed number are occasionally met with: thus, **triṣaptá** *thrice seven;* **triṇavá** *thrice nine;* **tridaçá** *thrice ten.*

d. Of course, the numbers to be added together may be expressed by independent words, with connecting *and:* thus, **náva ca navatíç ca,** or **náva navatíç ca** *ninety and nine;* **dvā́u ca viṅçatíç ca** *two and twenty.* But the connective is also (at least, in the older language) not seldom omitted: thus, **navatír náva** *99;* **triṅçátaṁ trī́n** *33;* **açītír aṣṭā́u** *88*.

478. The same methods are also variously used for forming the odd numbers above 100. Thus:

a. The added number is prefixed to the other, and takes the accent: for example, **ékaçatam** *101;* **aṣṭā́çatam** *108;* **triṅçácchatam** *130;* **aṣṭāviṅçatiçatam** *128;* **cátuḥsahasram** (RV.: unless the accent is wrong) *1004;* **açītisahasram** *1080*.

b. Or, the number to be added is compounded with **adhika** *redundant*, and the compound is either made to qualify the other number or is further compounded with it: thus, **pañcādhikaṁ çatam** or **pañcādhikaçatam** *105*. Of course, **ūna** *deficient* (as also other words equivalent to **ūna** or **adhika**) may be used in the same way: thus, **pañconaṁ çatam** *95*, **ṣaṣṭiḥ pañcavarjitā** *55*; **çatam abhyadhikaṁ ṣaṣṭitaḥ** *160*.

c. Syntactical combinations are made at convenience: for example, **dáça çatáṁ ca** *110*; **çatám ékaṁ ca** *101*.

479. Another usual method (beginning in the Brāhmaṇas) of forming the odd numbers above 100 is to qualify the larger number by an adjective derived from the smaller, and identical with the briefer ordinal (below, **487**): thus, **dvādaçáṁ çatám,** *112* (lit'ly *a hundred of a 12-sort*, or *characterised by 12*); **catuçcatvāriṅçáṁ çatám** *144*; **ṣaṭṣaṣṭáṁ çatám** *166*.

480. To multiply one number by another, among the higher or the lower denominations, the simplest and least ambiguous method is to make of the multiplied number a dual or plural, qualified by the other as any ordinary noun would be; and this method is a common one in all ages of the language. For example: **páñca pañcāçátas** *five fifties* (*250*); **náva navatáyas** *nine nineties* (*810*); **açītíbhis tisṛ́bhis** *with three eighties* (*240*); **páñca çatā́ni** *five hundreds*; **trī́ṇi sahásrāṇi** *three thousands*; **ṣaṣṭíṁ sahásrāṇi** *60,000*; **daça ca sahasrāṇy aṣṭāu ca çatāni** *10,800*: and, combined with addition, **trī́ṇi çatā́ni tráyastriṅçataṁ ca** *333*; **sahasre dve pañconaṁ çatam eva ca** *2095*.

a. In an exceptional case or two, the ordinal form appears to take the place of the cardinal as multiplicand in a like combination: thus, **ṣaṭtriṅçā́ṅç ca catúraḥ** (RV.) *36×4* (lit. *four of the thirty-six kind*); **trī́ṅr ekādaçā́n** (RV.) or **traya ekādaçāsaḥ** (ÇÇS. viii. 21. 1) *11×3*.

b. By a peculiar and wholly illogical construction, such a combination as **trīṇi ṣaṣṭiçatāni,** which ought to signify *480* ($3 \times \overline{100+60}$), is repeatedly used in the Brāhmaṇas to mean *360* ($3 \times 100 + 60$); so also **dvé catustriṅçé çaté** *234* (not *268*); **dvāṣaṣṭāni trīṇi çatāni** *362*; and other like cases. And even R. has **trayaḥ çataçatārdhāḥ** *350*.

481. But the two factors, multiplier and multiplied, are also, and in later usage more generally, combined into a compound (accented on the final); and this is then treated as an adjective, qualifying the numbered noun; or else its neuter or feminine (in ī) singular is used substantively: thus, **daçaçatā́s** *1000*; **ṣaṭçatāiḥ padātibhiḥ** (MBh.) *with 600 foot-soldiers*; **tráyastriṅçat triçatā́ḥ ṣaṭsahasrā́ḥ** (AV.) *6333*; **dviçatám** or **dviçatī́** *200*; **aṣṭādaçaçatī** *1800*.

a. In the usual absence of accentuation, there arises sometimes a question as to how a compound number shall be understood: whether **aṣṭaçatam,** for example, is **aṣṭáçatam** *108* or **aṣṭaçatám** *800*, and the like.

482. Inflection. **The inflection of the cardinal numerals is in many respects irregular. Gender is distinguished only by the first four.**

a. **Eka** *one* is declined after the manner of a pronominal adjective (like **sárva,** below, **524**); its plural is used in the sense of *some, certain ones.* Its dual does not occur.

b. Occasional forms of the ordinary declension are met with: thus, **éke** (loc. sing.), **ékāt** (**477 b**).

c. In the late literature, **eka** is used in the sense of *a certain,* or even sometimes almost of *a,* as an indefinite article. Thus, **eko vyāghraḥ** (H.) *a certain tiger;* **ekasmin dine** *on a certain day;* **haste daṇḍam ekam ādāya** (H.) *taking a stick in his hand.*

d. **Dva** *two* is dual only, and is entirely regular: thus, N. A. V. **dvāú** (**dvā́,** Veda) m., **dvé** f. n.; I. D. Ab. **dvā́bhyām;** G. L. **dváyos.**

e. **Tri** *three* is in masc. and neut. nearly regular, like an ordinary stem in **i;** but the genitive is as if from **trayá** (only in the later language: the regular **trīṇā́m** occurs once in RV.). For the feminine it has the peculiar stem **tisṛ́,** which is inflected in general like an **ṛ**-stem; but the nom. and accus. are alike, and show no strengthening of the **ṛ;** and the **ṛ** is not prolonged in the gen. (excepting in the Veda). Thus:

	m.	n.	f.
N.	**tráyas**	**trī́ṇi**	**tisrás**
A.	**trī́n**	**trī́ṇi**	**tisrás**
I.	**tribhís**		**tisṛ́bhis**
D. Ab.	**tribhyás**		**tisṛ́bhyas**
G.	**trayāṇā́m**		**tisṛṇā́m**
L.	**triṣú**		**tisṛ́ṣu**

f. The Veda has the abbreviated neut. nom. and accus. **trī́.** The accentuation **tisṛbhís, tisṛbhyás, tisṛ́ṇām,** and **tisṛṣú** is said to be also allowed in the later language. The stem **tisṛ** occurs in composition in **tisṛdhanvá** (B.) *a bow with three arrows.*

g. **Catúr** *four* has **catvā́r** (the more original form) in the strong cases; in the fem. it substitutes the stem **cátasṛ,** apparently akin with **tisṛ́,** and inflected like it (but with anomalous change of accent, like that in the higher numbers: see below, **483**). Thus:

	m.	n.	f.
N.	**catvā́ras**	**catvā́ri**	**cátasras**
A.	**catúras**	**catvā́ri**	**cátasras**
I.	**catúrbhis**		**catasṛ́bhis**
D. Ab.	**catúrbhyas**		**catasṛ́bhyas**
G.	**caturṇā́m**		**catasṛṇā́m**
L.	**catúrṣu**		**catasṛ́ṣu.**

h. The use of **n** before **ām** of the gen. masc. and neut. after a final consonant of the stem is (as in **ṣaṣ**: below, **483**) a striking irregularity. The more regular gen. fem. **catasṝṇām** also sometimes occurs. In the later language, the accentuation of the final syllable instead of the penult is said to be allowed in inst., dat.-abl., and loc.

483. The numbers from *5* to *19* have no distinction of gender, nor any generic character. They are inflected, somewhat irregularly, as plurals, save in the nom.-acc., where they have no proper plural form, but show the bare stem instead. Of **ṣáṣ** (as of **catúr**), **nām** is the gen. ending, with mutual assimilation (**198**b) of stem-final and initial of the termination. **Aṣṭá** (as accented in the older language) has an alternative fuller form, **aṣṭā́**, which is almost exclusively used in the older literature (V. and B.), both in inflection and in composition (but some compounds with **aṣṭa** are found as early as the AV.); its nom.-acc. is **aṣṭá** (usual later: found in RV. once, and in AV.), or **aṣṭā́** (RV.), or **aṣṭāú** (most usual in RV.; also in AV., B., and later).

a. The accent is in many respects peculiar. In all the accented texts, the stress of voice lies on the penult before the endings **bhis, bhyas,** and **su,** from the stems in **a,** whatever be the accent of the stem: thus, **pañcábhis** from **páñca, navábhyas** from **náva, daçásu** from **dáça, navadaçábhis** from **návadaça, ekādaçábhyas** from **ékādaça, dvādaçásu** from **dvā́daça** (according to the grammarians, either the penult or the final is accented in these forms in the later language). In the gen. pl., the accent is on the ending (as in that of i-, u-, and ṛ-stems): thus, **pañcadaçānā́m, saptadaçānā́m.** The cases of **ṣaṣ,** and those made from the stem-form **aṣṭā,** have the accent throughout upon the ending.

b. Examples of the inflection of these words are as follows:

N. A.	**páñca**	**ṣáṭ**	**aṣṭāú**	**aṣṭá**
I.	**pañcábhis**	**ṣaḍbhís**	**aṣṭābhís**	**aṣṭábhis**
D. Ab.	**pañcábhyas**	**ṣaḍbhyás**	**aṣṭābhyás**	**aṣṭábhyas**
G.	**pañcānā́m**	**ṣaṇṇā́m**	**aṣṭānā́m**	
L.	**pañcásu**	**ṣaṭsú**	**aṣṭāsú**	**aṣṭásu.**

c. Saptá (in the later language **sápta,** as **áṣṭa** for **aṣṭá**) and **náva** and **dáça,** with the compounds of **dáça** (*11—19*), are declined like **páñca,** and with the same shift of accent (or with alternative shift to the endings, as pointed out above).

484. The Hindu grammarians give to the stems for *5* and *7—19* a final **n**: thus, **pañcan, saptan, aṣṭan, navan, daçan,** and **ekādaçan** etc. This, however, has nothing to do with the demonstrably original final nasal of *7*, *9*, and *10* (compare *septem, novem, decem; seven, nine, ten*); it is only owing to the fact that, starting from such a stem-form, their inflection is made to assume a more regular aspect, the nom.-acc. having the form of a neut. sing. in **an,** and the instr., dat.-abl., and loc. that of a neut. or masc. pl. in **an**: compare **nā́ma, nā́mabhis, nā́ma-**

bhyas, nā́masu — the gen. alone being, rather, like that of an **a**-stem: compare **daçānā́m** with **índrāṇām** and **nā́mnām** or **ātmánām.** No trace whatever of a final **n** is found anywhere in the language, in inflection or derivation or composition, from any of these words (though ÇB. has twice **daçaṁdaçín,** for the usual **daçadaçín**).

485. a. The tens, **viṅçatí** and **triṅçát** etc., with their compounds, are declined regularly, as feminine stems of the same endings, and in all numbers.

b. Çatá and **sahásra** are declined regularly, as neuter (or, rarely, in the later language, as masculine) stems of the same final, in all numbers.

c. The like is true of the higher numbers — which have, indeed, no proper numeral character, but are ordinary nouns.

486. Construction. As regards their construction with the nouns enumerated by them —

a. The words for *1* to *19* are in the main used adjectively, agreeing in case, and, if they distinguish gender, in gender also, with the nouns: thus, **daçábhir vīrāíḥ** *with ten heroes;* **yé devā́ divy ékādaça sthá** (AV.) *what eleven gods of you are in heaven;* **pañcásu jáneṣu** *among the five tribes;* **catasṛ́bhir gīrbhíḥ** *with four songs.* Rarely occur such combinations as **dáça kaláçānām** (RV.) *ten pitchers,* **ṛtūnāṁ ṣaṭ** (R.) *six seasons.*

b. The numerals above *19* are construed usually as nouns, either taking the numbered noun as a dependent genitive, or standing in the singular in apposition with it: thus, **çataṁ dāsīḥ** or **çataṁ dāsīnām** *a hundred slaves* or *a hundred of slaves;* **viṅçatyā́ háribhiḥ** *with twenty bays;* **ṣaṣṭyā́ṁ çarátsu** *in 60 autumns;* **çaténa pā́çāiḥ** *with a hundred fetters;* **çatáṁ sahásram ayútaṁ nyàrbudaṁ jaghā́na çakró dásyūnām** (AV.) *the mighty* [Indra] *slew a hundred, a thousand, a myriad, a hundred million, of demons.* Occasionally they are put in the plural, as if used more adjectively: thus, **pañcāçadbhir bāṇāiḥ** *with fifty arrows.*

c. In the older language, the numerals for *5* and upward are sometimes used in the nom.-acc. form (or as if indeclinably) with other cases also: thus, **páñca kṛṣṭíṣu** *among the five races;* **saptá ṛṣīṇām** *of seven bards;* **sahásram ṛ́ṣibhiḥ** *with a thousand bards;* **çatám pūrbhíḥ** *with a hundred strongholds.* Sporadic instances of a like kind are also met with later.

487. Ordinals. Of the classes of derivative words coming from the original or cardinal numerals, the ordinals are by far the most important; and the mode of their formation may best be explained here.

Some of the first ordinals are irregularly made: thus,

a. éka *1* forms no ordinal; instead is used **prathamá** (i. e. **pratama** *foremost*); **ādya** (from **ādi** *beginning*) appears first in the Sūtras, and **ādima** much later;

b. from **dvá** *2*, and **trí** *3*, come **dvitīya** and **tṛtīya** (secondarily, through **dvita** and abbreviated **trita**);

c. catúr *4*, **ṣáṣ** *6*, and **saptá** *7*, take the ending **tha**: thus, **caturthá, ṣaṣṭhá, saptátha**; but for *fourth* are used also **turīya** and **túrya**, and **saptátha** belongs to the older language only; **pañcatha**, for *fifth*, is excessively rare;

d. the numerals for *5* and *7* usually, and for *8, 9, 10*, add **ma**, forming **pañcamá, saptamá, aṣṭamá, navamá, daçamá**;

e. for *11th* to *19th*, the forms are **ekādaçá, dvādaçá**, and so on (the same with the cardinals, except change of accent); but **ekādaçama** etc. occasionally occur also;

f. for the tens and intervening odd numbers from *20* onward, the ordinal has a double form — one made by adding the full (superlative) ending **tamá** to the cardinal: thus, **viñçatitamá, triñçattamá, açītitamá**, etc.; the other, shorter, in **a**, with abbreviation of the cardinal: thus, **viñçá** *20th*; **triñçá** *30th*; **catvāriñçá** *40th*; **pañcāçá** *50th*; **ṣaṣṭá** *60th*; **saptatá** *70th*; **açītá** *80th*; **navatá** *90th*; and so likewise **ekaviñçá** *21st*, **catustriñçá** *34th*; **aṣṭācatvāriñçá** *48th*; **dvāpañcāçá** *52d*; **ekaṣaṣṭá** *61st*; and **ekānnaviñçá** and **ūnaviñçá** and **ekonaviñçá** *19th*; — and so on. Of these two forms, the latter and briefer is by far the more common, the other being not quotable from the Veda, and extremely rarely from the Brāhmaṇas. From *50th* on, the briefer form is allowed by the grammarians only to the odd numbers, made up of tens and units; but it is sometimes met with, even in the later language, from the simple ten.

g. Of the higher numbers, **çatá** and **sahásra** form **çatatamá** and **sahasratamá**; but their compounds have also the simpler form: thus, **ekaçatá** or **ekaçatatama** *101st*.

h. Of the ordinals, **prathamá** (and **ādya**), **dvitīya, tṛtīya**, and **turīya** (with **túrya**) form their feminine in **ā**; all the rest make it in **ī**.

488. The ordinals, as in other languages, have other than ordinal offices to fill; and in Sanskrit especially they are general adjectives to the cardinals, with a considerable variety of meanings, as fractionals, as signifying *composed of so many parts* or *so-many-fold*, or *containing so many*, or (as was seen above, **479**) *having so many added*.

a. In a fractional sense, the grammarians direct that their accent be shifted to the first syllable: thus, **dvítīya** *half*; **tṛ́tīya** *third part*; **cáturtha** *quarter*; and so on. But in accented texts only **tṛ́tīya** *third*, and **cáturtha** (ÇB.) and **túrīya** *quarter*, are found so treated; for *half* occurs only **ardhá**; and **caturthá** (MS. etc.), **pañcamá**, and so on, are accented as in their ordinal use.

489. There are other numeral derivatives: thus —

a. multiplicative adverbs, as **dvís** *twice*, **trís** *thrice*, **catús** *four times*;

b. adverbs with the suffixes **dhā** (1104) and **ças** (1106): for example, **ekadhā́** *in one way*, **çatadhā́** *in a hundred ways*; **ekaças** *one by one*, **çataçás** *by hundreds*;

c. collectives, as **dvítaya** or **dvayá** *a pair*, **dáçataya** or **daçát** *a decade*;

d. adjectives like **dvika** *composed of two*, **pañcaka** *consisting of five* or *fives*;

and so on; but their treatment belongs rather to the dictionary, or to the chapter on derivation.

CHAPTER VII.

PRONOUNS.

490. THE pronouns differ from the great mass of nouns and adjectives chiefly in that they come by derivation from another and a very limited set of roots, the so-called pronominal or demonstrative roots. But they have also many and marked peculiarities of inflection — some of which, however, find analogies in a few adjectives; and such adjectives will accordingly be described at the end of this chapter.

Personal Pronouns.

491. The pronouns of the first and second persons are the most irregular and peculiar of all, being made up of fragments coming from various roots and combinations of roots. They have no distinction of gender.

a. Their inflection in the later language is as follows:

Singular:

	1st pers.	2d pers.
N.	अहम् **ahám**	त्वम् **tvám**
A.	माम्, मा **mā́m, mā**	त्वाम्, त्वा **tvā́m, tvā**
I.	मया **máyā**	त्वया **tváyā**
D.	मह्यम्, मे **máhyam, me**	तुभ्यम्, ते **túbhyam, te**
Ab.	मत् **mát**	त्वत् **tvát**
G.	मम, मे **máma, me**	तव, ते **táva, te**
L.	मयि **máyi**	त्वयि **tváyi**

Dual:

N. A. V.	आवाम् **āvā́m**	युवाम् **yuvā́m**
I. D. Ab.	आवाभ्याम् **āvā́bhyām**	युवाभ्याम् **yuvā́bhyām**
G. L.	आवयोस् **āváyos**	युवयोस् **yuváyos**
and A.D.G.	नौ **nāu**	वाम् **vām**

Plural:

N.	वयम् **vayám**	यूयम् **yūyám**
A.	अस्मान्, नस् **asmā́n, nas**	युष्मान्, वस् **yuṣmā́n, vas**
I.	अस्माभिस् **asmā́bhis**	युष्माभिस् **yuṣmā́bhis**
D.	अस्मभ्यम्, नस् **asmábhyam, nas**	युष्मभ्यम्, वस् **yuṣmábhyam, vas**

Ab.	अस्मत् **asmát**	युष्मत् **yuṣmát**
G.	अस्माकम्, नस् **asmākam, nas**	युष्माकम्, वस् **yuṣmākam, vas**
L.	अस्मासु **asmā́su**	युष्मासु **yuṣmā́su**

b. The briefer second forms for accus., dat., and gen., in all numbers, are accentless; and hence they are not allowed to stand at the beginning of a sentence, or elsewhere where any emphasis is laid.

c. But they may be qualified by accented adjuncts, as adjectives: e. g. **te jáyataḥ** *of thee when a conqueror*, **vo vṛtā́bhyaḥ** *for you that were confined*, **nas tribhyáḥ** *to us three* (all RV.).

d. The ablative **mat** is accentless in one or two AV. passages.

492. Forms of the older language. All the forms given above are found also in the older language; which, however, has also others that afterward disappear from use.

a. Thus, we find a few times the instr. sing. **tvā́** (only RV.: like **manīṣā́** for **manīṣáyā**); further, the loc. or dat. sing. **mé** (only VS.) and **tvé**, and the dat. or loc. pl. **asmé** (which is by far the commonest of these **e**-forms) and **yuṣmé**: their final **e** is uncombinable (or **pragṛhya**: **138 b**). The VS. makes twice the acc. pl. fem. **yuṣmā́s** (as if **yuṣmā́n** were too distinctively a masculine form). The datives in **bhyam** are in a number of cases written, and in yet others to be read as if written, with **bhya,** with loss of the final nasal; and in a rare instance or two we have in like manner **asmā́ka** and **yuṣmā́ka** in the gen. plural. The usual resolutions of semivowel to vowel are made, and are especially frequent in the forms of the second person (**tuám** for **tvám** etc.).

b. But the duals, above all, wear a very different aspect earlier. In Veda and Brāhmaṇa and Sūtra the nominatives are (with occasional exceptions) **āvám** and **yuvám,** and only the accusatives **āvā́m** and **yuvā́m** (but in RV. the dual forms of 1st pers. chance not to occur, unless in **vā́m**[?], once, for **āvám**); the instr. in RV. is either **yuvábhyām** (occurs also once in AÇS.) or **yuvā́bhyām**; an abl. **yuvát** appears once in RV., and **āvát** twice in TS.; the gen.-loc. is in RV. (only) **yuvós** instead of **yuváyos.** Thus we have here a distinction (elsewhere unknown) of five different dual cases, by endings in part accordant with those of the other two numbers.

493. Peculiar endings. The ending **am,** appearing in the nom. sing. and pl. (and Vedic du.) of these pronouns, will be found often, though only in sing., among the other pronouns. The **bhyam** (or **hyam**) of dat. sing. and pl. is met with only here; its relationship with the **bhyām, bhyas, bhis** of the ordinary declension is palpable. The **t** (or

d) of the abl., though here preceded by a short vowel, is doubtless the same with that of the **a**-declension of nouns and adjectives. That the nom., dat., and abl. endings should be the same in sing. and pl. (and in part in the earlier du. also), only the stem to which they are added being different, is unparalleled elsewhere in the language. The element **sma** appearing in the plural forms will be found frequent in the inflection of the singular in other pronominal words: in fact, the compound stem **asma** which underlies the plural of **aham** seems to be the same that furnishes part of the singular forms of **ayam** (501), and its value of *we* to be a specialisation of the meaning *these persons*. The genitives singular, **máma** and **táva**, have no analogies elsewhere; the derivation from them of the adjectives **māmaka** and **tāvaka** (below, 516 a) suggests the possibility of their being themselves stereotyped stems. The gen. pl., **asmā́kam** and **yuṣmā́kam**, are certainly of this character: namely, neuter sing. case-forms of the adjective stems **asmāka** and **yuṣmāka**, other cases of which are found in the Veda.

494. Stem-forms. To the Hindu grammarians, the stems of the personal pronouns are **mad** and **asmad**, and **tvad** and **yuṣmad**, because these are forms used to a certain extent, and allowed to be indefinitely used, in derivation and composition (like **tad**, **kad**, etc.: see below, under the other pronouns). Words are thus formed from them even in the older language — namely, **mátkṛta** and **mátsakhi** and **asmátsakhi** (RV.), **tvádyoni** and **mattás** (AV.), **tvátpitṛ** and **tvádvivācana** (TS.), **tvátprasūta** and **tvaddevatyà** and **yuvad-devatyà** and **yuṣmaddevatyà** (ÇB.), **asmaddevatya** (PB.); but much more numerous are those that show the proper stem in **a**, or with the **a** lengthened to **ā**: thus, **mā́vant**; **asmatrā́**, **asmadrúh**, etc.; **tvā́yata**, **tvā́vant**, **tvā́datta**, **tvānid**, **tvā́vasu**, **tvā́hata**, etc.; **yuṣmā́datta**, **yuṣméṣita**, etc.; **yuvā́vant**, **yuvā́ku**, **yuvā́dhita**, **yuvā́datta**, **yuvā́nīta**, etc. And the later language also has a few words made in the same way, as **mādṛç**.

a. The Vedas have certain more irregular combinations, with complete forms: thus, **tvā́ṁkāma**, **tvāmāhuti**, **māmpaçyá**, **mamasatyá**, **asméhiti**, **ahampūrvá**, **ahamuttará**, **ahaṁyú**, **ahaṁsana**.

b. From the stems of the grammarians come also the derivative adjectives **madīya**, **tvadīya**, **asmadīya**, **yuṣmadīya**, having a possessive value: see below, 516.

c. For **sva** and **svayám**, see below, 513.

Demonstrative Pronouns.

495. The simplest demonstrative, त **ta**, which answers also the purpose of a personal pronoun of the third person, may be taken as model of a mode of declension usual in so many pronouns and pronominal adjectives that it is fairly to be called the general pronominal declension.

a. But this root has also the special irregularity that in the nom. sing. masc. and fem. it has **sás** (for whose peculiar euphonic treatment see **176 a, b**) and **sā́**, instead of **tás** and **tā́** (compare Gr. ὁ, ἡ, το, and Goth. *sa, so, thata*). Thus:

Singular:	m.	n.	f.
N.	सस् **sás**	तत् **tát**	सा **sā́**
A.	तम् **tám**	तत् **tát**	ताम् **tā́m**
I.	तेन **téna**		तया **táyā**
D.	तस्मै **tásmāi**		तस्यै **tásyāi**
Ab.	तस्मात् **tásmāt**		तस्यास् **tásyās**
G.	तस्य **tásya**		तस्यास् **tásyās**
L.	तस्मिन् **tásmin**		तस्याम् **tásyām**
Dual:			
N. A. V.	तौ **tāú**	ते **té**	ते **té**
I. D. Ab.	ताभ्याम् **tā́bhyām**		ताभ्याम् **tā́bhyām**
G. L.	तयोस् **táyos**		तयोस् **táyos**
Plural:			
N.	ते **té**	तानि **tā́ni**	तास् **tā́s**
A.	तान् **tā́n**	तानि **tā́ni**	तास् **tā́s**
I.	तैस् **tāís**		ताभिस् **tā́bhis**

D. Ab.	तेभ्यस् tébhyas	ताभ्यस् tā́bhyas
G.	तेषाम् téṣām	तासाम् tā́sām
L.	तेषु téṣu	तासु tā́su

b. The Vedas show no other irregularities of inflection than those which belong to all stems in **a** and **ā**: namely, **ténā** sometimes; usually **tā́** for **tāú**, du.; often **tā́** for **tā́ni**, pl. neut.; usually **tébhis** for **tāís**, instr. pl.; and the ordinary resolutions. The RV. has one more case-form from the root **sa**, namely **sásmin** (occurring nearly half as often as **tásmin**); and ChU. has once **sasmāt**.

496. The peculiarities of the general pronominal declension, it will be noticed, are these:

a. In the singular, the use of **t** (properly **d**) as ending of nom.-acc. neut.; the combination of another element **sma** with the root in masc. and neut. dat., abl., and loc., and of **sy** in fem. dat., abl.-gen., and loc.; and the masc. and neut. loc. ending **in**, which is restricted to this declension (except in the anomalous **yādṛ́çmin**, RV., once). The substitution in B. of **āi** for **ās** as fem. ending (**307 h**) was illustrated at **365 d.**

b. The dual is precisely that of noun-stems in **a** and **ā**.

c. In the plural, the irregularities are limited to **té** for **tā́s** in nom. masc., and the insertion of **s** instead of **n** before **ām** of the gen., the stem-final being treated before it in the same manner as before **su** of the loc.

497. The stem of this pronoun is by the grammarians given as **tad**; and from that form come, in fact, the derivative adjective **tadīya**, with **tattvá**, **taḍvat**, **tanmaya**; and numerous compounds, such as **tacchīla**, **tajjña**, **tatkara**, **tadanantara**, **tanmātra**, etc. These compounds are not rare even in the Veda: so **tádanna**, **tadvíd**, **tadvaçá**, etc. But derivatives from the true root **ta** are also many: especially adverbs, as **tátas**, **tátra**, **táthā**, **tadā́**; the adjectives **tā́vant** and **táti**; and the compound **tādṛ́ç** etc.

498. Though the demonstrative root **ta** is prevailingly of the third person, it is also freely used, both in the earlier language and in the later, as qualifying the pronouns of the first and second person, giving emphasis to them: thus, **sò 'hám**, *this I*, or *I here;* **sá** or **sā́ tvám** *thou there;* **te vayam**, *we here;* **tasya mama** *of me here,* **tasmiṅs tvayi** *in thee there,* and so on.

499. Two other demonstrative stems appear to contain **ta** as an element; and both, like the simple **ta**, substitute **sa** in the nom sing. masc. and fem.

a. The one, **tya**, is tolerably common (although only a third of its possible forms occur) in RV., but rare in AV., and almost unknown later, its nom. sing., in the three genders, is **syás, syā́, tyát**, and it makes the accusatives **tyám, tyā́m, tyát**, and goes on through the remaining cases in the same manner as **ta**. It has in RV. the instr. fem. **tyā́** (for **tyáyā**). Instead of **syā** as nom. sing. fem. is also found **tyā**.

b. The other is the usual demonstrative of nearer position, *this here*, and is in frequent use through all periods of the language. It prefixes **e** to the simple root, forming the nominatives **eṣás, eṣā́, etát** — and so on through the whole inflection.

c. The stem **tya** has neither compounds nor derivatives. But from **eta** are formed both, in the same manner as from the simple **ta**, only much less numerous: thus, **etaddā́** (ÇB.), **etadartha**, etc., from the so-called stem **etat**; and **etādṛ́ç** and **etā́vant** from **eta**. And **eṣa**, like **sa** (498), is used to qualify pronouns of the 1st and 2d persons: e. g. **eṣā 'ham, ete vayam.**

500. There is a defective pronominal stem, **ena**, which is accentless, and hence used only in situations where no emphasis falls upon it. It does not occur elsewhere than in the accusative of all numbers, the instr. sing., and the gen.-loc. dual: thus,

		m.	n.	f.
Sing.	A.	**enam**	**enat**	**enām**
	I.	**enena**		**enayā**
Du.	A.	**enāu**	**ene**	**ene**
	G. L.	**enayos**		**enayos**
Pl.	A.	**enān**	**enāni**	**enās**

a. The RV. has **enos** instead of **enayos**, and in one or two instances accents a form: thus, **enā́m, enā́s** (?). AB. uses **enat** also as nom. neut.

b. As **ena** is always used substantively, it has more nearly than **ta** the value of a third personal pronoun, unemphatic. Apparent examples of its adjectival use here and there met with are doubtless the result of confusion with **eta** (499 b).

c. This stem forms neither derivatives nor compounds.

501. The declension of two other demonstratives is so irregularly made up that they have to be given in full. The one, अयम् **ayám** etc., is used as a more indefinite demonstrative, *this* or *that;* the other, असौ **asāú** etc., signifies especially the remoter relation, *yon* or *yonder*.

a. They are as follows:

	m.	n.	f.	m.	n.	f.
Singular:						
N.	अयम् ayám	इदम् idám	इयम् iyám	असौ asāú	अदस् adás	असौ asāú
A.	इमम् imám	इदम् idám	इमाम् imā́m	अमुम् amúm	अदस् adás	अमूम् amū́m
I.	अनेन anéna		अनया anáyā	अमुना amúnā		अमुया amúyā
D.	अस्मै asmāí		अस्यै asyāí	अमुष्मै amúṣmāi		अमुष्यै amúṣyāi
Ab.	अस्मात् asmā́t		अस्यास् asyā́s	अमुष्मात् amúṣmāt		अमुष्यास् amúṣyās
G.	अस्य asyá		अस्यास् asyā́s	अमुष्य amúṣya		अमुष्यास् amúṣyās
L.	अस्मिन् asmín		अस्याम् asyā́m	अमुष्मिन् amúṣmin		अमुष्याम् amúṣyām
Dual:						
N. A.	इमौ imāú	इमे imé	इमे imé		अमू amū́	
I. D. Ab.		आभ्याम् ābhyā́m			अमूभ्याम् amū́bhyām	
G. L.		अनयोस् anáyos			अमुयोस् amúyos	
Plural:						
N.	इमे imé	इमानि imā́ni	इमास् imā́s	अमी amī́	अमूनि amū́ni	अमूस् amū́s
A.	इमान् imā́n	इमानि imā́ni	इमास् imā́s	अमून् amū́n	अमूनि amū́ni	अमूस् amū́s
I.	एभिस् ebhís		आभिस् ābhís	अमीभिस् amī́bhis		अमूभिस् amū́bhis
D. Ab.	एभ्यस् ebhyás		आभ्यस् ābhyás	अमीभ्यस् amī́bhyas		अमूभ्यस् amū́bhyas
G.	एषाम् eṣā́m		आसाम् āsā́m	अमीषाम् amī́ṣām		अमूषाम् amū́ṣām
L.	एषु eṣú		आसु āsú	अमीषु amī́ṣu		अमूषु amū́ṣu

b. The same forms are used in the older language, without variation, except that (as usual) **imā́** occurs for **imāú** and **imā́ni**, and **amū́** for **amū́ni**; **amuyā** when used adverbially is accented on the final, **amuyā́**; **asāu** (with accent, of course, on the first, **ásāu**, or without accent, **asāu**: 314) is used also as vocative; **amī**, too, occurs as vocative.

502. a. The former of these two pronouns, **ayám** etc., plainly shows itself to be pieced together from a number of defective stems. The majority of forms come from the root **a**, with which, as in the ordinary pronominal declension, **sma** (f. **sy**) is combined in the singular. All these forms from **a** have the peculiarity that in their substantive use they are either accented, as in the paradigm, or accentless (like **ena** and the second forms from **ahám** and **tvám**). The remaining forms are always accented. From **aná** come, with entire regularity, **anéna, anáyā, anáyos.** The strong cases in dual and plural, and in part in singular, come not less regularly from a stem **imá**. And **ayám, iyám, idám** are evidently to be referred to a simple root **i** (**idám** being apparently a double form: **id**, like **tad** etc., with ending **am**).

b. The Veda has from the root **a** also the instrumentals **enā́** and **ayā́** (used in general adverbially), and the gen. loc. du. **ayós**; from **ima**, **imásya** occurs once in RV., **imasmāi** in AA., and **imāis** and **imeṣu** later. The RV. has in a small number of instances the irregular accentuation **ásmāi, ásya, ā́bhis**.

c. In analogy with the other pronouns, **idám** is by the grammarians regarded as representative stem of this pronominal declension; and it is actually found so treated in a very small number of compounds (**idammáya** and **idáṁrūpa** are of Brāhmaṇa age). As regards the actual stems, **ana** furnishes nothing further; from **ima** comes only the adverb **imáthā** (RV., once); but **a** and **i** furnish a number of derivatives, mostly adverbial: thus, for example, **átas, átra, átha, ad-dhā́** (?); **itás, íd** (Vedic particle), **idā, ihá, ítara, īm** (Vedic particle), **īdṛ́ç**, perhaps **evá** and **evám**, and others.

503. The other pronoun, **asāú** etc., has **amú** for its leading stem, which in the singular takes in combination, like the **a**-stems, the element **sma** (f. **sy**), and which shifts to **amī** in part of the masc. and neut. plural. In part, too, like an adjective **u**-stem, it lengthens its final in the feminine. The gen. sing. **amúṣya** is the only example in the language of the ending **sya** added to any other than an **a**-stem. The nom. pl. **amī́** is unique in form; its **ī** is (like that of a dual) **pragṛhya**, or exempt from combination with a following vowel (**138b**). **Asāú** and **adás** are also without analogies as regards their endings.

a. The grammarians, as usual, treat **adás** as representative stem of the declension, and it is found in this character in an extremely small number of words, as **adomūla**; **adomáya** is of Brāhmaṇa age. The ÇB. has also **asāunāman**. But most of the derivatives, as of the cases, come from **amu**: thus, **amútas, amútra, amúthā, amudā, amúrhi, amuvát, amuka.**

b. In the older language occurs the root **tva** (accentless), meaning *one, many a one;* it is oftenest found repeated, as *one* and *another.* It follows the ordinary pronominal declension. From it is made the (also accentless) adverb **tvadānīm** (MS.).

c. Fragments of another demonstrative root or two are met with: thus, **ámas** *he* occurs in a formula in AV. and in Brāhmaṇas etc.; **avós** as gen.-loc. dual is found in RV.; the particle **u** points to a root **u.**

Interrogative Pronoun.

504. The characteristic part of the interrogative pronominal root is क् **k**; it has the three forms क **ka,** कि **ki,** कु **ku**; but the whole declensional inflection is from क **ka,** excepting the nom.-acc. sing. neut., which is from कि **ki,** and has the anomalous form किम् **kím** (not elsewhere known in the language from a neuter **i**-stem). The nom. and accus. sing., then, are as follows:

	m.	n.	f.
N.	कस् **kás**	किम् **kím**	का **kā́**
A.	कम् **kám**	किम् **kím**	काम् **kā́m**

and the rest of the declension is precisely like that of त **ta** (above, **495**).

a. The Veda has its usual variations, **kā́** and **kébhis** for **kā́ni** and **kāís.** It also has, along with **kím,** the pronominally regular neuter **kád**; and **kám** (or **kam**) is a frequent particle. The masc. form **kis,** corresponding to **kim,** occurs as a stereotyped case in the combinations **nákis** and **mā́kis.**

505. The grammarians treat **kim** as representative stem of the interrogative pronoun; and it is in fact so used in a not large number of words, of which a few — **kimmáya, kiṁkará, kiṁkāmyā́, kíṁdevata, kiṁçīlá,** and the peculiar **kiṁyú** — go back even to the Veda and Brāhmaṇa. In closer analogy with the other pronouns, the form **kad,** a couple of times in the Veda (**katpayá, kádartha**), and not infrequently later, is found as first member of compounds. Then, from the real roots **ka, ki, ku** are made many derivatives; and from **ki** and **ku,** especially the latter, many compounds: thus,

káti, kathā́, kathám, kadā́, katará, katamá, kárhi; kíyant, kīdṛ́ç; kútas, kútra, kúha, kvà, kucará, kukarman, kumantrin, etc.

506. Various forms of this pronoun, as **kad, kim,** and **ku** (and, rarely, **ko**), at the beginning of compounds, have passed from an interrogative meaning, through an exclamatory, to the value of prefixes signifying an unusual quality — either something admirable, or, oftener, something contemptible. This use begins in the Veda, but becomes much more common in later time.

507. The interrogative pronoun, as in other languages, turns readily in its independent use also to an exclamatory meaning. Moreover, it is by various added particles converted to an indefinite meaning: thus, by **ca, caná, cid, ápi, vā,** either alone or with the relative **ya** (below, **511**) prefixed: thus, **káç caná** *any one;* **ná kó 'pi** *not any one;* **yā́ni kā́ni cit** *whatsoever;* **yatamát katamác ca** *whatever one.* Occasionally, the interrogative by itself acquires a similar value.

Relative Pronoun.

508. The root of the relative pronoun is य **ya,** which from the earliest period of the language has lost all trace of the demonstrative meaning originally (doubtless) belonging to it, and is used as relative only.

509. It is inflected with entire regularity according to the usual pronominal declension: thus,

	Singular.			Dual.			Plural.		
	m.	n.	f.	m.	n.	f.	m.	n.	f.
N.	यस् **yás**	यत् **yát**	या **yā́**	यौ **yāú**	ये **yé**	ये **yé**	ये **yé**	यानि **yā́ni**	यास् **yā́s**
A.	यम् **yām**	यत् **yát**	याम् **yā́m**				यान् **yā́n**	यानि **yā́ni**	यास् **yā́s**
I.	येन **yéna**		यया **yáyā**		याभ्याम् **yā́bhyām**		यैस् **yāís**		याभिस् **yā́bhis**
D.	यस्मै **yásmāi**		यस्यै **yásyāi**				येभ्यस् **yébhyas**		याभ्यस् **yā́bhyas**
	etc.		etc.		etc.		etc.		etc.

a. The Veda shows its usual variations of these forms: **yā́** for **yāú** and for **yā́ni,** and **yébhis** for **yāís; yós** for **yáyos** also occurs once; **yénā,** with prolonged final, is in RV. twice as common as **yéna.** Resolutions occur in **yā́bhias,** and **yéṣaam** and **yā́saam.** The conjunction **yā́t** is an ablative form according to the ordinary declension.

510. The use of **yát** as representative stem begins very early: we have **yátkāma** in the Veda, and **yatkārín, yaddevatyà** in the Brāhmaṇa; later it grows more general. From the proper root come also a considerable series of derivatives: **yátas, yáti, yátra, yáthā, yádā, yádi, yárhi, yā́vant, yatará, yatamá;** and the compound **yādṛ́ç.**

511. The combination of **ya** with **ka** to make an indefinite pronoun has been noticed above (**507**). Its own repetition — as **yád-yat** — gives it sometimes a like meaning, won through the distributive.

512. One or two marked peculiarities in the Sanskrit use of the relative may be here briefly noticed:

a. A very decided preference for putting the relative clause before that to which it relates: thus, **yáḥ sunvatáḥ sákhā tásmā índrāya gāyata** (RV.) *who is the friend of the soma-presser, to that Indra sing ye;* **yáṁ yajñám paribhū́r ási sá íd devéṣu gacchati** (RV.) *what offering thou protectest, that in truth goeth to the gods;* **yé triṣaptā́ḥ pariyánti bálā téṣāṁ dadhātu me** (AV.) *what thrice seven go about, their strength may he assign to me;* **asāú yó adharā́d gṛhás tátra santv arāyyàḥ** (AV.) *what house is yonder in the depth, there let the witches be;* **sahá yán me ásti téna** (TB.) *along with that which is mine;* **haṅsānāṁ vacanaṁ yat tu tan māṁ dahati** (MBh.) *but what the words of the swans were, that burns me;* **sarvasya locanaṁ çāstraṁ yasya nā 'sty andha eva saḥ** (H.) *who does not possess learning, the eye of everything, blind indeed is he.* The other arrangement, though frequent enough, is notably less usual.

b. A frequent conversion of the subject or object of a verb by an added relative into a substantive clause: thus, **mé 'mám prā́ "pat pā́uruṣeyo vadhó yáḥ** (AV.) *may there not reach him a human deadly weapon* (lit'ly, *what is such a weapon*); **pári ṇo pāhi yád dhánam** (AV.) *protect of us what wealth* [*there is*]; **apāmārgó 'pa mārṣṭu kṣetriyáṁ çapáthaç ca yáḥ** (AV.) *may the cleansing plant cleanse away the disease and the curse;* **puṣkareṇa hṛtaṁ rājyaṁ yac cā 'nyad vasu kiṁcana** (MBh.) *by Pushkara was taken away the kingdom and whatever other property* [*there was*].

Other Pronouns: Emphatic, Indefinite.

513. a. The isolated and uninflected pronominal word स्वयम् **svayam** (from the root **sva**) signifies *self, own self.* By its form it appears to be a nom. sing., and it is oftenest used as nominative, but along with words of all persons and numbers; and not seldom it represents other cases also.

b. **Svayam** is also used as a stem in composition: thus, **svayaṁjā́, svayambhū́**. But **sva** itself (usually adjective: below, **516** e) has the same value in composition; and even its inflected forms are (in the older language very rarely) used as reflexive pronoun.

c. In RV. alone are found a few examples of two indefinite pronouns, **sama** (accentless) *any, every*, and **simá** *every, all*.

Nouns used pronominally.

514. **a.** The noun **ātmán** *soul* is widely employed, in the singular (extremely rarely in other numbers), as reflexive pronoun of all three persons.

b. The noun **tanū́** *body* is employed in the same manner (but in all numbers) in the Veda.

c. The adjective **bhavant**, f. **bhavatī**, is used (as already pointed out: **456**) in respectful address as substitute for the pronoun of the second person. Its construction with the verb is in accordance with its true character, as a word of the third person.

Pronominal Derivatives.

515. From pronominal roots and stems, as well as from the larger class of roots and from noun-stems, are formed by the ordinary suffixes of adjective derivation certain words and classes of words, which have thus the character of pronominal adjectives.

Some of the more important of these may be briefly noticed here.

516. Possessives. **a.** From the representative stems **mad** etc. are formed the adjectives **madīya, asmadīya, tvadīya, yuṣmadīya, tadīya,** and **etadīya,** which are used in a possessive sense: *relating to me, mine,* and so on.

b. Other possessives are **māmaká** (also **mámaka**, RV.) and **tāvaká**, from the genitives **máma** and **táva**. And RV. has once **mā́kīna**.

c. An analogous derivative from the genitive **amúṣya** is **āmuṣyāyaṇá** (AV. etc.) *descendant of such and such a one*.

d. It was pointed out above (**493**) that the "genitives" **asmā́kam** and **yuṣmā́kam** are really stereotyped cases of possessive adjectives.

e. Corresponding to **svayám** (**513**) is the possessive **svá**, meaning *own*, as relating to all persons and numbers. The RV. has once the corresponding simple possessive of the second person, **tvá** *thy*.

f. For the use of **sva** as reflexive pronoun, see above, **513 b.**

g. All these words form their feminines in **ā**.

h. Other derivatives of a like value have no claim to be mentioned here. But (excepting **sva**) the possessives are so rarely used as to make but a small figure in the language, which prefers generally to indicate the possessive relation by the genitive case of the pronoun itself.

517. By the suffix **vant** are formed from the pronominal roots, with prolongation of their final vowels, the adjectives **mā́vant, tvā́vant, yuṣmā́vant, yuvā́vant, tā́vant, etā́vant, yā́vant**, meaning *of my sort, like me*, etc. Of these, however, only the last three are in use in the later language, in the sense of *tantus* and *quantus*. They are inflected like other adjective stems in **vant**, making their feminines in **vatī** (**452 ff.**).

a. Words of similar meaning from the roots **i** and **ki** are **íyant** and **kíyant**, inflected in the same manner: see above, **451**.

518. The pronominal roots show a like prolongation of vowel in combination with the root **dṛç** *see, look*, and its derivatives **-dṛça** and (quite rarely) **dṛkṣa**: thus, **mādṛç, -dṛça; tvādṛç, -dṛça; yuṣmādṛç, -dṛça; tādṛ́ç, -dṛ́ça, -dṛkṣa; etādṛ́ç, -dṛ́ça, -dṛ́kṣa; yādṛ́ç, -dṛ́ça; īdṛ́ç, -dṛ́ça, -dṛ́kṣa; kīdṛ́ç, -dṛça, -dṛkṣa.** They mean *of my sort, like* or *resembling me*, and the like, and **tādṛç** and the following are not uncommon, with the sense of *talis* and *qualis*. The forms in **dṛç** are unvaried for gender; those in **dṛça** (and **dṛkṣa**?) have feminines in **ī**.

519. From **ta, ka, ya** come **táti** *so many*, **káti** *how many?* **yáti** *as many*. They have a quasi-numeral character, and are inflected (like the numerals **páñca** etc.: above, **483**) only in the plural, and with the bare stem as nom. and accus.: thus, N.A. **táti**; I. etc. **tátibhis, tátibhyas, tátīnām, tátiṣu.**

520. From **ya** (in V. and B.) and **ka** come the comparatives and superlatives **yatará** and **yatamá**, and **katará** and **katamá**; and from **i**, the comparative **ítara**. For their inflection, see below, **523**.

521. Derivatives with the suffix **ka**, sometimes conveying a diminutive or a contemptuous meaning, are made from certain of the pronominal roots and stems (and may, according to the grammarians, be made from them all): thus, from **ta, takám, takát, takā́s**; from **sa, sakā́**; from **ya, yakás, yakā́, yaké**; from **asāú, asakāú**; from **amu, amuka.**

a. For the numerous and frequently used adverbs formed from pronominal roots, see Adverbs (below, **1097 ff.**).

Adjectives declined pronominally.

522. A number of adjectives — some of them coming from pronominal roots, others more or less analogous with pronouns in use — are inflected, in part or wholly, according to the pronominal declension (like त **ta, 495**), with feminine stems in **ā**. Thus:

523. The comparatives and superlatives from pronominal roots — namely, **katará** and **katamá, yatará** and **yatamá**, and **ítara**; also **anyá** *other*, and its comparative **anyatará** — are declined like **ta** throughout.

a. But even from these words forms made according to the adjective declension are sporadically met with (e. g. **itarāyām** K.).

b. **Anya** takes occasionally the form **anyat** in composition: thus, **anyatkāma, anyatsthāna.**

524. Other words are so inflected except in the nom.-acc.-voc. sing. neut., where they have the ordinary adjective form **am**, instead of the pronominal **at** (**ad**). Such are **sárva** *all*, **víçva** *all, every*, **éka** *one*.

a. These, also, are not without exception, at least in the earlier language (e. g. **víçvāya, víçvāt, víçve** RV.; **éke** loc. sing., AV.).

525. Yet other words follow the same model usually, or in some of their significations, or optionally; but in other senses, or without known rule, lapse into the adjective inflection.

a. Such are the comparatives and superlatives from prepositional stems: **ádhara** and **adhamá, ántara** and **ántama, ápara** and **apamá, ávara** and **avamá, úttara** and **uttamá, úpara** and **upamá.** Of these, pronominal forms are decidedly more numerous from the comparatives than from the superlatives.

b. Further, the superlatives (without corresponding comparatives) **paramá, caramá, madhyamá**; and also **anyatama** (whose positive and comparative belong to the class first mentioned: **523**).

c. Further, the words **pára** *distant, other;* **pū́rva** *prior, east;* **dákṣiṇa** *right, south;* **paçcima** *behind, western;* **ubháya** (f. **ubháyī** or **ubhayī́**) *of both kinds* or *parties;* **néma** *the one, half;* and the possessive **svá.**

526. Occasional forms of the pronominal declension are met with from numeral adjectives: e. g. **prathamásyās, tṛtīyasyām**; and from other words having an indefinite numeral character: thus, **álpa** *few;* **ardhá** *half;* **kévala** *all;* **dvítaya** *of the two kinds;* **bāhya** *outside* — and others. RV. has once **samānásmāt.**

CHAPTER VIII.

CONJUGATION.

527. THE subject of conjugation or verbal inflection involves, as in the other languages of the family, the distinctions of voice, tense, mode, number, and person.

a. Further, besides the simpler or ordinary conjugation of a verbal root, there are certain more or less fully developed secondary or derivative conjugations.

528. Voice. There are (as in Greek) two voices, active and middle, distinguished by a difference in the personal endings. This distinction is a pervading one: there is no active personal form which does not have its corresponding middle, and *vice versa;* and it is extended also in part to the participles (but not to the infinitive).

529. An active form is called by the Hindu grammarians **parasmāi padam** *a word for another*, and a middle form is called **ātmane padam** *a word for one's self:* the terms might be best paraphrased by *transitive* and *reflexive*. And the distinction thus expressed is doubtless the original foundation of the difference of active and middle forms; in the recorded condition of the language, however, the antithesis of transitive and reflexive meaning is in no small measure blurred, or even altogether effaced.

a. In the epics there is much effacement of the distinction between active and middle, the choice of voice being very often determined by metrical considerations alone.

530. Some verbs are conjugated in both voices, others in one only; sometimes a part of the tenses are inflected only in one voice, others only in the other or in both; of a verb usually inflected in one voice sporadic forms of the other occur; and sometimes the voice differs according as the verb is compounded with certain prepositions.

531. The middle forms outside the present-system (for which there is a special passive inflection: see below, **768 ff.**), and sometimes also within that system, are liable to be used likewise in a passive sense.

532. Tense. The tenses are as follows: 1. a present, with 2. an imperfect, closely related with it in form, having a prefixed augment; 3. a perfect, made with reduplication (to which in the Veda is added, 4. a so-called pluperfect. made from it with prefixed augment); 5. an aorist, of three different formations: **a.** simple; **b.** reduplicated; **c.** sigmatic or sibilant; 6. a future, with 7. a conditional, an augment-tense, standing to it in the relation of an imperfect to a present; and 8. a second, a periphrastic, future (not found in the Veda).

a. The tenses here distinguished (in accordance with prevailing usage) as imperfect, perfect, pluperfect, and aorist receive those names from their correspondence in mode of formation with tenses so called in other languages of the family, especially in Greek, and not at all from differences of time designated by them. In no period of the Sanskrit language is there any expression of imperfect or pluperfect time — nor of perfect time, except in the older language, where the "aorist" has this value; later, imperfect, perfect, and aorist are so many undiscriminated past tenses or preterits: see below, under the different tenses.

533. Mode. In respect to mode, the difference between the classical Sanskrit and the older language of the Veda — and, in a less degree, of the Brāhmaṇas — is especially great.

a. In the Veda, the present tense has, besides its indicative inflection, a subjunctive, of considerable variety of formation, an optative, and an imperative (in 2d and 3d persons). The same three modes are found, though of much less frequent occurrence, as belonging to the perfect; and they are made also from the aorists, being of especial frequency from the simple aorist. The future has no modes (an occasional case or two are purely exceptional).

b. In the classical Sanskrit, the present adds to its indicative an optative and an imperative — of which last, moreover, the first persons are a remnant of the old subjunctive. And the aorist has also an optative, of somewhat peculiar inflection, usually called the precative (or benedictive).

534. The present, perfect, and future tenses have each of them, alike in the earlier and later language, a pair of participles, active and middle, sharing in the various peculiarities of the tense-formations; and in the Veda are found such participles belonging also to the aorist.

535. Tense-systems. The tenses, then, with their accompanying modes and participles, fall into certain well-marked groups or systems:

I. The present-system, composed of the present tense with its modes, its participle, and its preterit which we have called the imperfect.

II. The perfect-system, composed of the perfect tense (with, in the Veda, its modes and its preterit, the so-called pluperfect) and its participle.

III. The aorist-system, or systems, simple, reduplicated, and sibilant, composed of the aorist tense along with, in the later language, its "precative" optative (but, in the Veda, with its various modes and its participle).

IV. The future-systems: 1. the old or sibilant future, with its accompanying preterit, the conditional, and its participle; and 2. the new periphrastic future.

536. Number and Person. The verb has, of course, the same three numbers with the noun: namely, singular, dual, and plural; and in each number it has the three persons, first, second, and third. All of these are made in every tense and mode — except that the first persons of the imperative numbers are supplied from the subjunctive.

537. Verbal adjectives and nouns: Participles. The participles belonging to the tense-systems have been already spoken of above (534). There is besides, coming directly from the root of the verb, a participle, prevailingly of past and passive (or sometimes neuter) meaning. Future passive participles, or gerundives, of several different formations, are also made.

538. Infinitives. In the older language, a very considerable variety of derivative abstract nouns — only in a few sporadic instances having anything to do with the tense-systems — are used in an infinitive or quasi-infinitive sense; most often in the dative case, but sometimes also in the accusative, in the genitive and ablative, and (very rarely) in the locative. In the classical Sanskrit, there remains a single infinitive, of accusative case-form, having nothing to do with the tense-systems.

539. Gerunds. A so-called gerund (or absolutive) — being, like the infinitive, a stereotyped case-form of a derivative noun — is a part of the general verb-system in both the earlier and later language, being especially frequent in the later language, where it has only two forms, one for simple verbs, and the other for compound. Its value is that of an indeclinable active participle, of indeterminate but prevailingly past tense-character.

a. Another gerund, an adverbially used accusative in form, is found, but only rarely, both earlier and later.

540. Secondary conjugations. The secondary or derivative conjugations are as follows: 1. the passive; 2. the intensive; 3. the desiderative; 4. the causative. In these, a conjugation-stem, instead of the simple root, underlies the whole system of inflection. Yet there is clearly to be seen in them the character of a present-system, expanded into a more or less complete conjugation; and the passive is so purely a present-system that it will be described in the chapter devoted to that part of the inflection of the verb.

a. Under the same general head belongs the subject of denominative conjugation, or the conversion of noun and adjective-stems into conjugation-stems. Further, that of compound conjugation, whether by the prefixion of prepositions to roots or by the addition of auxiliary verbs to noun and adjective-stems. And finally, that of periphrastic conjugation, or the looser combination of auxiliaries with verbal nouns and adjectives.

541. The characteristic of a proper (finite or personal) verb-form is its personal ending. By this alone is determined its character as regards number and person — and in part also as regards mode and tense. But the distinctions of mode and tense are mainly made by the formation of tense and mode-stems, to which, rather than to the pure root, the personal endings are appended.

a. In this chapter will be given a general account of the personal endings, and also of the formation of mode-stems from tense-stems, and of those elements in the formation of tense-stems — the augment and the reduplication — which are found in more than one tense-system. Then, in the following chapters, each tense-system will be taken up by itself, and the methods of formation of its stems, both tense-stems and mode-stems, and their combination with the endings, will be described and illustrated in detail. And the complete conjugation of a few model verbs will be exhibited in systematic arrangement in Appendix **C**.

Personal Endings.

542. The endings of verbal inflection are, as was pointed out above, different throughout in the active and middle voices. They are also, as in Greek, usually of two somewhat varying forms for the same person in the same voice: one fuller, called primary; the ther briefer, called secondary. There are also less pervading differences, depending upon other conditions.

a. In the epics, exchanges of primary and secondary active endings eespecially the substitution of **ma, va, ta,** for **mas, vas, tha**) are not infrequent.

b. A condensed statement of all the varieties of ending for each person and number here follows.

543. Singular: First person. **a.** The primary ending in the active is **mi**. The subjunctive, however (later imperative), has **ni** instead; and in the oldest Veda this **ni** is sometimes wanting, and the person ends in **ā** (as if the **ni** of **āni** were dropped). The secondary ending is properly **m**; but to this **m** an **a** has come to be so persistently prefixed, appearing regularly where the tense-stem does not itself end in **a** (**vam** for **varm** or **varam** in RV., once, and **abhūm** MS., **avadhīm** TS. etc., **sanem** TB., are rare anomalies), that it is convenient to reckon **am** as ending, rather than **m**. But the perfect tense has neither **mi** nor **m**; its ending is simply **a** (sometimes **ā**: **248c**); or, from **ā**-roots, **āu**.

b. The primary middle ending, according to the analogy of the other persons, would be regularly **me**. But no tense or mode, at any period of the language, shows any relic whatever of a **m** in this person; the primary ending, present as well as perfect, from **a**-stems and others alike, is **e**; and to it corresponds **i** as secondary ending, which blends with the final of an **a**-stem to **e**. The optative has, however, **a** instead of **i**; and in the subjunctive (later imperative) appears **āi** for **e**.

544. Second person. **a.** In the active, the primary ending is **si**, which is shortened to **s** as secondary; as to the loss of this **s** after a final radical consonant, see below, **555**. But the perfect and the imperative desert here entirely the analogy of the other forms. The perfect ending is invariably **tha** (or **thā**: **248c**). The imperative is far less regular. The fullest form of its ending is **dhi**; which, however, is more often reduced to **hi**; and in the great majority of verbs (including all **a**-stems, at every period of the language) no ending is present, but the bare stem stands as personal form. In a very small class of verbs (**722—3**), **āna** is the ending. There is also an alternative ending **tāt**; and this is even used sporadically in other persons of the imperative (see below, **570—1**).

b. In the middle voice, the primary ending, both present and perfect, is **se**. The secondary stands in no apparent relation to this, being **thās**; and in the imperative is found only **sva** (or **svā**: **248c**), which in the Veda is not seldom to be read as **sua**. In the older language, **se** is sometimes strengthened to **sāi** in the subjunctive.

545. Third person. **a.** The active primary ending is **ti**; the secondary, **t**; as to the loss of the latter after a final radical consonant, see below, **555**. But in the imperative appears instead the peculiar ending **tu**; and in the perfect no characteristic consonant is present, and the third person has the same ending as the first.

b. The primary middle ending is **te**, with **ta** as corresponding secondary. In the older language, **te** is often strengthened to **tāi** in the subjunctive. In the perfect, the middle third person has, like the active, the same ending with the first, namely e simply; and in the older language, the third person present also often loses the distinctive part of its termination, and comes to coincide in form with the first (and MS. has aduha for adugdha). To this e perhaps corresponds, as secondary, the i of the aorist 3d pers. passive (842 ff.). The imperative has tām (or, in the Veda, rarely ām) for its ending.

546. Dual: First person. Both in active and in middle, the dual first person is in all its varieties precisely like the corresponding plural, only with substitution of v for the m of the latter: thus, vas (no vasi has been found to occur), va, vahe, vahi, vahāi. The person is, of course, of comparatively rare use, and from the Veda no form in vas, even, is quotable.

547. Second and Third persons. a. In the active, the primary ending of the second person is thas, and that of the third is tas; and this relation of th to t appears also in the perfect, and runs through the whole series of middle endings. The perfect endings are primary, but have u instead of a as vowel; and an a has become so persistently prefixed that their forms have to be reckoned as athus and atus. The secondary endings exhibit no definable relation to the primary in these two persons; they are tam and tām; and they are used in the imperative as well.

b. In the middle, a long ā — which, however, with the final a of a-stems becomes e — has become prefixed to all dual endings of the second and third persons, so as to form an inseparable part of them (dīdhīthām AV., and jihīthām ÇB., are isolated anomalies). The primary endings, present and perfect, are āthe and āte; the secondary (and imperative) are āthām and ātām (or, with stem-final a, ethe etc.).

c. The Rig-Veda has a very few forms in āithe and āite, apparently from ethe and ete with subjunctive strengthening (they are all detailed below: see 615, 701, 737, 752, 836, 1008, 1043).

548. Plural: First person. a. The earliest form of the active ending is masi, which in the oldest language is more frequent than the briefer mas (in RV., as five to one; in AV., however, only as three to four). In the classical Sanskrit, mas is the exclusive primary ending; but the secondary abbreviated ma belongs also to the perfect and the subjunctive (imperative). In the Veda, ma often becomes mā (248 c), especially in the perfect.

b. The primary middle ending is mahe. This is lightened in the secondary form to mahi; and, on the other hand, it is regularly (in the Veda, not invariably) strengthened to mahāi in the subjunctive (imperative).

549. Second person. a. The active primary ending is tha. The secondary, also imperative, ending is ta (in the Veda, tā only

once in impv.). But in the perfect any characteristic consonant is wanting, and the ending is simply a. In the Veda, the syllable na, of problematic origin, is not infrequently added to both forms of the ending, making thana (rarely thanā) and tana. The forms in which this occurs will be detailed below, under the different formations; the addition is very rarely made excepting to persons of the first general conjugation.

b. The middle primary ending is dhve, which belongs to the perfect as well as the present. In the subjunctive of the older language it is sometimes strengthened to dhvāi. The secondary (and imperative) ending is dhvam (in RV., once dhva); and dhvāt is once met with in the imperative (570). In the Veda, the v of all these endings is sometimes to be resolved into u, and the ending becomes dissyllabic. As to the change of **dh** of these endings to **ḍh,** see above, **226 c.**

550. Third person. **a. The full primary ending is anti in the active, with ante as corresponding middle. The middle secondary ending is anta, to which should correspond an active ant; but of the t only altogether questionable traces are left, in the euphonic treatment of a final n (207); the ending is an. In the imperative, antu and antām take the place of anti and ante. The initial a of all these endings is like that of am in the 1st sing., disappearing after the final a of a tense-stem.**

b. Moreover, **anti, antu, ante, antām, anta** are all liable to be weakened by the loss of their nasal, becoming **ati** etc. In the active, this weakening takes place only after reduplicated non-**a**-stems (and after a few roots which are treated as if reduplicated: **639** ff.); in the middle, it occurs after all tense-stems save those ending in **a.**

c. Further, for the secondary active ending **an** there is a substitute **us** (or **ur**: **169 b**; the evidence of the Zend favors the latter form), which is used in the same reduplicating verbs that change **anti** to **ati** etc., and which accordingly appears as a weaker correlative of **an.** The same **us** is also used universally in the perfect, in the optative (not in the subjunctive), in those forms of the aorist whose stem does not end in **a,** and in the imperfect of root-stems ending in **ā,** and a few others (**621**).

d. The perfect middle has in all periods of the language the peculiar ending **re,** and the optative has the allied **ran,** in this person. In the Veda, a variety of other endings containing a **r** as distinctive consonant are met with: namely, **re** (and **ire**) and **rate** in the present; **rata** in the optative (both of present and of aorist); **rire** in the perfect; **ranta, ran,** and **ram** in aorists (and in an imperfect or two); **rām** and **ratām** in the imperative; **ra** in the imperfect of duh (MS.). The three **rate, ratām,** and **rata** are found even in the later language in one or two verbs (**629**).

551. Below are given, for convenience, in tabular form, the schemes of endings as accepted in the classical or later language: namely, a. the regular primary endings, used in the present indicative and the future (and the subjunctive in part); and b. the regular secondary endings, used in the imperfect, the conditional, the aorist, the optative (and the subjunctive in part); and further, of special schemes, c. the perfect endings (chiefly primary, especially in the middle); and d. the imperative endings (chiefly secondary). To the so-called imperative endings of the first person is prefixed the ā which is practically a part of them, though really containing the mode-sign of the subjunctive from which they are derived.

552. Further, a part of the endings are marked with an accent, and a part are left unaccented. The latter are those which never, under any circumstances, receive the accent; the former are accented in considerable classes of verbs, though by no means in all. It will be noticed that, in general, the unaccented endings are those of the singular active; but the 2d sing. imkerative has an accented ending; and, on the other hand, the whole series of 1st persons imperative, active and middle, have unaccented endings (this being a characteristic of the subjunctive formation which they represent).

553. The schemes of normal endings, then, are as follows:

	active.			middle.		
	s.	d.	p.	s.	d.	p.
			a. Primary Endings.			
1	mi	vás	más	é	váhe	máhe
2	si	thás	thá	se	ā́the	dhvé
3	ti	tás	ánti, áti	té	ā́te	ánte, áte
			b. Secondary Endings.			
1	am	vá	má	í, á	váhi	máhi
2	s	tám	tá	thā́s	ā́thām	dhvám
3	t	tā́m	án, ús	tá	ā́tām	ánta, áta, rán
			c. Perfect Endings.			
1	a	vá	má	é	váhe	máhe
2	tha	áthus	á	sé	ā́the	dhvé
3	a	átus	ús	é	ā́te	ré
			d. Imperative Endings.			
1	āni	āva	āma	āi	āvahāi	āmahāi
2	dhí, hí, —	tám	tá	svá	ā́thām	dhvám
3	tu	tā́m	ántu, átu	tā́m	ā́tām	ántām, átām

554. In general, the rule is followed that an accented ending, if dissyllabic, is accented on its first syllable — and the constant union-vowels are regarded, in this respect, as integral parts of the endings. But the

3d pl. ending **ate** of the pres. indic. middle has in RV. the accent **até** in a number of verbs (see **613, 685, 699, 719**); and an occasional instance is met with in other endings: thus, **mahé** (see **719, 735**).

555. The secondary endings of the second and third persons singular, as consisting of an added consonant without vowel, should regularly (**150**) be lost whenever the root or stem to which they are to be added itself ends in a consonant. And this rule is in general followed; yet not without exceptions. Thus:

a. A root ending in a dental mute sometimes drops this final mute instead of the added **s** in the second person; and, on the other hand, a root or stem ending in **s** sometimes drops this **s** instead of the added **t** in the third person — in either case, establishing the ordinary relation of **s** and **t** in these persons, instead of **s** and **s**, or **t** and **t**. The examples noted are: 2d sing. **aves** (to 3d sing. **avet**), √**vid**, AB.; 3d sing. **akat**, √**kṛ**, ÇB. **aghat**, √**ghas**, JB. AÇS.; **acakāt**, √**cakās**, RT.; **açāt**, √**çās**, AB. MBh. R.; **asrat**, √**sras**, VS.; **ahinat**, √**hiṅs**, ÇB. TB. GB. Compare also the **s**-aorist forms **ayās** and **srās** (**146a**), in which the same influence is to be seen; and further, **ajāit** etc. (**889a**), and precative **yāt** for **yās** (**837**). A similar loss of any other final consonant is excessively rare; AV. has once **abhanas**, for **-nak**, √**bhañj**. There are also a few cases where a 1st sing. is irregularly modeled after a 3d sing.: thus, **atṛṇam** (to **atṛ́ṇat**), √**tṛd**, KU., **acchinam** (to **acchinat**), √**chid**, MBh.: compare urther the 1st sing. in **m** instead of **am**, **543a**.

b. Again, a union-vowel is sometimes introduced before the ending, either **a** or **i** or **ī**: see below, **621b, 631, 819, 880, 1004a, 1068a.**

c. In a few isolated cases in the older language, this **ī** is changed to **āi**: see below, **904b, 936, 1068a.**

556. The changes of form which roots and stems undergo in their combinations with these endings will be pointed out in detail below, under the various formations. Here may be simply mentioned in advance, as by far the most important among them, a distinction of stronger and weaker form of stem in large classes of verbs, standing in relation with the accent — the stem being of stronger form when the accent falls upon it, or before an accentless ending, and of weaker form when the accent is on the ending.

a. Of the endings marked as accented in the scheme, the **ta** of 2d pl. is not infrequently in the Veda treated as unaccented, the tone resting on the stem, which is strengthened. Much less often, the **tam** of 2d du. is treated in the same way; other endings, only sporadically. Details are given under the various formations below.

Subjunctive Mode.

557. Of the subjunctive mode (as was pointed out above) only fragments are left in the later or classical language: namely, in the so-called first persons imperative, and in the use (579) of the imperfect and aorist persons without augment after mā́ prohibitive. In the oldest period, however, it was a very frequent formation, being three or four times as common as the optative in the Rig-Veda, and nearly the same in the Atharvan; but already in the Brāhmaṇas it becomes comparatively rare. Its varieties of form are considerable, and sometimes perplexing.

558. In its normal and regular formation, a special mode-stem is made for the subjunctive by adding to the tense-stem an **a** — which combines with a final **a** of the tense-stem to **ā**. The accent rests upon the tense-stem, which accordingly has the strong form. Thus, from the strong present-stem **doh** (√**duh**) is made the subjunctive-stem **dóha**; from **juhó** (√**hu**), **juháva**; from **yunáj** (√**yuj**), **yunája**; from **sunó** (√**su**), **sunáva**; from **bháva** (√**bhū**), **bhávā**; from **tudá** (√**tud**), **tudā́**; from **ucyá** (pass., √**vac**), **ucyā́**; and so on.

559. The stem thus formed is inflected in general as an **a**-stem would be inflected in the indicative, with constant accent, and **ā** for **a** before the endings of the first person (**733** i) — but with the following peculiarities as to ending etc.:

560. a. In the active, the 1st sing. has **ni** as ending: thus, **dóhāni, yunájāni, bhávāni.** But in the Rig-Veda sometimes **ā** simply: thus, **áyā, brávā.**

b. In 1st du., 1st pl., and 3d pl., the endings are the secondary: thus, **dóhāva, dóhāma, dóhan; bhávāva, bhávāma, bhávān.**

c. In 2d and 3d du. and 2d pl., the endings are primary: thus, **dóhathas, dóhatas, dóhatha; bhávāthas, bhávātas, bhávātha.**

d. In 2d and 3d sing., the endings are either primary or secondary: thus, **dóhasi** or **dóhas, dóhati** or **dóhat; bhávāsi** or **bhávās, bhávāti** or **bhávāt.**

e. Occasionally, forms with double mode-sign **ā** (by assimilation to the more numerous subjunctives from tense-stems in **a**) are met with from non-**a**-stems: thus, **ásātha** from **as; áyās, áyāt, áyān** from **e** (√**i**).

561. In the middle, forms with secondary instead of primary endings are very rare, being found only in the 3d pl. (where they are more frequent than the primary), and in a case or two of the 3d sing. (and AB. has once **asyāthās**).

a. The striking peculiarity of subjunctive middle inflection is the frequent strengthening of **e** to **āi** in the endings. This is less general in the very earliest language than later. In 1st sing., **āi** alone is found as ending, even in RV.; and in 1st du. also (of rare occurrence), only **āvahāi** is met with. In 1st pl., **āmahāi** prevails in RV. and AV. (**āmahe** is found a few times), and is alone known later. In 2d sing., **sāi** for **se** does not occur in RV., but is the only form in AV. and the Brāhmaṇas. In 3d sing., **tāi** for **te** occurs once in RV., and is the predominant form in AV., and the only one later. In 2d pl., **dhvāi** for **dhve** is found in one word in RV., and a few times in the Brāhmaṇas. In 3d pl., **ntāi** for **nte** is the Brāhmaṇa form (of far from frequent occurrence); it occurs neither in RV. nor AV. No such dual endings as **thāi** and **tāi**, for **the** and **te**, are anywhere found; but RV. has in a few words (nine: above, **547 c**) **āithe** and **āite**, which appear to be a like subjunctive strengthening of **ethe** and **ete** (although found in one indicative form, **kṛṇvāite**). Before the **āi**-endings, the vowel is regularly long **ā**; but **antāi** instead of **āntāi** is two or three times met with, and once or twice (TS. AB.) **atāi** for **ātāi**.

562. The subjunctive endings, then, in combination with the subjunctive mode-sign, are as follows:

	active.			middle.		
	s.	d.	p.	s.	d.	p.
1	**āni**	**āva**	**āma**	**āi**	**āvahāi** / **āvahe**	**āmahāi** / **āmahe**
2	**asi** / **as**	**athas**	**atha**	**ase** / **āsāi**	**āithe**	**adhve** / **ādhvāi**
3	**ati** / **at**	**atas**	**an**	**ate** / **ātāi**	**āite**	**ante, anta** / **āntāi**

a. And in further combination with final **a** of a tense-stem, the initial **a** of all these endings becomes **ā**: thus, for example, in 2d pers., **āsi** or **ās**, **āthas**, **ātha**, **āse**, **ādhve**.

563. Besides this proper subjunctive, with mode-sign, in its triple form — with primary, with strengthened primary, and with secondary endings — the name of subjunctive, in the forms "imperfect subjunctive" and "improper subjunctive", has been also given to the indicative forms of imperfect and aorist when used, with the augment omitted, in a modal sense (below, **587**): such use being quite common in RV., but rapidly dying out, so that in the Brāhmaṇa language and later it is hardly met with except after **mā** prohibitive.

a. As to the general uses of the subjunctive, see below, **574** ff.

Optative Mode.

564. a. As has been already pointed out, the optative is of comparatively rare occurrence in the language of the Vedas; but it gains rapidly in frequency, and already in the Brāhmaṇas greatly outnumbers the subjunctive, and still later comes almost entirely to take its place.

b. Its mode of formation is the same in all periods of the language.

565. a. The optative mode-sign is in the active voice a different one, according as it is added to a tense-stem ending in **a**, or to one ending in some other final. In the latter case, it is **yā́**, accented, this **yā** is appended to the weaker form of the tense-stem, and takes the regular series of secondary endings, with, in 3d plur., **us** instead of **an**, and loss of the **ā** before it. After an **a**-stem, it is **ī**, unaccented; this **ī** blends with the final **a** to **e** (which then is accented or not according to the accent of the **a**); and the **e** is maintained unchanged before a vowel-ending (**am, us**), by means of an interposed euphonic **y**.

b. In the middle voice, the mode-sign is **ī** throughout, and takes the secondary endings, with **a** in 1st sing., and **ran** in 3d pl. After an **a**-stem, the rules as to its combination to **e**, the accent of the latter, and its retention before a vowel-ending with interposition of a **y**, are the same as in the active. After any other final, the weaker form of stem is taken, and the accent is on the ending (except in one class of verbs, where it falls upon the tense-stem: see **645**); and the **ī** (as when combined to **e**) takes an inserted **y** before the vowel-endings (**a, āthām, ātām**).

c. It is, of course, impossible to tell from the form whether **i** or **ī** is combined with the final of an **a**-stem to **e**; but no good reason appears to exist for assuming **i**, rather than the **ī** which shows itself in the other class of stems in the middle voice.

566. The combined mode-sign and endings of the optative, then, are as follows, in their double form, for **a**-stems and for others:

a. for non-a-stems.

	active.			middle.		
	s.	d.	p.	s.	d.	p.
1	**yā́m**	**yā́va**	**yā́ma**	**īyá**	**īváhi**	**īmáhi**
2	**yā́s**	**yā́tam**	**yā́ta**	**īthā́s**	**īyā́thām**	**īdhvám**
3	**yā́t**	**yā́tām**	**yús**	**ītá**	**īyā́tām**	**īrán**

b. combined with the final of a-stems.

1	**eyam**	**eva**	**ema**	**eya**	**evahi**	**emahi**
2	**es**	**etam**	**eta**	**ethās**	**eyāthām**	**edhvam**
3	**et**	**etām**	**eyus**	**eta**	**eyātām**	**eran**

c. The **yā** is in the Veda not seldom resolved into **iā**.

d. The contracted **sanem**, for **saneyam**, is found in TB. and Āpast. Certain Vedic 3d pl. middle forms in **rata** will be mentioned below, under the various formations.

567. Precative. Precative forms are such as have a sibilant inserted between the optative-sign and the ending. They are made almost only from the aorist stems, and, though allowed by the grammarians to be formed from every root — the active precative from the simple aorist, the middle from the sibilant aorist — are

practically of rare occurrence at every period of the language, and especially later.

a. The inserted **s** runs in the active through the whole series of persons; in the middle, it is allowed only in the 2d and 3d persons sing. and du. and the 2d pl., and is quotable only for the 2d and 3d sing. In the 2d sing. act., the precative form, by reason of the necessary loss of the added **s**, is not distinguishable from the simple optative; in the 3d sing. act., the same is the case in the later language, which (compare **555 a**) saves the personal ending **t** instead of the precative-sign **s**; but the RV. usually, and the other Vedic texts to some extent, have the proper ending **yās** (for **yāst**). As to **ḍh** in the 2d pl. mid., see **226 c.**

b. The accent is as in the simple optative.

568. The precative endings, then, accepted in the later language (including, in brackets, those which are identical with the simple optative), are as follows:

	active.			middle.		
	s.	d.	p.	s.	d.	p.
1	**yā́sam**	**yā́sva**	**yā́sma**	[**īyá**]	[**īváhi**]	[**īmáhi**]
2	[**yā́s**]	**yā́stam**	**yā́sta**	**īṣṭhā́s**	**īyā́sthām**	**īḍhvam**
3	[**yā́t**]	**yā́stām**	**yā́sus**	**īṣṭá**	**īyā́stām**	[**īrán**]

a. Respecting the precative, see further **921** ff.

b. As to the general uses of the optative, see below, **573** ff.

Imperative Mode.

569. The imperative has no mode-sign; it is made by adding its own endings directly to the tense-stem, just as the other endings are added to form the indicative tenses.

a. Hence, in 2d and 3d du. and 2d pl., its forms are indistinguishable from those of the augment-preterit from the same stem with its augment omitted.

b. The rules as to the use of the different endings — especially in 2d sing., where the variety is considerable — will be given below, in connection with the various tense-systems. The ending **tāt**, however, has so much that is peculiar in its use that it calls for a little explanation here.

570. The Imperative in **tāt**. An imperative form, usually having the value of a 2d pers. sing., but sometimes also of other persons and numbers, is made by adding **tāt** to a present tense-stem — in its weak form, if it have a distinction of strong and weak form.

a. Examples are: **brūtāt, hatāt, vittā́t; pipṛtāt, jahītāt, dhattā́t; kṛṇutāt, kurutāt; gṛhṇītāt, jānītāt; ávatāt, rákṣatāt, vasatāt; viçatāt, sṛjatāt; asyatāt, naçyatāt, chyatāt; kriyatāt;**

gamayatā́t, cyāvayatā́t, vārayatā́t; īpsatāt; jāgṛtā́t. No examples have been found from a nasal-class verb (**690**), nor any other than those here given from a passive, intensive, or desiderative. The few accented cases indicate that the formation follows the general rule for one made with an accented ending (**552**).

b. The imperative in **tāt** is not a very rare formation in the older language, being made (in V., B., and S.) from about fifty roots, and in toward a hundred and fifty occurrences. Later, it is very unusual: thus, only a single example has been noted in MBh., and one in R.; and correspondingly few in yet more modern texts.

571. As regards its meaning, this form appears to have prevailingly in the Brāhmaṇas, and traceably but much less distinctly in the Vedic texts, a specific tense-value added to its mode-value — as signifying, namely, an injunction to be carried out at a later time than the present: it is (like the Latin forms in **to** and **tote**) a posterior or future imperative.

a. Examples are: **ihāì 'vá mā tíṣṭhantam abhyèhī́ 'ti brūhi tā́ṁ tú na ā́gatām pratiprábrūtāt** (ÇB.) *say to her "come to me as I stand just here," and [afterward] announce her to us as having come;* **yád ūrdhvás tíṣṭhā dráviṇe 'há dhattāt** (RV.) *when thou shalt stand upright, [then] bestow riches here* (and similarly in many cases); **utkū́lam udvahó bhavo 'dúhya práti dhāvatāt** (AV.) *be a carrier up the ascent; after having carried up, run back again;* **vánaspátir ádhi tvā sthāsyati tásya vittāt** (TS.) *the tree will ascend thee, [then] take note of it.*

b. Examples of its use as other than 2d sing. are as follows: 1st sing., **āvyuṣáṁ jāgṛtād ahám** (AV.; only case) *let me watch till daybreak;* as 3d sing., **púnar mā́ " viçatād rayíḥ** (TS.) *let wealth come again to me,* **ayáṁ tyásya rā́jā mūrdhā́naṁ ví pātayatāt** (ÇB.) *the king here shall make his head fly off;* as 2d du., **nā́satyāv abruvan devā́ḥ púnar ā́ vahatād íti** (RV.) *the gods said to the two Açvins "bring them back again";* as 2d pl., **ā́paḥ . . . devéṣu naḥ sukṛ́to brūtāt** (TS.) *ye waters, announce us to the gods as well-doers.* In the later language, the prevailing value appears to be that of a 3d sing.: thus, **bhavān prasādaṁ kurutāt** (MBh.) *may your worship do the favor,* **enam bhavān abhirakṣatāt** (DKC.) *let your excellency protect him.*

c. According to the native grammarians, the imperative in **tāt** is to be used with a benedictive implication. No instance of such use appears to be quotable.

d. In a certain passage repeated several times in different Brāhmaṇas and Sūtras, and containing a number of forms in **tāt** used as 2d pl., **vārayadhvāt** is read instead of **vārayatāt** in some of the texts (K. AB. AÇS. ÇÇS.). No other occurrence of the ending **dhvāt** has been anywhere noted.

Uses of the Modes.

572. Of the three modes, the imperative is the one most distinct and limited in office, and most unchanged in use throughout the whole history of the language. It signifies a command or injunction — an attempt at the exercise of the speaker's will upon some one or something outside of himself.

a. This, however (in Sanskrit as in other languages), is by no means always of the same force; the command shades off into a demand, an exhortation, an entreaty, an expression of earnest desire. The imperative also sometimes signifies an assumption or concession; and occasionally, by pregnant construction, it becomes the expression of something conditional or contingent; but it does not acquire any regular use in dependent-clause-making.

b. The imperative is now and then used in an interrogative sentence: thus, **bravīhi ko 'dyāi 'va mayā viyujyatām** (R.) *speak! who shall now be separated by me?* **katham ete guṇavantaḥ kriyantām** (H.) *how are they to be made virtuous?* **kasmāi piṇḍaḥ pradīyatām** (Vet.) *to whom shall the offering be given?*

573. The optative appears to have as its primary office the expression of wish or desire; in the oldest language, its prevailing use in independent clauses is that to which the name "optative" properly belongs.

a. But the expression of desire, on the one hand, passes naturally over into that of request or entreaty, so that the optative becomes a softened imperative; and, on the other hand, it comes to signify what is generally desirable or proper, what should or ought to be, and so becomes the mode of prescription; or, yet again, it is weakened into signifying what may or can be, what is likely or usual, and so becomes at last a softened statement of what is.

b. Further, the optative in dependent clauses, with relative pronouns and conjunctions, becomes a regular means of expression of the conditional and contingent, in a wide and increasing variety of uses.

c. The so-called precative forms (**567**) are ordinarily used in the proper optative sense. But in the later language they are occasionally met with in the other uses of the optative: thus, **na hi prapaçyāmi mamā 'panudyād yac chokam** (BhG.) *for I do not perceive what should dispel my grief;* **yad bhūyāsur vibhūtayaḥ** (BhP.) *that there should be changes.* Also rarely with **mā**: see **579 b**.

574. The subjunctive, as has been pointed out, becomes nearly extinct at an early period in the history of the language; there are left of it in classical usage only two relics: the use of its first persons in an imperative sense, or to signify a necessity or obligation resting on the speaker, or a peremptory intention on his part; and the use of unaugmented forms (579), with the negative particle मा **mā́**, in a prohibitive or negative imperative sense.

a. And the general value of the subjunctive from the beginning was what these relics would seem to indicate: its fundamental meaning is perhaps that of requisition, less peremptory than the imperative, more so than the optative. But this meaning is liable to the same modifications and transitions with that of the optative; and subjunctive and optative run closely parallel with one another in the oldest language in their use in independent clauses, and are hardly distinguishable in dependent. And instead of their being (as in Greek) both maintained in use, and endowed with nicer and more distinctive values, the subjunctive gradually disappears, and the optative assumes alone the offices formerly shared by both.

575. The difference, then, between imperative and subjunctive and optative, in their fundamental and most characteristic uses, is one of degree: command, requisition, wish; and no sharp line of division exists between them; they are more or less exchangeable with one another, and combinable in coördinate clauses.

a. Thus, in AV., we have in impv.: **çatáṁ jīva çarádaḥ** *do thou live a hundred autumns;* **ubhāú tāú jīvatāṁ jarádaṣṭī** *let them both live to attain old age;* — in subj., **adyá jīvāni** *let me live this day;* **çatáṁ jīvāti çarádaḥ** *he shall live a hundred autumns;* — in opt., **jī́vema çarádāṁ çatā́ni** *may we live hundreds of autumns;* **sárvam ā́yur jīvyāsam** (prec.) *I would fain live out my whole term of life.* Here the modes would be interchangeable with a hardly perceptible change of meaning.

b. Examples, again, of different modes in coördinate construction are: **iyám agne nā́rī pátiṁ videṣṭa . . . súvānā putrā́n máhiṣī bhavāti gatvā́ pátiṁ subhágā ví rājatu** (AV.) *may this woman, O Agni! find a spouse; giving birth to sons she shall become a chieftainess; having attained a spouse let her rule in happiness;* **gopāyá naḥ svastáye prabúdhe naḥ púnar dadaḥ** (TS.) *watch over us for* *our welfare; grant unto us to wake again;* **syā́n naḥ sūnúḥ . . . sā́ te sumatír bhūtv asmé** (RV.) *may there be to us a son; let that favor of thine be ours.* It is not very seldom the case that versions of the same passage in different texts show different modes as various readings.

c. There is, in fact, nothing in the earliest employment of these modes to prove that they might not all be specialized uses of forms originally equivalent — having, for instance, a general future meaning.

576. As examples of the less characteristic use of subjunctive and optative in the older language, in independent clauses, may be quoted the following: **ā́ ghā tā́ gacchān úttarā yugā́ni** (RV.) *those later ages will doubtless come;* **yád . . . ná marā íti mányase** (RV.) *if thou thinkest "I shall not die";* **ná tā́ naçanti ná dabhāti táskaraḥ** (RV.) *they do not become lost; no thief can harm them;* **kásmāi devā́ya havíṣā vidhema** (RV.) *to what god shall we offer oblation?* **agnínā rayím açnavat . . . divé-dive** (RV.) *by Agni one may gain wealth every day;* **utāí 'nām brahmáṇe dadyāt táthā syonā́ çivā́ syāt** (AV.) *one should give her, however, to a Brahman; in that case she will be propitious and favorable;* **áhar-ahar dadyāt** (ÇB.) *one should give every day.*

577. The uses of the optative in the later language are of the utmost variety, covering the whole field occupied jointly by the two modes in earlier time. A few examples from a single text (MBh.) will be enough to illustrate them: **ucchiṣṭaṁ nāi 'va bhuñjīyāṁ na kuryām pādadhāvanam** *I will not eat of the remnant of the sacrifice, I will not perform the foot-lavation;* **jñātīn vrajet** *let her go to her relatives;* **nāi 'vaṁ sā karhicit kuryāt** *she should not act thus at any time;* **kathaṁ vidyāṁ nalaṁ nṛpam** *how can I know king Nala?* **utsarge saṁçayaḥ syāt tu vindetā 'pi sukhaṁ kvacit** *but in case of her abandonment there may be a chance; she may also find happiness somewhere;* **kathaṁ vāso vikarteyaṁ na ca budhyeta me priyā** *how can I cut off the garment and my beloved not wake?*

578. The later use of the first persons subjunctive as so-called imperative involves no change of construction from former time, but only restriction to a single kind of use: thus, **dīvyāva** *let us two play;* **kiṁ karavāṇi te** *what shall I do for thee?*

579. The imperative negative, or prohibitive, is from the earliest period of the language regularly and usually expressed by the particle **mā́** with an augmentless past form, prevailingly aorist.

a. Thus, **prá pata mé 'há raṁsthāḥ** (AV.) *fly away, do not stay here;* **dviṣáñç ca máhyaṁ radhyatu mā́ cā 'háṁ dviṣaté radham** (AV.) *both let my foe be subject to me, and let me not be subject to my foe;* **urv àçyām ábhayaṁ jyótir indra mā́ no dīrghā́ abhí naçan tamisrā́ḥ** (RV.) *I would win broad fearless light, O Indra; let not the long darknesses come upon us;* **mā́ na ā́yuḥ prá moṣīḥ** (RV.) *do not* *steal away our life;* **samāçvasihi mā çucaḥ** (MBh.) *be comforted; do not grieve;* **mā bhāiṣīḥ** or **bhāiḥ** (MBh. R.) *do not be afraid;* **mā bhūt kālasya paryayaḥ** (R.) *let not a change of time take place.* Examples with the imperfect are: **mā́ bibher ná mariṣyasi** (RV.) *do not fear; thou wilt not die;* **mā́ smāi 'tā́nt sákhīn kuruthāḥ** (AV.) *do not make friends of them;* **mā putram anutapyathāḥ** (MBh.) *do not sorrow for thy son.* The relation of the imperfect to the aorist construction, in point of frequency, is in RV. about as one to five, in AV. still less, or about one to six; and though instances of the imperfect are quotable from all the older texts, they are exceptional and infrequent; while in the epics and later they become extremely rare.

b. A single optative, **bhujema,** is used prohibitively with **mā́** in RV.; the older language presents no other example, and the construction is very rare also later. In an example or two, also, the precative (**bhūyāt,** R. Pañc.) follows **mā.**

c. The RV. has once apparently **mā́** with an imperative; but the passage is probably corrupt. No other such case is met with in the older language (unless **sṛpa,** TA. i. 14; doubtless a bad reading for **sṛpas**); but in the epics and later the construction begins to appear, and becomes an ordinary form of prohibition: thus, **mā prayacche 'çvare dhanam** (H.) *do not bestow wealth on a lord;* **sakhi māi 'vaṁ vada** (Vet.) *friend, do not speak thus.*

d. The ÇB. (xi. 5. 1[1]) appears to offer a single example of a true subjunctive with **mā, ní padyāsāi;** there is perhaps something wrong about the reading.

e. In the epics and later, an aorist form not deprived of augment is occasionally met with after **mā:** thus, **mā tvāṁ kālo 'tyagāt** (MBh.) *let not the time pass thee;* **mā vālipatham anv agāḥ** (R.) *do not follow Vāli's road.* But the same anomaly occurs also two or three times in the older language: thus, **vyàpaptat** (ÇB.), **agās** (TA.), **anaçat** (KS.).

580. But the use also of the optative with **ná** *not* in a prohibitive sense appears in the Veda, and becomes later a familiar construction: thus, **ná riṣyema kadā́ caná** (RV.) *may we suffer no harm at any time;* **ná cā 'tisṛjén ná juhuyāt** (AV.) *and if he do not grant permission, let him not sacrifice;* **tád u táthā ná kuryāt** (ÇB.) *but he must not do that so;* **na divā çayīta** (ÇGS.) *let him not sleep by day;* **na tvāṁ vidyur janāḥ** (MBh.) *let not people know thee.* This in the later language is the correlative of the prescriptive optative, and both are extremely common; so that in a text of prescriptive character the optative forms may come to outnumber the indicative and imperative together (as is the case, for example, in Manu).

581. In all dependent constructions, it is still harder even in the oldest language to establish a definite distinction between subjunctive and optative; a method of use of either is scarcely to be found to which the other does not furnish a practical equivalent —

and then, in the later language, such uses are represented by the optative alone. A few examples will be sufficient to illustrate this:

a. After relative pronouns and conjunctions in general: **yā́ vyūṣúr yā́ç ca nunaṁ vyucchā́n** (RV.) *which have shone forth [hitherto], and which shall hereafter shine forth;* **yó 'to jā́yātā asmā́kaṁ sá éko 'sat** (TS.) *whoever shall be born of her, let him be one of us;* **yó vāí tā́n vidyā́t pratyákṣaṁ sá brahmā́ véditā syāt** (AV.) *whoever shall know them face to face, he may pass for a knowing priest;* **putrā́ṇāṁ . . . jātā́nāṁ janáyāç ca yā́n** (AV.) *of sons born and whom thou mayest bear;* **yásya . . . átithir gṛhā́n āgácchet** (AV.) *to whosesoever house he may come as guest;* **yatamáthā kāmáyeta táthā kuryāt** (ÇB.) *in whatever way he may choose, so may he do it;* **yárhi hótā yájamānasya nā́ma gṛhṇīyā́t tárhi brūyāt** (TS.) *when the sacrificing priest shall name the name of the offerer, then he may speak;* **svarūpaṁ yadā draṣṭum icchethāḥ** (MBh.) *when thou shalt desire to see thine own form.*

b. In more distinctly conditional constructions: **yájāma devā́n yádi çaknávāma** (RV.) *we will offer to the gods if we shall be able;* **yád agne syā́m ahám tvám tvám vā ghā syā́ ahám syúṣ ṭe satyā́ ihā́ "çíṣaḥ** (RV.) *if I were thou, Agni, or if thou wert I, thy wishes should be realized on the spot;* **yó dyā́m atisárpāt parástān ná sá mucyātāi váruṇasya rā́jñaḥ** (AV.) *though one steal far away beyond the sky, he shall not escape king Varuna;* **yád ánāçvān upaváset kṣódhukaḥ syād yád açnīyā́d rudrò 'sya paçū́n abhí manyeta** (TS.) *if he should continue without eating, he would starve; if he should eat, Rudra would attack his cattle;* **prārthayed yadi māṁ kaçcid daṇḍyaḥ sa me pumān bhavet** (MBh.) *if any man soever should desire me, he should suffer punishment.* These and the like constructions, with the optative, are very common in the Brāhmaṇas and later.

c. In final clauses: **yáthā 'hám çatruhó 'sāni** (AV.) *that I may be a slayer of my enemies;* **gṛṇānā́ yáthā píbātho ándhaḥ** (RV.) *that being praised with song ye may drink the draught;* **urāú yáthā táva çárman mádema** (RV.) *in order that we rejoice in thy wide protection;* **upa jānīta yáthe 'yám púnar āgácchet** (ÇB.) *contrive that she come back again;* **kṛpāṁ kuryād yathā mayi** (MBh.) *so that he may take pity on me.* This is in the Veda one of the most frequent uses of the subjunctive; and in its correlative negative form, with **néd** *in order that not* or *lest* (always followed by an accented verb), it continues not rare in the Brāhmaṇas.

d. The indicative is also very commonly used in final clauses after **yathā**: thus, **yáthā 'yám púruṣo 'ntárikṣam anucárati** (ÇB.) *in order that this man may traverse the atmosphere;* **yathā na vighnaḥ kriyate** (R.) *so that no hindrance may arise;* **yathā 'yaṁ naçyati tathā vidheyam** (H.) *it must be so managed that he perish.*

e. With the conditional use of subjunctive and optative is further to be compared that of the so-called conditional tense: see below, **950.**

f. As is indicated by many of the examples given above, it is usual in a conditional sentence, containing protasis and apodosis, to employ always the same mode, whether subjunctive or optative (or conditional), in each of the two clauses. For the older language, this is a rule well-nigh or quite without exception.

582. No distinction of meaning has been established between the modes of the present-system and those (in the older language) of the perfect and aorist-systems.

Participles.

583. Participles, active and middle, are made from all the tense-stems — except the periphrastic future, and, in the later language, the aorist (and aorist participles are rare from the beginning).

a. The participles unconnected with the tense-systems are treated in chap. XIII. (**952** ff.).

584. The general participial endings are अन्त् **ant** (weak form अत् **at**; fem. अन्ती **antī** or अती **atī**: see above, **449**) for the active, and आन **āna** (fem. आना **ānā**) for the middle. But —

a. After a tense-stem ending in **a**, the active participial suffix is virtually **nt**, one of the two **a**'s being lost in the combination of stem-final and suffix.

b. After a tense-stem ending in **a**, the middle participial suffix is **māna** instead of **āna**. But there are occasional exceptions to the rule as to the use of **māna** and **āna** respectively, which will be pointed out in connection with the various formations below. Such exceptions are especially frequent in the causative: see **1043 f**.

c. The perfect has in the active the peculiar suffix **vāṅs** (weakest form **uṣ**, middle form **vat**; fem. **uṣī**: see, for the inflection of this participle, above, **458** ff.).

d. For details, as to form of stem etc., and for special exceptions, see the following chapters.

Augment.

585. The augment is a short अ **a**, prefixed to a tense-stem — and, if the latter begin with a vowel, combining with that vowel irregularly into the heavier or **vṛddhi** diphthong

(136 a). It is always (without any exception) the accented element in the verbal form of which it makes a part.

a. In the Veda, the augment is in a few forms long **ā**: thus, **ā́naṭ**, **ā́var**, **āvṛṇi**, **ā́vṛṇak**, **āvidhyat**, **āyunak**, **ā́yukta**, **ā́yukṣātām**, **ā́riṇak**, **ā́rāik** (and **yás ta ā́vidhat**, RV. ii. 1. 7, 9?).

586. The augment is a sign of past time. And an augment-preterit is made from each of the tense-stems from which the system of conjugation is derived: namely, the imperfect, from the present-stem; the pluperfect (in the Veda only), from the perfect-stem; the conditional, from the future-stem; while in the aorist such a preterit stands without any corresponding present indicative.

587. In the early language, especially in the RV., the occurrence of forms identical with those of augment-tenses save for the lack of an augment is quite frequent. Such forms lose in general, along with the augment, the specific character of the tenses to which they belong; and they are then employed in part non-modally, with either a present or a past sense; and in part modally, with either a subjunctive or an optative sense — especially often and regularly after **mā** prohibitive (579); and this last mentioned use comes down also into the later language.

a. In RV., the augmentless forms are more than half as common as the augmented (about 2000 and 3300), and are made from the present, perfect, and aorist-systems, but considerably over half from the aorist. Their non-modal and modal uses are of nearly equal frequency. The tense value of the non-modally used forms is more often past than present. Of the modally used forms, nearly a third are construed with **mā** prohibitive; the rest have twice as often an optative as a proper subjunctive value.

b. In AV., the numerical relations are very different. The augmentless forms are less than a third as many as the augmented (about 475 to 1450), and are prevailingly (more than four fifths) aoristic. The non-modal uses are only a tenth of the modal. Of the modally used forms, about four fifths are construed with **mā** prohibitive; the rest are chiefly optative in value. Then, in the language of the Brāhmaṇas (not including the **mantra**-material which they contain), the loss of augment is, save in occasional sporadic cases, restricted to the prohibitive construction with **mā**; and the same continues to be the case later.

c. The accentuation of the augmentless forms is throughout in accordance with that of unaugmented tenses of similar formation. Examples will be given below, under the various tenses.

d. Besides the augmentless aorist-forms with **mā** prohibitive, there are also found occasionally in the later language augmentless imperfect-forms (very rarely aorist-forms), which have the same value as if they were augmented, and are for the most part examples of metrical license. They are especially frequent in the epics (whence some scores of them are quotable).

Reduplication.

588. The derivation of conjugational and declensional stems from roots by reduplication, either alone or along with other formative elements, has been already spoken of (259), and the formations in which reduplication appears have been specified: they are, in primary verb-inflection, the present (of a certain class of verbs), the perfect (of nearly all), and the aorist (of a large number); and the intensive and desiderative secondary conjugations contain in their stems the same element.

589. The general principle of reduplication is the prefixion to a root of a part of itself repeated — if it begin with consonants, the initial consonant and the vowel; if it begin with a vowel, that vowel, either alone or with a following consonant. The varieties of detail, however, are very considerable. Thus, especially, as regards the vowel, which in present and perfect and desiderative is regularly shorter and lighter in the reduplication than in the root-syllable, in aorist is longer, and in intensive is strengthened. The differences as regards an initial consonant are less, and chiefly confined to the intensive; for the others, certain general rules may be here stated, all further details being left to be given in connection with the account of the separate formations.

590. The consonant of the reduplicating syllable is in general the first consonant of the root: thus, पप्रक् **paprach** from √प्रक् **prach**; शिश्रि **çiçri** from √श्रि **çri**; बुबुध् **bubudh** from √बुध्. But —

a. A non-aspirate is substituted in reduplication for an aspirate: thus, दधा **dadhā** from √धा; बिभृ **bibhṛ** from √भृ **bhṛ**.

b. A palatal is substituted for a guttural or for ह् **h**:

thus, चकृ cakṛ from √कृ kṛ; चिखिद् cikhid from √खिद् khid; जग्रभ् jagrabh from √ग्रभ् grabh; जह्ृ jahṛ from √हृ hṛ.

c. The occasional reversion, on the other hand, of a palatal in the radical syllable to guttural form has been noticed above (216 l).

d. Of two initial consonants, the second, if it be a non-nasal mute, preceded by a sibilant, is repeated instead of the first: thus, तस्तृ tastṛ from √स्तृ stṛ; तस्था tasthā from √स्था sthā; चस्कन्द् caskand from √स्कन्द् skand; चस्खल् caskhal from √स्खल् skhal; चुश्चुत् cuçcut from √श्चुत् çcut; पस्पृध् paspṛdh from √स्पृध् spṛdh; पुस्फुट् pusphuṭ from √स्फुट् sphuṭ: — but सस्ना sasnā from √स्ना snā; सस्मृ sasmṛ from √स्मृ smṛ; सुस्रु susru from √स्रु sru; शिश्लिष् çiçliṣ from √श्लिष् çliṣ.

Accent of the Verb.

591. The statements which have been made above, and those which will be made below, as to the accent of verbal forms, apply to those cases in which the verb is actually accented.

a. But, according to the grammarians, and according to the invariable practice in accentuated texts, the verb is in the majority of its occurrences unaccented or toneless.

b. That is to say, of course, the verb in its proper forms, its personal or so-called finite forms. The verbal nouns and adjectives, or the infinitives and participles, are subject to precisely the same laws of accent as other nouns and adjectives.

592. The general rule, covering most of the cases, is this: The verb in an independent clause is unaccented, unless it stand at the beginning of the clause — or also, in metrical text, at the beginning of a pāda.

a. For the accent of the verb, as well as for that of the vocative case (above, 314 c), the beginning of a pāda counts as that of a sentence, whatever be the logical connection of the pāda with what precedes it.

b. Examples of the unaccented verb are: agním īḍe puróhitam *Agni I praise, the house-priest;* sá íd devéṣu gacchati *that, truly, goes to the gods;* ágne sūpāyanó bhava *O Agni, be easy of access;* idám indra çṛṇuhi somapa *this, O Indra, soma-drinker, hear;* námas te rudra kṛṇmaḥ *homage to thee, Rudra, we offer;* yájamānasya paçū́n pāhi *the sacrificer's cattle protect thou.*

c. Hence, there are two principal situations in which the verb retains its accent:

593. **First, the verb is accented when it stands at the beginning of a clause — or, in verse, of a pāda.**

a. Examples of the verb accented at the head of the sentence are, in prose, **çúndhadhvaṁ dāívyāya kármaṇe** *be pure for the divine ceremony;* **āpnótī 'máṁ lokám** *he wins this world;* — in verse, where the head of the sentence is also that of the **pāda, syā́mé 'd índrasya çármaṇi** *may we be in Indra's protection;* **darçáya mā yātudhā́nān** *show me the sorcerers;* **gámad vā́jebhir ā́ sá naḥ** *may he come with good things to us;* — in verse, where the head of the clause is within the **pāda, téṣām pāhi çrudhí hávam** *drink of them, hear our call;* **sástu mātā́ sástu pitā́ sástu çvā́ sástu viçpátiḥ** *let the mother sleep, let the father sleep, let the dog sleep, let the master sleep;* **víçvakarman námas te pāhy àsmā́n** *Viçvakarman, homage to thee; protect us!* **yuvā́m… rā́jña ūce duhitā́ pṛcché vāṁ narā** *the king's daughter said to you "I pray you, ye men";* **vayáṁ te váya indra viddhí ṣu ṇaḥ prá bharāmahe** *we offer thee, Indra, strengthening; take note of us.*

b. Examples of the verb accented at the head of the **pāda** when this is not the head of the sentence are: **áthā te ántamānāṁ vidyā́ma sumatīnā́m** *so may we enjoy thy most intimate favors;* **dhātā́ 'syā́ agrúvāi pátiṁ dádhātu pratikāmyàm** *Dhātar bestow upon this girl a husband according to her wish;* **yātudhā́nasya somapa jahí prajā́m** *slay, O Soma-drinker, the progeny of the sorcerer.*

594. Certain special cases under this head are as follows:

a. As a vocative forms no syntactical part of the sentence to which it is attached, but is only an external appendage to it, a verb following an initial vocative, or more than one, is accented, as if it were itself initial in the clause or **pāda**: thus, **ā́çrutkarṇa çrudhí hávam** *O thou of listening ears, hear our call!* **síte vándāmahe tvā** *O Sītā, we reverence thee;* **víçve devā vásavo rákṣate 'mám** *all ye gods, ye Vasus, protect this man;* **utā́ "gaç cakrúṣaṁ devā dévā jīváyathā púnaḥ** *likewise him, O gods, who has committed crime, ye gods, ye make to live again.*

b. If more than one verb follow a word or words syntactically connected with them all, only the first loses its accent, the others being treated as if they were initial verbs in separate clauses, with the same adjuncts understood: thus, **taráṇir íj jayati kṣéti púṣyati** *successful he conquers, rules, thrives;* **amítrān… párāca indra prá mṛṇā jahí ca** *our foes, Indra, drive far away and slay;* **asmábhyaṁ jeṣi yótsi ca** *for us conquer and fight;* **ágnīṣomā havíṣaḥ prásthitasya vītáṁ háryataṁ vṛṣaṇā juṣéthām** *O Agni and Soma, of the oblation set forth partake, enjoy, ye mighty ones, take pleasure.*

c. In like manner (but much less often), an adjunct, as subject or object, standing between two verbs and logically belonging to both, is reckoned to the first alone, and the second has the initial accent: thus, **jahí prajā́ṁ náyasva ca** *slay the progeny, and bring [it] hither;* **çṛṇótu naḥ subhágā bódhatu tmánā** *may the blessed one hear us, [and may she] kindly regard [us].*

d. It has even come to be a formal rule that a verb immediately following another verb is accented: thus, **sá yá etám evám upā́ste pūryáte prajáyā paçúbhiḥ** (ÇB.) *whoever worships him thus is filled with offspring and cattle.*

595. Second, the verb is accented, whatever its position, in a dependent clause.

a. The dependency of a clause is in the very great majority of cases conditioned by the relative pronoun **ya**, or one of its derivatives or compounds. Thus: **yáṁ yajñám paribhū́r ási** *what offering thou protectest;* **ó té yanti yé aparī́ṣu páçyān** *they are coming who shall behold her hereafter;* **sahá yán me ásti téna** *along with that which is mine;* **yátra naḥ pū́rve pitáraḥ pareyúḥ** *whither our fathers of old departed;* **adyā́ murīya yádi yātudhā́no ásmi** *let me die on the spot, if I am a sorcerer;* **yáthā́ 'hāny anupūrvám bhávanti** *as days follow one another in order;* **yā́vad idám bhúvanaṁ víçvam ásti** *how great this whole creation is;* **yátkāmās te juhumás tán no astu** *what desiring we sacrifice to thee, let that become ours;* **yatamás títṛpsāt** *whichever one desires to enjoy.*

b. The presence of a relative word in the sentence does not, of course, accent the verb, unless this is really the predicate of a dependent clause: thus, **ápa tyé tāyávo yathā yanti** *they make off like thieves (as thieves do);* **yát sthā́ jágac ca rejate** *whatever [is] immovable and movable trembles;* **yathākā́maṁ ní padyate** *he lies down at his pleasure.*

c. The particle **ca** when it means *if*, and **céd** (**ca**+**id**) *if*, give an accent to the verb: thus, **brahmā́ céd dhástam ágrahīt** *if a Brahman has grasped her hand;* **tváṁ ca soma no váço jīvā́tuṁ ná marāmahe** *if thou, Soma, willest us to live, we shall not die;* **ā́ ca gácchān mitrám enā dadhāma** *if he will come here, we will make friends with him.*

d. There are a very few passages in which the logical dependence of a clause containing no subordinating word appears to give the verb its accent: thus, **sám áçvaparṇāç cáranti no náro 'smā́kam indra rathíno jayantu** *when our men, horse-winged, come into conflict, let the chariot-fighters of our side, O Indra, win the victory.* Rarely, too, an imperative so following another imperative that its action may seem a consequence of the latter's is accented: thus, **tū́yam ā́ gahi káṇveṣu sú sácā píba** *come hither quickly; drink along with the Kanvas* (i. e. *in order to drink*).

e. A few other particles give the verb an accent, in virtue of a slight subordinating force belonging to them: thus, especially **hí** (with its negation **nahí**), which in its fullest value means *for*, but shades off from that into a mere asseverative sense; the verb or verbs connected with it are always accented: thus, **ví té muñcantā́m vimúco hí sánti** *let them release him, for they are releasers;* **yác cid dhí... anāçastā́ iva smási** *if we, forsooth, are as it were unrenowned;* — also **néd** (**ná**+**íd**), meaning *lest, that not:* thus, **nét tvā tápāti sū́ro arcíṣā** *that the sun may not burn thee with his beam;* **virā́jaṁ néd vicchinádānī 'ti** *saying to himself,* *"lest I cut off the virāj"* (such cases are frequent in the Brāhmaṇas); — and the interrogative **kuvíd** *whether?* thus, **ukthébhiḥ kuvíd ā́gámat** *will he come hither for our praises?*

596. But further, the verb of a prior clause is not infrequently accented in antithetical construction.

a. Sometimes, the relation of the two clauses is readily capable of being regarded as that of protasis and apodosis; but often, also, such a relation is very indistinct; and the cases of antithesis shade off into those of ordinary coördination, the line between them appearing to be rather arbitrarily drawn.

b. In many cases, the antithesis is made distincter by the presence in the two clauses of correlative words, especially **anya — anya, eka— eka, vā—vā, ca—ca**: thus, **prá-prā 'nyé yánti páry anyá āsate** *some go on and on, others sit about* (as if it were *while some go* etc.); **úd vā siñcádhvam úpa vā pṛṇadhvam** *either pour out, or fill up;* **sáṁ ce 'dhyásvā 'gne prá ca vardhaye 'mám** *both do thou thyself become kindled, Agni, and do thou increase this person.* But it is also made without such help: thus, **prā́ 'jātāḥ prajā́ janáyati pári prájātā gṛhṇāti** *the unborn progeny he generates, the born he embraces;* **ápa yuṣmád ákramīn nā́ 'smā́n upā́vartate** *[though] she has gone away from you, she does not come to us;* **nā́ 'ndhò 'dhvaryúr bhávati ná yajñáṁ rákṣāṅsi ghnanti** *the priest does not become blind, the demons do not destroy the sacrifice;* **kéna sómā gṛhyánte kéna hūyante** *by whom [on the one hand] are the somas dipped out? by whom [on the other hand] are they offered?*

597. Where the verb would be the same in the two antithetical clauses, it is not infrequently omitted in the second: thus, beside complete expressions like **urvī́ cā́ 'si vásvī cā 'si** *both thou art broad and thou art good,* occur, much oftener, incomplete ones like **agnír amúṣmiṅ loká ā́sīd yamò 'smín** *Agni was in yonder world, Yama [was] in this;* **asthnā́ 'nyā́ḥ prajā́ḥ pratitíṣṭhanti māṅsénā 'nyā́ḥ** *by bone some creatures stand firm, by flesh others;* **dvipā́c ca sárvaṁ no rákṣa cátuṣpād yác ca naḥ svám** *both protect everything of ours that is biped, and also whatever that is quadruped belongs to us.*

a. Accentuation of the verb in the former of two antithetical clauses is a rule more strictly followed in the Brāhmaṇas than in the Veda, and least strictly in the RV.: thus, in RV., **abhí dyā́m mahinā́ bhuvam** (not **bhúvam**) **abhī̀ 'mā́m pṛthivī́m mahī́m** *I am superior to the sky in greatness, also to this great earth;* and even **índro vidur áñgirasaç ca ghorā́ḥ** *Indra knows, and the terrible Angirases.*

598. There are certain more or less doubtful cases in which a verb-form is perhaps accented for emphasis.

a. Thus, sporadically before **caná** *in any wise,* and in connection with asseverative particles, as **kíla, añgá, evá,** and (in ÇB., regularly) **hánta**: thus, **hánte 'mā́m pṛthivī́ṁ vibhájāmahāi** *come on! let us share up this earth.*

CHAPTER IX.

THE PRESENT-SYSTEM.

599. THE present-system, or system of forms coming from the present-stem, is composed (as was pointed out above) of a present indicative tense, together with a subjunctive (mostly lost in the classical language), an optative, an imperative, and a participle, and also a past tense, an augment-preterit, to which we give (by analogy with the Greek) the name of imperfect.

a. These forms often go in Sanskrit grammars by the name of "special tenses", while the other tense-systems are styled "general tenses" — as if the former were made from a special tense-stem or modified root, while the latter came, all alike, from the root itself. There is nó reason why such a distinction and nomenclature should be retained; since, on the one hand, the "special tenses" come in one set of verbs directly from the root, and, on the other hand, the other tense-systems are mostly made from stems — and, in the case of the aorist, from stems having a variety of form comparable with that of present-stems.

600. Practically, the present-system is the most prominent and important part of the whole conjugation, since, from the earliest period of the language, its forms are very much more frequent than those of all the other systems together.

a. Thus, in the Veda, the occurrences of personal forms of this system are to those of all others about as three to one; in the Aitareya Brāhmaṇa, as five to one; in the Hitopadeça, as six to one; in the Çakuntalā, as eight to one; in Manu, as thirty to one.

601. And, as there is also great variety in the manner in which different roots form their present-stem, this, as being their most conspicuous difference, is made the basis of their principal classification; and a verb is said to be of this or of that conjugation, or class, according to the way in which its present-stem is made and inflected.

602. In a small minority of verbs, the present-stem is identical with the root. Then there are besides (excluding the passive and causative) seven more or less different methods of forming a present-stem from the root, each method being followed by a larger or smaller number of verbs. These are the "classes" or "conjugation-classes", as laid down by the native Hindu grammarians. They are arranged by the latter in a certain wholly artificial and unsystematic order (the ground of which has never been discovered); and they are wont to be designated in European works according to this order, or else, after Hindu example, by the root standing at the head of each class in the Hindu lists. A different arrangement and nomenclature will be followed here, namely as below — the classes being divided (as is usual in European grammars) into two more general classes or conjugations, distinguished from one another by wider differences than those which separate the special classes.

603. The classes of the FIRST OR NON-**a**-CONJUGATION are as follows:

I. The root-class (second class, or **ad**-class, of the Hindu grammarians); its present-stem is coincident with the root itself: thus, अद् **ad** *eat;* इ **i** *go;* आस् **ās** *sit;* या **yā** *go;* द्विष् **dviṣ** *hate;* दुह् **duh** *milk.*

II. The reduplicating class (third or **hu**-class); the root is reduplicated to form the present-stem: thus, जुहु **juhu** from √हु **hu** *sacrifice;* ददा **dadā** from √दा **dā** *give;* बिभृ **bibhṛ** from √भृ **bhṛ** *bear.*

III. The nasal class (seventh or **rudh**-class); a nasal, extended to the syllable न **na** in strong forms, is inserted before the final consonant of the root: thus, रुन्ध् **rundh** (or रुणध् **ruṇadh**) from √रुध् **rudh** *obstruct;* युञ्ज् **yuñj** (or युनज् **yunaj**) from √युज् **yuj** *join.*

IV. **a.** The **nu-class** (fifth or su-class); the syllable नु **nu** is added to the root: thus, सुनु **sunu** from √सु **su** *press out;* श्राप्नु **āpnu** from √श्राप् **āp** *obtain.*

b. A very small number (only half-a-dozen) of roots ending already in न् **n**, and also one very common and, quite irregularly inflected root not so ending (कृ **kṛ** *make*), add उ **u** alone to form the present-stem. This is the eighth or tan-class of the Hindu grammarians; it may be best ranked by us as a sub-class, the **u-class**: thus, तनु **tanu** from √तन् **tan** *stretch.*

V. The **nā-class** (ninth or krī-class); the syllable ना **nā** (or, in weak forms, नी **nī**) is added to the root: thus, क्रीणा **krīṇā** (or क्रीणी **krīṇī**) from √क्री **krī** *buy;* स्तभ्ना **stabhnā** (or स्तभ्नी **stabhnī**) from √स्तभ् **stabh** *establish.*

604. These classes have in common, as their most fundamental characteristic, a shift of accent: the tone being now upon the ending, and now upon the root or the class-sign. Along with this goes a variation in the stem itself, which has a stronger or fuller form when the accent rests upon it, and a weaker or briefer form when the accent is on the ending these: forms are to be distinguished as the strong stem and the weak stem respectively (in part, both have been given above). The classes also form their optative active, their 2d sing. imperative, their 3d pl. middle, and their middle participle, in a different manner from the others.

605. In the classes of the SECOND OR **a**-CONJUGATION, the present-stem ends in **a**, and the accent has a fixed place, remaining always upon the same syllable of the stem, and never shifted to the endings. Also, the optative, the 2d sing. impv., the 3d pl. middle, and the middle participle, are (as just stated) unlike those of the other conjugation.

606. The classes of this conjugation are as follows:

VI. The **a**-class, or unaccented **a**-class (first or **bhū**-class); the added class-sign is **a** simply; and the root, which has the accent, is (if capable of it) strengthened by **guṇa** throughout: thus, भव **bháva** from √भू **bhū** *be;* नय **náya** from √नी **nī** *lead;* बोध **bódha** from √बुध् **budh** *wake;* वद **váda** from √वद् **vad** *speak.*

VII. The **á**-class, or accented **a**-class (sixth or **tud**-class); the added class-sign is **a**, as in the preceding class; but it has the accent, and the unaccented root remains unstrengthened: thus, तुद **tudá** from √तुद् **tud** *thrust;* सृज **sṛjá** from √सृज् **sṛj** *let loose;* सुव **suvá** from √सू **sū** *give birth.*

VIII. The **ya**-class (fourth or **div**-class); **ya** is added to the root, which has the accent: thus, दीव्य **dī́vya** from √दिव् **div** (more properly दीव् **dīv**: see **765**) *play;* नह्य **náhya** from √नह् **nah** *bind;* क्रुध्य **krúdhya** from √क्रुध् **krudh** *be angry.*

IX. The passive conjugation is also properly a present-system only, having a class-sign which is not extended into the other systems; though it differs markedly from the remaining classes in having a specific meaning, and in being formable in the middle voice from all transitive verbs. Its inflection may therefore best be treated next to that of the **ya**-class, with which it is most nearly connected, differing from it as the **a**-class from the **á**-class. It forms its stem, namely, by adding an accented **yá** to the root: thus, अद्य **adyá** from √अद् **ad** *eat;* रुध्य **rudhyá** from √रुध् **rudh** *obstruct;* बुध्य **budhyá** from √बुध् **budh** *wake;* तुद्य **tudyá** from √तुद् **tud** *thrust.*

607. The Hindu grammarians reckon a tenth class or cur-class, having a class-sign **áya** added to a strengthened root (thus, **coráya** from √**cur**), and an inflection like that of the other a-stems. Since, however, this stem is not limited to the present-system, but extends also into the rest of the conjugation — while it also has to a great extent a causative value, and may be formed in that value from a large number of roots — it will be best treated in full along with the derivative conjugations (chap. XIV., 1041 ff.).

608. A small number of roots add in the present-system a **ch**, or substitute a **ch** for their final consonant, and form a stem ending in **cha** or **chá**, which is then inflected like any a-stem. This is historically, doubtless, a true class-sign, analogous with the rest; but the verbs showing it are so few, and in formation so irregular, that they are not well to be put together into a class, but may best be treated as special cases falling under the other classes.

a. Roots adding **ch** are **ṛ** and **yu**, which make the stems **ṛcchá** and **yúccha**.

b. Roots substituting **ch** for their final are **iṣ**, **uṣ** (or **vas** *shine*), **gam**, **yam**, which make the stems **icchá**, **ucchá**, **gáccha**, **yáccha**.

c. Of the so-called roots ending in **ch**, several are more or less clearly stems, whose use has been extended from the present to other systems of tenses.

609. Roots are not wholly limited, even in the later language, to one mode of formation of their present-stem, but are sometimes reckoned as belonging to two or more different conjugation-classes. And such variety of formation is especially frequent in the Veda, being exhibited by a considerable proportion of the roots there occurring; already in the Brāhmaṇas, however, a condition is reached nearly agreeing in this respect with the classical language. The different present-formations sometimes have differences of meaning; yet not more important ones than are often found belonging to the same formation, nor of a kind to show clearly a difference of value as originally belonging to the separate classes of presents. If anything of this kind is to be established, it must be from the derivative conjugations, which are separated by no fixed line from the present-systems.

610. We take up now the different classes, in the order in which they have been arranged above, to describe more in detail, and with illustration, the formation of their present-systems, and to notice the irregularities belonging under each class.

I. Root-class (second, ad-class).

611. In this class there is no class-sign; the root itself is also present-stem, and to it are added directly the personal endings — but combined in subjunctive and optative with the respective mode-signs; and in the imperfect the augment is prefixed to the root.

a. The accented endings (**552**) regularly take the accent — except in the imperfect, where it falls on the augment — and before them the root remains unchanged; before the unaccented endings, the root takes the guṇa-strengthening.

b. It is only in the first three classes that the endings come immediately in contact with a final consonant of the root, and that the rules for consonant combination have to be noted and applied. In these classes, then, additional paradigms will be given, to illustrate the modes of combination.

1. Present Indicative.

612. The endings are the primary (with अते **áte** in 3d pl. mid.), added to the bare root. The root takes the accent, and has guṇa, if capable of it, in the three persons sing. act.

Examples of inflection: **a.** active, root इ **i** *go:* strong form of root-stem, ए **é**; weak form, इ **i**; middle, root **ās** *sit*, stem **ā́s** (irregularly accented throughout: **628**).

	active.			middle.		
	s.	d.	p.	s.	d.	p.
1	एमि **émi**	इवस् **ivás**	इमस् **imás**	आसे **ā́se**	आस्वहे **ā́svahe**	आस्महे **ā́smahe**
2	एषि **éṣi**	इथस् **ithás**	इथ **ithá**	आस्से **ā́sse**	आसाथे **ā́sāthe**	आद्ध्वे **ā́ddhve**
3	एति **éti**	इतस् **itás**	यन्ति **yánti**	आस्ते **ā́ste**	आसाते **ā́sāte**	आसते **ā́sate**

b. root **dviṣ** *hate:* strong stem-form, **dvéṣ**; weak, **dviṣ**. For rules of combination for the final **ṣ**, see **226**.

1	**dvéṣmi**	**dviṣvás**	**dviṣmás**	**dviṣé**	**dviṣváhe**	**dviṣmáhe**
2	**dvékṣi**	**dviṣṭhás**	**dviṣṭhá**	**dvikṣé**	**dviṣā́the**	**dviḍḍhvé**
3	**dvéṣṭi**	**dviṣṭás**	**dviṣánti**	**dviṣṭé**	**dviṣā́te**	**dviṣáte**

c. root **duh** *milk:* strong stem-form, **dóh**; weak, **duh**. For rules of combination for the final **h**, and for the conversion of the initial to **dh**, see **222 a, 155, 160**.

1	**dóhmi**	**duhvás**	**duhmás**	**duhé**	**duhváhe**	**duhmáhe**
2	**dhókṣi**	**dugdhás**	**dugdhá**	**dhukṣé**	**duhā́the**	**dhugdhvé**
3	**dógdhi**	**dugdhás**	**duhánti**	**dugdhé**	**duhā́te**	**duháte**

d. root **lih** *lick:* strong stem, **léh**; weak, **lih**. For rules of combination of the final **h**, see **222 b.**

1	**léhmi**	**lihvás**	**lihmás**	**lihé**	**lihváhe**	**lihmáhe**
2	**lékṣi**	**līḍhás**	**līḍhá**	**likṣé**	**lihā́the**	**līḍhvé**
3	**léḍhi**	**līḍhás**	**lihánti**	**līḍhé**	**lihā́te**	**lihā́te**

613. Examples of the 3d sing. mid. coincident in form with the 1st sing. are not rare in the older language (both V. and B.): the most frequent examples are **ī́çe, duhé, vidé, çáye**; more sporadic are **cité, bruve, huvé.** To **tha** of the 2d pl. is added **na** in **sthána, pāthánā, yāthána.** The irregular accent of the 3d pl. mid. is found in RV. in **rihaté, duhaté.** Examples of the same person in **re** and **rate** also occur: thus (besides those mentioned below, **629—30, 635**), **vidré,** and, with auxiliary vowel, **arhire** (unless these are to be ranked, rather, as perfect forms without reduplication: **790 b**).

2. Present Subjunctive.

614. Subjunctive forms of this class are not uncommon in the older language, and nearly all those which the formation anywhere admits are quotable, from Veda or from Brāhmaṇa. A complete paradigm, accordingly, is given below, with the few forms not actually quotable for this class enclosed in brackets. We may take as models (as above), for the active the root **i** *go,* and for the middle the root **ās** *sit,* from both of which numerous forms are met with (although neither for these nor for any others can the whole series be found in actual use).

a. The mode-stems are **áya** (**é+a**) and **ā́sa** (**ā́s+a**) respectively.

	active.			middle.		
	s.	d.	p.	s.	d.	p.
1	**áyāni** / **áyā**	**áyāva**	**áyāma**	**ā́sāi**	**ā́sāvahāi** / [**ā́sāvahe**]	**ā́sāmahāi** / [**ā́sāmahe**]
2	**áyasi** / **áyas**	**áyathas**	**áyatha**	**ā́sase** / **ā́sāsāi**	[**ā́sāithe**]	[**ā́sadhve**] / **ā́sādhvāi**
3	**áyati** / **áyat**	**áyatas**	**áyan**	**ā́sate** / **ā́sātāi**	**ā́sāite**	[**ā́sante**]-**nta** / **ā́sāntāi**

615. The RV. has no middle forms in **āi** except those of the first person. The 1st. sing. act. in **ā** occurs only in RV., in **ayā, bravā, stávā.** The 2d and 3d sing. act. with primary endings are very unusual in the Brāhmaṇas. Forms irregularly made with long **ā,** like those from present-stems in **a,** are not rare in AV. and B.: thus, **ayās, ayāt, áyān; ā́sāt, brávāt; bravāthas; asātha, ayatha, bravātha, hanātha; ádān, dohān.** Of middle forms with secondary endings are found **hánanta,** 3d pl., and **ī́çata,** 3d sing. (after **mā́** prohibitive), which is an isolated example. The only dual person in **āite** is **brávāite.**

3. Present Optative.

616. The personal endings combined with the mode-signs of this mode (या **yā** in act., ई **ī** in mid.) have been given in full above (**566**). The stem-form is the unaccented and unstrengthened root.

	active.			middle.		
	s.	d.	p.	s.	d.	p.
1	इयाम् **iyā́m**	इयाव **iyā́va**	इयाम **iyā́ma**	आसीय **ā́sīya**	आसीवहि **ā́sīvahi**	आसीमहि **ā́sīmahi**
2	इयास् **iyā́s**	इयातम् **iyā́tam**	इयात **iyā́ta**	आसीथास् **ā́sīthās**	आसीयाथाम् **ā́sīyāthām**	आसीध्वम् **ā́sīdhvam**
3	इयात् **iyā́t**	इयाताम् **iyā́tām**	इयुस् **iyús**	आसीत **ā́sīta**	आसीयाताम् **ā́sīyātām**	आसीरन् **ā́sīran**

a. In the same manner, from √dviṣ, **dviṣyā́m** and **dviṣīyá**; from √**duh, duhyā́m** and **duhīyá**; from √**lih, lihyā́m** and **lihīyá**. The inflection is so regular that the example above given is enough, with the addition of **dviṣīyá**, to show the normal accentuation in the middle; thus, sing. **dviṣīyá, dviṣīthā́s, dviṣītá**; du. **dviṣīváhi, dviṣīyā́thām**, dviṣīyā́tām; pl. **dviṣīmáhi, dviṣīdhvám, dviṣīrán.**

b. The RV. has once **tana** in 2d pl. act. (in **syātana**).

4. Present Imperative.

617. The imperative adds, in second and third persons, its own endings (with अताम् **atām** in 3d pl. mid.) directly to the root-stem. The stem is accented and strengthened in 3d sing. act.; elsewhere, the accent is on the ending and the root remains unchanged. The first persons, so called, of the later language are from the old subjunctive, and have its strengthened stem and accent; they are repeated here from where they were given above (**614 a**). In the 2d sing. act., the ending is regularly (as in the two following classes) धि **dhi** if the root end with a consonant, and हि **hi** if it end with a vowel. As examples we take the roots already used for the purpose.

a. Thus, from the roots इ i and आस् ās:

	active.			middle.		
	s.	d.	p.	s.	d.	p.
1	अयानि áyāni	अयाव áyāva	अयाम áyāma	आसै ā́sāi	आसावहै ā́sāvahāi	आसामहै ā́sāmahāi
2	इहि ihí	इतम् itám	इत itá	आस्स्व ā́ssva	आसाथाम् ā́sāthām	आद्ध्वम् ā́ddhvam
3	एतु étu	इताम् itā́m	यन्तु yántu	आस्ताम् ā́stām	आसाताम् ā́sātām	आसताम् ā́satām

b. From the roots dviṣ and duh and lih:

1	dvéṣāṇi	dvéṣāva	dvéṣāma	dvéṣāi	dvéṣāvahāi	dvéṣāmahāi
2	dviḍḍhí	dviṣṭám	dviṣṭá	dvikṣvá	dviṣā́thām	dviḍḍhvám
3	dvéṣṭu	dviṣṭā́m	dviṣántu	dviṣṭā́m	dviṣā́tām	dviṣátām
1	dóhāni	dóhāva	dóhāma	dóhāi	dóhāvahāi	dóhāmahāi
2	dugdhí	dugdhám	dugdhá	dhukṣvá	duhā́thām	dhugdhvám
3	dógdhu	dugdhā́m	duhántu	dugdhā́m	duhā́tām	duhátām
1	léhāni	léhāva	léhāma	léhāi	léhāvahāi	léhāmahāi
2	līḍhí	līḍhám	līḍhá	likṣvá	lihā́thām	līḍhvám
3	léḍhu	līḍhā́m	lihántu	līḍhā́m	lihā́tām	lihátām

618. The 2d sing. act. ending **tāt** is found in the older language in a few verbs of this class: namely, **vittā́t, vītāt, brūtā́t, hatāt, yātāt, stutāt.** In 3d sing. mid., two or three verbs have in the older language the ending **ām**: thus, **duhā́m** (only RV. case), **vidām, çayām**; and in 3d pl. mid. AV. has **duhrā́m** and **duhratām.** The use of **tana** for **ta** in 2d pl. act. is quite frequent in the Veda: thus, **itana, yātána, attana,** etc. And in **stota, éta étana, bravītana, çāstána, hantana,** we have examples in the same person of a strong (and accented) stem.

5. Present Participle.

619. a. The active participle has the ending अन्त् **ánt** (weak stem-form अत् at) added to the unstrengthened root. Mechanically, it may be formed from the 3d pl. by dropping the final इ i. Thus, for the verbs inflected above, the active participles are यन्त् **yánt**, दुहन्त् **duhánt**, द्विषन्त् **dviṣánt**, लिहन्त् **lihánt**. The feminine stem ends usually in अती **atī́**: thus, यती **yatī́**, दुहती **duhatī́**, द्विषती **dviṣatī́**, लिहती **lihatī́**: but, from roots in ā, in आन्ती **ā́ntī** or आती **ātī́** (**449 g**).

b. The middle participle has the ending आन **āná**, added to the unstrengthened root: thus, इयान **iyāná**, दुहान **duhāná**, द्विषाण **dviṣāṇá**, लिहान **lihāná**.

c. The root **ās** forms the anomalous and isolated **ā́sīna** (in RV. also **āsāná**).

d. But a number of these participles in the older language have a double accent, either on the ending or on the radical syllable: thus, **īçāná** and **ī́çāna**, **ohāná** and **óhāna**, **duhāná** and **dúhāna** (also **dúghāna**), **rihāṇá** and **ríhāṇa**, **vidāná** and **vídāna**, **suvāná** and **súvāna**, **stuvāná** and **stavāná** and **stávāna** — the last having in part also a strong form of the root.

6. Imperfect.

620. This tense adds the secondary endings to the root as increased by prefixion of the augment. The root has the guṇa-strengthening (if capable of it) in the three persons of the singular active, although the accent is always upon the augment. Examples of inflection are:

a. From the roots इ **i** and आस् **ās**:

	active.			middle.		
	s.	d.	p.	s.	d.	p.
1	आयम् **ā́yam**	ऐव **ā́iva**	ऐम **ā́ima**	आसि **ā́si**	आस्वहि **ā́svahi**	आस्महि **ā́smahi**
2	ऐस् **ā́is**	ऐतम् **ā́itam**	ऐत **ā́ita**	आस्थास् **ā́sthās**	आसाथाम् **ā́sāthām**	आद्धम् **ā́ddhvam**
3	ऐत् **ā́it**	ऐताम् **ā́itām**	आयन् **ā́yan**	आस्त **ā́sta**	आसाताम् **ā́sātām**	आसत **ā́sata**

b. From the roots **dviṣ** and **duh** and **lih**:

1	**ádveṣam**	**ádviṣva**	**ádviṣma**	**ádviṣi**	**ádviṣvahi**	**ádviṣmahi**
2	**ádveṭ**	**ádviṣṭam**	**ádviṣṭa**	**ádviṣṭhās**	**ádviṣāthām**	**ádviḍḍhvam**
3	**ádveṭ**	**ádviṣṭām**	**ádviṣan**	**ádviṣṭa**	**ádviṣātām**	**ádviṣata**
1	**ádoham**	**áduhva**	**áduhma**	**áduhi**	**áduhvahi**	**áduhmahi**
2	**ádhok**	**ádugdham**	**ádugdha**	**ádugdhās**	**áduhāthām**	**ádhugdhvam**
3	**ádhok**	**ádugdhām**	**áduhan**	**ádugdha**	**áduhātām**	**áduhata**
1	**áleham**	**álihva**	**álihma**	**álihi**	**álihvahi**	**álihmahi**
2	**áleṭ**	**álīḍham**	**álīḍha**	**álīḍhās**	**álihāthām**	**álīḍhvam**
3	**áleṭ**	**álīḍhām**	**álihan**	**álīḍha**	**álihātām**	**álihata**

621. a. Roots ending in **ā** may in the later language optionally take **us** instead of **an** in 3d pl. act. (the **ā** being lost before it); and in the older they always do so: thus, **áyus** from √**yā**, **ápus** from √**pā** *protect*, **abhus** from √**bhā**. The same ending is also allowed and met with in the case of a few roots ending in consonants: namely **vid** *know*, **cakṣ**, **dviṣ**, **duh**, **mṛj**. RV. has **atviṣus**.

b. The ending **tana**, 2d pl. act., is found in the Veda in **áyātana**, **ásastana**, **áítana**, **ábravītana**. A strong stem is seen in the 1st pl. **homa**, and the 2d pl. **abravīta** and **ábravītana**.

c. To save the characteristic endings in 2d and 3d sing. act., the root **ad** inserts **a**: thus, **ā́das**, **ā́dat**; the root **as** inserts **ī**: thus, **ā́sīs**, **ā́sīt** (see below, **636**); compare also **631—4**.

622. The use of the persons of this tense, without augment, in the older language, has been noticed above (**587**). Augmentless imperfects of this class are rather uncommon in the Veda: thus, **hán**, **vés**, 2d sing.; **han**, **vet**, **stāut**, **dán** (?), 3d sing.; **bruvan**, **duhús**, **cakṣus**, 3d pl.; **vasta**, **sūta**, 3d sing. mid.

623. The first or root-form of aorist is identical in its formation with this imperfect: see below, **829** ff.

624. In the Veda (but hardly outside of the RV.) are found certain 2d sing. forms, having an imperative value, made by adding the ending **si** to the (accented and strengthened) root. In part, they are the only root-forms belonging to the roots from which they come: thus, **jóṣi** (for **jóṣṣi**, from √**juṣ**), **dhákṣi**, **párṣi** (√**pṛ** *pass*), **prā́si**, **bhakṣi**, **ratsi**, **sátsi**, **hoṣi**; but the majority of them have forms (one or more) of a root-present, or sometimes of a root-aorist, beside them: thus, **kṣéṣi** (√**kṣi** *rule*), **jéṣi**, **dárṣi**, **nakṣi** (√**naç** *attain*), **néṣi**, **mátsi**, **māsi** (√**mā** *measure*), **yákṣi**, **yáṅsi**, **yāsi**, **yótsi**, **rā́si**, **vákṣi** (√**vah**), **véṣi**, **çróṣi**, **sakṣi**. Their formal character is somewhat disputed; but they are probably indicative persons of the root-class, used imperatively.

625. Forms of this class are made from nearly 150 roots, either in the earlier language, or in the later, or in both: namely, from about 50 through the whole life of the language, from 80 in the older period (of Veda, Brāhmaṇa, and Sūtra) alone, and from a few (about 15) in the later period (epic and classical) only*. Not a few of these roots, however, show only sporadic root-forms, beside a more usual conjugation of some other class; nor is it in all cases possible to separate clearly root-present from root-aorist forms.

a. Many roots of this class, as of the other classes of the first conjugation, show transfers to the second or **a**-conjugation, forming a conjugation-stem by adding **a** to their strong or weak stem, or

---

* Such statements of numbers, with regard to the various parts of the system of conjugation, are in all cases taken from the author's Supplement to this grammar, entitled "Roots, Verb-Forms, and Primary Derivatives of the Sanskrit Language", where lists of roots, and details as to forms etc., are also given.

even to both: thus, from √mṛj, both mārja (627) and mṛja. Such transfers are met with even in the oldest language; but they usually become more frequent later, often establishing a new mode of present inflection by the side of, or in substitution for, the earlier mode.

b. A number of roots offer irregularities of inflection; these are, in the main, pointed out in the following paragraphs.

Irregularities of the Root-class.

626. The roots of the class ending in **u** have in their strong forms the **vṛddhi** instead of the **guṇa**-strengthening before an ending beginning with a consonant: thus, from √**stu, stāúmi, ástāut,** and the like: but **ástavam, stávāni,** etc.

a. Roots found to exhibit this peculiarity in actual use are **kṣṇu, yu** *unite*, **su** (or **sū**) *impel*, **sku, stu, snu** (these in the earlier language), **nu, ru,** and **hnu.** RV. has once **stoṣi,** and **anāvan.** Compare also **633.**

627. The root **mṛj** also has the **vṛddhi**-vowel in its strong forms: thus, **mā́rjmi, ámārjam, ámārṭ** (**150 b**); and the same strengthening is said to be allowed in weak forms before endings beginning with a vowel: thus, **mārjantu, amārjan;** but the only quotable case is **mārjīta** (ĹÇS.). Forms from **a**-stems begin to appear already in AV.

a. In the other tense-systems, also, and in derivation, **mṛj** shows often the **vṛddhi** instead of the **guṇa**-strengthening.

628. A number of roots accent the radical syllable throughout, both in strong and in weak forms: thus, all those beginning with a long vowel, **ās, īḍ, īr, īç;** and also **cakṣ, takṣ, trā, niṅs, vas** *clothe*, **çiñj, çī** *lie*, and **sū.** All these, except **takṣ** and **trā** (and **trā** also in the Vedic forms), are ordinarily conjugated in middle voice only. Forms with the same irregular accent occur now and then in the Veda from other verbs: thus, **mátsva, yákṣva, sákṣva, sā́kṣva, ṛ́dhat.** Middle participles so accented have been noticed above (**619 d**).

629. Of the roots mentioned in the last paragraph, **çī** *lie* has the **guṇa**-strengthening throughout: thus, **çáye, çéṣe, çáyīya, çáyāna,** and so on. Other irregularities in its inflection (in part already noticed) are the 3d pl. persons **çérate** (AV. etc. have also **çére**), **çératām, áçerata** (RV. has also **áçeran**), the 3d sing. pres. **çáye** (R.) and impv. **çáyām.** The isolated active form **áçayat** is common in the older language; other **a**-forms, active and middle, occur later.

630. Of the same roots, **īḍ** and **īç** insert a union-vowel **i** before certain endings: thus, **īçiṣe, ī́çidhve, ī́ḍiṣva** (these three being the only forms noted in the older language); but RV. has **ī́kṣe** beside **ī́çiṣe;** the ÇvU. has once **īçite** for **īṣṭe.** The 3d pl. **ī́çire** (on account of its accent) is also apparently present rather than perfect. The MS. has once the 3d sing. impf. **āiça** (like **aduha: 635**).

631. The roots rud *weep*, svap *sleep*, an *breathe*, and çvas *blow* insert a union-vowel i before all the endings beginning with a consonant, except the s and t of 2d and 3d sing. impf., where they insert instead either a or ī: thus, svápimi, çvásiṣi, ániti, and ā́nat or ā́nīt. And in the other forms, the last three are allowed to accent either root or ending: thus, svápantu and çvásantu (AV.), or svapántu etc. The AV. has sváptu instead of svápitu.

a. In the older language, √vam makes the same insertions: thus, vamiti, avamīt; and other cases occasionally occur: thus, jániṣva, vasiṣva (√vas *clothe*), çnathihi, stanihi (all RV.), yamiti (JB.), çocimi (MBh.). On the other hand, √an early makes forms from an a-stem: thus, ánati (AV.); pple ánant (ÇB.); opt. anet (AB.).

632. The root brū *speak, say* (of very frequent use) takes the union-vowel ī after the root when strengthened, before the initial consonant of an ending: thus, brávīmi, brávīṣi, brávīti, ábravīs, ábravīt; but brūmás, brūyā́m, ábravam, ábruvan, etc. Special occasional irregularities are brūmi, bravīhi, abruvam, abrūvan, bruyā́t, and sporadic forms from an a-stem. The subj. dual brávāite has been noticed above (**615**); also the strong forms abravīta, ábravītana (**621 a**).

633. Some of the roots in u are allowed to be inflected like brū: namely, ku, tu, ru, and stu; and an occasional instance is met with of a form so made (in the older language, only tavīti noted; in the later, only stavīmi, once).

634. The root am (hardly found in the later language) takes ī as union-vowel: thus, amīṣi (RV.), amīti and āmīt and amīṣva (TS). From √çam occur çamīṣva (VS.; TS. çamiṣva) and çamīdhvam (TB. etc.).

635. The irregularities of √duh in the older language have been already in part noted: the 3d pl. indic. mid. duhaté, duhré, and duhráte; 3d sing. impv. duhā́m, pl. duhrā́m and duhratām; impf. act. 3d sing. áduhat (which is found also in the later language), 3d pl. aduhran (beside áduhan and duhús); the mid. pple dúghāna; and (quite unexampled elsewhere) the opt. forms duhīyát and duhīyán (RV. only). The MS. has aduha 3d sing. and aduhra 3d pl. impf. mid., apparently formed to correspond to the pres. duhe (**613**) and duhre as adugdha and aduhata correspond to dugdh eand duhate: compare āíça (**630**), related in like manner to the 3d sing. īçe.

Some of the roots of this class are abbreviated or otherwise weakened in their weak forms: thus —

636. The root अस् as *be* loses its vowel in weak forms (except where protected by combination with the augment). Its 2d sing. indic. is असि ási (instead of assi); its 2d sing. impv. is एधि edhi (irregularly from asdhi). The insertion of

ई ī in 2d and 3d sing. impf. has been noticed already above.

a. The forms of this extremely common verb are, then, as follows:

	Indicative. s.	d.	p.	Optative. s.	d.	p.
1	अस्मि **ásmi**	स्वस् **svás**	स्मस् **smás**	स्याम् **syā́m**	स्याव **syā́va**	स्याम **syā́ma**
2	असि **ási**	स्थस् **sthás**	स्थ **sthá**	स्यास् **syā́s**	स्यातम् **syā́tam**	स्यात **syā́ta**
3	अस्ति **ásti**	स्तस् **stás**	सन्ति **sánti**	स्यात् **syā́t**	स्याताम् **syā́tām**	स्युस् **syús**
	Imperative.			**Imperfect.**		
1	असानि **ásāni**	असाव **ásāva**	असाम **ásāma**	आसम् **ā́sam**	आस्व **ā́sva**	आस्म **ā́sma**
2	एधि **edhí**	स्तम् **stám**	स्त **stá**	आसीस् **ā́sīs**	आस्तम् **ā́stam**	आस्त **ā́sta**
3	अस्तु **ástu**	स्ताम् **stā́m**	सन्तु **sántu**	आसीत् **ā́sīt**	आस्ताम् **ā́stām**	आसन् **ā́san**

Participle सन्त् **sánt** (fem. सती **satī́**).

b. Besides the forms of the present-system, there is made from this root only a perfect, **ā́sa** etc. (**800**), of wholly regular inflection.

c. The Vedic subjunctive forms are the usual ones, made upon the stem **ása**. They are in frequent use, and appear (**asat** especially) even in late texts where the subjunctive is almost lost. The resolution **siā́m** etc. (opt.) is common in Vedic verse. As 2d and 3d sing. impf. is a few times met with the more normal **ās** (for **ās-s**, **ās-t**). **Sthána**, 2d pl., was noted above (**613**).

d. Middle forms from √**as** are also given by the grammarians as allowed with certain prepositions (**vi+ati**), but they are not quotable; **smahe** and **syāmahe** (!) occur in the epics, but are merely instances of the ordinary epic confusion of voices (**529 a**). Confusions of primary and secondary endings — namely, **sva** and **sma** (not rare), and, on the other hand, **syāvas** and **syāmas** — are also epic. A middle present indicative is said to be compounded (in 1st and 2d persons) with the *nomen agentis* in **tṛ** (**tar**) to form a periphrastic future in the middle voice (but see below, **947**). The 1st sing. indic. is **he**; the rest is in the usual relation of middle to active forms (in 2d pers., **se, dhve, sva, dhvam,** with total loss of the root itself).

637. **The root han** ***smite, slay*** **is treated somewhat after the manner of noun-stems in an in declension (421): in weak forms, it loses its n before an initial consonant (except m and v) of a personal ending (not in the optative), and its a before an initial vowel — and in the latter case its h, in contact with the n, is changed to gh (compare 402). Thus, for example:**

	Present Indicative.			Imperfect.		
	s.	d.	p.	s.	d.	p.
1	**hánmi**	**hanvás**	**hanmás**	**áhanam**	**áhanva**	**áhanma**
2	**háṅsi**	**hathás**	**hathá**	**áhan**	**áhatam**	**áhata**
3	**hánti**	**hatás**	**ghnánti**	**áhan**	**áhatām**	**ághnan**

a. Its participle is **ghnánt** (fem. **ghnatī́**). Its 2d sing. impv. is **jahí** (by anomalous dissimilation, on the model of reduplicating forms).

b. Middle forms from this root are frequent in the Brāhmaṇas, and those that occur are formed in general according to the same rules: thus, **hate, hanmahe, ghnate; ahata, aghnātām, aghnata** (in AB., also **ahata**); **ghnīta** (but also **hanīta**). Forms from transfer-stems, **hana** and **ghna**, are met with from an early period.

638. The root **vaç** *be eager* is in the weak forms regularly and usually contracted to **uç** (as in the perfect: **794b**): thus, **uçmási** (V.: once apparently abbreviated in RV. to **çmasi**), **uçánti**; pple **uçánt, uçāná**. Middle forms (except the pple) do not occur; nor do the weak forms of the imperfect, which are given as **āuçva, āuṣṭam,** etc.

a. RV. has in like manner the participle **uṣāṇá** from the root **vas** *clothe*.

639. The root **çās** *order* shows some of the peculiarities of a reduplicated verb, lacking (**646**) the **n** before **t** in all 3d persons pl. and in the active participle. A part of its active forms — namely, the weak forms having endings beginning with consonants (including the optative) — are said to come from a stem with weakened vowel, **çiṣ** (as do the aorist, **854**, and some of the derivatives); but, excepting the optative (**çiṣyām** etc., U. S. and later), no such forms are quotable.

a. The 3d sing. impf. is **açāt** (**555 a**), and the same form is said to be allowed also as 2d sing. The 2d sing. impv. is **çādhí** (with total loss of the **s**); and RV. has the strong 2d pl. **çāstána** (with anomalous accent); and **a**-forms, from stem **çāsa,** occasionally occur.

b. The middle inflection is regular, and the accent (apparently) always upon the radical syllable (**çā́ste, çā́sate, çā́sāna**).

c. The root **dāç** *worship* has in like manner (RV.) the pple **dā́çat** (not **dā́çant**).

640. The double so-called root **jakṣ** *eat, laugh* is an evident reduplication of **ghas** and **has** respectively. It has the absence of **n** in act.

3d persons pl. and pple, and the accent on the root before vowel-endings, which belong to reduplicated verbs; and it also takes the union-vowel **i** in the manner of **rud** etc. (above, **631**). For its forms and derivatives made with utter loss of the final sibilant, see **233 f.**

641. Certain other obviously reduplicated verbs are treated by the native grammarians as if simple, and referred to this conjugation: such are the intensively reduplicated **jāgṛ** (**1020 a**), **daridrā** (**1024 a**), and **vevī** (**1024 a**), **dīdhī** etc. (**676**), and **cakās** (**677**).

II. Reduplicating Class (third, hu-class).

642. This class forms its present-stem by prefixing a reduplication to the root.

643. a. As regards the consonant of the reduplication, the general rules which have already been given above (**590**) are followed.

b. A long vowel is shortened in the reduplicating syllable: thus, ददा **dadā** from √दा **dā**; बिभी **bibhī** from √भी **bhī**; जुहू **juhū** from √हू **hū**. The vowel ऋ **ṛ** never appears in the reduplication, but is replaced by इ **i**: thus, बिभृ **bibhṛ** from √भृ **bhṛ**; पिपृच् **pipṛc** from √पृच् **pṛc**.

c. For verbs in which **a** and **ā** also are irregularly represented in the reduplication by **i**, see below, **660**. Thero ot **vṛt** (V. B.) makes **vavartti** etc.; **cakránt** (RV.) is very doubtful.

d. The only root of this class with initial vowel is **ṛ** (or **ar**); it takes as reduplication **i**, which is held apart from the root by an interposed **y**: thus, **iyar** and **iyṛ** (the latter has not been found in actual use).

644. The present-stem of this class (as of the other classes belonging to the first or non-a-conjugation) has a double form: a stronger form, with gunated root-vowel; and a weaker form, without **guṇa**: thus, from √हु **hu**, the two forms are जुहो **juho** and जुहु **juhu**; from √भी **bhī**, they are बिभे **bibhe** and बिभी **bibhī**. And the rule for their use is the same as in the other classes of this conjugation: the strong stem is found before the unaccented endings (**552**), and the weak stem before the accented.

645. According to all the analogies of the first general conjugation, we should expect to find the accent upon the root-syllable when this is strengthened. That is actually the case, however, only in a small minority of the roots composing the class: namely, in **hu**, **bhī** (no test-forms in the older language), **hrī** (no test-forms found in the older language), **mad** (very rare), **jan** (no forms of this class found to occur), **ci** *notice* (in V.), **yu** *separate* (in older language only), and in **bhṛ** in the later language (in V. it goes with the majority: but RV. has **bibhárti** once, and AV. twice; and this, the later accentuation, is found also in the Brāhmaṇas); and RV. has once **iyárṣi**. In all the rest — apparently, by a recent transfer — it rests upon the reduplicating instead of upon the radical syllable. And in both classes alike, the accent is anomalously thrown back upon the reduplication in those weak forms of which the ending begins with a vowel; while in the other weak forms it is upon the ending (but compare **666a**).

a. Apparently (the cases with written accent are too few to determine the point satisfactorily) the middle optative endings, **īya** etc. (**566**), are reckoned throughout as endings with initial vowel, and throw back the accent upon the reduplication.

646. The verbs of this class lose the न् **n** in the 3d pl. endings in active as well as middle, and in the imperfect have उस् **us** instead of अन् **an** — and before this a final radical vowel has **guṇa**.

1. Present Indicative.

647. The combination of stem and endings is as in the preceding class.

Examples of inflection: **a.** √हु **hu** *sacrifice:* strong stem-form, जुहो **juhó**; weak form, जुहु **juhu** (or **júhu**).

	active. s.	d.	p.	middle. s.	d.	p.
1	जुहोमि **juhómi**	जुहुवस् **juhuvás**	जुहुमस् **juhumás**	जुह्वे **júhve**	जुहुवहे **juhuváhe**	जुहुमहे **juhumáhe**
2	जुहोषि **juhóṣi**	जुहुथस् **juhuthás**	जुहुथ **juhuthá**	जुहुषे **juhuṣé**	जुह्वाथे **júhvāthe**	जुहुध्वे **juhudhvé**
3	जुहोति **juhóti**	जुहुतस् **juhutás**	जुह्वति **júhvati**	जुहुते **juhuté**	जुह्वाते **júhvāte**	जुह्वते **júhvate**

b. Root भृ **bhṛ** *bear* (given with Vedic accentuation): strong stem-form, बिभर् **bíbhar**; weak, बिभृ **bibhṛ** (or **bíbhṛ**).

1	बिभर्मि **bíbharmi**	बिभृवस् **bibhṛvás**	बिभृमस् **bibhṛmás**	बिभ्रे **bíbhre**	बिभृवहे **bibhṛváhe**	बिभृमहे **bibhṛmáhe**
2	बिभर्षि **bíbharṣi**	बिभृथस् **bibhṛthás**	बिभृथ **bibhṛthá**	बिभृषे **bibhṛṣé**	बिभ्राथे **bíbhrāthe**	बिभृध्वे **bibhṛdhvé**
3	बिभर्ति **bíbharti**	बिभृतस् **bibhṛtás**	बिभ्रति **bíbhrati**	बिभृते **bibhṛté**	बिभ्राते **bíbhrāte**	बिभ्रते **bíbhrate**

c. The **u** of **hu** (like that of the class-signs **nu** and **u**: see below, **697 a**) is said to be omissible before **v** and **m** of the endings of 1st du. and pl.: thus, **juhvás, juhváhe,** etc.; but no such forms are quotable.

2. Present Subjunctive.

648. It is not possible at present to draw a distinct line between those subjunctive forms of the older language which should be reckoned as belonging to the present-system and those which should be assigned to the perfect — or even, in some cases, to the reduplicated aorist and intensive. Here will be noticed only those which most clearly belong to this class; the more doubtful cases will be treated under the perfect-system. Except in first persons (which continue in use as "imperatives" down to the later language), subjunctives from roots having unmistakably a reduplicated present-system are of far from frequent occurrence.

649. The subjunctive mode-stem is formed in the usual manner, with the mode-sign **a** and **guṇa** of the root-vowel, if this is capable of such strengthening. The evidence of the few accented forms met with indicates that the accent is laid in accordance with that of the strong indicative forms: thus, from √**hu**, the stem would be **juháva**; from √**bhṛ**, it would be **bíbhara** (but **bibhára** later). Before the mode-sign, final radical **ā** would be, in accordance with analogies elsewhere, dropped: thus, **dáda** from √**dā**, **dádha** from √**dhā** (all the forms actually occurring would be derivable from the secondary roots **dad** and **dadh**).

650. Instead of giving a theoretically complete scheme of inflection, it will be better to note all the examples quotable from the older language (accented when found so occurring).

a. Thus, of 1st persons, we have in the active **juhávāni, bibharāṇi, dadāni, dadhāni, jahāni; juhavāma, dádhāma, jáhāma;** — in the middle, **dadhāi, mimāi; dadhāvahāi; juhavāmahāi, dadāmahe, dadāmahāi, dadhāmahāi.**

b. Of other persons, we have with primary endings in the active **bibharāsi** (with double mode-sign: **560 e**), **dádhathas, juhavātha** (do.)

and juhavatha; in the middle, dádhase; dádhate, rárate, dádhātāi, dadātāi; — with secondary endings, dádhas, víveṣas, juhavat, bibharat, yuyávat, dádhat, dadhánat, babhasat; dadhan, yuyavan, juhavan.

3. Present Optative.

651. To form this mode, the optative endings given above (**566 a**), as made up of mode-sign and personal endings, are added to the unstrengthened stem. The accent is as already stated (**645 a**). The inflection is so regular that it is unnecessary to give here more than the first persons of a single verb: thus,

	active. s.	d.	p.	middle. s.	d.	p.
1	जुहुयाम् **juhuyā́m** etc.	जुहुयाव **juhuyā́va** etc.	जुहुयाम **juhuyā́ma** etc.	जुह्वीय **júhvīya** etc.	जुह्वीवहि **júhvīvahi** etc.	जुह्वीमहि **júhvīmahi** etc.

4. Present Imperative.

652. The endings, and the mode of their combination with the root, have been already given. In 2d sing. act., the ending is हि hi after a vowel, but धि dhi after a consonant: हु **hu**, however, forms जुहुधि **juhudhí** (apparently, in order to avoid the recurrence of ह् h in two successive syllables): and other examples of धि dhi after a vowel are found in the Veda.

653. a. Example of inflection:

	active. s.	d.	p.	middle. s.	d.	p.
1	जुहवानि **juhávāni**	जुहवाव **juhávāva**	जुहवाम **juhávāma**	जुहवै **juhávāi**	जुहवावहै **juhávāvahāi**	जुहवामहै **juhávāmahāi**
2	जुहुधि **juhudhí**	जुहुतम् **juhutám**	जुहुत **juhutá**	जुहुष्व **juhuṣvá**	जुह्वाथाम् **júhvāthām**	जुहुध्वम् **juhudhvám**
3	जुहोतु **juhótu**	जुहुताम् **juhutā́m**	जुह्वतु **júhvatu**	जुहुताम् **juhutā́m**	जुह्वाताम् **júhvātām**	जुह्वताम् **júhvatām**

b. The verbs of the other division differ here, as in the indicative, in the accentuation of their strong forms only: namely, in all the first persons (borrowed subjunctives), and in the 3d sing. act.: thus, (in the older language) **bíbharāṇi** etc., **bíbhartu, bíbharāi** etc.

654. Vedic irregularities of inflection are: 1. the occasional use of strong forms in 2d persons: thus, **yuyodhí, çiçādhi** (beside **çiçīhí**); **yuyotam** (beside **yuyutám**); **íyarta, dádāta** and **dadātana, dádhāta** and **dádhātana** (see below, **668**), **pipartana, juhóta** and **juhótana, yuyota** and **yuyotana; rarāsva** (**666**); 2. the use of **dhi** instead of **hi** after a vowel (only in the two instances just quoted); 3. the ending **tana** in 2d pl. act.: namely, besides those just given, in **jigātana, dhattana, mamáttana, vivaktana, didiṣṭana, bibhītana, jujuṣṭana, juhutana, vavṛttana**: the cases are proportionally much more numerous in this than in any other class; 4. the ending **tāt** in 2d sing. act., in **dattāt, dhattāt, pipṛtāt, jahītāt.**

5. Present Participle.

655. As elsewhere, the active participle-stem may be made mechanically from the 3d pl. indic. by dropping इ **i**: thus, जुह्वत् **júhvat**, बिभ्रत् **bíbhrat**. In inflection, it has no distinction of strong and weak forms (**444**). The feminine stem ends in अती **atī**. The middle participles are regularly made: thus, जुह्वान **júhvāna**, बिभ्राण **bíbhrāṇa**.

a. RV. shows an irregular accent in **pipāná** (√**pā** *drink*).

6. Imperfect.

656. As already pointed out, the 3d pl. act. of this class takes the ending उस् **us**, and a final radical vowel has **guṇa** before it. The strong forms are, as in present indicative, the three singular active persons.

657. Examples of inflection:

	active.			middle.		
	s.	d.	p.	s.	d.	p.
1	अजुहवम् **ájuhavam**	अजुहुव **ájuhuva**	अजुहुम **ájuhuma**	अजुह्वि **ájuhvi**	अजुहुवहि **ájuhuvahi**	अजुहुमहि **ájuhumahi**
2	अजुहोस् **ájuhos**	अजुहुतम् **ájuhutam**	अजुहुत **ájuhuta**	अजुहुथास् **ájuhuthās**	अजुह्वाथाम् **ájuhvāthām**	अजुहुध्वम् **ájuhudhvam**
3	अजुहोत् **ájuhot**	अजुहुताम् **ájuhutām**	अजुहवुस् **ájuhavus**	अजुहुत **ájuhuta**	अजुह्वाताम् **ájuhvātām**	अजुह्वत **ájuhvata**

a. From √भृ **bhṛ**, the 2d and 3d sing. act. are अबिभर् **ábibhar** (for **abibhar-s** and **abibhar-t**) — and so in all other cases where the strong stem ends in a consonant. The 3d pl. act. is अबिभरुस् **ábibharus**; and other like cases are **ábibhayus, acikayus, asuṣavus.**

b. In MS., once, **abibhrus** is doubtless a false reading.

658. The usual Vedic irregularities in 2d pl. act. — strong forms, and the ending **tana** — occur in this tense also: thus, **ádadāta, ádadhāta; ádattana, ájahātana.** The RV. has also once **apiprata** for **apipṛta** in 3d sing. mid., and **abibhran** for **abibharus** in 3d pl. act. Examples of augmentless forms are **çiçās, vivés, jígāt; jíhīta, çíçīta, jihata;** and, with irregular strengthening, **yuyoma** (AV.), **yuyothās, yuyota.**

659. The roots that form their present-stem by reduplication are a very small class, especially in the modern language; they are only 50, all told, and of these only a third (16) are met with later. It is, however, very difficult to determine the precise limits of the class, because of the impossibility (referred to above, under subjunctive: **648**) of always distinguishing its forms from those of other reduplicating conjugations and parts of conjugations.

a. Besides the irregularities in tense-inflection already pointed out, others may be noticed as follows.

Irregularities of the Reduplicating Class.

660. Besides the roots in **ṛ** or **ar** — namely, **ṛ, ghṛ** (usually written **ghar**), **tṛ, pṛ, bhṛ, sṛ, hṛ, pṛc** — the following roots having **a** or **ā** as radical vowel take **i** instead of **a** in the reduplicating syllable: **gā** *go*, **mā** *measure*, **mā** *bellow*, **çā, hā** *remove* (mid.), **vac, sac; vaç** has both **i** and **a; rā** has **i** once in RV.; for **sthā, pā** *drink* **ghrā, han, hi,** see below (**670–4**).

661. Several roots of this class in final **ā** change the **ā** in weak forms to **ī** (occasionally even to **i**), and then drop it altogether before endings beginning with a vowel.

a. This is in close analogy with the treatment of the vowel of the class-sign of the **nā**-class: below, **717.**

These roots are:

662. **çā** *sharpen*, act. and mid.: thus, **çiçāti, çiçīmasi, çiçīhí** (also **çiçādhi**: above, **654**), **çiçātu, açiçāt, çíçīte, çíçīta.**

663. **mā** *bellow*, act., and **mā** *measure*, mid. (rarely also act.): thus, **mimāti, mimīyāt; mímīte, mimate, ámimīta; mimīhi, mímātu.** RV. has once **mimanti** 3d pl. (for **mimati**).

664. hā *remove*, mid.: thus, **jíhīte, jihīdhve, jíhate; jihīṣva, jihatām; ájihīta, ajihata.** ÇB. has **jihīthām** (for **jihāthām**).

665. hā *quit*, act. (originally identical with the former), may further shorten the **ī** to **i**: thus, **jahāti, jahīta, jahītāt** (AV.); **jahimas** (AV.), **jahitas** (TB.), **jahitam** (TA.), **ajahitām** (TS. AB.). In the optative, the radical vowel is lost altogether; thus, **jahyām, jahyus** (AV.). The 2d sing. impv., according to the grammarians, is **jahīhi** or **jahihi** or **jahāhi**; only the first appears quotable.

a. Forms from an **a**-stem, **jaha**, are made for this root, and even derivatives from a quasi-root **jah**.

666. rā *give*, mid.: thus, **rarīdhvam, rarīthās** (impf. without augment); and, with **i** in reduplication, **rirīhi**. But AV. has **rarāsva.**

a. In these verbs, the accent is generally constant on the reduplicating syllable.

667. The two roots **dā** and **dhā** (the commonest of the class) lose their radical vowel altogether in the weak forms, being shortened to **dad** and **dadh**. In 2d sing. impv. act., they form respectively **dehí** and **dhehí**. In combination with a following **t** or **th**, the final **dh** of **dadh** does not follow the special rule of combination of a final sonant aspirate (becoming **ddh** with the **t** or **th**: **160**), but — as also before **s** and **dhv** — the more general rules of aspirate and of surd and sonant combination; and its lost aspiration is thrown back upon the initial of the root (**155**).

668. The inflection of √**dhā** is, then, as follows:

Present Indicative.

	active. s.	d.	p.	middle. s.	d.	p.
1	**dádhāmi**	**dadhvás**	**dadhmás**	**dadhé**	**dádhvahe**	**dádhmahe**
2	**dádhāsi**	**dhatthás**	**dhatthá**	**dhatsé**	**dadhāthe**	**dhaddhve**
3	**dádhāti**	**dhattás**	**dádhati**	**dhatté**	**dadhā́te**	**dádhate**

Present Optative.

1	**dadhyā́m**	**dadhyā́va**	**dadhyā́ma**	**dádhīya**	**dádhīvahi**	**dádhīmahi**
	etc.	etc.	etc.	etc.	etc.	etc.

Present Imperative.

1	**dádhāni**	**dádhāva**	**dádhāma**	**dádhāi**	**dádhāvahāi**	**dádhāmahāi**
2	**dhehí**	**dhattám**	**dhattá**	**dhatsva**	**dadhāthām**	**dhaddhvam**
3	**dádhātu**	**dhattā́m**	**dádhatu**	**dhattām**	**dadhātām**	**dadhatām**

Imperfect.

1	**ádadhām**	**ádadhva**	**ádadhma**	**ádadhi**	**ádadhvahi**	**ádadhmahi**
2	**ádadhās**	**ádhattam**	**ádhatta**	**ádhatthās**	**ádadhāthām**	**ádhaddhvam**
3	**ádadhāt**	**ádhattām**	**ádadhus**	**ádhatta**	**ádadhātām**	**ádadhata**

Participles: act. **dádhat**; mid. **dádhāna.**

a. In the middle (except impf.), only those forms are here accented for which there is authority in the accentuated texts, as there is discordance between the actual accent and that which the analogies of the class would lead us to expect. RV. has once **dhátse: dadhé** and **dadhā́te** might be perfects, so far as the form is concerned. RV. accents **dadhītá** once (**dádhīta** thrice); several other texts have **dádhīta, dádhīran, dádīta.**

b. The root **dā** is inflected in precisely the same way, with change everywhere of (radical) **dh** to **d.**

669. The older language has irregularities as follows: 1. the usual strong forms in 2d pl., **dádhāta** and **ádadhāta, dádāta** and **ádadāta**; 2. the usual **tana** endings in the same person, **dhattana, dádātana,** etc. (**654, 658**); 3. the 3d sing. indic. act. **dadhé** (like 1st sing.); 4. the 2d sing. impv. act. **daddhí** (for both **dehi** and **dhehi**). And R. has **dadmi.**

670. A number of roots have been transferred from this to the **a-** or **bhū-**class (below, **749**), their reduplicated root becoming a stereotyped stem inflected after the manner of **a**-stems. These roots are as follows:

671. In all periods of the language, from the roots **sthā** *stand*, **pā** *drink*, and **ghrā** *smell*, are made the presents **tíṣṭhāmi, píbāmi** (with irregular sonantizing of the second **p**), and **jíghrāmi** — which then are inflected not like **mímāmi**, but like **bhávāmi**, as if from the present-stems **tíṣṭha, píba, jíghra.**

672. In the Veda (especially; also later), the reduplicated roots **dā** and **dhā** are sometimes turned into the **a**-stems **dáda** and **dádha,** or inflected as if roots **dad** and **dadh** of the **a**-class; and single forms of the same character are made from other roots: thus, **mimanti** (√**mā** *bellow*), **rárate** (√**rā** *give*: 3d sing. mid.).

673. In the Veda, also, a like secondary stem, **jighna,** is made from √**han** (with omission of the radical vowel, and conversion, usual in this root, of **h** to **gh** when in contact with **n**: **637**); and some of the forms of **saçc,** from √**sac,** show the same conversion to an **a**-stem, **saçca.**

674. In AB. (viii. 28), a similar secondary form, **jighya,** is given to √**hi** or **hā**: thus, **jighyati, jighyatu.**

675. A few so-called roots of the first or root-class are the products of reduplication, more or less obvious: thus, **jakṣ** (**640**), and probably **çās** (from √**ças**) and **cakṣ** (from √**kāç** or a lost root **kas** *see*). In the Veda is found also **saçc,** from √**sac.**

676. The grammarians reckon (as already noticed, **641**) several roots of the most evidently reduplicate character as simple, and belonging to the root-class. Some of these (**jāgṛ, daridrā, vevī**) are regular intensive stems, and will be described below under Intensives (**1020 a, 1024 a**); **dīdhī** *shine*, together with Vedic **dīdī** *shine* and **pīpī** *swell*, are sometimes also classed as intensives; but they have not the proper reduplication of such, and may perhaps be best noticed here, as reduplicated present-stems with irregularly long reduplicating vowel.

a. Of pres. indic. occurs in the older language only **dīdyati,** 3d pl., with the pples **dī́dyat** and **dī́dhyat,** and mid. **dīdye, dīdhye, dīdhyāthām,** with the pples **dī́dyāna, dī́dhyāna, pī́pyāna.** The subj. stems are **dīdáya, dīdhaya, pīpáya,** and from them are made forms with both primary (from **dīdáya**) and secondary endings (and the irregularly accented **dī́dayat** and **dīdāyat** and **dī́dhayan**). No opt. occurs. In impv. we have **dīdihí** (and **didīhí**) and **pīpihí,** and **pipyatam, pipyatām, pipyata.** In impf., **adīdes** and **pīpes, ádīdet** and **ádīdhet** and **apīpet** (with augmentless forms), **apīpema** (with strong form of root), and **adīdhayus** and (irregular) **apīpyan.**

b. A few forms from all the three show transfer to an **a**-inflection: thus, **dīdhaya** and **pīpaya** (impv.), **ápīpayat,** etc.

c. Similar forms from √**mī** *bellow* are **amīmet** and **mīmayat.**

677. The stem **cakās** *shine* (sometimes **cakāç**) is also regarded by the grammarians as a root, and supplied as such with tenses outside the present-system — which, however, hardly occur in genuine use. It is not known in the older language.

678. The root **bhas** *chew* loses its radical vowel in weak forms, taking the form **baps:** thus, **bábhasti,** but **bápsati** (3d pl.), **bápsat** (pple). For **babdhām,** see **233 f.**

679. The root **bhī** *fear* is allowed by the grammarians to shorten its vowel in weak forms: thus, **bibhīmas** or **bibhimas, bibhīyām** or **bibhiyām;** and **bibhiyāt** etc. are met with in the later language.

680. Forms of this class from √**jan** *give birth,* with added **i** — thus, **jajñiṣe, jajñidhve** — are given by the grammarians, but have never been found in use.

681. The roots **ci** and **cit** have in the Veda reversion of **c** to **k** in the root-syllable after the reduplication: thus, **cikéṣi, cikéthe** (anomalous, for **cikyā́the**), **cikitām, aciket, cíkyat** (pple); **cikiddhi.**

682. The root **vyac** has **i** in the reduplication (from the **y**), and is contracted to **vic** in weak forms: thus, **viviktás, áviviktām.** So the root **hvar** (if its forms are to be reckoned here) has **u** in reduplication, and contracts to **hur:** thus, **juhūrthās.**

III. Nasal Class (seventh, rudh-class).

683. The roots of this class all end in consonants. And their class-sign is a nasal preceding the final consonant: in the weak forms, a nasal simply, adapted in character to the consonant; but in the strong forms expanded to the syllable न **ná,** which has the accent.

a. In a few of the verbs of the class, the nasal extends also into other tense-systems: they are **añj, bhañj, hiṅs**: see below, **694**.

1. Present Indicative.

684. Examples of inflection: **a.** the root युज् **yuj** *join:* strong stem-form, युनज् **yunáj**; weak, युञ्ज् **yuñj**.

For the rules of combination of final **j**, see **219**.

	active. s.	d.	p.	middle. s.	d.	p.
1	युनज्मि **yunájmi**	युञ्ज्वस् **yuñjvás**	युञ्ज्मस् **yuñjmás**	युञ्जे **yuñjé**	युञ्ज्वहे **yuñjváhe**	युञ्ज्महे **yuñjmáhe**
2	युनक्षि **yunákṣi**	युङ्क्थस् **yuñkthás**	युङ्क्थ **yuñkthá**	युङ्क्षे **yuñkṣe**	युञ्जाथे **yuñjā́the**	युङ्ग्ध्वे **yuṅgdhvé**
3	युनक्ति **yunákti**	युङ्क्तस् **yuñktás**	युञ्जन्ति **yuñjánti**	युङ्क्ते **yuñkté**	युञ्जाते **yuñjā́te**	युञ्जते **yuñjáte**

b. the root रुध् **rudh** *obstruct;* bases रुणध् **ruṇadh** and रुन्ध् **rundh**.

For rules of combination of final **dh**, see **153, 160**.

	s.	d.	p.	s.	d.	p.
1	रुणध्मि **ruṇádhmi**	रुन्ध्वस् **rundhvás**	रुन्ध्मस् **rundhmás**	रुन्धे **rundhé**	रुन्ध्वहे **rundhváhe**	रुन्ध्महे **rundhmáhe**
2	रुणत्सि **ruṇátsi**	रुन्द्धस् **runddhás**	रुन्द्ध **runddhá**	रुन्त्से **runtsé**	रुन्धाथे **rundhā́the**	रुन्द्ध्वे **runddhvé**
3	रुणद्धि **ruṇáddhi**	रुन्द्धस् **runddhás**	रुन्धन्ति **rundhánti**	रुन्द्धे **runddhé**	रुन्धाते **rundhā́te**	रुन्धते **rundháte**

c. Instead of **yuñkthas, yuṅgdhve,** and the like (here and in the impv. and impf.), it is allowed and more usual (**231**) to write **yuñthas, yuñdhve,** etc.; and, in like manner, **rundhas, rundhe,** for **runddhas, runddhe**; and so in other like cases.

685. Vedic irregularities of inflection are: 1. the ordinary use of a 3d sing. mid. like the 1st sing., as **vṛñje**; 2. the accent on **té** of 3d pl. mid. in **añjaté, indhaté, bhuñjaté.**

a. Yunañkṣi, in BhP., is doubtless a false reading.

2. Present Subjunctive.

686. The stem is made, as usual, by adding **a** to the strong present-stem: thus, **yunája, ruṇádha.** Below are given as if made from √yuj all the forms for which examples have been noted as actually occurring in the older language.

	active.			middle.		
	s.	d.	p.	s.	d.	p.
1	**yunájāni**	**yunájāva**	**yunájāma**	**yunajāi**		**yunájāmahāi**
2	**yunájas**					**yunajādhvāi**
3	**yunájat**	**yunájatas**	**yunájan**	**yunájate**		

687. The RV. has once **añjatas,** which is anomalous as being made from the weak tense-stem. Forms with double mode-sign are met with: thus, **tṛṇáhān** (AV.), **rādhnávāt** and **yunajān** (ÇB.); and the only quotable example of 3d du. act. (besides **añjatás**) is **hinásātas** (ÇB.). ÇB. has also **hinasāvas** as 1st du. act.: an elsewhere unexampled form.

3. Present Optative.

688. The optative is made, as elsewhere, by adding the compounded mode-endings to the weak form of present-stem. Thus:

	active.			middle.		
	s.	d.	p.	s.	d.	p.
1	युञ्ज्याम् **yuñjyā́m** etc.	युञ्ज्याव **yuñjyā́va** etc.	युञ्ज्याम **yuñjyā́ma** etc.	युञ्जीय **yuñjīyá** etc.	युञ्जीवहि **yuñjīváhi** etc.	युञ्जीमहि **yuñjīmáhi** etc.

a. AB. has once the anomalous 1st sing. act. **vṛñjīyam.** And forms like **bhuñjīyām -yāt, yuñjīyāt,** are here and there met with in the epics (**bhuñjīyātām** once in GGS.). MBh., too, has once **bhuñjītam.**

4. Present Imperative.

689. In this class as the roots all end in consonants) the ending of the 2d sing. act. is always धि **dhi.**

	active.			middle.		
	s.	d.	p.	s.	d.	p.
1	युनजानि **yunájāni**	युनजाव **yunájāva**	युनजाम **yunájāma**	युनजै **yunájāi**	युनजावहै **yunájāvahāi**	युनजामहै **yunájāmahāi**
2	युङ्ग्धि **yuñgdhí**	युङ्क्तम् **yuñktám**	युङ्क्त **yuñktá**	युङ्क्ष्व **yuñkṣvá**	युञ्जाथाम् **yuñjā́thām**	युङ्ग्ध्वम् **yuñgdhvám**
3	युनक्तु **yunáktu**	युङ्क्ताम् **yuñktā́m**	युञ्जन्तु **yuñjántu**	युङ्क्ताम् **yuñktā́m**	युञ्जाताम् **yuñjā́tām**	युञ्जताम् **yuñjátām**

690. There is no occurrence, so far as noted, of the ending **tāt** in verbs of this class. The Veda has, as usual, sometimes strong forms, and sometimes the ending **tana,** in the 2d pl. act.: thus, **unátta, yunákta, anaktana, pinaṣṭana.**

5. Present Participle.

691. The participles are made in this class as in the preceding ones: thus, act. युञ्जत् **yuñjánt** (fem. युञ्जती **yuñjatī́**); mid. युञ्जान **yuñjāná** (but RV. has **índhāna**).

6. Imperfect.

692. The example of the regular inflection of this tense needs no introduction:

	active. s.	d.	p.	middle. s.	d.	p.
1	अयुनजम् **áyunajam**	अयुञ्ज्व **áyuñjva**	अयुञ्ज्म **áyuñjma**	अयुञ्जि **áyuñji**	अयुञ्ज्वहि **áyuñjvahi**	अयुञ्ज्महि **áyuñjmahi**
2	अयुनक् **áyunak**	अयुङ्क्तम् **áyuñktam**	अयुङ्क्त **áyuñkta**	अयुङ्क्थास् **áyuñkthās**	अयुञ्जाथाम् **áyuñjāthām**	अयुङ्ग्ध्वम् **áyuñgdhvam**
3	अयुनक् **áyunak**	अयुङ्क्ताम् **áyuñktām**	अयुञ्जन् **áyuñjan**	अयुङ्क्त **áyuñkta**	अयुञ्जाताम् **áyuñjātām**	अयुञ्जत **áyuñjata**

a. The endings **s** and **t** are necessarily lost in the nasal class throughout in 2d and 3d sing. act., unless saved at the expense of the final radical consonant: which is a case of very rare occurrence (the only quotable examples were given at **555 a**).

693. The Veda shows no irregularities in this tense. Occurrences of augmentless forms are found, especially in 2d and 3d sing. act., showing an accent like that of the present: for example, **bhinát, pṛṇák, vṛṇák, piṇák, riṇák.**

a. The 1st sing. act. **atṛṇam** and **acchinam** (for **atṛṇadam** and **acchinadam**) were noted above, at **555 a.**

694. The roots of this class number about thirty, more than half of them being found only in the earlier language; no new ones make their first appearance later. Three of them, **añj** and **bhañj** and **hiṅs,** carry their nasal also into other tense-systems than the present. Two, **ṛdh** and **ubh,** make present-systems also of other classes having a nasal in the class-sign: thus, **ṛdhnoti** (**nu-class**) and **ubhnāti** (**nā-class**).

a. Many of the roots make forms from secondary a-stems: thus, from **añja, unda, umbhá, chinda, tṛṅhá, piṅṣa, pṛñcá, bhuñja, rundha, çiṅṣá**, etc.

Irregularities of the Nasal Class.

695. The root **tṛh** combines **tṛṇah** with **ti, tu**, etc. into **tṛṇeḍhi, tṛṇéḍhu**; and, according to the grammarians, has also such forms as **tṛṇehmi**: see above, **224 b.**

696. The root **hiṅs** (by origin apparently a desiderative from √**han**) accents irregularly the root-syllable in the weak forms: thus, **híṅsanti, híṅste, híṅsāna** (but **hinásat** etc. and **hiṅsyā́t** ÇB.).

IV. Nu- and u-classes (fifth and eighth, su- and tan-classes).

697. A. The present-stem of the nu-class is made by adding to the root the syllable नु **nu**, which then in the strong forms receives the accent, and is strengthened to नो **nó**.

B. The few roots of the u-class (about half-a-dozen) end in न् **n**, with the exception of the later irregular कृ **kṛ** (or **kar**) — for which, see below, **714**. The two classes, then, are closely correspondent in form; and they are wholly accordant in inflection.

a. The **u** of either class-sign is allowed to be dropped before **v** and **m** of the 1st du. and 1st pl. endings, except when the root (nu-class) ends in a consonant; and the **u** before a vowel-ending becomes **v** or **uv**, according as it is preceded by one or by two consonants (**129 a**).

1. Present Indicative.

698. Examples of inflection: A. nu-class; root सु **su** *press out:* strong form of stem, सुनो **sunó**; weak form, सुनु **sunu**.

	active.			middle.		
	s.	d.	p.	s.	d.	p.
1	सुनोमि **sunómi**	सुनुवस् **sunuvás**	सुनुमस् **sunumás**	सुन्वे **sunvé**	सुनुवहे **sunuváhe**	सुनुमहे **sunumáhe**
2	सुनोषि **sunóṣi**	सुनुथस् **sunuthás**	सुनुथ **sunuthá**	सुनुषे **sunuṣé**	सुन्वाथे **sunvā́the**	सुनुध्वे **sunudhvé**

3	सुनोति	सुनुतस्	सुन्वन्ति	सुनुते	सुन्वाते	सुन्वते
	sunóti	**sunutás**	**sunvánti**	**sunuté**	**sunvāte**	**sunváte**

a. The forms **sunvás, sunmás, sunváhe, sunmáhe** are alternative with those given here for 1st du. and pl., and in practice are more common. From √**āp**, however (for example), only the forms with **u** can occur: thus, **āpnuvás, āpnumáhe**; and also only **āpnuvánti, āpnuvé, āpnuváte.**

B. u-class; root तन् **tan** *stretch:* strong form of stem, तनो **tanó**; weak, तनु **tanu.**

1	तनोमि	तन्वस्	तन्मस्	तन्वे	तन्वहे	तन्महे
	tanómi	**tanvás**	**tanmás**	**tanvé**	**tanváhe**	**tanmáhe**
	etc.	etc.	etc.	etc.	etc.	etc.

b. The inflection is so precisely like that given above that it is not worth writing out in full. The abbreviated forms in 1st du. and pl. are presented here, instead of the fuller, which rarely occur (as no double consonant ever precedes).

699. a. In the older language, no strong 2d persons du. or pl., and no **thana**-endings, chance to occur (but they are numerous in the impv. and impf.: see below). The RV. has several cases of the irregular accent in 3d pl. mid.: thus, **kṛṇvaté, tanvaté, manvaté, vṛṇvaté, spṛṇvaté.**

b. In RV. occur also several 3d pl. mid. in **ire** from present-stems of this class: thus, **invire, ṛṇvire, pinvire, çṛṇviré, sunviré, hinviré.** Of these, **pinvire** and **hinviré** might be perfects without reduplication from the secondary roots **pinv** and **hinv** (below, **716**). The 2d sing. mid. (with passive value) **çṛṇviṣé** (RV.) is of anomalous and questionable character.

2. Present Subjunctive.

700. The subjunctive mode-stem is made in the usual manner, by adding **a** to the gunated and accented class-sign: thus, **sunáva, tanáva.** In the following scheme are given all the forms of which examples have been met with in actual use in the older language from either division of the class; some of them are quite numerously represented there.

active.			middle.		
s.	d.	p.	s.	d.	p.
sunávāni	**sunávāva**	**sunávāma**	**sunávāi**	**sunávāvahāi**	**sunávāmahāi**
sunávas		**sunávatha**	**sunávase**	**sunávāithe**	
sunávat		**sunávan**	{**sunávate** / **sunávātāi**}		**sunávanta**

701. Of the briefer 1st sing. act., RV. has **kṛṇavā** and **hinavā**. Forms with double mode-sign occur (not in RV.): thus, **kṛṇávāt** and **karavāt** (AV.); **açnavātha** (K.), **kṛṇavātha** (VS.; but **-vatha** in Kāṇva-text), **karavātha** (ÇB.). On the other hand, **açnavatāi** is found once (in TS.). Forms like **āpnuvāni, ardhnúvat, açnuvat,** met with now and then in the older texts, are doubtless to be regarded as false readings. RV. has in a single passage **kṛṇvāíte** (instead of **kṛṇávāite**); the only form in **āithe** is **açnávāithe.**

3. Present Optative.

702. The combined endings (**566**) are added, as usual, to the weak tense-stem: thus,

	active.			middle.		
	s.	d.	p.	s.	d.	p.
1	सुनुयाम् **sunuyā́m**	सुनुयाव **sunuyā́va**	सुनुयाम **sunuyā́ma**	सुन्वीय **sunvīyá**	सुन्वीवहि **sunvīváhi**	सुन्वीमहि **sunvīmáhi**
	etc.	etc.	etc.	etc.	etc.	etc.

a. From √**āp**, the middle optative would be **āpnuvīyá** — and so in other like cases.

4. Present Imperative.

703. The inflection of the imperative is in general like that in the preceding classes. As regards the 2d sing. act., the rule of the later language is that the ending हि **hi** is taken whenever the root itself ends in a consonant; otherwise, the tense- (or mode-) stem stands by itself as 2d person (for the earlier usage, see below, **704**). An example of inflection is:

	active.			middle.		
	s.	d.	p.	s.	d.	p.
1	सुनवानि **sunávāni**	सुनवाव **sunávāva**	सुनवाम **sunávāma**	सुनवै **sunávāi**	सुनवावहै **sunávāvahāi**	सुनवामहै **sunávāmahāi**
2	सुनु **sunú**	सुनुतम् **sunutám**	सुनुत **sunutá**	सुनुष्व **sunuṣvá**	सुन्वाथाम् **sunvā́thām**	सुनुध्वम् **sunudhvám**
3	सुनोतु **sunótu**	सुनुताम् **sunutā́m**	सुन्वन्तु **sunvántu**	सुनुताम् **sunutā́m**	सुन्वाताम् **sunvā́tām**	सुन्वताम् **sunvátām**

a. From √**āp**, the 2d sing. act. would be **āpnuhí**; from √**aç**, **açnuhí**; from √**dhṛṣ**, **dhṛṣṇuhí**; and so on. From √**āp**, too, would be made **āpnuvántu, āpnuváthām, āpnuvátām, āpnuvátām.**

704. In the earliest language, the rule as to the omission of **hi** after a root with final vowel does not hold good: in RV., such forms as **inuhi, kṛṇuhí, cinuhí, dhūnuhi, çṛṇuhí, spṛṇuhi, hinuhi,** and **tanuhi, sanuhi,** are nearly thrice as frequent in use as **inú, çṛṇu, sunú, tanu,** and their like; in AV., however, they are only one sixth as frequent; and in the Brāhmaṇas they appear only sporadically: even **çṛṇudhí** (with **dhi**) occurs several times in RV. RV. has the 1st sing. act. **hinavā.** The ending **tāt** is found in **kṛṇutāt** and **hinutāt,** and **kurutāt.** The strong stem-form is found in 2d du. act. in **hinotam** and **kṛṇotam**; and in 2d pl. act. in **kṛṇóta** and **kṛṇótana, çṛṇóta** and **çṛṇotana, sunóta** and **sunótana, hinóta** and **hinotana,** and **tanota, karóta.** The ending **tana** occurs only in the forms just quoted.

5. Present Participle.

705. The endings अन्त् **ánt** and आन **āná** are added to the weak form of tense stem: thus, from √सु **su** come act. सुन्वन्त् **sunvánt** (fem. सुन्वती **sunvatī́**), mid. सुन्वान **sunvāná**; from √तन् **tan,** तन्वन्त् **tanvánt** (fem. तन्वती **tanvatī́**), तन्वान **tanvāná**. From √आप् **āp**, they are आप्नुवन्त् **āpnuvánt** and आप्नुवान **āpnuvāná.**

6. Imperfect.

706. The combination of augmented stem and endings is according to the rules already stated: thus,

	active. s.	d.	p.	middle. s.	d.	p.
1	असुनवम् **ásunavam**	असुनुव **ásunuva**	असुनुम **ásunuma**	असुन्वि **ásunvi**	असुनुवहि **ásunuvahi**	असुनुमहि **ásunumahi**
2	असुनोस् **ásunos**	असुनुतम् **ásunutam**	असुनुत **ásunuta**	असुनुथास् **ásunuthās**	असुन्वाथाम् **ásunvāthām**	असुनुध्वम् **ásunudhvam**
3	असुनोत् **ásunot**	असुनुताम् **ásunutām**	असुन्वन् **ásunvan**	असुनुत **ásunuta**	असुन्वाताम् **ásunvātām**	असुन्वत **ásunvata**

a. Here, as elsewhere, the briefer forms **ásunva, ásunma, ásunvahi, ásunmahi** are allowed, and more usual, except from roots with final consonant, as **dhṛṣ**: which makes, for example, always **ádhṛṣṇuma** etc., and also **ádhṛṣṇuvan, ádhṛṣṇuvi, ádhṛṣṇuvāthām, ádhṛṣṇuvātām, ádhṛṣṇuvata.**

707. Strong stem-forms and **tana**-ending are found only in RV., in **akṛṇota, akṛṇotana.** Augmentless forms with accent are **minván, ṛṇutá.**

708. About fifty roots make, either exclusively or in part, their present-forms after the manner of the **nu**-class: half of them do so only in the older language; three or four, only in the later.

a. As to transfers to the **a**-conjugation, see below, **716**.

709. The roots of the other division, or of the **u**-class, are extremely few, not exceeding eight, even including **tṛ** on account of **tarutė** RV., and **han** on account of the occurrence of **hanomi** once in a Sūtra (PGS. i. 3.27). BR. refer the stem **inu** to **in** of the **u**-class instead of **i** of the **nu**-class.

Irregularities of the nu and u-classes.

710. The root **tṛp** *be pleased* is said by the grammarians to retain the **n** of its class-sign unlingualized in the later language — where, however, forms of conjugation of this class are very rare; while in the Veda the regular change is made: thus, **tṛpṇu.**

711. The root **çru** *hear* is contracted to **çṛ** before the class-sign, forming **çṛṇó** and **çṛṇu** as stem. Its forms **çṛṇviṣé** and **çṛṇviré** have been noted above (**699**b).

712. The root **dhū** *shake* in the later language (and rarely in B. and S.) shortens its vowel, making the stem-forms **dhunó** and **dhunu** (earlier **dhūnó, dhūnu**).

713. The so-called root **ūrṇu**, treated by the native grammarians as dissyllabic and belonging to the root-class (I.), is properly a present-stem of this class, with anomalous contraction, from the root **vṛ** (or **var**). In the Veda, it has no forms which are not regularly made according to the **nu**-class; but in the Brāhmaṇa language are found sometimes such forms as **ūrṇāuti,** as if from an **u**-root of the root class (**626**); and the grammarians make for it a perfect, aorist, future, etc. Its 2d sing. impv.. act. is **ūrṇu** or **ūrṇuhi**; its impf., **áurṇos, āurṇot**; its opt. mid., **ūrṇuvīta** (K.) or **ūrṇvītá** (TS.).

714. The extremely common root कृ **kṛ** (or **kar**) *make* is in the later language inflected in the present-system exclusively according to the **u**-class (being the only root of that class not ending in न् **n**). It has the irregularity that in the strong form of stem it (as well as the class-sign) has the **guṇa**-strengthening, and that in the weak form it is changed to **kur**, so that the two forms of stem are करो **karó** and कुरु **kuru.** The class-sign उ **u** is always dropped before व् **v** and म् **m** of the 1st du. and pl., and also before य् **y** of the opt. act. Thus:

1. Present Indicative.

	active. s.	d.	p.	middle. s.	d.	p.
1	करोमि **karómi**	कुर्वस् **kurvás**	कुर्मस् **kurmás**	कुर्वे **kurvé**	कुर्वहे **kurváhe**	कुर्महे **kurmáhe**
2	करोषि **karóṣi**	कुरुथस् **kuruthás**	कुरुथ **kuruthá**	कुरुषे **kuruṣé**	कुर्वाथे **kurvā́the**	कुरुध्वे **kurudhvé**
3	करोति **karóti**	कुरुतस् **kurutás**	कुर्वन्ति **kurvánti**	कुरुते **kuruté**	कुर्वाते **kurvā́te**	कुर्वते **kurváte**

2. Present Optative.

	s.	d.	p.	s.	d.	p.
1	कुर्याम् **kuryā́m**	कुर्याव **kuryā́va**	कुर्याम **kuryā́ma**	कुर्वीय **kurvīyá**	कुर्वीवहि **kurvīváhi**	कुर्वीमहि **kurvīmáhi**
	etc.	etc.	etc.	etc.	etc.	etc.

3. Present Imperative.

	s.	d.	p.	s.	d.	p.
1	करवाणि **karávāṇi**	करवाव **karávāva**	करवाम **karávāma**	करवै **karávāi**	करवावहै **karávāvahāi**	करवामहै **karávāmahāi**
2	कुरु **kurú**	कुरुतम् **kurutám**	कुरुत **kurutá**	कुरुष्व **kuruṣvá**	कुर्वाथाम् **kurvā́thām**	कुरुध्वम् **kurudhvám**
3	करोतु **karótu**	कुरुताम् **kurutā́m**	कुर्वन्तु **kurvántu**	कुरुताम् **kurutā́m**	कुर्वाताम् **kurvā́tām**	कुर्वताम् **kurvátām**

4. Present Participle.

कुर्वन्त् **kurvánt** (fem. कुर्वती **kurvatī́**) कुर्वाण **kurvāṇá**

5. Imperfect.

	s.	d.	p.	s.	d.	p.
1	अकरवम् **ákaravam**	अकुर्व **ákurva**	अकुर्म **ákurma**	अकुर्वि **ákurvi**	अकुर्वहि **ákurvahi**	अकुर्महि **ákurmahi**
2	अकरोस् **ákaros**	अकुरुतम् **ákurutam**	अकुरुत **ákuruta**	अकुरुथास् **ákuruthās**	अकुर्वाथाम् **ákurvāthām**	अकुरुध्वम् **ákurudhvam**
3	अकरोत् **ákarot**	अकुरुताम् **ákurutām**	अकुर्वन् **ákurvan**	अकुरुत **ákuruta**	अकुर्वाताम् **ákurvātām**	अकुर्वत **ákurvata**

715. In RV., this root is regularly inflected in the present-system according to the **nu**-class, making the stem-forms **kṛṇó** and **kṛṇu**; the only exceptions are **kurmas** once and **kuru** twice (all in the tenth book); in AV., the **nu**-forms are still more than six times as frequent as the **u**-forms (nearly half of which, moreover, are in prose passages); but in the Brāhmaṇa language and later, the **u**-forms are used to the exclusion of the others.

a. As 1st sing. pres. act. is found **kurmi** in the epos.

b. What irregular forms from **kṛ** as a verb of the **nu**-class occur in the older language have been already noticed above.

c. The isolated form **tarutė́**, from √**tṛ**, shows an apparent analogy with these **u**-forms from **kṛ**.

716. A few verbs belonging originally to these classes have been shifted, in part or altogether, to the **a**-class, their proper class-sign having been stereotyped as a part of the root.

a. Thus, in RV. we find forms both from the stem **inu** (√**i** or **in**), and also from **inva**, representing a derivative quasi-root **inv** (and these latter alone occur in AV.). So likewise forms from a stem **ṛṇva** beside those from **ṛṇu** (√**ṛ**); and from **hinva** beside those from **hinu** (√**hi**). The so-called roots **jinv** and **pinv** are doubtless of the same origin, although no forms from the stem **pinu** are met with at any period — unless **pinvire** (above, **699b**) be so regarded; and AV. has the participle **pinvánt**, f. **pinvatī**. The grammarians set up a root **dhinv**, but only forms from **dhi** (stem **dhinu**) appear to occur in the present-system (the aorist **adhinvīt** is found in PB.).

b. Occasional **a**-forms are met with also from other roots: thus, **cinvata** etc., **dunvasva**.

V. Nā-class (ninth or krī-class).

717. The class-sign of this class is in the strong forms the syllable ना **nā́**, accented, which is added to the root; in the weak forms, or where the accent falls upon the ending, it is नी **nī**; but before the initial vowel of an ending the ई **ī** of नी **nī** disappears altogether.

1. Present Indicative.

718. Example of inflection: root क्री **krī** *buy*: strong form of stem, क्रीणा **krīṇā́**; weak form, क्रीणी **krīṇī** (before a vowel, क्रीण् **krīṇ**).

	active.			middle.		
	s.	d.	p.	s.	d.	p.
1	क्रीणामि krīṇā́mi	क्रीणीवस् krīṇīvás	क्रीणीमस् krīṇīmás	क्रीणे krīṇé	क्रीणीवहे krīṇīváhe	क्रीणीमहे krīṇīmáhe
2	क्रीणासि krīṇā́si	क्रीणीथस् krīṇīthás	क्रीणीथ krīṇīthá	क्रीणिषे krīṇiṣé	क्रीणाथे krīṇā́the	क्रीणीध्वे krīṇīdhvé
3	क्रीणाति krīṇā́ti	क्रीणीतस् krīṇītás	क्रीणन्ति krīṇánti	क्रीणीते krīṇīté	क्रीणाते krīṇā́te	क्रीणते krīṇáte

719. In the Veda, the 3d sing. mid. has the same form with the 1st in gr̥ṇé; the peculiar accent of 3d pl. mid. is seen in punaté and riṇaté; and vr̥ṇīmahé (beside vr̥ṇīmáhe) occurs once in RV.

2. Present Subjunctive.

720. The subjunctive forms which have been found exemplified in Veda and Brāhmaṇa are given below. The subjunctive mode-stem is, of course, indistinguishable in form from the strong tense-stem. And the 2d and 3d sing. act. (with secondary endings) are indistinguishable from augmentless imperfects.

	active.			middle.		
	s.	d.	p.	s.	d.	p.
1	krīṇā́ni		krīṇā́ma	krīṇāí	krīṇā́vahāi	krīṇā́mahāi
2	krīṇā́s	krīṇā́tha	krīṇā́sāi			
3	krīṇā́t	krīṇā́n	krīṇā́tāi			krīṇāntāi

3. Present Optative.

721. This mode is formed and inflected with entire regularity; owing to the fusion of tense-sign and mode-sign in the middle, some of its persons are indistinguishable from augmentless imperfects. Its first persons are as follows:

	active.			middle.		
	s.	d.	p.	s.	d.	p.
1	क्रीणीयाम् krīṇīyā́m etc.	क्रीणीयाव krīṇīyā́va etc.	क्रीणीयाम krīṇīyā́ma etc.	क्रीणीय krīṇīyá etc.	क्रीणीवहि krīṇīváhi etc.	क्रीणीमहि krīṇīmáhi etc.

4. Present Imperative.

722. The ending in 2d sing. act., as being always preceded by a vowel, is हि hi (never धि dhi); and there are no examples of an omission of it. But this person is forbidden

to be formed in the classical language from roots ending in a consonant; for both class-sign and ending is substituted the peculiar ending आन **āná**.

	active.			middle.		
	s.	d.	p.	s.	d.	p.
1	क्रीणानि **krīṇā́ni**	क्रीणाव **krīṇā́va**	क्रीणाम **krīṇā́ma**	क्रीणै **krīṇāí**	क्रीणावहै **krīṇā́vahāi**	क्रीणामहै **krīṇā́mahāi**
2	क्रीणीहि **krīṇīhí**	क्रीणीतम् **krīṇītám**	क्रीणीत **krīṇītá**	क्रीणीष्व **krīṇīṣvá**	क्रीणाथाम् **krīṇā́thām**	क्रीणीध्वम् **krīṇīdhvám**
3	क्रीणातु **krīṇā́tu**	क्रीणीताम् **krīṇītā́m**	क्रीणन्तु **krīṇántu**	क्रीणीताम् **krīṇītā́m**	क्रीणाताम् **krīṇā́tām**	क्रीणताम् **krīṇátām**

a. Examples of the ending **āná** in 2d sing. act. are **açāna, gṛhāṇá, badhāná, stabhāná.**

723. The ending **āna** is known also to the earliest language; of the examples just given, all are found in AV., and the first two in RV.; others are **iṣāṇa, muṣāṇa, skabhāna.** But AV. has also **gṛbhṇīhi** (also AB.), and even **gṛhṇāhi,** with strong stem; BhP. has **badhnīhi.** Strong stems are further found in **gṛṇāhi** and **stṛṇāhi** (TS.), **pṛṇāhi** (TB.), and **çrīṇāhi** (Āpast.), and, with anomalous accent, **punāhí** and **çṛṇāhí** (SV.); and, in 2d pl. act., in **punā́ta** (RV.). The ending **tāt** of 2d sing. act. occurs in **gṛhṇītāt, jānītā́t, punītāt.** The ending **tana** is found in **punītána, pṛṇītana, çrīṇītana.**

5. Present Participle.

724. The participles are regularly formed: thus, for example, act. क्रीणन्त् **krīṇánt** (fem. क्रीणती **krīṇatī́**); mid. क्रीणान **krīṇāná.**

6. Imperfect.

725. There is nothing special to be noted as to the inflection of this tense: an example is —

	active.			middle.		
	s.	d.	p.	s.	d.	p.
1	अक्रीणाम् **ákrīṇām**	अक्रीणीव **ákrīṇīva**	अक्रीणीम **ákrīṇīma**	अक्रीणि **ákrīṇi**	अक्रीणीवहि **ákrīṇīvahi**	अक्रीणीमहि **ákrīṇīmahi**
2	अक्रीणास् **ákrīṇās**	अक्रीणीतम् **ákrīṇītam**	अक्रीणीत **ákrīṇīta**	अक्रीणीथास् **ákrīṇīthās**	अक्रीणाथाम् **ákrīṇāthām**	अक्रीणीध्वम् **ákrīṇīdhvam**
3	अक्रीणात् **ákrīṇāt**	अक्रीणीताम् **ákrīṇītām**	अक्रीणन् **ákrīṇan**	अक्रीणीत **ákrīṇīta**	अक्रीणाताम् **ákrīṇātām**	अक्रीणत **ákrīṇata**

726. It has been pointed out above that augmentless persons of this tense are in part indistinguishable in form from subjunctive and optative persons. Such as certainly belong here are (in V.) **kṣiṇām; açnan, riṇán; gṛbhṇata, vṛṇata.** The AV. has once **minīt** instead of **mināt.** MBh. has **açnīs** after **mā.**

a. AB. has the false form **ajānīmas,** and in AA. occurs **avṛṇīta** as 3d plural.

727. The roots which form their present-systems, wholly or in part, after the manner of this class, are over fifty in number: but, for about three fifths of them, the forms are quotable only from the older language, and for half-a-dozen they make their first appearance later; for less than twenty are they in use through the whole life of the language, from the Veda down.

a. As to secondary **a**-stems, see **731.**

Irregularities of the nā-class.

728. a. The roots ending in **ū** shorten that vowel before the class-sign: thus, from √**pū, punā́ti** and **punīté;** in like manner also **jū, dhū, lū.**

b. The root **vlī** (B.S.) forms either **vlīnā** or **vlinā.**

729. The root **grabh** or **grah** (the former Vedic) is weakened to **gṛbh** or **gṛh.**

a. As the perfect also in weak forms has **gṛbh** or **gṛh,** it is not easy to see why the grammarians should not have written **ṛ** instead of **ra** in the root.

730. a. A few of the roots have a more or less persistent nasal in forms outside the present-system; such are without nasal before the class-sign: thus, **grath** or **granth, badh** or **bandh, math** or **manth, skabh** or **skambh, stabh** or **stambh.**

b. The root **jñā** also loses its nasal before the class-sign: thus, **jānā́ti, jānīté.**

731. Not rarely, forms showing a transfer to the **a**-conjugation are met with: thus, even in RV., **minati, minat, aminanta,** from √**mi;** in AV., **çṛṇa** from √**çṛ;** later, **gṛhṇa, jāna, prīṇa, mathna,** etc. And from roots **pṛ** and **mṛ** are formed the stems **pṛṇá** and **mṛṇá,** which are inflected after the manner of the **á**-class, as if from roots **pṛṇ** and **mṛṇ.**

732. In the Veda, an apparently denominative inflection of a stem in **āyá** is not infrequent beside the conjugation of roots of this class: thus, **gṛbhāyá, mathāyáti, açrathāyas, skabhāyáta, astabhāyat, pruṣāyánte, muṣāyát,** and so on. See below, **1066** b.

Second or a-Conjugation.

733. We come now to the classes which compose the Second or a-Conjugation. These are more markedly similar in their mode of inflection than the preceding classes; their common characteristics, already stated, may be here repeated in summary. They are: 1. A final **a** in the present-stem; 2. a constant accent, not changing between stem and ending; 3. a briefer form of the optative mode-sign in the active, namely **ī** instead of **yā** (combining in both voices alike with **a** to **e**); 4. the absence of any ending (except when **tāt** is used) in 2d sing. impv. act.; 5. the conversion of initial **ā** of the 2d and 3d du. mid. endings to **e**; 6. the use of the full endings **ante, anta, antām** in 3d pl. mid. forms; 7. the invariable use of **an** (not **us**) in 3d pl. impf. act.; 8. and the use of **māna** instead of **āna** as ending of the mid. pple. Moreover, 9. the stem-final **a** becomes **ā** before **m** and **v** of 1st personal endings — but not before **am** of 1st sing. impf.: here, as before the 3d pl. endings, the stem-final is lost, and the short **a** of the ending remains (or the contrary): thus, **bhávanti** (**bháva + anti**), **bhávante** (**bháva + ánte**), **ábhavam** (**ábhava + am**).

a. All these characteristics belong not to the inflection of the a-present-systems alone, but also to that of the a-, reduplicated, and sa-aorists, the s-future, and the desiderative, causative, and denominative present-systems. That is to say, wherever in conjugation an a-stem is found, it is inflected in the same manner.

VI. A-class (first, bhū-class).

734. The present-stem of this class is made by adding अ **a** to the root, which has the accent, and, when that is possible (**235, 240**), is strengthened to **guṇa**. Thus, भव **bháva** from √भू **bhū**; जय **jáya** from √जि **ji**; बोध **bódha** from √बुध् **budh**; सर्प **sárpa** from √सृप् **sṛp**; — but वद **váda** from √वद् **vad**; क्रीड **krīḍa** from √क्रीड् **krīḍ**.

1. Present Indicative.

735. The endings and the rules for their combination with the stem have been already fully given, for this and the other parts of the present-system; and it only remains to illustrate them by examples.

a. Example of inflection root भू **bhū** *be;* stem भव **bháva** (bho + a: 131).

	active. s.	d.	p.	middle. s.	d.	p.
1	भवामि **bhávāmi**	भवावस् **bhávāvas**	भवामस् **bhávāmas**	भवे **bháve**	भवावहे **bhávāvahe**	भवामहे **bhávāmahe**
2	भवसि **bhávasi**	भवथस् **bhávathas**	भवथ **bhávatha**	भवसे **bhávase**	भवेथे **bhávethe**	भवध्वे **bhávadhve**
3	भवति **bhávati**	भवतस् **bhávatas**	भवन्ति **bhávanti**	भवते **bhávate**	भवेते **bhávete**	भवन्ते **bhávante**

b. The V. has but a single example of the **thana**-ending, namely **vádathana** (and no other in any class of this conjugation). The 1st pl. mid. **manāmahé** (RV., once) is probably an error. RV. has **çóbhe** once as 3d singular.

2. Present Subjunctive.

736. The mode-stem is **bhávā** (**bháva+a**). Subjunctive forms of this conjugation are very numerous in the older language; the following scheme instances all that have been found to occur.

	active. s.	d.	p.	middle. s.	d.	p.
1	**bhávāni**	**bhávāva**	**bhávāma**	**bhávāi**	**bhávāvahāi**	**bhávāmahāi**
2	**bhávāsi** / **bhávās**	**bhávāthas**	**bhávātha**	**bhávāse** / **bhávāsāi**		**bhávādhvāi**
3	**bhávāti** / **bhávāt**	**bhávātas**	**bhávān**	**bhávāte** / **bhávātāi**	**bhávāite**	**bhávanta** / **bhávāntāi**

737. The 2d du. mid (**bhávāithe**) does not chance to occur in this class; and **yátāite** is the only example of the 3d person. No such pl. mid. forms as **bhávādhve, bhávānte** are made from any class with stem-final **a**; such as **bhávanta** (which are very common) are, of course, properly augmentless imperfects. The Brāhmaṇas (especially ÇB.) prefer the 2d sing. act. in **āsi** and the 3d in **āt.** AB. has the 3d sing. mid. **haratāi;** and a 3d pl. in **antāi** (**vartantāi** KB.) has been noted once. RV. has examples, **arcā** and **madā,** of the briefer 1st. sing. act.

3. Present Optative.

738. The scheme of optative endings as combined with the final of an **a**-stem was given in full above (**566**).

	active. s.	d.	p.	middle. s.	d.	p.
1	भवेयम् **bháveyam**	भवेव **bháveva**	भवेम **bhávema**	भवेय **bháveya**	भवेवहि **bhávevahi**	भवेमहि **bhávemahi**
2	भवेस् **bháves**	भवेतम् **bhávetam**	भवेत **bháveta**	भवेथास् **bhávethās**	भवेयाथाम् **bháveyāthām**	भवेधम् **bhávedhvam**
3	भवेत् **bhávet**	भवेताम् **bhávetām**	भवेयुस् **bháveyus**	भवेत **bháveta**	भवेयाताम् **bháveyātām**	भवेरन् **bháveran**

a. The RV. has once the 3d pl. mid. **bharerata** (for one other example, see **752b**). AV. has **udeyam** from √**vad**.

b. A few instances are met with of middle 3d persons from **a**-stems in **īta** and (very rarely) **īran**, instead of **eta** and **eran**. For convenience, they may be put together here (excepting the more numerous causative forms, for which see **1043c**); they are (so far as noted) these: **nayīta** S. and later, **çaṅsīta** S., **çrayīta** S.; **dhayīta** S., **dhyāyīta** U., **hvayīta** AB. S. and **hvayīran** S., **dhmāyīta** U. An active form **çaṅsīyāt** C. is isolated and anomalous.

4. Present Imperative.

739. An example of the imperative inflection is:

	active. s.	d.	p.	middle. s.	d.	p.
1	भवानि **bhávāni**	भवाव **bhávāva**	भवाम **bhávāma**	भवै **bhávāi**	भवावहै **bhávāvahāi**	भवामहै **bhávāmahāi**
2	भव **bháva**	भवतम् **bhávatam**	भवत **bhávata**	भवस्व **bhávasva**	भवेथाम् **bhávethām**	भवध्वम् **bhávadhvam**
3	भवतु **bhávatu**	भवताम् **bhávatām**	भवन्तु **bhávantu**	भवताम् **bhávatām**	भवेताम् **bhávetām**	भवन्ताम् **bhávantām**

740. The ending **tana** in 2d pl. act. is as rare in this whole conjugation as is **thana** in the present: the V. affords only **bhajatana** in the **a**-class (and **nahyatana** in the **ya**-class: **760c**). The ending **tāt** of 2d sing. act., on the other hand, is not rare; the RV. has **avatāt, oṣatāt, dahatāt, bhavatāt, yacchatāt, yācatāt, rákṣatāt, vahatāt**; to which AV. adds **jinvatāt, dhāvatāt**; and the Brāhmaṇas bring other examples. MS. has twice **svadātu** (parallel texts both times **svadāti**): compare similar cases in the **á**-class: **752c**.

5. Present Participle.

741. The endings **अन्त् ant** and **मान māna** are added to the present-stem, with loss, before the former, of the final stem-vowel: thus, act. **भवन्त् bhávant** (fem. **भवन्ती bhávantī**); mid. **भवमान bhávamāna.**

a. A small number of middle participles appear to be made from stems of this class (as of other a-classes: see **752e, 1043f**) by the suffix **āna** instead of **māna**: thus, **namāna, pacāna, çikṣāṇa, svajāna, hvayāna** (all epic), **majjāna** and **kaṣāṇa** (later); and there are Vedic examples (as **cyávāna, prathāná, yátāna** or **yatāná, çúmbhāna,** all RV.) of which the character, whether present or aorist, is doubtful: compare **840, 852.**

6. Imperfect.

742. An example of the imperfect inflection is:

active. s.	d.	p.	middle. s.	d.	p.
अभवम् ábhavam	अभवाव ábhavāva	अभवाम ábhavāma	अभवे ábhave	अभवावहि ábhavāvahi	अभवामहि ábhavāmahi
अभवस् ábhavas	अभवतम् ábhavatam	अभवत ábhavata	अभवथास् ábhavathās	अभवेथाम् ábhavethām	अभवध्वम् ábhavadhvam
अभवत् ábhavat	अभवताम् ábhavatām	अभवन् ábhavan	अभवत ábhavata	अभवेताम् ábhavetām	अभवन्त ábhavanta

743. No forms in **tana** are made in this tense from any a-class. Examples of augmentless forms (which are not uncommon) are: **cyávam, ávas, dáhas, bódhat, bhárat, cáran, náçan; bādhathās, várdhata, çócanta.** The subjunctively used forms of 2d and 3d sing. act. are more frequent than those of either of the proper subjunctive persons.

744. A far larger number of roots form their present-system according to the a-class than according to any of the other classes: in the RV., they are about two hundred and forty (nearly two fifths of the whole body of roots); in the AV., about two hundred (nearly the same proportion); for the whole language, the proportion is still larger, or nearly one half the whole number of present-stems: namely, over two hundred in both earlier and later language, one hundred and seventy-five in the older alone, nearly a hundred and fifty in the later alone. Among these are not a few transfers from the classes of the first conjugation: see those classes above. There are no roots ending in long **ā** — except a few which make an a-stem in some anomalous way: below, **749a.**

Irregularities of the a-class.

745. A few verbs have irregular vowel-changes in forming the present-stem: thus,

a. **ūh** *consider* has **guṇa**-strengthening (against **240**): thus, **óhate**.

b. **kṛp** (or **krap**) *lament*, on the contrary, remains unchanged: thus, **kṛ́pate**.

c. **guh** *hide* has prolongation instead of **guṇa**: thus, **gū́hati**.

d. **kram** *stride* regularly lengthens its vowel in the active, but not in the middle: thus, **krā́mati, krámate**; but the vowel-quantities are somewhat mixed up, even from the oldest language down; — **klam** *tire* is said to form **klāmati** etc., but is not quotable; — **cam** with the preposition **ā** *rinse the mouth* forms **ā́cāmati**.

e. In the later language are found occasional forms of this class from **mṛj** *wipe*; and they show the same **vṛddhi** (instead of **guṇa**) which belongs to the root in its more proper inflection (**627**): thus, **mārjasva**.

f. The grammarians give a number of roots in **urv**, which they declare to lengthen the **u** in the present-stem. Only three are found in (quite limited) use, and they show no forms anywhere with short **u**. All appear to be of secondary formation from roots in **ṛ** or **ar**. The root **murch** or **mūrch** *coagulate* has likewise only **ū** in quotable forms.

g. The onomatopoetic root **ṣṭhīv** *spew* is written by the grammarians as **ṣṭhiv**, and declared to lengthen its vowel in the present-system: compare **240 b**.

746. The roots **daṅç** *bite*, **rañj** *color*, **sañj** *hang*, **svañj** *embrace*, of which the nasal is in other parts of the conjugation not constant, lose it in the present-system: thus, **dáçati** etc.; **sañj** forms both **sajati** and **sajjati** (probably for **sajyati**, or for **sasjati** from **sasajati**); **math** or **manth** has **mathati** later. In general, as the present of this class is a strengthening formation, a root that has such a nasal anywhere has it here also.

747. The roots **gam** *go* and **yam** *reach* make the present-stems **gáccha** and **yáccha**: thus, **gácchāmi** etc.: see **608**.

748. The root **sad** *sit* forms **sída** (conjectured to be contracted from **sisda** for **sisada**): thus, **sídāmi** etc.

749. Transfers to this class from other classes are not rare, as has been already pointed out above, both throughout the present-system and in occasional forms. The most important cases are the following:

a. The roots in **ā**, **sthā** *stand*, **pā** *drink*, and **ghrā** *smell*, form the present-stems **tíṣṭha** (**tíṣṭhāmi** etc.), **píba** (**píbāmi** etc.), and **jíghra** (**jíghrāmi** etc.): for these and other similar cases, see **671—4**.

b. Secondary root-forms like **inv, jinv, pinv**, from simpler roots of the nu-class, are either found alongside their originals, or have crowded these out of use: see **716**.

750. On the other hand, the root **dham** or **dhmā** *blow* forms its present-stem from the more original form of the root: thus, **dhámati** etc.

VII. Accented á-class (sixth, tud-class).

751. The present-stem of this class has the accent on the class-sign अ **á**, and the root remains unstrengthened. In its whole inflection, it follows so closely the model of the preceding class that to give the paradigm in full will be unnecessary (only for the subjunctive, all the forms found to occur will be instanced).

752. Example of inflection: root विश् **viç** *enter;* stem विश **viçá**:

1. Present Indicative.

	active.			middle.		
	s.	d.	p.	s.	d.	p.
1	विशामि viçā́mi etc.	विशावस् viçā́vas etc.	विशामस् viçā́mas etc.	विशे viçé etc.	विशावहे viçā́vahe etc.	विशामहे viçā́mahe etc.

2. Present Subjunctive.

	s.	d.	p.	s.	d.	p.
1	viçā́ni	viçā́va	viçā́ma	viçāí	viçā́vahāi	viçā́mahāi
2	viçā́si, viçā́s		viçā́tha	viçā́se, viçā́sāi	viçāíthe	
3	viçā́ti, viçā́t	viçā́tas	viçā́n	viçā́te, viçā́tāi	viçāíte	viçā́ntāi

a. A single example of the briefer 1st sing. act. is **mṛkṣā́**. The only forms in **āithe** and **āite** are **pṛṇāíthe** and **yuvāíte**.

3. Present Optative.

	s.	d.	p.	s.	d.	p.
1	विशेयम् viçéyam etc.	विशेव viçéva etc.	विशेम viçéma etc.	विशेय viçéya etc.	विशेवहि viçévahi etc.	विशेमहि viçémahi etc.

b. The RV. has the ending **tana** once in **tiretana** 2d pl. act., and **rata** in **juṣerata** 3d pl. mid.

4. Present Imperative.

The first persons having been given above as subjunctives, the second are added here:

2	विश	विशतम्	विशत	विशस्व	विशेथाम्	विशध्वम्
	viçá	**viçátam**	**viçáta**	**viçásva**	**viçéthām**	**viçádhvam**
	etc.	etc.	etc.	etc.	etc.	etc.

c. The ending **tāt** is found in RV. and AV. in **mṛḍatāt, vṛhatāt, suvatāt**; other examples are not infrequent in the Brāhmaṇa language: thus, **khidatāt, chyatāt, pṛcchatāt, viçatāt, sṛjatāt**; and later, **spṛçatāt.** The 3d sing. act. **nudātu** and **muñcātu** occur in Sūtras (cf. **740**).

5. Present Participle.

The active participle is विशत् **viçánt**; the middle is विशमान **viçámāna**.

d. The feminine of the active participle is usually made from the strong stem-form: thus, **viçántī**; but sometimes from the weak: thus, **siñcántī** and **siñcatī́** (RV. and AV.), **tudántī** and **tudatī́** (AV.): see above, **449 d, e**.

e. Middle participles in **āna** instead of **māna** are **dhuvāná, dhṛṣāṇá, liçāna, çyāna,** in the older language; **kṛçāna, muñcāna, spṛçāna** in the later (cf. **741 a**).

6. Imperfect.

1	अविशम्	अविशाव	अविशाम	अविशे	अविशावहि	अविशामहि
	áviçam	**áviçāva**	**áviçāma**	**áviçe**	**áviçāvahi**	**áviçāmahi**
	etc.	etc.	etc.	etc.	etc.	etc.

f. Examples of augmentless forms accented are **sṛjás, sṛját, tiránta.**

g. The **a**-aorist (**846** ff.) is in general the equivalent, as regards its forms, of an imperfect of this class.

753. Stems of the **á**-class are made from nearly a hundred and fifty roots: for about a third of these, in both the earlier and the later language; for a half, in the earlier only; for the remainder, nearly twenty, only in the later language. Among them are a number of transfers from the classes of the non-a-conjugation.

a. In some of these transfers, as **pṛṇ** and **mṛṇ** (**731**), there takes place almost a setting-up of independent roots.

b. The stems **icchá, ucchá,** and **ṛcchá** are reckoned as belonging respectively to the roots **iṣ** *desire*, **vas** *shine*, and **ṛ** *go*.

c. The roots written by the Hindu grammarians with final **o** — namely, **cho, do, ço,** and **so** — and forming the present-stems **chyá,**

dyá, çyá, syá, are more properly (as having an accented á in the stem) to be reckoned to this class than to the **ya**-class, where the native classification puts them (see **761 g**). They appear to be analogous with the stems **kṣya, sva, hva,** noted below (**755**).

754. The roots from which **á**-stems are made have certain noticeable peculiarities of form. Hardly any of them have long vowels, and none have long interior vowels; very few have final vowels; and none (save two or three transfers, and √**lajj** *be ashamed*, which does not occur in any accentuated text, and is perhaps to be referred rather to the **a**-class) have **a** as radical vowel, except as this forms a combination with **r**, which is then reduced with it to **ṛ** or some of the usual substitutes of **ṛ**.

Irregularities of the á-class.

755. The roots in **i** and **u** and **ū** change those vowels into **iy** and **uv** before the class-sign: thus, **kṣiyá, yuvá, ruvá; suvá,** etc.; and **sva, hva** occur, instead of **suva** and **huva,** in the older language, while TS. has the participle **kṣyánt.** K. has **dhūva** from √**dhū.**

756. The three roots in **ṛ** form the present-stems **kirá, girá** (also **gila**), **tirá,** and are sometimes written as **kir̥** etc.; and **gur, jur, tur** are really only varieties of **gṛ, jṛ, tṛ;** and **bhur** and **sphur** are evidently related with other **ar** or **ṛ** root-forms.

a. The common root **prach** *ask* makes the stem **pṛcchá.**

757. As to the stems **-driyá** and **-priya,** and **mriyá** and **dhriyá,** sometimes reckoned as belonging to this class, see below, **773.**

758. Although the present-stem of this class shows in general a weak form of the root, there are nevertheless a number of roots belonging to it which are strengthened by a penultimate nasal. Thus, the stem **muñcá** is made from √**muc** *release;* **siñcá** from √**sic** *sprinkle;* **vindá** from √**vid** *find;* **kṛntá** from √**kṛt** *cut;* **piñçá** from √**piç** *adorn;* **tṛmpá** from √**tṛp** *enjoy;* **lumpá** from √**lup** *break;* **limpá** from √**lip** *smear;* and occasional forms of the same kind are met with from a few others, as **tunda** from √**tud** *thrust;* **bṛṅhá** from √**bṛh** *strengthen;* **dṛṅhá** (beside **dṛ́ṅha**) from √**dṛh** *make firm;* **çumbhá** (beside **çúmbha**) from √**çubh** *shine;* TS. has **çṛnthati** from √**çrath** (instead of **çrathnāti**); **uñcha, vindhá, sumbha,** are of doubtful character.

a. Nasalized **á**-stems are also in several instances made by transfer from the nasal class: thus, **unda, umbha, ṛñjá, piṅṣá, yuñja, rundha, çiṅṣa.**

VIII. Ya-class (fourth, div-class).

759. The present-stem of this class adds य **ya** to the accented but unstrengthened root. Its inflection is also precisely like that of the a-class, and may be presented in the same abbreviated form as that of the á-class.

760. Example of inflection: root नह् nah *bind;* stem नह्य náhya.

1. Present Indicative.

	active.			middle.		
	s.	d.	p.	s.	d.	p.
1	नह्यामि	नह्यावस्	नह्यामस्	नह्ये	नह्यावहे	नह्यामहे
	náhyāmi	náhyāvas	náhyāmas	náhye	náhyāvahe	náhyāmahe
	etc.	etc.	etc.	etc.	etc.	etc.

2. Present Subjunctive.

1	náhyāni		náhyāma	náhyāi	náhyāvahāi	náhyāmahāi
2	{náhyāsi / náhyās}			náhyāsāi		náhyādhvāi
3	{náhyāti / náhyāt}	náhyātas	náhyān	náhyātāi		náhyāntāi

a. A 3d pl. mid. in antāi (jāyantāi) occurs once in TS.

3. Present Optative.

1	नह्येयम्	नह्येव	नह्येम	नह्येय	नह्येवहि	नह्येमहि
	náhyeyam	náhyeva	náhyema	náhyeya	náhyevahi	náhyemahi
	etc.	etc.	etc.	etc.	etc.	etc.

b. For two or three 3d sing. mid. forms in īta (for eta), see 738 b.

4. Present Imperative.

2	नह्य	नह्यतम्	नह्यत	नह्यस्व	नह्येथाम्	नह्यध्वम्
	náhya	náhyatam	náhyata	náhyasva	náhyethām	náhyadhvam
	etc.	etc.	etc.	etc.	etc.	etc.

c. Of the ending tana, RV. has one example, nahyatana; the ending tāt is found in asyatāt, khyāyatāt, naçyatāt.

5. Present Participle.

The active participle is नह्यन्त् náhyant (fem. नह्यन्ती náhyantī); the middle is नह्यमान náhyamāna.

6. Imperfect.

1	अनह्यम्	अनह्याव	अनह्याम	अनह्ये	अनह्यावहि	अनह्यामहि
	ánahyam	ánahyāva	ánahyāma	ánahye	ánahyāvahi	ánahyāmahi
	etc.	etc.	etc.	etc.	etc.	etc.

d. Examples of augmentless forms showing the accent belonging to the present-system are **gā́yat, páçyat, páçyan, jā́yathās.**

761. The **ya**-class stems are more than a hundred and thirty in number, and nearly half of them have forms in use in all periods of the language, about forty occurring only in the earlier, and about thirty only in the modern period.

a. Of the roots making **ya**-stems, a very considerable part (over fifty) signify a state of feeling, or a condition of mind or body: thus, **kup** *be angry*, **klam** *be weary*, **kṣudh** *be hungry*, **muh** *be confused*, **lubh** *be lustful*, **çuṣ** *be dry*, etc. etc.

b. A further number have a more or less distinctly passive sense, and are in part evident and in part presumable transfers from the passive or **yá**-class, with change of accent, and sometimes also with assumption of active endings. It is not possible to draw precisely the limits of the division; but there are in the older language a number of clear cases, in which the accent wavers and changes, and the others are to be judged by analogy with them. Thus, √**muc** forms **múcyate** once or twice, beside the usual **mucyáte,** in RV. and AV.; and in the Brāhmaṇas the former is the regular accent. Similar changes are found also in **ya**-forms from other roots: thus, from **kṣi** *destroy*, **jī** or **jyā** *injure*, **tap** *heat*, **dṛh** *make firm*, **pac** *cook*, **pṛ** *fill*, [illegible] *damage*, **ric** *leave*, **lup** *break*, **hā** *leave*. Active forms are early made from some of these, and they grow more common later. It is worthy of special mention that, from the Veda down, **jā́yate** *is born* etc. is found as altered passive or original **ya**-formation by the side of √**jan** *give birth*.

c. A considerable body of roots (about forty) differ from the above in having an apparently original transitive or neuter meaning: examples are **as** *throw*, **nah** *bind*, **paç** *see*, **pad** *go*, **çliṣ** *clasp*.

d. A number of roots, of various meaning, and of somewhat doubtful character and relations, having present-stems ending in **ya,** are by the native grammarians written with final diphthongs, **āi** or **e** or **o.** Thus:

e. Roots reckoned as ending in **āi** and belonging to the **a**- (or **bhū**-) class, as **gāi** *sing* (**gā́yati** etc.). As these show abundantly, and for the most part exclusively, **ā**-forms outside the present-system, there seems to be no good reason why they should not rather be regarded as **ā**-roots of the **ya**-class. They are **kṣā** *burn*, **gā** *sing*, **glā** *be weary*, **trā** *save*, **dhyā** *think*, **pyā** *fill up*, **mlā** *relax*, **rā** *bark*, **vā** *be blown*, **çyā** *coagulate*, **çrā** *boil*, **styā** *stiffen*. Some of them are evident extensions of simpler roots by the addition of **ā**. The secondary roots **tāy** *stretch* (beside **tan**), and **cāy** *observe* (beside **ci**) appear to be of similar character.

f. Roots reckoned as ending in **e** and belonging to the **a**- (or **bhū**-) class, as **dhe** *suck* (**dháyati** etc.). These, too, have **ā**-forms, and sometimes **ī**-forms, outside the present system, and are best regarded as **ā**-roots, either with **ā** weakened to **a** before the class-sign of this class, or with **ā**

weakened to ī or i and inflected according to the **a**-class. They are **dhā** *suck*, **mā** *exchange*, **vā** *weave*, **vyā** *envelop*, **hvā** *call* (secondary, from **hū**). As of kindred form may be mentioned **day** *share* and **vyay** *expend* (probably denominative of **vyaya**).

g. A few roots artificially written with final **o** and reckoned to the **ya**-class, with radical vowel lost before the class-sign: thus, **do** *cut, bind*, pres. **dyáti** etc. These, as having an accented **á** in the sign, have plainly no right to be put in this class; and they are better referred to the **á**-class (see above, **753 c**). Outside the present-system they show **ā**- and **i**-forms; and in that system the **ya** is often resolved into **ia** in the oldest language.

762. The **ya**-class is the only one thus far described which shows any tendency toward a restriction to a certain variety of meaning. In this tendency, as well as in the form of its sign, it appears related with the class of distinctly defined meaning which is next to be taken up — the passive, with **yá**-sign. Though very far from being as widely used as the latter beside other present-systems, it is in some cases an intransitive conjugation by the side of a transitive of some other class.

Irregularities of the ya-class.

763. The roots of this class ending in **am** lengthen their vowel in forming the present-stem: they are **klam, tam, dam, bhram, çam** *be quiet,* **çram**: for example, **tā́myati, çrā́myati.** From **kṣam,** however, only **kṣamyate** occurs; and **çam** *labor* makes **çamyati** (B.).

764. The root **mad** has the same lengthening: thus, **mā́dyati.**

765. The roots in **īv** — namely, **dīv, sīv, srīv** or **çrīv,** and **ṣṭhīv** (from which no forms of this class are quotable) — are written by the grammarians with **iv,** and a similar lengthening in the present-system is prescribed for them.

a. They appear to be properly **dīū** etc., since their vocalized final in other forms is always **ū**; **dīv** is by this proved to have nothing to do with the assumed root **div** *shine*, which changes to **dyu** (**361 d**): compare **240 b.**

766. From the roots **jṝ** and **tṝ** (also written as **jur** and **tir** or **tur**) come the stems **jī́rya** and **tī́rya,** and **jū́rya** and **tū́rya** (the last two only in RV.); from **pṝ** comes **pū́rya.**

767. The root **vyadh** is abbreviated to **vidh**: thus, **vídhyati.** And any root which in other forms has a penultimate nasal loses it here: thus, **dṛ́hya** from **dṛṅh** or **dṛh**; **bhraçya** from **bhrañç** or **bhraç**; **rajya** from **rañj** or **raj.**

IX. Accented yá-class: Passive conjugation.

768. A certain form of present-stem, inflected with middle endings, is used only in a passive sense, and is formed from all roots for which there is occasion to make a passive conjugation. Its sign is an accented य **ya** added to the root: thus, हन्य **hanyá** from √हन् **han** *slay*, आप्य **āpyá** from √आप् **āp** *obtain*, गृह्य **gṛhyá** from √गृह् **gṛh** (or **grah**) *seize*: and so on, without any reference to the class according to which the active and middle forms are made.

769. The form of the root to which the passive-sign is added is (since the accent is on the sign) the weak one: thus, a penultimate nasal is dropped, and any abbreviation which is made in the weak forms of the perfect (**794**), in the aorist optative (**922b**), or before **ta** of the passive participle (**954**), is made also in the passive present-system: thus, **ajyá** from √**añj**, **badhyá** from √**bandh**, **ucyá** from √**vac**, **ijyá** from √**yaj**.

770. On the other hand, a final vowel of a root is in general liable to the same changes as in other parts of the verbal system where it is followed by **y**: thus —

a. Final **i** and **u** are lengthened: thus, **mīyá** from √**mi**; **sūyá** from √**su**;

b. Final **ā** is usually changed to **ī**: thus, **dīyá** from √**dā**; **hīya** from √**hā**: but **jñāyá** from √**jñā**, and so **khyāyá, khāyá, mnāyá**, etc.;

c. Final **ṛ** is in general changed to **ri**: thus, **kriyá** from √**kṛ**; but if preceded by two consonants (and also, it is claimed, in the root **ṛ**), it has instead the **guṇa**-strengthening: thus, **smaryá** from √**smṛ** (the only quotable case); — and in those roots which show a change of **ṛ** to **ir** and **ur** (so-called **ṝ**-verbs: see **242**), that change is made here also, and the vowel is lengthened: thus, **çīryá** from √**çṝ**; **pūryá** from √**pṝ**.

771. The inflection of the passive-stem is precisely like that of the other **a**-stems; it differs only in accent from that of the class last given. It may be here presented, therefore, in the same abbreviated form:

a. Example of inflection: root कृ **kṛ** *make;* passive-stem क्रिय **kriyá**:

1. Present Indicative.

	s.	d.	p.
1	क्रिये **kriyé** etc.	क्रियावहे **kriyā́vahe** etc.	क्रियामहे **kriyā́mahe** etc.

2. Present Subjunctive.

b. The forms noticed as occurring in the older language are alone here instanced:

	s.	d.	p.
1	**kriyāí**		**kriyā́mahāi**
2			**kriyā́dhvāi**
3	**kriyā́te** **kriyā́tāi**		**kriyā́ntāi**

c. The 3d pl. ending **antāi** is found once (**ucyantāi** K.).

3. Present Optative.

	s.	d.	p.
1	क्रियेय **kriyéya** etc.	क्रियेवहि **kriyévahi** etc.	क्रियेमहि **kriyémahi** etc.

d. No forms of the passive optative chance to occur in RV. or AV.; they are found, however, in the Brāhmaṇas. ChU. has once **dhmāyīta**.

4. Present Imperative.

	s.	d.	p.
2	क्रियस्व **kriyásva** etc.	क्रियेथाम् **kriyéthām** etc.	क्रियध्वम् **kriyádhvam** etc.

5. Present Participle.

e. This is made with the suffix मान **māna**: thus, क्रियमाण **kriyámāṇa**.

f. In use, this participle is well distinguished from the other passive participle by its distinctively present meaning: thus, **kṛtá** *done*, but **kriyámāṇa** *in process of doing*, or *being done*.

6. Imperfect.

	s.	d.	p.
1	अक्रिये **ákriye** etc.	अक्रियावहि **ákriyāvahi** etc.	अक्रियामहि **ákriyāmahi** etc.

g. The passive-sign is never resolved into **ia** in the Veda.

772. The roots **tan** and **khan** usually form their passives from parallel roots in **ā**: thus, **tāyáte, khāyáte** (but also **tanyate, khan-**

yate); and **dham**, in like manner, makes either **dhamyate** or **dhmāyáte**. The corresponding form to √**jan**, namely **jā́yate** (above, **761 b**), is apparently a transfer to the preceding class.

773. By their form, **mriyáte** *dies*, and **dhriyáte** *maintains itself, is steadfast*, are passives from the roots **mṛ** *die* and **dhṛ** *hold;* although neither is used in a proper passive sense, and **mṛ** is not transitive except in the derivative form **mṛṇ** (above, **731**). With them are to be compared the stems **ā-driyá** *heed* and **ā-priyá** *be busy*, which are perhaps peculiar adaptations of meaning of passives from the roots **dṛ** *pierce* and **pṛ** *fill*.

774. Examples of the transfer of stems from the **yá-** or passive class to the **ya-** or intransitive class were given above (**761 b**); and it was also pointed out that active instead of middle endings are occasionally, even in the earlier language, assumed by forms properly passive: examples are **ā́ dhmāyati** and **vy àpruṣyat** (ÇB.), **bhūyati** (MāiU.). In the epics, however (as a part of their general confusion of active and middle forms: **529 a**), active endings are by no means infrequently taken by the passive: thus, **çakyati, çrūyanti, bhriyantu, ijyant-**, etc.

The so-called Tenth or cur-Class.

775. As was noticed above (**607**), the Hindu grammarians — and, after their example, most European also — recognize yet another conjugation-class, coördinate with those already described; its stems show the class-sign **áya**, added to a generally strengthened root (for details as to the strengthening, see **1042**). Though this is no proper class, but a secondary or derivative conjugation (its stems are partly of causative formation, partly denominative with altered accent), an abbreviated example of its forms may, for the sake of accordance with other grammars, be added here.

a. Example: root **cint** *think, meditate;* stem **cintáya**:

	active.	middle.
Pres. Indic.	**cintáyāmi**	**cintáye**
Subj.	**cintáyāni**	**cintáyāi**
Opt.	**cintáyeyam**	**cintáyeya**
Pple.	**cintáyant**	**cintáyamāna**
Impf.	**ácintayam**	**ácintaye**

b. The inflection, of course, is the same with that of other forms from **a**-stems (**733 a**).

c. The middle participle, in the later language, is more often made with **āna** instead of **māna**: thus, **cintayāna**: see **1043 f**.

Uses of the Present and Imperfect.

776. The uses of the mode-forms of the present-system have been already briefly treated in the preceding chapter (**572** ff.). The tense-uses of the two indicative tenses, present and imperfect, call here for only a word or two of explanation.

777. The present has, besides its strictly present use, the same subsidiary uses which belong in general to the tense: namely, the expression of habitual action, of future action, and of past action in lively narration.

a. Examples of future meaning are: **imáṁ céd vā́ imé cinváte táta evá no 'bhíbhavanti** (ÇB.) *verily if these build this up, then they will straightway get the better of us;* **agnir ātmabhavam prādād yatra vāñchati nāiṣadhaḥ** (MBh.) *Agni gave his own presence wherever the Nishadhan should desire;* **svāgataṁ te 'stu kiṁ karomi tava** (R.) *welcome to thee; what shall I do for thee?*

b. Examples of past meaning are: **úttarā sū́r ádharaḥ putrá āsīd dā́nuḥ çaye sahávatsā ná dhenúḥ** (RV.) *the mother was over, the son under; there Dānu lies, like a cow with her calf;* **prahasanti ca tāṁ kecid abhyasūyanti cā 'pare akurvata dayāṁ kecit** (MBh.) *some ridicule her, some revile her, some pitied her;* **tato yasya vacanāt tatrā 'valambitās taṁ sarve tiraskurvanti** (H.) *thereupon they all fall to reproaching him by whose advice they had alighted there.*

778. In connection with certain particles, the present has rather more definitely the value of a past tense. Thus:

a. With **purā́** *formerly:* thus, **saptarṣī́n u ha sma vāí purá ṛkṣā́ íty ā́cakṣate** (ÇB.) *the seven sages, namely, are of old called the bears;* **tanmātram api cen mahyaṁ na dadāti purā bhavān** (MBh.) *if you have never before given me even an atom.*

b. With the asseverative particle **sma**: thus, **çrámeṇa ha sma vāí tád devā́ jayanti yád eṣāṁ jáyyam ā́sá ṛṣayaç ca** (ÇB.) *in truth, both gods and sages were wont to win by penance what was to be won;* **āviṣṭaḥ kalinā dyūte jīyate sma nalas tadā** (MBh.) *then Nala, being possessed by Kali, was beaten in play.*

c. No example of this last construction is found in either RV. or AV., or elsewhere in the metrical parts of the Veda. In the Brāhmaṇas, only habitual action is expressed by it. At all periods of the language, the use of **sma** with a verb as pure asseverative particle, with no effect on the tense-meaning, is very common; and the examples later are hardly to be distinguished from the present of lively narration — of which the whole construction is doubtless a form.

779. The imperfect has remained unchanged in value through the whole history of the language: it is the tense of narration; it expresses simple past time, without any other implication.

a. Compare what is said later (end of chap. X. and chap. XI.) as to the value of the older past tenses, the perfect and aorist.

CHAPTER X.

THE PERFECT-SYSTEM.

780. THE perfect-system in the later language, as has been seen above (**535**), consists only of an indicative tense and a participle — both of them in the two voices, active and middle.

a. In the oldest language, the perfect has also its modes and its augment-preterit, or pluperfect, or is not less full in its apparatus of forms than is the present-system (see **808** ff.).

781. The formation of the perfect is essentially alike in all verbs, differences among them being of only subordinate consequence, or having the character of irregularities. The characteristics of the formation are these:

1. a stem made by reduplication of the root;

2. a distinction between stronger and weaker forms of stem, the former being used (as in presents of the First or non-a-conjugation) in the singular active, the latter in all other persons;

3. endings in some respects peculiar, unlike those of the present;

4. the frequent use, especially in the later language, of a union-vowel इ **i** between stem and endings.

782. Reduplication. In roots beginning with a consonant, the reduplication which forms the perfect-stem is of the same character with that which forms the present-stem of the reduplicating conjugation-class (see **643**) — but with this exception, that radical अ **a** and आ **ā** and ऋ **ṛ** (or अर् **ar**) have only अ **a**, and never इ **i**, as vowel of the reduplicating syllable: thus, from √पृ **pṛ** *fill* comes the present-stem पिपृ **pipṛ**, but the perfect-stem पपृ **papṛ**; from √मा **mā**

measure comes the present-stem मिमा **mimā**, but the perfect-stem ममा **mamā**; and so on.

a. Irregularities of roots with initial consonants will be given below, **784**.

783. For roots beginning with a vowel, the rules of reduplication are these:

a. A root with initial अ **a** before a single final consonant repeats the अ **a**, which then fuses with the radical vowel to आ **ā** (throughout the whole inflection): thus, आद् **ād** from √अद् **ad** *eat;* and in like manner आज् **āj**, आन् **ān**, आस् **ās**, आह् **āh**. The root ऋ **ṛ** forms likewise throughout आर् **ār** (as if from अर् **ar**).

b. A root with इ **i** or उ **u** before a single final consonant follows the same analogy, except in the strong forms (sing. act.); here the vowel of the radical syllable has **guṇa**, becoming ए **e** or ओ **o**; and before this, the reduplicating vowel maintains its independent form, and is separated from the radical syllable by its own semivowel: thus, from √इष् **iṣ** comes ईष् **īṣ** in weak forms, but इयेष् **iyeṣ** in strong; from √उच् **uc**, in like manner, come ऊच् **ūc** and उवोच् **uvoc**. The root इ **i**, a single vowel, also falls under this rule, and forms ईय् **īy** (**y** added before a vowel) and इये **iye**.

c. Roots which begin with vowels long by nature or by position do not in general make a perfect-system, but use instead a periphrastic formation, in which the perfect tense of an auxiliary verb is added to the accusative of a verbal noun (see below, chap. XV.: **1070** ff.).

d. To this rule, however, √**āp** *obtain* (probably originally **ap**: **1087 f**) constitutes an exception, making the constant perfect-stem **āp** (as if from **ap**: above, **a**). Also are met with **īḍé** (RV.) and **īḍire** from √**īḍ**, and **īriré** (V.) from √**īr**.

e. For the peculiar reduplication **ān**, belonging to certain roots with initial vowels, see below, **788**.

784. A number of roots beginning with **va** and ending with a single consonant, which in various of their verbal forms and derivatives abbreviate the **va** to **u**, do it also in the perfect, and are treated like roots with initial **u** (above, **783 b**), except that they retain

the full form of root in the strong persons of the singular active. Thus, from √vac *speak* come ūc and uvac; from √vas *dwell* come ūṣ and uvas; and so on.

a. The roots showing this abbreviation are vac, vap, vad, vaç, vas, vah; and vā *weave* is said to follow the same rule.

b. A single root beginning with ya, namely yaj *offer*, has the same contraction, forming the stems iyaj and īj.

c. Occasional exceptions are met with: as, **vavāca** and **vavakṣé** (RV.); **vavāpa** and **vavāha** and **vavāhatus** (E. and later); **yejé** (V.).

785. A number of roots having **ya** after a first initial consonant take **i** (from the **y**) instead of **a** in the reduplicating syllable: thus, from √**vyac** comes **vivyac**; from √**pyā** comes **pipyā**.

a. These roots are **vyac, vyath, vyadh, vyā, jyā, pyā, syand**; and, in the Veda, also **tyaj**, with **cyu** and **dyu**, which have the root-vowel **u**. Other sporadic cases occur.

b. A single root with **va** is treated in the same way: namely **svap**, which forms **suṣvap**.

c. These roots are for the most part abbreviated in the weak forms: see below, **794**.

786. A considerable number of roots have in the Veda a long vowel in their reduplication.

a. Thus, of roots reduplicating with **ā**: **kan, kḷp, gṛdh, tṛp, tṛṣ, dṛh, dhṛ, dhṛṣ, nam, mah, mṛj, mṛç, ran, radh, rabh, vañc, van, vaç, vas** *clothe*, **vāç, vṛj, vṛt, vṛdh, vṛṣ, çad** *prevail*, **sah, skambh.** Some of these occur only in isolated cases; many have also forms with short vowel. Most are Vedic only; but **dādhāra** is common also in the Brāhmaṇa language, and is even found later. As to **jāgṛ**, see **1020 a.**

b. Of roots reduplicating with **ī**: the so-called roots (**676**) **dīdhī** and **dīdī**, which make the perfect from the same stem with the present: thus, **dīdétha, dīdā́ya; dīdhima, dīdhyus** (also **dīdhiyus, dīdiyus**). But **pīpī** has **pipye, pipyus**, etc., with short **i.** In AV. occurs once **jīhīḍa**, and in AB. (and AA.) **bībhāya**.

c. Of roots reduplicating with **ū**: **tu, jū**, and **çū** (or **çvā́**).

787. A few roots beginning with the (derivative: **42**) palatal mutes and aspiration show a reversion to the more original guttural in the radical syllable after the reduplication: thus, √**ci** forms **ciki**; √**cit** forms **cikit**; √**ji** forms **jigi**; √**hi** forms **jighi**; √**han** forms **jaghan** (and the same reversions appear in other reduplicated forms of these roots: **216 1**). A root **dā** *protect* is said by the grammarians to form **digi**; but neither root nor perfect is quotable.

788. A small number of roots with initial **a** or **ṛ** (**ar**) show the anomalous reduplication **ān** in the perfect.

a. Thus (the forms occurring mainly in the older language only):

√**añj** or **aj**, which forms the pres. **anákti**, has the perfect **ānañja** and **ānajé** etc. (with **anajā** and **anajyāt**);

√**aç** *attain* (from which comes once in RV. **anáçāmahāi**), has the weak forms **ānaçma** etc. (with opt. **ānaçyām**), **ānaçé** etc. (and LÇS. has **ānaçadhve**), and the strong forms **ānáñça** and **ānāça** — along with the regular **āça** etc.;

√**ṛdh** (from which comes once **ṛṇádhat**) has **ānṛdhús** and **ānṛdhe**;

√**ṛc** or **arc** has **ānṛcús** and **ānṛcé**, and later **ānarca** and **ānarcus**;

√**arh** has (in TS.) **ānṛhús**;

anāha (RV., once) has been referred to a root **ah**, elsewhere unknown, and explained as of this formation; but with altogether doubtful propriety.

b. The later grammar, then, sets up the rule that roots beginning with **a** and ending with more than one consonant have **ān** as their regular reduplication; and such perfects are taught from roots like **akṣ**, **arj**, and **añc** or **ac**; but the only other quotable forms appear to be **ānarchat** (MBh.) and **ānarṣat** (TA.); which are accordingly reckoned as "pluperfects".

789. One or two individual cases of irregularity are the following:

a. The extremely common root **bhū** *be* has the anomalous reduplication **ba**, forming the stem **babhū**; and, in the Veda, √**sū** forms in like manner **sasū**.

b. The root **bhṛ** *bear* has in the Veda the anomalous reduplication **ja** (as also in intensive: **1002**); but RV. has once also the regular **babhre**, and pple **babhrāṇá**.

c. The root **ṣṭhīv** *spew* forms either **tiṣṭhīv** (ÇB. et al.) or **ṭiṣṭhīv** (not quotable).

d. **Vivakvā́n** (RV., once) is doubtless participle of √**vac**, with irregular reduplication (as in the present, **660**).

790. Absence of reduplication is met with in some cases. Thus:

a. The root **vid** *know* has, from the earliest period to the latest, a perfect without reduplication, but otherwise regularly made and inflected: thus, **véda**, **véttha**, etc., pple **vidvā́ṅs**. It has the meaning of a present. The root **vid** *find* forms the regular **vivéda**.

b. A few other apparently perfect forms lacking a reduplication are found in RV.: they are **takṣathus** and **takṣus**, **yamátus**, **skambháthus** and **skambhus**, **nindima** (for **ninidima**?), **dhiṣe** and **dhire** (? √**dhā**), and **vidré** and **arhire** (? see **613**). And AV. VS. have **cetatus**. The participial words **dāçvā́ṅs**, **mīḍhvā́ṅs**, **sāhvā́ṅs** are common in the oldest language; and RV. has once **jānúṣas** (√**jñā**), and **khidvas** (voc.), perhaps for **cikhidvas**.

c. A few sporadic cases also are quotable from the later language, especially from the epics: thus, **karṣatus**, **ceṣṭa** and **ceṣṭatus**, **bhrājatus**, **sarpa**, **çaṅsus** and **çaṅsire**, **dhvaṅsire**, **sraṅsire**, **jalpire**, **edhire**; also the pples **çaṅsivāṅs** and **darçivāṅs**, the latter being not infrequent.

791. For an anomalous case or two of reduplicated preposition, see below, **1087 f.**

792. Strong and weak stem-forms. In the three persons of the singular active, the root-syllable is accented, and exhibits usually a stronger form than in the rest of the tense-inflection. The difference is effected partly by strengthening the root in the three persons referred to, partly by weakening it in the others, partly by doing both.

793. As regards the strengthening:

a. A final vowel takes either the **guṇa** or **vṛddhi** change in 1st sing. act., **guṇa** in 2d, and **vṛddhi** in 3d: thus, from √भी **bhī**, 1st बिभे **bibhé** or बिभै **bibhāí**; 2d बिभे **bibhé**; 3d बिभै **bibhāí**; from √कृ **kṛ**, 1st चकर् **cakár** or चकार् **cakā́r**, 2d चकर् **cakár**, 3d चकार् **cakā́r**.

b. But the ū of √**bhū** remains unchanged, and adds **v** before a vowel-ending: thus, **babhū́va** etc.

c. Medial अ **a** before a single final consonant follows the analogy of a final vowel, and is lengthened or vriddhied in the 3d. sing., and optionally in the first: thus, from √तप् **tap**, 1st ततप् **tatáp** or ततāप् **tatā́p**, 2d ततप् **tatáp**, 3d ततāप् **tatā́p**.

d. In the earlier language, however, the weaker of the two forms allowed by these rules in the first person is almost exclusively in use: thus, 1st only **bibháya, tatápa**; 3d **bibhā́ya, tatā́pa.** Exceptions are **cakāra** and **jagrā́ha** (doubtful reading) in AV., **cakāra** in AÇS. and BAU. (ÇB. **cakara**), **jigāya** in AÇS., as first persons.

e. A medial short vowel has in all three persons alike the **guṇa**-strengthening (where this is possible: **240**): thus, from √द्रुह् **druh** comes दुद्रोह् **dudróh**; from √विश् **viç** comes विवेश् **vivéç**; from √कृत् **kṛt** comes चकर्त् **cakárt**.

f. An initial short vowel before a single final consonant is to be treated like a medial, but the quotable examples are very few: namely, **iyeṣa** from √**iṣ** *seek*, **uvocitha** and **uvoca** from √**uc**, **uvoṣa** from √**uṣ**. As to roots **i** and **ṛ**, whose vowels are both initial and final, see above, **783 a, b.**

g. These rules are said by the grammarians to apply to the **2d** sing. always when it has simple **tha** as ending; if it has **itha** (below, **797 d**), the accent is allowed to fall on any one of the syllables of the word, and the root-syllable if unaccented has sometimes the weak form (namely, in contracted stems with **e** for medial **a**: below, **794e**; and in certain other verbs, as **vivijitha**). The earlier language, however, affords no example of a 2d sing., whatever its ending, accented on any other than the radical syllable, or failing to conform to the rules of strengthening as given above (in **a**, **c**, **e**).

h. Occasional instances of strengthening in other than the singular persons are met with: thus, **yuyopima** and **viveçus** (RV.), **pasparçus** (KeU.), and, in the epics, **cakartus** and **cakartire, cakarṣatus, jugūhire, nanāmire, bibhedus, vavāhatus, viveçatus, vavarṣus.** The roots **dṛ**, **pṛ**, and **çṛ**, and optionally **jṛ**, are said by the grammarians to have the strong stem in weak forms; but no examples appear to be quotable. AV., however, has once **jaharus** (probably a false reading); and in the later language occur **caskare** (√**kṛ** *scatter*) and **tastare.**

i. The root **mṛj** has (as in the present-system: **627**) **vṛddhi** instead of **guṇa** in strong forms: thus, **mamā́rja**; and √**guh** (also as in present: **745c**) has **ū** instead of **o** (but also **juguhe** E.).

794. As regards the weakening in weak forms:

a. It has been seen above (**783b**) that roots beginning with **i** or **u** fuse reduplicating and radical syllable together to **ī** or **ū** in the weak forms; and (**784**) that roots contracting **va** and **ya** to **u** or **i** in the reduplication do it also in the root in weak forms, the two elements here also coalescing to **ū** or **ī**.

b. A few roots having **ya** and **va** after a first initial consonant, and reduplicating from the semivowel (**785**), contract the **ya** and **va** to **i** and **u**: thus, **vivic** from √**vyac**, **vividh** from √**vyadh** (but **vivyadhus** MBh.), **suṣup** from √**svap**. The extended roots **jyā, pyā, vyā, çvā, hvā** show a similar apparent contraction, making their weak forms from the simpler roots **jī, pī, vī, çū, hū**, while **hvā** must and **çvā** may get their strong forms also from the same (and only **jijyāú** is quotable from the others).

c. The root **grabh** or **grah** (if it be written thus: see **729a**) contracts to **gṛh**, making the three forms of stem **jagráh** (1st and 2d sing. act.), **jagrā́h** (3d), and **jagṛh**; but **prach** (if it be so written: see **756a**) remains unchanged throughout.

d. Some roots omit in weak forms of this tense, or in some of them, a nasal which is found in its strong forms: thus, we have **cakradé** etc. (RV.) from √**krand**; **tatasré** (RV.) from √**taṅs**; **dadaçvā́ṅs** (RV.) from √**daṅç**; **bedhús, bedhé**, etc. (AV.) from √**bandh**; **sejus** (ÇB.) from √**sañj**; **caskabhāná** (AV.) from √**skambh**; **tastabhús** etc. (V.), **tastabhāná** (V.B.), from √**stambh**. Compare also **788a.**

e. A number of roots having medial **a** between single consonants drop that vowel. These are, in the later language, **gam, khan, jan,**

han, ghas; they form the weak stems **jagm, cakhn, jajñ, jaghn** (compare **637**), **jakṣ** (compare **640**): but RV. has once **jajanús.**

f. In the old language are found in like manner **mamnāthe** and **mamnāte** from √**man**; **vavné** from √**van**; **tatne, tatniṣe, tatnire** from √**tan** (beside **tatane,** and **tate,** as if from √**tā**); **paptima** and **paptús** and **paptivāṅs** from √**pat** (beside **pet**-forms; below, **g**); **pap-né** from √**pan**; **saçcima** and **saçcus, saçce** and **saçciré,** from √**sac.**

g. Roots in general having medial **a** before a single final consonant, and beginning also with a single consonant that is repeated unchanged in the reduplication — that is, not an aspirate, a guttural mute, or **h** — contract their root and reduplication together into one syllable, having **e** as its vowel: thus, √**sad** forms the weak stem **sed,** √**pac** forms **pec,** √**yam** forms **yem;** and so on.

h. Certain roots not having the form here defined are declared by the grammarians to undergo the same contraction — most of them optionally; and examples of them are in general of very rare occurrence. They are as follows: **rāj** (E.C.) and **rādh** (**radh?**), notwithstanding their long vowel; **phaṇ, phal** (**phelire** C.), **bhaj** (occurs from RV. down), though their initial is changed in reduplication; **trap, tras** (**tresus** E.C.), **çrath, syam, svan,** though they begin with more than one consonant; **dambh** (**debhús,** RV., from the weaker **dabh**), though it ends with more than one; and **bhram** (**bhremus** etc. KSS.), **bhrāj, granth, svañj,** in spite of more reasons than one to the contrary. And ÇB. has **sejus** from √**sañj,** and KB. has **çremus** from √**çram.** On the other hand, RV. has once **rarabh-má,** and R. has **papatus,** for **petus,** from √**pat.**

i. This contraction is allowed also in 2d sing. act. when the ending is **itha**: thus, **tenitha** beside **tatantha** (but no examples are quotable from the older language).

j. The roots **çaç** and **dad** (from **dā**: **672**) are said to reject the contraction; but no perfect forms of either appear to have been met with in use.

k. From √**tṛ** (or **tar**) occurs **terus** (R.); and **jerus** from √**jṛ** is authorized by the grammarians — both against the general analogy of roots in **ṛ.**

l. Roots ending in **ā** lose their **ā** before all endings beginning with a vowel, including those endings that assume the union-vowel **i** (**796**) — unless in the latter case it be preferred to regard the **i** as a weakened form of the **ā.**

795. Endings, and their union with the stem. The general scheme of endings of the perfect indicative has been already given (**553 c**); an dit has also been pointed out (**543 a**) that roots ending in आ **ā** have औ **āu** in 1st and 3d sing. active.

a. The ending **mas instead** of ma is found in **çuçrumas** (E.C.). For the alleged occurrence of **ḍhve instead** of dhve in 2d pl. mid., see **226 c.**

796. Those of the endings which **begin with** a consonant — namely थ tha, व va, म ma in active; से **se**, वहे vahe, महे mahe, ध्वे dhve, रे re in middle — are very often, and in the later language usually, joined to the base with the help of an interposed union-vowel इ i.

a. The union-vowel i is found widely used also in other parts of the general verbal system: namely, in the sibilant aorist, the futures, and the verbal nouns and adjectives (as also in other classes of derivative stems). In the later language, a certain degree of correspondence is seen among the different parts of the same verb, as regards their use or non-use of the connective; but this correspondence is not so close that general rules respecting it can be given with advantage; and it will be best to treat each formation by itself.

b. The perfect is the tense in which the use of i has established itself most widely and firmly in the later language.

797. The most important rules as to the use of इ i in the later language are as follows:

a. The रे re of 3d pl. mid. has it always.

b. The other consonant-endings, except थ **tha** of 2d sing. act., take it in nearly all verbs.

c. But it is rejected throughout by eight verbs — namely kṛ *make*, bhṛ *bear*, sṛ *go*, vṛ *choose*, dru *run*, çru *hear*, stu *praise*, sru *flow*; and it is allowably (not usually) rejected by some others, in general accordance with their usage in other formations.

d. In 2d sing. act., it is rejected not only by the eight verbs just given, but also by many others, ending in vowels or in consonants, which in other formations have no इ i; but it is also taken by many verbs which reject it in other formations: — and it is optional in many verbs, including those in आ ā (of which the आ ā is lost when the ending is इथ itha), and most of those in इ i, ई ī, and उ u.

e. The rules of the grammarians, especially as regards the use of **tha** or **itha**, run out into infinite detail, and are not wholly consistent with one another; and, as the forms are very infrequent, it is not possible to criticise the statements made, and to tell how far they are founded on the facts of usage.

f. With this **i**, a final radical **i** or **ī** is not combined, but changed into **y** or **iy**. The **ū** of √**bhū** becomes **ūv** throughout before a vowel.

798. In the older language, the usage is in part quite otherwise. Thus:

a. In the RV., the union-vowel **i** is taken by roots ending in consonants provided the last syllable of the stem is a heavy one, but not otherwise: thus, **ā́sitha, uvócitha, vivéditha,** but **tatántha** and **vivyáktha; ūcimá, paptima, sedima, yuyopimá,** but **jaganma, jagṛbhmá, yuyujma; ūciṣé, jajñiṣé, sasāhiṣe,** but **vivitse** and **dadṛkṣé; bubhujmáhe** and **çāçadmahe** etc. (no examples of **ivahe** or **imahe** chance to occur, nor any of either **idhve** or **dhve**); **ījiré, jajñiré, yetiré, tataksiré,** but **cākḷpré, vividré, duduhré, paspṛdhré, tatasré** (and so on: twenty-two forms). The only exception in RV. is **véttha** from √**vid,** without **i** (in Br., also **āttha** from √**ah**: below, **801 a**). The other Vedic texts present nothing inconsistent with this rule, but in the Brāhmaṇas 3d pl. forms in **ire** are made after light syllables also: thus, **sasṛjire, bubudhire, yuyujire, rurudhire.**

b. In roots ending with a vowel, the early usage is more nearly like the later. Thus: for roots in **ā** the rule is the same (except that no 2d sing. in **itha** is met with), as **dadhimá, dadhiṣé, dadhidhvé, dadhiré** (the only persons with **i** quotable from RV. and AV.; and RV. has **dadhre** twice); — roots in **ṛ** appear also to follow the later rule: as **cakṛṣé, papṛṣe, vavṛṣé, vavṛmáhe,** but **dadhriṣe** and **jabhriṣe,** and in 3d pl. mid. both **cakriré** and **dadhrire;** — √**bhū** has both **babhū́tha** (usually) and **babhū́vitha,** but only **babhūvimá** (AV.). But there are found, against the later rules, **suṣuma, cicyuṣe, juhuré,** and **juhūré,** without **i**: the instances are too few to found a rule upon.

799. The ending **riré** of 3d pl. mid. is found in RV. in six forms: namely, **cikitrire, jagṛbhriré, dadrire, bubhujriré, vividrire, sasṛjrire;** to which SV. adds **duduhrire,** and TB. **dadṛçrire.**

800. Examples of inflection. By way of illustration of the rules given above may be given in full the perfect indicative inflection of the following verbs:

a. As example of the normal inflection of a root with final consonant, we take the root बुध् **budh** *know:* its strong form of perfect-stem is बुबोध् **bubódh;** weak form, बुबुध् **bubudh.**

	active.			middle.		
	s.	d.	p.	s.	d.	p.
1	बुबोध **bubódha**	बुबुधिव **bubudhivá**	बुबुधिम **-dhimá**	बुबुधे **bubudhé**	बुबुधिवहे **-dhiváhe**	बुबुधिमहे **-dhimáhe**

2	बुबोधिथ **bubódhitha**	बुबुधथुस् **-dháthus**	बुबुध **-dhá**	बुबुधिषे **bubudhiṣé**	बुबुधाथे **-dhā́the**	बुबुधिध्वे **-dhidhvé**
3	बुबोध **bubódha**	बुबुधतुस् **-dhátus**	बुबुधुस् **-dhús**	बुबुधे **bubudhé**	बुबुधाते **-dhā́te**	बुबुधिरे **-dhiré**

b. The asserted variety of possible accent in 2d sing. act. (above, **793 g**) needs to be noted both in this and in the remaining paradigms.

c. As example of the normal inflection of a root with final i or u-vowel, we may take the root नी **nī** *lead:* its forms of stem are निनय् **ninay** or निनाय् **ninā́y**, and निनी **ninī**.

1	निनय, निनाय **ninaya, ninā́ya**	निन्यिव **ninyivá**	निन्यिम **ninyimá**	निन्ये **ninyé**	निन्यिवहे **ninyiváhe**	निन्यिमहे **ninyimáhe**
2	निनेथ, निनयिथ **ninétha, ninayitha**	निन्यथुस् **ninyáthus**	निन्य **ninyá**	निन्यिषे **ninyiṣé**	निन्याथे **ninyā́the**	निन्यिध्वे **ninyidhvé**
3	निनाय **ninā́ya**	निन्यतुस् **ninyátus**	निन्युस् **ninyús**	निन्ये **ninyé**	निन्याते **ninyā́te**	निन्यिरे **ninyiré**

d. The root **krī** would make (**129 a**) in weak forms **cikriyivá, cikriyátus, cikriyús,** etc.; and √**bhū** is inflected as follows in the active (middle forms not quotable):

1	**babhū́va**	**babhūvivá**	**babhūvimá**
2	**babhū́tha, babhū́vitha**	**babhūváthus**	**babhūvá**
3	**babhū́va**	**babhūvátus**	**babhūvús**

Other roots in ū or u change this to uv before the initial vowel of an ending.

e. As example of the inflection of a root ending in आ **ā**, we may take दा **dā** *give:* its forms of stem are ददा **dadā́** and दद् **dad** or ददि **dadi**: see above, **794 l**).

1	ददौ **dadāú**	ददिव **dadivá**	ददिम **dadimá**	ददे **dadé**	ददिवहे **dadiváhe**	ददिमहे **dadimáhe**
2	ददाथ, ददिथ **dadā́tha, dadithá**	ददथुस् **dadáthus**	दद **dadá**	ददिषे **dadiṣé**	ददाथे **dadā́the**	ददिध्वे **dadidhvé**
3	ददौ **dadāú**	ददतुस् **dadátus**	ददुस् **dadús**	ददे **dadé**	ददाते **dadā́te**	ददिरे **dadiré**

f. The RV. has once **paprā́** for **paprāú** (and **jahā́** for **jahāú**?).

g. As example of a root with medial अ **a** showing fusion of root and reduplication, resulting in medial ए **e**, in the weak forms (**794 g**), we may take तन् **tan** *stretch:* its forms of stem are ततन् **tatán** or ततान् **tatā́n**, and तेन् **ten**.

1	ततन, ततान **tatána, tatā́na**	तेनिव **tenivá**	तेनिम **tenimá**	तेने **tené**	तेनिवहे **teniváhe**	तेनिमहे **tenimáhe**
2	ततन्थ, तेनिथ **tatántha, tenithá**	तेनथुस् **tenáthus**	तेन **tená**	तेनिषे **teniṣé**	तेनाथे **tenā́the**	तेनिध्वे **tenidhvé**
3	ततान **tatā́na**	तेनतुस् **tenátus**	तेनुस् **tenús**	तेने **tené**	तेनाते **tenā́te**	तेनिरे **teniré**

h. The root **jan**, with the others which expel medial **a** in weak forms (**794 e**), makes **jajántha** or **jajñithá, jajñivá, jajñús; jajñé, jajñimáhe, jajñiré**; and so on.

i. As example of a root with initial व **va** contracted to उ **u** in the reduplication, and contracted with the reduplication to ऊ **ū** in weak forms (**784**), we may take वच् **vac** *speak:* its forms of stem are उवच् **uvác** or उवाच् **uvā́c**, and ऊच् **ūc**.

1	उवच, उवाच **uváca, uvā́ca**	ऊचिव **ūcivá**	ऊचिम **ūcimá**	ऊचे **ūcé**	ऊचिवहे **ūciváhe**	ऊचिमहे **ūcimáhe**
2	उवक्थ, उवचिथ **uváktha, uvácitha**	ऊचथुस् **ūcáthus**	ऊच **ūcá**	ऊचिषे **ūciṣé**	ऊचाथे **ūcā́the**	ऊचिध्वे **ūcidhvé**
3	उवाच **uvā́ca**	ऊचतुस् **ūcátus**	ऊचुस् **ūcús**	ऊचे **ūcé**	ऊचाते **ūcā́te**	ऊचिरे **ūciré**

j. In like manner, √**yaj** forms **iyája** or **iyā́ja, iyáṣṭha** or **iyájitha; ījé, ījiṣé,** and so on; √**uc** has **uvóca** and **uvócitha** in the strong forms, and all the rest like **vac**.

k. Of the four roots in ऋ **ṛ** mentioned at **797 c**, the inflection is as follows:

1	चकर, चकार **cakára, cakā́ra**	चकृव **cakṛvá**	चकृम **cakṛmá**	चक्रे **cakré**	चकृवहे **cakṛváhe**	चकृमहे **cakṛmáhe**
2	चकर्थ **cakártha**	चक्रथुस् **cakráthus**	चक्र **cakrá**	चकृषे **cakṛṣé**	चक्राथे **cakrā́the**	चकृढ्वे **cakṛdhvé**
3	चकार **cakā́ra**	चक्रतुस् **cakrátus**	चक्रुस् **cakrús**	चक्रे **cakré**	चक्राते **cakrā́te**	चक्रिरे **cakriré**

l. Of the roots in ऋ ṛ in general, the first persons are made as follows:

दधर, दधार	दध्रिव	दध्रिम	दध्रे	दध्रिवहे	दध्रिमहे
dadhára, dadhā́ra	**dadhrivá**	**dadhrimá**	**dadhré**	**dadhriváhe**	**dadhrimáhe**

m. We may further add here, finally, the active inflection (the middle is not in use) of the perfect of **as** *be*, which (like **babhū́va** and **cakā́ra,** given above) is frequently employed as an auxiliary.

1	**ā́sa**	**āsivá**	**āsimá**
2	**ā́sitha**	**āsáthus**	**āsá**
3	**ā́sa**	**āsátus**	**āsús**

801. A few miscellaneous irregularities call still for notice:

a. The root **ah** *speak* occurs only in the perfect indicative, and only in the 3d persons of all numbers and in the 2d sing. and du., in active (and in 2d sing. the **h** is irregularly changed to **t** before the ending): thus, **āttha, ā́ha; āhathus, āhatus; āhús** (in V., only **ā́ha** and **āhús** are met with).

b. From √**vā** *weave*, the 3d pl. act. **ūvus** occurs in RV., and no other perfect form appears to have been met with in use. It is allowed by the grammarians to be inflected regularly as **vā**; and also as **vay** (the present-stem is **váya: 761 f**), with contraction of **va** to **u** in weak forms; and further, in the weak forms, as simple **u.**

c. The root **vyā** *envelop* has in RV. the perfect-forms **vivyathus** and **vivyé,** and no others have been met with in use; the grammarians require the strong forms to be made from **vyay,** and the weak from **vī.**

d. The root **i** *go* forms in RV. and AV. the 2d sing. act. **iyátha** beside the regular **iyétha**; and beside **īriré** from √**īr,** RV. has several times **eriré.**

e. RV. has an anomalous accent in **dádṛçe** and **dádṛçre** (beside **dadṛkṣé**) and the pple **dádṛçāna.** And **cíketa** (once, beside **cikéta**) is perhaps a kindred anomaly.

f. Persons of the perfect from the **ir**-forms of roots in changeable **ṛ** (**242**) are **titirus** and **tistire** (both RV.); and they have corresponding participles.

g. The bastard root **ūrṇu** (**713**) is said by the grammarians to make the perfect-stem **ūrṇunu;** the roots **majj** and **naç** are said to insert a nasal in the 2d sing. active, when the ending is simple **tha:** thus, **mamaṅktha, nanaṅṣṭha** (also **mamajjitha** and **neçitha**).

h. Further may be noted **sasajjatus** (MBh.: √**sañj,** which has in passive the secondary form **sajj**), **rurundhatus** (R.), and **dudūhus** (BhP).

i. The anomalous **ajagrabhāiṣam** (AB. vi. 35) seems a formation on the perfect-stem (but perhaps for **ajigrabhiṣan,** desid.?).

Perfect Participle.

802. The ending of the active participle is वांस् **vā́ṅs** (that is to say, in the strong forms: it is contracted to उष् **úṣ** in the weakest, and replaced by वत् **vát** in the middle forms: see above, **458 ff.**). It is added to the weak form of the perfect stem — as shown, for example, in the dual and plural of the active inflection of the given verb; and, mechanically, the weakest participle-stem is identical with the 3d pl. active. Thus, बुबुध्वांस् **bubudhvā́ṅs**, निनीवांस् **ninīvā́ṅs**, चकृवांस् **cakṛvā́ṅs**.

803. If the weak form of the perfect stem is monosyllabic, the ending takes the union-vowel इ i (which, however, disappears in the weakest cases): thus, तेनिवांस् **tenivā́ṅs**, ऊचिवांस् **ūcivā́ṅs**, जज्ञिवांस् **jajñivā́ṅs**, आदिवांस् **ādivā́ṅs** (from √अद् **ad**: **783a**), and so on; ददिवांस् **dadivā́ṅs** and its like, from roots in आ **ā**, are to be reckoned in the one class or the other according as we view the इ i as weakened root-vowel or as union-vowel (**794 l**).

a. But participles of which the perfect-stem is monosyllabic by absence of the reduplication do not take the union-vowel: thus, **vidvā́ṅs**, and in V., **dāçvā́ṅs** (SV. **dāçivā́ṅs**), **mīḍhvā́ṅs**, **sāhvā́ṅs**, **khidvā́ṅs** (?); and RV. has also **dadvā́ṅs** (AV. **dadivā́ṅs** and once **dadāvā́ṅs**) from √**dā** (or **dad**: **672**); and **án-āçvāṅs** (√**aç** *eat*) occurs in TS. and TB. But AV. has **viçivā́ṅs** and **varjivā́ṅs** (in negative fem. **ávarjuṣī**).

804. Other Vedic irregularities calling for notice are few. The long vowel of the reduplication (**786**) appears in the participle as in the indicative: thus, **vāvṛdhvā́ṅs**, **sāsahvā́ṅs**, **jūjuvā́ṅs**. RV. and AV. have **sasavā́ṅs** from √**san** or **sā**. RV. makes the participial forms of √**tṛ** or **tar** from different modifications of the root: thus, **titirvā́ṅs**, but **tatarúṣas**. Respecting the occasional exchanges of strong and weak stem in inflection, see above, **462c**.

805. a. From roots **gam** and **han** the Veda makes the strong stems **jaganvā́ṅs** (as to the **n**, see **212a**) and **jaghanvā́ṅs**; the later language allows either these or the more regular **jagmivā́ṅs** and **jaghnivā́ṅs** (the weakest stem-forms being everywhere **jagmúṣ** and **jaghnúṣ**). RV. has also **tatanvā́ṅs**.

b. From three roots, **vid** *find*, **viç**, and **dṛç**, the later language allows strong participle-stems to be made with the union-vowel, as well as in the regular manner without it: thus, **viviçivāṅs** or **viviçvāṅs**; **dadṛçivāṅs** occurs in KṭhU. PB. has once **cicchidivāṅs**.

806. The ending of the middle participle is **āna**. It is added to the weak form of perfect-stem, as this appears in the middle inflection: thus, बुबुधान **bubudhāna**, निन्यान **ninyāná**, ददान **dadāná**, तेनान **tenāná**, जज्ञान **jajñāná**, ऊचान **ūcāná**.

a. In the Veda, the long reduplicating vowel is shown by many middle participles: thus, **vāvṛdhāná**, **vāvasāná**, **dādṛhāṇá**, **tūtujāná**, etc. RV. has **çaçayāná** from √**çī** (with irregular **guṇa**, as in the present-system: **629**); **tistirāṇá** from √**stṛ**; and once, with **māna**, **sasṛmāṇá** from √**sṛ**. A few participles with long redupl. vowel have it irregularly accented (as if rather intensive: **1013**): thus, **tū́tujāna** (also **tūtujāná**), **bā́badhāna**, **çā́çadāna**, **çū́çujāna**, **çū́çuvāna**.

807. In the later language, the perfect participles have nearly gone out of use; even the active appears but rarely, and is made from very few verbs, and of the middle hardly any examples are quotable, save such as the proper name **yuyudhāna**, the adjective **anūcāna** *learned in scripture*, etc.

Modes of the Perfect.

808. Modes of the perfect belong only to the Vedic language, and even are seldom found outside of the Rig-Veda.

a. To draw the line surely and distinctly between these and the mode-forms from other reduplicated tense-stems — the present-stem of the reduplicating class, the reduplicated aorist, and the intensive — is not possible, since no criterion of form exists which does not in some cases fail, and since the general equivalence of modal forms from all stems (**582**), and the common use of the perfect as a present in the Veda (**823**), deprive us of a criterion of meaning. There can be no reasonable doubt, however, that a considerable body of forms are to be reckoned here; optatives like **ānaçyām** and **babhūyās** and **babhūyā́t**, imperatives like **babhūtu**, subjunctives like **jabhárat**, show such distinctive characteristics of the perfect formation that by their analogy other similar words are confidently classed as belonging to the perfect.

809. The normal method of making such forms would appear to be as follows: from a reduplicated perfect-stem, as (for example) **mumuc**, an imperative would be made by simply appending, as usual, the imperative endings; the derived subjunctive mode-stem would be **mumóca** accented after the analogy of the strong forms of the perfect indicative), and would take either primary or secondary endings; and the optative mode-stems would be **mumucyā́** in the active, and **mumucī** (accent on personal endings) in the middle.

And the great majority of the forms in question (about three quarters) are made in these ways. Thus:

810. Examples of the regular subjunctive formation are:

a. with secondary endings, active: 2d sing., **paprā́thas, cākánas, māmáhas, pipráyas, bubodhas, rārā́ṇas**; 3d sing., **cākánat, jabhárat, rārā́ṇat, sāsáhat, paspárçat, pipráyat**; 1st pl., **cākánāma, tatánāma, çūçávāma**; 3d pl., **tatánan, paprā́than** (other persons do not occur). This is the largest class of cases.

b. with primary endings, active: here seem to belong only **dadhárṣati** and **vavártati**: compare the formation with different accent below, **811 a.**

c. of middle forms occur only the 3d sing. **tatápate, çaçámate, yuyójate, jujóṣate** (SV.; RV. has **júj oṣate**); and the 3d pl. **cākánanta, tatánanta** (and perhaps two or three others: below, **811 b,** end).

811. But not a few subjunctives of other formation occur; thus:

a. With strengthened root-syllable, as above, but with accent on the reduplication (as in the majority of present-forms of the reduplicating class: above, **645**). Here the forms with primary endings, active, preponderate, and are not very rare: for example, **júj oṣasi, júj oṣati, júj oṣathas, júj oṣatha** (other persons do not occur). With secondary endings, **júj oṣas, júj oṣat,** and **júj oṣan** are the forms that belong most distinctly here (since **dádāças** and **súṣūdas** etc. are perhaps rather aorists). And there is no middle form but **júj oṣate** (RV.: see above, **810 c**).

b. With unstrengthened root-syllable occur a small body of forms, which are apparently also accented on the reduplication (accented examples are found only in 3d pl. mid.): thus, active, for example, **mumucas; vavṛtat, vividat, çūçuvat**; the only middle forms are **dadhṛṣate, vāvṛdhate**, 3d sing.; and **cákramanta, dádhṛṣanta, rúrucanta** (with **dadabhanta, paprathanta, māmahanta, juhuranta,** which might also belong elsewhere: **810 c**).

c. Accented on the ending are **vāvṛdhánta** and **cakṛpánta** (which are rather to be called augmentless pluperfects).

d. As to forms with double mode-sign, or transfers to an **a**-conjugation, see below, **815.**

812. Examples of the regular optative formation are:

a. In active: 1st sing., **ānaçyām, jagamyām, papṛcyām, riricyām**; 2d sing., **vavṛtyās, viviçyās, çuçrūyā́s, babhūyā́s**; 3d sing., **jagamyāt, vavṛtyāt, tutujyā́t, babhūyā́t**; 2d du., **jagmyātam, çuçrūyā́tam**; 1st pl., **sāsahyāma, vavṛtyāma, çūçuyāma**; 3d pl., **tatanyus, vavṛjyús, vavṛtyus.** The forms are quite numerous.

b. In middle, the forms are few: namely, 1st sing., **vavṛtīya**; 2d sing., **vāvṛdhīthās**, **cakṣamīthās**; 3d sing., **jagrasīta**, **vavṛtīta**, **māmṛjīta**, **dudhuvīta**, **çuçucīta**; 1st pl., **vavṛtīmahi**. And **sāsahīṣṭhās** and **ririṣīṣṭa** appear to furnish examples of precative optative forms.

c. There is no irregular mode of formation of perfect optatives. Individual irregularities are shown by certain forms: thus, **cakriyās**, **papīyāt**, **çuçrūyā́s** and **çuçrūyā́tam**, with treatment of the final as before the passive-sign **yá** (770); **anajyāt** with short initial; **çiçrītá** from √**çri**; **jakṣīyāt** is anomalous: **ririṣes** is the only form that shows a union-vowel **a** (unless also **siṣet**, from √**sā**).

813. Of regular imperative forms, only a very small number are to be quoted: namely, active, **cākandhi**, **rārandhí**, **cikiddhi**, **titigdhi**, **mumugdhí**, **çuçugdhí**, and **piprīhí**; **cākantu**, **rārantu**, **mumoktu**, and **babhūtu**; **mumuktam** and **vavṛktam**; **jujuṣṭana** and **vavṛttana** (unless we are to add **mamaddhí**, **mamattu**, **mamáttana**); — middle, **vavṛtsva** and **vavṛddhvam**. AV. has once **dadṛçrām**.

814. As irregular imperatives may be reckoned several which show a union-vowel **a**, or have been transferred to an **a**-conjugation. Such are, in the active, **mumócatam** and **jujoṣatam** (2d du.), and **mumócata** (2d pl.); in the middle, **pipráyasva** (only one found with accent), and **māmahasva**, **vāvṛdhasva**, **vāvṛṣasva** (2d sing.), and **māmahantām** (3d pl.: probably to be accented **-ásva** and **-ántām**).

815. Such imperatives as these, taken in connection with some of the subjunctives given above (and a few of the "pluperfect" forms: below, **820**), suggest as plausible the assumption of a double present-stem, with reduplication and added **a** (with which the desiderative stems would be comparable: below, **1026** ff.): for example, **jujoṣa** from √**juṣ**, from which would come **jújoṣasi** etc. and **jújoṣate** (**811 a**) as indicative, **jújoṣas** etc. as subjunctively used augmentless imperfect, and **jujoṣatam** as imperative. Most of the forms given above as subjunctives with primary ending lack a marked and constant subjunctive character, and would pass fairly well as indicatives. And it appears tolerably certain that from one root at least, **vṛdh**, such a double stem is to be recognized; from **vāvṛdha** come readily **vāvṛdhate**, **vāvṛdhánta**, and from it alone can come regularly **vāvṛdhasva**, **vāvṛdhéte** and **vāvṛdhāti** (once, RV.) — and, yet more, the participle **vavṛdhánt** (RV.; AV. **vāvṛdhánt**: an isolated case): yet even here we have also **vāvṛdhīthā́s**, not **vāvṛdhéthās**. To assume double present-stems, however, in all the cases would be highly implausible; it is better to recognize the formation as one begun, but not carried out.

a. Only one other subjunctive with double mode-sign — namely, **papṛcāsi** — is found to set beside **vāvṛdhāti**.

816. Forms of different model are not very seldom made from the same root: for example, from √**muc**, the subjunctives **mumócas**, **múmo-**

cati, and **mumucas**; from √**dhṛṣ dadhárṣati** and **dadhṛṣate**; from √**prī**, the imperatives **piprīhí** and **pipráyasva.**

Pluperfect.

817. Of an augment-preterit from the perfect-stem, to which the name of pluperfect is given on the ground of its formation (though not of its meaning), the Veda presents a few examples; and one or two forms of the later language (mentioned above, **788 b**) have also been referred to it.

a. There is much of the same difficulty in distinguishing the pluperfect as the perfect modes from kindred reduplicated formations. Between it and the aorist, however, a difference of meaning helps to make a separation.

818. The normal pluperfect should show a strong stem in the singular active, and a weak one elsewhere — thus, **mumoc** and **mumuc** — with augment prefixed and secondary endings added (**us** in 3d pl. act., **ata** in 3d pl. mid.).

a. Of forms made according to this model, we have, in the active: 1st sing., **ajagrabham** and **açacakṣam** (which, by its form, might be aorist: **860**); 2d sing. **ájagan**; 3d sing., **ajagan** and **aciket**; 2d du., **amumuktam**; 2d pl. **ájaganta**, and **ájagantana** and **ajabhartana** (a strong form, as often in this person: **556 a**); 3d pl. (perhaps), **amamandus** and **amamadus**. To these may be added the augmentless **cākán** and **rārán**, **cikétam** and **cakaram**. In the middle, the 3d pl. **acakriran** and **ajagmiran** (with **iran** instead of **ata**), and the augmentless 2d sing. **jugūrthās** and **suṣupthās**, are the most regular forms to be found.

819. Several forms from roots ending in consonants save the endings in 2d and 3d sing. act. by inserting an **ī** (**555 b**): thus, **ábubhojīs**, **aviveçīs**; **arirecīt**, **ájagrabhīt** (**avāvarīt** and **avāvaçītām** are rather intensives); and the augmentless **jíhiṅsīs** (accent?) and **dadharṣīt** belong with them.

820. A few forms show a stem ending in **a**: they are, in the active: 3d sing., **asasvajat**, **acikitat**, **acakrat**; in the middle: 3d sing., **ápiprata**; 2d du., **ápaspṛdhethām**; 3d pl., **atitviṣanta** (which by its form might be aorist), **ádadṛhanta**; and **cakradat**, **cakṛpánta**, **vāvṛdhánta**, **jihuranta**, would perhaps be best classified here as augmentless forms (compare **811**, above).

Uses of the Perfect.

821. Perfects are quotable as made from more than half the roots of the language, and they abound in use at every period and in almost all branches of the literature, though not always with the same value.

a. According to the Hindu grammarians, the perfect is used in the narration of facts not witnessed by the narrator; but there is no evidence of its being either exclusively or distinctively so employed at any period.

b. In the later language, it is simply a preterit or past tense, equivalent with the imperfect, and freely interchangeable or coördinated with it. It is on the whole less common than the imperfect, although the preferences of different authors are diverse, and it sometimes exceeds the imperfect in frequency (compare (**927**).

c. The perfects **veda** and **āha** are everywhere used with present value. In the Brāhmaṇas, also others, especially **dādhāra**, also **dīdāya**, **bibhāya**, etc.

822. In the Brāhmaṇas, the distinction of tense-value between perfect and imperfect is almost altogether lost, as in the later language. But in most of the texts the imperfect is the ordinary tense of narration, the perfect being only exceptionally used. Thus in PB., the imperfects are to the perfects as more than a hundred to one; in the Brāhmaṇa parts of TS. and TB., as over thirty-four to one; and in those of MS. in about the same proportion; in AB., as more than four to one, the perfect appearing mostly in certain passages, where it takes the place of imperfect. It is only in ÇB. that the perfect is much more commonly used, and even, to a considerable extent, in coördination with the imperfect. Throughout the Brāhmaṇas, however, the perfect participles have in general the true "perfect" value, indicating a completed or proximate past.

823. In the Veda, the case is very different. The perfect is used as past tense in narration, but only rarely; sometimes also it has a true "perfect" sense, or signifies a completed or proximate past (like the aorist of the older language: **928**); but oftenest it has a value hardly or not at all distinguishable in point of time from the present. It is thus the equivalent of imperfect, aorist, and present; and it occurs coördinated with them all.

a. Examples are: of perfect with present, **ná çrāmyanti ná ví muñcanty éte váyo ná paptuḥ** (RV.) *they weary not nor stop, they fly like birds;* **sé 'd u rā́jā kṣayati carṣaṇīnā́m arā́n ná nemíḥ pári tā́ babhūva** (RV.) *he in truth rules king of men; he embraces them all, as the wheel the spokes;* — of perfect with aorist, **úpo ruruce yuvatír ná yóṣā... ábhūd agníḥ samídhe mā́nuṣāṇām ákar jyótir bā́dhamānā támāṅsi** (RV.) *she is come beaming like a young maiden; Agni hath appeared for the kindling of mortals; she hath made light, driving away the darkness;* — of perfect with imperfect, **áhann áhim ánv apás tatarda** (RV.) *he slew the dragon, he penetrated to the waters.* Such a coördination as this last is of constant occurrence in the later language: e. g. **mumude 'pūjayac cāi 'nām** (R.) *he was glad, and paid honor to her;* **vastrānte jagrāha skandhadeçe 'sṛjat tasya srajam** (MBh.) *she took hold of the end of his garment, and dropped a garland on his shoulders.*

CHAPTER XI.

THE AORIST SYSTEMS.

824. UNDER the name of aorist are included (as was pointed out above, **532**) three quite distinct formations, each of which has its sub-varieties: namely —

I. A SIMPLE AORIST (equivalent to the Greek "second aorist"), analogous in all respects as to form and inflection with the imperfect. It has two varieties: 1. the root-aorist, with a tense-stem identical with the root (corresponding to an imperfect of the root-class); 2. the **a**-aorist, with a tense-stem ending in अ **á**, or with union-vowel अ **a** before the endings (corresponding to an imperfect of the **á**-class).

II. 3. A REDUPLICATING AORIST, perhaps in origin identical with an imperfect of the reduplicating class, but having come to be separated from it by marked peculiarities of form. It usually has a union-vowel अ **a** before the endings, or is inflected like an imperfect of one of the **a**-classes; but a few forms occur in the Veda without such vowel.

III. A SIGMATIC OR SIBILANT AORIST (corresponding to the Greek "first aorist"), having for its tense-sign a स् **s** added to the root, either directly or with a preceding auxiliary इ **i**; its endings are usually added immediately to the tense-sign, but in a small number of roots with a union-vowel अ **a**; a very few roots also are increased by स् **s** for its formation; and according to these differences it falls into four varieties: namely, **A.** without union-vowel अ **a** before endings: 4. **s**-aorist, with स् **s** alone added to the root; 5. **iṣ**-aorist, the same with interposed इ **i**; 6. **siṣ**-aorist, the same as the preceding with स् **s** added at the end of the root; **B.** with union-vowel अ **a**, 7. **sa**-aorist.

825. All these varieties are bound together and made into a single complex system by certain correspondences of form and meaning. Thus, in regard to form, they are all alike, in the indicative, augment-preterits to which there does not exist any corresponding present; in regard to meaning, although in the later or classical language they are simply preterits, exchangeable with imperfects and perfects, they all alike have in the older language the general value of a completed past or "perfect", translatable by *have done* and the like.

826. The aorist-system is a formation of infrequent occurrence in much of the classical Sanskrit (its forms are found, for example, only twenty-one times in the Nala, eight in the Hitopadeça, seven in Manu, six each in the Bhagavad-Gītā and Çakuntalā, and sixty-six times, from fourteen roots, in the first book, of about 2600 lines, of the Rāmāyaṇa: compare **927 b**), and it possesses no participle, nor any modes (excepting in the prohibitive use of its augmentless forms: see **579**; and the so-called precative: see **921** ff.); in the older language, on the other hand, it is quite common, and has the whole variety of modes belonging to the present, and sometimes participles. Its description, accordingly, must be given mainly as that of a part of the older language, with due notice of its restriction in later use.

827. a. In the RV., nearly half the roots occurring show aorist forms, of one or another class; in the AV., rather less than one third; and in the other texts of the older language comparatively few aorists occur which are not found in these two.

b. More than fifty roots, in RV. and AV. together, make aorist forms of more than one class (not taking into account the reduplicated or "causative" aorist); but no law appears to underlie this variety; of any relation such as is taught by the grammarians, between active of one class and middle of another as correlative, there is no trace discoverable.

c. Examples are: of classes 1 and 4, **adhām** and **dhāsus** from √**dhā**, **ayuji** and **ayukṣata** from √**yuj**; — of 1 and 5, **agrabham** and **agrabhīṣma** from √**grabh**, **mṛṣṭhās** and **marṣiṣṭhās** from √**mṛṣ**; — of 1 and 2, **ārta** and **ārat** from √**ṛ**; — of 2 and 4, **avidam** and **avitsi** from √**vid** *find*, **anijam** and **anāikṣīt** from √**nij**; — of 2 and 5, **sanéma** and **asāniṣam** from √**san**; — of 2 and 7, **aruham** and **arukṣat** from √**ruh**; — of 4 and 5, **amatsus** and **amādiṣus** from √**mad**; — of 4 and 6, **hāsmahi** and **hāsiṣus** from √**hā**; — of 1 and 2 and 4, **atnata** and **atanat** and **atān** from √**tan**; — of 1 and 4 and 5, **abudhran** and **ábhutsi** and **bódhiṣat** from √**budh**, **ástar** and **stṛṣīya** and

astarīs from √**stṛ**. Often the second, or second and third, class is represented by only an isolated form or two.

I. Simple Aorist.

828. This is, of the three principal divisions of aorist, the one least removed from the analogy of forms already explained; it is like an imperfect, of the root-class or of the **á**-class, without a corresponding present indicative, but with (more or less fragmentarily) all the other parts which go to make up a complete present-system.

1. Root-aorist.

829. a. This formation is in the later language limited to a few roots in आ **ā** and the root भू **bhū**, and is allowed to be made in the active only, the middle using instead the **s**-aorist (4), or the **iṣ**-aorist (5).

b. The roots in आ **ā** take उस् **us** as 3d pl. ending, and, as usual, lose their आ **ā** before it; भू **bhū** (as in the perfect: **793a**) retains its vowel unchanged throughout, inserting व् **v** after it before the endings अम् **am** and अन् **an** of 1st sing. and 3d pl. Thus:

	s.	d.	p.	s.	d.	p.
1	अदाम् **ádām**	अदाव **ádāva**	अदाम **ádāma**	अभूवम् **ábhūvam**	अभूव **ábhūva**	अभूम **ábhūma**
2	अदास् **ádās**	अदातम् **ádātam**	अदात **ádāta**	अभूस् **ábhūs**	अभूतम् **ábhūtam**	अभूत **ábhūta**
3	अदात् **ádāt**	अदाताम् **ádātām**	अदुस् **ádus**	अभूत् **ábhūt**	अभूताम् **ábhūtām**	अभूवन् **ábhūvan**

For the classical Sanskrit, this is the whole story.

830. In the Veda, these same roots are decidedly the most frequent and conspicuous representatives of the formation: especially the roots **gā, dā, dhā, pā** *drink*, **sthā, bhū**; while sporadic forms are made from **jñā, prā, sā, hā**. As to their middle forms, see below, **834a**.

a. Instead of **abhūvam,** RV. has twice **abhuvam.** BhP. has **agan,** 3d pl., instead of **agus.**

831. But aorists of the same class are also made from a number of roots in **ṛ**, and a few in **i**- and **u**-vowels (short or long) —

with, as required by the analogy of the tense with an imperfect of the root-class, **guṇa**-strengthening in the three persons of the singular.

a. Thus (in the active), from √**çru**, **áçravam** and **áçrot**; from √**çri**, **áçres** and **áçret**; from √**kṛ** *make*, **ákaram** and **ákar** (for **akars** and **akart**); from **vṛ** *enclose*, **ā́var** (**585 a**); and so **ástar**, **aspar**. Dual and plural forms are much less frequent than singular; but for the most part they also show an irregular strengthening of the root-vowel: thus (including augmentless forms), **ákarma** and **karma** and **ákarta**, **vartam**, **spartam**, **áhema** and **áhetana**, **bhema**, **açravan**; regular are only **avran**, **ákran**, **ahyan**, and **áçriyan**.

832. Further, from a few roots with medial (or initial) vowel capable of **guṇa**-strengthening and having in general that strengthening only in the singular.

a. Thus, **ábhedam** and **abhet** from √**bhid**; **ámok** from √**muc**; **yojam** from √**yuj**; **rok** (VS.) from √**ruj**; **arodham** and **arudhma** from √**rudh**; **avart** from √**vṛt**; **várk** from √**vṛj** (AV. has once **avṛk**); **adarçam** from √**dṛç**; **ā́rdhma** from √**ṛdh**; and **adṛçan**, **avṛjan**, **açvitan**. But **chedma**, with **guṇa**, from √**chid**, and **adarçma** (TS.) from √**dṛç**.

833. Again, from a larger number of roots with **a** as radical vowel:

a. Of these, **gam** (with **n** for **m** when final or followed by **m**: **143 a**, **212 a**) is of decidedly most frequent occurrence, and shows the greatest variety of forms: thus, **ágamam**, **ágan** (2d and 3d sing.), **áganma**, **aganta** (strong form), **ágman**. The other cases are **akran** from √**kram**; **átan** from √**tan**; **abhrāṭ** from √**bhrāj**; **askan** from √**skand**; **asrat** from √**sraṅs** (? VS.); **dhak** and **daghma** from √**dagh**; **ā́naṭ** (**585 a**) and **anaṣṭām** from √**naç**; **ághas** or **aghat**, **ághastām**, **aghasta**, and **ákṣan** (for **aghsan**, like **agman**) from √**ghas**; and the 3d pll. in **us**, **ákramus**, **ayamus**, **dabhús**, **nṛtus** (pf.?), **mandús**.

834. So far only active forms have been considered. In the middle, a considerable part of the forms are such as are held by the grammarians (**881**) to belong to the **s**-aorist, with omission of the **s**: they doubtless belong, however, mostly or altogether, here. Thus:

a. From roots ending in vowels, we have **adhithās**, **adhita** (also **ahita**), and **adhīmahi**; **adithās**, **adita**, and **adimahi** (and **adīmahi** from √**dā** *cut*); **áçīta** (?); **sīmáhi**; **ásthithās** and **ásthita** and **ásthiran**, forms of **ā**-roots; — of **ṛ**-roots, **akri**, **ákṛthās**, **ákṛta**, **akrātām**, **ákrata** (and the anomalous **kránta**); **avri**, **avṛthās**, **avṛta**; **ārta**, **ārata**; **mṛthās**, **amṛta**; **dhṛthās**; **adṛthās**; **astṛta**; **ahṛthās**; **gūrta**; — of **i** and **u** roots, the only examples are **ahvi** (? AV., once), **áhūmahi**, and **ácidhvam**. The absence of any analogies whatever for the omission of a **s** in such forms, and the occurrence of **avri** and **akri** and **ákrata**, show that their reference to the **s**-aorist is probably without sufficient reason.

b. As regards roots ending in consonants, the case is more questionable, since loss of **s** after a final consonant before **thās** and **ta** (and, of course, **dhvam**) would be in many cases required by euphonic rule (**233 c** ff.). We find, however, such unmistakable middle inflection of the root-aorist as **ayuji, áyukthās, áyukta, ayujmahi, áyugdhvam, áyujran; ā́ṣṭa** and **ā́çata; náñçi; apadi** (1st sing.) and **apadmahi** and **apadran; ámanmahi; gánvahi** and **áganmahi** and **ágmata; atnata; ájani** (1st sing.) and **ajñata** (3d pl.); from √**gam** are made **agathās** and **agata,** from √**tan, atathās** and **átata,** and from √**man, amata,** with treatment of the final like that of **han** in present inflection (**637**). The ending **ran** is especially frequent in 3d pl., being taken by a number of verbs which have no other middle person of this aorist: thus, **agṛbhran, ásṛgran, adṛçran, abudhran, ávṛtran, ajuṣran, akṛpran, aspṛdhran, avasran, áviçran;** and **ram** is found beside **ran** in **ádṛçram, ábudhram, ásṛgram.**

c. From roots of which the final would combine with **s** to **kṣ**, it seems more probable that aorist-forms showing **k** (instead of **ṣ**) before the ending belong to the root-aorist: such are **amukthās** (and **ámugdhvam**), **apṛkthās** and **apṛkta, ábhakta, avṛkta, asakthās** and **asakta, rikthās, vikthās** and **vikta, arukta; apraṣṭa, ayaṣṭa, áspaṣṭa, asṛṣṭhās** and **ásṛṣṭa,** and **mṛṣṭhās** would be the same in either case.

d. There remain, as cases of more doubtful belonging, and probably to be ranked in part with the one formation and in part with the other, according to their period and to the occurrence of other persons: **chitthās, nutthā́s** and **ánutta** and **ánuddhvam, patthās, bhitthās, amatta, atapthās, alipta, asṛpta;** and finally, **árabdha, alabdha, aruddha, abuddha, ayuddha,** and **drogdhās** (MBh.: read **drugdhās**): see **883.**

Modes of the Root-aorist.

835. Subjunctive. In subjunctive use, forms identical with the augmentless indicative of this aorist are much more frequent than the more proper subjunctives. Those to which no corresponding form with augment occurs have been given above; the others it is unnecessary to report in detail.

836. a. Of true subjunctives the forms with primary endings are quite few. In the active, **kárāṇi, gāni, gamāni** (for **bhuvāni,** see below, **c**); **kárasi; sthāti, dā́ti** and **dhā́ti** (which are almost indicative in value), **karati, joṣati, padāti, bhédati, rādhati, varjati; sthāthas, karathas** and **karatas, darçathas, çravathas** and **çrávatas;** and (apparently) **karanti, gámanti.** In the middle, **joṣase; idhaté** (?), **kárate, bhójate, yojate, várjate; dhéthe** and **dhāithe; karāmahe, dhāmahe, gámāmahāi.**

b. Forms with secondary endings are, in the active, **dárçam, bhojam, yojam; káras, tárdas, párcas, yámas, rādhās, váras; karat, gámat, garat, jóṣat, daghat, padāt, yamat, yodhat, rādhat, várat, vártat, çrávat, sághat, spárat; kárāma, gamāma, rādhāma; gáman,**

garan, dárçan, yaman. No middle forms are classifiable with confidence here.

c. The series **bhuvam, bhúvas, bhúvat, bhúvan,** and **bhuvāni** (compare **abhuvam: 830 a),** and the isolated **çrúvat,** are of doubtful belongings; with a different accent, they would seem to be of the next class; here, a **guṇa**-strengthening would be more regular (but note the absence of **guṇa** in the aorist indicative and the perfect of √**bhū**).

837. Optative. The optative active of this aorist constitutes, with a **s** interposed between mode-sign and personal endings (**567**), the precative active of the Hindu grammarians, and is allowed by them to be made from every verb, they recognizing no connection between it and the aorist. But in the 2d sing. the interposed **s** is not distinguishable from the personal ending; and, after the earliest period (see **838**), the ending crowds out the sibilant in the 3d sing., which thus comes to end in **yāt** instead of **yās** (compare **555 a**).

a. In the older language, however, pure optative forms, without the **s**, are made from this tense. From roots in **ā** occur (with change of **ā** to **e** before the **y**: **250 d**) **deyām, dheyām** and **dheyus,** and **stheyāma;** in **u**-vowels, **bhūyā́ma;** in **ṛ**, **kriyāma;** in consonants, **açyā́m** and **açyā́ma** and **açyus, vṛjyām, çakyām, yujyāva** and **yujyā́tām, sāhyāma,** and **tṛdyus.**

b. The optative middle of the root-aorist is not recognized by the Hindu grammarians as making a part of the precative formation. The RV. has, however, two precative forms of it, namely **padīṣṭá** and **mucīṣṭa.** Much more common in the older language are pure optative forms: namely, **açīya** and **açīmáhi** (this optative is especially common), **indhīya, gmīya, murīya, rucīya; arīta, uhīta, vurīta; idhīmahi, naçīmahi, nasīmahi, pṛcīmahi, mudīmahi, yamīmahi;** and probably, from **ā**-roots, **sīmáhi** and **dhīmahi** (which might also be augmentless indicative, since **adhīmahi** and **adhītām** also occur). All these forms except the three in 3d sing. might be precative according to the general understanding of that mode, as being of persons which even by the native authorities are not claimed ever to exhibit the inserted sibilant.

838. Precative active forms of this aorist are made from the earliest period of the language. In RV., they do not occur from any root which has not also other aorist forms of the same class to show. The RV. forms are: 1st sing., **bhūyāsam;** 2d sing., **avyās, jñeyās, bhūyā́s, mṛdhyās, sahyās;** 3d sing. (in **-yās,** for **-yāst;** RV. has no 3d sing. in **yāt,** which is later the universal ending), **avyās, açyās, ṛdhyās, gamyā́s, daghyās, peyās, bhūyā́s, yamyās, yūyās, vṛjyās, çrūyās, sahyās;** 1st pl., **kriyāsma** (beside **kriyāma: 837 a).** AV. has six 1st persons sing. in **-yā́sam,** one 2d in **-yā́s,** one 3d in **-yāt** (and one in **-yās,** in a RV. passage), three 1st pl. in **-yā́sma** (beside one in **yāma,** in a RV. passage), and the 2d **bhūyāstha** (doubtless a false reading: TB. has **-sta** in the corresponding passage). From this time on, the pure optative forms nearly disappear (the exceptions are given in **837 a**). But the precative forms are nowhere common, excepting as made from √**bhū**; and from no other root is anything like a complete series of persons quotable (only **bhūyāsva** and **bhūyāstām** being wanting; and these two persons have no representative from any root). All together, active optative or precative forms are made in the older language from over fifty roots; and the epic and classical texts add them from hardly a dozen more: see further **925**.

839. Imperative. Imperative forms of the root-aorist are not rare in the early language. In the middle, indeed, almost only the 2d sing. occurs: it is accented either regularly, on the ending, as **kṛṣvá, dhiṣvá, yukṣvá,** or on the root, as **mátsva, yákṣva, váṅsva, rā́sva, sákṣva; dīṣva** and **māsva** are not found with accent; the 2d pl. is represented by **kṛdhvam, voḍhvam.** In the active, all the persons (2d and 3d) are found in use; examples are: 2d sing., **kṛdhí, vṛdhi, çagdhí, çrudhí, gadhi, yaṁdhí, gahi, māhi, sāhi, mogdhi;** 3d sing., **gaṁtu, dātu, aṣṭu, çrótu, sótu;** 2d du., **dātam, jitam, çaktam, çrutám, bhūtám, spṛtám, gatám, riktám, voḍham, sitam, sutám;** 3d du., only **gaṁtām, dātām, voḍhā́m;** 2d pl., **gātá, bhūtá, çruta, kṛta, gata, dāta, dhātana;** 3d pl., only **dhāntu, çruvantu.** These are the most regular forms; but irregularities as to both accent and strengthening are not infrequent. Thus, strong forms in 2d du. and pl. are **yaṁtám, varktam, vartam; kárta, gáṁta** (once **gaṁtá**), **yaṁta, vartta, heta, çróta, sóta;** and, with **tana, kártana, gáṁtana, yaṁtana, sotana,** and the irregular **dhetana** (√**dhā**); in 3d du., **gāṁtām.** Much more irregular are **yódhi** (instead of **yuddhí**) from √**yudh,** and **bodhí** from both √**budh** and √**bhū** (instead of **buddhí** and **bhūdhí**). A single form (3d sing.) in **tāt** is found, namely **çastāt.** We find **kṛdhi** also later (MBh. BhP.).

a. As to 2d persons singular in **si** from the simple root used in an imperative sense, see above, **624**.

Participles of the Root-aorist.

840. In the oldest language, of the RV., are found a number of participles which must be reckoned as belonging to this formation.

a. In the active, they are extremely few: namely, **kránt, citánt** (?), **gmánt, sthā́nt, bhidánt, vṛdhánt, dyutant-** (only in composition), and probably **ṛdhánt.** And BhP. has **mṛṣant** (but probably by error, for **mṛṣyant**).

b. In the middle, they are in RV. much more numerous. The accent is usually on the final of the stem: thus, **arāṇá, idhāná, krāṇá, juṣāṇá, tṛṣāṇá, nidāná, piçāná, pṛcāná, prathāná, budhāná, bhiyāná, manāná, mandāná, yujāná, rucāná, vipāná, vrāṇá, urāṇá, çubhāná, sacāná, suvāná** or **svāná, sṛjāná, spṛdhāná, hiyāná;** — but sometimes on the root-syllable: thus, **cítāna, cyávāna, rúhāṇa, úhāna** (pres.?), **vásāna, çúmbhāna;** — while a few show both accentuations (compare **619 d**): thus, **dr̥çāná** and **dŕ̥çāna, dyutāná** and **dyútāna, yatāná** and **yátāna**; and **cetāna** and **hrayāṇa** occur only in composition. A very few of these are found once or twice in other texts, namely **citāna, dyutāna, ruhāṇa, vasāna, suvāna**; and **-kupāna** occurs once in Āpast. (xiv. 28. 4).

841. All together, the roots exhibiting in the older language forms which are with fair probability to be reckoned to the root-aorist-system are about a hundred and thirty; over eighty of them make such forms in the RV.

Passive Aorist third person singular.

842. A middle third person singular, of peculiar formation and prevailingly passive meaning, is made from many verbs in the older language, and has become a regular part of the passive conjugation, being, according to the grammarians, to be substituted always for the proper third person of any aorist middle that is used in a passive sense.

843. This person is formed by adding इ **i** to the root, which takes also the augment, and is usually strengthened.

a. The ending **i** belongs elsewhere only to the first person; and this third person apparently stands in the same relation to a first in **i** as do, in the middle voice, the regular 3d sing. perfect, and also the frequent Vedic 3d sing. present of the root-class (**613**), which are identical in form with their respective first persons. That a fuller ending has been lost off is extremely improbable; and hence, as an aorist formation from the simple root, this is most properly treated here, in connection with the ordinary root-aorist.

844. Before the ending इ **i**, a final vowel, and usually also a medial अ **a** before a single consonant, have the **vr̥ddhi**-strengthening; other medial vowels have the **guṇa**-strengthening if capable of it (**240**); after final आ **ā** is added य् **y**.

a. Examples (all of them quotable from the older language) are: from roots ending in **ā, ā́jñāyi, ádhāyi, ápāyi**; in other vowels, **áçrāyi, ástāvi, áhāvi, ákāri, ástāri**; — from roots with medial **i, u, r̥, aceti, ácchedi, açeṣi, ábodhi, ámoci, áyoji, ádarçi, asarji, varhi**; from roots with medial **a** strengthened, **agāmi, ápādi, ayāmi, avāci, vāpi, ásādi** (these are all the earlier cases); with **a** unchanged, only **ájani** (and RV. has once **jā́ni**), and, in heavy syllables, **ámyakṣi, vandi, çañsi, syandi**; with medial **ā, ábhrāji, árādhi**; — from roots with initial vowel, **ārdhi** (only case).

b. According to the grammarians, certain roots in **am**, and √**vadh**, retain the **a** unchanged: quotable are **ajani** (or **ajāni**), **agami** (or **agāmi**),

asvani, avadhi, also **araci**; and there are noted besides, from roots sometimes showing a nasal, **adañçi, arambhi, arandhi, ajambhi, abhañji** or **abhāji, alambhi** (always, with prepositions) or **alābhi, astambhi**; ÇB. has **asañji.**

c. Augmentless forms, as in all other like cases, are met with, with either indicative or subjunctive value: examples (besides the two or three already given) are: **dhā́yi, çrā́vi, bhāri, reci, védi, roci, jáni, pā́di, sā́di, ardhi.** The accent, when present, is always on the root-syllable (SV. **dhāyí** is doubtless a false reading).

845. These forms are made in RV. from forty roots, and all the other earlier texts combined add only about twenty to the number; from the later language are quotable thirty or forty more; in the epics they are nearly unknown. When they come from roots of neuter meaning, as **gam, pad, sad, bhrāj, rādh, ruc, sañj,** they have (like the so-called passive participle in **ta: 952**) a value equivalent to that of other middle forms; in a case or two (RV. vii. 73. 3 [?]; VS. xxviii. 15; TB. ii. 6. 10[2]) they appear even to be used transitively.

2. The a-aorist.

846. a. This aorist is in the later language allowed to be made from a large number of roots (near a hundred). It is made in both voices, but is rare in the middle, most of the roots forming their middle according to the s-class (**878** ff.) or the iṣ-class (**898** ff.).

b. Its closest analogy is with the imperfect of the á-class (**751** ff.); its inflection is the same with that in all particulars; and it takes in general a weak form of root — save the roots in ऋ ṛ (three or four only), which have the guṇa-strengthening.

c. As example of inflection may be taken the root सिच् **sic** *pour*. Thus:

	active.			middle.		
	s.	d.	p.	s.	d.	p.
1	असिचम् **ásicam**	असिचाव **ásicāva**	असिचाम **ásicāma**	असिचे **asice**	असिचावहि **ásicāvahi**	असिचामहि **ásicāmahi**
2	असिचस् **ásicas**	असिचतम् **ásicatam**	असिचत **ásicata**	असिचथास् **ásicathās**	असिचेथाम् **ásicethām**	असिचध्वम् **ásicadhvam**
3	असिचत् **ásicat**	असिचताम् **ásicatām**	असिचन् **ásican**	असिचत **ásicata**	असिचेताम् **ásicetām**	असिचन्त **ásicanta**

847. The **a**-aorist makes in the RV. a small figure beside the root-aorist, being represented by less than half the latter's number of roots. It becomes, however, more common later (it is the only form of aorist which is made from more verbs in AV. than in RV.); and in Veda and Brāhmaṇa together about eighty roots exhibit the formation more or less fully. Of these a large number (fully half) are of the type of the roots which make their present-system according to the **á**-class, having a vowel capable of **guṇa**-strengthening before a final consonant (**754**): thus, with **i**, **chid**, **bhid**, **nij**, **ric**, **riṣ**, **lip**, **vid**, 1**çiṣ** (**çās**), 2 **çiṣ**, **çriṣ**, **çliṣ**, **sic**, **sridh**; — with **u**, **krudh**, **kṣudh**, **guh**, **duṣ**, **dyut**, **druh**, **puṣ**, **budh**, **bhuj**, **muc**, **mruc**, **yuj**, **ruc**, **rud**, **rudh**, **muh**, **ruh**, **çuc**; — with **ṛ**, **ṛdh**, **kṛt**, **gṛdh**, **gṛh**, **tṛp**, **tṛṣ**, **tṛh**, **dṛp**, **dṛç**, **dhṛṣ**, **nṛt**, **mṛdh**, **mṛṣ**, **vṛt**, **vṛdh**, **vṛṣ**, **sṛp**, **hṛṣ**. A small number end in vowels: thus, **ṛ**, **kṛ**, **sṛ** (which have the **guṇa**-strengthening throughout), **hi** (? **ahyat** once in AV.), and several in **ā**, apparent transfers from the root-class by the weakening of their **ā** to **a**: thus, **khyā**, **hvā**, **vyā**, **çvā**, and **dā** and **dhā**; and **āsthat**, regarded by the grammarians as aorist to √**as** *throw*, is doubtless a like formation from √**sthā**. A few have a penultimate nasal in the present and elsewhere, which in this aorist is lost: thus, **bhrañç**, **taṅs**, **dhvaṅs**, **sraṅs**, **krand**, **randh**. Of less classifiable character are **aç**, **kram**, **gam**, **ghas**, **tam**, **çam**, **çram**, **tan**, **san**, **sad**, **āp**, **das**, **yas**, **çak**, **dagh**. The roots **pat**, **naç**, **vac** form the tense-stems **papta**, **neça**, **voca**, of which the first is palpably and the other two are probably the result of reduplication; but the language has lost the sense of their being such, and makes other reduplicated aorists from the same roots (see below, **854**).

a. Many of these aorists are simply transfers of the root-aorist to an **a**-inflection. Conspicuous examples are **akarat** etc. and **agamat** etc. (in the earliest period only **akar** and **agan**).

848. The inflection of this aorist is in general so regular that it will be sufficient to give only examples of its Vedic forms. We may take as model **avidam**, from √**vid** *find*, of which the various persons and modes are more frequent and in fuller variety than those of any other verb. Only the forms actually quotable are instanced; those of which the examples found are from other verbs than **vid** are bracketed. Thus:

	active.			middle.		
	s.	d.	p.	s.	d.	p.
1	**ávidam**	**ávidāva**	**ávidāma**	**ávide**	[**ávidāvahi**]	**ávidāmahi**
2	**ávidas**		[**ávidata**]	[**ávidathās**]		
3	**ávidat**		**ávidan**	[**avidata**]	[**avidetām**]	**ávidanta**

a. The middle forms are rare in the earlier language, as in the later: we have **áhve** etc., **ákhye** etc., **ávide** (?) and **avidanta**, **avocathās** and **avocāvahi** (and **avidāmahe** GB. and **asicāmahe** KB. are doubtless to be amended to **-mahi**).

b. Augmentless forms, with indicative or subjunctive value, are not infrequent. Examples, showing accent on the tense-sign, according to the general analogies of the formation, are: **ruhám, sṛpas, bhuját, vidát, aratām, vocata, çakan; vidata** and **vyáta** (3d sing.), **arāmahi, çiṣāmahi, vidánta, budhánta, mṛṣanta** (for exceptions as regards accent, see below, **853**).

Modes of the a-aorist.

849. The subjunctive forms of this aorist are few; those which occur are instanced below, in the method which was followed for the indicative:

1	[vidā́va]	vidāma	[vidāmahe]
2	vidā́si / vidā́s	vidāthas	vidātha	
3	vidā́t		[vidātāi?]

a. The ending **thana** is found once, in **riṣāthana.** Of middle forms occur only **çiṣātāi** (AV.: but doubtless misreading for **çíṣyātāi**) and **çiṣāmahe** (AV., for RV. **çiṣāmahi**). The form **sádathas** seems an indicative, made from a secondary present-stem.

850. The optatives are few in the oldest language, but become more frequent, and in the Brāhmaṇas are not rare. Examples are: in active, **bhideyam, vidéyam, sanéyam** (TB. once **sanem**); **vidés, games; gamet, vocet; gametam; gaméma, çakéma, sanéma; vareta;** in middle, (only) **videya; gamemahi, vanemahi: ruhethās** etc. in the epics must be viewed rather as present forms of the **á**-class.

a. A single middle precative form occurs, namely **videṣṭa** (AV., once); it is so isolated that how much may be inferred from it is very questionable.

851. A complete series of active imperative forms are made from √**sad** (including **sadatana**, 2d pl.), and the middle **sadantām.** Other imperatives are very rare: namely, **sána, sára, ruha, vidá; ruhátam, vidátam; khyáta.** TS. has once **vṛdhātu** (compare **740**).

Participles of the a-aorist.

852. a. The active participles **tṛpánt, ríṣant** or **rīṣant, vṛdhánt, çiṣánt, çucánt, sádant,** and (in participial compounds, **1309**) **kṛtant-, guhant-, vidant-** (all RV.), are to be assigned with plausibility to this aorist.

b. Likewise the middle participles **guhámāna, dhṛṣámāṇa, dásamāna** (?), **nṛtámāna, çucámāna,** and perhaps **vṛdhāná, sridhāná.**

Irregularities of the a-aorist.

853. A few irregularities and peculiarities may be noticed here.

The roots in **ṛ**, which (**847**) show a strengthening like that of the present of the unaccented **a**-class, have likewise the accent upon the radical syllable, like that class: thus, from √ṛ, **áranta** (augmentless 3d pl.), **sárat** and **sára**. The root **sad** follows the same rule: thus, **sádatam**; and from √**san** are found **sánas** and **sánat** and **sánema** and **sána**, beside **sanéyam** and **sanéma**. It is questionable whether these are not true analogues of the **bhū**-class (unaccented **a**-class) present-system. On the other hand, **rúhat** (beside **ruhám, ruhā́va, ruhátam**), **çíṣat** and **çíṣātāi** (?), and **ríṣant** or **ríṣant** are more isolated cases. In view of such as these, the forms from the stem **bhúva** and **çrúva** (**836**c) are perhaps to be referred hither. From √**vac**, the optative is accented **vocéyam, vocés, vocéma, vocéyus**; elsewhere the accent is on the root-syllable: thus, **vóce, vócat, vócati, vócanta.**

854. a. The stem **voc** has in Vedic use well-nigh assumed the value of a root; its forms are very various and of frequent use, in RV. especially far outnumbering in occurrences all other forms from √**vac**. Besides those already given, we find **vocā** (1st sing. impv.) and **vocāti, vocāvahāi; voces, voceya, vocemahi; vocatāt** (2d sing.), **vocatu, vocatam, vocata.**

b. Of the stem **neça** from √**naç** only **neçat** occurs.

c. The root **çās** (as in some of its present forms: **639**) is weakened to **çiṣ**, and makes **açiṣam.**

855. Isolated forms which have more or less completely the aspect of indicative presents are made in the oldest language from some roots beside the aorist-systems of the first two classes. It must be left for maturer research to determine how far they may be relics of original presents, and how far recent productions, made in the way of conversion of the aorist-stem to a root in value.

a. Such forms are the following: from √**kṛ** *make*, **kárṣi, kṛthas, kṛtha, kṛṣe**; from √**gam, gathá**; from √**ci** *gather*, **ceti**; from √**dā** *give*, **dā́ti, dātu**; from √**dhā** *put*, **dhāti**; from √**pā** *drink*, **pāthás, pānti**; from √**bhṛ, bharti**; from √**muc, mucánti**; from √**rudh, rudhmas** (?); from √**vṛt, vartti.**

II. (3) Reduplicated Aorist.

856. The reduplicated aorist is different from the other forms of aorist in that it has come to be attached in almost all cases to the derivative (causative etc.) conjugation in अय **áya**, as the aorist of that conjugation, and is therefore liable to be made from all roots which have such a conjugation, beside the aorist or aorists which belong to their primary conjugation. Since, however, the connection of the two is not a formal one (the aorist being made directly from the root, and not from the causative stem), but rather a matter of established association, owing to kinship of meaning, the formation and inflection of this kind of aorist is best treated here, along with the others.

857. Its characteristic is a reduplication of the radical syllable, by which it is assimilated, on the one hand, to the imperfect of the reduplicating class (**656** ff.), and, on the other hand, to the so-called pluperfect (**817** ff.). But the aorist reduplication has taken on a quite peculiar character, with few traces left even in the Veda of a different condition which may have preceded this.

858. a. As regards, indeed, the consonant of the reduplication, it follows the general rules already given (**590**). And the quality of the reduplicated vowel is in general as in the formations already treated: it needs only to be noted that an **a**-vowel and **ṛ** (or **ar**) are usually (for exceptions, see below, **860**) repeated by an **i**-vowel — as they are, to a considerable extent, in the reduplicated present also (**660**).

b. But in regard to quantity, this aorist aims always at establishing a diversity between the reduplicating and radical syllables, making the one heavy and the other light. And the preference is very markedly for a heavy reduplication and a light root-syllable — which relation is brought about wherever the conditions allow. Thus:

859. If the root is a light syllable (having a short vowel followed by a single consonant), the reduplication is made heavy.

a. And this, usually by lengthening the reduplicating vowel, with **ī** for radical **a** or **ṛ** or **ḷ** (in the single root containing that vowel): thus, **arīriṣam, adūduṣam, ajījanam, avīvṛdham, acīkḷpam.** The great majority of reduplicated aorists are of this form.

b. If, however, the root begins with two consonants, so that the reduplicating syllable will be heavy whatever the quantity of its vowel, the vowel remains short: thus, **acikṣipam, acukrudham, atitrasam, apispr̥çam.**

860. If the root is a heavy syllable (having a long vowel, or a short before two consonants), the vowel of the reduplication is short: and in this case अ **a** or आ **ā**, and ऋ **r̥** (if it occurs), are reduplicated by अ **a.**

a. Thus, **adidīkṣam, abubhūṣam** (not quotable), **adadakṣam, adadhāvam, atatañsam.** And, in the cases in which a root should both begin and end with two consonants, both syllables would be necessarily heavy, notwithstanding the short vowel in the former: thus, **apapraccham, acaskandam** (but no such forms are found in use).

b. A medial **r̥** is allowed by the grammarians to retain the strengthening of the causative stem, together with, of course, reduplication by **a**: thus, **acakarṣat, avavartat** (beside **acīkr̥ṣat, avīvr̥tat**); but no such forms have been met with in use.

c. These aorists are not distinguishable in form from the so-called pluperfects (**817** ff.).

861. a. In order, however, to bring about the favored relation of heavy reduplication and light radical syllable, a heavy root is sometimes made light: either by shortening its vowel, as in **arīradham** from √**rādh, avīvaçam** from √**vāç, asīṣadham** from √**sādh, ajījivam** from √**jīv, adīdipam** (K. and later: RV. has **didipas**) from √**dīp, abībhiṣam** from √**bhīṣ, asūsucam** from √**sūc**; or by dropping a penultimate nasal, as in **acikradam** from √**krand, asiṣyadam** from √**syand.**

b. In those cases in which (**1047**) an aorist is formed directly from a causal stem in **āp**, the **ā** is abbreviated to **i**: thus, **atiṣṭhipam** etc., **ajijñipat** (but KSS. **ajijñapat**), **jīhipas, ajījipata** (but VS. **ajījapata**); but from **çrap** comes **açiçrapāma** (ÇB.).

862. Examples of this aorist from roots with initial vowel are very rare: the older language has only **āmamat** (or **amamat**) from √**am, āpipan** (ÇB.: BAU. **āpipipat**) from √**āp**, and **arpipam** (augmentless) from the causative stem **arp** of √**r̥** — in which latter the root is excessively abbreviated. The grammarians give other similar formations, as **ārcicam** from √**arc, āubjijam** from √**ubj, ārjiham** from √**arh, āicikṣam** from √**īkṣ, ārdidham** from √**r̥dh.** Compare the similar reduplication in desiderative stems: **1029 b.**

863. Of special irregularities may be mentioned:

a. From √**dyut** is made (V.B.) the stem **didyuta**, taking its reduplicating vowel from the radical semivowel. From √**gup**, instead of **jūgupa** (B.S.), JB. has **jugūpa**, and some texts (B.S.) have **jugupa**; and **jīhvara** (B.) is met with beside the regular **jihvara** (V.B.). In **caccha-**

da (Nir.), and the more or less doubtful **paprátha** and **çaçvacá** and **sasvaja** (RV.) we have **a** instead of **i** in the reduplication.

b. In support of their false view of this aorist as made from the causative stem instead of directly from the root, the native grammarians teach that roots ending in an **u**-vowel may reduplicate with **i**, as representing the **ā** of the strengthened stem: thus, **bībhava** from **bhāv-aya,** as well as **būbhuva** from **bhū.** No example of such a formation, however, is met with except **ápiplavam** (ÇB., once); against it we find **dudruva, būbhuva, rūruva, çuçruva,** and others.

c. As to **apaptam, avocam,** and **aneçam,** see above, **847.**

864. The inflection of the reduplicated aorist is like that of an imperfect of the second general conjugation: that is to say, it has अ **a** as final stem-vowel, with all the peculiarities which the presence of that vowel conditions (733 a). Thus, from √जन् **jan** *give birth* (stem **jījana**):

	active.			middle.		
	s.	d.	p.	s.	d.	p.
1	अजीजनम्	अजीजनाव	अजीजनाम	अजीजने	अजीजनावहि	अजीजनामहि
	ájījanam	**ájījanāva**	**ájījanāma**	**ájījane**	**ájījanāvahi**	**ájījanāmahi**
2	अजीजनस्	अजीजनतम्	अजीजनत	अजीजनथास्	अजीजनेथाम्	अजीजनध्वम्
	ájījanas	**ájījanatam**	**ájījanata**	**ájījanathās**	**ájījanethām**	**ájījanadhvam**
3	अजीजनत्	अजीजनताम्	अजीजनन्	अजीजनत	अजीजनेताम्	अजीजनन्त
	ájījanat	**ájījanatām**	**ájījanan**	**ájījanata**	**ájījanetām**	**ájījananta**

865. The middle forms are rare in the older language (the 3d pl. is decidedly the most common of them, being made from eleven roots; the 3d s. from seven); but all, both active and middle, are quotable except 1st and 2d du. middle and 1st du. active.

a. **Atītape** appears to be once used (RV.) as 3d sing., with passive sense.

866. A final **ṛ** has the guṇa-strengthening before the endings: thus, **acīkarat, apīparam, atītaras, dīdaras, adīdharat, amīmarat, avīvaran, jihvaras.** Of similar strengthened forms from **ī** and **u**-roots are found **apiprayan** (TS.), **abībhayanta** (RV.), **apiplavam** (ÇB.), **acucyavat** (K.), **açuçravat** (MS.), **atuṣṭavam** (RV.). Not many roots ending in other vowels than **ṛ** make this aorist: see below, **868.**

867. Forms of the inflection without union-vowel are occasionally met with: namely, from roots ending in consonants, **síṣvap** (2d sing., augmentless) from √**svap,** and **açiçnat** from √**çnath;** from roots in **ṛ** or **ar, dīdhar** (2d sing.), and **ajīgar** (2d and 3d sing.); for roots in **i**- and **u**-vowels, see **868.** Of 3d pl. in **us** are found almost only a form or two from **i-** and **u-**roots, with **guṇa** before the ending: thus, **açiçrayus, áсucyavus, açuçravus, asuṣavus**; but also **abībhajus** (ÇB.), and **nīnaçus** (MBh.).

868. In the later language, a few roots are said by the grammarians to make this aorist as a part of their primary conjugation: they are **çri** and **çvi, dru** and **sru, kam,** and **dhā** *suck* (**çvi** and **dhā** optionally).

a. In the older language are found from √**çri açiçret** and **açiçrayus** (noticed in the preceding paragraph) and **açiçriyat** (ÇB.); from √**dru, adudrot** and **adudruvat** (TB.: not used as aorist); from √**sru, asusrot** and (augmentless) **susros** and **susrot**; from √**kam, acīkametām** and **-manta** (B.S.). Of forms analogous with these occur a number from roots in **u** or **ū**: thus, **anūnot** and **nūnot** from √**nu**; **yūyot** from √**yu** *separate;* **dūdhot** from √**dhū**; **apupot** from √**pū**; **tūtos** and **tūtot** from √**tu**; **asuṣot** from √**sū**; — and one or two from roots in **i** or **ī**: thus, **siṣet** from √**si** (or **sā**) *bind;* **amīmet** from √**mā** *bellow;* **apipres** (with **apiprayan,** noticed above) from √**prī** (and the "imperfects" from **dīdhī** etc., **676**, are of corresponding form). And from √**cyu** are made, with union-vowel **ī**, **acucyavīt** and **acucyavītana.** Few of these forms possess a necessarily causative or a decidedly aoristic value, and it is very doubtful whether they should not be assigned to the perfect-system.

b. From the later language are quotable only **açiçriyat** etc. (3d pl., **-yan** or **-yus**) and **adudruvat.**

Modes of the Reduplicated Aorist.

869. a. As in other preterit formations, the augmentless indicative persons of this aorist are used subjunctively, and they are very much more frequent than true subjunctives.

b. Of the latter are found only **rīradhā** (1st sing.); **tītapāsi; cīkḷpāti** and **sīṣadhāti,** and **pispṛçati** (as if corresponding to an indicative **apispṛk,** like **açiçnat**); and perhaps the 1st sing. mid. **çaçvacāí.**

c. The augmentless indicative forms are accented in general on the reduplication: thus, **dī́dharas, nī́naças; jī́janat, pī́parat; jī́janan;** also **síṣvap;** but, on the other hand, we have also **pīpárat, çiçráthas** and **çiçnáthat,** and **dudrávat** and **tuṣṭávat** (which may perhaps belong to the perfect: compare **810**). According to the native grammarians, the accent rests either on the radical syllable or on the one that follows it.

870. Optative forms are even rarer. The least questionable case is the middle "precative" **rīriṣīṣṭa** (**ririṣīṣṭa** has been ranked above with **sāsahīṣṭa,** as a perfect: **812b**). **Cucyuvīmahi** and **cucyavīrata** belong either here or to the perfect-system.

871. Of imperatives, we have the indubitable forms **pūpurantu** and **çiçrathantu.** And **jigṛtám** and **jigṛtá,** and **didhṛtam** and **didhṛtá,**

and **jajastám** (all RV. only), and perhaps **suṣūdáta** (AV.), are to be referred hither, as corresponding to the indicatives (without union-vowel) **ajīgar** and **adīdhar**: their short reduplicating vowel and their accent assimilate them closely to the reduplicated imperfects (**656** ff.), with which we are probably to regard this aorist as ultimately related.

872. No participle is found belonging to the reduplicated aorist.

873. The number of roots from which this aorist is met with in the earlier language is about a hundred and twenty. In the later Sanskrit it is unusual; in the series of later texts mentioned above (**826**) it occurs only twice; and it has been found quotable from hardly fifty roots in the whole epic and classical literature.

III. Sigmatic or Sibilant Aorist.

874. **a.** The common tense-sign of all the varieties of this aorist is a स् **s** (convertible to ष् **ṣ**: **180**) which is added to the root in forming the tense-stem.

b. This sibilant has no analogues among the class-signs of the present-system; but it is to be compared with that which appears (and likewise with or without the same union-vowel **i**) in the stems of the future tense-system (**932** ff.) and of the desiderative conjugation (**1027** ff.).

c. To the root thus increased the augment is prefixed and the secondary endings are added.

875. In the case of a few roots, the sibilant tense-stem (always ending in क्ष् **kṣ**) is further increased by an अ **a**, and the inflection is nearly like that of an imperfect of the second or **a**- conjugation.

876. **a.** In the vast majority of cases, the sibilant is the final of the tense-stem, and the inflection is like that of an imperfect of the first or non-**a**-conjugation.

b. And these, again, fall into two nearly equal and strongly marked classes, according as the sibilant is added immediately to the final of the root, or with an auxiliary vowel इ **i**, making the tense-sign इष् **iṣ**. Finally, before this इष् **iṣ** the root is in a very small number of cases increased by a स् **s**, making the whole addition सिष् **siṣ**.

877. We have, then, the following classification for the varieties of sibilant-aorist:

A. With endings added directly to the sibilant:

4. with स् **s** simply after the root: **s-aorist**;

5. with इ **i** before the स् **s**: **iṣ-aorist**;

6. the same, with स् **s** at end of root: **siṣ-aorist**.

B. With अ **a** added to the sibilant before the endings:

7. with sibilant and अ **a**: **sa-aorist**.

a. As regards the distinction between the fourth and fifth forms, it may be said in a general way that those roots incline to take the auxiliary i in the aorist which take it also in other formations; but it is impossible to lay down any strict rules as to this accordance. Compare **903**.

4. The s-aorist.

878. The tense-stem of this aorist is made by adding स् **s** to the augmented root, of which also the vowel is usually strengthened.

879. The general rules as to the strengthening of the root-vowel are these:

a. A final vowel (including ऋ **ṛ**) has the vṛddhi-change in the active, and (excepting ऋ **ṛ**) guṇa in the middle: thus, from √नी *lead*, active stem अनैष **anāiṣ**, middle stem अनेष् **aneṣ**; from √श्रु **çru** *hear*, अश्रौष् **açrāuṣ** and अश्रोष् **açroṣ**; from √कृ **kṛ** *make*, अकार्ष् **akārṣ** and अकृष् **akṛṣ**.

b. A medial vowel has the vṛddhi-change in the active, and remains unaltered in the middle: thus, from √छन्द् **chand** *seem*, active stem अच्छान्त्स् **acchānts**, middle stem अच्छन्त्स् **acchants**; from √रिच् **ric** *leave*, अरैक्ष् **arāikṣ** and अरिक्ष् **arikṣ**; from √रुध् **rudh** *obstruct*, अरौत्स् **arāuts** and अरुत्स् **aruts**; from √सृज् **sṛj** *pour out*, अस्राक्ष् **asrākṣ** and असृक्ष् **asṛkṣ**.

880. a. The endings are the usual secondary ones, with उस् **us** (not अन् **an**) in 3d pl. act., and अत **ata** (not अन्त **anta**) in 3d pl. mid.

b. But before स् s and त् t of 2d and 3d sing. act. is in the later language always inserted an ई ī, making the endings ईस् īs and ईत् īt.

c. This insertion is unknown in the earliest language (of the RV.): see below, **888**.

881. a. Before endings beginning with t or th, the tense-sign s is (**233 c—e**) omitted after the final consonant of a root — unless this be r, or n or m (converted to **anusvāra**).

b. The same omission is of course made before **dhvam** after a consonant; and after a vowel the sibilant is either omitted or assimilated (the equivalence of **dhv** and **ddhv** in the theories of the grammarians and the practice of the manuscripts makes it impossible to say which: **232**); and then the ending becomes **ḍhvam,** provided the sibilant, if retained, would have been ṣ (**226 c**): thus, **astoḍhvam** and **avṛḍhvam** (beside **astoṣata** and **avṛṣata**); **dṛḍhvam** (√dṛ *regard:* ÇB., once), which is to **dṛthās** (2d sing.) as **avṛḍhvam** and **avṛṣata** to **avri** and **avṛthās**; and **kṛḍhvam** (M.).

c. According to the grammarians, the omission of **s** before **t** and **th** takes place also after a short vowel (the case can occur only in the 2d and 3d sing. mid.); but we have seen above (**834 a**) that this is to be viewed rather as a substitution in those persons of the forms of the root-aorist. Neither in the earlier nor in the later language, however, does any example occur of an aorist-form with **s** retained after a short vowel before these endings.

d. After the final sonant aspirate of a root, the sibilant before the same endings is said by the Hindu grammarians to disappear altogether, the combination of the aspirate with the **th** or **t** of the ending being then made according to the ordinary rule for such cases (**160**): thus, from the stem **arāuts,** for **arāudh-s,** is made **arāuddha,** as if from **arāudh+ta** directly. No example of such a form is quotable from the literature; but the combination is established by the occurrence of other similar cases (**233 f**). In the middle, in like manner, **aruts+ta** becomes **aruddha,** as if from **arudh+ta;** but all such forms admit also of being understood as of the root-aorist. Those that have been found to occur were given above (**834 d**); probably they belong at least in part to this aorist.

e. From the three nasal roots **gam, tan, man** are made the 2d and 3d sing. mid. persons **agathās** and **agata, atathās** and **atata,** and **amata** (**amathās** not quotable), reckoned by the native grammarians as **s**-aorist forms, made, after loss of their final root-nasal, with loss also of the sibilant after a short vowel. They are doubtless better referred to the root-aorist. But JB. has a corresponding 1st sing. **atasi** from √**tan.**

882. As examples of the inflection of this variety of

sibilant aorist we may take the roots नी **nī** *lead*, and छिद् **chid** *cut off*. Thus:

	active.			middle.		
	s.	d.	p.	s.	d.	p.
1	अनैषम्	अनैष्व	अनैष्म	अनेषि	अनेष्वहि	अनेष्महि
	ánāiṣam	**ánāiṣva**	**ánāiṣma**	**áneṣi**	**áneṣvahi**	**áneṣmahi**
2	अनैषीस्	अनैष्टम्	अनैष्ट	अनेष्ठास्	अनेषाथाम्	अनेढ्वम्
	ánāiṣīs	**ánāiṣṭam**	**ánāiṣṭa**	**áneṣṭhās**	**áneṣāthām**	**áneḍhvam**
3	अनैषीत्	अनैष्टाम्	अनैषुस्	अनेष्ट	अनेषाताम्	अनेषत
	ánāiṣīt	**ánāiṣṭām**	**ánāiṣus**	**áneṣṭa**	**áneṣātām**	**áneṣata**

	active.		
	s.	d.	p.
1	अच्छैत्सम्	अच्छैत्स्व	अच्छैत्स्म
	ácchāitsam	**ácchāitsva**	**ácchāitsma**
2	अच्छैत्सीस्	अच्छैत्तम्	अच्छैत्त
	ácchāitsīs	**ácchāittam**	**ácchāitta**
3	अच्छैत्सीत्	अच्छैत्ताम्	अच्छैत्सुस्
	ácchāitsīt	**ácchāittām**	**ácchāitsus**
	middle.		
1	अच्छित्सि	अच्छित्स्वहि	अच्छित्स्महि
	ácchitsi	**ácchitsvahi**	**ácchitsmahi**
2	अच्छित्थास्	अच्छित्साथाम्	अच्छिद्ध्वम्
	ácchitthās	**ácchitsāthām**	**ácchiddhvam**
3	अच्छित्त	अच्छित्साताम्	अच्छित्सत
	acchitta	**ácchitsātām**	**ácchitsata**

a. From √**rudh** *obstruct*, the 2d and 3d du. and 2d pl. act. and the 2d and 3d sing. mid. would be **árāuddham, árāuddhām, árāuddha, áruddhās, áruddha**; from √**sṛj** *pour out*, **ásrāṣṭam, ásrāṣṭām, asrāṣṭa, asṛṣṭhās, asṛṣṭa**; from √**dṛç** *see*, **ádrāṣṭam** etc. (as from **sṛj**). But from √**kṛ** *do* the same persons in the active are **ákārṣṭam, ákārṣṭām, ákārṣṭa**; from √**tan** *stretch* they are **átāṅstam, átāṅstām, átāṅsta.**

883. The omission of **s** in the active persons (**ácchāittam, ácchāittām, ácchāitta**) is a case of very rare occurrence; all the quotable examples were given above (**233 e**). As to the like omission in middle persons, see **881**. The ChU. has twice **ávāstam** for **avāts-tam** (√**vas** *dwell*): this may be viewed as another case of total disappearance of the sibilant, and consequent restoration of the final radical to its original form.

884. Certain roots in ā weaken the ā in middle inflection to i (as also in the root-aorist: above, **834a**): these are said to be **sthā**, **dā**, and **dhā**; in the older language have been noted **ádiṣi** and **adiṣata** from √**dā** *give* (and **adiṣi** perhaps once from √**dā** *bind*), **adhiṣi** and **adhiṣata** (with the optative **dhiṣīya**) from √**dhā** *put*, and **asthiṣata**; also **agīṣṭhās** and **agīṣata** from √**gā** *go* (with **adhi**).

a. The middle inflection of the aorist of √**dā** would be, then, according to the grammarians: **ádiṣi, ádithās, ádita; ádiṣvahi, ádiṣāthām, ádiṣātām; ádiṣmahi, ádiḍhvam, ádiṣata.**

885. Roots ending in changeable **ṛ** (so-called roots in **ṝ**: **242**) are said by the grammarians to convert this vowel to **īr** in middle forms: thus, **astīrṣi, astīrṣṭhās** etc. (from √**stṛ**); of such forms, however, has been found in the older language only **akīrṣata**, PB.

886. The s-aorist is made in the older language from about a hundred and forty roots (in RV., from about seventy; in AV., from about fifty, of which fifteen are additional to those in RV.); and the epic and classical literature adds but a very small number. It has in the Veda certain peculiarities of stem-formation and inflection, and also the full series of modes — of which the optative middle is retained also later as a part of the "precative" (but see **925 b**).

887. Irregularities of stem-formation are as follows:

a. The strengthening of the root-syllable is now and then irregularly made or omitted: thus, **ayokṣīt** (AB.), **chetsīs** (B.S.; also occurs in MBh., which has further **yotsīs**), **rotsīs** (KU.); **amatsus** (RV.); **ayāṁsi** and **arāutsi** (AB.), **asākṣi** etc. (V.B.: √**sah**), **mān̄sta** (AV.) and **mān̄stām** (TA.); **lopsīya** (U.); and MBh. has **drogdhās**. From √**saj** is made **sāñkṣīt** (U. etc.), and from √**majj**, **amāñkṣīt** (not quotable). The form **ayuñkṣmahi** (BhP.) is doubtless a false reading.

b. A radical final nasal is lost in **agasmahi** (RV.) and **gasāthām** (TA.) from √**gam**, and in the optatives **masīya** and **vasīmahi** (RV.) from √√**man** and **van**.

c. The roots **hū, dhū,** and **nū** have **ū** instead of **o** in the middle: thus, **ahūṣata, adhūṣata, anūṣi** and **anūṣātām** and **anūṣata**; √**dhur** (or **dhūrv**) makes **adhūrṣata**.

d. ÇB. has once **atrāsatām** for **atrāstām** (√**trā**).

888. The principal peculiarity of the older language in regard to inflection is the frequent absence of **ī** in the endings of 2d and 3d sing. act., and the consequent loss of the consonant-ending, and sometimes of root-finals (**150**). The forms without **ī** are the only ones found in RV. and K., and they outnumber the others in AV. and TS.; in the Brāhmaṇas they grow rarer (only one, **adrāk**, occurs in GB.; one, **ayāṭ**, in KB.; and two, **adrāk** and **ayāṭ**, in ÇB.; PB. has none).

889. If the root ends in a vowel, only the consonant of the ending is necessarily lost: thus, **aprās** (for both **aprās-s** and **aprās-t**) from √**prā**; and in like manner **ahās** from √**hā**; — **ajāis** (for **ajāiṣ-t**) from √**ji**; and in like manner **acāis** from √**ci**, and **nāis** (augmentless) from √**nī**; — and **yāus** (for **ayāuṣ-t**) from √**yu**.

a. But (as in other like cases: **555a**) the ending is sometimes preserved at the expense of the tense-sign; and we have in 3d sing. **ajāit** (beside **ajāis** and **ajāiṣīt**) from √**ji**; and in like manner **acāit, açrāit, ahāit, nāit** (no examples have been noted except from roots in **i** and **ī**): compare **ayās** and **srās**, 2d sing., **890a.**

890. a. If the root (in either its simple or strengthened form) ends in a consonant, the tense-sign is lost with the ending. Thus, **abhār** (for **abhārṣ-t**: beside **abhārṣam, abhārṣṭām**) from √**bhṛ**; other like cases are **ahār**, and (from roots in **ar**) **akṣār, atsār, asvār, hvār.** Further, **ārāik** (**585a**: for **arāikṣ-t**) from √**ric**; like cases are **açvāit** from √**çvit**, and (from roots with medial **u**) **adyāut** from √**dyut, arāut** from √**rudh**, and **māuk** from √**muc**. Further, from roots ending in the palatals and **h**, **aprāk** from √**pṛc, asrāk** from √**sṛj, abhāk** from √**bhaj, adrāk** from √**dṛç, adhāk** from √**dah**; but, with a different change of the final, **ayāṭ** from √**yaj, aprāṭ** from √**pṛch, avāṭ** from √**vah**, and **asrāṭ** from √**sṛj**; and (above, **146a**) **srās** appears to stand twice in AV. for **srāṣ-s** from √**sṛj**; RV. has also twice **ayās** from √**yaj.** Further, from roots ending in a nasal, **atān** from √**tan, khān** from √**khan, ayān** and **anān** from √√**yam** and **nam** (**143a**).

b. If, again, the roots end in a double consonant, the latter of the two is lost along with tense-sign and ending: thus, **acchān** (for **acchānts-t**; beside **acchāntta** and **acchāntsus**) from √**chand**; and other like cases are **akrān, askān**, and **asyān.**

891. A relic of this peculiarity of the older inflection has been preserved to the later language in the 2d sing. **bhāis,** from √**bhī.**

Modes of the s-aorist.

892. The indicative forms without augment are used in a subjunctive sense, especially after **mā́** prohibitive, and are not uncommon. Examples with accent, however, are extremely rare; there has been noted only **váṅsi**, middle; judging from this, the tone would be found on the radical syllable. According to the Hindu grammarians, it may be laid on either root or ending.

893. Proper subjunctive forms are not rare in RV., but are markedly less common in the later Vedic texts, and very seldom met with in the Brāhmaṇas. They are regularly made with guṇa-strengthening of the radical vowel, in both active and middle, and with accent on the root.

a. The forms with primary endings are: in active, **stoṣāṇi; darṣasi; neṣati, parṣati, pāsati, matsati, yoṣati, vakṣati, sakṣati; dā́sathas, dhāsathas, párṣathas, vakṣathas, varṣathas; pāsatas, yaṁsatas, yakṣatas, vakṣatas; dhāsatha, neṣatha, párṣatha, mátsatha;** — in middle, **naṁsāi, máṅsāi; máṅsase; kraṁsate, trāsate, darṣate, máṅsate, yakṣate, rāsate, vaṅsate, sākṣate, hāsate; trā́sāthe** (not **trāsāithe,** as we should rather expect); **náṁsante, máṅsante:** and, with the fuller ending in 3d sing., **mā́sātāi.**

b. The forms with secondary endings are (active only): **jéṣas, vákṣas; dárṣat, néṣat, pákṣat, párṣat, préṣat, yákṣat, yóṣat, váṅsat, vákṣat, véṣat, sátsat, chantsat,** etc. (some twenty others); **yakṣatām; váṅsāma, sā́kṣāma; stoṣāma; parṣan, yaṁsan, yoṣan, rā́san, vakṣan, çéṣan, çróṣan.** Of these, **yakṣat** and **vakṣat** are found not rarely in the Brāhmaṇas; any others, hardly more than sporadically.

894. Of irregularities are to be noted the following:

a. The forms **dṛ́kṣase** and **pṛkṣase** (2d sing. mid.) lack the **guṇa**-strengthening.

b. Jeṣam, stoṣam, and **yoṣam** (AV. **yūṣam,** with **ū** for **o** as in **anūṣata** etc.) appear to be first persons formed under government of the analogy of the second and third — unless they are relics of a state of things anterior to the **vṛddhi**-strengthening: in which case **jeṣma** is to be compared with them (we should expect **jāiṣma** or **jeṣāma**).

c. From roots in **ā** are made a few forms of problematic character: namely, **yeṣam** (only case in RV.), **khyeṣam, jñeṣam, geṣam** and **geṣma, deṣma, seṣam** and **set, stheṣam** and **stheṣus.** Their value is optative. The analogy of **jeṣam** and **jeṣma** suggests the possibility of their derivation from **i**-forms of the **ā**-roots; or the sibilant might be of a precative character (thus, **yā-ī-s-am**). That they really belong to the **iṣ**-aorist appears highly improbable.

d. The RV. has a few difficult first persons middle in **se,** which are perhaps best noted here. They are: 1. from the simple root, **kṛṣe, hiṣe** (and **ohiṣe?**), **stuṣé;** 2. from present-stems, **arcase, ṛñjase, yajase, gāyiṣe, gṛṇīṣé** and **punīṣé.** They have the value of indicative present. Compare below, **897 b.**

895. Optative forms of this aorist are made in the middle only, and they have in 2d and 3d sing. always the precative **s** before the endings. Those found to occur in the older language are: **diṣīya, dhiṣīya, bhakṣīyá, masīya** (for **maṅsīya**), **mukṣīya, rāsīya, lopsīya, sākṣīya, stṛṣīya; maṅsīṣṭhās; darṣīṣṭa, bhakṣīṣṭa, maṅsīṣṭa, mṛkṣīṣṭa; bhakṣīmahi, dhukṣīmáhi, maṅsīmáhi, vaṅsīmáhi, vasīmahi, sakṣīmáhi; maṅsīrata.** PB. has **bhukṣiṣīya,** which should belong to a **siṣ**-aorist. The RV. form **trā́sīthām** (for **trāsīyāthām** or **trāsāthām**) is an isolated anomaly.

a. This optative makes a part of the accepted "precative" of the later language: see below, **923, 925 b.**

896. Imperative persons from this aorist are extremely rare: we find the 2d sing. act. **neṣa** and **parṣa** and the 2d pl. **yaṅsata** (from **a**-stems, and showing rather, therefore, a treatment of the aorist-stem as a root), and the 3d sing. mid. **rāsatām** and pl. **rāsantām** (of which the same may be said).

Participles of the s-aorist.

897. a. Active participles are **dákṣat** or **dhákṣat,** and **sákṣat** (both RV.).

b. If **ṛñjase** (above, **894 d**) is to be reckoned as an **s**-aorist form, **ṛñjasāná** is an **s**-aorist participle; and of a kindred character, apparently, are **arçasāná, óhasāna, jrayasāná, dhiyasāná, mandasāná, yamasāná, rabhasāná, vṛdhasāná, sahasāná, çavasāná,** all in RV.; with **namasāná, bhiyásāna,** in AV. In RV. occurs also once **dhíṣamāṇa,** apparently an **a**-form of an **s**-aorist of √**dhī.**

5. The iṣ-aorist.

898. The tense-stem of this aorist adds the general tense-sign स् **s** by help of a prefixed auxiliary vowel इ **i**, making इष् **iṣ**, to the root, which is usually strengthened, and which has the augment.

899. The rules as to the strengthening of the root are as follows:

a. A final vowel has **vṛddhi** in the active, and **guṇa** in the middle: thus, अपाविष् **apāviṣ** and अपविष् **apaviṣ** from √पू **pū** *cleanse;* अतारिष् **atāriṣ**, act., from √तॄ **tṝ** *pass;* अशयिष् **açayiṣ**, mid., from √शी **çī** *lie.*

b. A medial vowel has **guṇa**, if capable of it, in both voices: thus, अलेशिष् **aleçiṣ**, act. and mid., from √लिश् **liç** *tear;* अरोचिष् **arociṣ** from √रुच् **ruc** *shine;* अवर्षिष् **avarṣiṣ** from √वृष् **vṛṣ** *rain;* but अजीविष् **ajīviṣ** from √जीव् **jīv** *live.*

c. Medial अ **a** is sometimes lengthened in the active; but it more usually remains unchanged in both voices.

d. The roots in the older language which show the lengthening are **kan, tan, ran, stan, svan, han, vraj, sad, mad, car, tsar, svar, jval, das, tras.** From **ran, san, kram, vad, rakṣ,** and **sah** occur forms of both kinds. From √**math** or **manth** are made the two stems **mathiṣ** and **manthiṣ.**

900. a. Of exceptions may be noted: √**mṛj** has (as elsewhere: **627**) **vṛddhi** instead of **guṇa**: thus, **amārjiṣam**; √**stṛ** has **astarīs**, and √**çṝ** has **açarīt** (also **açarāit** in AV.), with **guṇa** in active.

b. The root **grabh** or **grah** has (as in future etc., below, **936e**, **956**) long **ī** instead of **i** before the sibilant: thus, **agrabhīṣma, agrahīṣṭa, agrabhīṣata.** The roots in changeable **ṝ** (so-called roots in **ṝ**: **242**), and √**vṛ** are said by the grammarians to do the same optionally; but no forms with long **ī** from such roots have been found quotable. A Sūtra (PGS.) has once **anayīṣṭa** from √**nī** (doubtless a false reading).

901. The endings are as in the preceding formation (उस् **us** and अत **ata** in 3d pl.). But in 2d and 3d sing., the combinations **iṣ-s** and **iṣ-t** are from the earliest period of the language contracted into ईस् **īs** and ईत् **īt**.

a. The 2d pl. mid. should end always in **iḍhvam** (or **iḍḍhvam**, from **iṣ-dhvam**: **226**); and this is in fact the form in the only examples quotable, namely **ajaniḍhvam, artiḍhvam, āindhiḍhvam, vepiḍhvam**; as to the rules of the native grammarians respecting the matter, see **226c**.

902. As examples of the inflection of the iṣ-aorist may be taken the roots पू **pū** *cleanse*, and बुध् **budh** *wake*. Thus:

	active.			middle.		
	s.	d.	p.	s.	d.	p.
1	अपाविषम् **ápāviṣam**	अपाविष्व **ápāviṣva**	अपाविष्म **ápāviṣma**	अपविषि **ápaviṣi**	अपविष्वहि **ápaviṣvahi**	अपविष्महि **ápaviṣmahi**
2	अपावीस् **ápāvīs**	अपाविष्टम् **ápāviṣṭam**	अपाविष्ट **ápāviṣṭa**	अपविष्ठास् **ápaviṣṭhās**	अपविषाथाम् **ápaviṣāthām**	अपविढ्वम् **ápaviḍhvam**
3	अपावीत् **ápāvīt**	अपाविष्टाम् **ápāviṣṭām**	अपाविषुस् **ápāviṣus**	अपविष्ट **ápaviṣṭa**	अपविषाताम् **ápaviṣātām**	अपविषत **ápaviṣata**
1	अबोधिषम् **ábodhiṣam**	अबोधिष्व **ábodhiṣva**	अबोधिष्म **ábodhiṣma**	अबोधिषि **ábodhiṣi**	अबोधिष्वहि **ábodhiṣvahi**	अबोधिष्महि **ábodhiṣmahi**
	etc.	etc.	etc.	etc.	etc.	etc.

903. The number of roots from which forms of this aorist have been noted in the older language is nearly a hundred and fifty (in RV., about eighty; in AV., more than thirty, of which a dozen are additional to those in RV.); the later texts add less than twenty. Among these are no roots in ā; but otherwise they are of every variety of form (rarest in final i and ī). Active and middle persons are freely made, but sparingly from the same root; only about fifteen roots have both active and middle forms in the older language, and of these a part only exceptionally in the one voice or the other.

a. No rule appears to govern the choice of usage between the **iṣ-** and the **s**-aorist; and in no small number of cases the same root shows forms of both classes.

904. Irregularities are to be noticed as follows:

a. The contracted forms **akramīm, agrabhīm,** and **avadhīm** (with augmentless **vádhīm**) are found in 1st sing. act.

b. For **áçarīt** occurs in AV. **áçarāit;** also (in a part of the manuscripts) **çarāis** for **çarīs; agrahāiṣam** is found in AB. (also the monstrous form **ajagrabhāiṣam:** see **801 i**). **Ajayit,** with short **i** in the ending, occurs in TS.

c. AV. has once **nudiṣṭhās,** without **guṇa.**

d. The forms **atārima** (RV.), **avādiran** (AV.), and **bādhithās** (TA.), though they lack the sibilant, are perhaps to be referred to this aorist: compare **avitá, 908.** A few similar cases occur in the epics, and are of like doubtful character: thus, **jānithās, mādithās, vartithās, çaṅkithās,** and (the causative: **1048**) **aghātayithās. Agṛhītām** and **gṛhīthās** and **gṛhīta,** if not false readings for **gṛhṇī-,** are probably irregular present-formations.

Modes of the iṣ-aorist.

905. As usual, augmentless indicative forms of this aorist are more common than proper subjunctives. Examples, of all the persons found to occur (and including all the accented words), are, in the active: **çáṅsiṣam, vádhīm; máthīs, vádhīs, yā́vīs, sā́vīs; ávīt, jū́rvīt, máthīt, vádhīt, veçīt; mardhiṣṭam, doṣiṣṭam, hiṅsiṣṭam; aviṣṭām, jániṣṭām, bādhiṣṭām; çramiṣma, vādiṣma; vadhiṣṭa** and **vadhiṣṭana, mathiṣṭana, hiṅsiṣṭa; hvāriṣus, grahīṣus;** — in the middle: **rādhiṣi; jániṣṭhās, marṣiṣṭhās, vyathiṣṭhās; krámiṣṭa, jániṣṭa, paviṣṭa, práthiṣṭa, mándiṣṭa; vyathiṣmahi.** The accent is on the root-syllable (**tāriṣús,** AV. once, is doubtless an error).

906. a. Of subjunctive forms with primary endings occur only the 1st sing. act. **daviṣāṇi,** and the 1st pl. mid. (with unstrengthened **e**) **yāciṣāmahe** and **saniṣāmahe.**

b. Forms with secondary endings are almost limited to 2d and 3d sing. act. There are found: **aviṣas, kā́niṣas, tāriṣas, rakṣiṣas, vádhiṣas, vā́diṣas, véṣiṣas, çaṅsiṣas; kā́riṣat, jambhiṣat, jóṣiṣat, takṣiṣat, tāriṣat, níndiṣat, pā́riṣat, bódhiṣat, márdhiṣat, yāciṣat, yodhiṣat, rakṣiṣat, vaniṣat, vyathiṣat, çaṅsiṣat, saniṣat, sāviṣat.** They are made, it will be noticed, with entire regularity, by adding **a** to the tense-stem in **iṣ** before the endings. The only other persons found to occur are the 3d pl. act. **saniṣan** and mid. **sániṣanta** (and TS. has **vaniṣanta,**

for the problematic **vanuṣanta** of RV.), which are also regular. **Bhaviṣāt** (AB. once) is a solitary example of a form with double mode-sign; **cániṣṭhat** (RV.; SV. instead **jániṣṭhat**) seems hopelessly corrupt. The radical syllable always has the accent, and its vowel usually accords with that of the indicative: but we have **san-** in the subjunctive against **asāniṣam** (as to **cay-** and **ran-**, see below, **908**).

907. The middle optative of this aorist also forms a part of the accepted "precative" of the later language (**923, 925b**). It is very rare at all periods, being made in RV. from only five roots, and in AV. from two of the same and from three additional ones (six of the eight have other **iṣ**-forms); and the remaining texts add, so far as noticed, only four other roots. All the forms found to occur are as follows: **janiṣīya, indhiṣīya, edhiṣīyá,ruciṣīya** and **rociṣīya, gmiṣīya; modiṣīṣṭhās; janiṣīṣṭa; vaniṣīṣṭa; sahiṣīvahi; idhiṣīmahi, edhiṣīmáhi, janiṣīmahi, tāriṣīmahi, mandiṣīmahi, vandiṣīmáhi, vardhiṣīmáhi, sahiṣīmahi** and **sāhiṣīmáhi.** The accent is on the ending, and this would lead us to expect a weak form of root throughout; but the usage in this respect appears to be various, and the cases are too few to allow of setting up any rule. The forms **janiṣeyam** and **-ya,** from a secondary **a**-stem, occur in K.

908. Of imperative forms, we have from √**av** a series: namely, **aviḍḍhí, aviṣṭu, aviṣṭám, avitá** (if this, as seems probable, stands anomalously for **aviṣṭá**) and **aviṣṭána;** two of these are of unmistakably imperative form. Other forms occur only in 2d du. and 2d pl., and are accordingly such as might also be subjunctives used imperatively (which is further made probable for two of them by their accentuation on the root-syllable): they are **kramiṣṭam, gamiṣṭam, caniṣṭám, cayiṣṭam** (against **acāyiṣam**), **tā́riṣṭam, yodhiṣṭam, vadhiṣṭam, çnathiṣṭam; ráṇiṣṭana** (against **arāṇiṣus**), **çnathiṣṭana.**

909. No words having a participial ending after **iṣ** are found anywhere to occur.

910. This is the only aorist of which forms are made in the secondary and denominative conjugations: see below, **1035, 1048, 1068.**

6. The siṣ-aorist.

911. According to the grammarians, this aorist is made from roots in आ **ā** (including मि **mi** *fix*, मि **mi** (or **mī**) *damage* and ली **lī** *cling*, which substitute forms in **ā**), and from नम् **nam** *bow*, यम् **yam** *reach*, and रम् **ram** *be content*, and is used only in the active; the corresponding middle being of the **s**-form (**878** ff.). Its inflection is precisely like that of the **iṣ**-aorist; it is unnecessary, then, to give more than

its first persons, which we may form from the roots या yā *go* and नम् nam *bow*. Thus:

	s.	d.	p.	s.	d.	p.
1	अयासिषम्	अयासिष्व	अयासिष्म	अनंसिषम्	अनंसिष्व	अनंसिष्म
	áyāsiṣam	áyāsiṣva	áyāsiṣma	ánaṁsiṣam	ánaṁsiṣva	ánaṁsiṣma
	etc.	etc.	etc.	etc.	etc.	etc.

912. The **siṣ-aorist** is properly only a sub-form of the **iṣ-aorist**, having the tense-sign and endings of the latter added to a form of root increased by an added **s**. It is of extreme rarity in the older language, being made in RV. only from the roots **gā** *sing* and **yā** *go*, and in AV. only from **hā** *leave*, and doubtless also from **pyā** *fill up* and **van** *win* (see below, **914b**); the remaining older texts add **jñā** *know* (B.), **jyā** *overpower*, **dhyā** *think* (ÇB. once: the edition reads **-dhā-**), and **ram** *be content* (SV.: a bad variant for RV. **rāsīya**); other Brāhmaṇa forms which might be also of the s-aorist are **adrāsīt, avāsīt,** and **ahvāsīt**; and **bhukṣiṣīya** (PB. S.) must be regarded as an anomalous formation from √**bhuj**, unless we prefer to admit a secondary root **bhukṣ**, like **bhakṣ** from **bhaj**. In the later language have been found quotable from other roots only **glāsīs, adhmāsīt, anaṁsīt, apāsīt, mlāsīs,** and **amnāsiṣus.**

a. The participle **hā́samāna** and causative **hāsayanti** (RV.) show that **hās** had assumed, even at a very early period, the value of a secondary root beside **hā** for other forms than the aorist.

913. The whole series of older indicative forms (omitting, as doubtful, the 2d and 3d sing.) is as follows: **agāsiṣam, ajñāsiṣam, ayāsiṣam, adhyāsiṣam; ajyāsiṣṭām, ayāsiṣṭām; ajñāsiṣma; ajñāsiṣṭa, áyāsiṣṭa; agāsiṣus, ayāsiṣus** (**ākṣiṣus** is from √**akṣ** *attain*).

a. Forms without augment are these: **jñāsiṣam, raṁsiṣam, hāsiṣam; hāsiṣṭam; hāsiṣṭām; hāsiṣṭa; hāsiṣus, gāsiṣus, jñāsiṣus.** The accent would doubtless be upon the root-syllable.

914. a. Of proper subjunctives are found two, **gāsiṣat** and **yāsiṣat** (both RV.).

b. Optatives are not less rare: namely, **yāsisīṣṭhās** and **pyāsiṣīmahi** (for which the AV. manuscripts read **pyāçiṣīmahi**, altered in the edition to **pyāyiṣ-**); and doubtless **vañçiṣīya** (AV., twice) is to be corrected to **vaṅsiṣīya**, and belongs here. As to **bhukṣiṣīya**, see above, **912.**

c. The accent of **yāsiṣṭā́m** (like **aviṣṭám, 908**) shows it to be a true imperative form; and **yāsīṣṭa** (RV., once) is doubtless the same, with anomalous **ī** for **i**.

915. Middle forms of this aorist, it will be noticed, occur from the optative only; but, considering the great rarity of the whole formation, we are hardly justified in concluding that in the ancient language the middle persons in **-siṣi, -siṣṭhās,** etc., were not allowable, like those in **-iṣi, -iṣṭhās,** and the others of the **iṣ-aorist.**

7. The sa-aorist.

916. In the later language, the roots allowed to form this aorist end in श् **ç**, ष् **ṣ**, or ह् **h** — all of them sounds which in combination with the tense-sign make क्ष् **kṣ**; and they have इ **i**, उ **u**, or ऋ **ṛ** as radical vowel.

a. They are as follows: **diç, riç, liç, viç, kliç, kruç, ruç, mṛç, spṛç; tviṣ, dviṣ, çliṣ, viṣ, kṛṣ; dih, mih, lih, guh, duh, ruh, tṛh, vṛh, stṛh**; from about half of them **sa**-forms, earlier or later, are quotable. Some of them may, or with certain meanings must, take aorists of other forms. And a few are allowed to drop both tense-sign and union-vowel **a** in certain persons of the middle: that is, they may make instead forms of the root-aorist.

917. As the tense-stem ends in अ **a**, the inflection is in the main like that of an imperfect of the second general conjugation. But (according to the grammarians: the forms unfortunately have not been found quotable) the 1st sing. mid. ends in इ **i** instead of ए **e**, and the 2d and 3d du. mid. in आथाम् **āthām** and आताम् **ātām**, as in imperfects of the other conjugation. Both active and middle inflection is admitted. The root is throughout unstrengthened.

918. As example of inflection we may take the root दिश् **diç** *point*. Thus:

	active.			middle.		
	s.	d.	p.	s.	d.	p.
1	अदिक्षम् **ádikṣam**	अदिक्षाव **ádikṣāva**	अदिक्षाम **ádikṣāma**	अदिक्षि **ádikṣi**	अदिक्षावहि **ádikṣāvahi**	अदिक्षामहि **ádikṣāmahi**
2	अदिक्षस् **ádikṣas**	अदिक्षतम् **ádikṣatam**	अदिक्षत **ádikṣata**	अदिक्षथास् **ádikṣathās**	अदिक्षाथाम् **ádikṣāthām**	अदिक्षध्वम् **ádikṣadhvam**
3	अदिक्षत् **ádikṣat**	अदिक्षताम् **ádikṣatām**	अदिक्षन् **ádikṣan**	अदिक्षत **ádikṣata**	अदिक्षाताम् **ádikṣātām**	अदिक्षन्त **ádikṣanta**

919. In the earlier language, the forms of the **sa**-aorist are hardly more than sporadic. They are made in RV. from seven roots; in AV., from two of these and from two others; and the remaining texts add ten more, making nineteen in all (the later language makes no additions to this number). As later, all have **i** or **u** or **ṛ** as root-vowel, and a final consonant which combines with **s** to **kṣ**; but there are in the list also two ending in **j**, namely **mṛj** and **vṛj**. All the examples noted are given below.

a. So far as the middle forms are concerned, this aorist would be fully explained as a transfer of certain **s**-aorists to an **a**-inflection. The marked difference in the strength of radical vowel in the active, however, stands in the way of the successful application of such an explanation to the active forms.

920. a. In the indicative, we find, in the active: **avṛkṣam**; **adrukṣas, adhukṣas, arukṣas, akrukṣas, aspṛkṣas** (and MBh. adds **amṛkṣas**); **adikṣat, amikṣat, alikṣat, avikṣat, ákrukṣat, aghukṣat, adukṣat** and **ádhukṣat, árukṣat, avṛkṣat, akṛkṣat, ámṛkṣat, áspṛkṣat**; **aghukṣatām**; **arukṣāma, amṛkṣāma, avṛkṣāma**; **ádhukṣan, apikṣan** (√**piṣ**), **arukṣan, aspṛkṣan**; — in the middle, only **akṛkṣathās** (√**kṛṣ**), **ádhukṣata**, and **amṛkṣanta** (and MBh. adds **amṛkṣata**?).

b. Forms without augment (no true subjunctives occur) are, in the active: **dṛkṣam, mṛkṣam**; **dukṣas, rukṣas, mṛkṣas**; **dvikṣat**; **mṛkṣata**; **dhukṣán** and **dukṣán**; — in the middle, **dvikṣata, dukṣata** and **dhúkṣata, dhukṣánta**.

c. There are no optative forms.

d. Imperative are: in the active, **mṛkṣatam**; in the middle, **dhukṣásva**.

e. The few accented forms without augment which occur have the tone on the tense-sign **sá**, in analogy with the **a**-aorist (2) and the imperfect of the **á**-class: a single exception is **dhúkṣata**, which probably needs emendation to **dhukṣáta**.

f. The aspiration of initial **d** and **g**, after loss of the aspirated quality of the root-final (**155**), is seen in forms from the roots **duh** and **guh**, but not from **druh** (only a single case, AB.); RV., however, has also **adukṣat** and **dukṣas, dukṣán, dukṣata**.

Precative.

921. As the so-called precative is allowed by the grammarians to be made in the later language from every root, and in an independent way, without reference to the mode of formation of the aorist from the same root, it is desirable to put together here a brief statement of the rules given for it.

922. The precative active is made by adding the active precative endings (above, **568**) directly to the root. But:

a. Of final root-vowels (as before the passive-sign **yá**: **770**), **i** and **u** are lengthened; **ṛ** is usually changed to **ri**, but to **īr** and **ūr** in those roots which elsewhere show **ir**- and **ur**- forms (so-called **ṝ**-roots: **242**), and to **ar** in **ṛ** and **smṛ**; **ā** is changed to **e** in the roots **dā, dhā, sthā, pā** *drink*, **gā** *sing*, and a few others, in part optionally.

b. The root in general assumes its weakest form: a penultimate nasal is lost, as in **badhyāsam** from √**bandh**; the roots which are abbreviated in the weak persons of the perfect (**794**) have the same abbreviation here, as in **ucyāsam, ijyāsam, vidhyāsam, supyāsam, gṛhyāsam**; √**çās** forms **çiṣyāsam** (compare **639, 854c**): and so on.

c. It has been pointed out above (**837**) that the active precative is an optative of the root-aorist, with a problematic insertion of a sibilant between mode-sign and ending.

923. a. The precative middle is made by adding the middle precative endings (above, **568**) to the root increased by स् **s** or इष् **iṣ** — that is, to the tense-stem of an **s**-aorist or of an **iṣ**-aorist (but without augment).

b. The root is strengthened according to the rules that apply in forming the middle-stem of the **s** and of the **iṣ**-aorists respectively: in general, namely, a final vowel is gunated in both formations; but a medial vowel, only before इष् **iṣ**.

c. As was pointed out above (**567**) the middle precative is really the optative of certain aorists, with the insertion of a sibilant between mode-sign and ending only (so far as authenticated by use) in the 2d and 3d singular. In the older language, such forms are oftenest made from the **s**-aorist (**895**) and the **iṣ**-aorist (**907**); but also from the root-aorist (**837b**), the **a**-aorist (**850a**), the reduplicated aorist (**870**), and the **siṣ**-aorist (**914b**); and even from the perfect (**812b**).

924. As example of inflection, we may take the root भू **bhū** *be*, which is said (no middle aorist or precative from it is quotable) to form its middle on the **iṣ**-stem. Thus:

active.

	s.	d.	p.
1	भूयासम् **bhūyā́sam**	भूयास्व **bhūyā́sva**	भूयास्म **bhūyā́sma**
2	भूयास् **bhūyā́s**	भूयास्तम् **bhūyā́stam**	भूयास्त **bhūyā́sta**
3	भूयात् **bhūyā́t**	भूयास्ताम् **bhūyā́stām**	भूयासुस् **bhūyā́sus**

middle.

	s.	d.	p.
1	भविषीय **bhaviṣīyá**	भविषीवहि **bhaviṣīváhi**	भविषीमहि **bhaviṣīmáhi**
2	भविषीष्ठास् **bhaviṣīṣṭhā́s**	भविषीयास्थाम् **bhaviṣīyā́sthām**	भविषीढ्वम् **bhaviṣīḍhvám**
3	भविषीष्ट **bhaviṣīṣṭá**	भविषीयास्ताम् **bhaviṣīyā́stām**	भविषीरन् **bhaviṣīrán**

a. The forms given by the grammarians as 2d and 3d dual are of very questionable value, as regards the place assigned to the sibilant. Those persons, and the 2d pl., have never been met with in use. For the question respecting the ending of the 2d pl., as **dhvam** or **ḍhvam,** see **226 c**.

925. a. The precative active is a form of very rare occurrence in the classical language. In each of the texts already more than once referred to (Manu, Nala, Bhagavad-Gītā, Çakuntalā, Hitopadeça) it occurs once and no more, and not half-a-dozen forms have been found quotable from the epics. As to its value, see **573 c**.

b. The precative middle is virtually unknown in the whole later literature, not a single occurrence of it having been brought to light. The BhP. has once **rīriṣīṣṭa,** which is also a RV. form, belonging probably to the reduplicated aorist: see **870**.

Uses of the Aorist.

926. The uses of the aorist mode-forms (as has been already pointed out: **582**) appear to accord with those of the mode-forms of the present-system. The predilection of the earlier language, continued sparingly in the later, for the augmentless forms in prohibitive expression after **mā́** was sufficiently stated and illustrated above (**579**).

a. The tense-value of the aorist indicative has also been more than once referred to, and calls only for somewhat more of detail and for illustration here.

927. The aorist of the later language is simply a preterit, equivalent to the imperfect and perfect, and frequently coördinated with them.

a. Thus, **tataḥ sa gardabhaṁ laguḍena tāḍayāmāsa; tenā 'sāu pañcatvam agamat** (H.) *thereupon he beat the donkey with a stick; and hereof the latter died;* **tataḥ sā vidarbhān agamat punaḥ; tāṁ tu bandhujanaḥ samapūjayat** (MBh.) *thereupon she went back to Vidarbha; and her kindred paid her reverence;* **prītimān abhūt, uvāca**

cāi 'nam (MBh.) *he was filled with affection, and said to him;* **tam adahat kāṣṭhāiḥ so 'bhūd divyavapus tadā** (R.) *he burned him with wood, and he became then a heavenly form.*

928. The aorist of the older language has the value of a proper "perfect": that is, it signifies something past which is viewed as completed with reference to the present; and it requires accordingly to be rendered by our tense made with the auxiliary *have.* In general, it indicates what has just taken place; and oftenest something which the speaker has experienced.

a. Examples from the Veda are: **párī 'mé gam aneṣata páry agním ahṛṣata, devéṣv akrata çrávaḥ ká imā́ñ ā́ dadharṣati** (RV.) *these here have led about a cow, they have carried around the fire, they have done honor to the gods — who shall venture anything against them?* **yám āíchāma manasā so 'yám ā́ 'gāt** (RV.) *he whom we (formerly,* impf.) *sought with our mind has (now,* aor.) *come;* **yéné 'ndro havíṣā kṛtvy ábhavad dyumny ùttamáḥ, idáṁ tád akri devā asapatnáḥ kílā 'bhuvam** (RV.) *that libation by which Indra, making it, became* (impf.) *of highest glory, I have now made, ye gods; I have become free from enemies.*

b. Examples from the Brāhmaṇa language are: **sā́ hā 'smiñ jyóg uvāsa... táto ha gandharvaḥ sám ūdire: jyóg vā́ iyám urváçī manuṣyèṣv avātsīt** (ÇB.) *she lived with him a long time. Then the Gandharvas said to one another, "this Urvaçī, forsooth, hath dwelt a long time among mortals";* **tasya ha dantāḥ pedire: taṁ ho 'vāca: apatsata vā asya dantāḥ** (AB.) *his teeth fell out. He said to him: "his teeth truly have fallen out";* **índrasya vṛtráṁ jaghnúṣa indriyáṁ vīryàm pṛthivī́m ánu vy ā̀rchat tád óṣadhayo vīrúdho 'bhavan sá prajā́patim úpā 'dhāvad vṛtrám me jaghnúṣa indriyáṁ vīryàm pṛthivī́m ánu vy ā̀rat tád óṣadhayo vīrúdho 'bhūvann íti** (TS.) *of Indra, when he had slain Vritra, the force and might went away into the earth, and became the herbs and plants; he ran to Prajāpati, saying: "my force and might, after slaying Vritra, have gone away into the earth, and have become the herbs and plants";* **svayám enam abhyudétya brūyād vrā́tya kvā̀ 'vātsīḥ** (AV., in prose passage) *going up to him in person, let him say: "Vrātya, where hast thou abode"?* **yád idā́nīṁ dvāú vivádamānāv eyā́tām ahám adarçam ahám açrāuṣam íti yá evá brūyā́d ahám adarçam íti tásmā evá çráddadhyāma** (ÇB.) *if now two should come disputing with one another, [the one] saying "I have seen", [the other] "I have heard", we should believe the one who said "I have seen".*

929. a. This distinction of the aorist from the imperfect and perfect as tenses of narration is very common in the Brāhmaṇalanguage (including the older Upanishads and the Sūtras), and is closely observed; violation of it is very rare, and is to be regarded as either due to corruption of text or indicative of a late origin.

b. In the Vedic hymns, the same distinction is prevalent, but is both less clear and less strictly maintained; many passages would admit an interpretation implying either sense; and evident aorist-forms are sometimes used narratively, while imperfect-forms are also occasionally employed in the aorist sense.

930. The boundary between what has just been and what is is an evanescent one, and is sometimes overstepped, so that an aorist appears where a present might stand, or was even rather to be expected. Thus: **svāsasthe bhavatam indave na iti somo vāi rāje 'nduḥ somāyāi 'vāi 'ne etad rājña āsade 'cīkḷpat** (AB. i. 29. 7) *"be ye comfortable seats for our Indu", he says; Indu is king Soma; by this means he has made them* (instead of *makes them*) *suitable for king Soma to sit upon;* **vāruṇīr ā́po yád adbhír abhiṣiñcáti váruṇam evāí 'nam akar** (MS. iv. 3. 10) *the waters are Varuna's; in that he bepours him with waters, he has made him Varuna;* **pañcábhir vyā́ghārayati pā́ñkto yajñó yā́vān evá yajñás tám ā́labdhā́ 'tho yā́vān evá yajñás tásmād rákṣāṅsy ápahanti** (MS. iii. 2. 6) *he smears with five; fivefold is the offering; as great as is the offering, of it he has [thereby] taken hold; then, as great as is the offering, from it he smites away the demons.* This idiom is met with in all the Brāhmaṇas; but it is especially frequent in the MS.

CHAPTER XII.

THE FUTURE-SYSTEMS.

931. THE verb has two futures, of very different age and character. The one has for tense-sign a sibilant followed by **य ya,** and is an inheritance from the time of Indo-European unity. The other is a periphrastic formation, made by appending an auxiliary verb to a derivative noun of agency, and it is a recent addition to the verb-system; its beginnings only are met with in the earliest language. The former may be called the s-future (or the old future, or simply the future); the latter may be distinguished as the periphrastic future.

I. The s-future.

932. The tense-sign of this future is the syllable स्य **syá**, added to the root either directly or by an auxiliary vowel इ **i** (in the latter case becoming इष्य **iṣyá**). The root has the **guṇa**-strengthening. Thus, from √दा **dā** *give* is formed the future tense-stem दास्य **dāsyá**; from √इ **i** *go*, the stem एष्य **eṣya**; from √दुह् **duh** *milk*, the stem धोक्ष्य **dhokṣyá**; from √भू **bhū** *be*, the stem भविष्य **bhaviṣyá**; from √ऋध् **ṛdh** *thrive*, the stem अर्धिष्य **ardhiṣyá**; and so on.

a. But from √**jīv** *live* the stem is **jīviṣya**, from √**ukṣ** *sprinkle* it is **ukṣiṣyá**, and so on (**240**).

b. There are hardly any Vedic cases of resolution of the tense-sign **sya** into **sia**; RV. has **kṣeṣiántas** once.

933. This tense-stem is then inflected precisely like a present-stem ending in अ **a** (second general conjugation: **733a**). We may take as models of inflection the future of √दा **dā** *give*, and that of √कृ **kṛ** *make*. Thus:

	active.			middle.		
	s.	d.	p.	s.	d.	p.
1	दास्यामि **dāsyā́mi**	दास्यावस् **dāsyā́vas**	दास्यामस् **dāsyā́mas**	दास्ये **dāsyé**	दास्यावहे **dāsyā́vahe**	दास्यामहे **dāsyā́mahe**
2	दास्यसि **dāsyási**	दास्यथस् **dāsyáthas**	दास्यथ **dāsyátha**	दास्यसे **dāsyáse**	दास्येथे **dāsyéthe**	दास्यध्वे **dāsyádhve**
3	दास्यति **dāsyáti**	दास्यतस् **dāsyátas**	दास्यन्ति **dāsyánti**	दास्यते **dāsyáte**	दास्येते **dāsyéte**	दास्यन्ते **dāsyánte**

1	करिष्यामि **kariṣyā́mi**	करिष्यावस् **kariṣyā́vas**	करिष्यामस् **kariṣyā́mas**	करिष्ये **kariṣyé**	करिष्यावहे **kariṣyā́vahe**	करिष्यामहे **kariṣyā́mahe**
	etc.	etc.	etc.	etc.	etc.	etc.

a. In the epics are found occasional cases of 1st du. and pl. in **va** and **ma**: e. g. **raṁsyāva** (R.), **bhakṣayiṣyāva** (causative: MBh.); **eṣyāma** (MBh.), **vatsyāma** (R.).

934. With regard to the use or non-use of the auxiliary vowel **i** before the sibilant, there is a degree of general accordance between this tense and the other future and the desiderative; but it is by no means absolute, nor are any definite rules to be laid down with regard to it (and so much the less, because of the infrequency of the two latter formations in actual use): between this and the aorist (s-aorist on the one side, or iṣ-aorist on the other), any correspondence is still less traceable. Practically, it is necessary to learn, as a matter of usage, how any given root makes these various parts of its conjugational system.

935. Below is added a statement of the usage, as regards the auxiliary vowel, of all the roots found quotable — for the most part, in the form of a specification of those which add the tense-sign directly to the root; in brackets are further mentioned the other roots which according to the grammarians also refuse the auxiliary vowel.

a. Of roots ending in vowels, the great majority (excepting those in **ṛ**) take no **i**. Thus, all in **ā** (numerous, and unnecessary to specify: but compare **c** below); — those in **i**, as **kṣi** *possess*, **ci** *gather*, **ci** *note*, **mi**, **si** or **sā** *bind* (**siṣya**), **hi**; from **i**, **kṣi** *destroy*, and **ji** occur forms of both classes; **çri** [and **çvi**] has **i**; — those in **ī**, as **krī**, **bhī**, **mī**, **vlī**; but **çī** *lie* and **nī** have both forms [and **ḍī** takes **i**]; — those in **u**, as **cyu**, **dru**, **plu**, **çru**, **hu**; but **su** *press out* and **stu** have both forms [and **kṣu**, **kṣṇu**, **nu**, **yu**, **ru**, **snu** take **i**]; — of those in **ū**, **dhū** and **bhū** take **i**; **sū** has both forms. But all in **ṛ** (numerous, and unnecessary to specify) take **i** [those in changeable **ṛ**, or so-called **ṝ**-roots (**242**), are said by the grammarians to take either **i** or **ī**; no **ī**-forms, however, are quotable].

b. Of roots ending in mutes, about half add the tense-sign directly. Thus, of roots ending in gutturals, **çak**; — in palatals: in **c**, **pac**, **muc**, **ric**, **vac**, **vic**, **vraçc**, **sic** (but **yāc** takes **i**); in **ch**, **prach**; in **j**, **bhañj**, **mṛj** (**mārkṣya** and **mrakṣya**), **yaj**, **bhuj**, **yuj**, **vṛj**, **sṛj** [also **bhrajj**, **rañj**, **sañj**, **svañj**, **nij**, **ruj**], while **tyaj**, **bhaj**, and **majj** (**mañkṣya** and **majjiṣya**) have both forms, and **vij** (**vijiṣya** and **vejiṣya**) and **vraj** take **i**; — in dentals: in **t**, **kṛt** *cut* and **vṛt** [also **cṛt** and **nṛt**] make both forms; in **d**, **ad**, **pad**, **çad** *fall*, **skand**, **syand**, **chid**, **bhid**, **vid** *find*, **nud** [also **had**, **khid**, **svid**, **kṣud**, **tud**]; while **sad** (**satsya** and **sīdiṣya**) and **vid** *know* make both forms [also **chṛd** and **tṛd**], and **vad** has **i**; in **dh**, **vyadh** (**vetsya**), **rādh**, **sidh** *succeed*, **budh**, **yudh**, **rudh**, **vṛdh** [also **sādh**, **krudh**, **kṣudh**, **çudh**], and **bandh** and **sidh** *repel* have both forms; in **n**, **tan**, while **man** and **han** have both forms; — in labials: in **p**, **āp**, **kṣip**, **gup**, **tṛp**, **sṛp** (**srapsya** and **sarpsya**) [also **çap**, **lip**, **lup**], while **tap**, **vap**, **svap**, **dṛp**, and **kḷp** have both forms; in **bh**, **yabh** and **rabh**, **labh** having both forms; in **m**, **ram**, while **kram**, **kṣam**, **nam**, and **yam** make both forms.

c. Of the roots reckoned by the grammarians as ending in semivowels (**761 d—g**) all take **i**. And **vā** or **vi** *weave*, **vyā** or **vī** *envelop*, and **hvā** or **hū** *call* take a **y**-form, as in their present-system, to which then **i** is added: thus, **vayiṣya**, **vyayiṣya**, **hvayiṣya** (but also **hvāsya**).

d. Of roots ending in spirants, the minority (about a third) are without the auxiliary vowel. They are: roots in **ç**, **diç**, **viç**, **dṛç** (**drakṣya**), **spṛç** (**sprakṣya**) [also **dañç**, **riç**, **liç**, **kruç**, **mṛç**], while **naç** *be lost* has both forms (**nañkṣya** and **naçiṣya**); — in **ṣ**, **piṣ**, **viṣ**, **çiṣ** [also

tviṣ, dviṣ, çliṣ, tuṣ, duṣ, puṣ, çuṣ], while **kṛṣ** has both forms (**krakṣya** and **karṣiṣya**); — in **s, vas** *shine*, **vas** *clothe* [also **ghas**], while **vas** *dwell* has both forms; — in **h, mih, duh, druh** [also **nah, dih, lih**], while **dah, vah, sah,** and **ruh** have both forms.

e. In the older language, a majority (about five ninths) of simple roots add the **sya** without auxiliary **i**; of the futures occurring in the later language only, nearly three quarters have the **i**, this being generally taken by any root of late origin and derivative character — as it is also uniformly taken in secondary conjugation (**1019, 1036, 1050, 1068**).

936. As the root is strengthened to form the stem of this future, so, of a root that has a stronger and a weaker form, the stronger form is used: thus, from √**bandh** or **badh** *bind*, **bhantsya** or **bandhiṣya.**

a. By an irregular strengthening, **nañkṣya** (beside **naçiṣya**) is made from √**naç** *be lost*, and **mañkṣya** (beside **majjiṣya**) from √**majj** *sink*.

b. But a few roots make future-stems in the later language without strengthening: thus, **likhiṣya, miliṣya** (also TS.), **vijiṣya** (also **vejiṣya**), **siṣya** (√**sā** or **si**), **sūṣya** (**939 b**), **sphuṭiṣya**; and √**vyadh** makes **vetsya** from the weaker form **vidh.**

c. The ÇB. has once the monstrous form **açnuviṣyāmahe,** made upon the present-stem **açnu** (**697**) of √**aç** *attain*. And the later language makes **sīdiṣya** and **jahiṣya** from the present-stems of √**sad** and √**hā.** Compare further **hvayiṣya** etc., **935 c.** Also **khyāyiṣya** from √**khyā** (beside **khyāsya**) appears to be of similar character.

d. A number of roots with medial **ṛ** strengthen it to **ra** (**241**): thus, **krakṣya, trapsya, drapsya, drakṣya, mrakṣya** (beside **mārkṣya**), **sprakṣya, srakṣya, srapsya** (beside **sarpsya**), and **mradiṣya** (beside **mardiṣya**); and √**kḷp** forms **klapsya** (beside **kalpiṣya**).

e. The root **grah** (also its doublet **glah**) takes **ī** instead of **i,** as it does also in the aorist and elsewhere.

937. This future is comparatively rare in the oldest language — in part, apparently, because the uses of a future are to a large extent answered by subjunctive forms — but becomes more and more common later. Thus, the RV. has only seventeen occurrences of personal forms, from nine different roots (with participles from six additional roots); the AV. has fifty occurrences, from twenty-five roots (with participles from seven more); but the TS. has occurrences (personal forms and participles together) from over sixty roots; and forms from more than a hundred and fifty roots are quotable from the older texts.

Modes of the s-future.

938. Mode-forms of the future are of the utmost rarity. The only example in the older language is **kariṣyā́s,** 2d sing. subj. act., occurring once (or twice) in RV. (AB. has once **notsyāvahāi,** and GB. has **eṣyāmahāi, taṅsyāmahāi, sthāsyāmahāi,** but they are doubtless false readings for **-he**. Two or three optative forms are found in the epics: thus, **dhakṣyet** and **maṅsyeran** (MBh.), and **drakṣyeta** (R.); also an imperative **patsyantu** (Har.). And several 2d pl. mid. in **dhvam** are quotable from the epics: thus, **vetsyadhvam, saviṣyadhvam,** and (the causative) **kālayiṣyadhvam** (PB.) and **jīvayiṣyadhvam** (MBh.: and one text has **mokṣyadhvam** at i. 133.13, where the other reads **mokṣayadhvam**), and **bhaviṣyadhvam** (MBh. R.): it is a matter of question whether these are to be accounted a real imperative formation, or an epic substitution of secondary for primary endings (compare **542a**).

Participles of the s-future.

939. Participles are made from the future-stem precisely as from a present-stem in अ **a**: namely, by adding in the active the ending त् **nt**, in the middle the ending मान **māna**; the accent remains upon the stem. Thus, from the verbs instanced above, दास्यत् **dāsyánt** and दास्यमान **dāsyámāna,** करिष्यत् **kariṣyánt** and करिष्यमाण **kariṣyámāṇa.**

a. According to the grammarians, the feminine of the active participle is made either in **ántī** or in **atī́**; but only the former has been noted as occurring in the older language, and the latter is everywhere extremely rare: see above, **449e, f.**

b. In RV. occurs once **sū́ṣyantī,** from √**sū**, with anomalous accentuation.

Preterit of the s-future: Conditional.

940. From the future-stem is made an augment-preterit, by prefixing the augment and adding the secondary endings, in precisely the same manner as an imperfect from a present-stem in अ **a**. This preterit is called the conditional.

a. It stands related to the future, in form and meaning, as the French conditional *aurais* to the future *aurai*, or as the English *would have* to *will have* — nearly as the German *würde haben* to *werde haben.*

b. Thus, from the roots already instanced:

	active.			middle.		
	s.	d.	p.	s.	d.	p.
1	अदास्यम् **ádāsyam**	अदास्याव **ádāsyāva**	अदास्याम **ádāsyāma**	अदास्ये **ádāsye**	अदास्यावहि **ádāsyāvahi**	अदास्यामहि **ádāsyāmahi**

2	अदास्यस्	अदास्यतम्	अदास्यत	अदास्यथास्	अदास्येथाम्	अदास्यध्वम्
	ádāsyas	ádāsyatam	ádāsyata	ádāsyathās	ádāsyethām	ádāsyadhvam
3	अदास्यत्	अदास्यताम्	अदास्यन्	अदास्यत	अदास्येताम्	अदास्यन्त
	ádāsyat	ádāsyatām	ádāsyan	ádāsyata	ádāsyetām	ádāsyanta
1	अकरिष्यम्	अकरिष्याव	अकरिष्याम	अकरिष्ये	अकरिष्यावहि	अकरिष्यामहि
	ákariṣyam	ákariṣyāva	ákariṣyāma	ákariṣye	ákariṣyāvahi	ákariṣyāmahi
	etc.	etc.	etc.	etc.	etc.	etc.

941. The conditional is the rarest of all the forms of the Sanskrit verb. The RV. has but a single example, **ábhariṣyat** *was going to carry off*, and none of the Vedic texts furnishes another. In the Brāhmaṇas it is hardly more common — except in ÇB., where it is met with more than fifty times. Nor does it, like the future, become more frequent later: not an example occurs in Nala, Bhagavad-Gītā, or Hitopadeça; only one in Manu; and two in Çakuntalā. In the whole MBh. (Holtzmann) it is found about twenty-five times, from thirteen roots. The middle forms are extremely few.

II. The Periphrastic Future.

942. a. This formation contains only a single indicative active tense (or also middle: see **947**), without modes, or participle, or preterit.

b. It consists in a derivative *nomen agentis*, having the value of a future active participle, and used, either with or without an accompanying auxiliary, in the office of a verbal tense with future meaning.

943. The noun is formed by the suffix तृ **tṛ** (or तर् **tar**); and this (as in its other than verbal uses: see **1182**) is added to the root either directly or with a preceding auxiliary vowel इ **i**, the root itself being strengthened by guṇa, but the accent resting on the suffix: thus, दातृ **dātṛ́** from √दा **dā** *give;* कर्तृ **kartṛ́** from √कृ **kṛ** *make;* भवितृ **bhavitṛ́** from √भू **bhū** *be.*

a. As regards the presence or absence of the vowel **i**, the usage is said by the grammarians to be generally the same as in the **s**-future from the same root (above, **935**). The most important exception is that the roots in **ṛ** take no **i**: thus, **kartṛ** (against **kariṣya**); roots **han** and **gam** show the same difference; while **vṛt, vṛdh,** and **syand** have **i** here, though not in the s-future. The few forms which occur in the older language agree with these statements.

944. In the third persons, the nom. masc. of the noun, in the three numbers respectively (373), is used without auxiliary: thus, भविता **bhavitā́** *he* or *she* or *it will be;* भवितारौ **bhavitā́rau** *both will be;* भवितारस् **bhavitā́ras** *they will be.* In the other persons, the first and second persons present of √अस् **as** *be* (636) are used as auxiliary; and they are combined, in all numbers, with the singular nom. masc. of the noun.

a. Thus, from √दा **dā** *give:*

active.

	s.	d.	p.
1	दातास्मि **dātā́smi**	दातास्वस् **dātā́svas**	दातास्मस् **dātā́smas**
2	दातासि **dātā́si**	दातास्थस् **dātā́sthas**	दातास्थ **dātā́stha**
3	दाता **dātā́**	दातारौ **dātā́rāu**	दातारस् **dātā́ras**

b. Occasionally, in the epics and later (almost never in the older language), the norm of the tense as given above is in various respects departed from: thus, by use of the auxiliary in the 3d person also; by its omission in the 1st or 2d person; by inversion of the order of noun and auxiliary; by interposition of other words between them; by use of a dual or plural nom. with the auxiliary; and by use of a feminine form of the noun. Examples are: **vaktā 'sti** (MBh.) *he will speak;* **nihantā** (MBh.) *I shall* or *thou wilt strike down*, **yoddhā 'ham** (R.) *I shall fight*, **ahaṁ draṣṭā** (MBh.) *I shall see*, **kartā 'haṁ te** (BhP.) *I will do for thee*, **tvam bhavitā** (MBh. Megh.) *thou wilt be;* **asmi gantā** (MBh.) *I shall go;* **pratigrahītā tām asmi** (MBh.) *I will receive her*, **hantā tvam asi** (MBh.) *thou wilt slay;* **kartārāu svaḥ** (MBh.) *we two shall do;* **draṣṭry asmi** (MBh.) *I* (f.) *shall see*, **udbhavitrī** (Nāiṣ.) *she will increase*, **gantrī** (Y.) *she will go.* AB. has once **sotā** as 2d sing., *thou wilt press;* JUB. makes the combination **çmaçānāni bhavitāras** *the cemeteries will be.*

c. An optative of the auxiliary appears to be once used, in **yoddhā syām** *I would fight* (R. i. 22. 25 Peterson; but the Bombay edition reads **yoddhuṁ yāsyāmi**).

945. The accent in these combinations, as in all the ordinary cases of collocation of a verb with a preceding predicate noun or

adjective (592), is on the noun itself; and, unlike all the true verbal forms, the combination retains its accent everywhere even in an independent clause: thus, tárhi vā́ atinā̄ṣṭró bhavitā́smi (ÇB.) *then I shall be out of danger* (where bhaviṣyāmi, if used, would be accentless). Whether in a dependent clause the auxiliary verb would take an accent (595), and whether, if so, at the expense of the accent of the noun (as in the case of a preposition compounded with a verb-form: 1083b), we are without the means of determining.

946. In the Veda, the *nomina agentis* in **tṛ** or **tar**, like various other derivative nouns (**271**), but with especial frequency, are used in participial construction, governing the accusative if they come from roots whose verbal forms do so (**1182**). Often, also, they are used predicatively, with or without accompanying copula; yet without any implication of time; they are not the beginnings, but only the forerunners, of a new tense-formation. Generally, when they have a participial value, the root-syllable (or a prefix preceding it) has the accent. The tense-use begins, but rather sparingly, in the Brāhmaṇas (from which about thirty forms are quotable); and it grows more common later, though the periphrastic future is nowhere nearly so frequent as the **s**-future (it is quotable later from about thirty additional roots).

947. a. A few isolated attempts are made in the Brāhmaṇas to form by analogy middle persons to this future, with endings corresponding after the usual fashion to those of the active persons. Thus, TS. has once **prayoktā́se** *I will apply* (standing related to **prayoktā́smi** as, for example, **çā́se** to **çā́smi**); ÇB. has **çayitā́se** *thou shalt lie* (similarly related to **çayitā́si**); and TB. has **yaṣṭā́smahe** *we will make offering*. But in TA. is found (i.11) **yaṣṭā́he** as 1st sing., showing a phonetic correspondence of a problematic character, not elsewhere met with in the language.

b. On the basis of such tentative formations as these, the native grammarians set up a complete middle inflection for the periphrastic future, as follows:

	s.	d.	p.
1	**dātā́he**	**dātā́svahe**	**dātā́smahe**
2	**dātā́se**	**dātā́sāthe**	**dātā́dhve**
3	**dātā́**	**dātā́rāu**	**dātā́ras**

c. Only a single example of such a middle has been brought to light in the later language, namely (the causative) **darçayitā́he** (Nāiṣ.).

Uses of the Futures and Conditional.

948. As the **s**-future is the commoner, so also it is the one more indefinitely used. It expresses in general what is going to take place at some time to come — but often, as in other languages, adding on the one hand an implication of will or intention, or on the other hand that of promise or threatening.

a. A few examples are: **varṣiṣyáty āiṣámaḥ parjányo vṛ́ṣṭimān bhaviṣyati** (ÇB.) *it is going to rain; Parjanya is going to be rich in rain this year;* **yás tán ná véda kím ṛcā́ kariṣyati** (RV.) *whoever does not know that, what will he do with verse?* **ā́ vāí vayám agnī́ dhāsyāmahé 'tha yūyáṁ kíṁ kariṣyatha** (ÇB.) *we are going to build the two fires; then what will you do?* **tám índro 'bhyā́dudrāva haniṣyán** (ÇB.) *him Indra ran at, intending to slay;* **yády evā́ kariṣyátha sākáṁ devāír yajñíyāso bhaviṣyatha** (RV.) *if ye will do thus, ye shall be worthy of the sacrifice along with the gods;* **dántās te çatsyanti** (AV.) *thy teeth will fall out;* **ná mariṣyasi mā́ bibheḥ** (AV.) *thou shalt not die; be not afraid;* **brūhi kva yāsyasi** (MBh.) *tell us; where are you going to go?* **yadi mām pratyākhyāsyasi viṣam āsthāsye** (MBh.) *if you shall reject me, I will resort to poison.* As in other languages, the tense is also sometimes used for the expression of a conjecture or presumption: thus: **ko 'yaṁ devo gandharvo vā bhaviṣyati** (MBh.) *who is this? he is doubtless a god, or a Gandharva;* **adya svapsyanti** (MBh.) *they must be sleeping now.*

b. The spheres of future and desiderative border upon one another, and the one is sometimes met with where the other might be expected. Examples of the future taken in a quasi-desiderative sense are as follows: **yád dāçúṣe bhadráṁ kariṣyási távé 't tát satyám** (RV.) *what favor thou willest to bestow on thy worshiper, that of thee becometh actual (is surely brought about);* **yáthā 'nyád vadiṣyánt sò 'nyád vádet** (ÇB.) *as if, intending to say one thing, one were to say another.*

949. The periphrastic future is defined by the grammarians as expressing something to be done at a definite time to come. And this, though but faintly traceable in later use, is a distinct characteristic of the formation in the language where it first makes its appearance. It is especially often used along with **çvás** *tomorrow.*

a. A few examples are: **adyá varṣiṣyati ... çvó vraṣṭā́** (MS.) *it is going to rain today; it will rain tomorrow;* **yatarān vā ime çvaḥ kamitāras te jetāras** (K.) *whichever of the two parties these shall choose tomorrow, they will conquer;* **prātár yaṣṭā́smahe** (TB.) *we shall sacrifice tomorrow morning;* **ityahé vaḥ paktā̀smi** (ÇB.) *on such and such a day I will cook for you;* **tán ma ékāṁ rā́trim ánte çayitā́se jātá u te 'yáṁ tárhi putró bhavitā́** (ÇB.) *then you shall lie with me one night, and at that time this son of yours will be born.* In other cases, this definiteness of time is wanting, but an emphasis, as of special certainty, seems perhaps to belong to the form: thus, **bibhṛhí mā pārayiṣyā́mi tvé 'ti: kásmān mā pārayiṣyasī́ 'ty āughá imā́ḥ sárvāḥ prajā́ nirvoḍhā́, tátas tvā pārayitā̀smī́ 'ti** (ÇB.) *support me and I will save you, said it. From what will you save me? said he. A flood is going to carry off all these creatures; from that I will save you, said it;* **paridevayāṁ cakrire mahac chokabhayam prāptāsmaḥ** (GB.) *they set up a lamentation: "we are going to meet with great pain and dread";* **yaje 'yakṣi yaṣṭāhe ca** (TA.) *I sacrifice, I have sacrificed, and I shall sacrifice.* In yet other cases, in the older language even, and yet more in the later, this future appears to be equivalent to the other: thus, **prajāyām enaṁ vijñātāsmo yadi vidvān vā juhoty avidvān vā** (AB.) *in his children we shall know him, whether he is one that sacrifices with knowledge or without knowledge;* **vaktāsmo vā idaṁ devebhyaḥ** (AB.) *we shall tell this to the gods;* **yadi svārtho mamā 'pi bhavitā tata evaṁ svārthaṁ kariṣyāmi** (MBh.) *if later my own affair shall come up, then I will attend to my own affair;* **kathaṁ tu bhavitāsy eka iti tvāṁ nṛpa çocimi** (MBh.) *but how will you get along alone? that, O king, is the cause of my grief about you.*

950. The conditional would seem to be most originally and properly used to signify that something *was going to* be done. And this value it has in its only Vedic occurrence, and occasionally elsewhere. But usually it has the sense ordinarily called "conditional"; and in the great majority of its occurrences it is found (like the subjunctive and the optative, when used with the same value) in both clauses of a conditional sentence.

a. Thus, **yó vṛtrā́ya sínam átrā 'bhariṣyat prá tám jánitrī vidúṣa uvāca** (RV.) *him, who was going here to carry off Vritra's wealth, his mother proclaimed to the knowing one;* **çatāyuṁ gām akariṣyam** (AB.) *I was going to make (should have made) the cow live a hundred years* (in other versions of the same story is added the other clause, in which the conditional has a value more removed from its original: thus, in GB., *if you, villain, had not stopped* [**prā́grahīṣyaḥ**] *my mouth);* **táta evā̀ 'sya bhayáṁ vì 'yāya kásmād dhy ábheṣyad dvitī́yād vā́í bhayám bhavati** (ÇB.) *thereupon his fear departed; for of whom was he to be afraid? occasion of fear arises from a second person;* **útpapāta cirám tán mene yád vā́saḥ paryádhāsyata** (ÇB.) *he leaped up; he thought it long that he should put on a garment;* **sá tád evá nā́ 'vindat prajā́patir yátrā́ 'hoṣyat** (MS.) *Prajāpati, verily, did not then find where he was to (should) sacrifice;* **evaṁ cen nā 'vakṣyo mūrdhā te vyapatiṣyat** (GB.) *if you should not speak thus, your head would fly off;* **sá yád dhāi 'tā́vad evā́ 'bhaviṣyad yā́vatyo hāi 'vā́ 'gre prajā́ḥ sṛṣṭā́s tā́vatyo hāi 'vā̀ 'bhaviṣyan ná prā̀ 'janiṣyanta** (ÇB.) *if he had been only so much, there would have been only so many living creatures as were created at first; they would have had no progeny;* **kiṁ vā 'bhaviṣyad aruṇas tamasāṁ vibhettā taṁ cet sahasrakiraṇo dhuri nā 'kariṣyat** (Ç.) *would the Dawn, forsooth, be the scatterer of the darkness, if the thousand-rayed one did not set her on the front of his chariot?*

CHAPTER XIII.

VERBAL ADJECTIVES AND NOUNS: PARTICIPLES, INFINITIVES, GERUNDS.

951 a. THOSE verbal adjectives, or participles, which are made from tense-stems, and so constitute a part of the various tense-systems, have been already treated. It remains to describe certain others, which, being made directly from the root itself, belong to the verbal system as a whole, and not to any particular part of it.

b. The infinitive (with a few sporadic exceptions in the older language) also comes in all cases from the root directly, and not from any of the derived tense-stems.

c. The same is true of the so-called gerunds, or indeclinable participles.

Passive Participle in tá or ná.

952. By the accented suffix त **tá** — or, in a comparatively small number of verbs, न **ná** — is formed a verbal adjective which, when coming from transitive verbs, qualifies anything as having endured the action expressed by the verb: thus, दत्त **dattá** *given;* उक्त **uktá** *spoken.* Hence it is usually called the passive participle; or, to distinguish it from the participle belonging to the passive present-system (771), the past passive participle.

a. When made from an intransitive or neuter verb, the same participle, as in other languages, has no passive but only an indefinite past sense: thus, गत **gatá** *gone;* भूत **bhūtá** *been;* पतित **patitá** *fallen.*

953. In general, this participle is made by adding त **tá** to the bare verbal root, with observation of the ordinary rules of euphonic combination.

a. Some roots, however, require the prefixion of the auxiliary vowel **i** to the suffix. For these, and for the verbs that add **ná** instead of **tá**, see below, **956, 957**.

b. As to the accent when the root is preceded by a preposition, see **1085 a.**

954. The root before त **tá** has usually its weakest form, if there is anywhere in the verbal system a distinction of weak and strong forms. Thus:

a. A penultimate nasal is not seldom dropped: examples are **aktá** (√**añj**), **baddhá** (√**bandh**), **çrabdha** (√**çrambh**), **daṣṭá** (√**daṅç**), **srasta** (√**sraṅs**), **bāḍha** (√**baṅh**).

b. Roots which are abbreviated in the weak forms of the perfect (**794**) suffer the same abbreviation here: examples are **uktá** (√**vac**), **uṣṭá** (√**vas** *shine*), **uptá** (√**vap**: also **vapta**), **ūḍhá** (√**vah**), **suptá** (√**svap**), **iṣṭá** (√**yaj**), **viddhá** (√**vyadh**); — and, by a similar procedure, √**prach** (or **praç**) makes **pṛṣṭá**, √**bhraṅç** makes **bhṛṣṭa** (beside the regular **bhraṣṭá**), and √**çrā** *boil* makes **çṛtá** (beside **çrātá**).

c. Final **ā** is weakened to **ī** in **gītá** (√**gā** *sing*), **dhītá** (√**dhā** *suck*), **pītá** (√**pā** *drink*), **sphīta**; and **jītá**, **vītá**, **çītá** are made from the roots **jyā**, **vyā**, **çyā**, (or **jī** etc.); — and further to **i** in **chitá** (beside **chātá**), **dita** (√**dā** *divide* and **dā** *bind*), **drita** (? √**drā** *sleep*), **hitá** (√**dhā** *put*: with **h** for **dh**; but **dhita** also occurs in V.), **mitá** (√**mā** *measure*), **çitá** (also **çāta**), **sitá**, **sthitá**.

d. A final **m** is lost after **a** in **gatá**, **natá**, **yatá**, **ratá** (from √**gam** etc.); and a final **n** in **kṣata**, **tatá**, **matá**, **hatá**. As to the other roots in **am** and **an** taking **ta**, see **955 a, b.**

e. More isolated cases are **-ūta** (RV.: √**av**), **utá** or **ūta** (√**vā** *weave*), **çiṣṭá** (also **çāsta**: √**çās**), **mūrtá** (referred to √**mūrch**). As to **-gdha** and **jagdhá**, see **233 f.**

f. On the other hand, √**svad** makes **svāttá**.

955. Of more irregular character are the following:

a. A number of roots ending in **am** retain the nasal, and lengthen the radical vowel (as also in some others of their verbal forms): thus, **kāṁta**, **krāṁtá**, **klāṁtá**, **kṣāṁta**, **cāṁta**, **tāṁtá**, **dāṁtá**, **bhrāṁta**, **vāṁtá**, **çāṁtá** (√**çam** *be quiet*), **çrāṁtá** (from √**kam** etc.); and one in **an**, **dhvan** *sound*, makes **dhvāntá**.

b. A few roots in **an** make their participle from another root-form in **ā**: thus, **khātá**, **jātá**, **-vāta**, **sātá**; **dham** has both **dhamitá** and **dhmātá**.

c. Certain roots in **īv** take their **yū**-form (**765 a**): thus, **dyūtá** (√**dīv** *play*), **ṣṭhyūta**, **syūtá**; but √**mīv** makes **-mūta**.

d. From roots in changeable **ṛ** (generally taking **na**: **957 b**) are made also **pūrtá** (√**pṛ** *fill*: beside **pṛta**), **cīrta** and **çūrtá** (√**çṛ** *crush*); and **çīrta** is further made from √**çrī** *mix*.

e. Double forms are **mugdhá** and **mūḍha**, **sāḍhá** and **soḍha**, **dhūrta** and **dhruta**, **hvṛta** and **hrutá**.

f. The root **dā** *give* makes **dattá** (from the secondary root-form **dad**; but **dāta** also in V.). But the anomalously contracted form **-tta** (as if for **dāta**, with the radical vowel lost) is also frequent in composition, especially with prepositions: thus, **ā́tta**, **ánutta**, **párītta**, **prátta**, **prátītta**; rarely with other elements, as **devátta**, **punartta**, **marútta** (?). And the same abbreviated form comes from √**dā** *divide* in **ávatta**.

g. The roots making participles in both **ta** and **ita**, or **ta** and **na**, or in all three, will be noted in the next two paragraphs.

956. The suffix with इ **i**, or in the form इत **itá**, is used especially with roots having finals that are only with difficulty, if at all, combinable with त् **t** according to the usual analogies of the language, and often with roots of a secondary, derivative, or late character; but also not seldom with original roots.

a. Thus, of roots presenting difficulties of combination: — 1. all that end in two consonants (save those of which one consonant is lost by a weakening process: **954** a, b): e. g. **çañk**, **valg**, **vāñch**, **lajj**, **ubj**, **ceṣṭ**, **ghūrṇ**, **katth**, **nind**, **jalp**, **cumb**, **umbh**, **khall**, **pinv**, **çaṅs** (also **çastá**), **rakṣ**, **hiṅs**, **garh** (in all, over fifty); but **takṣ** makes **taṣṭá**; — 2. all that end in linguals (including **ṣ** after **a** or **ā**): e. g. **aṭ**, **truṭ**, **paṭh**, **luṭh**, **īḍ**, **vruḍ**, **bhaṇ**, **kaṣ**, **bhāṣ**; — 3. all that end in surd spirants: e. g. **likh**, **grath**, **nāth**, **kuth**, **riph**, **guph**; — 4. all that end in **l**: e. g. **cal**, **gil**, **mīl**, **lul**, **khel**: — 5. all that end in other persistent semivowels: namely, **carv** (also **cūrṇa**), **jīv** (for the other roots in **īv**, see **955** c), **dhāv** *run*, **sev**, **day**, **vyay**, **pūy**; — 6. **ujh**. — This class includes more than half of the whole number that take only **ita**.

b. Of other roots ending in consonants: — 1. in gutturals, **cak**, **ḍhāuk** (**çak** has both **ta** and **ita**); **çlāgh**; — 2. in palatals, **ac** (also **akná**), **uc**, **kuc**, **khac**, **yāc**, **ruc**; **aj**?, **kūj**, **vraj**, also **tyaj** and **mṛj** in late texts (usually **tyaktá** and **mṛṣṭá**); — 3. in dentals, **at**, **pat**, **çcut**, also **yat** in epos (elsewhere only **yattá**); **krad**, **khād**, **gad**, **cud**, **nad**, **mud**, **mṛd**, **rad**, **rud**, **vad**, **vid** *know*, **hrād**; also **nud** in epos (elsewhere **nuttá** and **nunna**); **mad** has both **mattá** and **maditá** (the majority of roots in **d** take **na**: **957** d); **edh**, **kṣudh**, **gadh**, **dudh**, **nādh**, **bādh**, **spardh**; **an**, **in**, **kvan**, **dhvan**, **pan**, **ran** *ring*, **van**, **stan**, **svan**, and **dhvan** (also **dhvāntá**); — 4. in labials, **cup**, **yup**, **rup**, and usually **kup** (**kupta** late) and **lap** (**lapta** epic), occasionally **kṣip**, **gup**, **tap**, **dṛp**, **vap**, **çap**, while **jap** has both **ta** and **ita**; **grabh** (**gṛbhītá**), **çubh**, **skabh**, and occasionally **lubh**, while **kṣubh** and **stabh** have both forms; **tim**, **dham**, **çam** *labor*, **stim**, and **kṣam** in epos (also **kṣāṁta**); — 5. in spirants, **aç** *eat*, **īç**, **kāç**, **kṛç**, **vāç**, **çaç**, while **piç** has both forms, and **mṛç** takes **ita** only late; **iṣ** *send*, **īṣ, kuṣ, tṛṣ, tviṣ, pruṣ, miṣ, rūṣ, heṣ, hreṣ,** also **muṣ** except late, while **dhṛṣ, ruṣ,** and **hṛṣ** show both forms; **ās, bhas, bhās, ras, las, vas** *clothe*, **has,** also **as** *throw* occasionally, while **kas, gras, yas, vas** *shine*, **vas** *dwell*, **çās** (with **çiṣṭá** and **çāsta**), **çvas,** and **hras** make both forms; **īh, grah** (**gṛhītá**), **jah** (secondary form of **hā**), **mah, rah,** and occasionally **ūh** *remove*, while **gāh** has both forms.

c. Of roots ending in vowels, only **çī** *lie*, which makes **çayita** (with **guṇa** of root, as elsewhere: **629**).

d. In general, a root maintains its full form before **ita**; but there are a few exceptions: thus, **gṛbhītá** and **gṛhītá** (the root being reckoned as **grabh** and **grah**: see **729**), **uditá** (also **vadita** in the later language), **uṣita** (√**vas** *shine;* beside **uṣṭá**), **uṣita** (√**vas** *dwell:* also sporadically **vasita** and **uṣṭa**), **ukṣitá** (√**vakṣ** *increase*), **çṛthitá** (√**çrath**). From √**mṛj** are made both **mṛjita** and **mārjita** (with strengthening as in present and elsewhere: **627**), beside **mṛṣṭá.**

e. Instead of **i,** long **ī** is taken in **gṛbhītá** and **gṛhītá.**

957. The suffix न **ná** (always without auxiliary इ **i**) is taken instead of त **tá** by a number of roots (about seventy). Thus:

a. Certain roots in **ā**: thus, **kṣā, glā, drā** *run*, **drā** *sleep*, (also **drita**?), **mlā** (also **mlātá**), **vā** *blow* (also **vāta**), **çyā** (also **çīná**), **styā, hā** *leave* (also **hīná** and **hāta**), **hā** *go forth;* and **dā** *divide* makes **diná** (also **dita** and **-tta**). Further, certain roots in **i-** and **u-**vowels: thus, **kṣi** *destroy* (**kṣīṇa**; also **kṣitá**), **ḍī, pī, lī** *cling*, **vlī, çī** or **çyā** *coagulate* (beside **çyāna** and **çīta**), **hrī** (beside **hrīta**); **dū** *burn* (also **duta**), **lū, çū**; and **dīv** *lament* makes **dyūna** (compare **765**).

b. Roots in **ṛ**, which before the suffix becomes **īr** or **ūr**: the forms are, **arṇa** (late; beside **ṛtá**), **kīrṇa** (√**kṛ** *scatter*), **gīrṇá** (√**gṛ** *swallow*), **jīrṇá** and **jūrṇá** (√**jṛ** *waste away*), **tīrṇá** and **tūrṇa** (also **tūrtá**), **dīrṇá** (√**dṛ** *pierce:* also **dṛta**), **pūrṇá** (√**pṛ** *fill:* also **pūrtá** and **pṛta**), **mūrṇá** (√**mṛ** *crush*), **çīrṇá** (√**çṛ** *crush:* also **çīrta** and **çūrtá**?), **stīrṇá** (also **stṛta**). Of like character with these are **īrṇá** from √**īr**, **cīrṇa** (beside **carita**) from √**car**, **gūrṇa** (beside **gūrtá**) from √**gur**, a secondary form of **gṛ**, and **cūrṇa** (beside **carvita**) from √**carv**, which is also plainly a secondary root.

c. A few roots ending in **j** (which becomes **g** before the suffix, against the usual rule of internal combination: **216 f**): thus, **bhagna** (√**bhañj**), **bhugna** (√**bhuj** *bend*), **magná** (√**majj**), **rugṇá, vigna** (beside **vikta**). Further, two or three ending in **c** (similarly treated): thus, **akná** (√**ac** or **añc**: also **acita** and **añcita**), **vṛkṇá** (√**vraçc**), and apparently **-pṛgṇa** (RV., once: with doubly irregular change of root-final, from √**pṛc**). And one root in **g, lagna.**

d. A considerable number, some of them very common ones, of roots in **d** (which, against ordinary rule, becomes **n** before the suffix: **157 b**). The forms are: **unna** (also **utta**), **arṇṇa**?, **klinna**, **kṣuṇṇa**, **kṣviṇṇa**, **khinna**, **channa**, **chinná**, **chṛṇṇá**, **tunná**, **tṛṇṇá**, **nunna** (also **nuttá** and **nudita**), **panná**, **bhinná**, **vinna** (√**vid** *find*: also **vittá**), **çanna** (√**çad** *fall*), **sanná** (also **sattá**), **skanná** (√**skand**), **syanná** (√**syand**), **svinná**, **hanna**. And **ánna** *food*, in spite of its different accent, appears to be a like formation from √**ad** *eat*.

958. The native grammarians reckon as participles of this formation a few miscellaneous derivative adjectives, coming from roots which do not make a regular participle: such are **kṣāma** *burnt*, **kṛçá** *emaciated*, **pakvá** *ripe*, **phullá** *expanded*, **çúṣka** *dry*.

Past Active Participle in tavant (or navant).

959. From the past passive participle, of whatever formation, is made, by adding the possessive suffix वत् **vant**, a secondary derivative having the meaning and construction of a perfect active participle: for example, तत् कृतवान् **tát kṛtávān** *having done that;* **taṁ nigīrṇavān** *having swallowed him down.* Its inflection is like that of other derivatives made with this suffix (**452** ff.); its feminine ends in वती **vatī**; its accent remains on the participle.

960. Derivative words of this formation are found in RV., but without anything like a participial value. The AV. has a single example, with participial meaning: **açitā́vaty átithāu** *one's guest having eaten* (loc. abs.). In the Brāhmaṇas also it is hardly met with. In the later language, however, it comes to be quite common. And there it is chiefly used predicatively, and oftenest without copula expressed, or with the value of a personal verb-form in a past tense: primarily, and not seldom, signifying immediate past, or having a true "perfect" value; but also (like the old perfect and the old aorist in later use) coming to be freely used for indefinite time, or with the value of the imperfect (**779**). For example: **māṁ na kaçcid dṛṣṭavān** *no one has seen* (or *saw*) *me;* **sa nakulaṁ vyāpāditavān** *he destroyed the ichneumon;* or, with copula, **mahat kṛcchram prāptavaty asi** *thou hast fallen upon great misery.* Although originally and properly made only from transitive verbs (with an object, to which the participle in **ta** stands in the relation of an objective predicate), it is finally found also from intransitives: thus, **cūtena saṁçritavatī** (Ç.) *has become united with the mango-tree;* **gatavatī** (ib.) *she has gone.*

a. The same participle is also made in the secondary conjugations: e. g. **darçitavant** *having shown*, **prabodhitavant** *having awakened.*

b. Possessives also in **in** made from passive participles are sometimes found used in an analogous manner, nearly as perfect active participles: e. g. **iṣṭín** *having sacrificed*, **vijitino manyamānāḥ** (AB.) *thinking themselves to have conquered.*

Future Passive Participles: Gerundives.

961. Certain derivative adjectives (for the most part more or less clearly secondary derivatives) have acquired in the language a value as qualifying something which is to, or which ought to, suffer the action expressed by the root from which they come; and they are allowed to be made from every verb. Hence they are, like more proper participles, sometimes treated as a part of the general verbal system, and called future passive participles, or gerundives (like the Latin forms in *ndus*, to which they correspond in meaning).

962. The suffixes by which such gerundives are regularly and ordinarily made are three: namely य **ya**, तव्य **tavya**, and अनीय **anīya**.

a. Derivatives in **ya** having this value are made in all periods of the language, from the earliest down; the other two are of more modern origin, being entirely wanting in the oldest Veda (RV.), and hardly known in the later. Other derivatives of a similar character, which afterward disappear from use, are found in the Veda (**966**).

963. The suffix **ya** in its gerundive use has nothing to distinguish it from the same suffix as employed to make adjectives and nouns of other character (see below, **1213**). And it exhibits also the same variety in the treatment of the root.

a. The original value of the suffix is **ia**, and as such it has to be read in the very great majority of its Vedic occurrences. Hence the conversion of **e** and **o** to **ay** and **av** before it (see below).

b. Thus: 1. Final **ā** becomes **e** before the suffix: **déya, dhyeya, khyéya, méya** (perhaps **dā́-ia** etc, with euphonic **y** interposed); but RV. has once **-jñāya.** — 2. The other vowels either remain unchanged, or have the **guṇa** or the **vṛddhi** strengthening; and **e** usually and **o** always are treated before the **ya** as they would be before a vowel: thus, **-kṣayya, jáyya, bháyya, lāyya; návya, bhávya, hávya, bhāvyá; vā́rya**: and, in the later language, **nīya, jeya, dhūya** (such cases are wanting earlier). In a few instances, a short vowel adds **t** before the suffix: thus, **itya, mitya, çrútya, stútya, kṛtya** (the only Vedic examples). — 3. Medial **a** remains unchanged or is lengthened: thus, **dábhya, vándya, sádya; mā́dya, vā́cya.** — 4. Medial **i-, u-,** and **ṛ**-vowels are unchanged or have the **guṇa**-strengthening: thus, **ī́ḍya, gúhya, dhṛṣya; dvéṣya, yódhya, márjya.**

c. The RV. has about forty examples of this gerundive, and the AV. adds half as many more. Except in **bhāviá** (once), the accent in RV. is always on the root; AV. has several cases of accent on the **i** of the suffix (hence written **ādyà, āçyà, -vyādhyà, -dharṣyà**). According to the grammarians, the accent is on the root or else the ending is circumflexed: always the former, if the **ya** follow a vowel.

964. a. The suffix **tavya** is a secondary adjective derivative from the infinitival noun in **tu** (below, **968**), made by adding the suffix **ya** (properly **ía**, whence the accent **yà**), before which the final **u**, as usual (**1203 a**), has **guṇa**-strengthening, and is resolved into **av.**

b. Hence, as regards both the form taken by the root and the use or omission of an auxiliary vowel **i** before the **tavya**, the rules are the same as for the formation of the infinitive (below, **968**).

c. No example of this formation is found in RV., and in AV. occur only two, **janitavyà** and **hiṅsitavyà.** In the Brāhmaṇa language it begins to be not rare, and is made both from the simple root and from the derived conjugational stems (next chapter); in the classical language it is still more frequent. According to the grammarians, the accent of the word is either circumflex on the final or acute on the penult: thus, **kartavyà** or **kartávya;** in the accentuated texts, it is always the former (the accent **távya** given to certain gerundives in the Petersburg lexicons is an error, growing out of the ambiguous accentuation of ÇB.: **88 c**).

965. a. The suffix **anīya** is in like manner the product of secondary derivation, made by adding the adjective suffix **īya** (**1215**) to a *nomen actionis* formed by the common suffix **ana.**

b. It follows, then, as regards its mode of formation, the rules for the suffix **ana** (below, **1150**).

c. This derivative also is unknown in RV., and in AV. is found only in **upajīvanī́ya** and **āmantranī́ya** (in both of which, moreover, its distinct gerundive value admits of question). In the Brāhmaṇas (where less than a dozen examples of it have been noted), and in the later language, it is less common than the gerundive in **tavya.** Its accent, as in all the derivatives with the suffix **īya,** is on the penult: thus, **karaṇī́ya.**

966. Other formations of kindred value are found in the Veda, as follows:

a. Gerundives in **tua** or **tva,** apparently made from the infinitival noun in **tu** with the added suffix **a** (**1209**). They are **kártua** (in two occurrences **kártva**), **-gaṁtva, jántua, jétua, náṁtua, váktua, sótua,**

snā́tua, hántua, hétua, hótva; and, with auxiliary i (or ī), jánitva, **sánitva, bhávītva.**

b. Gerundives in **enia** or **enya** (compare **1217**): they are **īkṣeṇía, īḍénia, caréṇia,** dṛçénia, -dviṣeṇia, bhūṣéṇya, **yudhénia, váreṇia** (and bhajenya BhP.); with one example from an apparent aorist-stem, **yaṁsénya,** and three or four from secondary verb-stems (see below, **1019, 1038, 1068 a**).

c. Gerundives in **ā́yia** (once **ā́yya**: compare **1218**): they are **dakṣā́yia, panā́yia, vidā́yia, çravā́yia, hnavāyia**; with a few from secondary conjugation-stems (below, **1019, 1038, 1051, 1068 a**); and **stuṣéyia** is of close kindred with them.

d. A few adjectives in **elima**, as **pacelima, bhidelima** (only these quotable), are reckoned as gerundives by the grammarians.

967. The division-line between participial and ordinary adjectives is less strictly drawn in Sanskrit than in the other Indo-European languages. Thus, adjectives in **u**, as will be seen later (**1178**), from secondary conjugational stems, have participial value; and in the Brāhmaṇas (with an example or two in AV.) is found widely and commonly used a participial adjective formed with the suffix **uka** (**1180**).

Infinitives.

968. The later language has only a single infinitive, which is the accusative case of a verbal noun formed by the suffix तु **tu**, added to the root usually directly, but often also with aid of the preceding auxiliary vowel इ **i**. The form of the infinitive ending, therefore, is तुम् **tum** or इतुम् **itum**. The root has the **guṇa**-strengthening, and is accented. Thus, for example, एतुम् **étum** from √इ **i**; कर्तुम् **kártum** from √कृ **kṛ**; चरितुम् **cáritum** from √चर् **car**; भवितुम् **bhávitum** from √भू **bhū**.

a. As regards the use or omission of **i**, the infinitive (as also the gerund in **tvā**: **991**) follows in general the analogy of the passive participle (**956**). Examples are (with the gerund added) as follows: **dagdhá, dágdhum, dagdhvā́** from √**dah**; **bhinná, bhéttum, bhittvā́** from √**bhid**; **matá, mántum, matvā́** from √**man**; **ūḍhá, vóḍhum, ūḍhvā́** from √**vah**; **patitá, pátitum, patitvā́** from √**pat**; **yācitá, yā́citum, yācitvā́** from √**yāc**; **çayitá, çáyitum, çayitvā́** from √**çī**. But certain exceptions and special cases require notice. Thus:

b. Of roots having no quotable participle, infinitive stems in **tu** are made from **ad, sagh**; in **itu** from **uñch, ūh** *consider*, **kṣap, luṇṭh, lok, svar**; and in both from **yabh.**

c. Of roots making participles of both forms, an infinitive stem in **tu** only is quotable for **kṣip, kṣubh, tap, tyaj, mṛç, lubh, vas** *shine*, **çak, stabh**; only in **itu** for **gāh, carv, jap, mad, yat, van, çaṅs, çvas**; in both for **as** *throw*, **ūh** *remove*, **gup, car, mṛj (mărṣṭu, mārjitu), lap, vas** *dwell*, **çap, çās.**

d. Also in a number of other cases (besides those already noticed) an infinitive stem is made both with and without **i**. Thus, in addition to the more regular form, a stem in **itu** is occasionally met with from roots **aç** *attain*, **iṣ** *seek*, **bandh, bhaj, yaj (ījitum), rudh** *obstruct*, **ruh, vṛṣ, sad (sīditum), sah, han, hṛ**; and one in **tu** from roots **ās, bhāṣ, vid** *know*. Both forms occur also from certain **am**-roots, namely **nam, yam, ram,** and, with **ā** before **tu** as in the pple, **kram** and **bhram** (**kṣam** has only **kṣaṁtu,** against the analogy of **kṣāṁta**); further, from certain roots in variable **ṛ**, namely **tṛ (tartu, tarĭtu), vṛ** *cover* **(vártu, varĭtu),** and **stṛ (stártu, staritu, stárītu)** (but from **çṛ** *crush* occur only **çárītu, çaritu,** and from **vṛ** *choose* only **varītu**; while **gṛ** *swallow* and **pṛ** *fill* make their infinitive from other root-forms, namely **giritum, pūritum**); further, from a few vowel-roots, namely **nī, cyu, sū (sū́tu)**; and finally from **kṛṣ, nṛt, çuc.**

e. Against the analogy of the participle, infinitive-stems in **itu** after a final consonant are made from the roots **av, kṣan, khan** and **jan** (the pples coming from **khā** and **jā**), **guh, jabh, tam, dīv** *play* and **dīv** *lament* (both **devitu**), **majj, vṛt, vṛdh, sṛp**; and after a final vowel, from roots in **ū**, namely **pū, bhū, sū** (also **sūtu**), and from **çri** and **çvi**; as to roots in variable **ṛ**, see just above, **d.**

f. As the infinitive is made from the (accented and) strengthened root, so it naturally has, as a rule, the stronger or fuller root-form where a weaker or contracted form is taken by the participle (and gerund in **tvā́**): e. g. **váktu** against **uktá** (and **uktvā́**), **yáṣṭu** against **iṣṭá** (and **iṣṭvā́**), **banddhum** against **baddhá** (and **baddhvā́**), and so on. Deserving special notice are **gātu** (√**gā** *sing*) against **gītá,** and **dhā́tu** (√**dhā** *suck*) against **dhītá**; and so from **dā** *give* and **hā** *leave* are made only **dā́tu** and **hātu**; but **dhā** *put*, **mā** *measure*, and **sthā** add to the regular **dhātu, mātu, sthātu** the late forms **-dhitu, -mitu, -sthitu**; and **sā** or **si** has **sātu, sétu,** and **-situ**; **vā** *weave* (pple **utá**) has both **vā́tu** and **ótu**; **hū** or **hvā** has **havītu, hváyitu,** and **hvātu.** The root **vyadh** makes its only quotable infinitive, **veddhum,** from its **vidh**-form; from **sañj** or **saj** occur both **sañktu** and **saktu.** The anomalous epic forms **ījitum** (√**yaj**) and **sīditum** (√**sad**), were mentioned above. The root **grah** makes **gráhītum.**

g. In the later language, the infinitive-stem forms possessive compounds with **kāma** and **manas** (especially the former): e. g. **svaptukāma** *having the wish to sleep*, **yaṣṭukāma** *desirous of sacrificing*, **vaktumanas** *minded to speak*.

h. In very rare instances, dative infinitives in **tave** or **tavāi** are made from the infinitive stem in the later language (as abundantly in the earlier: **970b**): thus, **pratihartave** (BhP.). And **jīvase** (**973a**) is once found in MBh. (i. 3. 67 = 732), in a quasi-Vedic hymn to the Açvins.

969. In the Veda and Brāhmaṇa, however, a number of verbal nouns, *nomina actionis*, in various of their cases, are used in constructions which assimilate them to the infinitive of other languages — although, were it not for these other later and more developed and pronounced infinitives, the constructions in question might pass as ordinary case-constructions of a somewhat peculiar kind.

970. The nouns thus used infinitively are the following:

a. The root-noun, without derivative suffix, is so used in its accusative in **am**, its dative in **e** or (from **ā**-roots) **āi**, its genitive and ablative in **as**, and its locative in **i**.

b. The verbal noun in **tu** is so used in its accusative in **tum**, its dative in **tave** or **tavāí**, and its ablative and genitive in **tos**.

Of other nouns only single cases, generally datives, are reckoned as used with infinitive value; thus:

c. From the verbal noun in **as**, the dative in **ase**; and also, in an extremely small number of instances, a dative in **se** (or **ṣe**), from a noun formed with **s** simply.

d. From nouns in **man** and **van**, datives in **mane** and **vane**.

e. From nouns in **ti**, datives in **taye**, or (from one or two verbs) in **tyāi**.

f. From nouns in **i**, datives in **áye**.

g. From nouns in **dhi** and **ṣi**, datives in **dhyāi** and **ṣyāi**.

h. A few infinitives in **ṣaṇi** are perhaps locatives from nouns in **an** added to a root increased by **s**.

i. From a single root, **dhṛ**, are made infinitively used forms in **tári**, of which the grammatical character is questionable.

j. Among all these, the forms which have best right to special treatment as infinitives, on account of being of peculiar formation, or from suffixes not found in other uses, or for both reasons, are those in **ṣe**, **ṣaṇi**, **tari**, **dhyāi**, and **tavāi**.

k. Except the various cases of the derivative in **tu**, and of the root-noun, these infinitives are almost wholly unknown outside the Rig-Veda.

l. Other suffixes and forms than those noticed above might be added; for it is impossible to draw any fixed line between the uses classed as infinitive and the ordinary case-uses: thus, **prajā́patim praçnám āitām** (TS.) *they went to ask Prajāpati;* **víçvaṁ jīvám prasuvántī carā́yāi** (RV.) *quickening every living being to motion;* **apáḥ sármāya codáyan** (RV.) *impelling the waters to flow;* **çaknuyā́d gráhaṇāya** (instead of the usual **gráhītum**: ÇB.) *may be able to apprehend;* **ā tamanāt** (instead of the usual **tamitoḥ**: S.) *until exhaustion.* And the so-called infinitives are found coördinated in the same sentence with common nouns, and even with compound nouns: e. g. **cáritave... ābhogáya iṣṭáye rāyé** (RV.) *to go abroad, to enjoy, to seek wealth;* **ārtatrāṇāya na prahartum anāgasi** (Ç.) *for the rescue of the distressed, not for hurling at the innocent.*

More special rules as to the various formations are as follows:

971. The root-noun used as infinitive has the same form (except that it does not take an added **t**: **383 f**), and the same accent, both when simple and when combined with prepositions, as in its other uses. In the very great majority of instances, it is made from roots ending in a consonant; but also from a few in **ā** (**khyā, dā, dhā, pā?, mā, yā**), from two or three in **i-** and **u-**vowels (**hi, mī, bhū**), and from one or two in changeable **ṛ**, which takes the **ir**-form (**tir, stir**).

a. The roots in **ā** form the accus. in **ām**, the dat. in **āi**, the abl. in **ās** (understanding **avasā́** before **ā́** as for **avasā́s** and not **avasāí** in RV. iii. 53. 20), and the locative in **e** (only two examples, of which one is perhaps better understood as dative).

972. The infinitive noun in **tu** is made freely from roots of every form. The root takes the **guṇa**-strengthening, if capable of it, and often adds the auxiliary vowel **i** before the suffix (according to the rules already stated, **968**). The root is accented, unless the noun be combined with a preposition, in which case the latter has the accent instead: thus, **kártum, étave, hántos**; but **níkartum, níretave, nírhantos.**

a. The dative in **tavāi** is in two respects anomalous: in having the heavy feminine ending **āi** along with a strengthened **u**; and in taking a double accent, one on the root or on the prefixed preposition, and the other on the ending **āi**: thus, **étavāí, hántavāí, átyetavāí, ápabhartavāí.**

973. a. The infinitive in **ase** is made in RV. from about twenty-five roots; in AV. and later there have been noted no other examples of it. In near three quarters of the cases, the accent is on the suffix: e. g. **ṛñjáse, jīváse, bhiyáse, tujáse**; the exceptions are **cákṣase**; **dhā́yase** (with **y** inserted before the suffix: **258**); and **áyase, bhárase, spárase, hárase** (with **guṇa**-strengthening of the root). Strengthening of the root is also shown by **javáse, doháse, bhojáse, çobháse.** In **puṣyáse** is seen, apparently, the present-stem instead of the root.

b. The ending **se** is extremely rare, being found only in **jiṣé** and perhaps **stuṣé,** and one or two still more doubtful cases.

974. Infinitives in **mane** are made from only five roots: thus, **trā́maṇe, dā́mane, dármaṇe, bhármaṇe,** and (with different accent) **vidmáne.** From √**dā** comes **dāváne**; **turváṇe** may come directly from √**tṛ**, or through the secondary root **turv**; **dhū́rvaṇe** is rather from √**dhūrv** than from √**dhvṛ**.

975. a. The infinitives in **taye** are **iṣṭáye** (√**iṣ**), **pītáye** (√**pā** *drink*), **vītáye, sātáye,** and perhaps **ūtáye** (**ūtáye nṝn** *to help his men:*

(RV.). In **tyāi**, the only examples noted are **ityāí** (RV.) and **sā́ḍhyāi** (MS. AB.).

b. With **aye** are formed **iṣáye, tujáye, dṛçáye, maháye, yudháye, sanáye**; and **citáye** (VS.), **gṛhaye** (K.).

976. The ending **dhyāi** is, more than any other, irregular and various in its treatment. It has always an **a** before it; and in the majority of cases it is accented upon this **a**, and added to a weak form of root: thus, **çucádhyāi, pṛṇádhyāi, dhiyádhyāi, huvádhyāi.** But the form of root is the strong one in a few cases: namely, **çayádhyāi, stavádhyāi, tarádhyāi, jarádhyāi, mandádhyāi, vandádhyāi.** In half-a-dozen forms, again, the root has the accent: namely, **kṣáradhyāi, gámadhyāi, yájadhyāi** (but once or twice also **yajádhyāi**), **váhadhyāi, sáhadhyāi, bháradhyāi.** In a single instance, **píbadhyāi,** the suffix is added distinctly to a present-stem; and in one, **vāvṛdhádhyāi,** to a perfect stem. Finally, in a number of instances (ten), this infinitive is made from a causative stem in **ay**: thus, **mādayádhyāi, riṣayádhyāi,** etc.

a. This infinitive is by no means rare in RV., being made in thirty-five different forms (with seventy-two occurrences). But it is hardly known outside of the RV.; the AV. has it but once (in a passage found also in RV.); and elsewhere half-a-dozen examples have been noticed, in **mantra**-passages (one of them TS. falsely reads **gámadhye**); in the Brāhmaṇa language proper it appears to be entirely wanting.

977. An example or two are met with of an infinitive in **ṣyāi**: thus, **róhiṣyāi** (TS.), **avyathiṣyāi** (K. Kap.; MS. **avyáthiṣe**; VS. **vyathiṣat**), and perhaps **-dhāsyāi** (PGS.).

978. The infinitives in **ṣaṇi** are: **iṣáṇi** (?) from √**iṣ** *send*, **-bhūṣáṇi** from √**bhū**; **çūṣáṇi** from √**çū** or **çvā**; **neṣáṇi** from √**nī**; **sakṣáṇi** from √**sah**; **parṣáṇi** from √**pṛ**, **tarīṣáṇi** from √**tṛ**; and **gṛṇīṣáṇi** and **-stṛṇīṣáṇi** from √√**gṛ** and **stṛ** — the last containing evident present tense-signs (compare the 1st sing. **gṛṇīṣé, 894 d**).

979. The only infinitive in **tari** is **dhartári** (with its compound **vidhartári**), from √**dhṛ**.

Uses of the Infinitives.

980. The uses of the so-called infinitives are for the most part closely accordant with those of the corresponding cases from other abstract nouns. Thus:

981. The accusative, which is made only from the root-noun and the noun in **tu**, is used as object of a verb.

a. Especially, of forms from the root **çak** *be able*, and **arh** *be worthy, have the right* or *the power*. Thus, **çakéma tvā samídham** (RV.) *may we accomplish thy kindling;* **mā́ çakan pratidhā́m íṣum** (AV.) *may they not be able to fit the arrow to the string;* **máno vā́ imā́ṁ sadyáḥ pāry-**

āptum arhati mánaḥ páribhavitum (TS.) *the mind, forsooth, can at once attain and surpass her;* **kó hy ètásyā́ 'rhati gúhyaṁ nā́ma gráhītum** (ÇB.) *for who is worthy to take his secret name?* In the Veda, the construction with these verbs is only one among others; in the Brāhmaṇa, it becomes the greatly prevalent one (three quarters or more of all the cases).

b. Further, of verbs of motion (next most frequent case): thus, **dā́kṣiṇāni hótum eti** (TS.) *he goes to sacrifice things pertaining to sacrificial gifts;* **índram pratíram emy ā́yuḥ** (RV.) *I go to Indra for* (i. e. *beseech of him*) *the lengthening out of life;* — of √**dhṛ** *persist in, undertake:* as, **sá idáṁ jātáḥ sárvam evá dágdhuṁ dadhre** (ÇB.) *he, as soon as born, began to burn this universe;* — of verbs meaning *desire, hope, notice, know*, and the like: as, **pā́çān vicṛ́taṁ vettha sárvān** (AV.) *thou knowest how to loosen all bonds;* **tásmād agníṁ nā́ "driyeta párihantum** (ÇB.) *therefore one should not be careful to smother the fire;* — and of others.

982. Of the infinitive datives, the fundamental and usual sense is that expressed by *for, in order to, for the purpose of.*

Examples are: **víçvaṁ jīváṁ caráse bodháyantī** (RV.) *awakening every living creature to motion;* **tā́n úpa yāta píbadhyāi** (RV.) *come to drink them;* **nāí 'tā́ṁ te devā́ adadur áttave** (AV.) *the gods did not give her to thee for eating;* **prāí "d yudháye dásyum índraḥ** (RV.) *Indra went forward to fight the demon;* **cákṣur no dhehi vikhyāí** (RV.) *give us sight for looking abroad.*

Some peculiar constructions, however, grow out of this use of the infinitive dative. Thus:

a. The noun which is logically the subject or the object of the action expressed by the infinitive is frequently put beside it in the dative (by a construction which is in part a perfectly simple one, but which is stretched beyond its natural boundaries by a kind of attraction): thus, **cakāra sū́ryāya pánthām ánvetavā́ u** (RV.) *he made a track for the sun to follow (made for the sun a track for his following);* **çíçīte çṛ́ñge rákṣobhyo viníkṣe** (RV.) *he whets his horns to pierce the demons;* **rudrā́ya dhánur ā́ tanomi brahmadvíṣe çárave hántavā́ u** (RV.) *I stretch the bow for Rudra, that with his arrow he may slay the* **brahma**-*hater;* **asmábhyaṁ dṛçáye sū́ryāya púnar dātām ásum** (RV.) *may they grant life again, that we may see the sun.*

b. An infinitive with √**kṛ** *make* is used nearly in the sense of a causative verb: thus, **prā́ 'ndháṁ çroṇáṁ cákṣasa étave kṛthaḥ** (RV.) *ye make the blind and lame to see and go;* **agníṁ samídhe cakártha** (RV.) *thou hast made the fire to be kindled.* Of similar character is an occasional construction with another verb: as, **yád īm uçmási kártave kárat tát** (RV.) *what we wish to be done, may he do that;* **kavī́ṅr icchāmi saṁdṛ́çe** (RV.) *I desire to see the sages.*

c. A dative infinitive is not seldom used as a predicate, sometimes with, but more usually without, a copula expressed: thus, **agnír iva ná pratidhṛ́ṣe bhavati** (TS.) *like fire, he is not to be resisted;* **mahimā́ te anyéna ná saṁnáçe** (VS.) *thy greatness is not to be attained by another;* **nákīm índro níkartave ná çakráḥ páriçaktave** (RV.) *Indra is not to be put down, the mighty one is not to be overpowered.*

d. Sometimes an infinitive so used without a copula has quite nearly the value of an imperative: thus, **tyā́ me yaçásā... āuçijó huvádhyāi** [asti] (RV.) *these glorious ones shall the son of Uçij invoke for me;* **sūktébhir vaḥ... índrā nv àgní ávase huvádhyāi** [staḥ] (RV.) *with your hymns shall ye call now on Indra and Agni for aid;* **vandádhyā agním námobhiḥ** [asmi] (RV.) *let me greet Agni with homage;* **asmākā́saç ca sūráyo víçvā ā́çās tarīṣáṇi** (RV.) *and let our sacrificers cross all regions;* **tán nāí 'váṁ kártavāí** (MS.) *that must not be done so;* **brahmadvíṣaḥ çárave hántavā́ u** (RV.) *let the arrow slay the brahma-haters.* The infinitives in **dhyāi** and **ṣaṇi** (which latter is in all its uses accordant with datives) are those in which the imperative value is most distinctly to be recognized.

e. In the Brāhmaṇas and Sūtras (especially in ÇB.) the dative in **tavāi** is not seldom used with a verb signifying *speak* (**brū, vac, ah**), to express the ordering of anything to be done: thus, **tásmād óṣadhīnām evá mū́lāny úcchettavāí brūyāt** (ÇB.) *therefore let him direct the roots of the plants to be cut up (speak in order to their cutting up:* cf. **yé vaçā́yā ádānāya vádanti** *who dissuade from giving the cow:* AV.).

983. The ablative infinitive — which, like the accusative, is made only from the root-noun and that in **tu** — is found especially with the prepositions **ā́** *until* and **purā́** *before.*

a. Thus, **ā́ támitoḥ** (TS. etc.) *until exhaustion;* **purā́ vācáḥ právaditoḥ** (TS.) *before utterance of the voice.* In the Brāhmaṇa language, this is the well-nigh exclusive construction of the ablative (it occurs also with **prāk, arvāk,** etc.); in the Veda, the latter is used also after **ṛté** *without,* and after several verbs, as **trā** and **pā** *protect,* **yu** *separate,* **bhī,** etc.

b. In a few instances, by an attraction similar to that illustrated above for the dative (**982a**), a noun dependent on this infinitive is put in the ablative beside it: thus, **purā vāgbhyaḥ sampravaditoḥ** (PB.) *before the utterance together of the voices;* **trā́dhvaṁ kartā́d avapádaḥ** (RV.) *save us from falling down into the pit;* **purā dakṣiṇābhyo netoḥ** (Āpast.) *before the gifts are taken away.*

984. The genitive infinitive (having the same form as the ablative) is in common use in the Brāhmaṇa language as dependent on **īçvará** *lord, master,* employed adjectively in the sense of *capable* or *likely* or *exposed to.*

a. Examples are: **tā́** [**devátāḥ**] **īçvarā́ enam pradáhaḥ** (TS.) *they are likely to burn him up;* **átha ha vā́ īçvarò 'gníṁ citvā́ kíṁcid dāuritám ā́pattor ví vā hválitoḥ** (ÇB.) *so in truth he is liable,* *after piling the fire, to meet with some mishap or other, or to stagger;* **īçvaraṁ vāi rathantaram udgātuç cakṣuḥ pramathitoḥ** (PB.) *the rathantara is liable to knock out the eye of the chanter.*

b. The dative is used in ÇB. instead of the genitive in a single phrase (**īçvarāú jánayitavāí**); and, in the later language, sometimes the accusative in **tum**. In a case or two the masc. sing. nom. **īçvaraḥ** is used, without regard to the gender or number of the word which it qualifies: thus, **tásye "çvaráḥ prajā́ pā́pīyasī bhávitoḥ** (ÇB.) *his progeny is liable to deteriorate.* And in a very few instances the word **īçvara** is omitted, and the genitive has the same value without it: thus, **dve madhyaṁdinam abhi pratyetoḥ** (AB.) *two may be added to the noon libation;* **táto dīkṣitáḥ pāmanó bhávitoḥ** (ÇB.) *then the consecrated is liable to get the itch.*

c. This construction with **īçvara**, which is the only one for the genitive infinitive in the Brāhmaṇa, is unknown in the Veda, where the genitive is found in a very small number of examples with **madhyā́**, and with the root **īç**: thus, **madhyā́ kártoḥ** (RV.) *in the midst of action;* **íçe rāyó dā́toḥ** (RV.) *he is master of the giving of wealth;* **íçe yótoḥ** (RV.) *is able to keep away.*

985. Unless the infinitives in **ṣaṇi** and **tari** are locative in form (their uses are those of datives), the locative infinitive is so rare, and has so little that is peculiar in its use, that it is hardly worth making any account of. An example is **uṣáso budhí** (RV.) *at the awakening of the dawn.*

986. In the Veda, the dative infinitive forms are very much more numerous than the accusative (in RV., their occurrences are twelve times as many; in AV., more than three times); and the accusative in **tum** is rare (only four forms in RV., only eight in AV.). In the Brāhmaṇas, the accusative has risen to much greater comparative frequency (its forms are nearly twice as many as those of the dative); but the ablative-genitive, which is rare in the Veda, has also come to full equality with it. The disappearance in the classical language of all excepting the accusative in **tum** (but see **968h**) is a matter for no small surprise.

987. The later infinitive in **tum** is oftenest used in constructions corresponding to those of the earlier accusative: thus, **na vāṣpam açakat soḍhum** *he could not restrain his tears;* **taṁ draṣṭum arhasi** *thou oughtest to see it;* **prāptum icchanti** *they desire to obtain;* **saṁkhyātum ārabdham** *having begun to count.* But also, not infrequently, in those of the other cases. So, especially, of the dative: thus, **avasthātuṁ sthānāntaraṁ cintaya** *devise another place to stay in;* **tvām anveṣṭum ihā "gataḥ** *he has come hither to seek for thee;* — but likewise of the genitive: thus, **samartho gantum** *capable of going;* **saṁdhātum īçvaraḥ** *able to mend.* Even a construction as nominative is not unknown: thus, **yuktaṁ tasya mayā samāçvā-**

sayitum bhāryām (MBh.) *it is proper for me to comfort his wife;* **na naptāraṁ svayaṁ nyāyyaṁ çaptum evam** (R.) *it is not suitable thus to curse one's own grandson;* **tad vaktuṁ na pāryate** (Çatr.) *it is not possible to say that.*

988. In the later language, as in the earlier, the infinitive in certain connections has what we look upon as a passive value. Thus, **kartum ārabdhaḥ** *begun to be made;* **çrotuṁ na yujyate** *it is not fit to be heard (for hearing).* This is especially frequent along with the passive forms of √**çak**: thus, **tyaktuṁ na çakyate** *it cannot be abandoned;* **çakyāv ihā 'netum** *they two can be brought hither;* **na ca vibhūtayaḥ çakyam avāptum ūrjitāḥ** *nor are mighty successes a thing capable of being attained.*

Gerunds.

989. The so-called gerund is a stereotyped case (doubtless instrumental) of a verbal noun, used generally as adjunct to the logical subject of a clause, denoting an accompanying or (more often) a preceding action to that signified by the verb of the clause. It has thus the virtual value of an indeclinable participle, present or past, qualifying the actor whose action it describes.

a. Thus, for example: **çrutvāi 'va cā 'bruvan** *and hearing* (or *having heard*) *they spoke;* **tebhyaḥ pratijñāyā 'thāi 'tān paripapraccha** *having given them his promise, he then questioned them.*

990. The gerund is made in the later language by one of the two suffixes त्वा **tvā** and य **ya**, the former being used with a simple root, the latter with one that is compounded with a prepositional prefix — or, rarely, with an element of another kind, as adverb or noun.

a. To this distribution of uses between the two suffixes there are occasional exceptions. Thus, gerunds in **ya** from simple roots are not very rare in the epic language (e. g. **gṛhya, uṣya** [√**vas** *dwell*], **arcya, īkṣya, cintya, tyajya, lakṣya;** also from causatives and denominatives, as **vācya, yojya, plāvya**), and are not unknown elsewhere (e. g. **arcya** and **īkṣya** M., **prothya** AGS., **sthāpya** ÇvU.). And gerunds in **tvā** from compounded roots are met with in considerable numbers from AV. (only **pratyarpayitvā́**) down: e. g. **samīrayitvā́** MS., **virocayitvā́** TA., **utkṣiptvā** U., **pratyuktvā** E., **pratyasitvā** S., **prahasitvā** MBh., **saṁdarçayitvā** MBh., **vimuktvā** R., **nivedayitvā** R., **proktvā** Pañc., **anupītvā** VBS.: the great majority of them are made from the causative stem.

b. The prefixion of the negative particle, **a** or **an**, does not cause the gerund to take the form in **ya**: thus, **akṛtvā́**, **anīrayitvā́** (but R. has **acintya**). Of compounds with other than verbal prefixes, RV. has **punardā́ya**, **karṇagṛ́hya**, **pādagṛ́hya**, **hastagṛ́hya**, **araṁkṛ́tya**, **akkhalīkṛ́tya**, **mithaspṛ́dhya**; AV. has further **namaskṛ́tya**.

991. The suffix त्वा **tvā** has the accent. It is usually added directly to the root, but often also with interposition of the auxiliary vowel इ **i** — with regard to which, as well as to the form of the root before it, the formation nearly agrees with that of the participle in त **ta** (**952** ff.).

a. Examples of the general accordance of passive participle, infinitive, and gerund in regard to the use of **i** were given above, **968 a**; further specifications are called for, as follows:

b. The quotable roots in variable **ṛ** (**242**) change it to **īr**: thus, **tīrtvā́**, **stīrtvā́** (also **stṛtvā́**); and **car** makes also **cīrtvā** (like **cīrṇa**); — roots in **ā** show in general the same weakening as in the participle; but from **dhā** *put* is quotable only **dhitvā́**, from **mā** *measure* **mitvā́** and **mītvā́**, from **dā** *give* only **dattvā́**, from **chā** **chāyitvā**; — of roots in **am**, **kram** and **bhram** and **yam** make forms both with and without **i** (as in the infinitive), but **ram** has **ratvā́** and **raṁtvā**, and **dam** and **vam** make **damitvā** and **vamitvā**.

c. The auxiliary vowel is taken by roots **gras**, **muṣ**, **çap**, and **çās** (**çāsitvā**) (whose participles have both forms); also by **cāy**, **nṛt** (**nartitvā**), **lag**, and **svaj** (against analogy of pple); and **çuc** makes **çocitvā**. On the other hand, from **ruj** (**rugṇa**) and **vraçc** (**vṛkṇa**) come **ruktvā́** and **vṛṣṭvā́**. And both forms are made (as also in infinitive or participle) from **car**, **vas** *dwell* (**uṣṭvā**, **uṣitvā́**), **nī** (**nītvā**, **nayitvā**), and **mṛj** (**mṛṣṭvā́**, **mārjitvā**).

d. While the formation is in general one requiring, like the passive participle (e. g. **uptvā**, like **uptá**; **uditvā́**, like **uditá**), a weak or weakened root, there are some cases in which it is made from a strong or strengthened root-form. Thus (besides the instances already given: **chāyitvā**, **raṁtvā**, **çāsitvā**, **cāyitvā**, **çocitvā**, **nayitvā**, **mārjitvā**), we find **charditvā** (Āpast.), **daṅṣṭvā**, and **spharitvā**, and, from a number of roots, a second strong form beside the more regular weak one: namely, **añktvā**, **bhañktvā**, **bhuñktvā**, **syanttvā** (beside **aktvā́** etc.); **cayitvā**, **smayitvā**, **smaritvā** (beside **citvā́** etc.); **roditvā** (beside **ruditvā**), and **siñcitvā** (beside **siktvā**). The last shows the influence of the present-stem; as do also **mārjitvā** (above) and **jighritvā** (√**ghrā**). The form **ṣṭhutvā** (Āpast.) is doubtless a false reading, for **ṣṭhyūtvā**.

992. The suffix य **ya** is added directly to the root, which is accented, but has its weak form. A root ending in a short vowel takes त्य **tya** instead of य **ya**: thus, जित्य **-jítya**, स्तुत्य **-stútya**, कृत्य **-kṛ́tya**.

a. Roots in variable **ṝ** (**242**) change that vowel to **īr** or **ūr**: thus, **kīrya, gírya, tīrya** (and **tū́rya**), **dírya, pūrya, çírya, stírya** (also **stṛtya**); — roots in **ā** have for the most part **-āya**; but **dhā** *suck* makes **dhīya**, and double forms are found from **gā** *sing* (**gāya, gíya**), **pā** *drink* (**pā́ya, pīya**), **dā** *give* (**dā́ya, dádya**), **dā** *divide* (**dā́ya, ditya**), **mā** *measure, exchange* (**mā́ya, mítya**), **sā** *bind* (**sā́ya, sya**); **lī** *cling* has **lā́ya** or **līya**, as if an **ā**-verb; and **khan** and **dham** make **khāya** and **dhmā́ya**, from their **ā**-forms; — the roots in **an** and **am** making their participle in **ata** (**954 d**) make the gerund in **atya**, but also later in **anya, amya** (e. g. **gátya, gamya; hátya, hanya**; but **tan** makes as second form **tāya**, and from **ram** only **ramya** is quotable) — the roots in **īv** add **ya** to their **īv**-form: thus, **ṣṭhīvya, sívya**; - a few roots in **i** and **u** add **ya** to the lengthened vowel besides adding **ya**: thus, **i** *go* (**īya, ítya**; also **ayya**), **ci** *gather* (**cīya, cítya**), and **pṛ u, yu** *unite*, **su, stu** (**plū́ya, plutya**, etc.); while **kṣi** *destroy* has only **kṣīya**.

b. This gerund, though accented on the root-syllable, is generally a weakening formation: thus are made, without a strengthening nasal found in some other forms, **ácya, ájya, idhya, údya, ubhya, grathya, tácya, daçya, bádhya, bhajya, lípya, lúpya, vlágya, çrabhya, sajya, skábhya, stábhya, syadya, svajya**; with weakening of other kinds, **gṛ́hya** and **gṛ́bhya, pṛcchya, úcya, udya, úpya, úṣya** (**vas** *dwell*), **úhya, vidhya, vīya, vṛçcya, spṛ́dhya, hū́ya**; — but from a number of roots are made both a stronger and a weaker form: thus, **manthya** and **máthya, mārjya** and **mṛ́jya, rundhya** (and **rúdhya, çaṅsya** and **çás-ya, çāsya** and **çiṣya, skándya** and **skádya, sráṅsya** and **srasya**; — and only strong forms are found from roots **arc, av, cāy, çī** (**çayya**), as well as from certain roots with a constant nasal: e. g. **uñch, kamp, nand, lamb, çaṅk**; isolated cases are **oṣya** (√**uṣ** *burn*), **prothya** (also **prúthya**).

c. Other special cases are **úhya** and **ūhya** (√**ūh** *remove*), **gurya** and **gū́rya, gúhya** and **gūhya, rúhya** and **rūhya, bhramya** and **bhrāmya, áyya** (beside **ítya, īya**), **ghrāya** and **jighrya**; and **ūrṇutya** (beside **vṛ́tya**).

993. The older language has the same two gerund formations, having the same distinction, and used in the same way.

a. In RV., however, the final of **ya** is in the great majority of instances (fully two thirds) long (as if the instrumental ending of a derivative noun in **i** or **ti**). In AV., long **ā** appears only once in a RV. passage.

b. Instead of **tvā** alone, the Veda has three forms of the suffix, namely **tvā́, tvā́ya**, and **tvī́**. Of these three, **tvī́** is decidedly the commonest in RV. (thirty-five occurrences, against twenty-one of **tvā**); but it is unknown in AV., and very rare elsewhere in the older language; **tvā́ya** is found nine times in RV. (only once outside the tenth Book), twice in AV., and but half-a-dozen times elsewhere (in ÇB., once from a causative stem: **spāçayitvā́ya**). The historical relation of the three forms is obscure.

c. Two other gerund suffixes, **tvānam** and **tvīnam**, are mentioned by the grammarians as of Vedic use, but they have nowhere been found to occur.

994. The use of this gerund, though not changing in its character, becomes much more frequent, and even excessive, in the later language.

a. Thus, in the Nala and Bhagavad-Gītā, which have only one tenth as many verb-forms as RV., there are more than three times as many examples of the gerund as in the latter.

b. In general, the gerund is an adjunct to the subject of a sentence, and expresses an act or condition belonging to the subject: thus, **vajreṇa hatvā́ nír apáḥ sasarja** (RV.) *smiting with his thunderbolt, he poured forth the waters;* **pītvī́ sómasya vāvṛdhe** (RV.) *having drunk of the soma, he waxed strong;* **té yajñásya rásaṁ dhītvā́ vidúhya yajñáṁ yūpéna yopayitvā́ tirò 'bhavan** (ÇB.) *having sucked out the sap of the offering, having milked the offering dry, having blocked it with the sacrificial post, they disappeared;* **çrutvāi 'va cā 'bruvan** (MBh.) *and having heard, they said;* **taṁ ca dūre dṛṣṭvā gardabhī 'yam iti matvā dhāvitaḥ** (H.) *and having seen him in the distance, thinking 'it is a she-ass', he ran.*

c. But if the logical subject, the real agent, is put by the construction of the sentence in a dependent case, it is still qualified by the gerund: thus, **stríyaṁ dṛṣṭvā́ya kitaváṁ tatāpa** (RV.) *it distresses the gambler* (i. e. *the gambler is distressed*) *at seeing a woman;* **táṁ hāi 'naṁ dṛṣṭvā́ bhī́r viveda** (ÇB.) *fear came upon him* (i. e. *he was afraid*) *when he saw him;* **vidhāya proṣite vṛttim** (M.) *when he stays away after providing for her support;* **kiṁ nu me syād idaṁ kṛtvā** (MBh.) *what, I wonder, would happen to me if I did this;* — and especially, when a passive form is given to the sentence, the gerund qualifies the agent in the instrumental case (**282a**): thus, **tataḥ çabdād abhijñāya sa vyāghreṇa hataḥ** (H.) *thereupon he was slain by the tiger, who recognized him by his voice;* **tvayā sa rājā çakuntalām puraskṛtya vaktavyaḥ** (Ç.) *presenting Çakuntalā, thou must say to the king;* **haṅsānāṁ vacanaṁ çrutvā yathā me** (gen. for instr.) **nāiṣadho vṛtaḥ** (MBh.) *as the Nishadhan was chosen by me on hearing the words of the swans:* this construction is extremely common in much of the later Sanskrit.

d. Occasionally, the gerund qualifies an agent, especially an indefinite one, that is unexpressed: thus, **tadā 'trāi 'va paktvā khāditavyaḥ** (H.) *then he shall be eaten [by us] cooking him on the spot;* **yad anyasya parijñāya punar anyasya dīyate** (M.) *that, after being promised* (lit. *when one has promised her*) *to one, she is given again to another;* **sucintya co 'ktaṁ suvicārya yat kṛtam** (H.) *what one says after mature thought,* *and does after full deliberation.* Hence, still more elliptically, after **alam**: thus, **alaṁ vicārya** (Ç.) *enough of hesitation;* **tad alaṁ te vanaṁ gatvā** (R.) *so have done with going to the forest.*

e. Other less regular constructions are met with, especially in the older language: thus, in the manner of a participle with **man** and the like (**268 a**), as **táṁ hiṅsitvè 'va mene** (ÇB.) *he thought he had hurt him;* **tā adbhir abhiṣicya nijāsyāi 'vā 'manyata** (AB.) *having sprinkled them with water, he believed himself to have exhausted them;* — in the manner of a participle forming a continuous tense with √**i** (**1075 a**), as **indram evāi 'tāir ārabhya yanti** (AB.) *by means of them they keep taking hold of Indra;* — as qualifying a subordinate member of the sentence, as **puroḍā́çam evá kūrmám bhūtvā́ sárpantam** (ÇB.) *to the sacrificial cake creeping about, having become a tortoise;* **ayodhyām ... saphenām sasvanām bhūtvā jalormim iva** (R.) *into Ayodhyā, like a surge that had been foamy and roaring;* — even absolutely, as **ātithyéna vā́i devā́ iṣṭvā́ tā́nt samád avindat** (ÇB.) *when the gods had sacrificed with the guest-offering, strife befel them.*

f. As in the two examples before the last, a predicate word with **bhūtvā** is put in the same case with the subject: thus, further, **tád iyám evāi 'tád bhūtvā́ yajati** (ÇB.) *so having thus become this earth he makes offering;* **yena vāmanenā 'pi bhūtvā** (Vet.) *by whom, even when he had become a dwarf.* The construction is a rare one.

g. A number of gerunds have their meaning attenuated sometimes to the semblance of a preposition or adverb: such are **adhikṛtya** *making a subject of,* i. e. *respecting, of;* **ādāya, upagṛhya** *taking,* i. e. *with;* **uddiçya** *pointing toward,* i. e. *at;* **āsādya,** *arriving at,* i. e. *along, by;* **ārabhya** *beginning,* i. e. *from;* **sambhūya** *being with,* i. e. *with;* **saṁhatya** *striking together,* i. e. *in unison;* **prasahya** *using force,* i. e. *violently;* **tyaktvā, parityajya, muktvā, vihāya, uddhṛtya, varjayitvā** *leaving out* etc., i. e. *excepting, without;* and others. Examples are: **çakuntalām adhikṛtya bravīmi** (Ç.) *I am speaking of Çakuntalā;* **tam uddiçya kṣiptalaguḍaḥ** (H.) *having thrown the cudgel at him;* **nimittaṁ kiṁcid āsādya** (H.) *for some reason or other.*

h. The gerund is in the later language sometimes found in composition, as if a noun-stem: e. g. **prasahyaharaṇa** *taking with violence;* **pretyabhāva** *existence after death;* **vibhajyapāṭha** *separate enunciation;* **sambhūyagamana** *going together.* It is also often repeated (**1260**), in a distributive sense: e. g. **sá vā́i sammṛ́jya-sammṛjya pratápya-pratapya prá yacchati** (ÇB.) *in each case, after wiping and warming them, he hands them over;* **gṛhītvā-gṛhītvā** (KÇS.) *at each taking;* **unnamyo-'nnamya** (Pañc.) *every time that they arise.*

Adverbial Gerund in am.

995. The accusative of a derivative *nomen actionis* in **a**, used adverbially, assumes sometimes a value and construction so accord ant with that of the usual gerund that it cannot well be called by a different name.

a. No example of a peculiar gerundial construction with such a form occurs either in RV. or AV., although a dozen adverbial accusatives are to be classed as representing the formation: thus, **abhyākrámam, pratáñkam, praṇódam, niláyam, abhiskándam,** etc. This gerund is found especially in the Brāhmaṇas and Sūtras, where it is not rare; in the epics it is extremely infrequent; later, also, it occurs very sparingly.

b. A final vowel has **vṛddhi**-strengthening before the suffix: thus, **nāyam, çrāvam, kāram**; final **ā** adds **y**: thus, **khyāyam, yāyam**; a medial vowel has **guṇa** (if capable of it: **240**): thus, **kṣepam, kroçam, vartam** (but **īkṣam, pūram**); a medial **a** before a single consonant is lengthened: thus, **krāmam, cāram, grāham, svādam** (but **grantham, lambham**). The accent is on the radical syllable. No uncompounded examples are found in the older language, and extremely few in the later.

c. Examples are: **kā́maṁ vā́ imā́ny áñgāni vyatyā́saṁ çete** (ÇB.) *he lies changing the position of these limbs at pleasure*; **úttarām-uttarāṁ çā́khāṁ samālámbhaṁ róhet** (ÇB.) *he would climb, taking hold of a higher and ever a higher limb*; **aparī́ṣu mahānāgám ivā 'bhisaṁsā́raṁ didṛkṣitā́raḥ** (ÇB.) *hereafter, running together as it were about a great snake, they will wish to see him*; **nā́māny āsām etā́ni nāmagrā́ham** (ÇB.) *with separate naming of these their names*; **yó viparyā́sam avagū́hati** (ÇB.) *whoever buries it upside down*; **bāhūtksepam kranditum pravṛttā** (Ç.) *she proceeded to cry, throwing up her arms (with arm-tossing)*; **navacūtapallavāni darçaṁ-darçam madhukarāṇāṁ kvanitāni çrāvaṁ-çrāvam paribabhrāma** (DKC.) *he wandered about, constantly seeing the young shoots of the mango, and hearing the humming of the bees.* Repeated forms, like those in the last example, are approved in the later language; they do not occur earlier (but instead of them the repeated ordinary gerund: **994 h**).

CHAPTER XIV.

DERIVATIVE OR SECONDARY CONJUGATION.

996. Secondary conjugations are those in which a whole system of forms, like that already described as made from the simple root, is made, with greater or less completeness, from a derivative conjugation-stem; and is also usually connected with a certain definite modification of the original radical sense.

a. We have seen, indeed, that the tense-systems are also for the most part made from derivative-stems; and even that, in some cases, such stems assume the appearance and value of roots, and are made the basis of a complete conjugational system. Nor is there any distinct division-line to be drawn between tense-systems and derivative conjugations; the latter are present-systems which have been expanded into conjugations by the addition of other tenses, and of participles, infinitives, and so on. In the earliest language, their forms outside of the present-system are still quite rare, hardly more than sporadic; and even later they are — with the exception of one or two formations which attain a comparative frequency — much less common than the corresponding forms of primary conjugation.

997. The secondary conjugations are: I. Passive; II. Intensive; III. Desiderative; IV. Causative; V. Denominative.

a. The passive is classed here as a secondary conjugation because of its analogy with the others in respect to specific value, and freedom of formation, although it does not, like them, make its forms outside the present system from its present-stem.

I. Passive.

998. The passive conjugation has been already in the main described. Thus, we have seen that —

a. It has a special present-system, the stem of which is present only, and not made the basis of any of the remaining forms: this stem is formed with the accented class-sign य **yá**, and it takes (with exceptions: **774**) the middle endings. This present-system is treated with the others, above, **768** ff.

b. There is a special passive 3d sing. of the aorist, ending in इ **i**: it is treated above, **842** ff.

c. In the remaining tenses, the middle forms are used also in a passive sense.

d. But the passive use of middle forms is not common; it is oftenest met with in the perfect. The participle to a great extent takes the place of a past passive tense, and the gerundive that of a future. On the other hand, in the oldest language (RV.), middle forms of other present-systems are in a considerable number of cases employed with passive meaning.

e. According to the grammarians, there may be formed from some verbs, for passive use, a special stem for the aorist and the two future systems, coinciding in form with the peculiar 3d sing. aorist.

f. Thus, from √**dā** (aor. 3d sing. **adāyi**), beside **ádāsi, dāsyé, dātā́he,** also **ádāyiṣi, dāyiṣyé, dāyitā́he.** The permission to make this double formation extends to all roots ending in vowels, and to **grah, dṛç,** and **han.** No such passive forms occur in the older language, and not half-a-dozen are quotable from the later (we find **adhāyiṣi** and **asthāyiṣi** in DKC., and **anāyiṣata** in Kuval.).

g. As to the alleged passive inflection of the periphrastic perfect, see below, **1072.**

h. Besides the participle from the present tense-stem (**771.** 5), the passive has a past participle in त **ta** (**952**), or न **na** (**957**), and future participles, or gerundives, of various formation (**961 ff.**), made directly from the root.

999. As already pointed out (**282 a**), the language, especially later, has a decided predilection for the passive form of the sentence. This is given in part by the use of finite passive forms, but oftener by that of the passive participle and of the gerundive: the participle being taken in part in a present sense, but more usually in a past (whether indefinite or proximate past), and sometimes with a copula expressed, but much oftener without it; and the gerundive representing either a pure future or one with the sense of necessity or duty added. A further example is: **tatrāi 'ko yuvā brāhmaṇo dṛṣṭaḥ: taṁ dṛṣṭvā kāmena pīḍitā saṁjātā: sakhyā agre kathitam: sakhi puruṣo 'yaṁ gṛhītvā mama mātuḥ samīpam ānetavyaḥ** (Vet.) *there she saw a young Brahman; at sight of him she felt the pangs of love; she said to her friend: 'friend, you must take and bring this man to my mother'*. In some styles of later Sanskrit, the prevailing expression of past time is by means of the passive participle (thus, in Vet., an extreme case, more than nine tenths).

a. As in other languages, a 3d sing. passive is freely made from intransitive as well as transitive verbs: thus, **ihā "gamyatām** *come hither;* **tvayā tatrāi 'va sthīyatām** *do you stand just there;* **sarvāir jālam ādāyo 'ḍḍīyatām** (H.) *let all fly up with the net.*

II. Intensive.

1000. The intensive (sometimes also called frequentative) is that one of the secondary conjugations which is least removed from the analogy of formations already described. It is, like the present-system of the second conjugation-class (**642** ff.), the inflection of a reduplicated stem, but of one that is peculiar in having a strengthened reduplication. It is decidedly less extended beyond the limits of a present-system than any other of the derivative conjugations.

a. The intensive conjugation signifies the repetition or the intensification of the action expressed by the primary conjugation of a root.

1001. According to the grammarians, the intensive conjugation may be formed from nearly all the roots in the language — the exceptions being roots of more than one syllable, those conjugated only causatively (below, **1056**), and in general those beginning with a vowel.

a. In fact, however, intensives in the later language are very rare, so rare that it is hard to tell precisely what value is to be given to the rules of the native grammar respecting them. Nor are they at all common earlier, except (comparatively) in the RV., which contains about six sevenths of the whole number (rather over a hundred) quotable from Veda and Brāhmaṇa and Sūtra-texts; AV. has less than half as many as RV., and many of them in RV. passages; from the later language are quotable about twenty of these, and about forty more, but for the most part only in an occurrence or two.

b. Hence, in the description to be given below, the actual aspect of the formation, as exhibited in the older language, will be had primarily and especially in view; and the examples will be of forms found there in use.

1002. The strong intensive reduplication is made in three different ways:

I. **a.** The reduplicating syllable is, as elsewhere, composed of a single consonant with following vowel, and, so far as the consonant is concerned, follows the rules for present and perfect reduplication (**590**); but the vowel is a heavy one, radical **a** and **ṛ** (or **ar**) being reduplicated with **ā**, an **i**-vowel by **e**, and an **u**-vowel by **o**.

Examples are: **vāvad, bābadh, çāçvas, rārandh; dādṛ, dādhṛ; cekit, tetij, nenī, vevlī; çoçuc, popruth, coṣku, johū.**

II. **b.** The reduplicating syllable has a final consonant, taken from the end of the root. With an exception or two, this consonant is either **r** (or its substitute **l**) or a nasal.

Examples are: **carcar, calcal, sarsṛ, marmṛj, jarhṛṣ; cañkram, jañghan, taṅstan, dandaç** (√**daṅç** or **daç**), **jañjabh** (√**jambh** or **jabh**), **tantas** (√**taṅs** or **tas**), **nannam** (√**nam**), **yaṁyam** (√**yam**). The nasal is assimilated to the initial consonant.

c. Only roots having **a** or **ṛ** as vowel make this form of reduplication, but with such roots it is more common than either of the other forms.

d. Irregular formations of this class are: with a final other than **r** or **n** in the reduplication, **badbadh**; with a final nasal in the reduplication which is not found in the root, **jañgah** (RV.), **jañjap** (ÇB.; and **jañgūyat** PB. is perhaps from √**gu**; the later language has further **dandah**); with an anomalous initial consonant in reduplication, **jarbhur** from √**bhur** (compare the Vedic perfect **jabhāra** from √**bhṛ, 789** b), **galgal** from √**gal**; with various treatment of an **ṛ** or **ar**-element, **dardar** and **dardir, carkar** and **carkir, tartar** and **tartur, carcar** and **carcur, jargur** and **jalgul.**

e. The roots **i** and **ṛ** are the only ones with vowel initial forming an intensive stem: **i** makes **iyāy** (? PU., once); **ṛ** makes the irregular **alar** or **alṛ.** As to the stem **íya**, see below, **1021** b.

III. **f.** The reduplication is dissyllabic, an i-vowel being added after a final consonant of the reduplicating syllable. This i-vowel is in the older language short before a double consonant, and long before a single.

Examples are: **ganīgam** (but **gánigmatam**), **varīvṛt, vanīvāh, caniṣkad, saniṣvan; navīnu, davidyut** (and the participles **dávidhvat** but **távītuạt**). A single exception as to the quantity of the **i** is **davidhāva.**

g. This method of reduplication is followed in the older language by about thirty roots. Thus, of roots having final or penultimate **n** (once **m**), and **n** in the reduplicating syllable, **pan, phan, san, svan, han; gam; krand, çcand, skand, syand**; of roots having final or medial **ṛ**, and **r** in the reduplicating syllable, **kṛ** *make*, **tṛ, bhṛ, vṛ, mṛj, mṛç, vṛj, vṛt, sṛp**: also **mluc** (**malimluc**); — further, of roots assuming in the reduplication a **n** not found in the root, only **vah** (ÇB.: the grammarians allow also **kas, pat, pad**; and **panīpad** is quotable later; and AÇS. has **canīkhudat**, for which TB. reads **kánīkhunat**); finally, of roots having **u** or **ū** as radical vowel, with **av** before the **i**-vowel, **tu, dhū, nu, dyut.**

h. In this class, the general rules as to the form of the reduplicating consonant (**590**) are violated in the case of **ghanīghan** and **bharībhṛ**, and of **ganīgam, karīkṛ** (but the regular **carīkṛ** also occurs), **kanikrand**, and **kaniṣkand** (but also **caniṣkand** occurs); also in **kanīkhun.**

i. The reversion to more original guttural form after the reduplication in **cekit**, and **jañghan** and **ghanīghan**, is in accordance with what takes place elsewhere (**216** l).

1003. The same root is allowed to form its intensive stem in more than one way.

Thus, in the older language, **dādṛ** and **dardṛ**; **dādhṛ** and **dardhṛ**; **cācal** and **carcar** (and **carcur**); **tartar** (and **tartur**) and **tarītṛ**; **jañgam** and **ganīgam**; **jañghan** and **ghanīghan**; **pamphan** and **panīphan**; **marmṛj** and **marīmṛj**; **marmṛç** and **marīmṛç**; **varvṛt** and **varīvṛt**; **jarbhṛ** and **bharībhṛ**; **dodhū** and **davīdhū**; **nonu** and **navīnu**; **bābadh** and **badbadh**.

1004. The model of normal intensive inflection is the present-system of the reduplicating conjugation-class (642 ff.); and this is indeed to a considerable extent followed, in respect to endings, strengthening of stem, and accent. But deviations from the model are not rare; and the forms are in general of too infrequent occurrence to allow of satisfactory classification and explanation.

a. The most marked irregularity is the frequent insertion of an ī between the stem and ending. According to the grammarians, this is allowed in all the strong forms before an ending beginning with a consonant; and before the ī a final vowel has guṇa-strengthening, but a medial one remains unchanged.

Present-System.

1005. We will take up the parts of the present-system in their order, giving first what is recognized as regular in the later language, and then showing how the formation appears in the earlier texts. As most grammarians do not allow a middle inflection, and middle forms are few even in the Veda, no attempt will be made to set up a paradigm for the middle voice.

1006. As example of inflection may be taken the root विद् vid *know*, of which the intensive stem is वेविद् vevid, or, in strong forms, वेवेद् véved.

a. Neither from this nor from any other root are more than a few scattering forms actually quotable.

1. Present Indicative.

	s.	d.	p.
1	वेवेद्मि, वेविदीमि **vévedmi, vévidīmi**	वेविद्वस् **vevidvás**	वेविद्मस् **vevidmás**

2	वेवेत्सि, वेविदीषि	वेवित्थस्	वेवित्थ
	vévetsi, vévidīṣi	vevitthás	vevitthá
3	वेवेत्ति, वेविदीति	वेवित्तस्	वेविदति
	vévetti, vévidīti	vevittás	vévidati

b. From √ह्नु hū, the singular forms with auxiliary vowel would be जोह्नवीमि **jóhavīmi**, जोह्नवीषि **jóhavīṣi**, जोह्नवीति **jóhavīti**.

1007. a. The forms found in the older language agree in general with the paradigm. Examples are: 1st sing., **carkarmi, veveṣmi**; 2d sing., **alarṣi, dárdarṣi**; 3d sing., **álarti, dādharti, veveti, nenekti, jañghanti, kánikrantti, ganīgaṁti**; 3d du., **jarbhṛtás**; 1st pl., **nonumas**; 2d pl., **jāgratha**; 3d pl., **dādhrati, nānadati, bharibhrati, várvṛtati, dávidyutati, nénijati**, and, irregularly, **veviṣanti**; and, with the auxiliary vowel, **jóhavīmi, cākaçīmi; cā́kaçīti, nónavīti, dardarīti, jarbhurīti.** No stem with dissyllabic reduplication takes the auxiliary ī in any of its forms.

b. A single dual form with ī and strong stem occurs: namely, **tartarīthas.**

c. The middle forms found to occur are: 1st sing., **jóguve, nenije**; 3d sing., **nenikté, sarsṛte**; and, with irregular accent, **tétikte, dédiṣṭe**; with irregular loss of final radical nasal, **nánnate**; with ending **e** instead of **te, cékite, jáñgahe, jóguve, yoyuve, bābadhe**, and (with irregular accent) **badbadhé**; 3d du., **sarsrāte**; 3d pl., **dédiçate.**

2. Present Subjunctive.

1008. a. Subjunctive forms with primary endings are extremely rare: there have been noticed only **jañghánāni, jāgarāsi** (AV.); and, in the middle, **tantasāíte** (3d du.).

b. Forms with secondary endings are more frequent: thus, 2d sing., **jañghanas, jalgulas**; 3d sing., **jāgarat, cékitat, bobhavat, cárkṛṣat, jañghanat, bárbṛhat, mármṛjat, mármṛçat, parpharat, dardirat, caniṣkadat, davidyutat, saniṣvaṇat**; 1st du., **jañghanāva**; 1st pl., **carkirāma, vevidāma**; 3d pl., **pā́patan, çóçucan, carkiran**; and, with double mode-sign, **cā́kaçān** (AV.). Of the middle are found only 3d persons plural: thus, **jáñghananta, jarhṛṣanta, marmṛjanta, nonuvanta, çoçucanta.**

3. Present Optative.

1009. This mode would show the unstrengthened stem, with the usual endings (**566**), accented. Thus:

	s.	d.	p.
1	वेविद्याम् **vevidyā́m** etc.	वेविद्याव **vevidyā́va** etc.	वेविद्याम **vevidyā́ma** etc.

a. The optative is represented by only an example or two in the older language: thus, active, **veviṣyāt** (AV.), **jāgr̥yās** (KB.), **jāgriyāt** (AB.), **jāgr̥̄yāma** (VS. MS.; but **jāgriyāma** TS.); RV. has only **cākanyāt** (pft.?); middle, **nenijīta** (K.).

4. Present Imperative.

1010. The regular forms of the imperative, including the usual subjunctive first persons, would be as follows:

	s.	d.	p.
1	वेविदानि **vévidāni**	वेविदाव **vévidāva**	वेविदाम **vévidāma**
2	वेविद्धि **veviddhí**	वेवित्तम् **vevittám**	वेवित्त **vevittá**
3	वेवेत्तु, वेविदीतु **vévettu, vévidītu**	वेवित्ताम् **vevittā́m**	वेविदतु **vévidatu**

1011. a. Older imperative forms are less rare than optative. The first persons have been given above (**jāngháñāni**, the only accented example, does not correspond with the model, but is in conformity with the subjunctive of the reduplicating present); the proper imperatives are: 2d sing., **dādr̥hí, dardr̥hi, carkr̥dhi, jāgr̥hi, nenigdhi, rāranddhí**; the ending **tāt** is found in **carkr̥tāt** and **jāgr̥tāt**; and the latter (as was pointed out above, **571 b**) is used in AV. as first person sing.; **barbr̥hi** shows an elsewhere unparalleled loss of **h** before the ending **hi**; 3d sing., **dādhartu, veveṣṭu, dardartu, marmarttu**; 2d du., **jāgr̥tam**; 3d du., **jāgr̥tām**; 2d pl., **jāgr̥tá**; **cañkramata** (RV., once) has an anomalous union-vowel. In the middle voice is found only **nenikṣva** (ÇB.).

b. Of imperative forms with auxiliary **ī**, RV. has none; AV. has **vāvadītu** and **johavītu**, and such are sometimes found in the Brāhmaṇas; AV. has also, against rule, **tañstanīhi** and **jañghanīhi**; VS. has **cākaçīhi**.

5. Present Participle.

1012. The intensive participles, both active and middle, are comparatively common in the older language. They are formed and inflected like those of the reduplicating present, and have the accent on the reduplicating syllable.

Examples are: active, **cā́kaçat, nā́nadat, cékitat, mémyat, çóçucat, róruvat, dárdrat, mármṛjat, jáñghanat, nánnamat, pánīphanat, kánikradat, dávidyutat**; — middle, **bā́badhāna, mémyāna, cékitāna, yóyuvāna, rórucāna, járbhurāṇa, sársrāṇa, jañjabhāna, nánnamāna, dándaçāna.** No middle participle shows the dissyllabic reduplication.

1013. a. On account of their accent, **rārahāṇá, rārakṣāṇá,** and **jāhṛṣāṇá** (beside **járhṛṣāṇa**) are probably to be regarded as perfect participles, although no other perfect forms with heavy reduplication from the same roots occur. The inference is, however, rendered uncertain by the unmistakably intensive **badbadhānā́** and **marmṛjānā́** (beside **mármṛjāna**). As to **çúçucāna** etc., see **806 a.**

b. The RV. has once **jáñghnatas,** gen. sing., with root-vowel cast out; **kánikrat** appears to be used once for **kánikradat**; if **cākát** is to be referred to √**kā** (Grassmann), it is the only example of an intensive from a root in **ā,** and its accent is anomalous. **Marmṛçantas** (AB.) is perhaps a false reading; but forms with the nasal irregularly retained are found repeatedly in the epics and later: thus, **lelihan, dedīpyantīm** (MBh.), **jājvalant** (MBh. R.), **sarīsṛpantāu** (BhP.), **rāraṭantī** (R.).

6. Imperfect.

1014. The imperfect is regularly inflected as follows:

	s.	d.	p.
1	अवेविदम् **ávevidam**	अवेविद्व **ávevidva**	अवेविद्म **ávevidma**
2	अवेवेत्, अवेविदीस् **ávevet, ávevidīs**	अवेवित्तम् **ávevittam**	अवेवित्त **ávevitta**
3	अवेवेत्, अवेविदीत् **ávevet, ávevidīt**	अवेवित्ताम् **ávevittām**	अवेविदुस् **ávevidus**

1015. The imperfect forms found in the earlier texts are not numerous. They are, including those from which the augment is omitted, as follows: in active, 1st sing., **acākaçam, dediçam**; 2d sing., **ajāgar, adardar, dárdar**; 3d sing., **adardar, adardhar, avarīvar, dardar, kániṣkan, dávidyot, návīnot**; 2d du., **adardṛtam**; 1st pl., **marmṛjmá**; 3d pl., **anannamus, adardirus, acarkṛṣus, ájohavus, anonavus**; and, with auxiliary **ī,** in 3d sing., **avāvacīt, ávāvaçīt, ávāvarīt, áyoyavīt, ároravīt, ájohavīt**; and, irregularly, in 3d du., **avāvaçītām.** The middle forms are extremely few: namely, 3d sing., **ádediṣṭa, ánannata** (with loss of the final radical in a weak form of root); 3d pl. **marmṛjata,** and **avāvaçanta** (which, if it belongs here, shows a transfer to an **a**-stem).

1016. Derivative Middle Inflection. From every intensive stem, as above described, may be formed in the present-system a further derivative conjugation which is formally identical with a passive, being made by the accented sign य **ya**, along with middle endings only. It has not, however, a passive value, but is in meaning and use indistinguishable from the simpler conjugation.

a. A final vowel before this **ya** is treated as before the passive-sign **ya** (770).

b. The inflection is precisely like that of any other stem ending in **a** in the middle voice: thus, from √**mṛj**, intensive stem **marmṛj**, is made the present indicative **marmṛjyé, marmṛjyáse, marmṛjyáte**, etc.; optative **marmṛjyeya, marmṛjyéthās, marmṛjyéta**, etc.; imperative **marmṛjyásva, marmṛjyátām**, etc.; participle **marmṛjyámāna**; imperfect **ámarmṛjye, ámarmṛjyathās, ámarmṛjyata**, etc.; subjunctive forms do not occur.

c. In a very few sporadic cases, these **yá**-forms are given a passive value: thus, **jañghanyamāna** in MdU.; **bambhramyate, dādhmāyamāna, pepīyamāna** in the later language. And active participles (**529** a) are not unknown: thus, **dedīpyantīm** (MBh.), **dodhūyant** (MBh. BhP.).

1017. This kind of intensive inflection is more common than the other in the later language; in the earlier, it is comparatively rare.

a. In RV., **ya**-forms are made from eight roots, five of which have also forms of the simpler conjugation; the AV. adds one more; the other earlier texts (so far as observed) about twenty more, and half of them have likewise forms of the simpler conjugation. Thus: from √**mṛj, marmṛjyáte** etc., and **marīmṛjyeta**; from √**tṛ, tartūryante**; from √**car, carcūryámāṇa**; from √**nī, nenīyéran**, etc.; from √**vī, vevīyate**; from √**rih, rerihyáte** etc.; from **vij, vevijyáte**; from √**sku, coṣkūyáse** etc.; from √**diç, dediçyate**; from √**kāç, cākaçyáte** etc.; from √**vad, vāvadyámāna**; from √**nam, nannamyadhvam**; from √**vah, vanīvāhyeta** etc. (with lengthened root-vowel, elsewhere unknown); from √**krand, kanikradyámāna**; from √**vṛt, varīvartyámāna** (ÇB.: should be **varīvṛty-**); from √**mṛç, amarīmṛçyanta** (ÇB.? the text reads **amarīmṛtsyanta**); from √**yup, yoyupyánte** etc.; from √**nud, anonudyanta**; from √**vlī, avevlīyanta**; from √**jabh, jañjabhyáte** etc.; from √**jap, jañjapyámāna**; and so on.

Perfect.

1018. The grammarians are at variance as to whether a perfect may be formed directly from the intensive stem, or whether only a periphrastic perfect (below, **1070** ff.) is to be admitted.

a. No example of an intensive periphrastic perfect has anywhere come to light (except from **jāgṛ**: **1020 a**). A few unmistakable perfect forms are made from the intensively reduplicated root in RV.: namely, **davidhāva** and **nónāva,** 3d sing., and **nonuvus,** 3d pl.; and there occur further **dodrāva** (TS.), **yoyāva** and **leláya** (MS.), and **leláya** (? ÇB.), all used in the sense of presents. To them may be added **jāgara** 1st sing. and **jāgā́ra** 3d sing.: but as to these, see below, **1020 a.**

Aorist, Future, etc.

1019. As to the remaining parts of a full verbal conjugation, also, the grammarians are not agreed (occurrences of such forms, apparently, being too rare to afford even them any basis for rules); in general, it is allowed to treat the intensive stem further as a root in filling up the scheme of forms, using always the auxiliary vowel इ i where it is ever used in the simple conjugation.

a. Thus, from √vid, intensive stem **vevid,** would be made the aorist **avevidiṣam** with precative **vevidyāsam,** the futures **vevidiṣyāmi** and **veviditāsmi,** the participles **vevidita, veviditavya,** etc., the infinitive **veviditum,** and the gerunds **veviditvā** and **-vevidya.** And, where the intensive conjugation is the derivative middle one, the aorist and futures would take the corresponding middle form.

b. Of all this, in the ancient language, there is hardly a trace. The RV. has **cárkṛṣe,** 3d sing. mid., of a formation like **hiṣe** and **stuṣé** (**894 d**), and the gerundives **vitantasā́yya,** and **marmṛjénya** and **vāvṛdhénya;** and ÇB. has the participle **vanīvāhitá,** and the infinitive **dédīyitavāí.** As to **jāgariṣyánt** and **jāgaritá,** see the next paragraph.

1020. There are systems of inflection of certain roots, the intensive character of which is questioned or questionable. Thus:

a. The root **gṛ** (or **gar**) *wake* has from the first no present-system save one with intensive reduplication; and its intensive stem, **jāgṛ,** begins early to assume the value of a root, and form a completer conjugation; while by the grammarians this stem is reckoned as if simple and belonging to the root-class, and is inflected throughout accordingly. Those of its forms which occur in the older language have been given along with the other intensives above. They are, for the present-system, the same with those acknowledged as regular later. The older perfect is like the other intensive perfects found in RV.: namely, **jāgara** etc., with the participle **jāgṛvā́ṅs**; and a future **jāgariṣyá-**, a passive participle **jāgaritá**, and a gerundive **jāgaritavyà**, are met with in the Brāhmaṇas. The old aorist (RV.) is the usual reduplicated or so-called causative aorist: thus, **ájīgar.** The grammarians give it in the later language a perfect with additional reduplication, **jajāgāra** etc., an **iṣ**-aorist, **ajāgariṣam**, with precative **jāgaryāsam**, and everything else that is needed to make up a complete conjugation. The perf. **jajāgāra** is quotable from the epics and later, as also the periphrastic **jāgarām āsa.** And MBh. has the mutilated **jāgṛmi**, and also **a**-forms, as **jāgarati** and **jāgramāṇa.**

1021. a. The stem **irajya** (active only) *regulate*, from which a number of forms are made in RV., has been viewed as an intensive from √**raj** or **ṛj.** It lacks, however, any analogy with the intensive formation. The same is true of **iradh** *propitiate* (only **iradhanta** and **irádhyāi**, apparently for **iradhadhyāi**).

b. The middle **stem ī́ya**, not infrequent in the oldest language, is often called an intensive of √**i** *go*, but without any propriety, as it has no analogy of form whatever with an intensive. The isolated 1st pl. **īmahe**, common in RV., is of questionable character.

1022. The root **lī** *totter*, with constant intensive reduplication, **lelī**, is quite irregular in inflection and accent: thus, pres., **lelā́yati** and **lelā́yate**, pples **lelāyántī** and **leláyatas** (gen. sing.) and **lelāyamāna**, impf. **alelāyat** and **alelet** and **alelīyata**, perf. **lelāya** and **leláya** (?).

1023. The RV. anomalous form **dart** (or **dard**), 2d and 3d sing. from √**dṛ** or **dar**, is doubtfully referred to the intensive, as if abbreviated from **dardar.** RV. has once **avarīvus** (or **-vur**) where the sense requires a form from √**vṛt**, as **avarīvṛtus.** The form **rarāṇátā** (RV., once) seems corrupt.

1024. A marked intensive or frequentative meaning is not always easily to be traced in the forms classed as intensive; and in some of them it is quite effaced. Thus, the roots **cit**, **nij**, **viṣ** use their intensive present-system as if it were an ordinary conjugation-class; nor is it otherwise with **gṛ** (**jāgṛ**). The grammarians reckon the inflection of **nij** and **viṣ** as belonging to the reduplicating present-system, with irregularly strengthened reduplication; and they treat in the same way **vic** and **vij**; **jāgṛ**, as we have seen, they account a simple root.

a. Also **daridrā**, intensive of √**drā** *run*, is made by the grammarians a simple root, and furnished with a complete set of conjugational forms: as **dadaridrāu**; **adaridrāsīt**, etc. etc. It does not occur in the older language (unless **dáridrat** TS., for which VS. MS. read **dáridra**). The so-called root **vevī** *flutter* is a pure intensive.

1025. It is allowed by the grammarians to make from the intensive stem also a passive, desiderative, causative, and so on: thus, from **vevid,** pass. **vevidyé;** desid. **vévidiṣāmi;** caus. **vevidáyāmi;** desid. of causative, **vévidayiṣāmi.** But such formations are excessively rare; quotable are **varīvarjáyantī** AV., **jāgaráyant** TB. etc.; **dādhārayati** JB., **dandaçayitvā** DKC.

III. Desiderative.

1026. By the desiderative conjugation is signified a desire for the action or condition denoted by the simple root: thus, पिबामि **píbāmi** *I drink*, desid. पिपासामि **pípāsāmi** *I wish to drink;* जीवामि **jī́vāmi** *I live*, desid. जिजीविषामि **jíjīviṣāmi** *I desire to live.* Such a conjugation is allowed to be formed from any simple root in the language, and also from any causative stem.

a. The desiderative conjugation, although its forms outside the present-system are extremely rare in the oldest language, is earlier and more fully expanded into a whole verbal system than the intensive. Its forms are also of increasing frequency: much fewer than the intensives in RV., more numerous in the Brāhmaṇas and later; not one third of the whole number of roots (about a hundred) noted as having a desiderative conjugation in Veda and Brāhmaṇa have such in RV.

1027. The desiderative stem is formed from the simple root by the addition of two characteristics: 1. a reduplication, which always has the accent; 2. an appended स **sa** — which, however (like the tense-signs of aorist and future), sometimes takes before it the auxiliary vowel इ **i**, becoming इष **iṣa.**

a. A few instances in the concluding part of ÇB. in which the accent is otherwise laid — thus, **tiṣṭhā́set, yiyāsántam, vividiṣánti, īpsántas** — must probably be regarded as errors.

1028. The root in general remains unchanged; but with the following exceptions:

a. A final **i** or **u** is lengthened before **sa**: thus, **cikṣiṣa, cikīṣa, jigīṣa; çuçrūṣa, juhūṣa, cukṣūṣa.**

b. A final **ṛ** becomes **īr** or **ūr** before **sa**: thus, **cikīrṣa, titīrṣa** (also irregularly **tūtūrṣa** RV.), **didhīrṣa, sisīrṣa, tistīrṣa** (also **tustūrṣa**), **jihīrṣa; bubhūrṣa, mumūrṣa** (the only examples quotable).

c. Before **iṣa**, a final **i-** or **u-** or **ṛ**-vowel necessarily, and a penultimate **i** or **u** or **ṛ** optionally, have the **guṇa**-strengthening; no examples are quotable from the older texts; later occur **çiçayiṣa, çiçariṣa; cikartiṣa, ninartiṣa, mimardiṣa, vivarṣiṣa, çuçobhiṣa;** but **rurudiṣa.**

More special exceptions are:

d. A few roots in **ā** weaken this vowel to **ī** or even **i**: thus, **jigīṣa** from √**gā** *go;* **pipīṣa** (beside **pipāsa**) from √**pā** *drink*, **jihīṣa** (AV.) from √**hā** *remove* (**jihīte**: **664**); **didhiṣa** (beside **dhitsa**) from √**dhā.**

e. A few roots in **an** or **am** lengthen the vowel: thus, **jigāṅsa** (beside **jigamiṣa**) from √**gam**; **jighāṅsa** from √**han**; **mīmāṅsa** from √**man**; and **titāṅsa** from √**tan.**

f. Reversion to guttural form of an initial after the reduplication is seen in **cikīṣa** from √**ci, cikitsa** from √**cit, jigīṣa** from √**ji, jighāṅsa** from √**han**; and √**hi** is said to make **jighīṣa** (no occurrence).

g. The roots **van** and **san** make **vivāsa** and **siṣāsa,** from the root-forms **vā** and **sā.**

h. The root **jīv** forms **jujyūṣa** (ÇB.: **jijīviṣa,** VS.); and the other roots in **īv** (**765**) are required to make the same change before **sa,** and to have **guṇa** before **iṣa**: thus, **susyūṣa** or **siseviṣa** from √**sīv. Svap** forms **suṣupsa. Dhūrv** forms **dudhūrṣa.**

i. Initial **s** is usually left unchanged to **ṣ** after the reduplication when the desiderative sign has **ṣ** (**184**e): thus, **sisaṅkṣa** (ÇB.: √**sañj**), and **susyūṣa** and **sisaniṣa,** according to the grammarians; but **tuṣṭūṣa** is met with.

j. Further may be mentioned as prescribed by the grammarians: **ninaṅkṣa** (or **ninaçiṣa**) from √**naç** *be lost;* **mimaṅkṣa** from √**majj** (occurs in **mimaṅkṣu**); **mimārjiṣa** (or **mimṛkṣa**) from √**mṛj.**

1029. The consonant of the reduplication follows the general rules (**590**); the vowel is इ **i** if the root has an a-vowel, or ऋ **ṛ**, or an i-vowel; it is उ **u** if the root has an u-vowel. But:

a. A few roots have a long vowel in the reduplicating syllable: thus, **bībhatsa** from √**badh** or **bādh**; **mīmāṅsa** from √**man**; and **tūtūrṣa** (RV.) from √**tur**; **dadhiṣu** (AV.) and **dadaṅkṣu** (C.) are probably false forms.

b. From √**aç** is made (ÇB.) **açiçiṣa,** and from √**edh** (VS.) **edidhiṣa** (with a mode of reduplication like that followed sometimes in the reduplicating aorist: **862**). In the older language, these are the only roots with initial vowel which form a desiderative stem, except **āp** and **ṛdh,** which have abbreviated stems: see the next paragraph. In the later language occur further **eṣiṣiṣa** (√**iṣ** *seek*) and **īcikṣiṣa** (√**īkṣ**); and the grammarians add others, as **arjihiṣa** (√**arh**), **undidiṣa** (√**und**), **ardidhiṣa** (√**ṛdh**).

c. RV. has the stems **ínakṣa** and **íyakṣa**, regarded as desideratives from √√**naç** *attain* and **yaj**, with mutilated reduplication.

1030. A number of roots, including some of very common use, form an abbreviated stem apparently by a contraction of reduplication and root together into one syllable: thus, ईप्स **īpsa** from √आप् **āp**; दित्स **ditsa** from √दा **dā**.

a. Such abbreviated stems are found in the older language as follows: **dhitsa** (beside **didhiṣa**) from √**dhā**; **ditsa** (beside **didāsa**) from √**dā**; **dipsa** (**dhīpsa** JB.) from √**dabh**; **çikṣa** from √**çak**; **sīkṣa** from √**sah**: these are found in RV.; in AV. are added **īpsa** from √**āp** (RV. has **apsa** once), and **īrtsa** from √**ṛdh**; the other texts furnish **lipsa** (ÇB.) or **līpsa** (TB.) from √**labh**, **ripsa** (GB.) from √**rabh**, **pitsa** (ÇB.) from √**pad**, and **dhīkṣa** (ÇB.) from √**dah** (not √**dih**, since no roots with **i** as medial vowel show the contracted form). In the later language are further found **pitsa** from √**pat** also, **jñīpsa** from the causative quasi-root **jñap** (below, **1042**j), and the anomalous **mitsa** from √**mā** *measure* (allowed also from roots **mi** and **mī**); and the grammarians give **ritsa** from √**rādh**. Also **mokṣa** is (very questionably) viewed as a desiderative stem from √**muc**.

1031. The use of the auxiliary vowel इ **i** is quite rare in the early language, but more common later; and it is allowed or prescribed by the grammarians in many stems which have not been found in actual use.

a. It is declared to follow in general, though not without exceptions, necessary or optional, the analogy of the futures (**934**, **943**a).

b. No example of the use of **i** is found in RV., and only one each in AV. (**pipatiṣa**), VS. (**jijīviṣa**), and TS. (**jigamiṣa**). The other examples noted in the early texts are **açiçiṣa**, **cikramiṣa**, **jigrahīṣa** (with **ī** for **i**, as elsewhere in this root), **cicariṣa**, **edidhiṣa**, **jijaniṣa**, **didīkṣiṣa**, **bibādhiṣa**, **ruruciṣa**, **vivadiṣa**, **vividiṣa**, **çiçāsiṣa**, **tiṣṭighiṣa**, **jihiṅsiṣa**: most of them are found only in ÇB. Stems also without the auxiliary vowel are made from roots **gam**, **grah**, **car**, **jīv**, **pat**, **bādh**, **vid**.

1032. Inflection: Present-System. The desiderative stem is conjugated in the present-system with perfect regularity, like other **a**-stems (**733**a), in both voices, in all the modes (including, in the older language, the subjunctive), and with participles and imperfect. It will be sufficient to give here the first persons only. We may take as active model ईप्स **īpsa** *seek to obtain*, from √आप् **āp** *obtain*; as middle, तितिक्ष **titikṣa** *endure*, from √तिज् **tij** *be sharp* (see below, **1040**).

1. Present Indicative.

	active.			middle.		
	s.	d.	p.	s.	d.	p.
1	ईप्सामि **ípsāmi**	ईप्सावस् **ípsāvas**	ईप्सामस् **ípsāmas**	तितिक्षे **títikṣe**	तितिक्षावहे **títikṣāvahe**	तितिक्षामहे **títikṣāmahe**
	etc.	etc.	etc.	etc.	etc.	etc.

2. Present Subjunctive.

1	ईप्सानि **ípsāni**	ईप्साव **ípsāva**	ईप्साम **ípsāma**	तितिक्षै **títikṣāi**	तितिक्षावहै **títikṣāvahāi**	तितिक्षामहै **títikṣāmahāi**
	etc.	etc.	etc.	etc.	etc.	etc.

3. Present Optative.

1	ईप्सेयम् **ípseyam**	ईप्सेव **ípseva**	ईप्सेम **ípsema**	तितिक्षेय **títikṣeya**	तितिक्षेवहि **títikṣevahi**	तितिक्षेमहि **títikṣemahi**
	etc.	etc.	etc.	etc.	etc.	etc.

4. Present Imperative.

2	ईप्स **ípsa**	ईप्सतम् **ípsatam**	ईप्सत **ípsata**	तितिक्षस्व **títikṣasva**	तितिक्षेथाम् **títikṣethām**	तितिक्षध्वम् **títikṣadhvam**
	etc.	etc.	etc.	etc.	etc.	etc.

5. Present Participle.

ईप्सन्त् **ípsant** (f. ईप्सन्ती **ípsantī**) तितिक्षमाण **títikṣamāṇa**

6. Imperfect.

1	ऐप्सम् **áipsam**	ऐप्साव **áipsāva**	ऐप्साम **áipsāma**	अतितिक्षे **átitikṣe**	अतितिक्षावहि **átitikṣāvahi**	अतितिक्षामहि **átitikṣāmahi**
	etc.	etc.	etc.	etc.	etc.	etc.

a. There are almost no irregularities of inflection to be reported from the older language. No 1st pl. in **masi**, or 2d pl. in **thana** or **tana**, is met with; of the impv. in **tāt**, only **īpsatāt**. The quotable subjunctive forms are those in **sāni**, **sāt** and **sat**, **sān**, and **santa**. KBU. has **jijñāsīta** (cf. **738b**). But the fem. pple **síṣāsatī** (instead of **siṣāsantī**) occurs once or twice in the older texts; and RV. has **dídhiṣāṇa**.

b. In the epics and later are found sporadic forms of the non-a-conjugation: thus, **sisṛkṣmas** (BhP.), **titikṣmahe** and **bubhūṣate** 3d pl. (MBh.); and the fem. participles **lipsatī** and **cikīrṣatī** (MBh.: against **449 b**). The anomalous **jighāṅsīyāt** occurs also in MBh. and Vas.

1033. a. Desiderative forms outside the present-system are extremely rare in the oldest language. The RV. has only perfect forms from a stem **mimikṣ** — thus, **mimikṣáthus, mimikṣátus, mimikṣús; mimikṣe, mimikṣire** — along with the present forms **mimikṣati, mimikṣa** etc., **mimikṣant** (pple): they show that **mimikṣ** or **mikṣ** has taken on the character of an independent root. In AV. are found two aorist forms, **īrtsīs** and **acikitsīs,** and a participle or two from **mīmāṅsa** (see below, **1037 a, 1039 a**) — all of them from stems which have lost their distinct desiderative meaning, and come to bear an independent value. The forms noted from the other earlier texts will be given in full below.

b. In the later language, a complete system of verbal forms is allowed to be made in the desiderative conjugation, the desiderative stem, less its final vowel, being treated as a root. Thus:

1034. Perfect. The desiderative perfect is the periphrastic (**1070 ff.**).

a. Thus, **īpsāṁ cakāra** etc.; **titikṣāṁ cakre** etc. Such forms are made in ÇB. from √√**kram, dhūrv, bādh, ruh**; and in ChU. from **man.**

b. Apparent perfect forms of the ordinary kind made from **mimikṣ** in RV. have been noticed in the preceding paragraph. And AB. (viii. 21. 10) has once **didāsitha** *thou hast desired to give.*

1035. Aorist. The aorist is of the **iṣ**-form: thus, ऐप्सिषम् **āipsiṣam,** अतितिक्षिषि **átitikṣiṣi.**

a. The AV. has **acikitsīs,** and **īrtsīs** (augmentless, with **mā́** prohibitive: **579**). TB. has **āipsīt**; ÇB. **āírtsīt, ācikīrṣīs** and **ajighāṅsīs,** and **amīmāṅsiṣṭhās**; KB. **jijñāsiṣi**; JUB. **āipsiṣma**; and AA. **adhitsiṣam.** No examples have been found in the later language.

b. A precative is also allowed — thus, **īpsyāsam, titikṣiṣīya**; but it never occurs.

1036. Futures. The futures are made with the auxiliary vowel इ **i**: thus, ईप्सिष्यामि **īpsiṣyā́mi** and ईप्सितास्मि **īpsitā́smi**; तितिक्षिष्ये **titikṣiṣyé** and तितिक्षिताहे **titikṣitā́he.**

a. The ÇB. has **titikṣiṣyate** and **didṛkṣitā́ras.** Such forms as **jijñāsyāmas** (MBh.), **didhakṣyāmi** (R.), and **mīmāṅsyant** (GGS.) are doubtless presents, with **-sya-** blunderingly for **-sa-.**

1037. Verbal Nouns and Adjectives. These too are made with the auxiliary vowel इ i, in all cases where that vowel is ever taken.

a. In the older language have been noted: participle in **ta, mīmāṅsitá** (AV., GB.), **jijyūṣita** (AB.), **çuçrūṣitá** and **dhīkṣitá** (ÇB.); — gerundive in **tavya, līpsitavya** (AB.), **didhyāsitavyà** (ÇB.); in **ya, jijñāsyà** (ÇB.); — gerund in **tvā, mīmāṅsitvā** (K.).

1038. Of other declinable stems derived from the desiderative stem, by far the most common are the adjective in **ú** — e. g. **titikṣu, dipsú, bībhatsú, siṣāsú** (RV. once **didṛ́kṣu**) — and the abstract noun in **ā́** — e. g. **īpsā, bībhatsā́, mīmāṅsā́, çuçrūṣā** — both of which are made with increasing freedom from an early epoch of the language: especially the former, which has the value and construction (**271 a**) of a present participle. A few adjectives in **enya** (having a gerundive character: **966 b**) occur in the earlier language: thus, **didṛkṣéṇya** (RV.), **çuçrūṣéṇya** (TS.), **ninīṣeṇya** (PB.), **jijñāsenya** (AB.), and, with irregular reduplication (apparently) **papṛkṣeṇya** (RV.), **dadhiṣeṇya** (JB.); and **didṛkṣéya** (RV.) is a similar formation. RV. has also **siṣāsáni** and **rurukṣáṇi**, and **siṣāsátu** (?). In the later language, besides some of the formations already instanced (those in **u** and **ā**, and in **sya** and **sitavya**), are found a few derivatives in **aka**, as **cikitsaka, bubhūṣaka**; in **ana**, as **jijñāsana, didhyāsana**; and, very rarely, in **anīya** (**cikitsanīya**) and **tṛ** (**çuçrūṣitṛ**); further, secondary derivatives (doubtless) in **in** from the noun in **ā**, as **īpsin, jigīṣin** (one or two of these occur in the older language). And of an adjective in **a** we have an example in **bībhatsá** (B.S., and later), and perhaps in **avalipsa** (AVP.); such words as **ajugupsa, duçcikitsa,** are rather to be understood as possessive compounds with the noun in **ā**. As to noun-stems in **is**, see **392 d**.

1039. Derivative or Tertiary Conjugations. A passive is allowed to be made, by adding the passive-sign य yá to the desiderative root (or stem without final **a**): thus, ईप्स्यते **īpsyáte** *it is desired to be obtained;* — and a causative, by adding in like manner the causative-sign अय áya (1041): thus, ईप्सयामि **īpsáyāmi** *I cause to desire obtainment.*

a. Of these formations in the older language are found **mīmāṅsyámāna** (doubtless to be read for **-sámāna**, AV.), **lipsyámāna** (ÇB.), and **rurutsyamāna** (K.). Half-a-dozen such passives are quotable later, and one or two causatives: e. g. **cikitsyate, vivakṣyate, jijñāsyate; cikīrṣayant, cikitsayiṣyati.**

b. For the desiderative conjugation formed on causative stems, which is found as early as the Brāhmaṇas, see below, **1052 b**.

1040. Some stems which are desiderative in form have lost the peculiarity of desiderative meaning, and assumed the value of independent roots: examples are **cikits** *cure*, **jugups** *despise*, **titikṣ** *endure*, **bībhats** *abhor*, **mīmāṅs** *ponder*, **çuçrūṣ** *obey*. Doubtless some of the apparent roots in the language with sibilant final are akin with the desideratives in origin: e. g. **çikṣ**, desiderative of **çak**.

a. On account of the near relation of desiderative and future (cf. **948 b**), the former is occasionally found where the latter was rather to be expected: thus, **rājānam prayiyāsantam** (ÇB.) *a king about to depart*; **prāṇa uccikramiṣan** (ChU.) *the breath on the point of expiring*; **mumūrṣur ivā 'bhavat** (H.) *he was fain to die*.

IV. Causative.

1041. a. In the later language is allowed to be made from most roots a complete causative conjugation. The basis of this is a causative stem, formed by appending the causative-sign अय **áya** to the, usually strengthened, root.

b. But by no means all conjugation-stems formed by the sign अय **áya** are of causative value; and the grammarians regard a part of them as constituting a conjugation-class, the tenth or **cur**-class, according to which roots may be inflected as according to the other classes, and either alone or along with others (**775**).

c. In RV., the proportion without causative value is fully one third. The formation is a more obviously denominative one than any of the other conjugation-classes, an intermediate between them and the proper denominatives. A causative meaning has established itself in connection with the formation, and become predominant, though not exclusive. A number of roots of late appearance and probably derivative character are included in the class, and some palpable denominatives, which lack only the usual denominative accent (below, **1056**).

d. The causative formation is of much more frequent use, and more decidedly expanded into a full conjugation, than either the intensive or the desiderative. It is made from more than three hundred roots in the early language (in RV., from about one hundred and fifty); but in the oldest, its forms outside the present-system are (apart from the attached reduplicated aorist: **1046**) exceedingly few.

1042. The treatment of the root before the causative-sign अय **aya** is as follows:

a. Medial or initial **i, u, ṛ, ḷ** have the **guṇa**-strengthening (if capable of it: **240**); thus, **vedaya** from √**vid**, **codaya** from √**cud**, **tarpaya** from √**tṛp**; and **kalpaya** from √**kḷp** (only example): but **cintaya, gulphaya, dṛṅhaya.**

b. But a few roots lack the strengthening: these are, in the older language, **cit (citaya** and **cetaya), iṣ, il, riṣ (riṣaya** and **reṣaya), vip (vipaya** and **vepaya), tuj, tur, tuṣ (tuṣaya** and **toṣaya), dyut (dyutaya** and **dyotaya), ruc (rucaya** and **rocaya), çuc (çucaya** and **çocaya), çubh (cubhaya** and **çobhaya), kṛp, mṛḍ, spṛh**; and **grabh** makes in RV. **gṛbhaya. Duṣ** and **guh** lengthen the vowel instead. **Mṛj** sometimes has **vṛddhi**, as in other forms: thus, **mārjaya** (beside **marjaya**). On the other hand, **guṇa** appears irregularly (**240 b**) in **srevaya** (beside **çrīvaya**), **heḍaya, mekṣaya.** Similar irregularities in the later language are **giraya, tulaya** (also **tolaya**), **churaya** (also **choraya**), **muṣaya, sphuraya.** No forms without strengthening have a causative value made in the older language.

c. A final vowel has the **vṛddhi**-strengthening: thus, **cāyaya, çāyaya, cyāvaya, bhāvaya, dhāraya, sāraya.**

d. But no root in **i** or **ī** has **vṛddhi** in the Veda (unless **pāyaya** [**k**, below] comes from **pī** rather than **pā**) — as, indeed, regular causatives from such roots are hardly quotable: only RV. has **kṣayaya** (beside **kṣepaya**) from √**kṣi** *possess*; for a few alternatively permitted forms, see below, **l.** In B. and S., however, occur **çāyaya** and **sāyaya** (√**si** or **sā**); and later **-āyaya, cāyaya, smāyaya, ḍāyaya, nāyaya.**

e. A few roots have a form also with **guṇa**-strengthening: thus, **cyu, dru, plu, yu** *separate*, **çru, pū, stu, sru; jṛ** *waste away*, **dṛ** *pierce*, **sṛ, smṛ, hṛ; vṛ** *choose* makes **varaya** later (it is not found in V.; epic also **vāraya**).

f. A medial or initial **a** in a light syllable is sometimes lengthened, and sometimes remains unchanged: thus, **bhājaya, svāpaya, ādaya; janaya, çrathaya, anaya** (but **mandaya, valgaya, bhakṣaya**).

g. The roots in the older language which keep their short **a** are **jan, pan, svan, dhan, ran, stan, gam (gāmaya** once in RV.), **tam, dam, raj** (usually **rañjaya**), **prath, çrath, çnath, vyath, svad, chad** *please* (also **chandaya**), **nad, dhvas** (also **dhvaṅsaya**), **rah, mah** (also **maṅhaya**), **nabh** (also **nambhaya**), **tvar, svar, hval.** In the later language, further, **kvaṇ, jvar, trap, day, paṇ, rac, ran** *ring*, **vadh, val, vaç, çlath, skhal, sthag.** Both forms are made (either in the earlier or in the later language, or in both taken together) by **ad, kal, kram, kṣam, khan, ghaṭ, cam, cal, jval, tvar, dal, dhvan, nad, nam, pat, bhram, math, mad, yam, ram, lag, lal, vam, vyadh, çam** *be quiet*, **çram, çvas, svap.** The roots which lengthen the vowel are decidedly the more numerous.

h. If a nasal is taken in any of the strong forms of a root, it usually appears in the causative stem: e. g. **dambhaya, daṅçaya, indhaya,**

limpaya, rundhaya, çundhaya, kṛntaya, dṛṅhaya. From a number of roots, stems both with and without the nasal are made: thus (besides those mentioned above, g), **kuñcaya** and **kocaya, granthaya** and **grathaya, bṛṅhaya** and **barhaya, bhrañçaya** and **bhrāçaya, çundhaya** and **çodhaya, sañjaya** and **sajjaya, siñcaya** and **secaya.** In a few of these is seen the influence of present-stems.

i. Most roots in final ā, and the root ṛ, add p before the conjugation-sign: thus, **dāpaya, dhāpaya, sthāpaya; arpaya.**

j. Such stems are made in the older language from the roots **kṣā, khyā, gā** *sing* (also **gāyaya**), **glā, ghrā, jñā, dā** *give*, **dā** *divide*, **drā** *run*, **dhā** *put* and **dhā** *suck*, **mā** *measure*, **mlā, yā, vā** *blow*, **sthā, snā, hā** *remove;* the later language adds **kṣmā, dhmā,** and **hā** *leave*. From **jñā** and **snā** are found in AV. and later the shortened forms **jñapaya** and **snapaya,** and from **çrā** only **çrapaya** (not in RV.). Also, in the later language, **glā** forms **glapaya,** and **mlā** forms **mlapaya.**

k. Stems from ā-roots showing no p are, earlier, **gāyaya** (also **gāpaya**) from √**gā** *sing*, **chāyaya, pāyaya** from √**pā** *drink* (or **pī**), **pyāyaya** from √**pyā** or **pyāy; sāyaya** from √**sā** (or **si**); also, later, **hvāyaya** from √**hvā** (or **hū**); — and further, from roots **vā** *weave*, **vyā,** and **çā** (or **çi**), according to the grammarians.

l. The same p is taken also by a few i- and ī-roots, with other accompanying irregularities: thus, in the older language, **kṣepaya** (RV., beside **kṣayaya**) from √**kṣi** *possess;* **jāpaya** (VS. and later) from √**ji**; **lāpaya** (TB. and later; later also **lāyaya**) from √**lī** *cling;* **çrāpaya** (VS., once) from √**çri; adhyāpaya** (S. and later) from **adhi**+√**i**; — in the later, **kṣapaya** (beside **kṣayaya**) from √**kṣi** *destroy;* **māpaya** from √**mī; smāpaya** (beside **smāyaya**) from √**smi; hrepaya** from √**hrī**; — and the grammarians make further **krāpaya** from √**krī; cāpaya** (beside **cāyaya**) from √**ci** *gather;* **bhāpaya** (beside **bhāyaya** and **bhīṣaya**) from √**bhī; repaya** from √**rī,** and **vlepaya** from √**vlī.** Moreover, √**ruh** makes **ropaya** (B. and later) beside **rohaya** (V. and later), and √**knū** makes **knopaya** (late).

m. More anomalous cases, in which the so-called causative is palpably the denominative of a derived noun, are: **pālaya** from √**pā** *protect;* **prīṇaya** from √**prī; līnaya** (according to grammarians) from √**lī; dhūnaya** (not causative in sense) from √**dhū; bhīṣaya** from √**bhī; ghātaya** from √**han; sphāvaya** from √**sphā** or **sphāy.**

n. In the Prakrit, the causative stem is made from all roots by the addition of (the equivalent of) **āpaya**; and a number (about a dozen) of like formations are quotable from Sanskrit texts, mostly of the latest period; but three, **krīḍāpaya, jīvāpaya,** and **dīkṣāpaya,** occur in the epics; and two, **açāpaya** and **kṣālāpaya,** even in the Sūtras.

1043. Inflection: Present-System. The causative stem is inflected in the present-system precisely like other stems in अ a (733a): it will be sufficient to give here in general the first persons of the different formations, taking as model the stem धारय dhāráya, from √धृ dhṛ. Thus:

1. Present Indicative.

active.

	s.	d.	p.
1	धारयामि dhāráyāmi etc.	धारयावस् dhāráyāvas etc.	धारयामस् dhāráyāmas etc.

middle.

	s.	d.	p.
1	धारये dhāráye etc.	धारयावहे dhāráyāvahe etc.	धारयामहे dhāráyāmahe etc.

a. The 1st pl. act. in **masi** greatly outnumbers (as ten to one) that in **mas** in both RV. and AV. No example occurs of 2d pl. act. in **thana**, nor of 3d sing. mid. in **e** for **ate**.

2. Present Subjunctive.

For the subjunctive may be instanced all the forms noted as occurring in the older language:

active.

	s.	d.	p.
1	dhāráyāṇi	dhāráyāva	dhāráyāma
2	dhāráyāsi dhāráyās	dhāráyāthas	dhāráyātha
3	dhāráyāti dhāráyāt	dhāráyātas	dhāráyān

middle.

	s.	d.	p.
1	dhāráyāi	dhāráyāvahāi	
2	dhāráyāse		dhāráyādhve dhāráyādhvāi
3	dhāráyāte dhāráyātāi	dhāráyāite	

b. Only one dual mid. form in **āite** occurs: **mādáyāite** (RV.). The only RV. mid. form in **āi**, except in 1st du., is **mādayādhvāi**. The primary endings in 2d and 3d sing. act. are more common than the secondary.

3. Present Optative.

active.

	s.	d.	p.
1	धारयेयम् dhāráyeyam etc.	धारयेव dhāráyeva etc.	धारयेम dhāráyema etc.

middle.

1 धारयेय	धारयेवहि	धारयेमहि
dhāráyeya	**dhāráyevahi**	**dhāráyemahi**
etc.	etc.	etc.

c. Optative forms are very rare in the oldest language (four in RV., two in AV.); they become more common in the Brāhmaṇas. A 3d sing. mid. in **īta** instead of **eta** (cf. **738 b**) occurs once in B. (**kāmayīta** AB.), is not very rare in S. (a score or two of examples are quotable), and is also found in MBh. and later. Of a corresponding 3d pl. in **īran** only one or two instances can be pointed out (**kāmayīran** AÇS., **kalpayīran** AGS.).

4. Present Imperative.

active.

2 धारय	धारयतम्	धारयत
dhāráya	**dhāráyatam**	**dhāráyata**
etc.	etc.	etc.

middle.

2 धारयस्व	धारयेथाम्	धारयध्वम्
dhāráyasva	**dhāráyethām**	**dhāráyadhvam**
etc.	etc.	etc.

d. Imperative persons with the ending **tāt** occur: **dhārayatāt** (AV.) and **cyāvayatāt** (ÇB.) are 2d sing.; **pātayatāt** (ÇB.) is 3d sing.; **gamayatāt** and **cyāvayatāt** (K. etc.), and **vārayatāt** (TB.) are used as 2d pl. **Vārayadhvāt** (K. etc.) is 2d pl., and the only known example of such an ending (see above, **549 b**).

5. Present Participle.

धारयन्त् **dhāráyant** धारयमाण **dhāráyamāṇa.**

e. The feminine of the active participle is regularly and usually made in **antī** (**449 c**). But a very few examples in **atī** are met with (one in the older language: **namayatī** Āpast.).

f. The middle participle in **māna** is made through the whole history of the language, from RV. (only **yātáyamāna**) down, and is the only one met with in the earlier language (for **írayānas** [sic!], MS. ii. 7.12, is evidently a false reading, perhaps for **írayā nas**). But decidedly more common in the epics and later is one formed with **āna**: e. g. **kāmayāna, cintayāna, pālayāna, vedayāna.** It is quotable from a larger number of roots than is the more regular participle in **māna.** As it occurs in no accentuated text, its accent cannot be given.

6. Imperfect.

active.

1	अधारयम् ádhārayam etc.	अधारयाव ádhārayāva etc.	अधारयाम ádhārayāma etc.

middle.

1	अधारये ádhāraye etc.	अधारयावहि ádhārayāvahi etc.	अधारयामहि ádhārayāmahi etc.

1044. As was above pointed out, the formations from the causative stem in **aya** outside the present-system are in the oldest language very limited. In RV. are found two forms of the future in **syāmi,** one passive participle (**coditá**), and ten infinitives in **dhyāi;** also one or two derivative nouns in **tṛ** (**bodhayitṛ́, codayitrī́**), five in **iṣṇu,** seven in **itnu,** and a few in **a** (**atipārayá, nidhārayá, vācamīn̄khayá, viçvamejaya**), and in **u** (**dhārayú, bhāvayú, mandayú**). In AV., also two **s**-future forms and four gerunds in **tvā;** and a few derivative noun-stems, from one of which is made a periphrastic perfect (**gamayā́m̐ cakāra**). In the Brāhmaṇas, verbal derivative forms become more numerous and various, as will be noted in detail below.

1045. Perfect. The accepted causative perfect is the periphrastic (**1071a**); a derivative noun in **ā́** is made from the causative stem, and to its accusative, in **ā́m,** is added the auxiliary: thus,

धारयां चकार **dhārayā́m̐ cakāra** (or **āsa: 1070b**)

धारयां चक्रे **dhārayā́m̐ cakre**

a. Of this perfect no example occurs in RV. or SV. or VS., only one — **gamayā́m̐ cakāra** — in AV., and but half-a-dozen in all the various texts of the Black Yajur-Veda, and these not in the **mantra**-parts of the text. They are also by no means frequent in the Brāhmaṇas, except in ÇB. (where they abound: chiefly, perhaps, for the reason that this work uses in considerable part the perfect instead of the imperfect as its narrative tense).

1046. Aorist. The aorist of the causative conjugation is the reduplicated, which in general has nothing to do with the causative stem, but is made directly from the root.

a. It has been already fully described (above, **856** ff.).

b. Its association with the causative is probably founded on an original intensive character belonging to it as a reduplicated form, and is a matter of gradual growth; in the Veda it is made from a considerable number of roots (in RV., more than a third of its instances; in AV., about a fifth) which have no causative stem in **aya**.

c. The causative aorist of √धृ **dhṛ**, then, is as follows:

1	अदीधरम् **ádīdharam** etc.	अदीधराव **ádīdharāva** etc.	अदीधराम **ádīdharāma** etc.
1	अदीधरे **ádīdhare** etc.	अदीधरावहि **ádīdharāvahi** etc.	अदीधरामहि **ádīdharāmahi** etc.

An example was inflected in full at **864**.

1047. In a few cases, where the root has assumed a peculiar form before the causative sign — as by the addition of a **p** or **ṣ** (above, **1042** i ff.) — the reduplicated aorist is made from this form instead of from the simple root: thus, **atiṣṭhipam** from **sthāp** (stem **sthāpaya**) for √**sthā**. Aorist-stems of this character from quasi-roots in **āp** are **arpipa** (√**ṛ**), **jījapa** or **jījipa**, **jijñapa** or **jijñipa**, **çiçrapa**, **tiṣṭhipa**, **jīhipa**; the only other example from the older language is **bībhiṣa** from **bhīṣ** for √**bhī**.

1048. But a few sporadic forms of an **iṣ**-aorist from causative conjugation-stems are met with: thus, **dhvanayīt** (RV.; TS. has instead the wholly anomalous **dhvanayit**), **vyathayīs** and **āilayīt** (AV.), **pyāyayiṣṭhās** and **avādayiṣṭhās** (KBU.), in the older language (RV. has also **ūnayīs** from a denominative stem); in the later, **ahlādayiṣata** (DKC.), and probably **aghātayithās** (MBh.; for **-iṣṭhās**: cf. **904** d). The passive 3d sing. **aropi**, from the causative **ropaya**, has a late occurrence (Çatr.).

1049. A precative is of course allowed by the grammarians to be made for the causative conjugation: in the middle, from the causative stem with the auxiliary **i** substituted for its final **a**; in the active, from the form of the root as strengthened in the causative stem, but without the causative sign: thus,

धार्यासम् **dhāryāsam** etc. धारयिषीय **dhārayiṣīya** etc.

This formation is to be regarded as purely fictitious.

1050. Futures. Both futures, with the conditional, are made from the causative stem, with the auxiliary इ **i**, which takes the place of its final अ **a**. Thus:

S-Future.

धारयिष्यामि **dhārayiṣyámi** etc. धारयिष्ये **dhārayiṣyé** etc.
धारयिष्यन्त् **dhārayiṣyánt** धारयिष्यमाण **dhārayiṣyámāṇa**

Conditional.

अधारयिष्यम् ádhārayiṣyam etc. अधारयिष्ये ádhārayiṣye etc.

Periphrastic Future.

धारयितास्मि dhārayitā́smi etc.

a. It has been mentioned above that RV. and AV. contain only two examples each of the s-future, and none of the periphrastic. The former begin to appear in the Brāhmaṇas more numerously, but still sparingly, with participles, and conditional (only **adhārayiṣyat** ÇB.; **alāpayiṣyathās** ChU.); of the latter, ÇB. affords two instances (**pārayitā́smi** and **janayitā́si**). Examples of both formations are quotable from the later language (including the middle form **darçayitāhe**: **947 c**).

1051. Verbal Nouns and Adjectives. These are made in two different ways: either 1. from the full causative stem (in the same manner as the futures, just described); or 2. from the causatively strengthened root-form (with loss of the causative-sign).

a. To the latter class belong the passive participle, as **dhārita**; the gerundive and gerund in **ya**, as **dhārya**, **-dhārya**; and the gerund in **am**, as **dhāram**; also, in the older language, the root-infinitive, as **-dhāram** etc. (**970 a**). To the former class belong the infinitive and the gerund in **tvā**, as **dhārayitum**, **dhārayitvā**, and the gerundive in **tavya**, as **dhārayitavya** (also, in the older language, the infinitives in **tavāi** and **dhyāi**, as **jánayitavāí**, **īrayádhyāi**, etc.). The auxiliary **i** is taken in every formation which ever admits that vowel.

b. Examples of the passive participle are **īritá**, **vāsita**, **çrāvitá**. But from the quasi-root **jñap** (**1042 j**) is made **jñapta**, without union-vowel.

c. Examples of the infinitive and gerund in **tvā** are **jóṣayitum**, **dhā́rayitum**; **kalpayitvā́**, **arpayitvā́**. But in the epics, and even later, infinitives are occasionally made with loss of the causative-sign: e. g. **çeṣitum**, **bhāvitum**, **dhāritum**, **mocitum**.

d. Examples of the gerunds in **ya** and **am** are **-bhā́jya**, **-ghārya**, **-pādya**, **-vāsya**, **nāyya**, **-sthāpya**; **-bhājam**, **-sthāpam**. But stems showing in the root-syllable no difference from the root retain **ay** of the causative-sign in the gerund, to distinguish it from that belonging to the primary conjugation: e. g. **-kramáyya**, **-gamáyya**, **-janáyya**, **-jvaláyya**, **-kalayya**, **-çamayya**, **-racayya**, **-āpayya**.

e. Examples of the gerundive in **tavya** are **tarpayitavyà**, **gamayitavya**, **hvāyayitavya**; of that in **ya**, **sthā́pya**, **hā́rya**, **yājya**; of that in **anīya**, **sthāpanīya**, **bhāvanīya**.

f. Examples of other formations occurring in the older language are as follows: root-infinitive, **-sthāpam, -vāsas**; — infinitive in **tu**, other cases than accusative, **-janayitave; jánayitavāí, pā́yayitavāí, -çotayitavāí; çā́mayitos**; — infinitive in **dhyāi, iṣayádhyāi, īrayádhyāi, taṅsayádhyāi, nāçayádhyāi, mandayádhyāi, mādayádhyāi, riṣayádhyāi, vartayádhyāi, vājayádhyāi, syandayádhyāi** (all RV.); — gerundive in **āyya, panayā́yya, spṛhayā́yya, trayayā́yya** (? √**trā**).

g. Other noun-derivatives from the causative stem are not infrequent, being decidedly more numerous and various than from any other of the secondary conjugation-stems. Examples (of other kinds than those instanced in **1044**) are: **árpaṇa, dāpana, prīṇana, bhī́ṣaṇa; jñāpaka, ropaka; patayālú, spṛhayālu; jánayati, jñapti.**

h. All the classes of derivatives, it will be noticed, follow in regard to accent the analogy of similar formations from the simple root, and show no influence of the special accent of the causative-stem.

1052. Derivative or Tertiary Conjugations. From the causative stem are made a passive and a desiderative conjugation. Thus:

a. The passive-stem is formed by adding the usual passive-sign य **ya** to the causatively strengthened root, the causative-sign being dropped: thus, धार्यते **dhāryáte.**

b. Such passives are hardly found in the Veda (only **bhājyá-** AV.), but some thirty instances are met with in the Brāhmaṇas and Sūtras: examples are **jñapyá-** (TS.), **sādya-** (K.), **pādya-** (AB.), **vādya-** (TB.), **sthāpya-** (GB.); and they become quite common later.

c. The desiderative stem is made by reduplication and addition of the sign इष **iṣa**, of which the initial vowel replaces the final of the causative stem: thus, दिधारयिषति **dídhārayiṣati.**

d. These, too, are found here and there in the Brāhmaṇas and later (about forty stems are quotable): examples are **pipāyayiṣa** (K.), **bibhāvayiṣa** and **cikalpayiṣa** and **lulobhayiṣa** (AB.), **dídrāpayiṣa** and **rirādhayiṣa** and **āpipayiṣa** (ÇB.), and so on.

e. As to causatives made from the intensive and desiderative stems, see above, **1025, 1039.**

V. Denominative.

1053. A denominative conjugation is one that has for its basis a noun-stem.

a. It is a view now prevailingly held that most of the present-systems of the Sanskrit verb, along with other formations analogous with a

present-system, are in their ultimate origin denominative; and that many apparent roots are of the same character. The denominatives which are so called differ from these only in that their origin is recent and undisguised.

1054. The grammarians teach that any noun-stem in the language may be converted, without other addition than that of an अ **a** (as union-vowel enabling it to be inflected according to the second general conjugation) into a present-stem, and conjugated as such.

a. But such formations are rare in actual use. The RV. has a few isolated and doubtful examples, the clearest of which is **bhiṣákti** *he heals*, from **bhiṣáj** *physician*; it is made like a form of the root-class; **abhiṣṇak** seems to be its imperfect according to the nasal class; and **pátyate** *he rules* appears to be a denominative of **páti** *master*; other possible cases are **iṣaṇas** etc., **kṛpáṇanta, taruṣema** etc., **vanuṣanta, bhurajanta, váṇanvati.** From the other older texts are quotable **kavyánt** (TS.), **áçlonat** (TB.), **unmūlati** (ṢB.), **svadhāmahe** (ÇÇS.). And a considerable number of instances, mostly isolated, are found in the later language: e. g. **kalahant** (MBh.), **arghanti** (Pañc.), **abjati** (Çatr.), **gardabhati** (SD.), **utkaṇṭhate** (SD.), **jagannetrati** (Pras.), **keliçvetasahasrapattrati** (Pras.).

1055. In general, the base of denominative conjugation is made from the noun-stem by means of the conjugation-sign य **yá**, which has the accent.

a. The identity of this **ya** with the **ya** of the so-called causative conjugation, as making with the final **a** of a noun-stem the causative-sign **aya,** is hardly to be questioned. What relation it sustains to the **ya** of the **ya**-class (**759**), of the passive (**768**), and of the derivative intensive stem (**1016**), is much more doubtful.

1056. Intermediate between the denominative and causative conjugations stands a class of verbs, plainly denominative in origin, but having the causative accent. Examples, beginning to appear at the earliest period of the language, are **mantráyate** *speaks, takes counsel,* (from **mantra,** √**man** + **tra**), **kīrtáyati** *commemorates* (from **kīrti,** √**kṛ** *praise*), **artháyati** or **-te** *makes an object of, seeks* (from **ártha** *goal, object*), **varṇayati** *depicts* (from **varṇa** *color*), **kathayati** or **-te** *gives the how of anything, relates* (from **katham** *how?*), and so on. These, along with like forms from roots which have no other present-system (though they may make scattering forms outside that system from the root directly), or which have this beside other present-systems without causative meaning, are reckoned by the grammarians as a separate conjugation-class, the **cur**-class (above, **607, 775**).

1057. Denominatives are formed at every period in the history of the language, from the earliest down.

a. They are frequent in RV., which contains over a hundred, of all varieties; AV. has only half as many (and personal forms from hardly a third as many: from the rest, present participles, or derivative nouns); AB., less than twenty; ÇB., hardly more than a dozen; and so on. In the later language they are quotable by hundreds, but from the vast majority of stems occur only an example or two; the oniy ones that have won any currency are those that have assumed the character of "cur-class" verbs.

1058. The denominative meaning is, as in other languages, of the greatest variety; some of the most frequent forms of it are: *be like, act as, play the part of; regard* or *treat as; cause to be, make into; use, make application of; desire, wish for, crave* — that which is signified by the noun-stem.

a. The modes of treatment of the stem-final are also various; and the grammarians make a certain more or less definite assignment of the varieties of meaning to the varieties of form; but this allotment finds only a dubious support in the usages of the words as met with even in the later language, and still less in the earlier. Hence the formal classification, according to the final of the noun-stem and the way in which this is treated before the denominative sign **yá**, will be the best one to follow.

1059. From stems in a. **a.** The final **a** of a noun-stem oftenest remains unchanged: thus, **amitrayáti** *plays the enemy, is hostile;* **devayáti** *cultivates the gods, is pious.*

b. But final **a** is also often lengthened: thus, **aghāyáti** *plans mischief;* **priyāyáte** *holds dear;* **açvāyáti** *seeks for horses;* **açanāyáti** *desires food.*

c. While in the Veda the various modes of denominative formation are well distributed, no one showing a marked preponderance, in the later language the vast majority of denominatives (fully seven eighths) are of the two kinds just noticed: namely, made from **a**-stems, and of the form **aya** or **āya**, the former predominating. And there is seen a decided tendency to give the denominatives in **aya** an active form and transitive meaning, and those in **āya** a middle form and intransitive or reflexive meaning. In not a few cases, parallel formations from the same stem illustrate this distinction: e. g. **kaluṣayati** *makes turbid,* **kaluṣāyate** *is* or *becomes urbid;* **taruṇayati** *rejuvenates,* **taruṇāyate** *is rejuvenated;* **çithilayati** *loosens,* **çithilāyate** *grows loose.* No distinct traces of this distinction are recognizable in the Veda, although there also corresponding forms with short **a** and with long **ā** sometimes stand side by side.

d. Final **a** is sometimes changed to **ī** (very rarely **i**): thus, **adhvarīyáti** *performs the sacrifice;* **taviṣīyáti** *is mighty;* **putrīyáti** or **putriyáti** *desires a son;* **mānsīyáti** *craves flesh;* **sajjīyate** *is ready;* **candrakāntīyati** *is moonstonelike.* Not fifty stems of this form are quotable.

e. It is occasionally dropped (after **n** or **r**): thus, **turaṇyáti** *is rapid;* **adhvaryáti** *performs the sacrifice.*

f. Other modes of treatment are sporadic: thus, the addition of **s**, as in **stanasyati** *seeks the breast;* the change of **a** to **e**, as in **vareyáti** *plays the wooer.*

1060. From stems in **ā**. Final **ā** usually remains, as in **gopāyáti** *plays the herdsman, protects;* **pṛtanāyati** *fights;* but it is sometimes treated in the other methods of an **a**-stem: thus, **pṛtanyati** *fights;* **tilottamīyati** *acts Tilottamā.*

1061. From stems in **i, ī,** and **u, ū**. Such stems are (especially those in **u, ū**) very rare. They show regularly **ī** and **ū** before **ya**: thus, **arātīyáti** (also **-tiy-**) *plots injury;* **janīyáti** (also **-niy-**) *seeks a wife;* **sakhīyáti** *desires friendship;* **nārīyate** *turns woman;* — **çatrūyáti** *acts the foe;* **ṛjūyáti** *is straight;* **vasūyáti** *desires wealth;* **asūyáti** *grumbles, is discontented:* with short **u**, **gātuyáti** *sets in motion.*

a. More rarely, **i** or **u** is treated as **a** (or else is gunated, with loss of a **y** or **v**): thus, **dhunayáti** *comes snorting;* **laghayati** *makes easier.* Sometimes, as to **a** (above, **1059 f**), a sibilant is added: thus, **aviṣyáti** *is vehement;* **uruṣyáti** *saves.* From **dhī**, RV. makes **dhiyāyáte**.

1062 From other vowel-stems. **a.** Final **ṛ** is changed to **rī**: thus, **mātrīyáti** *treats as a mother* (only quotable example).

b. The diphthongs, in the few cases that occur, have their final element changed to a semivowel: thus, **gavyáti** *seeks cattle, goes a-raiding.*

1063. From consonant-stems. A final consonant usually remains before **ya**: thus, **bhiṣajyáti** *plays the physician, cures;* **ukṣaṇyáti** *acts like a bull;* **apasyáti** *is active;* **namasyáti** *pays reverence;* **sumanasyáte** *is favorably disposed;* **taruṣyáti** *fights.*

a. But a final **n** is sometimes dropped, and the preceding vowel treated as a final: thus, **rājāyáte** or **rājīyáti** *is kingly,* from **rājan**; **-karmayati** from **-karman**; **svāmīyati** *treats as master,* from **svāmin**: **vṛṣāyáte** from **vṛṣan** is the only example quotable from the older language. Sporadic cases occur of other final consonants similarly treated: thus, **ojāyáte** from **ojas**, **-manāyate** from **-manas**; — while, on the other hand, an **a**-vowel is occasionally added to such a consonant before **ya**: thus, **iṣayáti** from **iṣ**, **satvanāyati** from **satvan**.

1064. The largest class of consonantal stems are those showing a **s** before the **ya**; and, as has been seen above, a sibilant is sometimes, by analogy, added to a final vowel, making the denominative-sign virtually **sya**

— or even, with **a** also added after an **i**- or **u**-vowel, **asya**; and this comes to be recognized by the grammarians as an independent sign, forming denominatives that express desire: thus, **sumakhasyáte** *is merry;* **jīvanasya-** (in **-syá** *love of life*); **vṛṣasyati** *desires the male* (the only quotable examples); **madhuṣyati** or **madhvasyati** *longs for honey;* **kṣīrasyati** *craves milk.*

1065. The grammarians reckon as a special class of denominatives in **kāmya** what are really only ordinary ones made from a compound noun-stem having **kāma** as its final member: thus, **rathakāmyati** *longs for the chariot* (K.: only example found in the older language); **arthakāmyati** *desires wealth;* **putrakāmyati** *wishes a son* (the only quotable examples); coming from the possessive compounds **rathakāma** etc. And **arthāpāyati** *treats as property* is a (sole quotable) example of a stem having the Prakritic causative form (**1042n**).

a. Stems of anomalous formation are **draghaya** from **dīrgha**, **draḍhaya** from **dṛḍha**, and perhaps **mradaya** from **mṛdu**.

1066. a. A number of denominative stems occur in the Veda for which no corresponding noun-stems are found, although for all or nearly all of them related words appear: thus, **aṅkūyá**, **stabhūyá**, **iṣudhya**; **dhiṣaṇyá**, **riṣaṇyá**, **ruvaṇya**, **huvanya**, **iṣaṇyá**; **ratharyá**, **çratharyá**, **saparyá**; **iyasya** (ÇB.), **irasyá**, **daçasyá**, **makhasyá**, **panasyá**, **sacasyá**. Those in **anya**, especially, look like the beginnings of a new conjugation-class.

b. Having still more that aspect, however, are a Vedic group of stems in **āya**, which in general have allied themselves to present-systems of the **nā**-class (**732**), and are found alongside the forms of that class: thus, **gṛbhāyáti** beside **gṛbhṇāti**. Of such, RV. has **gṛbhāyá**, **mathāyá**, **pruṣāyá**, **muṣāyá**, **çrathāya**, **skabhāyá**, **stabhāyá**. A few others have no **nā**-class companions: thus, **damāyá**, **çamāyá**, **tudāyá** (AV.); and **panāya**, **naçāya**, **vṛṣāya** (√**vṛṣ** *rain*), **vasāyá** (√**vas** *clothe*), and perhaps **açāya** (√**aç** *attain*).

c. Here may be mentioned also quasi-denominatives made from onomatopoetic combinations of sounds, generally with repetition: e. g. **kiṭakiṭāya**, **thatathatarāya**, **miṣamiṣāya**, **çaraçarāya**.

1067. The denominative stems in RV. and AV. with causative accentuation are: RV. **aṅkháya**, **artháya**, **iṣáya** (also **iṣayá**), **ūrjáya**, **ṛtáya**, **kṛpáya**, **mantráya**, **mṛgáya**, **vavráya**, **vājáya** (also **vājayá**), **vīḷáya**, **suṣváya** (also **suṣvayá**); AV. adds **kīrtáya**, **dhūpáya**, **pāláya**, **vīráya**, **sabhāgáya**.

a. The accent of **ánniya** and **hástaya** (RV.) is wholly anomalous.

1068. Inflection. The denominative stems are inflected with regularity like the other stems ending in अ **a** (**733a**) throughout the present-system. Forms outside of that system — except from the stems which are reckoned to the causative or cur-class, and which follow in all respects the rules for that class — are of the utmost rarity.

a. In RV. occurs no form not belonging to the present-system, except **ūnayīs** (with **mā́** prohibitive), an **iṣ**-aorist 2d sing. (cf. **1048**). Further examples of this aorist are **āsūyīt** (ÇB.), **pāpayiṣṭa** (TS.: pl., with **mā́** prohibitive), and **avṛṣāyiṣata** (VS. etc.). The form **ásaparyāit** (AV. xiv. 2. 20), with **āi** for **ī** (**555c**), might be aorist; but, as the metre shows, is probably a corrupt reading; **amanasyāit**, certainly imperfect, appears to occur in TB. (ii. 3. 8[3]). Other forms begin to appear in the Brāhmaṇas: e. g. the futures **gopāyiṣyati** (ÇB.), **meghāyiṣyánt, kaṇḍūyiṣyánt, çīkāyiṣyánt** (TS.), the participles **bhiṣajyitá** (? JB. **-jita**) and **iyasitá** (ÇB.), **kaṇḍūyitá, çīkitá,** and **meghitá** (TS.), the gerund **saṁçlákṣṇya** (ÇB.), and so on. In the later language, also, forms outside the present-system (except the participle in **ta**) are only sporadic; and of tertiary conjugation forms there are hardly any: examples are the causatives **dhūmāyaya** and **asūyaya** (MBh.), and the desiderative **abhiṣiṣenayiṣa** (Çiç.).

b. Noun-derivatives from denominative stems follow the analogy of those from causative stems (**1051g**). In the older language, those in **u** and **ā** (especially the former) are much the most numerous; later, that in **ana** prevails over all others.

CHAPTER XV.

PERIPHRASTIC AND COMPOUND CONJUGATION.

1069. ONE periphrastic formation, the periphrastic future, has been already described (**942** ff.), since it has become in the later language a recognized part of every verbal conjugation, and since, though still remaining essentially periphrastic, it has been so fused in its parts and altered in construction as to assume in considerable measure the semblance of an integral tense-formation.

By far the most important other formation of the class is —

The Periphrastic Perfect.

1070. This (though almost unknown in the Veda, and coming only gradually into use in the Brāhmaṇas) is a tense widely made and frequently used in the classical Sanskrit.

a. It is made by prefixing the accusative of a derivative noun-stem in आ ā́ (accented) to the perfect tense of an auxiliary verb: namely, of √कृ kṛ *make*, more often of √अस् as *be*, and very rarely of √भू bhū *be*.

b. In the older language (see below, 1073 d), kṛ is almost the only auxiliary used in making this tense, as occurring very few times, and bhū never. Later, also, bhū is quite rare (it is found nine times in MBh., six times in Rgh., and a few times elsewhere), but as gains very greatly in currency, having become the usual auxiliary, while kṛ is only exceptional.

c. Somewhat similar formations with yet other auxiliaries are not absolutely unknown in the later language: thus, varayām pracakramus (MBh.), pūrayām (etc.) vyadhus (Vīracaritra), mṛgayām avāsīt (ib.).

1071. The periphrastic perfect occurs as follows:

a. It is the accepted perfect of the derivative conjugations: intensive, desiderative, causative, and denominative; the noun in आ ā́ being made from the present-stem which is the general basis of each conjugation: thus, from √बुध् budh, intensive बोबुधाम् bobudhā́m, desiderative बुभुत्साम् bubhutsā́m, causative बोधयाम् bodhayā́m; denominative मन्त्रयाम् mantrayā́m.

b. The formation from causative stems (including those denominatives which have assumed the aspect of causatives: 1056) is by far the most frequent. Only a few desideratives are quotable (1034a), and of intensives only jāgarām āsa (1020a; beside jajāgāra).

c. Most roots beginning with a vowel in a heavy syllable (long by nature or long by position) make this perfect only, and not the simple one: thus, आसाम् āsām from √आस् ās *sit*, ईक्षाम् īkṣā́m from √ईक्ष् īkṣ *see*; उज्झाम् ujjhām from √उज्झ् ujh *forsake*; एधाम् edhā́m from √एध् edh *thrive* (the only examples quotable).

d. Excepted are the roots **āp** and **āñch**, and those beginning with **a** before two consonants (and taking **ān** as reduplication: **788**).

e. The roots (that is, stems reckoned by the grammarians as roots) of more than one syllable have their perfect of this formation: thus, **cakāsā́m**. But **ūrṇu** (**713**) is said to form **ūrṇonāva** only; while **jāgṛ** (**1020**) makes a perfect of either formation, and **daridrā** (**1024 a**) is said to do the same.

f. A few other roots make the periphrastic in addition to the usual reduplicated perfect. Thus, in the older language only are found the stems **cāyām, tāyām, nilayām, vāsām** (√**vas** *dwell*), **vidām** (√**vid** *know*), **vyayām**, and the reduplicated stems **bibhayām** and **juhavām**; the later language adds **ayām, jayām, dayām, nayām, smayām, hvayām**, and the reduplicated **bibharām**; and the grammarians teach like formations from **uṣ, kās**, and the reduplicating **hrī**. The stem is made in every case from the present-stem, with **guṇa** of a final vowel.

1072. The periphrastic perfect of the middle voice is made with the middle inflection of √कृ **kṛ**. For passive use, the auxiliaries अस् **as** and भू **bhū** are said to be allowed to take a middle inflection.

a. One or two late examples of **bhū** with middle inflection have been pointed out, but none of **as**.

b. It is unnecessary to give a paradigm of this formation, as the inflection of the auxiliaries is the same as in their independent use: for that of √**kṛ**, see **800 k**; of √**bhū**, see **800 d**; of √**as**, see **800 m**.

c. The connection of the noun and auxiliary is not so close that other words are not occasionally allowed to come between them: thus, **mīmāṅsā́m evá cakré** (ÇB.) *he merely speculated;* **vidāṁ vā idam ayaṁ cakāra** (JB.) *he verily knew this;* **prabhrañçayāṁ yo naghusaṁ cakāra** *who made Naghusha fall headlong* (Rgh.).

1073. The above is an account of the periphrastic formation with a derivative noun in **ām** as it appears especially in the later language; earlier, its aspect is rather that of a more general, but quite infrequent, combination of such a noun with various forms of the root **kṛ**. Thus:

a. Of the periphrastic perfect occurs only a single example in the whole body of Vedic texts (metrical): namely, **gamayā́ṁ cakāra** (AV.). In the Brāhmanas examples from causative stems begin to appear more freely, but are everywhere few in number, except in ÇB. (which has them from twenty-four roots, and a few of these in several occurrences). From desiderative stems they are yet rarer (only seven occurrences, five of them in ÇB.: see **1034 a**); and from intensives they are unknown. The periphrastic perfects of primary conjugation were noted above (**1071 f**: in ÇB., eight stems and about eighty occurrences, chiefly from **īkṣ, bhī,** and **vid;** that from **vid** is found in the greatest number of texts).

b. Forms with the aorist of the auxiliary are in the oldest Brāhmaṇas as numerous as those with the perfect. Thus, with **akar** occur **ramayām** (K.), **janayā́m** and **sādayā́m** and **svadayā́m** and **sthāpayā́m** (MS.); and with **akran, vidā́m** (TS. TB. MS.). With the aorist optative or precative has been found only **pāvayā́ṁ kriyāt** (MS.).

c. Like combinations with other tenses are not entirely unknown: thus, **juhavāṁ karoti** (ÇÇS.). So also in the later language, where have been found quotable half-a-dozen such cases as **vidāṁ karoti** (Pañc.), **vidāṁ karotu** and **kurvantu** (Pañc. etc.).

d. Only two or three cases of the use of **as** instead of **kṛ** as auxiliary are met with in the older language: they are **mantrayām āsa** (AB. GB.), **janayām āsa** (ÇvU.), and **īkṣām āsa** (ÇÇS.).

e. A single example of an accented auxiliary is met with in the accentuated texts: namely, **atirecayā́ṁ cakrús** (ÇB.). As was to be expected, from the nature of the combination, the noun also retains its accent (compare **945**).

Participial Periphrastic Phrases.

1074. The frequent use, especially in the later language, of a past or a future passive participle with the copula (or also without it) to make participial phrases having a value analogous to that of verb-tenses, has been already noticed (**999**). But other similar combinations are not unknown in any period of the language, as made with other auxiliaries, or with other participles.

a. They occur even in the Veda, but are far more common and conspicuous in the Brāhmaṇas, and become again of minor account in the later language.

1075. Examples of the various formations are as follows:

a. A (usually present) participle with the tenses of the verb **i** *go*. This is the combination, on the whole, of widest and most frequent occurrence. Thus: **áyajvano vibhájann éti védaḥ** (RV.) *he ever gives away the wealth of the non-offerer;* **yathā sūcyā vāsaḥ saṁdadhad iyād evam evāi 'tābhir yajñasya chidraṁ saṁdadhad eti** (AB.) *just as one would mend [habitually] a garment with a needle, so with these one mends any defect of the sacrifice;* **agnir vā idaṁ vāiçvānaro dahann āit** (PB.) *Agni Vaiçvānara kept burning this creation;* **té 'surāḥ párājitā yánto dyā́vāpṛthivī́ úpāçrayan** (TB.) *those Asuras, getting beaten, took refuge with heaven and earth;* **tè 'sya gṛhā́ḥ paçáva upamūryámāṇā īyuḥ** (ÇB.) *the animals, his family, would be continually destroyed.*

b. The same with the verb **car** *go (continually* or *habitually),* signifying still more distinctly than the preceding a continued or habitual action. Thus: **agnā́v agníç carati prā́viṣṭaḥ** (AV.) *Agni is constantly present in the fire;* **adaṇḍyaṁ daṇḍena ghnantaç caranti** (PB.) *they make a practice of beating with a rod what is undeserving of punishment.*

c. The same with the verbs **ās** *sit* and **sthā** *stand,* with a like meaning. Thus, **juhvata āsate** (K.) *they continue sacrificing;* **te 'pakramya prativāvadato 'tiṣṭhan** (AB.) *they, having gone off, kept vehemently refusing.* In the later language, **sthā** is the verb oftenest used, with predicates of various kind, to make a verbal phrase of continuance.

d. A present or future or perfect participle with **as** and **bhū** *be.* The participle is oftenest a future one; **as** only is used in the optative, **bhū** usually in other forms. Thus: **yaḥ pūrvam anījānaḥ syāt** (AB.) *whoever may not have made sacrifice before;* **samāvad eva yajñe kurvāṇā āsan** (GB.) *they did the same thing at the sacrifice;* **parikrī́ḍanta āsan** (MS.) *they were playing about;* **yátra suptvā́ púnar nā̀ 'vadrāsyán bhávati** (ÇB.) *when, after sleeping, he is not going to fall asleep again;* **havyaṁ hi vakṣyan bhavati** (AB.) *for he is intending to carry the sacrifice;* **dāsyant syāt** (K.) *may be going to give;* **yéna vā́hanena syantsyánt syā́t** (ÇB.) *with what vehicle he may be about to drive.* True expressions for perfect and pluperfect and future perfect time are capable of being made by such means, and now and then are made, but in no regular and continued fashion.

Composition with Prepositional Prefixes.

1076. All the forms, personal and other, of verbal conjugation — of both primary and secondary conjugation, and even to some extent of denominative (so far as the denominative stems have become assimilated in value to simple roots) — occur very frequently in combination with certain words of direction, elements of an adverbial character (see the next chapter), the so-called prepositions (according to the original use of that term), or the verbal prefixes.

a. Practically, in the later language, it is as if a compounded root were formed, out of root and prefix, from which then the whole conjugation (with derivatives: below, chap. XVII.) is made, just as from the simple root. Yet, even there (and still more in the older language: **1081 a—c**), the combination is so loose, and the members retain so much of their independent value, that in most dictionaries (that of Sir Monier Williams is an exception) the conjugation of each root with prefixes is treated under the simple root, and not in the alphabetic order of the prefix. Derivative words, however, are by universal agreement given in their independent alphabetic place, like simple words.

1077. Those verbal prefixes which have value as such throughout the whole history of the language are given below, in alphabetic order, with their fundamental meanings:

अति **áti** *across, beyond, past, over, to excess;*

अधि **ádhi** *above, over, on, on to;*

अनु **ánu** *after, along, toward;*

अन्तर् **antár** *between, among, within;*

अप **ápa** *away, forth, off;*

अपि **ápi** *unto, close upon* or *on;*

अभि **abhí** *to, unto, against* (often with implied violence);

अव **áva** *down, off;*

आ **á** *to, unto, at;*

उद् **úd** *up, up forth* or *out;*

उप **úpa** *to, unto, toward;*

नि **ní** *down; in, into;*

निस् **nís** *out, forth;*

परा **párā** *to a distance, away, forth;*

परि **pári** *round about, around;*

प्र **prá** *forward, onward, forth, fore;*

प्रति **práti** *in reversed direction, back to* or *against, against, in return;*

वि **ví** *apart, asunder, away, out;*

सम् **sám** *along, with, together.*

a. Some of these, of course, are used much more widely and frequently than others. In order of frequency in the older language (as estimated by the number of roots with which they are found used in RV. and AV.), they stand as follows: **pra, ā, vi, sam, abhi, ni, ud, pari, anu, upa, prati, ava, nis, ati, apa, parā, adhi, api, antar. Api** is of very limited use as prefix in the later language, having become a conjunction, *too, also.*

b. The meanings given above are only the leading ones. In combinations of root and prefix they undergo much modification, both literal and figurative — yet seldom in such a way that the steps of transition from the fundamental sense are not easy to trace. Sometimes, indeed, the value of a root is hardly perceptibly modified by the addition of the prefix. An intensive force is not infrequently given by **pari, vi,** and **sam.**

1078. Prefixes essentially akin with the above, but more distinctly adverbial, and of more restricted use, are these:

ácha (or **áchā**) *to, unto:* tolerably frequent in RV. (used with over twenty roots), but already unusual in AV. (only two roots), quite restricted in B., and entirely lost in the later language;

āvís *forth to sight, in view:* used only with the roots **bhū, as,** and **kṛ;**

tirás *through, crossways; out of sight:* hardly used except with **kṛ, dhā, bhū** (in RV., with three or four others);

purás *in front, forward:* used with only half-a-dozen roots, especially **kṛ, dhā, i;**

prādús *forth to view:* only with **bhū, as, kṛ.**

a. A few others, as **bahis** *outside,* **vinā** *without,* **alam** (with **bhū** and **kṛ**) *sufficiently, properly,* **sākṣāt** *in view,* are still less removed from ordinary adverbs.

1079. Of yet more limited use, and of noun-rather than adverb-value, are:

çrad (or **çrath?**), only with **dhā** (in RV., once also with **kṛ**): **çraddhā** *believe, credit;*

hiñ, only with **kṛ** (and obsolete in the classical language): **hiñkṛ** *make the sound,* **hing** *low, murmur.*

a. And beside these stand yet more fortuitous combinations: see below, **1091.**

1080. More than one prefix may be set before the same root. Combinations of two are quite usual; of three, much less common; of more than three, rare. Their order is in general determined only by the requirements of the meaning, each added prefix bringing a further modification to the combination before which it is set. But आ **á** is almost never allowed, either earlier or later, to be put in front of any of the others.

a. The very rare cases of apparent prefixion of **ā** to another prefix (as **āvihanti** MBh., **āvitanvānāḥ** BhP.) are perhaps best explained as having the **ā** used independently, as an adverb.

1081. In classical Sanskrit, the prefix stands immediately before the verbal form.

a. In the earlier language, however (especially in the Veda; in the Brāhmana less often and more restrictedly), its position is quite free: it may be separated from the verb by another word or words, and may even come after the form to which it belongs; it may also stand alone, qualifying a verb that is understood, or conjointly with another prefix one that is expressed.

b. Thus, sá devā́ṅ é 'há vakṣyati (RV.) *he shall bring the gods hither;* prá ṇa ā́yūṅṣi tāriṣat (AV.) *may he lengthen out our lives;* tā́v ā́ yātam úpa dravát (RV.) *do ye two come hither quickly;* gámad vā́jebhir ā́ sá naḥ (RV.) *may he come with gifts hither to us;* pári mā́m pári 'me prajā́m pári ṇaḥ pāhi yád dhánam (AV.) *protect me, my progeny, and what wealth we own;* yátaḥ sadyá ā́ ca párā ca yánti (AV.) *from whence every day they advance and retire;* vy ahā́ṁ sárveṇa pāpmánā [avr̥tam] ví yákṣmeṇa sám ā́yuṣā (AV.) *I have separated from all evil, from disease, [I have joined myself] with life;* vi hy enena paçyati (AB.) *for by it he sees;* ví vā́ eṣā́ prajā́yā paçúbhir r̥dhyate (TB.) *he is deprived of progeny and cattle.*

c. Three or four instances have been cited from the later language of a prefix separated from, or following, a verb; perhaps the prefix in every such case admits of being regarded as an adverb.

1082. As regards the accent of verb-forms compounded with prefixes, only the case needs to be considered in which the prefix stands (as always in the later language) immediately before the verb; otherwise, verb and prefix are treated as two independent words.

1083. a. A personal verbal form, as has been seen above (592), is ordinarily unaccented: before such a form, the prefix has its own accent; or, if two or more precede the same form, the one nearest the latter is so accented, and the others lose their accent.

b. If, however, the verb-form is accented, the prefix or prefixes lose their accent.

c. That is, in every case, the verb along with its normally situated prefix or prefixes so far constitutes a unity that the whole combination is allowed to take but a single accent.

d. Examples are: páre 'hi nāri púnar é 'hi kṣiprám (AV.) *go away, woman; come again quickly;* áthā́ 'staṁ vipáretana (RV.) *then scatter ye away to your home;* samā́cinuṣvā 'nusamprā́yāhi (AV.) *gather together, go forth together after;* yád gr̥hā́n upodáiti (AV.) *when he goes up to the house;* evā́ ca tvám sarama ājagántha (RV.) *now that you, Saramā, have thus come hither;* yénā́ "viṣṭitaḥ pravivéçithā 'páḥ (RV.) *enveloped in which thou didst enter the waters.*

1084. A prefix, however, not seldom has a more independent value, as a general adverb of direction, or as a preposition (in the usual modern sense of that term), belonging to and governing a noun; in such case, it is not drawn in to form part of a verbal compound, but has its own accent. The two kinds of use shade into one another, and are not divisible by any distinct and fixed line.

a. There is in RV. a considerable number of cases (some thirty) in which the **pada**-text gives unnecessarily, and probably wrongly, an independent accent to a prefix before an accented verb (or other prefix): resolving, for example, **ā́ruhat** into **ā́ áruhat, vyácet** into **ví ácet, abhyávarṣīt** into **abhí ávarṣīt, vyā́sarat** into **ví ā́ asarat** (instead of **ā-áruhat** etc.).

1085. In combination with the non-personal parts of the verb-system — with participles, infinitives, and gerunds — the general rule is that the prefix loses its accent, in favor of the other member of the compound. But the prefix instead has sometimes the accent: namely, when combined —

a. with the passive participle in **ta** or **na**: thus, **páreta** *gone forth;* **antárhita** *concealed;* **ávapanna** *fallen;* **sámpūrṇa** *complete* (cf. **1284**).

b. But some exceptions to this rule are met with: e. g., in RV., **nicitá, niṣkṛtá, praçastá, niṣattá**, etc.; in AV., **apakrītá**.

c. with the infinitive in **tu** (**972**), in all its cases: thus, **sáṁhartum** *to collect;* **ápidhātave** *to cover up;* **ávagantos** *of descending.* The doubly accented dative in **tavāí** retains its final accent, but throws the other back upon the prefix: thus, **ánvetavāí** *for following;* **ápabhartavāí** *for carrying off.*

1086. The closeness of combination between the root and the prefix is indicated not only by their unity of accent, but also by the euphonic rules (e. g. **185, 192**), which allow the mutual adaptations of the two to be made to some extent as if they were parts of a unitary word.

1087. A few special irregularities call for notice:

a. In the later language, **api, adhi**, and **ava**, in connection with certain roots and their derivatives, sometimes lose the initial vowel: namely, **api** with **nah** and **dhā, adhi** with **sthā, ava** with **gāh** etc.: e. g. **pinaddha, pihita, dhiṣṭhita, vagāhya, vataṅsa, vadānya, vaṣṭabhya, vamajjana, vekṣaṇa, valepana.** In the Veda, on the other hand, **iṣ** is in a few cases found instead (apparently) of **nis** with √**kṛ**.

b. The final vowel of a prefix, especially an **i**, is (oftenest in the older language) sometimes lengthened, especially in derivative words: e. g. **pratīkāra, nīvṛt, parīhāra, vīrúdh, adhīvāsá, ápīvṛta, abhīvartá; anūrúdh; avāyatī́, prāvṛ́ṣ, úpāvasu.** In the Veda, the initial of **anu** is sometimes lengthened after negative **an**: e. g. **anānudá, anānukṛtyá.**

c. In combination with √**i** *go*, the prefixes **parā, pari**, and **pra** sometimes change their **r** to **l**. In this way is formed a kind of derivative stem **palāy** *flee*, inflected according to the **a**-class, in middle voice, which is not uncommon from the Brāhmaṇas down, and has so lost the consciousness of its origin that it sometimes takes the augment prefixed: thus, **apalāyiṣṭhās** (ÇÇS.), **apalāyata** (R.), **apalāyanta** (MBh.); it makes the periphrastic perfect **palāyām cakre.** The stem **palyay,** similarly inflected, occurs only in one or two texts (ÇB. JB. JUB.); and **plāy** has been found nowhere except in MS. Also the imperfect **nílāyata** (TS. TB.: not separated in the **pada-text**) and perfect **nilayā́ṁ cakre** (ÇB.) are doubtless a corresponding formation from √**i** with **nis,** though nearly akin in form and meaning with forms from √**lī + ni.** So also **pari** becomes **pali** in the combination **palyaṅg** (ÇB. ÇÇS.), whether viewed as a denominative formation or as √**aṅg + pari.** And MS. has once **plā́kṣārayan** (iii. 10. 2; in an etymology).

d. The root **kṛ** *make* sometimes assumes (or retains from a more original condition) an initial **s** after the prefixes **sam, pari, nis,** and **upa:** thus, **saṁskurute, samaskurvan, saṁskṛta,** etc.; **pariṣkṛṇvanti, pariskṛta,** etc.; **nír askṛta; upaskṛta.** And √**kṝ** *scatter* is said by the grammarians to add **s** in the same manner, under certain circumstances, after **apa** and **prati** (only **apaskiramāṇa, praticaskare,** both late, are quotable).

e. The passive participle of the roots **dā** *give* and **dā** *cut* has often the abbreviated form **tta** after a prefix — of which the final vowel, if **i,** is lengthened (compare **955 f,** and the derivative in **ti,** below, **1157 c).**

f. In a few sporadic cases, the augment is taken before a prefix, instead of between it and the root: thus, **avaṣaṭkārṣīt** (GB.); **udaprapatat** (AB.); **anvasaṁcarat, pratyasaṁharat, pratyavyūhat, anvavīkṣetām, aprāiṣīt, asambhramat** (MBh.); **abhyanimantrayat** (Har.); **vyāvasthāpi** (SDS.); compare also the forms from **palāy,** above, **c.** And AB. has once **niniyoja** (for **niyuyoja,** as read in the corresponding passage of ÇÇS.). Some of the apparent roots of the language have been suspected of being results of a similar unification of root and prefix: e. g. **āp** from **ā + ap, vyac** from **vi + ac, tyaj** from **ati + aj.**

g. The loss of the initial **s** of **sthā** and **stambh** after the prefix **ud** has been noticed above (**233 c**). Also (**137 a, c**), certain peculiarities of combination of a prefix with the initial vowel of a root.

1088. As to the more general adverbial uses of the prefixes, and their prepositional uses, see the next chapter.

1089. As to the combination of the particles **a** or **an** privative, **dus** *ill,* and **su** *well,* with verb-forms, see **1121 b, g, i.** As to the addition of the comparative and superlative suffixes **tarām** and **tamām** to verbs, see above, **473 c.**

Other Verbal Compounds.

1090. It has been seen above that some of the prepositional prefixes are employed in combination with only very small classes of roots, namely those whose meaning makes them best fitted for auxiliary and periphrastic uses — such as **kṛ** *make,* **bhū** and **as** *be,* **dhā** *put,* **i** *go* — and that the first of these are widely used in combination with a derivative in **ām** to make a periphrastic conjugation. Such roots have also been, from the earliest period of the language, but with increasing frequency, used in somewhat analogous combinations with other elements, substantive and adjective as well as adverbial; and this has become, in part, developed finally into a regular and indefinitely extensible method of increasing the resources of verbal expression.

1091. a. The older language has a number of (mostly) reduplicative onomatopoetic compounds with roots **kṛ** and **bhū**, the prefixed element ending in **ā** or **ī** (generally the former): thus, in RV., **akkhalīkṛ́tya** *croaking*, **jañjanābhávant** *flimmering*, **alalābhávant** *making merry*, **kikirā́ kṛṇu** *tear;* in AV., **maṣmaṣā́ 'karam** *I have crushed;* in VS., **masmasā́** (also TS.; MS. **mṛsmṛsā́**) **kuru**; in TS., **malmalābhávant**; in K., **manmalābhavant, kikkitākāra**; in MS., **bibibābhávant, bharbharā́ 'bhavat**; in AB., **bababākurvant.** The accentuation, where shown, is like that of a verb-form with accompanying prefix.

b. Further, combinations with √**kṛ** of utterances used at the sacrifice, and mostly ending in **ā**: thus, **svā́hā, svadhā́, svagā́**; also **váṣaṭ.** In these, too, the accentuation is generally that of a verb with prefix: e. g. **svagākaróti** (ÇB.; but **svadhā́ karóti** [?] TA.), **vaṣaṭkuryā́t** (MS.); and, with another prefix, **anuváṣaṭkaroti** (ÇB.).

c. An instance or two also occur of ordinary words in such combinations, put in corresponding form: thus, **çūlā́ kuryāt** (ÇB.) *may roast on a spit* (**çū́la**); **anṛṇākartos** (AB.) *of getting clear of debt;* **āikyābhāvayant** (AA.) *uniting.*

1092. a. The noun **namas** *obeisance, homage,* in a still more purely noun-value, becomes combined with √**kṛ**: in the Veda, only with the gerund, in **namaskṛ́tya** (beside **hastagṛ́hya** and **karṇagṛ́hya**: above, **990 b**).

b. A solitary combination with √**i** *go* is shown by the accusative **ástam** *home:* which, appearing only in ordinary phrases in RV., is in AV. compounded with the participles — in **astaṁyánt, aṣtameṣyánt, ástamita** (with accent like that of ordinary compounds with a prefix) — and in the Brāhmaṇas and the later language is treated quite like a prefix: thus, **astaméti** (ÇB.).

c. Other ordinary accusative forms of adjectives in combination with verbal derivatives of **kṛ** and **bhū** are found here and there in the older language: thus, **çṛtaṁkṛ́tya** and **nagnaṁkṛ́tya** (TS.); **nagnambhā́vuka, pāmanambhā́vuka** etc. (TS. et al.); **ánaruṣkaroti** (ÇB.).

1093. In the early but not in the earliest language, a noun-stem thus compounded with **kṛ** or **bhū** (and very rarely with **as**), in verbal nouns and ordinary derivatives, and then also in verbal forms, begins to assume a constant ending **ī** (of doubtful origin).

a. There is no instance of this in RV., unless the **ī** of **akkhalīkṛ́tya** (above, **1091 a**) is to be so explained. In AV., besides the obscure

vātíkṛta and **vātīkārá**, is found only **phalīkáraṇa.** In the Brāhmaṇa language, examples begin to occur more often: thus, in TS., **çyetí, mithuní, muṣṭī**; in TB., further, **phalí, krūrí, udvāsī**; in ÇB., besides some of these, also **ekí, kālvālí, tīvrī, daridrī, brāhmaṇī, mithuní, sví**; and **açvābhidhānī,** of which (as of **muṣṭī**) the **ī** might be that of an ordinary grammatical form; in K., **dvī**; in GB., **pravaṇī**; in ṢB., **vajrī**; in AB., **matī** (from **matya**). From Upanishad and Sūtra are to be added **dvāitī** (MU.). **samī** (KÇS.), **navī** and **kuçalī** (AGS.). The accent is in general like that of the similar combinations treated above (**1091**): e.g. **krūrīkurvánti, svíkṛtya, brāhmaṇībhū́ya, mithunībhávantyāu, phalīkartavāí, krūrī́kṛta**; but sometimes a mere collocation takes place: thus, **mithuní bhávantīs** (TS.), **phalí kriyámāṇānām** (TB.), **vajrī bhūtvā́** (TA.). The **ī** is variously treated: now as an uncombinable final, as in **çyetī́ akuruta** and **mithunī́ abhavan** (TS.); now as liable to the ordinary conversions, as in **mithuny ènayā syām, mithuny àbhiḥ syām,** and **svyàkurvata** (ÇB.).

b. Out of such beginnings has grown in the later language the following rule:

1094. Any noun or adjective stem is liable to be compounded with verbal forms or derivatives of the roots √कृ **kṛ** and भू **bhū** (and of अस् **as** also; but such cases are extremely rare), in the manner of a verbal prefix. If the final of the stem be an **a-** or **i-**vowel, it is changed to ई **ī**; if an **u-**vowel, it is changed to ऊ **ū**.

a. Examples are: **stambhībhavati** *becomes a post;* **ekacittībhūya** *becoming of one mind;* **upahārīkaroṣi** *thou makest an offering;* **nakhaprahārajarjarīkṛta** *torn to pieces with blows of the claws;* **çithilībhavanti** *become loose;* **kuṇḍalīkṛta** *ring-shaped;* **surabhīkṛta** *made fragrant;* **ādhīkaraṇa** *pawning;* **ṛjūkṛtya** *straightening;* **hetūkaraṇa** *taking as cause.* As in the case of the denominatives (**1059 c**), the combinations with **a**-stems are the immense majority, and occur abundantly (hardly less than a thousand are quotable) in the later language, but for the most part only once or twice each; those made with **i-** and **u**-stems are a very small number. In a few instances, stems in **an** and **as,** with those finals changed to **ī,** are met with: e. g. **ātmī-kṛ, yuvī-bhū; unmanī-kṛ, amanī-bhū**; final **ya** after a consonant is contracted to **ī**: e. g. **kāṅsī-kṛ**; and anomalous cases like **kāṁdiçī-bhū** occur. Final **ṛ** is said to become **rī,** but no examples are quotable. The combinations with **kṛ** are about twice as frequent as those with **bhū,** and examples with **as** do not appear to have been brought to light.

b. Similar combinations are occasionally made with elements of questionable or altogether obscure character: e. g. **urarī-kṛ, urī-kṛ.**

c. Examples are not altogether wanting in the later language of **ā** as final of the compounded noun-stem (cf. 1091): thus, **duḥkhā-kṛ, niṣkulā-kṛ, çambā-kṛ,** and one or two others.

1095. **Of all the forms which constitute or are attached to the verbal system, the passive participle is the one most closely assimilated in its treatment as a combinable element to an ordinary adjective. Next to it come the gerund and the gerundives. Combinations of the kind above treated of are quite common with passive participles and gerunds.**

CHAPTER XVI.

INDECLINABLES.

1096. THE indeclinable words are less distinctly divided into separate parts of speech in Sanskrit than is usual elsewhere in Indo-European language — especially owing to the fact that the class of prepositions hardly has a real existence, but is represented by certain adverbial words which are to a greater or less extent used prepositionally. They will, however, be briefly described here under the usual heads.

Adverbs.

1097. Adverbs by Suffix. Classes of adverbs, sometimes of considerable extent, are formed by the addition of adverb-making suffixes especially to pronominal roots or stems, but also to noun and adjective stems.

a. There is no ultimate difference between such suffixes and the case-endings in declension; and the adverbs of this division sometimes are used in the manner of cases.

1098. With the suffix **tas** are made adverbs having an ablative sense, and not rarely also an ablative construction. Such are made:

a. From pronominal roots, in **átas, itás, tátas, yátas, kútas, amútas, svatas** (not found earlier); from the pronominal stems in **t** or d (494) of the personal pronouns: thus, **mattás** (only example in V.), **tvattas, asmattas, yuṣmattas**; and from pronominal derivatives: thus, **itarátas, katarátas.**

b. From noun and adjective stems of every class, since the earliest period, but more freely later: e. g. **mukhatás, agratás, ṛbhutás, ṛktás, hṛttás, çīrṣatás, janmatas, nastás, yajuṣṭas, pārátas, anyátas, anyatarátas, sarvátas, dakṣiṇatás, abhīpatás** (once, in RV., from a case-form: **patsutás**).

c. From a few prepositions: thus, **abhítas, parítas, ántitas.**

d. Examples of ablative construction are: **áto bhū́yaḥ** (RV.) *more than that;* **tátaḥ ṣaṣṭhā́t** (AV.) *from that sixth;* **áto 'nyéna** (ÇB.) *with any other than this;* **sarvato bhayāt** (AGS.) *from all fear;* **kutaç cid deçād ā́gatya** (H.) *arriving from some region or other;* **purād itaḥ** (R.) *from this city;* **tasmāt pretakāyataḥ** (KSS.) *from that dead body.*

e. But the distinctive ablative meaning is not infrequently effaced, and the adverb has a more general, especially a locative, value: thus, **agratás** *in front;* **asmatsamīpatas** *in our presence;* **dharmatas** *in accordance with duty;* **chāgatas** (H.) *with reference to the goat;* **guṇato 'dhikaḥ** (M.) *superior in virtue.*

1099. With the suffix **tra** (in the older language often **trā**) are made adverbs having a locative sense, and occasionally also a locative construction.

a. These adverbs are very few, compared with those in **tas.** They are formed chiefly from pronominal stems, and from other stems having a quasi-pronominal character: namely, in **tra, átra, tátra, yátra, kútra, amútra, anyátra, viçvátra, sarvátra, ubhayátra, aparatra, uttaratra, itarátra, anyataratra, pūrvatra, paratra, samānátra, ekatra, anekatra, ekāikatra**; in **trā, asmatrā́, satrā́, purutrā́, bahutrā́, dakṣiṇatrā́.** But a few in **trā** come from ordinary nouns: thus, **devatrā́, martyatrā́, puruṣatrā́, manuṣyatrā́, pākatrā́, çayutrā́, kurupañcālatrā́.** Those in **trā** are distinguished from the others by their accent.

b. Examples of locative construction are: **hásta ā́ dakṣiṇatrā́** (RV.) *in the right hand;* **yátrā́ 'dhi** (RV.) *in which;* **ekatra puruṣe** (MBh.) *in a single man;* **atra mārātmake** (H.) *in this murderous creature*; **prabhutvaṁ tatra yujyate** (H.) *sovereignty befits him.* And, as the locative case is used also to express the goal of motion (304), so the adverbs in **tra** have sometimes an accusative as well as a locative value: thus, **tatra gaccha** *go there* or *thither;* **pathó devatrā́ yā́nān** (RV.) *roads that go to the gods.*

1100. One or two other suffixes of locality are:

a. **ha**, in **ihá** *here*, **kúha** *where?* and the Vedic **viçváha** (also **viçváhā, viçvā́hā**) *always* (compare below, 1104b); and **ihá** (like **átra** etc.:

1099 b) is sometimes used with locative-case value: e. g. **iha samaye** (H.) *at this conjuncture.*

b. tāt, which is added to words having already a local or directive value: thus, to adverbial accusatives, **prāktāt, údaktāt, tā́vattāt**; to adverbial ablatives, **ārā́ttāt, uttarā́ttāt, parākā́ttāt**; and to prepositional adverbs, **paçcā́tāt, adhástāt, avástāt, parástāt, purástāt, bahíṣṭāt**. Apparently by analogy with these last, the suffix has the form **stāt** in **upáriṣṭāt** (and BhP. has **udastāt**).

c. hi, in **uttarāhi** (ÇB.) and **dakṣiṇāhi** (not quotable).

1101. By the suffix **thā** are made adverbs of manner, especially from pronominal roots or stems.

a. Thus, **táthā, yáthā; kathā́** and **itthā́** (by the side of which stand **kathám** and **itthám**; and ÇB. has **itthā́t**); and the rare **imáthā** and **amúthā**. And **átha** (V. often **áthā**) *so then* doubtless belongs with them. Further, from a few adjective and noun stems, mostly of quasi-pronominal character: thus, **viçváthā, sarváthā, anyáthā, ubhayáthā, aparathā, itaráthā, yataráthā, yatamáthā, katarathā, katamathā, pūrváthā, pratnáthā, ūrdhváthā, tiraçcáthā, ekathā** (JB.), **ṛtuthā́, nāmáthā** (once, AV.); and **eváthā**.

b. Yáthā becomes usually toneless in V., when used in the sense of **iva** after a noun forming the subject of comparison: thus, **tāyávo yathā** (RV.) *like thieves.*

1102. One or two other suffixes of manner are:

a. ti, in **íti** *thus*, very commonly used, from the earliest period, especially as particle of quotation, following the words quoted.

b. Examples are: **brahmajāyé 'yám íti céd ávocan** (RV.) *if they have said "this is a Brahman's wife"*; **táṁ devā́ abruvan vrā́tya kíṁ nú tiṣṭhasī́ 'ti** (AV.) *the gods said to him: "Vrātya, why do you stand?"* Often, the **iti** is used more pregnantly: thus, **yáḥ çraddádhāti sánti devā́ íti** (AV.) *whoever has faith that the gods exist;* **taṁ vyāghram munir mūṣiko 'yam iti paçyati** (H.) *the sage looks upon that tiger as being really a mouse;* **yūyaṁ kim iti sīdatha** (H.) *why* (lit. *alleging what reason*) *do you sit?*

c. But **iti** is sometimes used in a less specialized way, to mark an onomatopœia, or to indicate a gesture: e. g. **bahíṣ ṭe astu bā́l íti** (AV.) *let it come out of you with a splash;* **íty ágre kṛṣáty áthé 'ti** (ÇB.) *he ploughs first this way, then this way;* or it points forward to something to be said: e. g. **yan nv ity āhur anyāni chandāṅsi varṣīyāṅsi kasmād bṛhaty ucyata iti** (PB.) *when now they say thus: "the other metres are greater; why is the* **bṛhatī** *spoken?"* It also makes a number of derivatives and compounds: e. g. **ititha** *the so-many-eth;* **itivat** *in this fashion;* **ityartham** *for this purpose;* **itihāsa** *a story* or *legend* (lit. *thus forsooth it was*). As to the use of a nominative with **iti** as predicate to an accusative, see **268 b**.

d. With the suffix of **íti** is to be compared that of **táti** etc. (519). The word is abbreviated to **ti** two or three times in ÇB.

e. va in **iva** (toneless) *like, as*, and **evá** (in V. often **evā́**), earlier *thus*, later a particle emphasizing the preceding word; for *thus* is used later the related **evám**, which hardly occurs in RV., and in AV. only with √**vid**: as, **eváṁ vidvā́n** *knowing thus*.

f. In later Vedic (AV. etc., and the later parts of RV.) **iva** more often counts for only a single syllable, **'va**.

1103. **a.** By the suffix **dā** are made adverbs of time, but almost only from pronominal roots.

b. Thus, **tadā́**, **yadā́**, **kadā́** (in RV. also **kádā**), **idā́** (only in V.); and **sádā**, beside which is found earlier **sádam**. Besides these, in the older language, only **sarvadā́**; later a few others, **anyadā**, **ekadā**, **nityadā**. A quasi-locative case use is seen occasionally in such phrases as **kadācid divase** (R.) *on a certain day*.

c. By the perhaps related **dānīm** are made **idā́nīm**, **tadā́nīm**, **viçvadā́nīm**, **tvadānīm** (toneless). **Viçvadā́ni** occurs as adjective in TB.

d. With **rhi** are made, from pronominal roots, **tárhi**, **etárhi**, **yárhi**, **kárhi**, **amúrhi**.

e. The suffix **di**, found only in **yádi** *if*, is perhaps related with **dā**, in form as in meaning. **Sadadí** (MS.) is of doubtful character.

1104. By the suffix **dhā** are formed adverbs especially from numerals, signifying *-fold, times, ways*, etc.

a. Thus, **ekadhā́**, **dvidhā́** (also **dvídhā** and **dvedhā́**), **trídhā** (in the older language usually **tredhā́**), **ṣaḍḍhā́** (also **ṣoḍhā́** and **ṣaḍdhā**), **dvādaçadhā́**, **ekānnaviṅçatidhā́**, **sahasradhā́**, and so on. Also, naturally, from words having a quasi-numeral character: thus, **anekadhā**, **katidhā́**, **tatidhā́**, **bahudhā́**, **purudhā́**, **viçvádhā**, **çaçvadhā́**, **aparimitadhā**, **yāvaddhā́**, **etāvaddhā́**, **māsadhā**. In a very few cases, also from general noun and adjective stems: thus, **mitradhā́** (AV.), **priyadhā́** (TS.; **predhā́**, MS.), **ṛjudhā́** (TB.), **urudhā** and **citradhā** (BhP.); and from one adverb, **bahirdhā́**.

b. The particle **ádha** or **ádhā**, a Vedic equivalent of **átha**, probably belongs here (**purudhá** and **viçvádha**, with shortened final, occur a few times in RV.); also **addhā́** *in truth;* and perhaps **sahá** *with*, which has an equivalent **sadha-** in several Vedic compounds. And the other adverbs in **ha** (1100a) may be of like origin.

1105. From a few numerals are made multiplicative adverbs with **s**: namely, **dvís**, **trís**, and **catúr** (probably, for **catúrs**): **489a**.

a. The corresponding word for *once*, **sakṛ́t**, is a compound rather than a derivative; and the same character belongs still more evidently to **pañcakṛtvas**, **navakṛtvas**, **aparimitakṛtvas**, etc., though **kṛt** and **kṛtvas** are regarded by the native grammarians as suffixes; the earlier texts (AV. ÇB. MS.) have **saptá kṛ́tvas, dáça kṛ́tvas, dvā́daça kṛ́tvas, aṣṭā́v evá kṛ́tvas**, etc. AP. has the redundant combination **triṣ kṛtvaḥ**.

b. The quasi-suffix **dyus**, from a case-form of **div** *day*, is in a similar manner added to various determining words, generally made to end in **e**: e. g. **anyedyús** *another day*, **ubhayedyus** (AV. **-yadyús**) *on either day*, **pūrvedyús** *the day before*.

1106. By the suffix **çás** are made, especially from numeral or quantitative stems, many adverbs of quantity or measure or manner, generally used distributively:

a. Examples are: **ekaçás** *one by one*, **çataçás** *by hundreds*, **ṛtuçás** *season by season*, **pacchas** *foot by foot*, **akṣaraçás** *syllable by syllable*, **gaṇaçás** *in crowds*, **stambaçás** *by bunches*, **paruççás** *limb by limb*, **tāvacchás** *in such and such number* or *quantity*: and, in a more general way, **sarvaçás** *wholly*, **mukhyaças** *principally*, **kṛchraças** *stingily*, **manmaçás** *as minded*.

1107. By the suffix **vát** are made with great freedom, in every period of the language, adverbs signifying *after the manner of*, *like*, etc.

a. Thus, **aṅgirasvát** *like Angiras*, **manuṣvát** (RV.) *as Manu did*, **jamadagnivát** *after the manner of Jamadagni*; **pūrvavát** or **pratnavát** or **purāṇavát**, *as of old*, **kākatālīyavat** *after the fashion of the crow and the palm-fruit*.

b. This is really the adverbially used accusative (with adverbial shift of accent: below, **1111 g**) of the suffix **vant** (**1233 f**), which in the Veda makes certain adjective compounds of a similar meaning: thus, **tvā́vant** *like thee*, **mā́vant** *of my sort*, etc.

1108. By the suffix **sāt** are made from nouns quasi-adverbs signifying *in* or *into the condition* or *the possession of* what is indicated by the noun; they are used only with verbs of being, of becoming, and of making: namely, oftenest **kṛ** and **bhū**, but also **as, gam, yā**, and **nī** (and, according to the grammarians, **sam-pad**). Some twenty-five examples are quotable from the later literature; but none from the earlier, which also appears to contain nothing that casts light upon the origin of the formation. The **s** of **sāt** is not liable to conversion into **ṣ**. The connection with the verb is not so close as to require the use of the gerund in **ya** instead of that in **tvā** (**990**); and other words are sometimes interposed between the adverb and verb.

a. Examples are: **sarvakarmāṇi bhasmasāt kurute** (MBh.) *reduces all deeds to ashes*; **loko 'yam dasyusād bhaved** (MBh.) *this world would become a prey to barbarians*; **yasya brāhmaṇasāt sarvaṁ vittam āsīt** (MBh.) *whose whole property was given to Brahmans*; **niyataṁ bhasmasād yāti** (Har.) *it is inevitably reduced to ashes*; **agnīn ātmasāt kṛtvā** (Y.) *having taken the fires to one's self*.

1109. a. Suffixes, not of noun-derivation or of inflection, may be traced with more or less plausibility in a few other adverbs. Thus, for example, in **prātár** *early*, and **sanutár** *away;* in **dakṣiṇít** *with right hand*, and **cikitvít** *with consideration;* in **nūnám** *now*, and **nānānám** *variously*. But the cases are in the main too rare and doubtful to be worth notice here.

b. In the epics begin to be found a small class (about a dozen are quotable) of adverbs having the form of a repeated noun-stem with its first occurrence ending in **ā** and its second in **i**: e. g. **hastāhasti** *hand to hand*, **rathārathi** *chariot against chariot*, **karṇākarṇi** *ear to ear*.

c. The adverbs thus far described are almost never used prepositionally. Those of the next division, however, are in many instances so used.

1110. Case-forms used as Adverbs. A large number of adverbs are more or less evidently cases in form, made from stems which are not otherwise in use. Also many cases of known stems, pronominal or noun or adjective, are used with an adverbial value, being distinguished from proper cases by some difference of application, which is sometimes accompanied by an irregularity of form.

1111. The accusative is the case most frequently and widely used adverbially. Thus:

a. Of pronominal stems: as, **yád** *if, when, that*, etc.; **tád** *then* etc.; **kím** *why, whether*, etc.; **idám** *now, here;* **adás** *yonder;* and so on. Of like value, apparently, are the (mostly Vedic) particles **kád, kám** and **kam** (?), **íd, cid** (common at every period), **smád** and **sumád, īm** and **sīm** (by some regarded as still possessing pronoun-value), **-kīm**. Compounds with **íd** are **céd** *if*, **néd** *lest*, **éd, svid, kuvíd;** with **cid, kúcid;** with **-kīm, nákīm** and **mā́kīm**, and **ā́kīm**.

b. Of noun-stems: as, **nā́ma** *by name;* **súkham** *happily;* **kā́mam** *at will, if you please;* **náktam** *by night;* **ráhas** *secretly;* **oṣám** *quickly* (V.); and so on.

c. Of adjective stems, in unlimited numbers: as, **satyám** *truly*, **cirám** *long;* **pū́rvam** *formerly;* **nítyam** *constantly;* **bhū́yas** *more, again;* **viçrabdham** *confidently;* **prakāçam** *openly;* and so on.

d. The neuter singular is the case commonly employed in this way; and it is so used especially as made from great numbers of compound adjective stems, often from such as hardly occur, or are not at all found, in adjective use. Certain of these adverbial compounds, having an indeclinable as prior member, are made by the Hindu grammarians a special class of compounds, called **avyayībhāva** (1313).

e. But the feminine singular also is sometimes used, especially in the so-called adverbial endings of comparison, **tarām** and **tamām**, which are attached to particles (cf. 1119), and even (473c) to verb-forms:

e. g. **natarā́m, kathaṁtarā́m, uccaistarā́m, çanāistarā́m, jyoktamā́m.** In the oldest language (RV. and AV.), the neuter instead of the feminine form of these suffixes is almost alone in use: see **1119**.

f. Many adverbs of obscure form or connection are to be explained with probability as accusatives of obsolete noun or adjective stems: examples are **tūṣṇī́m** *in silence;* **sāyám** *at evening;* **sākám** *together, with* (prep.); **áram** or **álam** *sufficient* (in the later language used with √**kṛ** in the manner of a prefix: **1078 a**); **prāyas** *usually;* **īṣát** *somewhat;* **amnás** *unexpectedly;* **bahís** *outside;* **míthu** and **mitháṣ, múhu** and **múhus, jā́tu,** and so on. **Madrík** etc., and **niṇík** (in RV.), are perhaps contracted forms of adjectives having √**ac** or **añc** as their final (**407** ff.). The presence of other roots as final members is also probable for **uçádhak, ānuṣák** and **āyuṣák, anuṣṭhú** and **suṣṭhú, yugapát,** etc. Compare also the forms in **am** beside those in **ā**, above, **1101 a, 1102 e, 1103 b.**

g. In (Vedic) **dravát** *quickly* is to be seen a change of accent for the adverbial use (pple **drávant** *running*); and **drahyát** *stoutly* (RV., once) may be another example. The comparative and superlative suffixes (above, **e**) show a like change; and it is also to be recognized in the derivatives with **vát** (**1107**).

1112. The **instrumental** is also often used with adverbial value: generally in the singular, but sometimes also in the plural. Thus:

a. Of pronominal stems: as, **enā́** and **ayā́, káyā, anā́, amā́, amuyā́.**

b. Of noun-stems: as, **kṣaṇena** *instantly;* **açeṣeṇa** *completely;* **viçeṣeṇa** *especially;* **dívā** *by day;* **diṣṭyā** *fortunately;* **sáhasā** *suddenly;* **aktubhis** *by night;* and so on.

c. Of adjectives, both neuter (not distinguishable from masculine) and feminine: as, **akhilena** *wholly;* **prāyeṇa** *mostly;* **dákṣiṇena** *to the south;* **úttareṇa** *to the north;* **ántareṇa** *within;* **ciréṇa** *long;* — **çánāis** and **çanakāis** *slowly;* **uccāís** *on high;* **nīcāís** *below;* **parācāís** *afar;* **táviṣībhis** *mightily;* and so on.

d. More doubtful cases, mostly from the older language, may be instanced as follows: **tiraçcátā, devátā, bāhúta,** and **sasvártā** (all RV.), homonymous instrumentals from nouns in **tā**; **dvitā́, tādī́tnā, īrmā́, mṛṣā́, vṛ́thā, sácā, asthā́** (?), **mudhā** (not V.), **adhunā́** (B. and later).

e. Adverbially used instrumentals are (in the older language), oftener than any other case, distinguished from normal instrumentals by differences of form: thus, especially, by an irregular accent: as, **amā́** and **dívā** (given above); perhaps **gúhā**; **apākā́, āsayā́, kuhayā́** (?); **naktayā́, svapnayā́, samanā́; adatrayā́, ṛtayā́, ubhayā́, sumnayā́** (?); **dakṣiṇā́, madhyā́; nīcā́, prācā́, uccā́, paççā́, tiraççā́; vasántā;** — in a few **u**-stems, by a **y** inserted before the ending, which is accented: thus, **amuyā́** (given above), **āçuyā́, sādhuyā́, raghuyā́, dhṛṣṇuyā́, anuṣ-**

ṭhuyā́, mithuyā́; — and **urviyā́** (for **urvyā́**) and **víçvyā** (properly **víçvayā**) are more slightly irregular.

1113. The dative has only very seldom an adverbial use.

a. Examples are **aparā́ya** *for the future* (RV.; with changed accent); **cirāya** *long;* **arthāya** *for the sake of;* **ahnāya** *presently.*

1114. The ablative is not infrequently used adverbially. Thus:

a. Of pronominal stems: as, **kásmāt** *why?* **akasmāt** *casually, unexpectedly;* **ā́t, tā́t, yā́t** (V.: normal forms, instead of the pronominal **asmāt** etc.).

b. Of noun-stems: as, **āsā́t** *near;* **ārāt** *afar;* **balāt** *forcibly;* **kutūhalāt** *emulously;* **sakāçāt** *on the part of.*

c. Oftenest, of adjective stems: as, **dūrā́t** *afar;* **nīcā́t** *below;* **paçcā́t** *behind;* **sākṣā́t** *plainly, actually;* **samantāt** *completely;* **acirāt** *not long;* **pratyakṣatamāt** (AB.) *most obviously;* **pratyantāt** (S.) *to the end.*

d. In a few instances, adverbially used ablatives likewise show a changed accent in the early language: thus, **apākā́t** *from afar;* **amā́t** *from near by;* **sanā́t** *from of old* (but instr. **sánā**); **uttarā́t** *from the north;* **adharā́t** *below.*

1115. The genitive is almost never used adverbially.

a. In the older language occur **aktós** *by night*, and **vástos** *by day;* later, **cirasya** *long.*

1116. The locative is sometimes used with adverbial value. Thus:

a. From noun and adjective stems: **āké** *near;* **āré** and **dūré** *afar;* **abhisvaré** *behind;* **astamīké** *at home;* **ṛté** *without* (prep.); **ágre** *in front;* **sthāne** *suitably;* **sapadi** *immediately;* **-arthe** and **-kṛte** (common in composition) *for the sake of;* **aparíṣu** *in after time;* **ādāu** *first;* **rahasi** *in secret.*

1117. Even a nominative form appears to be stereotyped into an adverbial value in (Vedic) **kís**, interrogative particle, and its compounds **nákis** and **mā́kis**, negative particles. And masc. nominatives from **añc**-stems (as **parāñ** AB., **nyañ** Āpast.) are sometimes found used by substitution for neuters.

1118. Verbal Prefixes and kindred words. The verbal prefixes, described in the preceding chapter (1076 ff.), are properly adverbs, having a special office and mode of use in connection with verbal roots and their more immediate derivatives.

a. Their occasional looser connection with the verb has been noticed above (1084). In the value of general adverbs, however, they only rarely occur (except as ápi has mainly changed its office from prefix to adverb or conjunction in the later language); but their prepositional uses are much more frequent and important: see below, **1125b.**

b. In composition with nouns, they (like other adverbial elements) not infrequently have an adjective value: see below, **1281** ff., **1305**.

1119. Several of the prefixes (as noticed above, **473—4**) form comparative and superlative adjectives, by the suffixes **tara** and **tama,** or **ra** and **ma:** thus, **úttara** and **uttamá, ádhara** and **adhamá, ápara** and **apamá, ávara** and **avamá, úpara** and **upamá,** and **prathamá** is doubtless of the same character; also, **ántara** and **ántama.** And accusatives of such derivative adjectives (for the most part not otherwise found in use) have the value of comparatives, and rarely superlatives, to the prefixes themselves: thus, **sáṁçitaṁ cit saṁtaráṁ sáṁ çiçādhi** (AV.) *whatever is quickened do thou still further quicken;* **vitaráṁ ví kramasva** (RV.) *stride out yet more widely;* **prá táṁ naya prataráṁ vásyo ácha** (RV.) *lead him forward still further toward advantage;* **úd enam uttaráṁ naya** (ÁV.) *lead him up still higher.*

a. Besides those instanced, are found also **nitarám, apatarám, abhitarám, avatarám, parātarám, parastarám.** In the Brāhmaṇas and later (above, **1111e**), the feminine accusative is used instead: thus, **atitarā́m** and **atitamām, abhitarā́m, anutamā́m, ātamā́m, pratitarā́m, nitarā́m, uttarā́m, pratarā́m** and **pratamā́m, vitarā́m, saṁtarā́m** (also RV., once).

1120. Kindred in origin and character with the verbal prefixes, and used like them except in composition with verbs, are a few other adverbs: thus, **avás** *down;* **adhás** *below* (and **adhastarā́m**); **parás** *far off* (and **parastarā́m**); **purā́** *before;* **antarā́** (apparently, **antár + ā́**) *among, between;* **ánti** *near;* **upári** *above;* and **sahá** (already mentioned, **1104b**) *along, with,* and **sácā** *together, with,* may be noticed with them. **Vinā́** *without,* and **viṣu-** *apart,* appear to be related with **ví.**

1121. Inseparable Prefixes. A small number of adverbial prefixes are found only in combination with other elements. Thus:

a. The negative prefix **a** or **an** — **an** before vowels, **a** before consonants.

b. It is combined especially with innumerable nouns and adjectives; much more rarely, with adverbs, as **akútra** and **ápunar** (RV.), **áneva** (AV.), **ánadhas** (TB.), **akasmāt, asakṛt;** in rare cases, also with pronouns (as **atad, akiṁcit**); and even, in the later language, now and then with verbs, as **aspṛhayanti** (BhP. Çiç.) *they do not desire,* **alokayati** (SD.) *he does not view.* Now and then it is prefixed to itself: e. g. **anakāmamāra, anaviprayukta, anavadya** (?).

c. In a very few cases, the negative a appears to be made long: thus, **ā́sat** *non-existent*, **ā́deva** *godless*, **ā́rāti** *enemy*, **āçāuca** *impurity*, **ātura** *ill(?)*.

d. The independent negative adverbs, **ná** and **mā́**, are only in exceptional instances used in composition: see below, **1122 e**.

e. The comitative prefix **sa**, used instead of the preposition **sám**, and interchangeably with **sahá**, before nouns and adjectives.

f. The prefix of dispraise **dus** *ill*, *badly* (identical with √**duṣ**: **225 a**).

g. It is combined in the same manner as **a** or **an**. Of combinations with a verbal form, at least a single example appears to be quotable: **duçcaranti** (R.) *behave ill*.

h. The corresponding laudatory prefix **su** *well* is in general so closely accordant in its use with the preceding that it is best mentioned here though it occurs not rarely as an independent particle in the oldest language (in RV., more than two hundred times; in the peculiar parts of AV., only fourteen times), and even occasionally later.

i. The particle **su** sometimes appears in B. and later before a verbform, and considering its rapid loss of independent use in V., and the analogy of **a** and **dus** (above, **b**, **g**) it is probably at least in part to be regarded as in composition with the verb. The **pada**-text of AV. xix. 49. 10 reads **su-ápāyati**, but its testimony is of little or no value. K. has **na su vijñāyete** and **na vāi su viduḥ**, and KeU. has **su veda**; TB. has **susámbodháyati**(?); MBh. and BhP. have **sūpatasthe**; R. has **suçakyante**.

j. The exclamatory and usually depreciative prefixed forms of the interrogative pronoun (**506**) are most analogous with the inseparable prefixes.

1122. Miscellaneous Adverbs. Other words of adverbial character and office, not clearly referable to any of the classes hitherto treated, may be mentioned as follows:

a. Asseverative particles (in part, only in the older language): thus, **aṅgá**, **hánta**, **kíla**, **khálu**, **tú** (rare in older language), **vāí**, **vā́vá** (in Brāhmaṇa language only), **hi**, **hiná**, **u**, **áha**, **ha**, **gha**, **samaha**, **sma**, **bhala**.

b. Of these, **hánta** is a word of assent and incitement; **hí** has won also an illative meaning, and accents the verb with which it stands in connection (**595 e**); **sma** sometimes appears to give a past meaning to a present tense (**778 b**); **u** is often combined with the final **a** of other particles: thus, **átho**, **nó**, **mó**, **utó**, **úpo**, **pró**; but also with that of verbforms, as **dattó**, **vidmó**. The final **o** thus produced is **pragṛhya** or uncombinable (**138 c**). Particles of kindred value, already mentioned above, are **íd, kám** or **kam, cid, jā́tu, evá.** Some of the asseverative particles are much used in the later artificial poetry with a purely expletive value, as devices to help make out the metre (**pādapūraṇa** *verse-fillers*); so especially **ha, hi, tu, sma.**

c. Negative particles are: **ná**, signifying simple negation; **mā́**, signifying prohibition.

d. As to the construction of the verb with **mā́**, see above, **579**. In the Veda, **nú** (or **nū́**: **248 a**) has also sometimes a negative meaning. For the Vedic **ná** of comparison, see below, **g, h.**

e. In **nahí, ná** is combined with **hí**, both elements retaining their full meaning; also, with **íd** in **néd** *lest.* It is perhaps present in **nanú** and **caná,** but not in **hiná** (RV., once). In general, neither **ná** nor **mā́** is used in composition to make negative compounds, but, instead, the inseparable negative prefix **a** or **an** (**1121 a**): exceptions are the Vedic particles **nákis** and **mā́kis, nákīm** and **mā́kīm;** also **naciram** and **māciram, napuṅsaka,** and, in the later language, a number of others.

f. Interrogative particles are only those already given: **kád, kim, kuvíd, svid, nanú,** of which the last introduces an objection or expostulation.

g. Of particles of comparison have been mentioned the toneless **iva,** and **yathā** (also toneless when used in the same way). Of frequent occurrence in the oldest language is also **ná,** having (without loss of accent) the same position and value as the preceding.

h. Examples of the **ná** of comparison are: **ṛṣidvíṣa íṣuṁ ná sṛjata dvíṣam** (RV.) *let loose your enmity like an arrow at the enemy of the singer;* **váyo ná vṛkṣám** (AV.) *as birds to the tree;* **gāuró ná tṛṣitáḥ piba** (RV.) *drink like a thirsty buffalo.* This use is generally explained as being a modification or adaptation of the negative one: thus, *[although, to be sure] not [precisely] a thirsty buffalo;* and so on.

i. Of particles of place, besides those already mentioned, may be noticed **kvà** *where?* (in V., always to be read **kúa**).

j. Particles of time are: **nú** *now* (also **nū́: nūnám** was mentioned above, **1109 a**), **adyá** and **sadyás** and **sadívas** (RV., once) *today, at once* (all held to contain the element **div** or **dyu**), **hyás** *yesterday,* **çvás** *tomorrow,* **jyók** (also related with **dyu**) *long;* **púnar** *again.*

k. Of particles of manner, besides those already mentioned, may be noticed **nā́nā** *variously* (for **nānānám,** its derivative, see **1109 a**); **sasvár** (RV.) *secretly.*

l. In the above classifications are included all the Vedic adverbial words, and most of those of the later language: for the rest, see the dictionaries.

Prepositions.

1123. There is, as already stated, no proper class of prepositions (in the modern sense of that term), no body of words having for their prevailing office the "government" of nouns. But many of the adverbial words indicated above are used with nouns in a way which approximates them to the more fully developed prepositions of other languages.

a. If one and another of such words — as **vinā, ṛte** — occurs almost solely in prepositional use, this is merely fortuitous and unessential.

1124. Words are thus used prepositionally along with all the noun-cases excepting the dative. But in general their office is directive only, determining more definitely, or strengthening, the proper case-use of the noun. Sometimes, however, the case-use is not easy to trace, and the noun then seems to be more immediately "governed" by the preposition — that is, to have its case-form more arbitrarily determined by its association with the latter. This is oftenest true of the accusative; and also of the genitive, which has, here as elsewhere (**294 b**), suffered an extension of its normal sphere of use.

1125. a. The adverbs by derivative form (**1097** ff.) have least of a prepositional value (exceptions are especially a few made with the suffix **tas: 1098**).

b. Most of the verbal prefixes (exceptions are **ud, ni, parā, pra**; and **ava** and **vi** are almost such) have their prepositional or quasi-prepositional uses with cases; but much more widely in the older time than in the later: in the classical language the usage is mainly restricted to **prati, anu,** and **ā**.

c. Most of the directive words akin with the more proper prefixes are used prepositionally: some of them — as **saha, vinā, upari, antarā, purā** — freely, earlier and later.

d. The case-forms used adverbially are in many instances used prepositionally also: oftenest, as was to be expected, with the genitive; but frequently, and from an early time, with the accusative; more rarely with other cases.

e. We will take up now the cases for a brief exposition, beginning with those that are least freely used.

1126. The Locative. This case is least of all used with words that can claim the name of preposition. Of directives, **antár** and its later derivative **antarā́**, meaning *within, in,* are oftenest added to it, and in the classical language as well as earlier. Of frequent Vedic use with it are **ā́** and **ádhi**: thus, **mártyeṣv ā́** *among mortals;* **pṛthivyā́m ádhy óṣadhīḥ** *the plants upon the earth;* **téjo máyi dhārayā́ 'dhi** (AV.) *establish glory* *in me;* — **ápi** and **úpa** are much rarer: thus, **yā́ apā́m ápi vratè** [**sánti**] (RV.) *who are in the domain of the waters;* **amū́r yā́ úpa sū́rye** [**sánti**] (RV.) *who are up yonder in the sun;* — **sácā** *along with* is not rare in RV., but almost entirely unknown later: thus, **pitróḥ sácā satī́** *staying with her parents.*

1127. The Instrumental. The directives used with this case are almost only those which contain the associative pronominal root **sa**: as **sahá** (most frequent), **sākám, sārdhám, samám, samáyā, sarátham**; and, in the Veda, the prefix **sám**: as, **te sumatíbhiḥ sám pátnībhir ná vṛ́ṣaṇo nasīmahi** (RV.) *may we be united with thy favors as men with their spouses.* By substitution of the instrumental for the ablative of separation (**283 a**), **vinā** *without* (not Vedic) takes sometimes the instrumental; and so, in the Veda, **avás** *down* and **parás** *beyond*, with which the ablative is also, and much more normally, construed. And **ádhi**, in RV., is used with the instrumentals **snúnā** and **snúbhis**, where the locative would be expected.

1128. The Ablative. In the prepositional constructions of the ablative (as was pointed out and partly illustrated above, **293**), the ablative value of the case, and the merely directive value of the added particle, are for the most part clearly to be traced. Many of the verbal prefixes are more or less frequently joined in the older language with this case: oftenest, **ádhi** and **pári**; more sporadically, **ánu, ápa, áva, práti**, and the separatives **nís** and **ví**. The change of meaning of the ablative with **ā́** *hither*, by which it comes to fill the office of its opposite, the accusative, was sufficiently explained above (**293 c**). Of directive words akin with the prefixes, many — as **bahís, purás, avás, adhás, parás, purā́, vinā**, and **tirás** *out of knowledge of* — accompany this case by a perfectly regular construction. Also the case-forms **arvā́k, prā́k, paçcā́t, ūrdhvám, pū́rvam, páram**, and **ṛté** *without*, of which the natural construction with an ablative is predominant earlier.

1129. The Accusative. Many of the verbal prefixes and related words take an accompanying accusative. Most naturally (since the accusative is essentially the *to*-case), those that express a motion or action toward anything: as **abhí, práti, ánu, úpa, ā́, áti** and **ádhi** in the sense of *over on to*, or *across, beyond*, **tirás** *through*, **antár** and **antarā́** when meaning *between*, **pári** *around*. Examples are: **yā́ḥ pradíço abhí sū́ryo vicáṣṭe** (AV.) *what quarters the sun looks abroad unto;* **ábodhy agníḥ práty āyatī́m uṣā́sam** (RV.) *Agni has been awakened to meet the advancing dawn;* **gacchet kadācit svajanam prati** (MBh.) *she might go somewhither to her own people;* **imam prakṣyāmi nṛpatim prati** (MBh.) *him I will ask with reference to the king;* **máma cittám ánu cittébhir é 'ta** (AV.) *follow after my mind with your minds;* **é 'hy ā́ naḥ** (AV.) *come hither to us;* **úpa na é 'hy arvā́ṅ** (RV.) *come hither unto us;* **yó devó mártyāṅ áti** (AV.) *the god who is beyond mortals;* **adhiṣṭhā́ya várcasā́ 'dhy anyā́n** (AV.) *excelling above others in glory.* Also **abhítas** and **parítas**, which have a like value with the simple **abhí** and **pári**;

and **upári** *above* (oftener with genitive). Less accordant with ordinary accusative constructions is the use of this case with **adhas, paras, puras, vinā,** beside other cases which seem more suited to the meaning of those particles. And the same may be said of most of the adverbial case-forms with which the accusative is used. Thus, a number of instrumentals of situation or direction: as **yé 'vareṇā "dityám, yé páreṇā "dityám** (TB.) *those who are below the sun, those who are beyond the sun;* **ántareṇa yónim** (ÇB.) *within the womb;* **te hī 'dam antareṇa sarvam** (AB.) *for all this universe is between them;* **úttareṇa gā́rhapatyam** (ÇB.) *to the north of the householder's fire;* **dákṣiṇena védim** (ÇB.) *to the south of the sacrificial hearth;* **dakṣiṇena vṛkṣavāṭikām** (Ç.) *to the right of the orchard;* **nikaṣā́ yamunām** (Har.) *near the Yamunā.* Similarly, **ūrdhvam** and **pūrvam** have an accusative object as well as an ablative; and the same is true later of **ṛte. Abhimukham** *toward* has a more natural right to construction with this case.

1130. The Genitive. The words which are accompanied by the genitive are mostly case-forms of nouns, or of adjectives used substantively, retaining enough of the noun-character to take this case as their natural adjunct. Such are the locatives **agre** *in front of,* **abhyāçe** *near,* **arthe** and **kṛte** *for the sake of,* **nimitte** and **hetāu** *by reason of,* **madhye** *in the midst of;* and other cases, as **arthāya, kāraṇāt, sakāçāt, hetos.** And really, although less directly and obviously, of the same character are other adjective cases (some of them showing other constructions, already noticed): as **adhareṇa, uttareṇa** and **uttarāt, dakṣiṇena** and **dakṣiṇāt, paçcāt, ūrdhvam, anantaram, samakṣam, sākṣāt.** More questionable, and illustrations rather of the general looseness of use of the genitive, are its constructions (almost wholly unknown in the oldest language) with more proper words of direction: thus, with the derivative **paritas, paratas,** and **antitas,** and **parastāt** and **purastāt** (these found in the Brāhmaṇa language: as, **saṁvatsarasya parastāt** *after a year;* **sūktasya purastāt** *before the hymn* [AB.]); with **anti, adhas, avas, puras;** with **upari** *above* (common later); and with **antar.**

Conjunctions.

1131. The conjunctions, also, as a distinct class of words, are almost wanting.

a. The combination of clauses is in Sanskrit in general of a very simple character; much of what in other Indo-European languages is effected by subordinating conjunctions is here managed by means of composition of words, by the use of the gerunds (**994**), of iti (**1102**), of abstract nouns in case-forms, and so on.

1132. The relative derivative adverbs, already given

(1098 ff.), may properly be regarded as conjunctions; and a few other particles of kindred value, as **céd** and **néd** (**1111a**).

1133. Purely of conjunctive value are च **ca** *and*, and वा **vā** *or* (both toneless, and never having the first place in a sentence or clause).

a. Of copulative value, along with **ca**, is in the older language especially **utá** (later it becomes a particle of more indefinite use); and **ápi**, **tátas**, **táthā**, **kíṁ ca**, with other particles and combinations of particles, are used often as connectives of clauses.

b. Adversative is **tú** *but* (rare in the older language); also, less strongly, **u** (toneless).

c. Of illative value is **hí** *for* (originally, and in great part at every period, asseverative only): compare above, **1122 b**.

d. To **ca** (as well as to its compound **céd**) belongs occasionally the meaning *if*.

e. It is needless to enter into further detail with regard to those uses which may be not less properly, or more properly, called conjunctive than adverbial, of the particles already given, under the head of Adverbs.

Interjections.

1134. The utterances which may be classed as interjections are, as in other languages, in part voice-gestures, in part onomatopœias, and in part mutilations and corruptions of other parts of speech.

1135. a. Of the class of voice-gestures are, for example: **ā**, **hā**, **hāhā**, **ahaha**, **he**, **hāí** (AV.), **ayi**, **aye**, **hayé** (RV.), **aho**, **báṭ** (RV.), **bata** (RV.) or **vata**, and (probably) **híruk** and **hurúk** (RV.).

b. Onomatopoetic or imitative utterances are, for example (in the older language): **ciçcā́** *whiz* (of an arrow: RV.); **kikirā́** (palpitation: RV.); **bā́l** and **pháṭ** (**pháṣ**?) or **phál** *splash* (AV.); **bhúk** *bow-wow* (AV.); **çál** *pat* (AV.); **āṣ**, **hīṣ**, **as**, and **has** (PB.); and see the words already quoted in composition with the roots **kṛ** and **bhū**, above, **1091**.

c. Nouns and adjectives which have assumed an interjectional character are, for example: **bhos** (for the vocative **bhavas**, **456**); **are** or **re** (voc. of **ari** *enemy*); **dhik** *alas!* (may be mere voice-gesture, but perhaps related with √ **dih**); **kaṣṭam** *woe is me!* **diṣṭyā** *thank heaven!* **svasti** *hail!* **suṣṭhu**, **sādhu** *good, excellent!* None of these are Vedic in interjectional use.

CHAPTER XVII.

DERIVATION OF DECLINABLE STEMS.

1136. THE formation from roots of conjugable stems — namely, tense-stems, mode-stems, and stems of secondary conjugation (not essentially different from one another, nor, it is believed, ultimately from the formation of declined stems) — was most conveniently treated above, in the chapters devoted to the verb. Likewise the formation of adverbs by derivation (not essentially different from case-formation), in the chapter devoted to particles. And the formation of those declinable stems — namely, of comparison, and of infinitives and participles — which attach themselves most closely to the systems of inflection, has also been more or less fully exhibited. But the extensive and intricate subject of the formation of the great body of declinable stems was reserved for a special chapter.

a. Of course, only a brief and compendious exhibition of the subject can be attempted within the here necessary limits: no exhaustive tracing out of the formative elements of every period; still less, a complete statement of the varied uses of each element; least of all, a discussion of origins; but enough to help the student in that analysis of words which must form a part of his labor from the outset, giving a general outline of the field, and preparing for more penetrating investigation.

b. The material from accented texts, and especially the Vedic material, will be had especially in view (nothing that is Vedic being intentionally left unconsidered); and the examples given will be, so far as is possible, words found in such texts with their accent marked. No word not thus vouched for will be accented unless the fact is specifically pointed out.

1137. The roots themselves, both verbal and pronominal, are used in their bare form, or without any added suffix, as declinable stems.

a. As to this use of verbal roots, see below, 1147.

b. The pronominal roots, so-called, are essentially declinable; and hence, in their further treatment in derivation, they are throughout in accordance with other declinable stems, and not with verbal roots.

1138. Apart from this, every such stem is made by a suffix. And these suffixes fall into two general classes:

A. Primary suffixes, or those which are added directly to roots;

B. Secondary suffixes, or those which are added to derivative stems (also to pronominal roots, as just pointed out, and sometimes to particles).

a. The division of primary suffixes nearly corresponds to the **kṛt** (more regular) and **uṇādi** (less regular) suffixes of the Hindu grammarians; the secondary, to their **taddhita**-suffixes.

1139. But this distinction, though one of high value, theoretically and practically, is not absolute. Thus:

a. Suffixes come to have the aspect and the use of primary which really contain a secondary element — that is to say, the earliest words exhibiting them were made by addition of secondary suffixes to words already derivative.

b. Sundry examples of this will be pointed out below: thus, the gerundival suffixes, **tavya, anīya**, etc., the suffixes **uka** and **aka, tra**, and others. This origin is probable for more cases than admit of demonstration; and it is assumable for others which show no distinct signs of composition.

c. Less often, a suffix of primary use passes over in part into secondary, through the medium of use with denominative "roots" or otherwise: examples are **yu, iman, īyas** and **iṣṭha, ta.**

1140. Moreover, primary suffixes are added not only to more original roots, but, generally with equal freedom, to elements which have come to wear in the language the aspect of such, by being made the basis of primary conjugation — and even, to a certain extent, to the bases of secondary conjugation, the conjugation-stems, and the bases of tense-inflection, the tense-stems.

a. The most conspicuous examples of this are the participles, present and future and perfect, which are made alike from tense and conjugation-stems of every form. The infinitives (**968** ff.) attach themselves only in sporadic instances to tense-stems, and even from conjugation-stems are made but sparingly earlier; and the same is true of the gerundives.

b. General adjectives and nouns are somewhat widely made from conjugation-stems, especially from the base of causative conjugation: see below the suffixes **a** (**1148 j, k**), **ā** (**1149 c, d**), **ana** (**1150 m**), **as** (**1151 f**), **ani** (**1159 b**), **u** (**1178 g—i**), **ti** (**1157 g**), **tṛ** (**1182 e**), **tnu** (**1196 b**), **snu** (**1194 b**), **uka** (**1180 d**), **āku** (**1181 d**), **ālu** (**1192 b**), **tu** (**1161 d**).

c. From tense-stems the examples are far fewer, but not unknown: thus, from present-stems, occasional derivatives in **a** (**1148 j**), **ā** (**1149 d, e**), **ana** (**1150 n**), **i** (**1155 d**), **u** (**1178 f**), **ta** (**1176 e**), **tu** (**1161 d**), **uka** (**1180 d**), **tra** (**1185 e**), **ti** (**1157 g**), **vin** (or **in**: **1232 b**, **1183 a**); from stems in a **s** apparently of aoristic character (besides infinitives and gerundives), occasional derivatives in **a** (**1148 j**), **ana** (**1150 j**), **ani** (**1159 b**), **an** (**1160 a**), **āna** (**1175**), **as** (**1151 c**), **ī** (**1156 b**), **iṣṭha** (**1184 a**), **u** (**1178 f**), **us** (**1154 a**), **tṛ** (**1182 e**), **in** (**1183 a**).

1141. The primary suffixes are added also to roots as compounded with the verbal prefixes.

a. Whatever, namely, may have been originally and strictly the mode of production of the derivatives with prefixes, it is throughout the recorded life of the language as if the root and its prefix or prefixes constituted a unity, from which a derivative is formed in the same manner as from the simple root, with that modification of the radical meaning which appears also in the proper verbal forms as compounded with the same prefixes.

b. Not derivatives of every kind are thus made; but, in the main, those classes which have most of the verbal force, or which are most akin in value with infinitives and participles.

c. The occurrence of such derivatives with prefixes, and their accent, will be noted under each suffix below. They are chiefly (in nearly the order of their comparative frequency), besides root-stems, those in **a**, in **ana**, in **ti**, in **tar** and **tra**, and in **in**, **ya**, **van** and **man**, **i** and **u**, **as**, and a few others.

1142. The suffixes of both classes are sometimes joined to their primitives by a preceding union-vowel — that is to say, by one which wears that aspect, and, in our ignorance or uncertainty as to its real origin, may most conveniently and safely be called by that name. The line between these vowels and those deserving to be ranked as of organic suffixal character cannot be sharply drawn.

Each of the two great classes will now be taken up by itself, for more particular consideration.

A. Primary Derivatives.

1143. Form of root. The form of root to which a primary suffix is added is liable to more or less variation. Thus:

a. By far the most frequent is a strengthening change, by **guṇa**- or **vṛddhi**-increment. The former may occur under all circumstances (except, of course, where **guṇa**-change is in general forbidden: **235**, **240**): thus, **véda** from √**vid**, **móda** from √**mud**, **várdha** from √**vṛdh**;

áyana from √**i**, **sávana** from √**su**, **sáraṇa** from √**sṛ**; and so on. But the latter is only allowed under such circumstances as leave long **ā** as the resulting vowel: that is to say, with non-final **a**, and with a final **i**- or **u**-vowel and **ṛ** before a vowel: thus, **nādá** from √**nad**, **grābhá** from √**gṛbh** or **grabh**, **vāhá** from √**vah**, **nāyá** from √**nī**, **bhāvá** from √**bhū**, **kārá** from √**kṛ**; such strengthening as would make **vāida** and **māuda** does not accompany primary derivation.

b. Strengthening in derivation does not stand in any such evident connection with accent as strengthening in conjugation; nor can any general rules be laid down as to its occurrence; it has to be pointed out in detail for each suffix. So also with other vowel-changes, which are in general accordance with those found in inflection and in the formation of tense- and mode-stems.

c. The reversion of a final palatal or **h** to a guttural has been already noticed (**216**). A final **n** or **m** is occasionally lost, as in formations already considered.

d. After a short final vowel is sometimes added a **t**: namely, where a root is used as stem without suffix (**1147 d**), and before a following **y** or **v** of **van** (**1169**), **vara** and **varī** (**1171**), **yu** once (**1165 a**), and **ya** (**1213 a**). The presence of **t** before these suffixes appears to indicate an original secondary derivation from derivatives in **ti** and **tu**.

e. The root is sometimes reduplicated: rarely in the use without suffix (**1147 c, e**); oftenest before **a** (**1148 k**), **i** (**1155 e**), **u** (**1178 d**); but also before other suffixes, as **ā** (**1149 e**), **ana** (**1150 m**), **vana** (**1170 a**), **van** and **varī** (**1169 d**, **1171 a, b**), **vaṇi** (**1170 b**), **vi** (**1193**), **vit** (**1193 b**), **ani** (**1159 b**), **in** (**1183 a**), **tnu** (**1196 a**), **ta** (**1176 a**), **ti** (**1157 d**), **tha** (**1163 a**), **tṛ** (**1182 b**), **tra** (**1185 f**), **ūka** (**1180 f**), **aka** (**1181 a**), **īka** (**1186 c**), **ma** (**1166 b**).

1144. Accent. No general laws governing the place of the accent are to be recognized; each suffix must in this respect be considered by itself.

a. In connection with a very few suffixes is to be recognized a certain degree of tendency to accent the root in case of a *nomen actionis* or infinitival derivative, and the ending in the case of a *nomen agentis* or participial derivative: see the suffixes **a**, **ana**, **as**, **an**, and **man**, below, where the examples are considered. Differences of accent in words made by the same suffix are also occasionally connected with differences of gender: see the suffixes **as** and **man**.

1145. Meaning. As regards their signification, the primary derivatives fall in general into two great classes, the one indicating the action expressed by the verbal root, the other the person or thing in which the action appears, the agent or actor — the latter, either substantively or adjectively. The one class is more abstract, infinitival; the other is more concrete, participial. Other meanings

may in the main be viewed as modifications or specializations of these two.

a. Even the words indicating recipience of action, the passive participles, are, as their use also as neuter or reflexive shows, only notably modified words of agency. The gerundives are, as was pointed out above 961 ff.), secondary derivatives, originally indicating only *concerned with the action*.

1146. But these two classes, in the processes of formation, are not held sharply apart. There is hardly a suffix by which action-nouns are formed which does not also make agent-nouns or adjectives; although there are not a few by which are made only the latter. In treating them in detail below, we will first take up the suffixes by which derivatives of both classes are made, and then those forming only agent-nouns.

a. To facilitate the finding of the different suffixes is given the following list of them, in their order as treated, with references to paragraphs:

—	1147	yu	1165	in	1183
a	1148	ma	1166	īyas, iṣṭha	1184
ā	1149	mi	1167	tra	1185
ana	1150	man	1168	ka	1186
as	1151	van	1169	ya	1187
tas, nas, sas	1152	vana, -ni, -nu	1170	ra	1188
is	1153	vara	1171	la	1189
us	1154	ant	1172	va	1190
i	1155	vāṅs	1173	ri	1191
ī	1156	māna	1174	ru	1192
ti	1157	āna	1175	vi	1193
ni	1158	tā	1176	snu	1194
ani	1159	na, ina, una	1177	sna	1195
an	1160	u	1178	tnu	1196
tu	1161	ū	1179	sa	1197
nu	1162	uka	1180	asi	1198
tha	1163	aka	1181	abha	1199
thu	1164	tṛ or tar	1182	sundries	1200—1

1147. Stems without suffix; Root-words. These words and their uses have been already pretty fully considered above (**323**, **348** ff., **383** ff., **400**, **401**).

a. They are used especially (in the later language, almost solely) as finals of compounds, and have both fundamental values, as action-nouns (frequently as infinitives: **971**), and as agent-nouns and adjectives (often governing an accusative: **271** e). As action-nouns, they are chiefly feminines (**384**: in many instances, however, they do not occur in situations that determine the gender).

b. In a small number of words, mostly of rare occurrence, the reduplicated root is used without suffix.

c. The Vedic cases are: with simple reduplication, **sasyád**, **cikít**, **dadŕh**, **didyú** and **didyút**, **juhū́**, and perhaps **gáñgā** and **çíçu**; with intensive reduplication, **-nenī́**, **malimluc**, **yavīyúdh**, and **jógū** and **vánīvan** (with the intensive instead of the usual radical accent). In **dáridra** is seen a transfer to the a-declension. **Asūsū́** is probably to be understood as a compound, **asū-sū́**.

d. If the root end in a short vowel, a t is regularly and usually added (383f–h).

e. Examples have been given at the place just quoted. In **jágat** the t is added to the mutilated form of **√gam** reduplicated, and **ṛṇayā́t** (TS., once) appears to put it after a long vowel. In a single instance, **çrútkarṇa** (RV.) *of listening ears*, a stem of this class occurs as prior member of a compound.

f. Words of this form in combination with verbal prefixes are very numerous. The accent rests (as in combination of the same with other preceding elements) on the root-stem.

g. A few exceptions in point of accent occur: thus, **ávasā**, **úpastut**; and, with other irregularities of form, **párijri**, **upástha**, **uparístha**.

1148. अ **a.** With the suffix अ **a** is made an immensely large and heterogeneous body of derivatives, of various meaning and showing various treatment of the root: **guṇa**-strengthening, **vṛddhi**-strengthening, retention unchanged, and reduplication.

In good part, they are classifiable under the two usual general heads; but in part they have been individualized into more special senses.

1. a. With guṇa-strengthening of the root (where that is possible: 235, 240). These are the great majority, being more than twice as numerous as all others together.

b. Many *nomina actionis:* as, **çráma** *weariness*, **gráha** *seizure*, **áya** *movement*, **véda** *knowledge*, **háva** *call*, **kródha** *wrath*, **jóṣa** *enjoyment*, **tára** *crossing*, **sárga** *emission*.

c. Many *nomina agentis:* as, **kṣamá** *patient*, **svajá** *constrictor*, **jīvá** *living*, **meghá** *cloud*, **codá** *inciting*, **plavá** *boat*, **sará** *brook*, **sarpá** *serpent*, **bhojá** *generous*, **khādá** *devouring*.

d. Of the examples here given, those under b accent the radical syllable, and those under c the ending. And this is in perhaps a majority of cases the fact as regards the two classes of derivatives; so that, taken in connection with kindred facts as to other suffixes, it hints at such a difference of accent as a general tendency of the language. A few sporadic instances are met with of the same form having the one or the other value according to its accent: thus, **éṣa** *haste*, **eṣá** *hasting*; **çása** *order*, **çāsá** *orderer* (other examples are **coda, çāka, çoka**: compare a similar difference with other derivatives in **as, ana, an, man**). But exceptions are numerous — thus, for example, **jayá, javá, smará**, action-nouns; **çráva, mógha, stáva**, agent-nouns — and the subject calls for a much wider and deeper investigation than it has yet received, before the accentuation referred to can be set up as a law of the language in derivation.

2. **e.** With **vṛddhi**-strengthening of the root — but only where **ā** is the resulting radical vowel: that is, of medial **a**, and of final **ṛ** (most often), **u** or **ū**, **i** or **ī** (rare).

f. Examples of action-nouns are: **kā́ma** *love*, **bhāgá** *share*, **nādá** *noise*, **dāvá** *fire*, **tārá** *crossing*. Very few forms of clear derivation and meaning are quotable with accent on the root-syllable.

g. Examples of agent-nouns are: **grābhá** *seizing*, **vāhá** *carrying*, **nāyá** *leading*, **jārá** *lover*.

3. **h.** With unstrengthened root, the examples are few: e. g. **kṛçá** *lean*, **turá** *rapid*, **yugá** *yoke*, **sruvá** *spoon*, **priyá** *dear*, **vrá** *troop*, **çucá** *bright*.

i. A number of words of this class, especially as occurring in composition, are doubtless results of the transfer of root-stems to the **a**-declension: e. g. **-ghuṣa, -sphura, -tuda, -dṛça, -vida, -kira**.

j. A few **a**-stems are made, especially in the older language, from conjugation-stems, mostly causative: thus, **-āmaya, ilaya, -īṅkhaya, -ejaya, -dhāraya, -pāraya, -mṛḍaya, -çamaya** (compare the **ā**-stems, **1149 c,d**): also desiderative, as **bībhatsa** (compare **1038**). Occasional examples also occur from tense-stems: thus, from **nu**-stems, or secondary stems made from such, **hinvá, -inva, -jinva, -pinva, -sinva, -sunva, -açnuva**; from others, **-pṛṇa, -mṛṇa, -stṛṇa, -puna, -jāna, -paçya, -manya, -dasya, -jurya, -kṣudhya, -sya, -tiṣṭha, -jighra, -piba**; from future-stems, **kariṣya** (JB.), **janiṣya, bhaviṣya, ruciṣya** (?); apparently from aorist-stems, **jeṣá, néṣa-, parṣá, pṛkṣá** (?), **-hoṣa**.

4. **k.** Derivatives in **a** from a reduplicated root-form are a considerable class, mostly occurring in the older language. They are sometimes made with a simple reduplication: thus, **cacará, cikita, dṛdhrá, dadhṛṣá, babhasa, -babhra, vavrá, çiçayá, çiçnátha** (an action-noun), **sasrá**; but oftener with an intensive reduplication: thus, merely strengthened, **cākṣmá, -cācala, jāgara, nānada, lālasa, vīvadhá** (?), **-memiṣa, rerihá** and **leliha, vevijá, nonuva, momughá, -roruda, lolupa**; with consonant added, **-cañkaça-, -cañkrama, jañgama, cañcala, -jañjapa, dandhvana, -nannama, -jarjalpa, jarjara, -tartura, -dardira, múrmura, gadgada**; dissyllabic, **-karikra, kanikradá, carācará** and **calācalá, marīmṛçá, malimlucá, varīvṛtá, sarīsṛpá, paniṣpadá, saniṣyadá, sanisrasá, patāpata, madāmada, -vadāvada, ghanā-**

ghaná. Many of these are to be regarded as from an intensive conjugation-stem; but some of them show a form not met with in intensive conjugation.

5. l. Derivatives with this suffix from roots as compounded with the verbal prefixes are quite common, in all the modes of formation (in each, in proportion to the frequency of independent words): constituting, in fact, considerably the largest body of derivative stems with prefixes. They are of both classes as to meaning. The accent is, with few exceptions, on the ending — and that, without any reference to the value of the stem as action-noun or agent-noun.

m. Examples are: **saṁgamá** *assembly*, **nimeṣá** *wink*, **abhidrohá** *enmity*, **anukará** *assistance*, **udāná** *inspiration*, **pratyāçrāvá** *response*; — **paricará** *wandering*, **saṁjayá** *victorious*, **vibodhá** *wakeful*, **atiyājá** *over-pious*, **udārá** *inciting*, *elevated*, **uttudá** *rousing*, **saṁgirá** *swallowing*, **ādardirá** *crushing*, **adhicaṅkramá** *climbing*.

n. The only definite class of exceptions in regard to accent appears to be that of the adverbial gerunds in **am** (above, **995**), which are accented on the root-syllable. A very few other stems have the same tone: for example, **utpā́ta** *portent*, **āçréṣa** *plague*. A few others, mostly agent-nouns, have the accent on the prefix: for example, **vyòṣa** (i. e. **ví-oṣa**) *burning*, **prátiveça** *neighbor*, **ā́bhaga** *sharing*; but also **sáṁkāça** *appearance*.

o. For the remaining compounds of these derivatives, with the inseparable prefixes and with other elements, see the next chapter. It may be merely mentioned here that such compounds are numerous, and that the **a**-derivative has often an active participial value, and is frequently preceded by a case-form, oftenest the accusative.

p. Many words in the language appear to end with a suffix **a**, while yet they are referable to no root which can be otherwise demonstrated as such.

1149. आ **ā**. The vast majority of stems in आ **ā** are feminine adjectives, corresponding to masculines and neuters in अ **a** (**332, 334**). But also many suffixes ending in अ **a** have corresponding feminine forms in long आ **ā**, making a greater or less number of action-nouns. These will be given under the different suffixes below.

a. There is further, however, a considerable body of feminine action-nouns made by adding ā to a root, and having an independent aspect; though they are doubtless in part transfers from the root-noun (**1147**). Usually they show an unstrengthened form of root, and (such as occur in accented texts) an accented suffix.

b. Examples are **īçā́** *lordship*, **krīḍā** *play*, **dayā́** *pity*, **nindā́** *reproach*, **çaṅkā́** *doubt*, **hiṅsā́** *injury*, **kṣamā́** *patience*, **kṣudhā́** *hunger*, **bhāṣā́** *speech*, **sevā́** *service*, **spṛhā́** *eagerness*.

c. But especially, such nouns in **ā** are made in large numbers, and with perfect freedom, from secondary conjugation-stems.

d. Thus, especially from desiderative stems, as **jigīṣā́**, **bhikṣā́**, **vīrtsā́**, **bībhatsā́**, etc. (see **1038**); in the formation of periphrastic perfects, especially from causative stems, but also from desiderative and intensive, and even from primary present-stems (**1071 c—f**); from denominative stems, in the older language, as **açvayā́**, **sukratūyā́**, **apasyā́**, **uruṣyā́**, **asūyā́**, **açanayā́**, **jīvanasyā́**, etc., and quite rarely in the later, as **mṛgayā**.

e. The only example from a reduplicated stem is the late **paspaçā**; for **sūṣā́**, **jáṅghā**, and **jihvā́**, which have a reduplicated aspect, are of doubtful origin. From present-stems come **icchā** and probably **-ṛcchā**.

1150. अन **ana**. With this suffix (as with अ **a**) are formed innumerable derivatives, of both the principal classes of meaning, and with not infrequent specializations. The root has oftenest **guṇa**-strengthening, but not seldom **vṛddhi** instead; and in a few cases it remains unstrengthened. Derivatives of this formation are frequent from roots with prefixes, and also in composition with other elements.

a. The normal and greatly prevalent accent is upon the root-syllable, without regard to the difference of meaning; but cases occur of accented final, and a few of accented penult. The action-nouns are in general of the neuter gender. The feminine of adjectives is made either in **ā** or in **ī** (for details, see below). And a few feminine action-nouns in **anā** and **anī** occur, which may be ranked as belonging to this suffix.

1. **b.** With strengthened and accented root-syllable. Under this head fall, as above indicated, the great mass of forms.

c. With **guṇa**-strengthening: examples of action-nouns are **sádana** *seat*, **rákṣaṇa** *protection*, **dā́na** *giving*, **cáyana** *collection*, **védana** *property*, **hávana** *call*, **bhójana** *enjoyment*, **káraṇa** *deed*, **várdhana** *increase*; — of agent-nouns, **tápana** *burning*, **cétana** *visible*, **códana** *impelling*.

d. With **vṛddhi**-strengthening (only in such circumstances that **ā** remains as vowel of the radical syllable): examples are **-cā́tana**, **nā́çana**, **mā́dana**, **-vā́cana**, **-vā́sana**, **-vā́hana**, **sā́dana**, **-spā́çana**, **svā́dana**, **-ā́yana**, **-yā́vana**, **-srāvaṇa**, **-pā́raṇa**.

e. From roots with prefixes, the derivatives of this formation are very numerous, being exceeded in frequency only by those made with the suffix **a** (above, **1148 l, m**). A few examples are: **ākrámaṇa** *striding on*, **udyā́na** *upgoing*, **nidhā́na** *receptacle*, **prā́ṇana** *expiration*, **vimócana** *release* and *releasing*, **saṁgámana** *assembly* and *assembler*, **adhivikártana** *cutting off*, **avaprabhráñçana** *falling away down*. For other compounds of these derivatives, showing the same accent (and the same feminine stem), see the next chapter (below, **1271**). A few exceptions occur: **vicakṣaṇá**, **upariçayaná**, and the feminines **pramandanī́** and **nirdahanī́**.

f. The adjectives of this formation, simple or compound, make their feminine usually in **ī**: thus, **códanī**, **péçanī**, **spáraṇī**, **jámbhanī**; **prajñā́nī**, **prókṣaṇī**, **saṁgráhaṇī**, **abhiṣávaṇī**, **vidháraṇī** (**cetanī́** is of doubtful meaning: below, **i**). An adjective compound, however, having a noun in **ana** as final member, makes its feminine in **ā**: thus, **sūpasarpaṇā́** *of easy approach*, **ṣáḍvidhānā** *of sextuple order*, **anapavācanā́** *not to be ordered away*.

2. The more irregular formations may be classed as follows:

g. With accent on the final: a number of agent-nouns and adjectives, as **karaṇá** *active* (against **káraṇa** *act*), **kṛpaṇá** *miserable* (against **kṛpáṇa** *misery*), **tvaraṇá** *hasting*, **rocaná** *shining*, **kroçaná** *yelling*, **svapaná** *sleepy*, **kṣayaṇá** *habitable*.

h. These, unlike the preceding class, make their feminine in **ā**: e. g. **tvaraṇā́**, **spandanā́**. A few feminine action-nouns in the older language have the same form: thus, **açanā́**, **asanā́**, **mananā́**, **dyotanā́**, **rodhanā́**, **çvetanā́**, **hasanā́** (and compare **kapanā́**, **raçanā́**); those of the later language in **anā** (rather numerous) are doubtful as regards accent.

i. Beside these may be mentioned a few feminines in **anī́**, of more or less doubtful character: **arṣaṇī́**, **cetanī́** (to **cétana**), **tapanī́** (to **tápana**), **pṛçanī́**, **vṛjanī́** (with **vṛjána**), **rajanī**, **tedanī́**.

j. With accent on the penult: a small number of adjectives: as **turáṇa** *hasting*, **doháná** *milking*, **manána** *considerate*, **bhandána** and **mandána** *rejoicing*, **sakṣáṇa** *overcoming*, and perhaps **vakṣáṇā** *carrying* (the last two with aoristic **s**); and a still smaller number of neuter action-nouns: **daṅsána** *great deed*, **vṛjána** *enclosure, town*, **veṣáṇa** *service*. **kṛpáṇa** *misery* (against **kṛpaṇá** *miserable*), with the masculine **kiráṇa** *dust*.

k. The only noticed example of a feminine is in **ā**: **turáṇā**. And a few feminine nouns have the same form: **arháṇā**, **jaráṇā**, **barháṇā**, **bhandánā**, **maṅhánā**, **mehánā**, **vadhánā**, **vanánā**, **vakṣáṇā**. (And compare the anomalous masc. name **uçánā**: **355a**.)

l. Without strengthening of the root are made a small number of derivatives: thus (besides those already noted, **kṛpáṇa** and **kṛpaṇá**, **vṛjána** and **vṛjanī́**, **kiráṇa**, **turáṇa**), further accented examples are **úraṇa**, **dhúvana**, **pṛ́çana**, **bhúvana**, **vṛ́jana**, **vṛ́ṣaṇa**, **-súvana**; and later are found **sphuraṇa**, **sphuṭana**, **spṛhaṇa**, **-hnuvana**, **likhana**, **rudana**, etc. RV. makes denominatives from **riṣaṇa-**, **ruvaṇa-**, **vipana-**, **huvana-**.

m. Stems in **ana** are made also from secondary conjugation-stems: thus, from desideratives, as **cikitsana** (see **1038**); from causatives, as **hāpana, bhīṣaṇa** (see **1051 g**); from denominatives, with great freedom, in the later language, as **ākarṇana, unmūlana, çlakṣṇana, cihnana**; from intensives and other reduplicated stems, only **cañkramaṇa, jañgamana, jāgaraná, yoyupana.**

n. A few isolated cases may be further mentioned: from tense-stems, **-jighraṇa, -ūrṇavana, -paçyana, yacchana, -siñcana**; from prepositions, **antaraṇa** and **sámana**; **astamana** from the quasi-prefix (**1092 b**) **astam.** Feminines in **anā** of doubtful connection are **yóṣaṇā** *woman* (beside **yóṣan, yoṣā,** etc.) and **pṛ́tanā.**

1151. अस् **as.** By this suffix are made (usually with **guṇa**-strengthening of the root-vowel) especially a large class of neuter nouns, mostly abstract (action-nouns), but sometimes assuming a concrete value; and also, in the older language, a few agent-nouns and adjectives, and a considerable number of infinitives.

a. The accent in words of the first class is on the root, and in the second on the ending; and in a few instances words of the two classes having the same form are distinguished by their accent; the infinitives have for the most part the accent on the suffix.

1. **b.** Examples of the first and principal class are: **ávas** *aid, favor,* **tápas** *warmth,* **práyas** *pleasure,* **téjas** *splendor,* **çrávas** *fame,* **dóhas** *milking,* **káras** *deed,* **práthas** *breadth,* **cétas** and **mánas** *mind,* **cákṣas** *eye,* **sáras** *pond,* **vácas** *speech.*

c. A few words of this class are of irregular formation: thus, without strengthening of the root, **júvas** *quickness* (beside **jávas**), **úras** *breast,* **mṛ́dhas** *contempt;* and **iras-** (**irasy-**) and **vipas-**, and the adverbs **tirás, mithás, huras-**, also **çíras** *head,* are to be compared; — with **vṛddhi**-strengthening, **-vā́cas, vā́sas, vā́has, -svādas,** and, of doubtful connections, **pā́jas, pā́thas,** and **-hāyas**; — perhaps with an aoristic **s, héṣas** *missile;* — **pī́vas** contains a **v** apparently not radical.

d. After final **ā** of a root is usually inserted **y** before the suffix (**258**): thus, **dhā́yas, -gā́yas.** But there are in the oldest language apparent remains of a formation in which **as** was added directly to radical **ā**: thus, **bhā́s** and **-dās** (often to be pronounced as two syllables), **jñā́s, mā́s**; and **-dhas** and **-das,** from the roots **dhā** and **dā.**

2. **e.** The instances in which an agent-noun is differentiated by its accent from an action-noun are: **ápas** *work,* and **apás** *active;* **yáças** *beauty,* and **yaçás** *beauteous;* **táras** *quickness,* and **tarás** (VS., once) *quick;* **távas** *strength,* and **tavás** *strong:* **dúvas** *worship,* and **duvás** *lively(?);* **máhas** *greatness,* and **mahás** *great;* between **rákṣas** n. and

rakṣás m., both meaning *demon*, and between **tyájas** n. *abandonment(?)* and **tyajás** m. *descendant(?)*, the antithesis is much less clear.

f. Adjectives in **ás** without corresponding abstracts are: **toçás** *bestowing*, **yajás** *offering*, **vedhás** *pious*, probably **āhanás** *heady;* and a few other words of isolated occurence, as **veçás, dhvarás.** From a denominative stem is made **mṛgayás** *wild animal* (RV., once).

g. But there are also a very few cases of abstract nouns, not neuter, accented on the ending: thus, **jarás** *old age*, **bhiyás** *fear;* and doubtless also **havás** *call*, and **tveṣás** *impulse.* The feminine **uṣás** *dawn*, and **doṣás** *night*, might belong either here or under the last preceding head.

h. Apparently containing a suffix **as** are the noun **upás** *lap*, and certain proper names: **áñgiras, nodhás, bhalānás, arcanānás, naciketas.** The feminine **apsarás** *nymph* is of doubtful derivation.

i. The irregular formation of some of the words of this division will be noticed, without special remark.

3. **j.** The infinitives made by the suffix **as** have been explained above (**973**): they show various treatment of the root, and various accent (which last may perhaps mark a difference of gender, like that between **sáhas** and **jarás**).

4. **k.** The formation of derivatives in **as** from roots compounded with prefixes is very restricted -- if, indeed, it is to be admitted at all. No infinitive in **as** occurs with a prefix; nor any action-noun; and the adjective combinations are in some instances evidently, and in most others apparently, possessive compounds of the noun with the prefix used adjectively: the most probable exceptions are **-nyòkas** and **víṣpardhas.** As in these examples, the accent is always on the prefix.

l. Certain Vedic stems in **ar** may be noticed here, as more or less exchanging with stems in **as**, and apparently related with such. They were reported above, at **169 a.**

In connection with this, the most common and important suffix ending in **s**, may be best treated the others, kindred in office and possibly also in origin, which end in the same sibilant.

1152. **तस्** **tas,** **नस्** **nas,** **सस्** **sas.** With these suffixes are made an extremely small number of action-nouns. Thus:

a. With **tas** are made **rétas** *seed*, and **srótas** *stream.*

b. With **nas** are made **ápnas** *acquisition*, **árṇas** *wave*, **-bhárṇas** *offering*, **rékṇas** *riches;* and in **dráviṇas** *wealth*, and **párīṇas** *fulness*, is apparently to be seen the same suffix, with prefixed elements having the present value of union-vowels. Probably the same is true of **dámūnas** *house-friend*, and **ṛjūnas** (RV.) n. pr., **uçánas** (or **-nā**) n. pr.

c. With **sas** is perhaps made **vápsas** *beauty;* and **tárūṣas** may be mentioned with it (rather **tarus-a**?).

1153. इस् **is.** With the suffix **is** is formed a small number (about a dozen) of nouns.

a. They are in part nouns of action, but most are used concretely. The radical syllable has the **guṇa**-strengthening, and the accent is on the suffix (except in **jyótis** *light*, **vyáthis**, and **ā́mis**, *raw meat*). Examples are: **arcís**, **rocís**, and **çocís** *light*, **chadís** or **chardís** *cover*, **barhís** *straw*, **vartís** *track*, **sarpís** *butter*, **havís** *oblation*, **dyotis** *light*, and **kravís** *raw flesh*. **Avis-**, **pāthis**, **bhrājis-**, and **máhis-** are isolated variants of stems in **as**; and **túvis-**, **çucis-**, and **surabhis-** appear inorganically for **tuvi** etc. in a few compounds or derivatives.

1154. उस् **us.** With this suffix are made a few words, of various meaning, root-form, and accent.

a. They are words signifying both action and agent. A few have both meanings, without difference of accent: thus, **tápus** *heat* and *hot;* **árus** *wound* and *sore;* **cákṣus** *brightness* and *seeing, eye;* **vápus** *wonderful* and *wonder*. The nouns are mostly neuter, and accented on the root-syllable: thus, **ā́yus**, **tárus**, **púrus**, **múhus** (? only adverbial), **míthus** (do.), **yájus**, **çā́sus**; exceptions are: in regard to accent, **janús** *birth;* in regard to gender, **mánus** *man*, and **náhus**, proper name. Of adjectives, are accented on the ending **jayús**, **vanús**, and **dakṣús** *burning* (which appears to attach itself to the aorist-stem).

1155. इ **i.** With this suffix are formed a large body of derivatives, of all genders: adjectives and masculine agent-nouns, feminine abstracts, and a few neuters. They show a various form of the root: strong, weak, and reduplicated. Their accent is also various. Many of them have meanings much specialized; and many (including most of the neuters) are hardly to be connected with any root elsewhere demonstrable.

1. **a.** The feminine action-nouns are of very various form: thus, with weak root-form, **rúci** *brightness*, **tvíṣi** *sheen;* **kṛṣí** *ploughing*, **nṛtí** *dance;* — with **guṇa**-strengthening (where possible), **rópi** *pain*, **çocí** *heat*, **vaní** and **saní** *gain;* — with **vṛddhi**-strengthening, **grā́hi** *seizure*, **dhrā́ji** *course*, **ājí** *race;* from √**duṣ** comes **dū́ṣi** (compare **dūṣayati**, **1042 b**). The variety of accent, which seems reducible to no rule, is illustrated by the examples given. The few infinitively used words of this formation (above, **975 b**) have a weak root-form, with accent on the ending.

2. **b.** The adjectives and masculine agent-nouns exhibit the same variety. Thus:

c. With unstrengthened root: **çúci** *bright*, **bhṛ́mi** *lively* (√**bhram**), **gṛ́bhi** *container*.

d. With unstrengthened root (or root incapable of **guṇa**-change): **arí** *enemy*, **máhi** *great*, **arcí** *beam*, **granthí** *knot*, **krīḍí** *playing;* with **vṛddhi**-increment, **kā́rṣi, jā́ni, -dhāri, çā́ri, sācí, sādi, -sāhi,** and a few words of obscure connections: thus, **drāpí** *mantle*, **rāçí** *heap*, **pāṇí** *hand*, etc. The isolated **-ānaçi** appears to come from the perfect-stem (**788**) of √**aç**.

e. With reduplicated root. This is in the older language a considerable class, of quite various form. Thus: with weak or abbreviated root, **cákri, jághri** (√**ghar**), **pápri, sásri, -amri, babhrí, vavrí, jágmi, -jájñi** (√**jan**), **-tatni, jághni, sásni, súṣvi, -çiçvi**; and, with displacement of final **ā** (or its weakening to the semblance of the suffix), **dadí, papí, yayí** (with a case or two from **yayī́**), **-jajñi, dádhi**; — from the **ur**-form of roots in changeable **ṛ**, **jáguri, táturi, pápuri** (**púpuri** SV.); — with simple reduplication, **cíkiti, yúyudhi, vívici**; — with strengthened reduplication, **-cācali, tā́tṛpi, dā́dhṛṣi, vā́vahi, sāsahí, tū́tuji** and **tūtují, yū́yuvi, yū́yudhi**; and **jarbhári** and **bámbhāri**. And **karkarí** *lute* and **dundubhí** *drum* have the aspect of belonging to the same class, but are probably onomatopoetic. The accent, it will be noticed, is most often on the reduplication, but not seldom elsewhere (only once on the root). It was noticed above (**271 f**) that these reduplicated derivatives in **i** not seldom take an object in the accusative, like a present participle.

f. Formations in **i** from the root compounded with prefixes are not at all numerous. They are accented usually on the suffix. Examples are: **āyají, vyānaçí, nijaghní, parādadí, viṣāsahí**; but also **ājā́ni, āmúri, vívavri**. As compounded with other preceding words, the adjectives or agent-nouns in **i** are not rare, and are regularly accented on the root: see the next chapter, **1276**.

g. From √**dhā** comes a derivative **-dhi**, forming many masculine compounds, with the value both of an abstract and a concrete: thus, with prefixes, **antardhí, uddhí, nidhí, paridhí**, etc. From √**dā** is made in like manner **ādi** *beginning*, and from √**sthā**, **pratiṣṭhí** *resistance*. Opinions are at variance as to whether such forms are to be regarded as made with the suffix **i**, displacing the radical **ā**, or with weakening of **ā** to **i**.

3. h. Neuter nouns in **i** are few, and of obscure derivation: examples are **ákṣi** *eye*, **ásthi** *bone*, **dádhi** *curds*, etc.

1156. ई **ī**. Stems in ई **ī** (like those in आ **ā**, above, **1149**) are for the most part feminine adjectives, corresponding to masculines and neuters of other terminations.

a. Thus, feminines in **ī** are made from **a**-stems (**332, 334**: and see also the different suffixes), from **i**-stems (**344, 346**), from **u**-stems (**344 b**), from **ṛ**-stems (**376 a**), and from various consonant-stems (**378 a**).

b. But there are also a few stems in **ī** wearing the aspect of independent derivatives. Examples are **dakṣī́, dehī́, nadī́, nāndī́, péṣī,**

vakṣī (apparently with aoristic **s**), **veçí, çā́kī, çácī, çámī, çímī, tarī, vāpī**; they are either action-nouns or agent-nouns. In the later language (as noticed at **344a**) there is very frequent interchange of **i-** and **ī**-stems and the forms from them.

c. In the oldest language there are even a few masculines in **ī**. They were noticed, and their inflection illustrated, above, at **355b, 356.**

1157. ति **ti.** This suffix forms a large class of frequently used feminine nouns of action; and also a few agent-nouns (masculine) and adjectives. The root has in general the same form as before the suffix त **ta** of the passive participle (**952** ff.) — that is to say, a weak, and often a weakened or abbreviated, form.

a. The accent ought, it would appear, in analogy with that of the participle, to rest always upon the suffix; but in the recorded condition of the language it does so only in a minority of cases: namely, about fifty, against sixty cases of accent an the radical syllable, and a hundred and forty of undetermined accent; a number of words — **iti, ṛti, citti, tṛpti, pakti, puṣṭi, bhūti, bhṛti, vṛṣṭi, çakti, çruṣṭi, sṛṣṭi, sthiti** — have both accentuations.

1. **b.** Examples of the normal formation are: **rātí** *gift*, **ūtí** *aid*, **rītí** *flow*, **stutí** *praise*, **bhaktí** *division*, **viṣṭí** *service*, **stutí** *praise*, **kīrtí** *fame*, **pūrtí** *bestowal*, **matí** *thought*, **pītí** *drink* (√**pā**; pple **pīta**), **dhāutí** *stream* (√**dhāv**; pple **dhāuta**); — and with accented root, **gáti** *motion*, **çā́ṅti** *repose*, **díti** *division* (√**dā**; pple **ditá**), **dṛ́ṣṭi** *sight*, **íṣṭi** *offering* (√**yaj**: pple **iṣṭá**), **úkti** *speech* (√**vac**: pple **uktá**), **vṛ́ddhi** *increase*.

c. The roots which form their participle in **ita** (**956**) do not have the **i** also before **ti**: thus, only **gúpti, -dṛpti.** A few roots having their participle in **na** instead of **ta** (**957**) form the abstract noun also in **ni** (below, **1158**). And from the roots **tan** and **ran** occur **tantí** and **ránti**, beside the more regular **tati** and **ráti**; also **áhanti** (once, VS.) beside **áhati.** From roots having the form **dā**, the derivative in composition is sometimes **-tti** (for **dāti**, with loss of radical vowel: compare the participle-form **-tta**, above, **955f**): thus, **niravatti** (K.), **samprátti** (ÇB.), **páritti** (TB.), **vásutti, bhágatti, maghátti** (all RV.).

d. A few derivatives are made from reduplicated roots; their accent is various: thus, **carkṛtí, dī́dhiti** and **-dī́diti, jígarti,** and perhaps the proper name **yayā́ti**; also **jágdhi** from √**jakṣ** (**233f**).

e. Derivatives from roots with prefixes are numerous, and have (as in the case of the participles in **ta**, and the action-nouns in **tu**) the accent on the prefix: examples are **ánumati, abhī́ti, ā́huti, nírṛti, vyā́pti, sáṅgati.** The only exceptions noticed are **āsaktí** and **āsutí**, and **abhi-**

ṣṭí (beside abhíṣṭi). In other combinations than with prefixes, the accentuation is in general the same: see the next chapter (1274).

2. f. The adjectives and agent-nouns — which, as masculines, are to be connected with these rather than with the feminine abstracts — are very few: thus, pū́ti *putrid*, vā́ṣṭi *eager*, dhū́ti *shaker*, jñātí *relative*, pattí *footman*, páti *master;* and a few others, of more or less dubious character. The accent is various, as in the other class.

3. g. A few words show the suffix ti preceded by various vowels, union- or stem-vowels. The ordinary intermediate i of the ta-participle etc. is seen in sániti, ujhiti, -gṛhīti (ī, as usual with this root: 900 b), paṭhiti, bhaṇiti; and with them may be mentioned the adjective ṛ́jīti, the proper names turvī́ti and dabhī́ti, and snī́hitī and snéhitī, notwithstanding their long final. With ati are made a few derivatives, variously accented: thus, the action-nouns aṅhatí, dṛçatí, pakṣatí, mithatí, vasatí, ramáti, vratáti, amáti and ámati, -dhrajati; and the agent-words aratí, khalatí, vṛkáti, rámati, dahati. In some of these is to be seen with probability a stem-vowel, as also in jánayati and rasayati (and RV. has gopayátya). The grammarians' method of representing a root by its 3d sing. pres. indic., declining this as a ti-stem, begins in the older language: e. g. étivant (TB.), kṣetivant (AB.), yajati and juhoti and dadāti (S.), nandati (MBh.). The feminine yúvati *young, maiden* is of isolated character.

h. In some of the words instanced in the last paragraph, ti is perhaps applied as a secondary suffix. A kindred character belongs to it in the numeral derivatives from pronominal roots, káti, táti, yáti, and from numerals, as daçati, viṅçatí, ṣaṣṭí, etc., with paṅktí (from páñca); in padāti; and in addhātí, from the particle addhā́.

1158. नि **ni.** This suffix agrees in general in its uses and in the form of its derivatives with the preceding; but it makes a very much smaller number of words, among which the feminine abstracts are a minority.

a. As was noticed above (1157 c), a few verbs (ending in vowels) making their passive participle in na instead of ta make their action-noun in ni instead of ti. From the older language are quotable jyāní *injury*, jūrní *heat*, hāni *abandonment* (and the masculines ghṛ́ṇi and jī́rṇi); later occur glāni, -mlāni, sanni-.

b. Words of the other class are: açni *eating*, -uṣṇi *burning*, váhni *carrying*, jū́rṇi *singing*, tū́rṇi *hasty*, bhū́rṇi *excited*, dharṇí *sustaining*, preṇí *loving*, vṛṣṇí and vṛ́ṣṇi *virile;* and with them may be mentioned pṛ́çni *speckled*.

c. In preṇí, yóni, mení, çréṇi, çróṇi is seen a strengthening of the radical syllable, such as does not appear among the derivatives in ti.

d. Derivatives in ni from roots with prefixes do not appear to occur.

e. In **hrādúni** and **hlāduni** we have a prefixed **u**. In the words ending in **ani**, the **a** has probably the same value with that of **ati** (above, **1157g**); but **ani** has gained a more independent status, and may be best treated as a separate suffix.

1159. **अनि ani.** The words made by this suffix have the same double value with those made by the preceding suffixes. Their accent is various. Thus:

a. Feminine action-nouns, sometimes with concreted meaning: as, **iṣáṇi** *impulse*, **çaráṇi** *injury*, **dyotaní** *brightness*, **kṣipaṇí** *blow*, **açáni** *missile*, **vartaní** *track;* and **-arçani, udani-, jaraṇi-.**

b. Adjectives and other agent-words are: **aráṇi** *fire-stick*, **caráṇi** *movable*, **cakṣáṇi** *enlightener*, **taráṇi** *quick*, **dhamáni** *pipe*, **dhvasáni** *scattering*, **vakṣáṇi** *strengthener*, **saraṇi** *track*. **Dharaṇi** and one or two other late words are probably variants to stems in **anī**. From a reduplicated root-form comes **-paptani.** From desiderative stems are made **rurukṣáṇi, siṣāsáni,** and (with prefix) **ā-çuçukṣáṇi.** And a small number of words appear to attach themselves to an **s**-aorist stem: thus, **parṣáṇi, sakṣáṇi, carṣaṇí.**

c. It is questionable whether the infinitives in **ṣáṇi (978)** are to be put here, as accusatives of a formation in **ani,** or under the next suffix, as locatives of a formation in **an,** from roots and stems increased by an aoristic **s.**

1160. **अन् an.** Not many words are made with a suffix of this form, and of these few are plainly to be connected with roots. Certain rare neuters (along with the doubtful infinitives) are nouns of action; the rest are masculine and neuter agent-nouns. The accent is various.

a. The infinitives which admit of being referred to this suffix, as locative cases, are those in **ṣáṇi,** of which the sibilant may be the final of a tense-stem. They are all given above (**978**).

b. The other action-nouns in **an** are **mahán** *greatness*, **rājánˑ** *authority* (RV., once: compare **rā́jan**; the accent-relation is the reverse of the usual one), and **gámbhan** *depth* (VS., once); and PB. has **kṣepṇā** once.

c. Agent-nouns (in part of doubtful connection) are: **ukṣán** *ox*, **cákṣan** *eye*, **tákṣan** *carpenter*, **dhvasán** proper name, **pūṣán** name of a god, **majján** *marrow*, **rā́jan** *king*, **vṛ́ṣan** *virile*, *bull*, **sághan, snīhán** (**snūhan** Āpast.); also **-gman, jmán, -bhvan, -çvan,** with **çván, yúvan, yóṣan,** and the stems **áhan, ū́dhan,** etc. (**430—4**), filling up the inflection of other defective stems.

d. With prefixes occur **pratidī́van** and **átidīvan, vibhván, níkāman.**

1161. तु **tu.** The great mass of the words of this formation are the infinitives — accusatives in the later language, in the earlier likewise datives and ablative-genitives: see above, **970b**, **972.** But a few are also used independently, as action-nouns or with concreted meaning; and an extremely small number, of somewhat questionable character, appear to have the value of agent-words. They are of all genders, but chiefly masculine. The root has the **guṇa**-strengthening.

a. The infinitive words are accented on the radical syllable when simple, and most of the others have the same accent; but a few have the tone on the ending.

b. Examples are: of the regular formation, masc. **dā́tu** *share*, **jātu**-*birth*, **dhā́tu** *element*, **tántu** *thread*, **mántu** *counsel*, **ótu** *weft*, **sātu** *receptacle*, **sétu** *tie*, **sótu** *pressure;* also **krátu** *capacity*, and **sáktu** *grits;* fem. **vástu** *morning;* neut. **vastu** *thing*, **vā́stu** *abode;* — with accent on the ending, **aktú** *ray*, **jantú** *being*, **gātú** *way* and *song*, **yātú** (?) *demon*, **hetú** *cause*, **ketú** *banner* (all masc.); — with unstrengthened root, **ṛtú** *season*, **pitú** *drink*, **sū́tu** *birth*, and apparently **kṛ́tu** (in **kṛ́tvas** *times*); with **vṛddhi**-strengthening, **vā́stu** (above). Agent-nouns appear to be **dhā́tu** *drinkable* and **kroṣṭu** *jackal.*

c. The infinitives in **tu** have (**968**) often the union-vowel **i** before the suffix, and this in a few cases is lengthened to **ī**. In other use occur also **-stárītu** and **-dhárītu** (both with **dus**), **-hávītu** (with **su**); **turphárītu** seems of the same formation, but is obscure.

d. In a few instances, the suffix **tu** appears to be added to a tense- or conjugation-stem in **a**; thus, **edhatú** and **vahatú**; **tamyatú** and **tapyatú**; and **siṣāsátu.** The accent of the last is paralleled only by that of **jīvā́tu** *life*, which is further exceptional in showing a long **ā**; it is used sometimes in the manner of an infinitive.

1162. नु **nu.** This suffix forms a comparatively small body of words, generally masculine, and having both the abstract and the concrete value.

a. The accent is usually on the ending, and the root unstrengthened.

b. Thus: **kṣepnú** *jerk*, **bhānú** *light* (later *sun*), **vagnú** *sound*, **sūnú** *son*, **dā́nu** (with irregular accent) m. f. *demon*, n. *drop*, *dew;* **dhenú** f. *cow;* — **gṛdhnú** *hasty*, **tapnú** *burning*, **trasnu** *fearful*, **dhṛṣṇú** *bold:* — and **víṣṇu** *Vishnu*, and perhaps **sthāṇú** *pillar.* Compare also suffix **tnu**, **1196a.**

c. This also (like **tu**) appears sometimes with a prefixed **a**: thus, **kṣipaṇú** *missile*, **krandanu** and **nadanú** *roaring*, **nabhanú** (and **-nū́**, f.) *fountain*, **vibhañjanú** (only instance with prefix) *breaking to pieces*; and perhaps the proper names **dāsanu** and **kṛçā́nu** belong here.

1163. थ **tha.** The words made with this suffix are almost without exception action-nouns (though some have assumed a concrete value). They are of all genders. The root is of a weak (or even weakened) form, and the accent usually on the suffix.

a. Thus: masc., **-itha** *going*, **ártha** *goal*, **-kṛtha** *making*, **gāthá** *song*, **pakthá** n. pr., **bhṛthá** *offering*, **-yātha** *road*, **-çītha** *lying down*, **çotha** *swelling*, **siktha** *sediment*; and, of less clear connections, **yūthá** *herd*, **rátha** *chariot*; — neut., **ukthá** *saying*, **tīrthá** *ford*, **nīthá** *song*, **rikthá** *heritage*, and apparently **pṛṣṭhá** *back*; — fem. (with **ā**), **gā́thā** *song*, **nī́thā** *way*. Radical **ā** is weakened to **ī** in **gī́tha** *song* and **-pītha** *drink* and **-pītha** *protection*; a final nasal is lost in **-gatha** *going* and **hátha** *slaying*. In **vijigīthá** (ÇB.; but BAU. **-īta**) is apparently seen a formation from a reduplication of √**ji**, *victorious*.

b. A few examples of combination with prefixes occur, with accent on the final: thus, **nirṛthá** *destruction*, **saṁgathá** *union*, etc.

c. Still more common in the older language is a form of this suffix to which has become prefixed an **á**, which is probably of thematic origin, though become a union-vowel. Thus: **-anátha** *breathing*, **ayátha** *foot*, **carátha** *mobility*, **tveṣátha** *vehemence*, and so **prothátha, yajátha, ravátha, vakṣátha, ucátha, vidátha, çaṅsatha, çapátha, çayátha, çvayátha, çvasátha, sacátha, stanátha, stavátha, sravátha,** and, with weak root-form, **ruvátha**; the later language adds **karatha, taratha, çamatha, savatha.** With a prefix, the accent is thrown forward upon the final: thus, **āvasathá** *abode*, **pravasathá** *absence*; but **prāṇátha** *breath* is treated as if **prān** were an integral root.

d. Isolated combinations of **tha** with other preceding vowels occur: thus, **várūtha** *protection*, **járūtha** *wasting* (?); and **matútha** (√**man**?).

1164. थु **thu.** This suffix (like थ **tha**, above) has an अ **á** attached to it, and, in the very few derivatives which it makes, appears only as अथु **áthu**.

a. The only Vedic examples are **ejáthu** *quaking*, **vepáthu** *trembling*, **stanáthu** *roaring*. Later cases are **nandáthu** (TS.), **nadathu** (U.), **kṣavathu** (S.), **davathu, bhrañçathu, majjathu, vamathu, çvayathu, sphūrjathu.**

1165. यु **yu.** With this suffix are made a very few nouns, both of agent and of action, with unstrengthened root and various accent. Thus:

a. Abstracts (masc.) are **manyú** *wrath*, **mṛtyú** *death* (with **t** added to the short final of the root).

b. Adjectives etc. are **druhyú** n. pr., **bhujyú** *pliable*, **mucyu** (GB. i. 1. 7), **çundhyú** *pure*; **yájyu** *pious*, **sáhyu** *strong*, **dásyu** *enemy*; and, with **vṛddhi**-strengthening, **jāyú** *victorious*.

c. For other derivatives ending in **yu**, see the suffix **u**, below, **1178h,i.**

1166. म **ma.** The action-nouns made by this suffix are almost all masculine; and they are of various root-form and accent, as are also the agent-nouns and adjectives.

a. Examples of action-nouns are: **ajmá** *course*, **gharmá** *heat*; **éma** *progress*, **bhā́ma** *brightness*, **sárma** *flow*, **stóma** *song of praise*.

b. Examples of agent-nouns etc. are: **tigmá** *sharp*, **bhīmá** *terrible*, **çagmá** *mighty*, **idhmá** *fuel*, **yudhmá** *warrior*. A single instance from a reduplicated root is **tūtumá** *powerful*. **Sarámā** f., with **a** before the suffix, is of doubtful connection.

c. A number of stems in **ma** have stems in **man** beside them, and appear, at least in part, to be transfers from the **an-** to the **a**-declension. Such are **ajma, oma, ema, arma, tókma, darmá, dhárma, narmá, yā́ma, yugma, vema, çuṣma, sóma, sárma, hóma.**

1167. मि **mi.** A very small number of nouns, masculine and feminine, formed with **mi**, may be conveniently noticed here.

Thus, from **ṛ**-roots, **ūrmí** *wave*, **-kūrmi** *action*, **sūrmī́** f. *tube*; from others, **jāmí** *relation*, **bhū́mi** or **bhū́mī** f. *earth*, **lakṣmī́** *sign*; also probably **raçmí** *line, ray*; and the adjective **krúdhmi** (? RV., once).

1168. मन् **man.** The numerous derivatives made with this suffix are almost only action-nouns. The great majority of them are neuter, and accented on the root-syllable; a much smaller number are masculine, and accented on the suffix. The few agent-words are, if nouns, masculine, and have the latter accent: in several instances, a neuter and a masculine, of the one and the other value and accent, stand side by side. The root has in general the **guṇa**-strengthening.

1. **a.** Examples of regularly formed neuters are: **kárman** *action*, **jánman** *birth*, **nā́man** *name*, **vártman** *track*, **véçman** *dwelling*, **hóman** *sacrifice*, **-dyótman** *splendor*.

b. Examples of masculine abstracts are: **omán** *favor*, **ojmán** *strength*, **jemán** *conquest*, **svādmán** *sweetness*, **hemán** *impulse*.

c. Corresponding neuter action-nouns and masculine agent-nouns are: **bráhman** *worship* and **brahmán** *priest;* **dā́man** *gift* and **dāmán** *giver;* **dhárman** *rule* and **dharmán** *orderer;* **sádman** *seat* and **sadmán** *sitter*. But **óman** *friend* stands in the contrary relation to **omán** m. *favor*. Very few other agent-nouns occur; and all, except **brahmán**, are of rare occurrence.

d. On the other hand, **jeman** and **varṣman** and **svādman** (and **variman**) have the difference of gender and accent without a corresponding difference of meaning.

e. The noun **áçman** *stone*, though masculine, is accented on the radical syllable; and two or three other questionable cases of the same kind occur.

f. The derivatives in **man** used as infinitives (**974**) have for the most part the accent of neuters: the only exception is **vidmáne**.

g. A few words, of either class, have an irregular root-form: thus, **udman**, **ūṣmán** or **uṣman**, **bhū́man** *earth*, **bhūmán** *abundance*, **syū́man**, **sīmán**, **bhujmán**, **vidmán**, **çíkman**, **çuṣman**, **sidhman**; and **kā́rṣman**, **bhā́rman**, **çā́kman**.

h. Derivatives in **man** from roots with prefixes are not numerous. They are usually accented on the prefix, whether action-nouns or adjectives: thus, **prábhar̃man** *forthbringing*, **práyāman** *departure;* **ánuvartman** *following after:* the exceptions, **vijā́man**, **prativartmán**, **visarmán**, are perhaps of possessive formation.

2. i. The same suffix, though only with its abstract-making value, has in a number of cases before it a union-vowel, **i** or **ī**; and **imán** comes to be used as a secondary suffix, forming abstract nouns (masculine) from a considerable number of adjectives.

j. The neuters in **iman** and **īman** are primary formations, belonging almost only to the older language: thus, **jániman**, **dhariman** (M.), **váriman** (beside **varimán**, as noticed above); and **dárīman**, **dhárīman**, **párīman** (and **páreman** SV., once), **bhárīman**, **várīman**, **sárīman**, **stárīman**, **sávīman**, and **hávīman**. Those in **īman** are hardly met with outside the Rig-Veda.

k. The masculines in **imán** are in the oldest language less frequent than the neuters just described: they are **tániman** (?), **jarimán**, **prathimán**, **mahimán**, **varimán** (beside the equivalent **váriman** and **várīman**), **varṣimán** (beside the equivalent **várṣman** and **varṣmán**), **harimán**, and **drāghimán** (VS.) beside **drāghmán** (V.B.). Some of these, as well as of the derivatives in simple **man**, attach themselves in meaning, or in form also, to adjectives, to which they seem the accompanying abstracts: compare the similar treatment of the primary comparatives and superlatives (above, **468**): such are **pāpmán** (to **pāpá**, **pā́pīyas** etc.); **drāghmán** etc. (to **dīrghá**, **drā́ghīyas**, etc.); **váriman** etc. (to **urú**,

váríyas, etc.); **práthiman** (to **pṛthú**, **práthiṣṭha**); **harimán** (to **hári** or **hárita**); **várṣman** etc. (to **várṣīyas** etc.); **svádman** etc. (to **svādú**, **svā́dīyas**, etc.). Then in the Brāhmaṇa language are found further examples: thus, **dhūmrimán** (TS. K.), **draḍhimán** (MS. K.: to **dṛḍhá**, **dráḍhīyas**, etc.), **aṇimán** (ÇB.; and **áṇiman** n. *bit*), **sthemán**, **sthá-viman** (n. *big piece*), **taruṇiman** (K.), **paruṣiman** (AB.), **abaliman** (ChU.), **lohitiman** (KB.); and still later such as **laghiman**, **kṛṣṇiman**, **pūrṇiman**, **madhuriman**, **çoṇiman**, etc., etc.

1169. वन् **van.** By this suffix are made almost only agent-words, adjectives and nouns, the latter chiefly masculines. The root is unstrengthened, and to a short final vowel is added a त् **t** before the suffix. The accent is almost always on the root, both in the simple words and in their compounds.

a. The insertion of **t** is an intimation that the words of this form are originally made by the addition of **an** to derivatives in **u** and **tu**; yet **van** has the present value of an integral suffix in the language, and must be treated as such.

b. Examples of the usual formation are: masc. **yájvan** *offering*, **drúhvan** *harming*, **çákvan** *capable*, **-ríkvan** *leaving*, **-jítvan** *conquering*, **sútvan** *pressing*, **kṛ́tvan** *active*, **-gátvan** (like **-gat**, **-gatya**) *going*, **sát-van** (√**san**) *warrior*; neut. **párvan** *joint*, **dhánvan** *bow*. Irregular, with strengthened root, are **árvan** *courser*, **-yāvan** (? AV.) *driving off*; and, with accent on the suffix, **dṛván** (? VS.) and **vidván** (? AV.).

c. Examples from roots with prefixes (which are not rare) are: **atī́tvan** *excelling*, **upahásvan** *reviler*, **sambhṛ́tvan** *collecting*; and perhaps **vivás-van** *shining*: **abhísatvan** is a compound with governing preposition (**1310**). For the compounds with other elements, which, except in special cases, have the same accent, see below, **1277**.

d. The stems **muṣīván** *robber* and **sanítvan** (each RV., once) are the only ones with a union-vowel, and are perhaps better regarded as secondary derivatives — of which a few are made with this suffix: see below, **1234**. From a reduplicated root are made **rárāvan** and **cikitván** (and possibly **vivásvan**).

e. Action-nouns made with the suffix **van** are only the infinitival words mentioned at **974** — unless **bhurváṇi** (RV., once) is to be added, as locative of **bhurván**.

f. The feminines corresponding to adjectives in **van** are not made (apparently) directly from this suffix, but from **vara**, and end in **varī**; see below, **1171 b**.

1170. वन **vana**, वनि **vani**, वनु **vanu.** The very few words made with these suffixes may best be noticed here, in connection with वन् van (of which the others are probably secondary extensions).

a. With **vana** are made **vagvaná** *talkative*, **satvaná** *warrior* (beside **sátvan**, above); and, from a reduplicated root, **çuçukvaná** *shining*.

b. With **vani** are made from simple roots **turváṇi** *excelling*, and **bhurváṇi** *restless*, and, from reduplicated roots, **çuçukváni** *shining*, **dadhṛṣváṇi** *daring*, **tuturváni** *striving after*, and **jugurváṇi** *praising*; **ariṣvaṇi** is obscure.

c. With **vanu** is made only **vagvanú** *tone*, *noise*.

1171. वर् **vara.** With this suffix are made a few derivatives, of all genders, having for the most part the value of agent-nouns and adjectives. Much more common are the feminine stems in वरी varī, which, from the earliest period, serve as corresponding feminines to the masculine stems in वन् van.

a. A few masculine adjectives in **vará** occur, formally accordant (except in accent) with the feminines: thus, **itvará** *going*, **-advara** *eating*; and so, further, in the older language, **īçvará**, **-jāvara**, **phárvara**, **bhārvará**, **bhāsvará**, **vyadhvará** (?), **-sadvara**, **sthāvará**, and doubtless with them belongs **vidvalá**; later, **-kasvara**, **gatvara**, **ghasvara** (also **ghasmara**), **-jitvara**, **naçvara**, **pīvara**, **madvara**, **-sṛtvara**; from a reduplicated root, **yāyāvará** (B. and later). Many of these have feminines in **ā**.

b. The feminines in **varī** accord in treatment of the root and in accent with the masculines in **van** to which they correspond: thus, **yájvarī**, **-jítvarī**, **sṛ́tvarī**, **-çívarī**, **-yāvarī**, and so on (about twenty-five such formations in RV.); from a reduplicated root, **-çiçvarī**.

c. A very small number of neuters occur, with accent on the root: thus, **kárvara** *deed*, **gáhvara** (later also **gabhvara**) *thicket*; and a feminine or two, with accent on the penult: **urvárā** *field*, and **urvárī** *tow* (both of doubtful etymology).

We take up now the suffixes by which are made only stems having the value of agent-nouns and adjectives; beginning with a brief mention of the participial endings, which in general have been already sufficiently treated.

1172. अन्त् **ant** (or अत् **at**). The office of this suffix, in making present and future participles active, has been fully explained above, in connection with the various tense-stems and conjugation-stems (chaps. VIII.—XIV.), in combination with which alone it is employed (not directly with the root, unless this is also used as tense-stem).

a. A few words of like origin, but used as independent adjectives, were given at 450. With the same or a formally identical suffix are made from pronominal roots íyant and kíyant (451, 517 a). And ádvayant *not double-tongued* (RV., once), appears to contain a similar formation from the numeral dvi — unless we are to assume a denominative verb-stem as intermediate.

1173. वांस् vāṅs (or वस् vas). For the (perfect active) participles made with this suffix, see above, 802—6, and 458 ff.

a. A few words of irregular and questionable formation were noticed at 462, above. Also, apparent transfers to a form us or uṣa. RV. vocalizes the v once, in jujuruā́n.

b. The oldest language (RV.) has a very few words in vas, of doubtful relations: ṛ́bhvas and çíkvas *skilful* (beside words in va and van), and perhaps khidvas (√khād). The neuter abstract várivas *breadth, room* (belonging to urú *broad*, in the same manner with váriyas and varimán), is quite isolated. MBh. makes a nominative pīvān, as if from pīvāṅs instead of pīvan.

1174. मान māna. The participles having this ending are, as has been seen (584 b), present and future only, and have the middle, or the derived passive, value belonging in general to the stems to which the suffix is attached.

1175. आन āna. The participles ending in आन āna are of middle and passive value, like those just noticed, and either present, perfect, or (partly with the form सान sāna: above, 897 b) aorist.

a. A few other words ending in the same manner in the old language may be mentioned here. The RV. has the adjectives tákavāna, bhṛ́gavāṇa, vásavāna, ūrdhvasāná, apparently made on the model of participial stems. Also the proper names ápnavāna, pṛ́thavāna, and cyávāna and cyávatāna. Párçana *abyss* is doubtful; rujā́nā (RV., once) is probably a false reading; ā́pnāna is of doubtful character.

1176. त ta. The use of this suffix in forming participles directly from the root, or from a conjugational (not a tense) stem, was explained above, 952—6. The participles thus made are in part intransitive, but in great part passive in value (like those made by the two preceding suffixes, but in much larger measure, and more decidedly).

a. A few general adjectives, or nouns with concrete meaning, are adaptations of this participle. Examples are: **tṛṣṭá** *rough*, **çītá** *cold*, **dṛḍhá** (for **dṛḍhá: 224 a**) *firm;* **dūtá** *messenger*, **sūtá** *charioteer;* **ṛtá** *right*, **ghṛtá** *ghee*, **jātá** *kind*, **dyūtá** *gambling*, **nṛttá** *dance*, **jīvitá** *life*, **caritá** *behavior*, **smita** *smile*. The adjective **tigitá** (RV.) *sharp* shows anomalous reversion of palatal to guttural before the **i** (**216 d**). **Vāvā́ta** *dear* is a single example from a reduplicated root.

b. Doubtless after the example and model of participles from denominative stems (of which, however, no instances are quotable from the Veda — unless **bhāmita** RV.), derivatives in **ita** are in the later language made directly from noun and adjective-stems, having the meaning of *endowed with*, *affected by*, *made to be*, and the like (compare the similar English formation in *ed*, as *horned*, *barefooted*, *bluecoated)*. Examples are **rathita** *furnished with a chariot*, **duḥkhita** *pained*, **kusumita** *flowered*, **durbalita** *weakened*, **niḥsaṅçayita** *indubitable*, etc. etc.

c. A few words ending in **ta** are accented on the radical syllable, and their relation to the participial derivatives is very doubtful: such are **ásta** *home*, **márta** *mortal*, **vā́ta** *wind;* and with them may be mentioned **gárta** *high seat*, **nákta** *night*, **hásta** *hand*. **Vratá** is commonly viewed as containing a suffix **ta**, but it doubtless comes from √**vṛt** (**vrat-á**, like **tradá**, **vrajá**) and means originally *course*.

d. Several adjectives denoting color end in **ita**, but are hardly connectible with roots of kindred meaning: thus, **palitá** *gray*, **ásita** *black*, **róhita** and **lóhita** *red*, **hárita** *green;* akin with them are **éta** *variegated*, **çyetá** *white*. The feminines of these stems are in part irregular: thus, **énī** and **çyénī**; **róhiṇī** and **lóhinī**, and **háriṇī** (but the corresponding masc. **háriṇa** also occurs); and **ásiknī**, **páliknī**, and **hárikni**.

e. A small number of adjectives in the older language ending in **ata** are not to be separated from the participial words in **ta**, although their specific meaning is in part gerundive. They are: **pacatá** *cooked*, **darçatá** and **paçyata** *seen*, *to be seen*, *worth seeing;* and so **yajatá**, **haryatá**, **bharatá**. The **y** of **paçyata** and **haryatá** indicates pretty plainly that the **a** also is that of a present tense-stem. **Rajatá** *silvery* is of more obscure relation to √**raj** *color;* **párvata** *mountain* must be secondary.

1177. न **na** (and इन **ina**, उन **una**). The use of the suffix न **na** in forming from certain roots participles equivalent to those in त ta, either alongside the latter or instead of them, was explained above, at **957**.

a. With the same suffix are made a number of general adjectives, and of nouns of various gender (fem. in **nā**). The accent is on the suffix or on the root. A few examples are: **uṣṇá** *hot*, **çuná** *fortunate*, **áçna** *ravenous*, **çvítna** *white;* masc., **praçná** *question*, **yajñá** *offering*, **ghṛṇá** *heat*, **várṇa** *color*, **svápna** *sleep;* neut., **parṇá** *wing*, **rátna** *jewel* (?); fem. **tṛ́ṣṇā** *thirst*, **yācñā́** *supplication*. But many of the stems ending in **na** are not readily connectible with roots. An antithesis of accent is seen in **kárṇa** *ear* and **karṇá** *eared*.

b. The few words ending in **ina** are of doubtful connection, but may be mentioned here: thus, **aminá** *violent*, **vṛjiná** *crooked*, **dákṣiṇa** *right*, **dráviṇa** *property*, **druhiṇa**, **-çreṣiṇa**, **hariṇá**; and **kanī́na** may be added.

c. The words ending in **una** are of various meaning and accent, like those in **ana**: they are **árjuna**, **karúṇa**, **-cetúna**, **táruṇa**, **dāruṇá**, **dharúṇa**, **narúṇa**, **píçuna**, **mithuná**, **yatúna**, **vayúna**, **varuṇa**, **çalúna**, and the feminine **yamúnā**; and **bhrūṇá** may be added.

d. These are all the proper participial endings of the language. The gerundives, later and earlier, are in the main evident secondary formations, and will be treated under the head of secondary derivation.

We take up now the other suffixes forming agent-nouns and adjectives, beginning with those which have more or less a participial value.

1178. उ **u.** With this suffix are made a considerable body of derivatives, of very various character — adjectives, and agent-nouns of all genders, with different treatment of the root, and with different accent. It is especially used with certain conjugational stems, desiderative (particularly later) and denominative (mainly earlier), making adjectives with the value of present participles; and in such use it wins in part the aspect of a secondary suffix.

a. The root has oftenest a weak (or weakened) form; but it is sometimes vriddhied; least often (when capable of guṇa), it has the guṇa-strengthening — all without any apparent connection with either accent or meaning or gender. After final radical **ā** is usually added **y** (258) before the suffix. A few derivatives are made from the reduplicated root. But many words ending in **u** are not readily, or not at all, connectible with roots; examples will be given especially of those that have an obvious etymology.

b. Examples of ordinary adjectives are: **uru** *wide*, **ṛjú** *straight*, **pṛthú** *broad*, **mṛdú** *soft*, **sādhú** *good*, **svādú** *sweet*, **tápu** *hot*, **vásu** *good;* **jāyú** *conquering*, **dārú** *bursting;* **çayú** *lying*, **réku** *empty;* **dhāyú** *thirsty*, **pāyú** *protecting*. Final **ā** appears to be lost before the suffix in **-sthu** (**suṣṭhú**, **anuṣṭhú**), and perhaps in **yú**, **-gu** (**agregú**), and **-khu** (**ākhú**).

c. Examples of nouns are: masc., **añçú** *ray*, **ripú** *deceiver*, **vāyú**

wind-god, **ásu** *life*, **mánu** *man*, *Manu;* fem., **íṣu** (also masc.) *arrow*, **síndhu** (also masc.) *river*, **tanū́** or **tanú** *body;* neut., **kṣú** *food.*

d. Derivatives from reduplicated roots are: **cikitú, jágmu, jigyú, jijñu, siṣṇu, -tatnu** (unless this is made with **nu** or **tnu**), **didyu** (?), **dadru, yáyu** or **yayú** and **yíyu** (with final **ā** lost), **pípru** (proper name), **-dīdhayu;** and **títaü, babhrú, -raru** (**aráru**), **malimlú** (?) have the aspect of being similar formations.

e. A few derivatives are made from roots with prefixes, with various accentuation: for example, **upāyú** *on-coming*, **pramayú** *going to destruction*, **viklíndu** a certain disease, **abhíçu** *rein (directer)*, **sáṁvasu** *dwelling together.*

f. From tense-stems, apparently, are made **tanyú** *thundering*, **bhindú** *splitting*, **-vindu** *finding*, and (with aoristic **s**) **dákṣu** and **dhákṣu** (all RV.).

g. Participial adjectives in **u** from desiderative "roots" (stems with loss of their final **a**) are sufficiently numerous in the ancient language (RV. has more than a dozen of them, AV. not quite so many) to show that the formation was already a regular one, extensible at will; and later such adjectives may be made from every desiderative. Examples (older) are: **ditsú, dipsú, cikitsú, titikṣú, pipīṣu, mumukṣú, iyakṣú, çiçlikṣú;** with prefix, **abhidipsú;** with anomalous accent, **didṛ́kṣu.** These adjectives, both earlier and later, may take an object in the accusative (**271 a**).

h. A few similar adjectives are made in the older language from causatives: thus, **dhārayú** (*persistent*), **bhājayú, bhāvayú, maṅhayú, mandayú, çramayú:** and **mṛgayú** from the caus.-denom. **mṛgáya.**

i. Much more numerous, however, are such formations from the more proper denominatives, especially in the oldest language (RV. has toward eighty of them; AV. only a quarter as many, including six or eight which are not found in RV.; and they are still rarer in the Brāhmaṇas, and hardly met with later). In a majority of cases, personal verbal forms from the same denominative stem are in use: thus, for example, to **aghāyú, arātīyú, ṛjūyú, caraṇyú, manasyú, saniṣyú, uruṣyú, saparyú;** in others, only the present participle in **yánt,** or the abstract noun in **yā́** (**1149 d**), or nothing at all. A few are made upon denominative stems from pronouns: thus, **tvāyú** (beside **tvāyánt** and **tvāyā́**), **yuvayú** or **yuvāyú, asmayú, svayú,** and the more anomalous **ahaṁyú** and **kiṁyú.** Especially where no other denominative forms accompany the adjective, this has often the aspect of being made directly from the noun with the suffix **yu,** either with a meaning of *seeking* or *desiring*, or with a more general adjective sense: thus, **yavayú** *seeking grain*, **varāhayú** *boar-hunting*, **stanasyú** *desiring the breast;* **ūrṇāyú** *woolen*, **yuvanyú** *youthful*, **bhīmayú** *terrible.* And so the "secondary suffix **yu**" wins a degree of standing and application as one forming derivative adjectives (as in **ahaṁyú** and **kiṁyú,** above, and doubtless some others, even of the RV. words). In three RV. cases, the final **as** of a noun-stem is even changed to **o** before it: namely, **aṅhoyú, duvoyú** (and **duvoyā́;** beside **duvasyú**), **áskṛdhoyu.**

j. The words in **yu** do not show in the Veda resolution into **iu** (except **dhāsiús** AV., once).

1179. ऊ **ū.** Stems in ऊ **ū** are very few, even as compared with those in ई **ī** (**1156**). They are for the most part feminines corresponding to masculines in **u** (**344b**), with half-a-dozen more independent feminines (see **355c**).

a. To those already mentioned above are to be added **karṣū́** *pit*, **-calū** (in **puṁçcalū́**), **-janū** (in **prajanū́**), **çumbhū́**.

1180. उक **uka.** With this suffix are made derivatives having the meaning and construction (**271g**) of a present participle. The root is strengthened, and has the accent.

a. The derivatives in **uka** are hardly known in the Veda; but they become frequent in the Brāhmaṇas, of whose language they are a marked characteristic (about sixty different stems occur there); and they are found occasionally in the older language. In all probability, they are originally and properly obtained by adding the secondary suffix **ka** (**1222**) to a derivative in **u**; but they have gained fully the character of primary formations, and in only an instance or two is there found in actual use an **u**-word from which they should be made.

b. The root is only so far strengthened that the radical syllable is a heavy (**79**) one; and it has the accent, whether the derivative is made from a simple root or from one with prefix.

c. Examples, from the Brāhmaṇa language, are: **vā́duka, nā́çuka, upakrā́muka, prapā́duka, upasthā́yuka** (**258**), **vyā́yuka, véduka, bhā́vuka, kṣódhuka, hā́ruka, várṣuka, samárdhuka, dáṅçuka, ālambuka, çikṣuka** (GB.: RV. has **çikṣú**), **pramā́yuka** (ÇB. has **pramāyu**).

d. Exceptions as regards root-form are: **nirmā́rguka** (with **vṛddhi**-strengthening, as is usual with this root: **627**), **-kasuka, ṛdhnuka** (from a tense-stem; beside **árdhuka**). AV. accents **sáṁkasuka** (ÇB. has **saṁkásuka**) and **víkasuka**; RV. has **sānuká** (which is its only example of the formation, if it be one; AV. has also **ghā́tuka** from √**han**, and **ápramāyuka**); **vasuká** (TS. et al.) is probably of another character. **Açanāyuka** (PB. et al.) is the only example noticed from a conjugation-stem.

e. Of later occurrence are a few words whose relation to the others is more or less doubtful: **kārmuka** and **dhārmuka, tsāruka, tarkuka, nānduka, pādukā, pecuka, bhikṣuka, lāṣuka, seduka, hiṇḍuka, hreṣuka.** Of these, only **lāṣuka** appears like a true continuer of the formation; several are pretty clearly secondary derivatives.

f. A formation in **ūka** (a suffix of like origin, perhaps, with **uka**) may be mentioned here: namely, **indhūka, majjūka,** and, from reduplicated roots, **jāgarū́ka** *wakeful*, **jañjapūka** (later) *muttering*, **dandaçū́ka** *biting*, **yāyajū́ka** *sacrificing much*, **vāvadūka** (later) *talkative;* **salalū́ka** is questionable.

1181. अक **aka.** Here, as in the preceding case, we doubtless have a suffix made by secondary addition of क **ka** to a derivative in अ **a**; but it has, for the same reason as the other, a right to be mentioned here. Its free use in the manner of a primary suffix is of still later date than that of **uka**; it has very few examples in the older language.

a. In RV. is found (besides **pāvaká,** which has a different accent, and which, as the metre shows, is really **pavāka**) only **sā́yaka** *missile:* AV. adds **pī́yaka** and **vádhaka,** and VS. **abhikróçaka.** But in the later language such derivatives are common, more usually with raising of the root-syllable by strengthening to heavy quantity: thus, **nāyaka, dāyaka (258), pācaka, grāhaka, bodhaka, jāgaraka;** but also **janaka, khanaka.** They are declared by the grammarians to have the accent on the radical syllable. They often occur in copulative composition with gerundives of the same root: thus, **bhakṣyabhakṣaka** *eatable and eater*, **vācyavācaka** *designated and designation*, and so on.

b. That the derivatives in **aka** sometimes take an accusative object was pointed out above (**271 c**).

c. The corresponding feminine is made sometimes in **akā** or in **akī,** but more usually in **ikā:** thus, **nāyikā** (with **nāyakā**), **pācikā, bodhikā;** compare secondary **aka,** below, **1222.**

d. Derivatives in **āka** are made from a few roots: thus. **jalpāka, bhikṣāka;** but very few occur in the older language: thus, **pavāka** (above, a), **nabhāka, smayā́ka, jáhāka**(?), **-calāka, patākā.** With **āku** is made in RV. **mṛḍayā́ku,** from the causative stem: **pṛ́dāku** and the proper name **íkṣvāku** are of obscure connection.

e. Derivatives in **ika** and **īka** will be treated below, in connection with those in **ka** (**1186 c**).

1182. तृ **tṛ** (or तर् **tar**). The derivatives made by this suffix, as regards both their mode of formation and their uses, have been the subject of remark more than once above (see **369 ff., 942 ff.**). Agent-nouns are freely formed with it at every period of the language; these in the oldest language are very frequently used participially, governing an object in the accusative (**271 d**); later they enter into combination with an auxiliary verb, and, assuming a future meaning, make a periphrastic future tense (**942**). Their corresponding feminine is in **trī**.

a. The root has regularly the **guṇa**-strengthening. A union-vowel **i** (very rarely, one of another character) is often taken: as regards its presence or absence in the periphrastic future forms, see above (**943 a**).

b. Without **guṇa**-change is only **úṣṭṛ** *plough-ox* (no proper agent-noun: apparently **úkṣ-tṛ**: compare the nouns of relationship further on). The root **grah** has, as usual, **ī** — thus, **grahītṛ́**; and the same appears in **-tarītṛ́, -pavītṛ́, -marītṛ́, -varītṛ, -savītṛ**. An **u**-vowel is taken instead by **tárutṛ** and **tarutṛ́, dhánutṛ**, and **sánutṛ**; long in **varūtṛ́**; strengthened to **o** in **manótṛ** and **manotṛ́**. From a reduplicated root comes **vāvā́tṛ**.

c. The accent, in the older language, is sometimes on the suffix and sometimes on the root; or, from roots combined with prefixes, sometimes on the suffix and sometimes on the prefix.

d. In general, the accent on the root or prefix accompanies the participial use of the word; but there are exceptions to this: in a very few instances (four), a word with accented suffix has an accusative object; very much more often, accent on the root appears along with ordinary noun value. The accent, as well as the form, of **manótṛ** is an isolated irregularity. Examples are: **jétā dhánāni** *winning treasures*; **yūyám mártaṁ çrótāraḥ** *ye listen to a mortal*; but, on the other hand, **yaṁtā́ vásūni vidhaté** *bestcwing good things on the pious*; and **jétā jánānām** *conqueror of peoples*.

e. The formation of these nouns in **tṛ** from conjugation-stems, regular and frequent in the later language, and not very rare in the Brāhmaṇas, is met with but once or twice in the Veda (**bodhayitṛ́** and **codayitrī́**, RV.). In **néṣṭṛ** a certain priest (RV. and later), is apparently seen the aoristic **s**.

f. The words of relationship which, in whatever way, have gained the aspect of derivatives in **tṛ**, are **pitṛ́, mātṛ́, bhrā́tṛ, yā́tṛ, duhitṛ́, náptṛ, jā́mātṛ**. Of these, only **mātṛ́** and **yā́tṛ** are in accordance with the ordinary rules of the formation in **tṛ**.

g. Instead of **tṛ** is found **tur** in one or two RV. examples: **yaṁtúr, sthātúr**.

h. Apparently formed by a suffix **ṛ** (or **ar**) are **usṛ́, savyaṣṭhṛ, nánāndṛ, devṛ́**, the last two being words of relationship. For other words ending in **ṛ**, see **369**.

1183. इन् **in.** This is another suffix which has assumed a primary aspect and use, while yet evidently identical in real character with the frequent secondary suffix of the same form denoting possession (below, **1230**).

a. How far it had gained a primary value in the early language is not easy to determine. Most of the words in **in** occurring in RV. and AV. are explainable as possessives; in many the other value is possible, and in a few it is distinctly suggested: thus, **kevalādín, bhadravādín, nitodín, āçārāiṣín, ánāmin, vivyādhín**; from a tense-stem, **-açnuvin, -paçyin** (late); with aoristic **s, -sakṣín**; and, with reduplication, **niyayín, vadāvadin.** As the examples indicate, composition, both with prefixes and with other elements, is frequent; and, in all cases alike, the accent is on the suffix.

b. Later, the primary employment is unquestionable, and examples of it, chiefly in composition, are frequent. The radical syllable is usually strengthened, a medial **a** being sometimes lengthened and sometimes remaining unchanged. Thus, **satyavādin** *truth-speaking*, **abhibhāṣin** *addressing*, **manohārin** *soul-winning.* In **bhāvin** has established itself a prevailingly future meaning, *about to be.*

c. The use of an accusative object with words in **in** was noticed above (**271 b**).

1184. ईयस् **īyas** and इष्ठ **iṣṭha.** These suffixes, which, from forming intensive adjectives corresponding to the adjective of root-form, have come to be used, within somewhat narrow limits, as suffixes of adjective comparison, have been already sufficiently treated above, under the head of comparison (**466–470**).

a. It may be further noticed that **jyéṣṭha** has in the older language (only two or three times in RV.) the accent also on the final, **jyeṣṭhá**, and that its correlative also is **kaniṣṭhá** in the oldest language; **párṣiṣṭha** is made from a secondary form of root, with aoristic **s** added.

b. When the comparative suffix has the abbreviated form **yas** (**470 a**), its **y** is never to be read in the Veda as **i.**

c. No other suffixes make derivatives having participial value otherwise than in rare and sporadic cases; those that remain, therefore, will be taken up mainly in the order of their frequency and importance.

1185. त्र **tra.** With this suffix are formed a few adjectives, and a considerable number of nouns, mostly neuter, and often having a specialized meaning, as signifying the means or instrument of the action expressed by the root. The latter has usually the **guṇa**-strengthening, but sometimes remains unchanged. The accent is various, but more often on the radical syllable.

a. Here, as in certain other cases above, we have doubtless a suffix originally secondary, made by adding **a** to the primary **tṛ** or **tar** (1182); but its use is in great part that of a primary suffix.

b. Examples of neuter nouns are: **gā́tra** *limb*, **páttra** *wing*, **pā́tra** *cup*, **yóktra** *bond*, **vástra** *garment*, **çrótra** *ear*; **astrá** *missile*, **stotrá** *song of praise*, **potrá** *vessel*; of more general meaning, **dáttra** *gift*, **kṣétra** *field*, **mū́tra** *urine*, **hotrá** *sacrifice*. The words accented on the final have often an abstract meaning: thus, **kṣatrá** *authority*, **rāṣṭrá** *kingdom*, **çāstrá** *doctrine*, **sattrá** *sacrificial session* (also **jñā́tra** *knowledge*).

c. Masculines are: **dáṅṣṭra** *tusk*, **mántra** *prayer*, **attrá** (or **atrá**: **232**) *devourer*, **úṣṭra** *buffalo, camel*, and a few of questionable etymology, as **mitrá** *friend*, **putrá** *son*, **vṛtrá** *foe*. **Mitrá** and **vṛtrá** are sometimes neuters even in the Veda, and **mitra** comes later to be regularly of that gender.

d. Feminines (in **trā**) are: **áṣṭrā** *goad*, **mā́trā** *measure*, **hótrā** *sacrifice* (beside **hotrá**), **daṅṣṭrā** (later, for **dáṅṣṭra**); **nā́ṣṭrā** *destroyer*.

e. Not seldom, a "union-vowel" appears before the suffix; but this is not usually the equivalent of the union-vowel used with **tṛ** (above, **1182a**). For the words in **itra** have the accent on **i**: thus, **arítra** (**áritra** AV., once) *impelling, oar*, **khanítra** *shovel*, **pavítra** *sieve*, **janítra** *birth-place*, **sanítra** *gift*; and so **-avitra, açítra, carítra, -taritra, dhamitra, dhavítra, bhavítra, bharítra, vāditra** (with causative root-strengthening), **vahitra**: the combination **ítra** has almost won the character of an independent suffix. The preceding vowel is also in a few cases **a** (sometimes apparently of the present-stem): thus, **yájatra** *venerable*, **kṛntátra** *shred*, **gāyatrá** (f. **-trī́**) *song*, **-damatra, pátatra** *wing*; but also **ámatra** *violent*, **vádhatra** *deadly weapon*; and **varatrā́** f. *strap*. **Tárutra** *overcoming* corresponds to **tarutṛ**. **Nákṣatra** *asterism* is of very doubtful etymology. **Saṁskṛtatrá** (RV., once) seems of secondary formation.

f. The words still used as adjectives in **tra** are mostly such as have union-vowels before the suffix. A single example from a reduplicated root is **johū́tra** *crying out*.

g. A word or two in **tri** and **tru** may be added here, as perhaps of kindred formation with those in **tra**: thus, **áttri** *devouring*, **arcátri** *beaming*, **rā́tri** or **rā́trī** *night*; **çátru** (**çáttru**: **232**) *enemy*.

1186. क **ka.** The suffix क **ka** is of very common use in secondary derivation (below, **1222**); whether it is directly added to roots is almost questionable: at any rate, extremely few primary derivatives are made with it.

a. The words which have most distinctly the aspect of being made from roots are **puṣka-, -meka** (√**mi** *fix*), **yaska** n. pr., **çúṣka** *dry*, **çlóka** (√**çru** *hear*) *noise, report*, etc., and **-sphāka** *teeming*; and **stúkā** *flake* and **stoká** *drop* seem to belong together to a root **stu**; **rākā́** f., n. pr., may be added.

b. But **ka** enters, in its value as secondary, into the composition of certain suffixes reckoned as primary: see **aka** and **uka** (above, **1180, 1181**).

c. A few words in which **ika** and **īka** seem added to a root, though they are really of a kindred formation with the preceding, may be most conveniently noticed here: thus, **vṛ́çcika** (√**vraçc**) *scorpion;* **ánīka** (?) *face*, **dṛ́çīka** *aspect*, **dṛ́bhīka** n. pr., **mṛḍīká** *grace*, **vṛdhīká** *increaser*, **ā́çarīka** and **víçarīka** *gripes*, **-ṛjīka** *beaming*, **ṛṣīka; ṛkṣī́kā;** and, from reduplicated root, **parpharī́ka** *scattering* (?). Compare secondary suffix **ka** (below, **1222**).

1187. य **ya.** It is altogether probable that a part of the derivatives made with this suffix are not less entitled to be ranked as primary than some of those which are above so reckoned. Such, however, are with so much doubt and difficulty to be separated from the great mass of secondary derivatives made with the same suffix that it is preferred to treat them all together under the head of secondary formation (below, **1210—13**).

1188. र **ra.** With this suffix are made a large number of adjectives, almost always with weak root-form, and usually with accent on the suffix. Also, a few words used as nouns, of various gender. In some cases, the suffix is found with a preceding vowel, having the aspect of a union-vowel.

a. Examples of adjectives in **ra** are: **kṣiprá** *quick*, **chidrá** *split*, **turá** *strong*, **bhadrá** *pleasing*, **çakrá** *mighty*, **çukrá** *bright*, **hiṅsrá** *injurious;* — with accent on the root, only **gṛ́dhra** *greedy*, **túmra** *stout*, **dhī́ra** *wise* (secondary?), **vípra** *inspired*, **túgra** n. pr.

b. From roots with prefixes come only an example or two: thus, **niciŕá** *attentive*, **nímṛgra** *joining on*.

c. Nouns in **ra** are: masc., **ájra** *field*, **vīrá** *man*, **vájra** *thunderbolt*, **çū́ra** *hero;* neut., **ágra** *point*, **kṣīrá** *milk*, **rándhra** *hollow*, **riprá** *defilement;* fem., **dhā́rā** *stream*, **çíprā** *jaw*, **súrā** *intoxicating drink*.

The forms of this suffix with preceding vowel may best be considered here, although some of them have nearly or quite gained the value of independent endings. Thus:

d. With **ara** are made a few rare words: the adjectives **dravará** *running*, **patará** *flying*, (with prefix) **nyocará** *suiting;* and the nouns **gambhára** *depth*, **tásara** and **trasara** *shuttle*, **sánara** *gain*, **-ṛkṣara** *thorn:* **bhārvará** and **vāsará** are doubtless of secondary formation; and the same thing may be plausibly conjectured of others. As made with **āra** may be mentioned **mandāra** a tree, **mārjāra** *cat*.

e. With **ira** are made a few words, some of which are in common use: thus, **ajirá** *quick*, **khadirá** a tree, **timira** *dark*, **dhvasirá** *stirring up*, **madirá** *pleasing*, **mudira** *cloud*, **badhirá** *deaf*, **rucira** *bright*, **iṣirá**

lively, **ásira** *missile*, **sthávira** *firm;* and **sthira** *hard*, and **sphirá** *fat*, with displacement of final radical **ā**; also **sarirá** *wave* (usually **salilá**). With **īra** are made **gabhīrá** or **gambhīrá** *profound* and **çávīra** *mighty*, and perhaps **çárīra** *body*.

f. With **ura** are made a few words, of some of which the secondary character is probable: thus, **aṅhurá** (**aṅhu-ra**?) *narrow*, **ásura** (**ásu-ra**?) *living*, **chidura** *tearing*, **bhañgurá** *breaking*, **bhāsura** *shining*, **bhidura** *splitting*, **medura** *fat*, **yādura** *uniting*, **vithura** *tottering*, **vidura** *knowing*, **vidhura** *lacking*. With **ūra**, apparently, are made **sthūrá** *stout* (compare **sthávira**), **kharjúra** a tree, **mayúra** *peacock* (or imitative?).

1189. ल **la.** This suffix is only another form of the preceding, exchanging with it in certain words, in others prevalently or solely used from their first appearance.

a. Conspicuous examples of the interchange are **çuklá**, **sthūlá**, **-miçla**, **çithilá**, **salilá**.

b. Examples of the more independent use are: **pālá** *protecting*, **ánila** (or **aníla**) *wind*, **tṛpála** *joyous;* later **capala** and **tarala** (said to be accented on the final), and **harṣula** (the same). Many words ending in **la** are of obscure etymology.

1190. व **va.** Very few words of clear derivation are made with this suffix — too few to be worth classifying. They are of various meaning and accent, and generally show a weak root-form.

a. Thus: **ṛkvá** *praising*, **ṛṣvá** *lofty*, **takvá** *quick*, **dhruvá** *fixed*, **pakvá** *ripe*, **padva** *going*, **yahvá** *quick* (?), **çarvá** n. pr., **hrasvá** *short*, **çikvá** *artful*, **raṇvá** *joyful*, **ūrdhvá** *lofty*, **vákva** *twisting*, **ūrvá** *stall;* **éva** *quick*, *course*, **áçva** *horse*, **srákva** or **sṛkva** *corner;* and perhaps **úlba** *caul;* a feminine is **prúṣvā** (TS. **pṛ́ṣvā**, AV. **pruṣvā́**); with union-vowel are made **saciva** *companion*, **ámīva** *disease*, and **vidhávā** *widow*.

b. The words in **va** exhibit only in sporadic cases resolution of the ending into **ua**.

1191. रि **ri.** With this suffix are formed, directly or with preceding **u**, a small number of derivatives.

a. Thus: **áñghri** or **aṅhri** *foot*, **áçri** *edge*, **úsri** *dawn*, **tandri** or **-drī́** *weariness*, **bhū́ri** *abundant*, **váñkri** *rib*, **sūrí** *patron*, **-takri** *quick*, **vádhri** *eunuch*, **çubhrí** *beautiful*, **sthúri** *single (team);* and, with **uri**, **jásuri** *exhausted*, **dā́çuri** *pious*, **bhāguri** n. pr., **sáhuri** *mighty;* **añgúri** (or **añgúli**) *finger*.

1192. रु **ru.** This suffix makes a few adjectives and neuter nouns, either directly or with a preceding vowel.

a. Thus: **áçru** *tear*, **cáru** *dear*, **dhārú** *sucking*, **bhīrú** *timid;* — with preceding a-vowel: **aráru** *inimical*, **patáru** *flying*, **vandā́ru** *praising*, **píyāru** *scoffing*, **çarā́ru** *harming;* — with preceding **e**, **tameru** *relaxed*, **maderú** *rejoicing*, **sanéru** *obtaining*, **himerú** *chilly*, the evidently secondary **mitréru** *ally*, and **péru** (of doubtful meaning).

b. The secondary suffix **lu** (see **1227 b**) is apparently added to certain nouns in **ā** from conjugation-stems, making derivatives that have a primary aspect: thus, **patayālú** *flying*, **spṛhayālu** *desiring*.

1193. वि **vi.** By this suffix are made:

a. Two or three derivatives from reduplicated roots: **jā́gṛvi** *awake*, **dā́dhṛvi** *sustaining*, **dī́divi** *shining;* and a very few other words; **ghṛ́ṣvi** *lively*, **dhruví** *firm*, **jírvi** *worn out* (AV.; elsewhere **jívri**); **-pharvī** is doubtful.

b. Here may be mentioned **cikitvít** (RV., once), apparently made with a suffix **vit** from a reduplicated root-form.

1194. स्नु **snu.** With this suffix, with or without a union-vowel, are made a few adjective derivatives from roots, but also from causative stems.

a. From simple roots: direct, **kṣeṣṇú** *perishable*, **-glāsnu** *sick*, **jiṣṇú** *victorious*, **daṅkṣṇú** *biting*, **bhūṣṇu** *thriving*, **ni-ṣatsnú** *sitting down*, **sthāsnu** *fixed;* with union-vowel **i**, **kariṣṇu**, **kāçiṣṇu**, **kṣayiṣṇu**, **gamiṣṇú**, **grasiṣṇu**, **grahiṣṇu**, **cariṣṇú**, **-janiṣṇu**, **jayiṣṇu**, **tapiṣṇu**, **-trapiṣṇu**, **-patiṣṇu**, **-bhaviṣṇu**, **bhrājiṣṇu**, **madiṣṇu**, **-maviṣṇu**, **yajiṣṇu**, **yāciṣṇu**, **-vadiṣṇu**, **vardhiṣṇu**, **-sahiṣṇu**.

b. From secondary conjugation-stems: **kopayiṣṇu**, **kṣapayiṣṇu**, **cyāvayiṣṇú**, **janayiṣṇu**, **tāpayiṣṇu**, **namayiṣṇu**, **patayiṣṇu**, **poṣayiṣṇú**, **pārayiṣṇú**, **bodhayiṣṇu**, **mādayiṣṇu**, **yamayiṣṇú**, **ropayiṣṇu**, **-vārayiṣṇu**, **-çocayiṣṇú**; and **jāgariṣṇu**. An anomalous formation is **ulbaniṣṇu**.

c. These derivatives are freely compounded with prefixes: e. g. **niṣatsnú**, **prajaniṣṇú**, **abhiçocayiṣṇú**, **saṁvārayisṇu**.

d. It is not unlikely that the **s** of this suffix is originally that of a stem, to which **nu** was added. Such a character is still apparent in **kraviṣṇú** *craving raw flesh* (**kravis**); and also in **vadhasnú**, **vṛdhasnú** (?), and **prathasnu** (?).

1195. स्न **sna.** Extremely few words have this ending.

a. It is seen in **tīkṣṇá** *sharp*, and perhaps in **çlakṣṇá**, **-rūkṣṇá**, **-mārtsna**; and in **geṣṇa** and **deṣṇá** (usually trisyllabic: **daïṣṇa**) *gift*. Unless in the last, it is not found preceded by **i**; but it has (like **snu**, above) **a** before it in **vadhasná** *deadly weapon*, **karásna** *fore-arm;* **nadīṣṇa** *skilled* seems to be secondary. Feminines are **mṛtsnā** *loam*, **jyotsnā** *moonlight*.

1196. तु **tnu.** This suffix is used in nearly the same way with स्नु **snu** (above, **1194**).

a. As used with simple roots, the **t** is generally capable of being considered the adscititious **t** after a short root-final, to which **nu** is then added: thus, **kṛtnú** *active*, **gatnú** (? RV.), **hatnú** *deadly*, **-tatnu** (?) *stretching;* and, from reduplicated roots, **jigatnú** *hasting*, and **jighatnú** *harming;* but also **dartnú** *bursting*. Also, with union-vowel, **dravitnú** *running*, **dayitnu** (? LÇS.).

b. With causative stems: for example, **drāvayitnú** *hasting*, **poṣayitnú** *nourishing*, **mādayitnú** *intoxicating*, **tanayitnú** and **stanayitnú** *thunder*, **sūdayitnú** *flowing*, **-āmayitnú** *sickening*.

c. With preceding **a**, in **pīyatnú** *scoffing*, **mehatnú** a river, **ā-rujatnú** *breaking into;* and **kavatnú** *miserly* (obscure derivation).

1197. स **sa.** The words ending in suffixal स **sa**, with or without preceding union-vowel, are a heterogeneous group, and in considerable part of obscure derivation. Thus:

a. With **sa** simply: **gṛtsa** *clever*, **jeṣá** *winning* (rather, aoristic **s**? **1148j**), **-dṛkṣa** *looking*, **rukṣá** *shining*, **rūkṣá** *rough;* **útsa** n. *fountain;* **bhīṣā́** f. *fear* (or from the secondary root **bhiṣ**).

b. With preceding **i**-vowel: **taviṣá** (f. **táviṣī**) *strong*, **mahiṣá** (f. **máhiṣī**) *mighty*, **bhariṣá** (?) *seeking booty;* **ṛjīṣá** *rushing*, **púrīṣa** *rubbish*, **manīṣā́** f. *devotion;* and compare **rayīṣín** (? SV.).

c. With preceding **u**-vowel: **aruṣá** (f. **áruṣī**) *red*, **açúṣa** *ravenous*, **táruṣa** *overcomer*, **púruṣa** and **mánuṣa** (**-us-a**?) *man;* **pīyū́ṣa** *biestings*.

1198. असि **asi.** A few words in the oldest language are made with a suffix having this form (perhaps produced by the addition of **i** to **as**).

a. Thus, **atasí** *vagabond*, **dharnasí** *firm*, **sānasí** *winning;* and **dhāsí** m. *drink*, f. *station*, **sarasí** (?) *pool*.

1199. अभ **abha.** A few names of animals, for the most part of obscure derivation, show this ending.

a. Thus, **vṛṣabhá** and **ṛṣabhá** *bull*, **çarabhá** a certain fabulous animal, **çerabha** a certain snake, **gardabhá** and **rā́sabha** *ass;* further, **kanabha, karabha** and **kalabha, laṭabha, çalabha;** and, with other union-vowels, **tuṇḍibha, nuṇḍibha,** and **kukkubha.** The feminine, if occurring, is in **ī**; and **kaṭabhī** is found without corresponding masculine. AV. has the adjective **sthūlabhá,** equivalent to **sthūlá.**

1200. A few words ending in the consonants **t, d, j,** etc., and for the most part of doubtful root-connections, were given above, at **383k** (3–5,7); it is unnecessary to repeat them here. Certain of those in **at** are perhaps related to the participles in **ant** (**1172**).

1201. A number of other primary suffixes are either set up by the grammarians and supported with examples of questionable value, or are doubtfully deducible from isolated words traceable to known roots, or from words of obscure connection.

a. A few such may be mentioned here: **aṇḍa** in **karaṇḍa** and **váraṇḍa** and certain unquotable words (prakritized **a**-forms from the present participle); **era** and **ora** in unquotable words, and **elima** (above, **966 d**: perhaps a further derivative with secondary **ima** from **era**); **mara** (**ma** or **man** with secondary **ra** added) in **ghasmara, sṛmará**, etc.; — **sara** in **matsará, kara** in **púṣkara** and other obscure words, **pa** in **púṣpa, stupá, stū́pa**, and a number of other obscure words; and so on.

B. Secondary Derivatives.

1202. Words of secondary derivation are made by the addition of further suffixes to stems already ending in evident suffixes.

a. But also, as pointed out above (**1137 b**), to pronominal roots.

b. Further, in exceptional cases, to indeclinables, to case-forms, and to phrases: e. g. **antarvant, apitvá, paratastva, sahatva, sārvatrika, āikadhya, mā́maka, āmuṣmika, āmuṣyāyaṇá, apsumánt, apsavyà, kiṁcanya, kiṁkartavyatā, kvācitka, nāstika, akiṁcinmaya.**

1203. Changes of the stem. The stem to which the suffix is added is liable to certain changes of form.

a. Before a suffix beginning with a vowel or with **y** (which in this respect is treated as if it were **i**), final **a**- and **i**-vowels are regularly lost altogether, while a final **u**-vowel has the **guṇa**-strengthening and becomes **av**; **ṛ** and **o** and **āu** (all of rare occurrence) are treated in accordance with usual euphonic rule.

b. An **u**-vowel also sometimes remains unstrengthened: see **1208 e.**

c. A final **n** is variously treated, being sometimes retained, and sometimes lost, even along with a preceding **a**; and sometimes an **a** is lost, while the **n** remains: thus, **vṛṣaṇvant, vṛṣaṇa, vṛṣa, vṛṣatva, vṛṣṇya**, from **vṛṣan**. Of a stem ending in **ant**, the weak form, in **at**, is regularly taken: thus, **vāivasvata** (**vivasvant**).

d. In general, the masculine form of a primitive stem is that from which a further secondary derivative is made. But there are not very rare cases in which the feminine is taken instead; examples are **satītva, bhāryātva, pranītātvá, bhāratīvant, rakṣāvant, priyāvant.** On the other hand, a final long vowel — **ī**, much more rarely **ā** — generally of a feminine stem, is sometimes shortened in derivation: thus, **yājyàvant, praçākhavant, goṣátama, vaçátamā, sadhanitvá, jaratikā, annā-**

dítamā (cf. 471 b), **rohinitvá** (TB.; **-nītvá** ÇB.), **pṛthivitvá, pratipatnivat, sárasvativant.**

e. As was pointed out above (**111 c, d**), the combination of a secondary suffix with a stem is sometimes made according to the rules of external combination. Such cases are pointed out under the suffixes **īya** (**1215 e**), **ka** (**1222 m**), **maya** (**1225 a**), **min** (**1231 b**), **vin** (**1232 c**), **vant** (**1233 i**), **van** (**1234 c**), **mant** (**1235 f**), **tva** (**1239 c**), **taya** (**1245 a**), **tya** (**1245 c**), **tana** (**1245 i**).

1204. The most frequent change in secondary derivation is the **vṛddhi**-strengthening of an initial syllable of the stem to which a suffix is added.

a. The strengthened syllable may be of any character: radical, of a prefix, or of the first member of a compound: thus, **āçviná** (**açvín**), **sāumyá** (**sóma**), **pā́rthiva** (**pṛthivī́**), **āmitrá** (**amítra**), **sā́mrājya** (**samrā́j**), **sāúkṛtya** (**sukṛtá**), **māitrāvaruṇá** (**mitrā́váruṇā**), **āuccāiḥçravasá** (**uccā́iḥçravas**). As to the accompanying accent, see the next paragraph.

b. If a stem begins with a consonant followed by **y** or **v**, the semivowel is sometimes vriddhied, as if it were **i** or **u**, and the resulting **āi** or **āu** has **y** or **v** further added before the succeeding vowel.

c. This is most frequent where the **y** or **v** belongs to a prefix — as **ni, vi, su** — altered before a following initial vowel: thus, **nāiyāyika** from **nyāya** (as if **niyāya**), **vāiyaçvá** from **vyàçva** (as if **viyaçva**), **sāúvaçvya** from **sváçva** (as if **suvaçva**); but it occurs also in other cases, as **sāuvará** from **svára**, **çāuva** from **çvan**, against **svāyambhuva** (**svayambhū**), and so on. AV. has irregularly **kāveraká** from **kúvera** (as if from **kvèra**, without the euphonic **y** inserted).

d. This strengthening takes place especially, and very often, before the suffixes **a** and **ya**; also regularly before **i, āyana, eya** (with **ineya**), and later **īya**; before the compound **aka** and **ika**, and later **aki**; and, in single sporadic examples before, **na, ena, ra,** and **tva** (?): see these various suffixes below.

e. Sometimes an unstrengthened word is prefixed to one thus strengthened, as if the composition were made after instead of before the strengthening: e. g. **indradāivatya** *having Indra as divinity* (instead of **āindradevatya**), **caramaçāirṣika** *with head to the west*, **jīvalāukika** *belonging to the world of the living*, **antarbhāuma** *within the earth*, **somārāudra, gurulāghava** (cf. **tāmasaṁ guṇalakṣaṇam** M. xii. 35). But especially when the first word is of numeral value: as **çatáçārada** *of a hundred years*, **pañcaçāradīya, trisāṁvatsara, bahuvārṣika, aṣṭavārṣika, anekavarṣasāhasra, daçasāhasra, trisāhasrī, tripāuruṣa, caturādhyāyī** or **-yikā** *of four chapters*, etc. etc.

f. More often, both members of a compound word have the initial strengthening: e. g. **sāumāpāuṣṇá, kāúrupāñcāla, cāturvāidya, āihalāukika, āikabhāutika, trāiṣṭubjāgata, yājurvāidika.** Such cases are not rare.

g. The **guṇa**-strengthening (except of a final **u**-vowel: **1203 a**) is only in the rarest cases an accompaniment of secondary derivation. Exceptions are **dvayá** and **trayá** and **náva** (**1209 i**), **bheṣajá** and **devá** (**1209 j**), **dróna** (**1223 g**), **çekhara** (**1226 a**).

1205. Accent. a. The derivatives with initial **vṛddhi**-strengthening always have their accent on either the first or the last syllable. And usually it is laid, as between these two situations, in such a way as to be furthest removed from the accent of the primitive; yet, not rarely, it is merely drawn down upon the suffix from the final of the latter; much less often, it remains upon an initial syllable without change. Only in the case of one or two suffixes is the distinction between initial and final accent connected with any difference in the meaning and use of the derivatives (see below, suffix **eya**: **1216**).

b. No other general rules as to accent can be given. Usually the suffix takes the tone, or else this remains where it was in the primitive; quite rarely, it is thrown back to the initial syllable (as in derivation with initial **vṛddhi**); and in a single case (**tā**: **1237**) it is drawn down to the syllable preceding the suffix.

1206. Meaning. a. The great mass of secondary suffixes are adjective-making: they form from nouns adjectives indicating appurtenance or relation, of the most indefinite and varied character. But, as a matter of course, this indefiniteness often undergoes specialization: so, particularly, into designation of procedure or descent, so that distinctive patronymic and metronymic and gentile words are the result; or, again, into the designation of possession. Moreover, while the masculines and feminines of such adjectives are employed as appellatives, the neuter is also widely used as an abstract, denoting the quality expressed attributively by the adjective; and neuter abstracts are with the same suffixes made from adjectives. There are also special suffixes (very few) by which abstracts are made directly, from adjective or noun.

b. A few suffixes make no change in the part of speech of the primitive, but either change its degree (diminution and comparison), or make other modifications, or leave its meaning not sensibly altered.

1207. The suffixes will be taken up below in the following order. First, the general adjective-making suffixes, beginning with those of most frequent use (**a, ya** and its connections, **i, ka**); then, those of specific possessive value (**in, vant** and **mant**, and their connections); then, the abstract-making ones (**tā** and **tva**, and their connections); then, the suffixes of comparison etc.; and finally, those by which derivatives are made only or almost only from particles.

a. For convenience of reference, a list of them in their order as treated is here added:

a	1208—9	maya	1225	tva, tvatā	1239
ya	1210—13	ra, ira, etc.	1226	tvana	1240
iya	1214	la, lu	1227	tara, tama	1242
īya	1215	va, vala, vaya,		ra, ma	»
eya, eyya	1216	vya	1228	tha	»
enya	1217	ça	1229	titha	»
āyya	1218	in	1230	taya	1245
āyana	1219	min	1231	tya	»
āyī	1220	vin	1232	ta	»
i, aki	1221	vant	1233	na	»
ka, aka, ika	1222	van	1234	tana, tna	»
na, āna, īna, ina, ena	1223	mant	1235	vat	»
		tā	1237	kaṭa	»
ma, ima, mna	1224	tāti, tāt	1238	vana, āla	»

1208. अ **a.** With this suffix are made an immensely large class of derivatives, from nouns or from adjectives having a noun-value. Such derivatives are primarily and especially adjectives, denoting *having a relation* or *connection* (of the most various kind) *with* that denoted by the more primitive word. But they are also freely used substantively: the masculine and feminine as appellatives, the neuter, especially and frequently, as abstract. Often they have a patronymic or gentile value.

a. The regular and greatly prevailing formation is that which is accompanied with vṛddhi-strengthening of the first syllable of the primitive word, simple or compound. Examples of this formation are:

b. From primitives ending in consonants: with the usual shift of accent, **āyasá** *of metal* (**áyas**), **mānasá** *relating to the mind* (**mánas**), **sāumanasá** *friendliness* (**sumánas**), **brāhmaṇá** *priest* (**bráhman**), **hāimavatá** *from the Himalaya* (**himávant**), **āñgirasá** *of the Angiras family* (**áñgiras**); **hā́stina** *elephantine* (**hastín**), **mā́ruta** *pertaining to the Maruts* (**marút**); — with accent thrown forward from the final upon the suffix, **çāradá** *autumnal*, **vāirājá** *relating to the* **virā́j**, **pāuṣṇá** *belonging to Pūshán*; **gāirikṣitá** *son of Girikshít*; — with accent unchanged, **mā́nuṣa** *descendant of Mánus*.

c. The suffix is added (as above instanced) to the middle stem-form of stems in **vant**; it is added to the weakest in **mā́ghona** and **vā́rtraghna**; the ending **in** remains unchanged; **an** usually does the same, but sometimes loses its **a**, as in **pāuṣṇá, trāivṛṣṇá, dāçarājñá**; and sometimes its **n**, as in **brāhmá, āukṣá, bārhatsāma.**

d. From primitives in **ṛ**: **jāítra** *victorious* (**jetṛ́** or **jétṛ** *conqueror*), **tvāṣṭrá** *relating to Tváshtar*, **sāvitrá** *descendant of the sun* (**savitṛ́**), **āúdbhetra, pāitra.**

e. From primitives in **u**: usually with **guṇa**-strengthening of the **u**, as **vāsavá** *relating to the Vásus*, **ārtavá** *concerning the seasons* (**ṛtú**), **dānavá** *child of Dānu* (**dā́nu**), **sāindhavá** *from the Indus* (**síndhu**); — but sometimes without, as **mā́dhva** *full of sweets* (**mádhu**), **pārçvá** *side* (**párçu** *rib*), **pāidvá** *belonging to Pedú*, **tā́nva** *of the body* (**tanū́**), **yā́dva** of Yádu.

f. From primitives in **i** and **ī**, which vowels are supplanted by the added suffix: **pā́rthiva** *earthly* (**pṛthivī́**), **sārasvatá** *of the Sárasvatī*, **āindrāgná** *belonging to Indra and Agni* (**indrāgní**); **pā́ñkta** *five-fold* (**pañktí**), **nāirṛtá** *belonging to Nírṛti*, **pārthuraçmá** *of Pṛthuraçmi*, **pāçupatá** *of Paçupáti.*

g. From primitives in **ā**, which in like manner disappears: **yāmuná** *of the Yamúnā*, **sāraghá** *honey* etc. (**sarághā** *bee*), **kānīná** *natural child* (**kanī́nā** *girl*).

h. A large number (more than all the rest together) from primitives in **a**, of which the final is replaced by the suffix: for example, with the usual shift of accent, **āmitrá** *inimical* (**amítra** *enemy*), **vāruṇá** *of Váruṇa*, **vāiçvadevá** *belonging to all the gods* (**viçvádeva**), **nāirhastá** *handlessness* (**nírhasta**), **vāiyaçvá** *descendant of Vyàçva*; **gā́rdabha** *asinine* (**gardabhá**), **dāíva** *divine* (**devá**), **mā́dhyaṁdina** *meridional* (**madhyáṁdina**), **pāútra** *grandchild* (**putrá** *son*), **sāúbhaga** *good fortune* (**subhága**), **vā́dhryaçva** *of Vadhryaçvá's race*; with unchanged accent (comparatively few), **vāsantá** *vernal* (**vasantá** *spring*), **māitrá** *Mitrá's*, **ātithigvá** *of Atithigvá's race*, **dāívodāsa** *Dívodāsa's*. In a few instances, **ya** is replaced by the suffix: thus, **sāura, pāuṣá, yājñavalka.**

i. The derivatives of this last form are sometimes regarded as made by internal change, without added suffix. Considering, however, that other final vowels are supplanted by this suffix, that **a** disappears as stem-final also before various other suffixes of secondary derivation, and that no examples of derivation without suffix are quotable from primitives of any other final than **a**, it seems far too violent to assume here a deviation from the whole course of Indo-European word-making.

j. Adjectives of this formation make their feminines in **ī** (see **332 a**).

1209. The derivatives made by adding अ **a** without **vṛddhi**-change of the initial syllable are not numerous, and are in considerable part, doubtless, of inorganic make, results of the transfer to an **a**-declension of words of other finals.

a. A number of examples of stems in **a** made by transfer were noticed above (**399**). The cases of such transition occur most frequently in composition (**1315**): thus, further, **apa-** (for **ap** or **āp** *water*), **-ṛca, -nara,** etc.; from stems in **an, -aha, -vṛṣa,** etc., but also **-ahna** and **-vṛṣṇa** and **vṛ́ṣaṇa**; from stems in **i, -an̄gula, -rātra,** etc.; from the weakest forms of **añc**-stems (**407**) **uccá, nīcá, parācá,** etc.

b. Also occurring especially in composition, yet likewise as simple words often enough to have an independent aspect, are derivatives in **a** from nouns in **as** (rarely **is, us**): thus, for example, **tamasá, rajasá, payasá, brahmavarcasá, sarvavedasá, devāinasá, paruṣá, tryāyuṣá,** and probably **mánuṣa.**

c. Similar derivatives from adjectives in **in** are reckoned by the grammarians as made with the suffix **ina**: thus, **malina** *polluted*, **parameṣṭhína** etc. (see **441 b**).

d. A number of words formed with the so-called suffix **anta** are evident transfers from stems in **ant.** A few of them are found even from the earliest period: thus, **pánta** *draught*, **çvāntá** (?), **vasantá** *spring*, **hemantá** *winter*, **veçantá** etc. *tank*, **jīvantī́** a certain healing plant; and others occur later, as **jayanta, taranta, madhumanta,** etc. They are said to be accented on the final.

e. From **añc**-stems (**407**) are made a few nouns ending in **k-a**: thus, **ánūka, ápāka, upā́ka, prátīka, parāká,** etc.

f. From stems in **ṛ, hotrá, netrá, neṣṭrá, potrá, praçāstrá,** etc., from titles of priests; also **dhātrá, bhrātrá,** etc.

g. Other scattering cases are: **savidyutá, āvyuṣá, vī́rudha, kákuda, kakubhá, açúṣa, bhūmyá, sakhyá, ádhipatya, jāspatyá, araṭvá, pāṇḍvà.**

h. The Vedic gerundives in **tva** (**tua**), made by addition of **a** to abstract noun-stems in **tu,** have been already (**966 a**) fully given.

i. Trayá and **dvayá** come with **guna**-strengthening from numeral stems; **náva** *new* in like manner from **nú** *now;* and **ántara** apparently from **antár.**

j. Bheṣajá *medicine* is from **bhiṣáj** *healer*, with **guṇa**-change; and probably **devá** *heavenly, divine, god*, in like manner from **div** *sky, heaven* (there is no "root **div** *shine*" in the language).

1210. य **ya.** With this suffix are made a very large class of words, both in the old language and later.

a. The derivatives in **ya** exhibit a great and perplexing variety of form, connection, and application; and the relations of the suffix to others containing a **ya**-element — **iya, īya, eya, āyya, eyya, enya** — are also in part obscure and difficult. In the great majority of instances in the oldest language, the **ya** when it follows a consonant is dissyllabic in metrical value, or is to be read as **ia**. Thus, in RV., 266 words (excluding compounds) have **ia**, and only 75 have **ya** always; 46 are to be read now with **ia** and now with **ya**, but many of these have **ya** only in isolated cases. As might be expected, the value **ia** is more frequent after a heavy syllable: thus, in RV., there are 188 examples of **ia** and 27 of **ya** after such a syllable, and 78 of **ia** and 96 of **ya** after a light syllable (the circumflexed **yà** — that is to say, **ía** — being, as is pointed out below, **1212 l**, more liable to the resolution than **ya** or **yá**). It must be left for further researches to decide whether in the **ya** are not included more than one suffix, with different accent, and different quantity of the **i**-element; or with an **a** added to a final **i** of the primitive. It is also matter for question whether there is a primary as well as a secondary suffix **ya**; the suffix at least comes to be used as if primary, in the formation of gerundives and in that of action-nouns: but it is quite impossible to separate the derivatives into two such classes, and it has seemed preferable therefore to treat them all together here.

b. The derivatives made with **ya** may be first divided into those which do and those which do not show an accompanying **vṛddhi**-increment of the initial syllable.

c. Adjectives in **ya**, of both these divisions, make their feminines regularly in **yā**. But in a number of cases, a feminine in **ī** is made, either alone or beside one in **yā**: e. g. **cāturmāsī**, **āgniveçī**, **çāṇḍilī**, **ā́rī** (and **ā́ryā**), **dāívī** (and **dāívyā**), **sāumī** (and **sāumyā**); **dhīrī́**, **çīrṣaṇī**, **svarī**, etc.

1211. Derivatives in य **ya** with initial **vṛddhi**-strengthening follow quite closely, in form and meaning, the analogy of those in अ **a** (above, **1208**). They are, however, decidedly less common than the latter (in Veda, about three fifths as many).

a. Examples are: with the usual shift of accent, **dāívya** *divine* (**devá**), **pā́litya** *grayness* (**palitá**), **grāívya** *cervical* (**grīvā́**), **ā́rtvijya** *priestly office* (**ṛtvíj**), **gā́rhapatya** *householder's* (**gṛhápati**), **jā́narājya** *kingship* (**janarā́j**), **sā́ṅgrāmajitya** *victory in battle* (**saṅgrāmajít**), **sāúvaçvya** *wealth in horses* (**sváçva**), **āúpadraṣṭrya** *witness* (**upadraṣṭṛ́**); **ādityá** *Aditya* (**áditi**), **sāumyá** *relating to sóma*, **ātithyá** *hospitality* (**átithi**), **prājāpatyá** *belonging to Prajā́pati*, **vāimanasyá** *mindlessness* (**vímanas**), **sā́hadevya** *descendant of Sahā́deva*; — with accent thrown forward from the final upon the ending, **lāukyá** *of the world* (**loká**), **kāvyá** *of the Kaví-race*, **ārtvyá** *descendant of Ritú*, **vāyavyá** *belonging to the wind* (**vāyú**), **rāivatyá** *wealth* (**revánt**); — with unchanged accent (very few), **ā́dhipatya** *lordship* (**ádhipati**), **çrāíṣṭhya** *excellence* (**çréṣṭha**), **vāíçya** *belonging to the third class* (**víç** *people*), **pāúṅsya** *manliness* (**púṅs**).

b. The AV. has once **nāirbādhyà**, with circumflexed final; if not an error, it is doubtless made through **nāirbādha**; **vāiṣṇavyāù** (VS. i. 12) appears to be dual fem. of **vāiṣṇavī́**.

1212. Derivatives in य **ya** without initial vṛddhi-strengthening are usually adjectives, much less often (neuter, or, in या **yā**, feminine) abstract nouns. They are made from every variety of primitive, and are very numerous (in Veda, three or four times as many as the preceding class).

a. The general mass of these words may be best divided according to their accent, into: 1. Words retaining the accent of the primitive; 2. Words with retracted accent; 3. Words with acute **yá** (iá); 4. Words with circumflexed **yà** (ía). Finally may be considered the words, gerundives and action-nouns, which have the aspect of primary derivatives.

1. **b.** Examples of derivatives in **ya** retaining the accent of their primitives are: **áçvya** *equine* (**áçva**), **áñgya** *of the limbs* (**áñga**), **múkhya** *foremost* (**múkha** *mouth*), **ávya** *ovine* (**ávi**), **gávya** *bovine* (**gó**), **víçya** *of the people* (**víç**), **dúrya** *of the door* (**dúr**), **nárya** *manly* (**nṛ́**), **vṛ́ṣṇya** *virile* (**vṛ́ṣan**), **svarā́jya** *autocracy* (**svarā́j**), **suvī́rya** *wealth in retainers* (**suvī́ra**), **viçvájanya** *of all men*, **viçvádevya** *of all the gods* (**viçvádeva**), **mayū́raçepya** *peacock-tailed*.

c. In the last words, and in a few others, the **ya** appears to be used (like **ka, 1222h**: cf. **1212m**) as a suffix simply helping to make a possessive compound: and so further **suhástya** (beside the equivalent **suhásta**), **mádhuhastya**, **dáçamāsya**, **miçrádhānya**, **anyódarya**, **samānodarya**.

2. **d.** Examples with retraction of the accent to the first syllable (as in derivation with **vṛddhi**-increment) are: **káṇṭhya** *guttural* (**kaṇṭhá**), **skándhya** *humeral* (**skandhá**), **vrátya** *of a ceremony* (**vratá**), **méghya** *in the clouds* (**meghá**), **pítrya** *of the Fathers* (**pitṛ́**), **prátijanya** *adverse* (**pratijaná**). **Hiraṇyáya** *of gold* (**híraṇya**), is anomalous both in drawing the accent forward and in retaining the final **a** of the primitive; and **gavyáya** and **avyáya** (also **ávyaya**) are to be compared with it as to formation.

3. **e.** Examples with acute accent on the suffix are: **divyá** *heavenly* (**dív**), **satyá** *true* (**sánt**), **vyāghryá** *tigrine* (**vyāghrá**), **kavyá** *wise* (**kaví**), **grāmyá** *of the village* (**grā́ma**), **somyá** *relating to the sóma*, **anenasyá** *sinlessness* (**anenás**), **adakṣiṇyá** *not fit for* **dákṣiṇā**.

4. **f.** Of derivatives ending in circumflexed **yà** (which in the Veda are considerably more numerous than all the three preceding classes together), examples are as follows:

g. From consonant-stems: **viçyà** *of the clan* (RV.: **víç**), **hṛdyà** *of the heart* (**hṛ́d**), **vidyutyà** *of the lightning* (**vidyút**), **rājanyà** *of the royal class* (**rā́jan**), **doṣaṇyà** *of the arm* (**doṣán**), **çīrṣaṇyà** *of the head* (**çīrṣán**), **karmaṇyà** *active* (**kárman**), **dhanvanyà** *of the plain* (**dhánvan**), **namasyà** *reverend* (**námas**), **tvacasyà** *cuticular* (**tvácas**), **barhiṣyà** *of barhís*, **āyuṣyà** *giving life* (**ā́yus**), **bhasadyà** *of the buttocks* (**bhasád**), **prācyà** *eastern* (**prā́ñc**), etc. Of exceptional formation is **aryamyà** *intimate* (**aryamán**), with which doubtless belong **sātmya** (**sātman**) and **sākṣya** (**sākṣin**).

h. From u-stems: **hanavyà** *of the jaws* (**hánu**), **vāyavya** *belonging to Vāyú*, **paçavyà** *relating to cattle* (**paçú**), **iṣavyà** *relating to arrows* (**íṣu**), **madhavyà** *of the sweet* (**mádhu**), **apsavyà** *of the waters* (**apsú** loc.), **rajjavyà** *of rope* (**rájju**); **çaravyā̀** f. *arrow* (**çáru**, do.); and there may be added **nāvyà** *navigable* (especially in fem., **nāvyā̀** *navigable stream*: **nāú** *boat*). The RV. has **prāçavyà** *to be partaken of* (**pra**+√**aç**), without any corresponding noun **prāçu**; and also **ūrjavyà** *rich in nourishment* (**ūrj**), without any intermediate **ūrju**.

i. Under this head belong, as was pointed out above (**964**), the so-called gerundives in **tavyà**, as made by the addition of **yà** to the infinitive noun in **tu**. They are wholly wanting in the oldest language, and hardly found in later Vedic, although still later **tavya** wins the value of a primary suffix, and makes numerous verbal derivatives.

j. From i- and ī-stems hardly any examples are to be quoted. VS. has **dundubhyà** from **dundubhí**.

k. From a-stems: **svargyà** *heavenly* (**svargá**), **devatyà** *relating to a deity* (**devátā**), **prapathyà** *guiding* (**prapathá**), **budhnyà** *fundamental* (**budhná**), **jaghanyà** *hindmost* (**jaghána**), **varuṇyà** *Váruna's*, **vīryà** *might* (**vīrá**), **udaryà** *abdominal* (**udára**), **utsyà** *of the fountain* (**útsa**); and from ā-stems, **urvaryà** *of cultivated land* (**urvárā**), **svāhyà** *relating to the exclamation* **svā́hā**.

l. The circumflexed **yà** is more generally resolved (into **ía**) than the other forms of the suffix: thus, in RV. it is never to be read as **ya** after a heavy syllable ending with a consonant; and even after a light one it becomes **ía** in more than three quarters of the examples.

m. There are a few cases in which **yà** appears to be used to help make a compound with governing preposition (next chapter, **1310**: cf. **1212c**): thus, **apikakṣyà** *about the arm-pit*, **upapakṣyà** *upon the sides*, **udāpyà** *up-stream*; and perhaps **upatṛṇyà** *lying in the grass* (occurs only in voc.). But, with other accent, **ánvāntrya** *through the entrails*, **úpamāsya** *in each month*, **abhinabhyá** *up to the clouds*, **antaḥparçavyá** *between the ribs*, **ádhigartya** *on the chariot seat*; of unknown accent, **adhihastya**, **anupṛṣṭhya**, **anunāsikya**, **anuvañçya**.

1213. The derivatives in य **ya** as to which it may be

questioned whether they are not, a least in part, primary derivatives from the beginning, are especially the gerundives, together with action-nouns coincident with these in form; in the later language, the gerundive-formation (above, 963) comes to be practically a primary one.

a. In RV. occur about forty instances of gerundives in **ya**, of tolerably accordant form: the root usually unstrengthened (but **cétya, bhávya, -hávya, márjya, yódhya**; also **-mā́dya, -vā́cya, bhāvyá**); the accent on the radical syllable when the word is simple, or compounded with prepositions: thus, **praçásya, upasádya, vihávya** (but usually on the final after the negative prefix: thus, **anāpyá, anapavṛjyá**) — exceptions are only **bhāvyá** and the doubtful **ākāyyà**; the **ya** resolved into **ia** in the very great majority of occurrences; a final short vowel followed by **t** (in **-ítya, -kṛtya, -çrútya, -stútya**, and the reduplicated **carkṛ́tya**, beside **carkṛ́ti**: not in **návya** and **-hávya**), and **ā** changed to **e** (in **-deya** only). If regarded as secondary, they might be made with **ya**, in accordance with other formations by this suffix, in part from the root-noun, as **anukṛ́t-ya**, in part from derivatives in **a**, as **bhāvyá** (from **bhāva**).

b. The AV. has a somewhat smaller number (about twenty-five) of words of a like formation; but also a considerable group (fifteen) of derivatives in **yà** with the same value: thus, for example, **ādyà** *eatable*, **kāryà** *to be done*, **samāpyà** *to be obtained*, **atitāryà** *to be overpassed*, **nīvibhāryà** *to be carried in the apron*, **prathamavāsyà** *to be first worn*. These seem more markedly of secondary origin: and especially such forms as **parivargyà** *to be avoided*, **avimokyá** *not to be gotten rid of*, where the guttural reversion clearly indicates primitives in **ga** and **ka** (**216 h**).

c. Throughout the older language are of common occurrence neuter abstract nouns of the same make with the former of these classes. They are rarely found except in composition (in AV., only **cítya** and **stéya** as simple), and are often used in the dative, after the manner of a dative infinitive. Examples are: **brahmajyéya, vasudéya, bhāgadhéya, pūrvapéya, çataséya, abhibhū́ya, devahū́ya, mantraçrútya, karmakṛ́tya, vṛtratū́rya, hotṛvū́rya, ahihátya, sattrasádya, çīrṣabhídya, brahmacárya, nṛṣáhya.** Of exceptional form are **ṛtódya** (√**vad**) and **sahaçéyya** (√**çī**); of exceptional accent, **sadhástutya.** And AV. has one example, **raṇyà,** with circumflexed final.

d. Closely akin with these, in meaning and use, is a smaller class of feminines in **yā́**: thus, **kṛtyā́, vidyā́, ityā́, agnicityā́, vājajityā́, muṣṭihatyā́, devayajyā́,** etc.

e. There remain, of course, a considerable number of less classifiable words, both nouns and adjectives, of which a few from the older language may be mentioned, without discussion of their relations: thus, **sū́rya** (with fem. **sūryā́**), **ā́jya, púṣya, nábhya; yújya, gṛ́dhya, írya, aryá** and **ā́rya, márya, mádhya.**

The suffixes apparently most nearly akin with **ya** may best be next taken up.

1214. **इय iya.** This suffix is virtually identical with the preceding, being but another written form of the same thing. It is used only after two consonants, where the direct addition of **य ya** would create a combination of difficult utterance. It has the same variety of accent with **ya.** Thus:

a. With accent **íya** (= **ía** or **yà**): for example, **abhríya** (also **abhriyá**) *from the clouds* (**abhrá**), **kṣatríya** *having authority* (**kṣatrá**), **yajñíya** *reverend* (**yajñá**), **hotríya** *libational* (**hótrā**), **amitríya** *inimical* (**amítra**).

b. With accent **iyá** (= **iá** or **yá**): for example, **agriyá** (also **agríya**) *foremost* (**ágra**), **indriyá** *Indra's* (later, *sense:* **índra**), **kṣetriyá** *of the field* (**kṣétra**).

c. With accent on the primitive: **çrótriya** *learned* (**çrótra**), **ṛ́tviya** (also **ṛtvíya**) *in season* (**ṛtú**).

1215. **ईय īya.** This suffix also is apparently by origin a **ya** (**īa**) of which the first element has maintained its long quantity by the interposition of a euphonic **y.** It is accented always on the **ī́.**

a. In RV. occur, of general adjectives, only **ārjikī́ya** and **gṛhamedhī́ya,** and examples in the later Vedic are very few: e. g. **parvatī́ya** *mountainous* (AV., beside RV. **parvatyà**). In the Brāhmaṇas are found a number of adjectives, some of them from phrases (first words of verses and the like): thus, **anyarāṣṭrī́ya, pañcavātī́ya, mārjālī́ya, kayācubhī́ya, svāduṣkilī́ya, āpohiṣṭhī́ya,** etc.

b. It was pointed out above (**965**) that derivative adjectives in **īya** from action-nouns in **ana** begin in later Veda and in Brāhmaṇa to be used gerundivally, and are a recognized formation as gerundives in the classical language. But adjectives in **anīya** without gerundive character are also common.

c. Derivatives in **īya** with initial **vṛddhi** are sometimes made in the later language: e. g. **pārvatīya, pāitāputrīya, āparapakṣīya, vāirakīya.**

d. The pronominal possessives **madīya** etc. (**516 a**) do not occur either in Veda or in Brāhmaṇa; but the ordinals **dvitī́ya** etc. (**487 b, c:** with fractionals **tṛtī́ya** and **túrīya: 488 a**) are found from the earliest period.

e. The possessives **bhagavadīya** and **bhavadīya,** with the final of the primitive made sonant, have probably had their form determined by the pronominal possessives in **-dīya.**

1216. एय **eya.** With this suffix, accompanied by **vṛddhi**-increment of an initial syllable, are made adjectives, often having a patronymic or metronymic value. Their neuter is sometimes used as abstract noun. The accent rests usually on the final in adjectives of descent, and on the first syllable in others.

a. Examples are: **ārṣeyá** *descendant of a sage* (**ṛ́si**), **jānaçruteyá** son of *Jānaçruti*, **sārameyá** *of Saramā's race*, **çātavaneyá** *Çatavani's descendant*, **rāthajiteyá** *son of Rathajīt*; **ā́sneya** *of the blood* (**asán**), **vā́steya** *of the bladder* (**vastí**), **pāúruṣeya** *coming from man* (**púruṣa**), **pāitṛsvaseya** *of a paternal aunt* (**pitṛsvasṛ**), etc.

b. A more than usual proportion of derivatives in **eya** come from primitives in **i** or **ī**; and probably the suffix first gained its form by addition of **ya** to a gunated **i**, though afterward used independently.

c. The gerundive etc. derivatives in **ya** (above, **1213**) from **ā**-roots end in **éya**; and, besides such, RV. etc. have **sabhéya** from **sabhā́**, and **didṛkṣéya** *worth seeing*, apparently from the desiderative noun **didṛkṣā́**, after their analogy. M. has once **adhyeya** as gerund of √**i**.

d. Derivatives in the so-called suffix **ineyá** — as **bhāgineyá**, **jyāiṣṭhineya**, **kāniṣṭhineya** — are doubtless made upon proximate derivatives in **-inī** (fem.).

e. In **eyya** (i. e. **eyia**) end, besides the neuter abstract **sahaçéyya** (above, **1213 c**), the adjective of gerundival meaning **stuṣéyya** (with aoristic **s** added to the root), and **çapatheyyà** *curse-bringing* (or *accursed*), from **çapátha**.

1217. एन्य **enya.** This suffix is doubtless secondary in origin, made by the addition of य **ya** to derivatives in a **na**-suffix; but, like others of similar origin, it is applied in some measure independently, chiefly in the older language, where it has nearly the value of the later **anīya** (above, **1215 b**), as making gerundival adjectives.

a. The **y** of this suffix is almost always to be read as vowel, and the accent is (except in **váreṇya**) on the **e**: thus, **-énia**.

b. The gerundives have been all given above, under the different conjugations to which they attach themselves (**966 b**, **1019 b**, **1038**). The RV. has also two non-gerundival adjectives, **vīréṇya** *manly* (**vīrá**), and **kīrténya** *famous* (**kīrtí**), and TS. has **anabhiçastenyá** (**abhíçasti**); **vijenyà** (RV.) is a word of doubtful connections; **çikṣeṇya** *instructive* is found in a Sūtra; **prāvṛṣeṇya** *of the rainy season* occurs later.

1218. आय्य **āyya.** With this suffix are made gerundival adjectives, almost only in RV. They have been noticed above (**966** c). The ending is everywhere to be read as **ā́yia.**

a. A few adjectives without gerundival value, and neuter abstracts, also occur: thus, **bahupā́yya** *protecting many*, **nṛpā́yya** *men-guarding*; **kuṇḍapā́yya,** and **purumā́yya,** proper names; **pūrvapā́yya** *first drink*, **mahayā́yya** *enjoyment*; — and **rasā́yya** *nervous*, and **uttamā́yya** *summit*, contain no verbal root. **Alā́yya** is doubtful; also **ākā́yya,** which its accent refers to a different formation, along with **prahāyyà** (AV.: √**hi**) *messenger*, and **pravāyyà** (AV.), of doubtful value.

1219. आयन **āyana.** In the Brāhmaṇas and later, patronymics made by this suffix are not rare. They come from stems in अ **a,** and have vṛddhi-strengthening of the first syllable, and accent on the final.

a. In RV., the only example of this formation is **kāṇvāyana** (voc.: **káṇva**); AV. has in metrical parts **dākṣāyaṇá** and the fem. **rāmāyaṇī́**; and **āmuṣyāyaṇá** *son of so-and-so* (**516**) in its prose; ÇB. has **rājastambā́yana** beside **-bāyaná.** The RV. name **ukṣaṇyā́yana** is of a different make, elsewhere unknown.

1220. आयी **āyī.** Only a very few words are made with this suffix, namely **agnā́yī** (**agní**) *Agni's wife*, **vṛṣākapāyī** *wife of Vrishā-kapi*; and later **pūtakratāyī,** and **manāyī** *Manu's wife* (but **manāvī** ÇB.).

a. They seem to be feminines of a derivative in **a** made with vṛddhi-increment of the final **i** of the primitive.

1221. इ **i.** Derivatives made with this suffix are patronymics from nouns in **a.** The accent rests on the initial syllable, which has the vṛddhi-strengthening.

a. In RV. are found half-a-dozen patronymics in **i**: for example, **ā́gniveçi, pā́urukutsi, prā́tardani, sā́ṁvaraṇi**; AV. has but one, **prā́hrādi**; in the Brāhmaṇas they are more common: thus, in AB., **sāuyavasi, jānaṁtapi, āruṇi, jānaki,** etc. A single word of other value — **sārathi** *charioteer* (**sarátham**) — is found from RV. down.

b. The words made with the so-called suffix **aki** — as **vāiyāsaki** *descendant of Vyāsa* — are doubtless properly derivatives in **i** from others in **ka** or **aka.** That the secondary suffix **ika** is probably made by addition of **ka** to a derivative in **i** is pointed out below (**1222** j).

c. RV. has **tápuṣi,** apparently from **tápus** with a secondary **i** added, and the n. pr. **çucantí**; **bhuvantí** is found in B., and **jīvanti** later.

1222. क **ka.** This is doubtless originally one of the class of suffixes forming adjectives of appurtenance. And that value it still has in actual use; yet only in a small minority of occurrences. It has been, on the one hand, specialized into an element forming diminutives; and, on the other hand, and much more widely, attenuated into an element without definable value, added to a great many nouns and adjectives to make others of the same meaning — this last is, even in the Veda, and still more in the later language, its chief office.

a. Hence, **ka** easily associates itself with the finals of derivatives to which it is attached, and comes to seem along with them an integral suffix, and is further used as such. Of this origin are doubtless, as was seen above (**1180, 1181**), the so-called primary suffixes **uka** and **aka**; and likewise the secondary suffix **ika** (below, j).

b. The accent of derivatives in **ka** varies — apparently without rule, save that the words most plainly of diminutive character have the tone usually on the suffix.

c. Examples (from the older language) of words in which the suffix has an adjective-making value are: **ántaka** (**ánta**) *end-making*, **bálhika** (**bálhi**) *of Balkh*, **āṇḍīka** (**āṇḍá**) *egg-bearing*, **sūcī́ka** (**sūcī́**) *stinging*, **urvārukā́** *fruit of the gourd* (**urvārú**), **paryāyiká** (**paryāyá**) *strophic*; from numerals, **ekaká, dvaká, triká, áṣṭaka; tṛ́tīyaka** *of the third day*; from pronoun-stems, **asmā́ka** *ours*, **yuṣmā́ka** *yours*, **mámaka** *mine* (**516 d**); from prepositions, **ántika** *near*, **ánuka** *following*, **ávakā** a plant (later **adhika, utka**); and, with accent retracted to the initial syllable (besides **áṣṭaka** and **tṛ́tīyaka,** already given), **rū́paka** (**rūpá**) *with form*, **bábhruka** (**babhrú** *brown*) a certain lizard. **Bhāvatka** *your worship's* has an anomalous initial **vṛddhi.**

d. Of words in which a diminutive meaning is more or less probable: **açvaká** *nag*, **kanī́naka** and **kumāraká** *boy*, **kanīnakā́** or **kanī́nikā** *girl*, **pādaká** *little foot*, **putraká** *little son*, **rājaká** *princeling*, **çakuntaká** *birdling.* Sometimes a contemptuous meaning is conveyed by such a diminutive: for formations with this value from pronominal stems, see above, **521**; other examples are **anyaká** (RV.), **álakam** (RV.: from **álam**), and even the verb-form **yāmaki** (for **yāmi**: KB.).

e. The derivatives in **ka** with unchanged meaning are made from primitives of every variety of form, simple and compound, and have the same variety of accent as the adjective derivatives (with which they are at bottom identical). Thus:

f. From simple nouns and adjectives: **ástaka** *home*, **nā́sikā** *nostril*, **mákṣikā** *fly*, **avikā́** *ewe*, **iṣuká** *arrow*, **dūraká** *distant*, **sarvaká** *all*. **dhénukā** (**dhenú**) *cow*, **nágnaka** (**nagná**) *naked*, **báddhaka** (**baddhá**) *captive*, **abhinnataraka** *by no means different*, **anastamitaké** *before sun-*

set, **vamraká** *ant*, **arbhaká** *small*, **çiçuká** *young*, **aṇīyaska** *finer*, **ejatká** *trembling*, **abhimādyatká** *intoxicated*, **patayiṣṇuká** *flying*. Such derivatives in the later language are innumerable; from almost any given noun or adjective may be made an equivalent, ending in **ka** or **kā** (according to the gender).

g. From compound primitives: **svalpaká** *very small*, **vímanyuka** *removing wrath*, **vikṣiṇatká** *destroying*, **pravartamānaká** *moving forward*, **vikṣīṇaká** *destroyed*.

h. In the Brāhmaṇas and later, **ka** is often added to a possessive adjective compound (**1307**), sometimes redundantly, but usually in order to obtain a more manageable stem for inflection: thus, **anakṣíka** *eyeless*, **atvákka** *skinless*, **aretáska** *without seed*, **vyasthaka** *boneless*, **saçiraska** *along with the head*, **ekagāyatrīka** *containing a single* **gāyatrī**-*verse*, **gṛhītávasatīvarīka** *one who has taken yesterday's water*, **sapatnīka** *with his spouse*, **bahuhastíka** *having many elephants*, **sadīkṣopasátka** *with* **dīkṣā** and **upasad**, **āhitasamitka** *with his fuel laid on*, **abhinavavayaska** *of youthful age*, **aṅguṣṭhamātraka** *of thumb size*.

i. The vowel by which the **ka** is preceded has often an irregular character; and especially, a feminine in **ikā** is so common beside a masculine in **aka** as to be its regular correspondent (as is the case with the so-called primary **aka**: above, **1181**). In RV. are found beside one another only **iyattaká** and **iyattikā́**; but AV. has several examples.

j. Two suffixes made up of **ka** and a preceding vowel — namely, **aka** and **ika** — are given by the grammarians as independent secondary suffixes, requiring initial **vṛddhi**-strengthening of the primitive. Both of them are doubtless originally made by addition of **ka** to a final **i** or **a**, though coming to be used independently.

k. Of **vṛddhi**-derivatives in **aka** no examples have been noted from the older language (unless **māmaká** *mine* is to be so regarded); and they are not common in the later: thus, **āvaçyaka** *necessary*, **vārddhaka** *old age*, **rāmaṇīyaka** *delightfulness*.

l. Of **vṛddhi**-derivatives in **ika**, the Veda furnishes a very few cases: **vā́santika** *vernal*, **vā́rṣika** *of the rainy season*, **hāímantika** *wintry* (none of them in RV.); AV. has **kāirātikā́** *of the Kirātas*, apparent fem. to a masc. **kāirātaka**, which is not found till later. Examples from a more recent period (when they become abundant) are: **vāidika** *relating to the Vedas*, **dhārmika** *religious*, **āhnika** *daily*, **vāinayika** *well-behaved*, **dāuvārika** *doorkeeper*, **nāiyāyika** *versed in the Nyāya*.

m. Before the suffix **ka**, some finals show a form which is characteristic of external rather than internal combination. A final sonant mute, of course, becomes surd, and an aspirate loses its aspiration (**117 a, 114**): cf. **-upasatka, -samitka**, above, **h.** So also a palatal becomes guttural (as before **t** etc.: **217**): e. g. **-srukka, -rukka, -tvakka, anṛkka.** A **s** remains after **ă**, and becomes **ṣ** after an alterant vowel (**180**): e. g. **sadyaska, jyotiṣka, dīrghāyuṣka.** But the other sibilants take the form they would have in composition: thus, **adíkka** (**diç**), **ṣaṭka**, **-viṭka**, **-tviṭka** (**ṣaṣ** etc.). **Anāçīrka** (TS.: **āçis**) is anomalous; and so is **parutka** (Āpast.), if it comes from **parus**.

1223. Several suffixes, partly of rare occurrence and questionable character, contain a न् n as consonantal element, and may be grouped together here.

a. A few derivatives in **āna** in RV. were given above (**1175** a).

b. With **ānī** (which is perhaps the corresponding feminine) are made a small number of words, chiefly wife-names: thus, **indrāṇī**, **varuṇānī** (these, with **uçīnárāṇī**, **purukútsānī**, **mudgalā́nī**, **ūrjā́nī**, are found in RV.), **rudrāṇī**, **mātulānī** *maternal uncle's wife*, **çarvāṇī**, **bhavānī**, **īçānānī**, **çakrāṇī**, **upādhyāyānī**, **mṛḍānī**, **brahmāṇī**; and **yavānī**.

c. The feminines in **nī** and **knī** from masculine stems in **ta** have been already noticed above (**1176** d). From **páti** *master*, *husband* the feminine is **pátnī**, both as independent word, *spouse*, and as final of an adjective compound: thus, **devápatnī** *having a god for husband*, **síndhupatnī** *having the Indus as master*. And the feminine of **paruṣá** *rough* is in the older language sometimes **páruṣṇī**.

d. With **īna** are made a full series of adjective derivatives from the words with final **añc** (**407** ff.); they are accented usually upon the penult, but sometimes on the final; and the same word has sometimes both accents: for example, **apācī́na**, **nīcī́na**, **prācī́na**, **arvācī́na** and **arvācīná**, **praticī́na** and **pratīcīná**, **samīcīná**. Besides these, a number of other adjectives, earlier and later: examples are **saṁvatsarī́na** *yearly*, **prāvṛṣī́ṇa** *of the rainy season*, **viçvajanī́na** *of all people*, **jñātakulī́na** *of known family*, **adhvanī́na** *traveller* (**ádhvan** *way*), **āçvīna** *day's journey on horseback* (**áçva** *horse*). RV. has once **mā́kīna** *mine*.

e. With **ena** is made **sāmidhená** (f. **-nī́**), from **samídh**, with initial strengthening.

f. As to a few words in **ina**, compare **1209** c.

g. The adjectives made with simple **na** fall partly under another head (below, **1245** f); here may be noted **çū́raṇa** *heroic* (?), **phálguna**, **çmacruṇá**, **dadruṇa**, and, with **vṛddhi**-strengthening, **strāíṇa** *woman's* (its correlative, **pāuṁsna**, occurs late) and **cyāutná** *inciting*. If **dróṇa** comes from **dru** *wood*, it has the anomaly of a **guṇa**-strengthening.

1224. Certain suffixes containing a म् m may be similarly grouped.

a. With **ima** are made a small number of adjectives from nouns in **tra**: thus, **khanítrima** *made by digging*, **kṛtríma** *artificial*, **dattrima**, **paktrima**, **pūtríma**; in other finals, **kuṭṭima**, **ganima**, **talima**, **tulima**, **pākima**, **udgārima**, **vyāyogima**, **saṁvyūhima**, **nirvedhima**, **āsañgima**, all late. In **agrima** (RV.) *foremost* the **ma** has perhaps the ordinal value.

b. The uses of simple **ma** in forming superlatives (**474**) and ordinals (**487** d, e) have been already noticed, and the words thus made specified.

c. A few neuter abstracts end in **mna**: thus, **dyumná** *brightness*, **nṛmṇá** *manliness*; and, from particles, **nimná** *depth* and **sumná** *welfare*. The suffix comes perhaps from **man** with an added **a**.

d. For the words showing a final **min**, see below, **1231**.

1225. मय **maya.** With this suffix are formed adjectives signifying *made* or *composed* or *consisting of*, also *abounding in*, that which is denoted by the primitive.

a. The accent is always on the **má**, and the feminine is regularly and usually in **máyī**. In the oldest language (V.), final **as** remains unchanged before the suffix: thus, **manasmáya, nabhasmáya, ayasmáya**; but **d** is treated as in external combination: thus, **mṛnmáya**; and in the Brāhmaṇas and later, finals in general have the latter treatment: e. g. **tejomáya, adomáya, āpomáya, jyotirmaya, yajurmáya, etanmáya, asṛñmaya, vāñmáya, ammaya, prāvṛṇmaya.** RV. has **açmanmáya** (later **açmamaya**). In **hiraṇmáya** (B. and later) the primitive (**hiraṇya**) is peculiarly mutilated. RV. has **sūmáya** *of good make*, and **kimmáya** *made of what?*

b. A very few examples of a feminine in **yā** occur in the later language.

1226. र **ra.** A few derivative adjectives are made with this suffix. Accent and treatment of the primitive are various.

a. With simple addition of **ra** are made, for example: **pāṅsurá** *dusty*, **-çrīra** (also **-çlīla**) in **açrīrá** *ugly*, **dhūmrá** *dusky* (**dhūmá** *smoke*), **madhura** (late) *sweet*. In an example or two, there appears to be accompanying initial strengthening: thus, **ā́gnīdhra** *of the fire-kindler* (**agnī́dh**), **çāñkurá** *stake-like* (**çaṅkú**); and in **çekhara** (also **çikhara**), a **guṇa**-strengthening.

b. With an inorganic vowel before the ending are made, for example, **médhira** *wise*, **rathirá** *in a chariot*; **karmā́ra** *smith*; **dantura** (late) *tusked*; **acchéra** (? MS.), **çrāmaṇera, saṅgamanera.**

c. The use of **ra** in forming a few words of comparative meaning was noticed above (**474**), and the words so made were given.

1227. ल **la.** This and the preceding suffix are really but two forms of the same. In some words they exchange with one another, and ल **la** is usually, but not always, the later form in use.

a. Examples are: **bahulá** *abundant*, **madhulá** (later **madhura**) and **madhūla** *sweet*, **bhīmala** *fearful*, **jīvalá** *lively*, **açlīlá** (and **açrīrá**) *wretched*; with **ā**, **vācāla** *talkative* (late); with **i**, **phenila** *foamy* (late:

phéna); with **u**, **vātula** and **vātūla** *windy* (late: **vā́ta**); and **mātula** *maternal uncle* is a somewhat irregular formation from **mātṛ** *mother.*

b. In the later language are found a few adjectives in **lu**, always preceded by **ā**; examples are: **kṛpālu** and **dayālu** *compassionate*, **īrṣyālu** *jealous*, **uṣṇālu** *heated*, **çayālu** and **svapnālu** *sleepy*, **lajjālu** *modest*, **lālālu** *drooling*, **çraddhālu** *trusting*, **krodhālu** *passionate.* One or two such derivatives having a primary aspect were noticed at **1192b.**

1228. **व va.** A small number of adjectives have this ending (accented, added to an unaltered primitive).

a. Examples are: **arṇavá** *billowy*, **keçavá** *hairy*; **rāsnāvá** *girded*; **añjivá** *slippery*, **çantivá** *tranquillizing*, **çraddhivá** *credible*, **amaṇiva** *jewelless*, **rājīva** *striped.*

b. There are a very few adjectives in **vala** and **vaya** which may be noticed here: thus, **kṛṣīvalá** *peasant* (**kṛṣi** *ploughing*), **ūrṇāvalá** *wooly*, **rajasvala, ūrjasvala, payasvala, çādvala, naḍvala, çikhāvala, dantāvala**; **druváya** *wooden dish*, **caturvaya** *fourfold.*

c. With **vya** are made two or three words from names of relationship: thus, **pítṛvya** *paternal uncle*, **bhrā́tṛvya** *nephew, enemy.*

1229. **श ça.** A very few adjectives appear to be made by an added ending of this form.

a. Thus, **romaçá** or **lomaçá** *hairy*, **étaça** (also **etaçá**) *variegated*, **arvaçá** or **árvaça** *hasting*, **babhluçá** or **babhruçá** and **kapiça** *brownish*, **kṛṣṇaça** *blackish*, **yuváçá** *youthful*, **bāliça** *childish*, **karkaça** *harsh*, **karmaça** (?) n. pr.; and **giriça, vāriça** (?), **vṛkṣaça** are doubtless of the same character (not containing the root **çī**). The character of **harīmaçá, káçmaça, kaláça** is doubtful.

b. Many of the adjective derivatives already treated have sometimes a possessive value, the general meaning of *being concerned with, having relation to* being specialized into that of *being in possession of.* But there are also a few distinctively possessive suffixes; and some of these, on account of the unlimited freedom of using them and the frequency of their occurrence, are very conspicuous parts of the general system of derivation. These will be next considered.

1230. **इन् in.** Possessive adjectives of this ending may be formed almost unlimitedly from stems in **अ a** or **आ ā**, and are sometimes (but very rarely) made from stems with other finals.

a. A final vowel disappears before the suffix. The accent is on the suffix. As to the inflection of these adjectives, see above, **438 ff.** They are to be counted by hundreds in the older language, and are equally or more numerous in the later.

b. Examples from **a**-stems are: **açvín** *possessing horses*, **dhanín** *wealthy*, **pakṣín** *winged*, **balín** *strong*, **bhagín** *fortunate*, **vajrín** *wielding the thunderbolt*, **çikhaṇḍín** *crested*, **hastín** *possessing hands*, **ṣoḍaçín** *of sixteen*, **gardabhanādín** *having an ass's voice*, **brahmavarcasín** *of eminent sanctity*, **sādhudevín** *having luck at play*, **kūcidarthín** *having errands everywhither*; — from **ā**-stems, **manīṣín** *wise*, **çikhín** *crested*, **ṛtāyín** *pious*.

c. Derivatives from other stems are very few in comparison: thus, from **i**-stems, **atithin** (?), **abhimātín**, **arcín**, **açanin**, **ūrmin**, **kālanemin**, **khādín**, **-pāṇin**, **marīcin**, **mauñjin**, **māulin**, **-yonin**, **veṇin**, **saṁdhin**, **samṛddhin**, **surabhin** (of those found only at the end of a possessive compound the character is doubtful, since case-forms of **i**- and **in**-stems are not seldom exchanged); — from **u**-stems, **gurvin**, **çatagvín** (?), **veṇavin** (with **guna** of the **u**); — from stems in **an**, **varmín**, **karmin**, **carmin**, **-chadmin**, **janmin**, **dhanvin**, **-dharmin**, **nāmin**, **brahmin**, **yakṣmin**, **çarmin**, and **çvanín**; — in **as**, **retín** *rich in seed*, and probably **varcin** n. pr.; also (perhaps through stems in **-sa**) **çavasín** and **sahasin**, **manasín**, **-vayasín**; — isolated are **parisrajín** *garlanded*, and **hiranín** (**hiráṇya**).

d. It was pointed out above (**1183**) that derivatives in **in** have assumed on a large scale the aspect and value of primary derivatives, with the significance of present participles, especially at the end of compounds. The properly secondary character of the whole formation is shown, on the one hand, by the frequent use in the same manner of words bearing an unmistakably secondary form, as **praçnín**, **garbhín**, **jūrṇín**, **dhūmín**, **snānin**, **homin**, **matsarín**, **paripanthín**, **pravepanín**, **saṁgatin**; and, on the other hand, by the occurrence of reverted palatals (**216**) before the **in**, which could only be as **in** replaced **a**: thus, **arkín**, **-bhaṅgín**, **-saṅgín**, **-rokín**.

e. In a few cases, there appears before the **in** a **y** preceded by an **ā** of inorganic character: thus, **dhanvāyín**, **tantrāyin**, **çvetāyin**, **sṛkāyín**, **ātatāyín**, **pratihitāyín**, **marāyín**, **ṛtāyin**, **svadhāyín** (VS.: TB. **-vín**). The **y** in all such words is evidently the inserted **y** after **ā** (**258 a**), and to assume for them a suffix **yin** is quite needless.

f. The accentuation **pravrā́jin**, **prasyándin**, in the concluding part of ÇB., is doubtless false; and the same is to be suspected for **çā́kī**, **sárī**, **írī** (RV., each once).

g. A very few words in **in** have not suffered the possessive specialization. Such are **vanín** *tree*, *hermit*, **kapotín** *dovelike*, **aṇḍin** *scrotumike* (cf. **1233 f**).

1231. मिन् **min.** With this suffix are made an extremely small number of possessive adjectives.

a. In the old language, the words in **min** have the aspect of derivatives in **in** from nouns in **ma**, although in two or three cases — **iṣmín**

and **ṛgmín** in RV., **vāgmín** in ÇB. — no such nouns are found in actual use beside them. In the later language, **miṇ** is used as independent element in a very few words: thus, **gomin** *possessing cattle*, **svāmin** (Sūtras and later) *master*, *lord* (**sva** *own*), **kakudmin** *humped*.

b. The two words **ṛgmín** and **vāgmín** show not only reversion but also sonantizing of an original palatal.

1232. विन् **vin.** The adjectives made with this suffix are also not numerous. They have the same meanings with those in इन् **in.** The accent is on the suffix.

a. The RV. has ten adjectives in **vin**; they become rather more common later. Though for them may be suspected a similar origin to those in **yin** and **min** (above), signs of it are much less clearly traceable.

b. The great majority have **vin** added after **as**: e. g. **namasvín** *reverential*, **tapasvín** *heated*, **tejasvín** *brilliant*, **yaçasvín** *beautiful*, and so **retasvín, enasvín, harasvín**, etc.; and **çatasvín, çrotrasvín, rūpasvin** have an inserted **s**, by analogy with them. Most others have **ā** (sometimes, by lengthening): thus, **glāvín, medhāvín, māyāvín, sabhāvín, aṣṭrāvín** *obedient to the goad*, **dvayāvín** *double-minded*, **ubhayāvín** *possessing of both kinds*, **dhanvāvin, tandrāvin, āmayāvín, ātatāvín.** More rarely, **vin** is added after another consonant than **s**: thus, **vāgvín, dhṛṣadvín, ātmanvín, kumudvin, sragvin, yajvin, ajvin.** The doubtful word **vyaçnuvín** (VS., once: TB. **vyáçniya**) appears to add the ending (or **in**, with euphonic **v**) to a present tense-stem.

c. An external form of combination is seen only in **vāgvín** and **dhṛṣadvín** (both Vedic), with the common reversion of a palatal in **sragvin.**

1233. वत् **vant.** Very numerous possessive adjectives are made by this suffix, from noun-stems of every form, both in the earlier language and in the later.

a. The accent generally remains upon the primitive, without change; but an accent resting on a stem-final, if this be anything but **á** or **ā́**, is in the majority of cases thrown forward upon the suffix. As to inflection, formation of feminine, etc., see **452** ff.

b. A final vowel — oftenest **a**, very rarely **u** — is in many words lengthened in the older language (**247**) before this ending, as in composition. Nouns in **an** more often retain the **n.**

c. Examples of the normal formation are: with unchanged accent, **kéçavant** *hairy*, **putrávant** *having a son*, **prajánanavant** *procreative*, **puṇḍárīkavant** *rich in lotuses*, **híraṇyavant** *rich in gold*, **apūpávant** *having cakes*, **rājanyàvant** *allied with a kshatriya*; **prajā́vant** *having progeny*, **ū́rṇāvant** *wooly*, **dákṣiṇāvant** *rich in sacrificial gifts*; **sákhivant** *having friends*, **saptarṣívant** *accompanied by the seven sages*; **çácīvant** *powerful*, **táviṣīvant** *vehement*, **pátnīvant** *with spouse*, **dhī́vant** *devoted*,

dyā́vāpṛthivī́vant (**94b**) *with heaven and earth;* **víṣṇuvant** *accompanied by Vishnu;* **háritvant** *golden,* **āvṛ́tvant** *hither turned,* **āçī́rvant** *mixed with milk,* **svàrvant** *splendid,* **çarádvant** *full of years,* **púṅsvant** *having a male,* **páyasvant** *rich,* **támasvant** *dark,* **bráhmaṇvant** *accompanied with worship,* **rómaṇvant** *hairy* (but also **romavant, lómavant, vṛtrahavant,** etc.), **kakúbhvant** *containing a* **kakúbh**; — with accent on the suffix, **agnivánt** *having fire,* **rayivánt** *wealthy,* **nṛvánt** *manly,* **padvánt** *having feet,* **nasvánt** *with nose,* **āsanvánt** *having a mouth,* **çīrṣaṇvánt** *headed* (also **çī́rṣavant**).

d. With final stem-vowel lengthened: for example, **áçvāvant** (beside **áçvavant**) *possessing horses,* **sutā́vant** *having soma expressed,* **vṛ́ṣṇyāvant** *of virile force* (about thirty such cases occur in V.); **çáktīvant** *mighty,* **svádhitīvant** *having axes,* **ghṛ́ṇīvant** *hot;* **viṣūvánt** *dividing* (**víṣu** *apart*).

e. Certain special irregularities are as follows: an inserted **s** in **índrasvant, máhiṣvant**; inserted **n** in **vánanvant, búdhanvant, vádhanvant, gartanvánt, māṅsanvánt**; shortening of a final of the primitive in **māyávant, yājyàvant, puronuvākyàvant, āmíkṣavant, sarasvativant**; abbreviation in **hiraṇvant**; inserted **ā** in **çavasāvant, sahasāvant,** and the odd **mahimāvant**; anomalous accent in **kṛçanā́vant** (if from **kṛ́çana** *pearl*); derivation from particles in **antárvant** *pregnant,* **viṣūvánt** (above, **d**).

f. Instead of the specialized meaning of *possessing,* the more general one of *like to, resembling* is seen in a number of words, especially in the derivatives from pronominal stems, **mā́vant** *like me* etc. (**517**: add **ī́vant, kī́vant**). Other examples are **índrasvant** *like Indra,* **nīḍávant** *nestlike,* **nī́lavant** *blackish,* **nṛvánt** *manly,* **pṛ́ṣadvant** *speckled,* **kṣāítavant** *princely;* compare the later **paravant** *dependent.* It was pointed out above (**1107**) that the adverb of comparison in **vát** is the accusative neuter of a derivative of this class.

g. In a few words, **vant** has the aspect of forming primary derivatives: thus, **vivásvant** (or **vívasvant**) *shining,* also n. pr., **ánupadasvant, árvant, pípiṣvant** (?), **yahvánt.**

h. For the derivatives in **vat** from prepositions, which appear to have nothing to do with this suffix, see **1245j**.

i. While this suffix is generally added to a primitive according to the rules of internal combination (see examples above, **c**), treatment also as in external combination begins already in RV., in **pṛ́ṣadvant** (**pṛ́ṣat**), and becomes more common later: thus, **tapovant, tejovant, aṅgirovant** (beside **tápasvant** etc.); **vidyúdvant** (beside **vidyutvant**), **bṛhadvant, jagadvant, sadvant,** etc.; **triṣṭubvant** (against **kakúbhvant**), **samidvant, vimṛdvant**; **vāgvant** (against **ṛkvant**); **svarāḍvant**; **havyavāḍvant**; **āçīrvant.**

j. None of the suffixes beginning with **v** show in the Veda resolution of **v** to **u**.

1234. वन् **van.** The secondary derivatives in this suffix belong to the older language, and are a small number, of which extremely few have more than an occurrence or two.

a. They have the aspect of being produced under the joint influence of primary **van** and secondary **vant.** A final short vowel is usually lengthened before the suffix. The accent is various, but oftenest on the penult of the stem. The feminine (like that of the derivatives in primary **van**: **1169 f**) is in **varī.**

b. The Vedic examples are: from **a**-stems, **ṛṇāván** or **ṛṇaván, ṛtā́van** (and f. **-varī**), **ṛ́ghāvan, dhitā́van, satyā́van, sumnāvárī,** and **maghávan**; from **ā**-stems, **sūnṛ́tāvarī, svadhā́van** (and f. **-varī**); from **i**-stems, **amatīván, arātīván, çruṣṭīván, muṣīván,** and **kṛṣīvan** (only in the further derivative **kā́rṣīvaṇa**); **dhī́van**; from consonant-stems, **átharvan, samádvan, sáhovan** (bad AV. variant to RV. **sahā́van**); **hā́rdvan** (TA. also **hārdivan**). Somewhat anomalous are **sahā́van, índhanvan** (for **índhanavan**?), and **sanítvan** (for **sánitivan**?). The only words of more than sporadic occurrence are **ṛtā́van, maghávan, átharvan.**

c. Sáhovan (see **b**) is the only example of external combination with this suffix.

1235. मत् **mant.** This is a twin-suffix to वत् **vant** (above, **1233**); their derivatives have the same value, and are to some extent exchangeable with one another. But possessives in मत् **mant** are much less frequent (in the older language, about a third as many), and are only very rarely made from **a**-stems.

a. If the accent of the primitive word is on the final, it is in the great majority of instances (three quarters) thrown forward upon the added suffix; otherwise, it maintains its place unchanged. A final vowel before the suffix is in only a few cases made long. Examples are:

b. With the accent of the primitive unchanged: **káṇvamant, yávamant** *rich in barley*, and **vibhavamant** n. pr. (these alone from **a**-stems, and the first only occurring once); **ávimant** *possessing sheep*, **açánimant** *bearing the thunderbolt*, **óṣadhīmant** *rich in herbs*, **vā́çīmant** *carrying an axe*, **vásumant** *possessing good things*, **mádhumant** *rich in sweets*, **tváṣṭṛmant** *accompanied by Tvashtar*, **hótṛmant** *provided with priests*, **ā́yuṣmant** *long-lived*, **jyótiṣmant** *full of brightness*; — **ulkuṣī́mant** *accompanied with meteors*, **pīlúmant** (?), **prasū́mant** *having young shoots*, **gómant** *rich in kine*, **garútmant** *winged*, **vihútmant** *with libation*, **kakúdmant** *humped*, **vidyúnmant** (with irregular assimilation of **t**: VS. has also **kakúnmant**) *gleaming*, **virúkmant** *shining*, **havíṣmant** *with libations*. **vipruṣmant** *with drops*.

c. With the accent thrown forward upon the ending: **asimánt** *with knives*, **agnimánt** *having fire*, **iṣudhimánt** *with a quiver*, **paçumánt** *possessing cattle*, **vāyumánt** *with wind*, **pitṛmánt** (AV. **pitṝmant**) *accompanied by the Fathers*, **mātṛmánt** *having a mother*; no long final vowels are found before the suffix in this division, and only once a consonant, in **dasmát** (RV., once).

d. Protraction of a final vowel is seen in **tvíṣīmant, dhrájīmant, hírīmant**; in **jyótiṣīmant** is irregularly inserted an **ī** (after the analogy of **táviṣīmant**); in **çuciṣmant, mahiṣmant**, an **s**; **suṣumánt** (RV., once) appears to be primary.

e. The adverb **āçumát** appears to be related to adverbs in **vát** as the suffix **mant** to **vant**.

f. By the side of derivatives made with internal combination appears **vidyúnmant** even in RV.; [and other like cases occur later: thus, **parisrúnmant, kakunmant, kṣunmant, purorúṅmant, vāṅmant, kakummant, gudaliṇmant, yaçomant**.

1236. It has been seen above (especially in connection with the suffixes **a** and **ya**) that the neuter of a derivative adjective is frequently used as an abstract noun. There are, however, two suffixes which have in the later language the specific office of making abstract nouns from adjectives and nouns; and these are found also, more sparingly used, in the oldest language, each having there one or two other evidently related suffixes beside it.

a. For derivatives of the same value made with the suffix **iman**, see above, **1168 i—k**.

1237. ता tā. With this suffix are made feminine abstract nouns, denoting *the quality of being so and so*, from both adjectives and nouns.

a. The form of the primitive is unchanged, and the accent is uniformly on the syllable preceding the suffix.

b. Examples (from the older language) are: **devátā** *divinity*, **vīrátā** *manliness*, **puruṣátā** *human nature*, **agnítā** *firehood*, **apaçútā** *cattle-lessness*, **bandhútā** *relationship*, **vasútā** *wealth*; **nagnátā** *nakedness*, **suvīrátā** *wealth in retainers*, **anapatyátā** *lack of descendants*, **agótā** *poverty in cattle*, **abrahmátā** *lack of devotion*, **aprajástā** *absence of progeny*; also doubtless **sūnṛtā** (from **sūnára**), although the word is a few times used as an adjective (like **çaṁtāti** and **satyatāti**: see next paragraph).

c. Of special formation are **mamátā** *selfishness*, **trétā** *triplicity*, **astitā** *actuality*. RV. has **avīratā**, with exceptional accent. In **ekapatnitā** is seen a shortened final vowel of the primitive. **Janátā** has acquired a concrete meaning, *people, folk*; also **grāmatā** (once) *villages* collectively.

1238. ताति tāti, तात् tāt. These suffixes are Vedic only, and the latter is limited to RV. Their relationship to the preceding is evident, but opinions are at variance as to its nature. The accent is as in the derivatives with **tā**.

a. The quotable examples in **tāti** are: **ariṣṭátāti** *uninjuredness*, **ayakṣmátāti** *freedom from disease*, **gṛbhītátāti** *the being seized*, **jyeṣṭhátāti** *supremacy*, **devátāti** *divinity*, **vasútāti** *wealth*, **çáṁtāti** *good-fortune*, **sarvátāti** *completeness;* and, with exceptional accent, **ástatāti** *home*, and **dákṣatāti** *cleverness;* **çivatāti** and **çubhatāti** occur (once each) in the later language. Two words in **tāti** are used adjectively (inorganically, by apposition?): **çáṁtāti** (RV., twice; and AV. xix. 44. 1, in manuscripts), and **satyatāti** (RV., once: voc.).

b. The words in **tāt** (apparently made by abbreviation from **tāti**) occur in only one or two cases-forms; they were all mentioned above (**383 k.** 2).

1239. त्व **tva:** With this suffix are made neuter nouns, of the same value as the feminines in ता **tā** (above, **1237**).

a. The neuter abstracts in **tva** are in the older language considerably more common than the feminines in **tā**, although themselves also not very numerous. The accent is without exception on the suffix.

b. Examples (from the older language) are: **amṛtatvá** *immortality*, **devatvá** *divinity*, **subhagatvá** *good-fortune*, **ahamuttaratvá** *struggle for precedency*, **çucitvá** *purity*, **patitvá** *husbandship*, **taraṇitvá** *energy*, **dīrghāyutvá** *long life*, **çatrutvá** *enmity*, **bhrātṛtvá** *brotherhood*, **vṛṣatvá** *virility*, **sātmatvá** *soulfulness*, **maghavattvá** *liberality*, **rakṣastvá** *sorcery*. In **anāgāstvá** and **-prajāstvá** there is a lengthening of the final syllable of the primitive; and in **sāuprajāstvá** (AV., once) this appears to be accompanied by initial **vṛddhi** (**sāubhagatvá** is doubtless from **sāúbhaga**, not **subhága**); and in these and **pratyanastvá** there is an apparent insertion of **s**. In **sadhanitvá** (RV.), **vasatīvaritvá** (TS.), **rohiṇitvá** (TB.), there is shortening of final feminine **ī** before the suffix. Of peculiar formation are **astitva** *actuality* and **sahatva** *union*. The apparent feminine datives **yūthatvāyāi** and **gaṇatvāyāi** (KS.) are doubtless false forms.

c. Besides the usual guttural reversions in **samyaktva**, **sayuktva**, we have external combination in **samittva** (**-idh-**) and **pūrvavāṭtva** (**-vah-**).

d. In **iṣitatvátā** (RV., once) *incitedness*, and **puruṣatvátā** (RV., twice) *human quality*, appears to be a combination of the two equivalent suffixes **tva** and **tā**.

e. The **v** of **tva** is to be read in Veda as **u** only once (**rakṣastuá**).

1240. त्वन **tvana.** The derivatives made with this suffix are, like those in **tva**, neuter abstracts. They occur almost only in RV., and, except in a single instance (**martyatvaná**), have beside them equivalent derivatives in **tva**. The accent is on the final, and the **tva** is never resolved into **tua**.

a. The words are: **kavitvaná, janitvaná, patitvaná** (also JB.), **martyatvaná, mahitvaná, vasutvaná, vṛṣatvaná, sakhitvaná.**

1241. A few suffixes make no change in the character as part of speech of the primitive to which they are added, but either are merely formal appendages, leaving the value of the word what it was before, or make a change of degree, or introduce some other modification of meaning.

1242. The suffixes of comparison and ordinal suffixes have for the most part been treated already, and need only a reference here.

a. तर **tara** and तम **tama** are the usual secondary suffixes of adjective comparison: respecting their use as such, see above, **471—473**; respecting the use of **tama** as ordinal etc. suffix, see **487—8**; respecting that of their accusatives as adverbial suffixes to prepositions etc., see **1111 e.**

b. In **vṛtratára** and **purutáma** (RV.) the accent is anomalous; in **mṛḍayáttama,** it is drawn forward to the final of the participle, as often in composition (**1309**); **çaçvattamá** (RV.) has the ordinal accent; **saṁvatsaratamá** (ÇB.) is an ordinal; **dívātara** (RV., once: an error?) is an ordinary adjective, *of the day;* **surabhíṣṭama** and **tuvíṣṭama** insert a **s**; **kārotará** and **kāulitará** are probably **vṛddhi**-derivatives in **a.** In **vatsatará** (f. **-rī́**) *weanling*, **açvatará** *mule*, and **dhenuṣṭarī́** *cow losing her milk*, the application of the suffix is peculiar and obscure; so also in **rathaṁtará,** name of a certain *sāman.*

c. र **ra** and म **ma,** like **tara** and **tama,** have a comparative and superlative value; and the latter of them forms ordinals: see above, **474, 487.**

d. थ **tha,** like **tama** and **ma,** forms ordinals from a few numerals: see **487 c**; also (with fem. in **-thī́**) from **tati, kati, yati, iti**: thus, **tatithá** *so-many-eth* etc.

e. Apparently by false analogy with **tatithá** etc. (above, **d**), the quasi-ordinals **tāvatitha, yāvatitha, bahutitha** are made, as if with a suffix **titha** (also **katititha,** late, for **katithá**); and, it is said, from other words meaning *a number* or *collection*, as **gaṇa, pūga, saṁgha**; but none such are quotable.

1243. Of diminutive suffixes there are none in Sanskrit with clearly developed meaning and use. The occasional employment of **ka,** in a somewhat indistinct way, to make diminutives, has been noticed above (**1222**).

1244. Of the ordinary adjective-making suffixes, given above, some occasionally make adjectives from adjectives, with slight or imperceptible modification of value. The only one used to any considerable extent in this way is **ka**: as to which, see **1222.**

1245. A few suffixes are used to make derivatives from certain limited and special classes of words, as numerals and particles. Thus:

a. तय **taya** makes a few adjectives, meaning *of so many divisions* or *kinds* (used in the neuter as collectives), from numerals: thus, **ékataya** (MS.), **dvitaya, tritaya, cátuṣṭaya** (AV.), **ṣaṭtaya** (KB.: with external combination), **saptátaya** (ÇB.), **aṣṭātaya** (AB.), **dáçataya** (RV.), **bahútaya** (TS.). Their fem. is in **-yī**.

b. त्य **tya** makes a class of adjectives from particles: e. g. **nítya** *own*, **níṣṭya** *foreign*, **amā́tya** *companion*, etc. As the examples show, the accent of the primitive is retained. The fem. is in **-tyā**.

c. The other quotable examples are **ápatya, āvíṣṭya, sánutya, antastya, anyatastya-, tatastya, kutastya, atratya, tatratya, yatratya, kutratya, ihatya, upatya, adhitya, prātastya, dakṣiṇātya** (instead of which, the regular form, is generally found **dākṣiṇātya**, apparently a further **vṛddhi**-derivative from it: as if *belonging to the southerners*), and **pāçcāttya** and **pāurastya** (of a similar character: these three last are said by the grammarians to be accented on the final, as is proper for **vṛddhi**-derivatives); **aptyá** and **āptyá** perhaps contain the same suffix. In **antastya** and **prātastya** is seen external combination.

d. The **y** of **tya** is in RV. always to be read as **i** after a heavy syllable.

e. त **ta** forms **ekatá, dvitá**, and **tritá**, also **muhūrtá** *moment*, and apparently **avatá** *well* (for water).

f. With न **na** are made **purāṇá** *ancient*, **víṣuṇa** *various*, and perhaps **samāná** *like*.

g. With तन **tana** or (in a few cases) त्न **tna** are made adjectives from adverbs, nearly always of time: e. g. **pratná** *ancient*, **nūtana** or **nūtna** *present*, **sanātána** or **sanátna** *lasting*, **divātana** *of the day*, **çvástana** *of tomorrov*, **hyastana** *of yesterday*. The accent is various. The feminine is in **nī**.

h. The other quotable examples are: **agretana, adyatana, adhunātána, idaṁtana, idānīṁtana, etarhitana, ciraṁtana, tadānīṁtana, doṣātana, purātana, prāktana, prātastána, sadātana, sāyaṁtána**; from adverbs of place, **adhastana, arvāktana, uparitana, kutastana**; — with **tna, parastāttna, purastāttna**. A further **vṛddhi**-derivative, with equivalent meaning, **nāutana** (cf. above, **c**), occurs late. In PB. is once found **tvattana** *belonging to thee*.

i. Besides the obvious cases of an assimilated final **m** before this suffix, we have external combination in **prātastána**.

j. वत् **vat** makes from particles of direction the feminine nouns mentioned above (**383**k. 1).

k. कट **kaṭa**, properly a noun in composition, is reckoned by the grammarians as a suffix, in **utkaṭa, nikaṭa, prakaṭa, vikaṭa** (RV., once, voc.), and **saṁkaṭa** (all said to be accented on the final).

l. A suffix **vana** is perhaps to be seen in **nivaná, pravaṇa**; — and **āla** in **antarāla.**

m. Occasional derivatives made with the ordinary suffixes of primary and secondary derivation from numerals and particles have been noted above: thus, see **ana** (**1150n**), **ti** (**1157h**), **ant** (**1172a**), **u** (**1178i**), **a** (**1209i**), **ka** (**1222c**), **mna** (**1224c**), **maya** (**1225a**), **vant** (**1233e**).

CHAPTER XVIII.

FORMATION OF COMPOUND STEMS.

1246. The frequent combination of declinable stems with one another to form compounds which then are treated as if simple, in respect to accent, inflection, and construction, is a conspicuous feature of the language, from its earliest period.

a. There is, however, a marked difference between the earlier and the later language as regards the length and intricacy of the combinations allowed. In Veda and Brāhmaṇa, it is quite rare that more than two stems are compounded together — except that to some much used and familiar compound, as to an integral word, a further element is sometimes added. But the later the period, and, especially, the more elaborate the style, the more a cumbrous and difficult aggregate of elements, abnegating the advantages of an inflective language, takes the place of the due syntactical union of formed words into sentences.

1247. Sanskrit compounds fall into three principal classes:

I. **a.** Copulative or aggregative compounds, of which the members are syntactically coördinate: a joining together into one of words which in an uncompounded condition would be connected by the conjunction *and* (rarely *or*).

b. Examples are: **índrāváruṇāu** *Indra and Varuna*, **satyānṛté** *truth and falsehood*, **kṛtākṛtám** *done and undone*, **devagandharvamānuṣoragarakṣasās** *gods and Gandharvas and men and serpents and demons.*

c. The members of such a compound may obviously be of any number, two or more than two. No compound of any other class can contain more than two members — of which, however, either or both may be compound, or decompound (below, **1248**).

II. **d.** Determinative compounds, of which the former member is syntactically dependent on the latter, as its determining or qualifying adjunct: being either, 1. a noun (or pronoun) limiting it in a case-relation, or, 2. an adjective or adverb describing it. And, according as it is the one or the other, are to be distinguished the two sub-classes: A. Dependent compounds; and B. Descriptive compounds. Their difference is not an absolute one.

e. Examples are: of dependent compounds, **amitrasenā́** *army of enemies*, **pādodaka** *water for the feet*, **āyurdā́** *life-giving*, **hástakṛta** *made with the hands;* of descriptive compounds, **maharṣí** *great sage*, **priyasakhi** *dear friend*, **amítra** *enemy*, **súkṛta** *well done.*

f. These two classes are of primary value; they have undergone no unifying modification in the process of composition; their character as parts of speech is determined by their final member, and they are capable of being resolved into equivalent phrases by giving the proper independent form and formal means of connection to each member. That is not the case with the remaining class, which accordingly is more fundamentally distinct from them than they are from one another.

III. **g.** Secondary adjective compounds, the value of which is not given by a simple resolution into their component parts, but which, though having as final member a noun, are themselves adjectives. These, again, are of two sub-classes: A. Possessive compounds, which are noun-compounds of the preceding class, with the idea of *possessing* added, turning them from nouns into adjectives; B. Compounds in which the second member is a noun syntactically dependent on the first: namely, 1. Prepositional compounds, of a governing preposition and following noun;

2. **Participial** compounds (only Vedic), of a present participle and its following object.

h. The sub-class **B.** is comparatively small, and its second division (participial compounds) is hardly met with even in the later Vedic.

i. Examples are: **vīrasena** *possessing a hero-army*, **prajākāma** *having desire of progeny*, **tigmáçṛñga** *sharphorned*, **háritasraj** *wearing green garlands;* **atimātrá** *excessive;* **yāvayáddveṣas** *driving away enemies.*

j. The adjective compounds are, like simple adjectives, liable to be used, especially in the neuter, as abstract and collective nouns, and in the accusative as adverbs; and out of these uses have grown apparent special classes of compounds, reckoned and named as such by the Hindu grammarians. The relation of the classification given above to that presented in the native grammar, and widely adopted from the latter by the European grammars, will be made clear as we go on to treat the classes in detail.

1248. A compound may, like a simple word, become a member in another compound, and this in yet another — and so on, without definite limit. The analysis of any compound, of whatever length (unless it be a copulative), must be made by a succession of bisections.

a. Thus, the dependent compound **pūrvajanmakṛta** *done in a previous existence* is first divisible into **kṛta** and the descriptive **pūrvajanman**, then this into its elements; the dependent **sakalanītiçāstratattvajña** *knowing the essence of all books of behavior* has first the root-stem **jña** (for √**jñā**) *knowing* separated from the rest, which is again dependent; then this is divided into **tattva** *essence* and the remainder, which is descriptive; this, again, divides into **sakala** *all* and **nītiçāstra** *books of behavior*, of which the latter is a dependent compound and the former a possessive (**sa** and **kalā** *having its parts together*).

1249. a. The final of a stem is combined with the initial of another stem in composition according to the general rules for external combination: they have been given, with their exceptions, in chap. III., above.

b. If a stem has a distinction of strong and weak forms, it regularly enters into composition as prior member in its weak form; or, if it has a triple distinction (**311**), in its middle form.

c. That is, especially, stems in ṛ or ar, at or ant, ac or añc, etc., show in composition the forms in ṛ, at, ac, etc.; while those in an and in usually (exceptions sometimes occur, as **vṛṣaṇaçvá, vṛṣaṇvasú**) lose their final n, and are combined as if a and i were their proper finals.

d. As in secondary derivation (**1203 d**), so also as prior member of a compound, a stem sometimes shortens its final long vowel (usually ī, rarely ā): thus, in V., **rodasiprā́, pṛthiviṣṭhā́, pṛthiviṣád, dhā́rapūta, dhāravāká**; in B., **pṛthivi-dā, -bhāga, -loká, sarasvatikṛta, senānigrāmaṇyāù**; in S., **garbhiniprāyaçcitta, sāmidheniprāiṣa, vasatīvariparibaraṇa, ekādaçiniliñga, prapharvidā, devatalakṣaṇa, devatapradhānatva**; later, **devakinandana, lakṣmivardhana, kumāridatta, muhūrtaja, iṣṭakacita**, etc.

e. Occasionally, a stem is used as prior member of a compound which does not appear, or not in that form, as an independent word: examples are **mahā** *great* (apparently used independently in V. in accusative), **tuvi** *mighty* (V.), **dvi** *two*.

f. Not infrequently, the final member of a compound assumes a special form: see below, **1315**.

1250. But a case-form in the prior member of a compound is by no means rare, from the earliest period of the language. Thus:

a. Quite often, an accusative, especially before a root-stem, or a derivative in a of equivalent meaning: for example, **pataṁgá** *going by flight*, **dhanaṁjayá** *winning wealth*, **abhayaṁkará** *causing absence of danger*, **puṣṭimbhará** *bringing prosperity*, **vācamīñkhayá** *inciting the voice*; but also sometimes before words of other form, as **áçvamiṣṭi** *horse-desiring*, **çubhaṁyā́van** *going in splendor*, **subhāgaṁkáraṇa** *making happy*, **bhayaṁkartṛ** *causer of fear*. In a few cases, by analogy with these, a word receives an accusative form to which it has no right: thus, **hṛdaṁsáni, makṣúṁgama, vasuṁdhara, ātmambhari**.

b. Much more rarely, an instrumental: for example, **girāvṛ́dh** *increasing by praise*, **vācā́stena** *stealing by incantation*, **krátvāmagha** *gladly bestowing*, **bhāsā́ketu** *bright with light*, **vidmanā́pas** *active with wisdom*.

c. In a very few instances, a dative: thus, **nareṣṭhā́** *serving a man*, **asméhiti** *errand to us*, and perhaps **kiyedhā́** and **mahevṛ́dh**.

d. Not seldom, a locative; and this also especially with a root-stem or a-derivative: for example, **agregá** *going at the head*, **divikṣít** *dwelling in the sky*, **vaneṣáh** *prevailing in the wood*, **añgeṣṭhā́** *existing in the limbs*, **proṣṭheçayá** *lying on a couch*, **sutékara** *active with the soma*, **divícara** *moving in the sky*; **āréçatru** *having enemies far removed*, **sumnáāpi** *near in favor*, **máderaghu** *hasting in excitement*, **yudhiṣṭhira** *firm in battle*, **antevāsin** *dwelling near*; **apsujá** *born in the waters*, **hṛtsvás** *hurling at hearts*.

e. Least often, a genitive: thus, **rāyáskāma** *desirous of wealth*,

akasyavíd *knowing no one.* But the older language has a few examples of the putting together of a genitive with its governing noun, each member of the combination keeping its own accent: see below, **1267 d.**

f. Ablative forms are to be seen in **balātkāra** *violence* and **balātkṛta,** and perhaps in **parātpriya.** And a stem in **ṛ** sometimes appears in a copulative compound in its nominative form: thus, **pitāputrāu** *father and son,* **hotāpotārāu** *the invoker and purifier.* **Anyonya** *one another* is a fused phrase, of nominative and oblique case.

g. In a very few words, plural meaning is signified by plural form: thus, **apsuj́** etc. (in derivation, also, **apsu** is used as a stem), **hṛtsvás, nṝ́ṅhpraṇetra** *conducting men,* **rujaskara** *causing pains,* (and dual) **hanūkampa** *trembling of the two jaws.*

h. Much more often, of words having gender-forms, the feminine is used in composition, when the distinctive feminine sense is to be conveyed: e. g. **gopīnātha** *master of the shepherdesses,* **dāsīputra** *son of a female slave,* **mṛgīdṛç** *gazelle-eyed,* **praṇītāpraṇáyana** *vessel for consecrated water.*

1251. The accent of compounds is very various, and liable to considerable irregularity even within the limits of the same formation; and it must be left to be pointed out in detail below. All possible varieties are found to occur. Thus:

a. Each member of the compound retains its own separate accent. This is the most anomalous and infrequent method. It appears in certain Vedic copulative compounds chiefly composed of the names of divinities (so-called **devatā-dvandvas: 1255** ff.), and in a small number of aggregations partly containing a genitive case-form as prior member (**1267 d**).

b. The accent of the compound is that of its prior member. This is especially the case in the great class of possessive compounds; but also in determinatives having the participle in **ta** or **na** as final member, in those beginning with the negative **a** or **an,** and in other less numerous and important classes.

c. The accent of the compound is that of the final member. This is not on so large a scale the case as the preceding; but it is nevertheless quite common, being found in many compounds having a verbal noun or adjective as final member, in compounds beginning with the numerals **dvi** and **tri** or the prefixes **su** and **dus,** and elsewhere in not infrequent exceptions.

d. The compound takes an accent of its own, independent of that of either of its constituents, on its final syllable (not always, of course, to be distinguished from the preceding case). This method is largely followed: especially, by the regular copulatives, and by the great mass of dependent and descriptive noun-compounds, by most possessives beginning with the negative prefix; and by others.

e. The compound has an accent which is altered from that of one of its members. This is everywhere an exceptional and sporadically occurring case, and the instances of it, noted below under each formation, do not require to be assembled here. Examples are: **medhásāti** (**médha**), **tilámiçra** (**tíla**), **khā́dihasta** (**khādí**), **yāvayáddveṣas** (**yāváyant**); **çakadhū́ma** (**dhūmá**), **amŕ̥ta** (**mr̥tá**), **suvíra** (**vīrá**), **tuvigrī́va** (**grīvā́**). A few words — as **víçva**, **pū́rva**, and sometimes **sárva** — take usually a changed accent as prior members of compounds.

I. Copulative Compounds.

1252. Two or more nouns — much less often adjectives, and, in an instance or two, adverbs — having a coördinate construction, as if connected by a conjunction, usually *and*, are sometimes combined into compounds.

a. This is the class to which the Hindu grammarians give the name of **dvandva** *pair, couple;* a **dvandva** of adjectives, however, is not recognized by them.

b. Compounds in which the relation of the two members is alternative instead of copulative, though only exceptional, are not very rare: examples are **nyūnādhika** *defective or redundant*, **jayaparājaya** *victory or defeat*, **krītotpanna** *purchased or on hand*, **kāṣṭhaloṣṭasama** *like a log or clod*, **pakṣimr̥gatā** *the condition of being bird or beast*, **triñçadviñça** *numbering twenty or thirty*, **catuṣpañcakr̥tvas** *four or five times*, **dvyekāntara** *different by one or two.* A less marked modification of the copulative idea is seen in such instances as **priyasatya** *agreeable though true*, **prārthitadurlabha** *sought after but hard to obtain;* or in **çrāntāgata** *arrived weary!*

1253. The noun-copulatives fall, as regards their inflective form, into two classes:

1\. **a.** The compound has the gender and declension of its final member, and is in number a dual or a plural, according to its logical value, as denoting two or more than two individual things.

b. Examples are: **prāṇāpānāú** *inspiration and expiration*, **vrīhiyavāú** *rice and barley*, **r̥ksāmé** *verse and chant*, **kapotolūkāú** *dove and owl*, **candrādityāu** *moon and sun*, **hastyaçvāu** *the elephant and horse*, **ajāváyas** *goats and sheep*, **devāsurā́s** *the gods and demons*, **atharvāñgirásas** *the Atharvans and Angirases*, **sambādhatandryàs** *anxieties and fatigues*, **vidyākarmáṇī** *knowledge and action*, **hastyaçvās** *elephants and horses;* of more than two members (no examples quotable from the older language), **çayyāsanabhogās** *lying, sitting, and eating*, **brāhmaṇakṣatriyaviṭçūdrās** *a Brahman, Kshatriya, Vaiçya, and Çūdra*,

rogaçokaparītāpabandhanavyasanāni *disease, pain, grief, captivity, and misfortune.*

2. c. The compound, without regard to the number denoted, or to the gender of its constituents, becomes a neuter singular collective.

d. Examples are: **iṣṭāpūrtám** *what is offered and bestowed,* **ahorātrám** *a day and night,* **kṛtākṛtám** *the done and undone,* **bhūtabhavyám** *past and future,* **keçaçmaçrú** *hair and beard,* **oṣadhivanaspatí** *plants and trees,* **candratārakám** *moon and stars,* **ahinakulam** *snake and ichneumon,* **çirogrīvam** *head and neck,* **yūkāmakṣikamatkuṇam** *lice, flies, and bugs.*

1254. a. That a stem in **ṛ** as prior member sometimes takes its nominative form, in **ā**, was noticed above, **1250 f.**

b. A stem as final member is sometimes changed to an **a**-form to make a neuter collective: thus, **chattropānaham** *an umbrella and a shoe.*

c. The grammarians give rules as to the order of the elements composing a copulative compound: thus, that a more important, a briefer, a vowel-initial member should stand first; and that one ending in **a** should be placed last. Violations of them all, however, are not infrequent.

1255. In the oldest language (RV.), copulative compounds such as appear later are quite rare, the class being chiefly represented by dual combinations of the names of divinities and other personages, and of personified natural objects.

a. In these combinations, each name has regularly and usually the dual form, and its own accent; but, in the very rare instances (only three occurrences out of more than three hundred) in which other cases than the nom.-acc.-voc. are formed, the final member only is inflected.

b. Examples are: **índrāsómā, índrāvíṣṇū, índrābṛ́haspátī, agnī́ṣómāu, turváçāyádū, dyā́vāpṛthiví, uṣā́sānáktā** (and, with intervening words, **náktā... uṣā́sā**), **sū́ryāmā́sā.** The only plural is **índrāmarutas** (voc.). The cases of other than nominative form are **mitrā́váruṇābhyām** and **mitrā́váruṇayos** (also **mitráyor váruṇayoḥ**), and **índrāváruṇayos** (each once only).

c. From **dyā́vāpṛthiví** is made the very peculiar genitive **diváspṛthivyós** (4 times: AV. has **dyā́vāpṛthivíbhyām** and **dyā́vāpṛthivyós**).

d. In one compound, **parjányavā́tā,** the first member (RV., once) does not have the dual ending along with the double accent (**indranāsatyā,** voc., is doubtful as to accent). In several, the double accent is wanting, while yet the double designation of number is present: thus, **indrāpūṣṇós** (beside **índrāpūṣáṇā**), **somāpūṣábhyām** (**somāpūṣaṇā** occurs only as voc.), **vātāparjanyā́, sūryācandramásā,** and **indrāgnī́** (with **indrāgníbhyām** and **indrāgnyós**): **somārudrāú** is accented only in ÇB. And in one, **indravāyū́**, form and accent are both accordant with the usages of the later language.

e. Of other copulatives, like those made later, the RV. has the plural **ajāvā́yas**, the duals **ṛksāmé, satyānṛté, sāçanānaçané**; also the neuter collective **iṣṭāpūrtám**, and the substantively used neuter of a copulative adjective, **nīlalohitám**. Further, the neuter plurals **ahorātrā́ṇi** *nycthemera*, and **ukthārkā́** *praises and songs*, of which the final members as independent words are not neuter. No one of these words has more than a single occurrence.

1256. In the later Vedic (AV.), the usage is much more nearly accordant with that of the classical language, save that the class of neuter singular collectives is almost wanting.

a. The words with double dual form are only a small minority (a quarter, instead of three quarters, as in RV.); and half of them have only a single accent, on the final: thus, besides those in RV., **bhavārudrāú, bhavāçarvāú**; **agnāviṣṇū**, voc., is of anomalous form. The whole number of copulatives is more than double that in RV.

b. The only proper neuter collectives, composed of two nouns, are **keçaçmaçrú** *hair and beard*, **āñjanābhyañjanám** *salve and ointment*, and **kaçipūpabarhaṇám** *mat and pillow*, unified because of the virtual unity of the two objects specified. Neuter singulars, used in a similar collective way, of adjective compounds, are (besides those in RV.): **kṛtākṛtám** *what is done and undone* (instead of *what is done and what is undone*), **cittākūtám** *thought and desire*, **bhadrapāpám** *good and evil*, **bhūtabhavyám** *past and future*.

1257. Copulative compounds composed of adjectives which retain their adjective character are made in the same manner, but are in comparison rare.

a. Examples are: **çuklakṛṣṇa** *light and dark*, **sthalajāudaka** *terrestrial and aquatic*, **dāntarājatasāuvarṇa** *of ivory and silver and gold*, used distributively; and **vṛttapīna** *round and plump*, **çāntānukūla** *tranquil and propitious*, **hṛṣitasragrajohīna** *wearing fresh garlands and free from dust*, **niṣekādiçmaçānānta** *beginning with conception and ending with burial*, used cumulatively; **nā 'tiçītoṣṇa** *not over cold or hot*, used alternatively; **kṣaṇadṛṣṭanaṣṭa** *seen for a moment and then lost*, **cintitopasthita** *at hand as soon as thought of*, in more pregnant sense.

b. In the Veda, the only examples noted are the cumulative **nīlalohitá** and **iṣṭāpūrtá** etc., used in the neut. sing. as collectives (as pointed out above), with **tāmradhūmrá** *dark tawny*; and the distributive **dakṣiṇasavyá** *right and left*, **saptamāṣṭamá** *seventh and eighth*, and **bhadrapāpá** *good and bad* (beside the corresponding neut. collective). Such combinations as **satyānṛté** *truth and falsehood*, **priyāpriyā́ṇi** *things* *agreeable and disagreeable*, where each component is used substantively, are, of course, not to be separated from the ordinary noun-compounds.

c. A special case is that of the compound adjectives of direction: as **uttarapūrva** *north-east*, **prāgdakṣiṇa** *south-east*, **dakṣiṇapaçcima** *south-west*, etc.: compare **1291 b.**

1258. In accentuated texts, the copulative compounds have uniformly the accent (acute) on the final of the stem.

a. Exceptions are a case or two in AV., where doubtless the reading is false: thus, **vātāparjanyà** (once: beside **-nyáyos**), **devamanuṣyàs** (once: ÇB. **-ṣyá**), **brahmarājanyàbhyām** (also VS.); further, **vākopavākyà** (ÇB.), **açanāyā́pipāse** (ÇB.).

1259. An example or two are met with of adverbial copulatives: thus, **áhardivi** *day by day*, **sāyámprātar** *at evening and in the morning*. They have the accent of their prior member. Later occur also **bāhyantar**, **pratyagdakṣiṇā**, **pratyagudak.**

1260. Repeated words. In all ages of the language, nouns and pronouns and adjectives and particles are not infrequently repeated, to give an intensive, or a distributive, or a repetitional meaning.

a. Though these are not properly copulative compounds, there is no better connection in which to notice them than here. They are, as the older language shows, a sort of compound, of which the prior member has its own independent accent, and the other is without accent: hence they are most suitably and properly written (as in the Vedic **pada**-texts) as compounds. Thus: **jahy èṣāṁ váraṁ-varam** *slay of them each best man*; **divé-dive** or **dyávi-dyavi** *from day to day*; **áṅgād-aṅgāl lómno-lomnaḥ párvaṇi-parvaṇi** *from every limb, from every hair, in each joint*; **prá-pra yajñápatiṁ tira** *make the master of the sacrifice live on and on*; **bhū́yo-bhūyaḥ çváḥ-çvaḥ** *further and further, tomorrow and again tomorrow*; **ékayāi-'kayā** *with in each case one*; **vayáṁ-vayam** *our very selves.*

b. Exceptional and rare cases are those of a personal verb-form repeated: thus, **píbā-piba** (RV.), **yájasva-yajasva** (ÇB.), **véda-veda** (? ÇB.); — and of two words repeated: thus, **yā́vad vā-yāvad vā** (ÇB.), **yatamé vā-yatame vā** (ÇB.).

c. In a few instances, a word is found used twice in succession without that loss of accent the second time which makes the repetition a virtual composite: thus, **nū́ nú** (RV.), **sáṁ sám** (AV.), **ihé 'há** (AV.), **anáyā- 'náyā** (ÇB.), **stuhí stuhí** (RV., acc. to **pada**-text).

d. The class of combinations here described is called by the native grammarians **āmreḍita** *added unto* (?).

1261. Finally may be noticed in passing the compound numerals, **ékādaça** *11*, **dvā́viṅçati** *22*, **tríçata** *103*, **cátuḥsahasra** *1004*, and so on (**476** ff.), as a special and primitive class of copulatives. They are accented on the prior member.

II. Determinative Compounds.

1262. A noun or adjective is often combined into a compound with a preceding determining or qualifying word — a noun, or adjective, or adverb. Such a compound is conveniently called determinative.

1263. This is the class of compounds which is of most general and frequent occurrence in all branches of Indo-European language. Its two principal divisions have been already pointed out: thus, A. Dependent compounds, in which the prior member is a substantive word (noun or pronoun or substantively used adjective), standing to the other member in the relation of a case dependent on it; and B. Descriptive compounds, in which the prior member is an adjective, or other word having the value of an adjective, qualifying a noun; or else an adverb or its equivalent, qualifying an adjective. Each of these divisions then falls into two sub-divisions, according as the final member, and therefore the whole compound, is a noun or an adjective.

a. The whole class of determinatives is called by the Hindu grammarians **tatpuruṣa** (the term is a specimen of the class, meaning *his man*); and the second division, the descriptives, has the special name of **karmadhāraya** (of obscure application: the literal sense is something like *office-bearing*). After their example, the two divisions are in European usage widely known by these two names respectively.

A. Dependent Compounds.

1264. Dependent Noun-compounds. In this division, the case-relation of the prior member to the other may be of any kind; but, in accordance with the usual relations of one noun to another, it is oftenest genitive, and least often accusative.

a. Examples are: of genitive relation, **devasenā́** *army of gods*, **yamadūtá** *Yama's messenger*, **jīvaloká** *the world of the living*, **indra-**

dhanús *Indra's bow*, **brahmagaví** *the Brahman's cow*, **viṣagirí** *poison-mount*, **mitralābha** *acquisition of friends*, **mūrkhaçatāni** *hundreds of fools*, **vīrasenasuta** *Vīrasena's son*, **rājendra** *chief of kings*, **asmatputrās** *our sons*, **tadvacas** *his words*; — of dative, **pādodaka** *water for the feet*, **māsanicaya** *accumulation for a month*; — of instrumental, **ātmasādṛçya** *likeness with self*, **dhānyārtha** *wealth acquired by grain*, **dharmapatnī** *lawful spouse*, **pitṛbandhú** *paternal relation*; — of ablative, **apsaraḥsambhava** *descent from a nymph*, **madviyoga** *separation from me*, **cāurabhaya** *fear of a thief*; — of locative, **jalakrīḍā** *sport in the water*, **grāmavāsa** *abode in the village*, **puruṣānṛta** *untruth about a man*; — of accusative, **nagaragamana** *going to the city*.

1265. Dependent Adjective-compounds. In this division, only a very small proportion of the compounds have an ordinary adjective as final member; but usually a participle, or a derivative of agency with the value of a participle. The prior member stands in any case-relation which is possible in the independent construction of such words.

a. Examples are: of locative relation, **sthālīpakva** *cooked in a pot*, **açvakovida** *knowing in horses*, **vayaḥsama** *alike in age*, **yudhiṣṭhira** *steadfast in battle*, **tanū́çubhra** *beautiful in body*; — of instrumental, **mātṛsadṛça** *like his mother*; — of dative, **gohita** *good for cattle*; — of ablative, **bhavadanya** *other than you*, **garbhāṣṭama** *eighth from birth*, **dṛçyetara** *other than visible* (i. e. *invisible*); — of genitive, **bharataçreṣṭha** *best of the Bharatas*, **dvijottama** *foremost of Brahmans*: — with participial words, in accusative relation, **vedavíd** *Veda-knowing*, **annādá** *food-eating*, **tanūpā́na** *body-protecting*, **satyavādín** *truth-speaking*, **pattragata** *committed to paper* (lit. *gone to a leaf*); — in instrumental, **madhupū́** *cleansing with honey*, **svayáṁkṛta** *self-made*, **índragupta** *protected by Indra*, **vidyāhīna** *deserted by* (i. e. *destitute of*) *knowledge*; — in locative, **hṛdayāvídh** *pierced in the heart*, **ṛtvíj** *sacrificing in due season*, **divícara** *moving in the sky*; — in ablative, **rājyabhraṣṭa** *fallen from the kingdom*, **vṛkabhīta** *afraid of a wolf*; — in dative, **çaraṇāgata** *come for refuge*.

1266. We take up now some of the principal groups of compounds falling under these two heads, in order to notice their specialities of formation and use, their relative frequency, their accentuation, and so on.

1267. Compounds having as final member ordinary nouns (such, namely, as do not distinctly exhibit the character of verbal nouns, of action or agency) are quite common. They are regularly and usually accented on the final syllable, without reference to the accent of either constituent. Examples were given above (**1264 a**).

a. A principal exception with regard to accent is **páti** *master, lord* (and its feminine **pátnī**), compounds with which usually retain the accent of the prior member: thus, **prajā́pati, vásupati, átithipati, gópati, gṛhápatnī**, etc. etc. (compare the verbal nouns in **ti**, below, **1274**). But in a few words **páti** retains its own accent: thus, **viçpáti, rayipáti, paçupáti, vasupátnī**, etc.; and the more general rule is followed in **apsarāpatí** and **vrājapatí** (AV.), and **nadīpatí** (VS.), **citpatí** (MS.; elsewhere **citpáti**).

b. Other exceptions are sporadic only: for example, **janarā́jan, devavárman, hiraṇyatéjas, pṛtanāháva, godhū́ma** and **çakadhū́ma** (but **dhūmá**); **vācā́stena.**

c. The appearance of a case-form in such compounds is rare: examples are **dívodāsa, vācā́stena, uccā́iḥçravas, uccā́irghoṣa, dūrébhās** (the three last in possessive application).

d. A number of compounds are accented on both members: thus, **çácīpáti, sádaspáti, bṛ́haspáti, vánaspáti, ráthaspáti, jā́spáti** (also **jā́spati**), **nárāçáṅsa, tánūnáptṛ, tánūnápāt** (**tanū́** as independent word), **çúnaḥçépa.** And ÇB. has a long list of metronymics having the anomalous accentuation **kā́útsīpútra, gā́rgīpútra**, etc.

1268. The compounds having an ordinary adjective as final member are (as already noticed) comparatively few.

a. So far as can be gathered from the scanty examples occurring in the older language, they retain the accent of the prior member: thus, **gáviṣṭhira** (AV. **gavíṣṭhira**), **tanū́çubhra, máde**r**aghu, yajñádhīra, sā́mavipra, tilámiçra** (but **tíla**); but **kṛṣṭapacyá** *ripening in cultivated soil.*

1269. The adjective dependent compounds having as final member the bare root — or, if it end in a short vowel, generally with an added **t** — are very numerous in all periods of the language, as has been already repeatedly noticed (thus, **383f—h, 1147**). They are accented on the root.

a. In a very few instances, the accent of words having apparently or conjecturally this origin is otherwise laid: thus, **áṅsatra, ánarviç, svā́vṛj, pratyákṣadṛç, púraṁdhi, óṣadhi, áramiṣ, uçádagh, vatsápa, ábda.**

b. Before a final root-stem appears not very seldom a case-form: for example, **pataṁgá, girāvṛ́dh, dhiyājúr, akṣṇayādrúh, hṛdispṛ́ç, divispṛ́ç, vanesáh, diviṣád, añgeṣṭhā́, hṛtsvás, pṛtsutúr, apsujā́.**

c. The root-stem has sometimes a middle or passive value: for example, **manoyúj** *yoked (yoking themselves) by the will*, **hṛdayāvídh** *pierced to the heart*, **manuja** *born of Manu.*

1270. Compounds made with verbal derivatives in **a**, both of action and of agency, are numerous, and take the accent usually on their final syllable (as in the case of compounds with verbal prefixes: **1148m**).

a. Examples are: **hastagrābhá** *hand-grasping*, **devavandá** *god-praising*, **haviradá** *devouring the offering*, **bhuvanacyavá** *shaking the world*, **vrātyabruvá** *calling one's self a* **vrātya**; **akṣaparājayá** *failure at play*, **vaṣaṭkārá** *utterance of* **vashaṭ**, **gopoṣá** *prosperity in cattle*, **añgajvará** *pain in the limbs*.

b. In a few instances, the accent is (as in compounds with ordinary adjectives: above, **1268**) that of the prior member: thus, **marúdvṛdha, sutékara, divíçara** (and other more questionable words). And **dúgha** *milking, yielding* is so accented as final: thus, **madhudúgha, kāmadúgha.**

c. Case-forms are especially frequent in the prior members of compounds with adjective derivatives in **a** showing **guṇa**-strengthening of the root: thus, for example, **abhayaṁkará, yudhiṁgamá, dhanaṁjayá, puraṁdará, viçvambhará, divākará, talpeçayá, diviṣṭambhá.**

1271. Compounds with verbal nouns and adjectives in **ana** are very numerous, and have the accent always on the radical syllable (as in the case of compounds with verbal prefixes: **1150e**).

a. Examples are: **keçavárdhana** *hair-increasing*, **āyuṣpratáraṇa** *life-lengthening*, **tanūpā́na** *body-protecting*; **devahéḍana** *hatred of the gods*, **puṁsúvana** *giving birth to males*.

b. A very few apparent exceptions as regards accent are really cases where the derivative has lost its verbal character: thus, **yamasādaná** *Yama's realm*, **āchádvidhāna** *means of protection*.

c. An accusative-form is sometimes found before a derivative in **ana**: thus, **sarūpaṁkáraṇa, ayakṣmaṁkáraṇa, subhāgaṁkáraṇa, vanaṁkáraṇa.**

1272. a. The action-nouns in **ya** (**1213**) are not infrequent in composition as final member, and retain their own proper accent (as in combination with prefixes). Sufficient examples were given above (**1213**).

b. The same is true of the equivalent feminines in **yā́**: see above, **1213 d.**

c. The gerundives in **ya** (**1213**) hardly occur in the older language in combination with other elements than prefixes. The two **nīvibhāryà** and **prathamavāsyà** (the latter a descriptive) have the accent of the independent words of the same form; **balavijñāyá** and **áçvabudhya** (?) are inconsistent with these and with one another.

1273. Compounds made with the passive participle in **ta** or **na** have the accent of their prior member (as do the combinations of the same words with prefixes: **1085 a**).

a. Examples are: **hástakṛta** *made with the hand*, **vīrájāta** *born of a hero*, **ghóṣabuddha** *awakened by noise*, **prajā́patisṛṣṭa** *created by Prajāpati*, **devátta** *given by the gods*; and, of participles combined with prefixes, **índraprasūta** *incited by Indra*, **bṛ́haspátipraṇutta** *driven away by Brihaspati*, **ulkā́bhihata** *struck by a thunderbolt*, **vájravihata, saṁvat-**

sarásammita *commensurate with the year.* AV. has the anomalous **apsúsaṁçita** *quickened by the waters.*

b. A number of exceptions occur, in which the final syllable of the compound has the accent: for example, **agnitaptá, indrotá, pitṛvittá, rathakrītá, agnidagdhá** (beside **agnídagdha**), **kaviçastá** (beside **kavíçasta**), **kavipraçastá.**

c. One or two special usages may be noticed. The participle **gata,** *gone to,* as final of a compound, is used in a loose way in the later language to express relation of various kinds: thus, **jagatīgata** *existing in the world,* **tvadgata** *belonging to thee,* **sakhīgata** *relating to a friend,* **citragata** *in a picture,* **putragataṁ sneham** *affection toward a son,* etc. The participle **bhūta** *been, become* is used in composition with a noun as hardly more than a grammatical device to give it an adjective form: thus, **idaṁ tamobhūtam** *this creation, being darkness (existing in the condition of darkness)*; **tāṁ ratnabhūtāṁ lokasya** *her, being the pearl of the world;* **kṣetrabhūtā smṛtā nārī bījabhūtaḥ smṛtaḥ pumān** *a woman is regarded as a field; a man, as seed;* and so on.

d. The other participles only seldom occur as finals of compounds: thus, **prāsakārmukabibhrat** *bearing javelin and bow,* **açāstravidvāṅs** *not knowing the text-books,* **arjunadarçivāṅs** *having seen Arjuna,* **apriyaçaṅsivāṅs** *announcing what is disagreeable,* **gāutamabruvāṇá** *calling himself Gautama.*

1274. Compounds with derivatives in **ti** have (like combinations with the prefixes: **1157**e) the accent of the prior member.

a. Examples are: **dhánasāti** *winning of wealth,* **sómapīti** *soma-drinking,* **deváhūti** *invocation of the gods,* **námaükti** *utterance of homage,* **havyádāti** *presentation of offerings;* and so **tokásāti, deváhiti, rudráhūti, sūktókti, svagā́kṛti, díviṣṭi.**

b. In **nemádhiti, medhásāti, vanádhiti** (all RV.), the accent of the prior member is changed from penult to final.

c. Where the verbal character of the derivative is lost, the general rule of final accent (**1267**) is followed: thus, **devahetí** *weapon of the gods,* **devasumatí** *favor of the gods,* **brahmacití** *Brahman-pile.* Also in **sarvajyāní** *entire ruin,* the accent is that of compounds with ordinary nouns.

1275. Compounds with a derivative in **in** as final member have (as in all other cases) the accent on the **ín.**

a. Thus, **ukthaçaṅsín** *psalm-singing,* **vratacārín** *vow-performing,* **ṛṣabhadāyín** *bullock-giving,* **satyavādín** *truth-speaking,* **çroṇipratodín** *thigh-pounding.*

1276. There is a group of compounds with derivatives in **i,** having the accent on the penult or radical syllable.

a. Thus, **pathirákṣi** *road-protecting,* **havirmáthi** *sacrifice-disturbing,* **ātmadū́ṣi** *soul-harming,* **pathiṣádi** *sitting in the path,* **sahobhári** *strength-*

bearing, **vasuváni** *winning good-things*, **dhanasáni** *gaining wealth*, **manomúṣi** *mind-stealing*, **phalagráhi** *setting fruit*; and, from reduplicated root, **urucákri** *making room*. Compounds with **-sáni** and **-váni** are especially frequent in Veda and Brāhmaṇa; as independent words, nouns, these are accented **saní** and **vaní**. In many cases, the words are not found in independent use. Combinations with prefixes do not occur in sufficient numbers to establish a distinct rule, but they appear to be oftenest accented on the suffix (**1155f**).

b. From √**han** are made in composition **-ghni** and **-ghnī**, with accent on the ending: thus, **sahasraghní, ahighní, çvaghnī́**; **-dhi** from √dhā (**1155g**) has the accent in its numerous compounds: thus, **iṣudhí, garbhadhí, pucchadhí**.

1277. Compounds with derivatives in **van** have (like combinations with prefixes: **1169c**) the accent of the final member: namely, on the radical syllable.

a. Thus, **somapā́van** *soma-drinking*, **baladā́van** *strength-giving*, **pāpakṛ́tvan** *evil-doing*, **bahusū́van** *much-yielding*, **talpaçī́van** *lying on a couch*, **rathayā́van** *going in a chariot*, **druṣádvan** *sitting on a tree*, **agrétvarī** f. *going at the head*. The accent of the obscure words **mātaríçvan** and **mātaríbhvan** is anomalous.

b. The few compounds with final **man** appear to follow the same rule as those with **van**: thus, **svādukṣádman** *sharing out sweets*, **āçuhéman** *steed-impelling*.

1278. Compounds with other derivatives, of rare or sporadic occurrence, may be briefly noticed: thus, in **u, rāṣṭradipsú, devapīyú, govindú, vanargú** (?): compare **1178e**; — in **nu** or **tnu, lokakṛtnú, surūpakṛtnú**: compare **1196**; — in **tṛ, nṛpātṛ́, mandhātṛ́, haskartṛ́** (**vasudhā́taras**, AV., is doubtless a false reading). The derivatives in **as** are of infrequent occurrence in composition (as in combination with prefixes: above, **1151k**), and appear to be treated as ordinary nouns: thus, **yajñavacás** (but **híraṇyatéjas**, AV.).

B. Descriptive Compounds.

1279. In this division of the class of determinatives, the prior member stands to the other in no distinct case-relation, but qualifies it adjectively or adverbially, according as it (the final member) is noun or adjective.

a. Examples are: **nīlotpala** *blue lotus*, **sarvaguṇa** *all good quality*, **priyasakha** *dear friend*, **maharṣi** *great-sage*, **rajatapātrá** *silver cup*; **ájñāta** *unknown*, **súkṛta** *well done*, **duṣkṛ́t** *ill-doing*, **puruṣṭutá** *much praised*, **púnarṇava** *renewed*.

b. The prior member is not always an adjective before a noun, or an adverb before an adjective; other parts of speech are sometimes used adjectively and adverbially in that position.

c. The boundary between descriptive and dependent compounds is not an absolute one; in certain cases it is open to question, for instance, whether a prior noun, or adjective with noun-value, is used more in a case-relation, or adverbially.

d. Moreover, where the final member is a derivative having both noun and adjective value, it is not seldom doubtful whether an adjective compound is to be regarded as descriptive, made with final adjective, or possessive, made with final noun. Sometimes the accent of the word determines its character in this respect, but not always.

e. A satisfactorily simple and perspicuous classification of the descriptive compounds is not practicable; we cannot hold apart throughout the compounds of noun and of adjective value, but may better group both together, as they appear with prefixed elements of various kinds.

1280. The simplest case is that in which a noun as final member is preceded by a qualifying adjective as prior member.

a. In this combination, both noun and adjective may be of any kind, verbal or otherwise. The accent is (as in the corresponding class of dependent noun-compounds: **1267**) on the final syllable.

b. Thus, **ajñātayakṣmá** *unknown disease*, **mahādhaná** *great wealth*, **kṣipraçyená** *swift hawk*, **kṛṣṇaçakuní** *black bird*, **dakṣiṇāgní** *southern fire*, **urukṣití** *wide abode*, **adharahanú** *lower jaw*, **itarajaná** *other folks*, **sarvātmán** *whole soul*, **ekavīrá** *sole hero*, **saptarṣí** *seven sages*, **tṛtīyasavaná** *third libation*, **ekonaviṅçatí** *a score diminished by one*, **jāgratsvapná** *waking sleep*, **yāvayatsakhá** *defending friend*, **apakṣīyamāṇapakṣá** *waning half*.

c. There are not a few exceptions as regards accent. Especially, compounds with **viçva** (in composition, accented **viçvá**), which itself retains the accent: thus, **viçvádevās** *all the gods*, **viçvámānuṣa** *every man*. For words in **ti**, see below, **1287 d**. Sporadic cases are **madhyáṁdina**, **vṛṣā́kapi**, both of which show an irregular shift of tone in the prior member; and a few others.

d. Instead of an adjective, the prior member is in a few cases a noun used appositionally, or with a quasi-adjective value. Thus, **rājayakṣmá** *king-disease*, **brahmarṣi** *priest-sage*, **rājarṣi** *king-sage*, **rājadanta** *king-tooth*, **devajana** *god-folk*, **duhitṛjana** *daughter-person*, **çamīlatā** *creeper named* **çamī**, **muṣikākhyā** *the name "mouse"*, **jayaçabda** *the word "conquer"*, **ujhitaçabda** *the word "deserted"*; or, more figuratively, **gṛhanaraka** *house-hell* (*house which is a hell*), **çāpāgni** *curse-fire* (*consuming curse*).

e. This group is of consequence, inasmuch as in possessive application

it is greatly extended, and forms a numerous class of appositional compounds: see below, 1302.

f. This whole subdivision, of nouns with preceding qualifying adjectives, is not uncommon; but it is greatly (in AV., for example, more than five times) exceeded in frequency by the sub-class of possessives of the same form: see below, 1298.

1281. The adverbial words which are most freely and commonly used as prior members of compounds, qualifying the final member, are the verbal prefixes and the words of direction related with them, and the inseparable prefixes, **a** or **an**, **su**, **dus**, etc. (1121). These are combined not only with adjectives, but also, in quasi-adjectival value, with nouns; and the two classes of combinations will best be treated together.

1282. Verbal adjectives and nouns with preceding adverbs. As the largest and most important class under this head might properly enough be regarded the derivatives with preceding verbal prefixes. These, however, have been here reckoned rather as derivatives from roots combined with prefixes (1141), and have been treated under the head of derivation, in the preceding chapter. In taking up the others, we will begin with the participles.

1283. The participles belonging to the tense-systems — those in **ant** (or **at**), **māna**, **āna**, **vāṅs** — are only rarely compounded with any other adverbial element than the negative **a** or **an**, which then takes the accent.

a. Examples are: **ánadant, ádadat, ánaçnant, ásravant, álubhyant, ádāsyant, áditsant, ádevayant; ámanyamāna, áhiṅsāna, áchidyamāna; ádadivāṅs, ábibhīvāṅs, atasthāna**; and, with verbal prefixes, **ánapasphurant, ánāgamiṣyant, ánabhyāgamiṣyant, áviradhayant, ávicācalat, ápratimanyūyamāna.**

b. Exceptions in regard to accent are very few: **arundhatī́, ajárantī, acodánt** (RV., once: doubtless a false reading; the simple participle is **códant**); AV. has **anipádyamāna** for RV. **ánipadyamāna** (and the published text has **asaṁyánt**, with a part of the manuscripts); ÇB. has **akāmáyamāna.**

c. Of other compounds than with the negative prefix have been noted in the Veda **-punardīyamāna** (in **ápunard-**) and **súvidvāṅs**. In **alalābhávant** and **jañjanābhávant** (RV.), as in **astaṁyánt** and **astameṣyánt** (AV.), we have participles of a compound conjugation (1091), in which, as has been pointed out, the accent is as in combinations with the verbal prefixes.

1284. The passive (or past) participle in **ta** or **na** is much more variously compounded; and in general (as in the case of the verbal prefixes: **1085a**) the preceding adverbial element has the accent.

a. Thus, with the negative **a** or **an** (by far the most common case): **ákṛta, ádabdha, áriṣṭa, ánādhṛṣṭa, áparājita, ásaṁkhyāta, ánabhyārūḍha, áparimitasamṛddha;** — with **su, sújāta, súhuta, súsaṁçita, svàraṁkṛta;** — with **dus, dúçcarita, dúrdhita** and **dúrhita, dúḥçṛta;** — with other adverbial words, **dáṅsujūta, návajāta, sánaçruta, svayáṁkṛta, trípratiṣṭhita: áraṁkṛta** and **kakajā́kṛta** are rather participles of a compound conjugation.

b. Exceptions in regard to accent are: with **a** or **an, anāçastá, apraçastá,** and, with the accent of the participle retracted to the root, **amṛ́ta, adṛ́ṣṭa, acítta, ayúta** *myriad*, **atū́rta** (beside **átūrta**), **asū́rta** (? beside **sū́rta**); — with **su** (nearly half as numerous as the regular cases), **subhūtá, sūktá, supraçastá, svā́kta, sukṛtá** and **sujātá** (beside **súkṛta** and **sújāta**), and a few others; with **dus** (quite as numerous as the regular cases), **duritá** (also **dúrita**), **duruktá, duṣkṛtá** (also **dúṣkṛta**), **durbhūtá;** with **sa, sajātá;** with other adverbs, **amotá, ariṣṭutá, tuvijātá, prācīnopavītá, tadānīṁdugdhá, prātardugdhá,** etc., and the compounds with **puru, purujātá, purupraјātá, purupraçastá, puruṣṭutá,** etc., and with **svayam, svayaṁkṛtá** etc. The proper name **aṣāḍhá** stands beside **áṣāḍha;** and AV. has **abhinná** for RV. **ábhinna.**

1285. The gerundives occur almost only in combination with the negative prefix, and have usually the accent on the final syllable.

a. Examples are: **anāpyá, anindyá, abudhyá, asahyá, ayodhyá, amokyá; adviṣeṇyá; ahnavāyyá;** and, along with verbal prefixes, the cases are **asaṁkhyeyá, apramṛṣyá, anapavṛjyá, anatyudyá, anādhṛṣyá, avimokyá, anānukṛtyá** (the accent of the simple word being **saṁkhyéya** etc.).

b. Exceptions in regard to accent are: **ánedya, ádābhya, ágohya, ájoṣya, áyabhya.** The two **anavadharṣyà** and **anativyādhyà** (both AV.) belong to the **yà**-division (**1213b**) of gerundives, and have retained the accent of the simple word. And **ághnya** and **aghnyá** occur together.

c. The only compounds of these words with other adverbial elements in V. are **súyabhya** (accented like its twin **áyabhya**) and **prathamavāsyà** (which retains the final circumflex), and perhaps **ekavādyá.**

d. The neuter nouns of the same form (**1213c**: except **sadhástutya**) retain their own accent after an adverbial prior member: thus, **purvapā́yya, pūrvapéya, amutrabhū́ya;** and **sahaçéyya.** And the negatived gerundives instanced above are capable of being viewed as possessive compounds with such nouns.

e. Some of the other verbal derivatives which have rules of their own as to accent etc. may be next noticed.

1286. The root-stem (pure root, or with **t** added after a short final vowel: **1147 d**) is very often combined with a preceding adverbial word, of various kinds; and in the combination it retains the accent.

a. Examples are: with inseparable prefixes, **adrúh** *not harming*, **asū́** *not giving birth*, **arúc** *not shining*; **sukṛ́t** *well-doing*, **suçrút** *hearing well*; **duṣkṛ́t** *ill-doing*, **dūḍā́ç** (**199 d**) *impious*; **sayúj** *joining together*, **samád** *conflict*; **sahajā́** *boin together*, **sahaváh** *carrying together*; — with other adverbs, **amājúr** *growing old at home*, **uparispṛ́ç** *touching upward*, **punarbhū́** *appearing again*, **prātaryúj** *harnessed early*, **sadyaḥkrī́** *bought the same day*, **sākaṁvṛ́dh** *growing up together*, **sadaṁdí** *ever-binding*, **viṣūvṛ́t** *turning to both sides*, **vṛthāsáh** *easily overcoming*; — with adjectives used adverbially, **uruvyác** *wide-spreading*, **prathamajā́** *first-born*, **raghuṣyád** *swift-moving*, **navasū́** *newly giving birth*, **ekajá** *only born*, **çukrapíç** *brightly adorned*, **dvijá** *twice born*, **trivṛ́t** *triple*, **svarā́j** *self-ruling*; — with nouns used adverbially, **çambhū́** *beneficent*, **sūryaçvít** *shining like the sun*, **īçānakṛ́t** *acting as lord*, **svayambhū́** *self-existent*; and, with accusative case-form, **pataṁgá** *going by flight*.

b. When, however, a root-stem is already in composition, whether wtih a verbal prefix or an element of other character, the further added negative itself takes the accent (as in case of an ordinary adjective: below, **1288 a**): thus, for example, **ánākṣit** *not abiding*, **ánāvṛt** *not turning back*, **ávidviṣ** *not showing hostility*, **áduṣkṛt** *not ill-doing*, **ánaçvadā** *not giving a horse*, **ápaçuhan** *not slaying cattle* (**anāgā́s** would be an exception, if it contained √**gā**: which is very unlikely). Similar combinations with **su** seem to retain the radical accent: thus, **supratúr, svābhū́, svāyúj**: **svā́vṛj** is an unsupported exception.

c. A few other exceptions occur, mostly of doubtful character, as **prátiprāç, sadhástha, ádhrigu,** and the words having **añc** as final member (**407** ff.: if this element is not, after all, a suffix): compare **1269 a.**

1287. Other verbal derivatives, requiring to be treated apart from the general body of adjectives, are few and of minor importance. Thus:

a. The derivatives in **a** are in great part of doubtful character, because of the possibility of their being used with substantive value to make a possessive compound. The least ambiguous, probably, are the derivatives from present-stems (**1148 j**), which have the accent on the suffix: thus, **asunvá, apaçyá, akṣudhyá, avidasyá, anāmṛṇá, sadāpṛṇá, punarmanyá**; and with them belong such cases as **atṛpá, avṛdhá, araṁgamá, urukramá, evāvadá, satrāsahá, punaḥsará, puraḥsará**; and the nouns **sāyambhavá, sahacārá, prātaḥsāvá, mithoyodhá.** Differently accented, on the other hand, although apparently of the same formation, are such as **ánapasphura, ánavahvara** (compare the compounds noticed at **1286 b**), **sadā́vṛdha, sū́bharva, nyagródha, puroḍā́ça, sadhamā́da, sudúgha, supáca, suháva,** and others. Words like **adábha, durháṇa, sukára, suyáma,** are probably possessives.

b. The derivatives in **van** keep in general the accent of the final member, on the root (compare **1169 c, 1277**): thus, **āçupátvan** and **raghupátvan** *swift-flying*, **puroyā́van** *going in front*, **sukṛ́tvan** *well-doing;* and **sutárman** and **suváhman** and **raghuyā́man** are probably to be classed with them. But the negative prefix has the accent even before these: thus, **áyajvan, árāvan, ápṛayutvan;** and **satyámadvan** (if it be not possessive) has the accent of its prior member.

c. A few words in **i** seem to have (as in dependent compounds: **1276**) the accent on the radical syllable: thus, **durgṛ́bhi, ṛjuváni, tuviṣváṇi.**

d. The derivatives in **ti** are variously treated: the negative prefix has always the accent before them: as, **ácitti, ábhūti, ánāhūti;** with **su** and **dus,** the compound is accented now on the prefix and now on the final, and in some words on either (**súnīti** and **sunītí, dúṣṭuti** and **duṣṭutí**); with other elements, the accent of the prefix prevails: thus, **sáhuti, sadhástuti, puróhiti, pūrvápīti, pūrvyástuti.**

e. The derivatives in **in** have, as in general, the accent on the suffix: thus, **pūrvāsín, bahucārín, sādhudevín, savāsín, kevalādín.** But, with the negative prefix, **ánāmin, ávitārin.**

f. Other combinations are too various in treatment, or are represented by too few examples in accentuated texts, to justify the setting up of rules respecting them.

1288. Of the remaining combinations, those made with the inseparable prefixes form in some measure a class by themselves.

1. a. The negative prefix **a** or **an**, when it directly negatives the word to which it is added, has a very decided tendency to take the accent.

b. We have seen above (**1283**) that it does so even in the case of present and perfect and future participles, although these in combination with a verbal prefix retain their own accent (**1085**: but there are exceptions, as **avadánt, apaçyánt,** etc. ÇB.); and also in the case of a root-stem, if this be already compounded with another element (**1286 b**). And the same is true of its other combinations.

c. Thus, with various adjective words: **átandra, ádabhra, ádāçuri, ánṛju, ádevayu, átṛṣṇaj, átavyāṅs, ánāmin, ádvayāvin, ápracetas, ánapatyavant, ánupadasvant, ápramāyuka, ámamri, áprajajñi, ávidīdhayu, ánagnidagdha, ákāmakarçana, ápaççāddaghvan.** Further, with nouns, **ápati, ákumāra, ábrāhmaṇa, ávidyā, āçraddhā, ávrātya.**

d. But there are a number of exceptions, in which the accent is on the final syllable, without regard to the original accentuation of the final member: thus, for example, **acitrá, açrīrá, aviprá, ayajñiyá, anāsmāká, asthūrí, anāçú, ajarayú, anāmayitnú;** and in **amítra** *enemy*, and **avī́ra** *unmanly*, there is a retraction of the accent from the final syllable of the final member to its penult.

2. e. **The prefixes su and dus have this tendency in a much less degree, and their compounds are very variously accented, now on the prefix, now on the final syllable, now on the accented syllable of the final member; and occasionally on either of two syllables.**

f. Thus, for example, **súbhadra, súvipra, súpakva, súbrāhmaṇa, súbhiṣaj; sutīrthá, suvasaná, suṣārathí, supāçá, sucitrá; suçéva, suhótṛ: suvíra** is like **avíra; — durmitrá, duṣvápnya;** and **ducchúnā (168 b),** with irregular retraction of accent (**çuná**).

3. **g.** The compounds with sa are too few to furnish occasion for separate mention; and those with the interrogative prefix in its various forms are also extremely rare in the Veda: examples are **kucará, katpayá, kábandha, kunannamá, kumārá, kúyava, kuṣáva.**

1289. The verbal prefixes are sometimes used in a general adverbial way, qualifying a following adjective or noun.

a. Examples of such combinations are not numerous in the Veda. Their accentuation is various, though the tone rests oftenest on the preposition. Thus, **ádhipati** *over-lord*, **áparūpa** *mis-form*, **prátiçatru** *opposing foe*, **prápada** *fore part of foot*, **práṇapāt** *great-grandchild*, **vípakva** *quite done*, **sámpriya** *mutually dear;* **upajíhvikā** *side tongue* (with retraction of the accent of **jihvā́**); **antardeçá** *intermediate direction*, **pradív** *forward heaven*, **prapitāmahá** (also **prápitāmaha**) *great-grandfather*, **pratijaná** *opponent*, **vyadhvá** *midway*. These compounds are more frequent with possessive value (below, **1305**).

b. This use of the verbal prefixes is more common later, and some of them have a regular value in such compounds. Thus, **ati** denotes excess, as in **atidūra** *very far*, **atibhaya** *exceeding fear*, **átipūruṣa** (ÇB.) *chief man;* **adhi**, superiority, as in **adhidanta** *upper-tooth*, **adhistrī** *chief woman;* **abhi** is intensive, as in **abhinamra** *much incliving*, **abhinava** *span-new*, **abhirucira** *delightful;* **ā** signifies *somewhat*, as in **ākuṭila** *somewhat crooked*, **ānīla** *bluish;* **upa** denotes something accessory or secondary, as in **upapurāṇa** *additional Purāna;* **pari**, excess, as in **paridurbala** *very weak;* **prati**, opposition, as in **pratipakṣa** *opposing side*, **pratipustaka** *copy;* **vi**, variation or excess, as in **vidūra** *very far*, **vipāṇḍu** *greyish*, **vikṣudra** *respectively small;* **sam**, completeness, as in **sampakva** *quite ripe*.

1290. Other compounds with adverbial prior members are quite irregularly accented.

Thus, the compounds with **puru**, on the final (compare the participles with **puru**, **1284 b**): as, **purudasmá, purupriyá, puruçcandrá;** those with **púnar**, on the prior member, as **púnarṇava, púnarmagha, púnaryuvan, púnarvasu** (but **punaḥsará** etc.); those with **satás, satīná, satyá**, the same, as **satómahant, satīnámanyu, satyámugra;** a few combinations of nouns in **tṛ** and **ana** with adverbs akin with the prefixes, on the final syllable, as **puraëtṛ́, puraḥsthātṛ́, upariçayaná, prātaḥsavaná;** and miscellaneous cases are **mithóavadyapa, háriçcandra, álpaçayu, sādhvaryá, yācchreṣṭhá** and **yāvacchreṣṭhá, jyógāmayāvin.**

1291. One or two exceptional cases may be noted, as follows:

a. An adjective is sometimes preceded by a noun standing toward it in a quasi-adverbial relation expressive of comparison or likeness: e. g. **çúkababhru** (VS.) *parrot-brown*, **ū́rṇāmṛdu** (TB.) *soft as wool*, **prāṇapriya** *dear as life*, **kuçeçayarajomṛdu** *soft as lotus-pollen*, **bakālīna** *hidden like a heron*, **mattamātañgagāmin** *moving like a maddened elephant*.

b. An adjective is now and then qualified by another adjective: e. g. **kṛṣṇāita** *dark-gray*, **dhūmrárohita** *grayish red*: and compare the adjectives of intermediate direction, **1257 c.**

c. The adjective **pūrva** is in the later language frequently used as final member of a compound in which its logical value is that of an adverb qualifying the other member (which is said to retain its own accent). Thus, **dṛṣṭapūrva** *previously seen*, **pariṇītapūrva** *already married*, **aparijñātapūrva** *not before known*, **somapītapūrva** *having formerly drunk soma*, **strīpūrva** *formerly a woman*.

III. Secondary Adjective Compounds.

1292. a. A compound having a noun as its final member very often wins secondarily the value of an adjective, being inflected in the three genders to agree with the noun which it qualifies, and used in all the constructions of an adjective.

b. This class of compounds, as was pointed out above (**1247.** III.), falls into the two divisions of **A.** Possessives, having their adjective character given them by addition of the idea of *possessing*; and **B.** those in which the final member is syntactically dependent on or governed by the prior member.

A. Possessive Compounds.

1293. The possessives are noun-compounds of the preceding class, determinatives, of all its various subdivisions, to which is given an adjective inflection, and which take on an adjective meaning of a kind which is most conveniently and accurately defined by adding *having* or *possessing* to the meaning of the determinative.

a. Thus: the dependent **sūryatejás** *sun's brightness* becomes the possessive **sū́ryatejas** *possessing the brightness of the sun;* **yajñakāmá** *desire of sacrifice* becomes **yajñákāma** *having desire of sacrifice;* the descriptive **bṛhadratha** *great chariot* becomes the possessive **bṛhád-ratha** *having great chariots;* **áhasta** *not hand* becomes **ahastá** *handless;* **durgandhi** *ill savor* becomes **durgándhi** *of ill savor;* and so on.

b. A copulative compound is not convertible into an adjective directly, any more than is a simple noun, but requires, like the latter, a possessive suffix or other means: e. g. **vāgghastavant, doṣaguṇin, rajastamaska, açirogrīva, anṛgyajus.** A very small number of exceptions, however, are found: thus, **somendrá** (TS.), **stómapṛṣṭha** (VS. TS.), **hastyṛ̀ṣabha** (ÇB.), **dāsīniṣka** (ChU.), and, later, **cakramusala, sadānanda, saccid-ānanda, sāñkhyayoga** (as n. pr.), **balābala, bhūtabhāutika.**

c. The name given by the native grammarians to the possessive compounds is **bahuvrīhi**: the word is an example of the class, meaning *possessing much rice.*

d. The name "relative", instead of possessive, sometimes applied to this class, is an utter misnomer; since, though the meaning of such a compound (as of any attributive word) is easily cast into a relative form, its essential character lies in the possessive verb which has nevertheless to be added, or in the possessive case of the relative which must be used: thus, **mahākavi** and **āyurdā**, descriptive and dependent, are "relative" also, *who is a great poet*, and *that is life-giving*, but **bṛhadratha**, possessive, means *who has a great chariot*, or *whose is a great chariot*.

1294. a. That a noun, simple or compound, should be added to another noun, in an appositive way, with a value virtually attributive, and that such nouns should occasionally gain by frequent association and application an adjective form also, is natural enough, and occurs in many languages; the peculiarity of the Sanskrit formation lies in two things. First, that such use should have become a perfectly regular and indefinitely extensible one in the case of compounded words, so that any compound with noun-final may be turned without alteration into an adjective, while to a simple noun must be added an adjective-making suffix in order to adapt it to adjective use: for example, that while **hasta** must become **hastin** and **bāhu** must become **bāhumant, hiraṇyahasta** and **mahābāhu** change from noun to adjective value with no added ending. And second, that the relation of the qualified noun to the compound should have come to be so generally that of possession, not of likeness, nor of appurtenance, nor of any other relation which is as naturally involved in such a construction: that we may only say, for example, **mahābāhuḥ puruṣaḥ** *man with great arms*, and not also **mahābāhur maṇiḥ** *jewel for a great arm*, or **mahābāhavaḥ çākhāḥ** *branches like great arms.*

b. There are, however, in the older language a few derivative adjective compounds which imply the relation of appurtenance rather than that of possession, and which are with probability to be viewed as survivals of a state of things antecedent to the specialization of the general class as possessive (compare the similar exceptions under possessive suffixes, **1230 g**, **1233 f**). Examples are: **viçvā́nara** *of* or *for all men, belonging to all* (and so **viçvákṛṣṭi, -carṣaṇi, -kṣiti, -gotra, -manus, -āyu,** and **sarvápaçu, saptámānuṣa**), **viçváçārada** *of every autumn*, **vipathá** *for bad roads*, **dvirājá** *[battle] of two kings*, **áçvapṛṣṭha** *carried on horseback*, **vīrápastya** *abiding with heroes*, **pūrṇámāsa** *at full moon*, **adévaka** *for no divinity*, **bahudevata** or **-tyà** *for many divinities*, **aparisaṁvatsara** *not lasting a full year*, **ekādaçakapāla** *for eleven dishes*, **somendrá** *for Soma and Indra*. And the compounds with final member in **ana** mentioned at **1296 b** are probably of the same character. But also in the later language, some of the so-called **dvigu**-compounds (**1312**) belong with these: so **dvigu** itself, as meaning *worth two cows*, **dvināu** *bought for two ships;* also occasional cases like **devāsura** [**saṁgrāma**] *of the gods and demons*, **narahaya** *of man and horse*, **cakramusala** *with discus and club*, **gurutalpa** *violating the teacher's bed*.

1295. The possessive compound is distinguished from its substrate, the determinative, generally by a difference of accent. This difference is not of the same nature in all the divisions of the class; but oftenest, the possessive has as a compound the natural accent of its prior member (as in most of the examples given above).

1296. Possessively used dependent compounds, or possessive dependents, are very much less common than those corresponding to the other division of determinatives.

a. Further examples are: **mayū́raroman** *having the plumes of peacocks*, **agnítejas** *having the brightness of fire*, **jñātímukha** *wearing the aspect of relatives*, **pátikāma** *desiring a husband*, **hastipāda** *having an elephant's feet*, **rājanyàbandhu** *having kshatriyas for relatives*.

b. The accent is, as in the examples given, regularly that of the prior member, and exceptions are rare and of doubtful character. A few compounds with derivatives in **ana** have the accent of the final member: e. g. **indrapā́na** *serving as drink for Indra*, **devasádana** *serving as seat for the gods*, **rayisthā́na** *being source of wealth;* but they contain no implication of possession, and are possibly in character, as in accent, dependent (but compare **1294 b**). Also a few in **as**, as **nṛcákṣas** *menbeholding*, **nṛvā́has** *men-bearing*, **kṣetrasā́dhas** *field-prospering*, are probably to be judged in the same way.

1297. Possessively used descriptive compounds, or possessive descriptives, are extremely numerous and of every variety of character; and some kinds of combination which are rare in proper descriptive use are very common as possessives.

a. They will be taken up below in order, according to the character of the prior member — whether the noun-final be preceded by a qualifying adjective, or noun, or adverb.

1298. Possessive compounds in which a noun is preceded by a qualifying ordinary adjective are (as pointed out above, **1280 f**) very much more common than descriptives of the same form.

a. They regularly and usually have the accent of their prior member: thus, **anyárūpa** *of other form*, **ugrábāhu** *having powerful arms*, **jīváputra** *having living sons*, **dīrgháçmaçru** *longbearded*, **bṛhácchravas** *of great renown*, **bhū́rimūla** *many-rooted*, **mahā́vadha** *bearing a great weapon*, **viçvárūpa** *having all forms*, **çukrávarṇa** *of bright color*, **çivā́bhimarçana** *of propitious touch*, **satyásaṁdha** *of true promises*, **sárvāñga** *whole-limbed*, **sváyaças** *having own glory*, **háritasraj** *wearing yellow garlands*.

b. Exceptions, however, in regard to accent are not rare (a seventh or eighth of the whole number, perhaps). Thus, the accent is sometimes that of the final member; especially with derivatives in **as**, as **tuvirā́dhas, purupéças, pṛthupákṣas**, and others in which (as above, **1296 b**) a determinative character may be suspected: thus, **urujráyas** beside **urujrí, uruvyácas** beside **uruvyác**, and so on; but also with those of other final, as **ṛjuhásta, çitikákṣa** etc., **kṛṣṇakárṇa, citradṛ́çīka, tuviçúṣma, ṛjukrátu, pṛthupárçu, puruvártman, raghuyā́man, vīḍupátman**. In a very few cases, the accent is retracted from the final to the first syllable of the second member: thus, **aṅhubhéda, tuvigrī́va, puruvī́ra, pururū́pa, çitibā́hu** (also **çitibāhú**). The largest class is that of compounds which take the accent upon their final syllable (in part, of course, not distinguishable from those which retain the accent of the final member): for example, **bahvanná, nīlanakhá, puruputrá, viçvāñgá, svapatí, tuvipratí, pṛçniparṇī́** f., **darçataçrī́, pūtirajjú, asitajñú, pṛthugmán, bahuprajás**.

c. The adjective **víçva** *all*, as prior member of a compound (and also in derivation), changes its accent regularly to **viçvá**; **sárva** *whole, all* does the same in a few cases.

1299. Possessive compounds with a participle preceding and qualifying the final noun-member are numerous, although such a compound with simple descriptive value is almost unknown. The accent is, with few exceptions, that of the prior member.

a. The participle is oftenest the passive one, in **ta** or **na**. Thus, **chinnápakṣa** *with severed wing*, **dhṛtárāṣṭra** *of firmly held royalty*, **hatámātṛ** *whose mother is slain*, **iddhā́gni** *whose fire is kindled*, **uttānáhasta** *with outstretched hand*, **práyatadakṣiṇa** *having presented sacrificial gifts*; and, with prefixed negative, **áriṣṭavīra** *whose men are unharmed*, **átaptatanu** *of unburned substance*, **ánabhimlātavarṇa** *of untarnished color*. Exceptions in regard to accent are very few: there have been noticed only **paryastākṣá, vyastakeçī́** f., **achinnaparṇá**.

b. Examples occur of a present participle in the same situation. In about half the (accentuated) instances, it gives its own accent to the compound: thus, **dyutádyāman, dhṛṣádvarṇa** etc., **çucádratha, rúçadvatsa** etc., **bhrā́jajjanman** etc., **saṁyádvīra, stanáyadama, sā́dhadiṣṭi**; in the others, the accent is drawn forward to the final syllable of the participle (as in the compounds with governing participle: below, **1309**): thus, **dravátpāṇi** etc. (**dravát** also occurs as adverb), **rapçádūdhan, svanádratha, arcáddhūma, bhandádiṣṭi, krandádiṣṭi.** With these last agrees in form **jarádaṣṭi** *attaining old age, long-lived;* but its make-up, in view of its meaning, is anomalous.

c. The RV. has two compounds with the perfect middle participle as prior member: thus, **yuyujānásapti** *with harnessed coursers* (perhaps rather *having harnessed their coursers*), and **dadṛçānápavi** (with regular accent, instead of **dádṛçāna**, as elsewhere irregularly in this participle) *with conspicuous wheel-rims.*

d. Of a nearly participial character is the prior element in **çrútkarṇa** (RV.) *of listening ear;* and with this are perhaps accordant **dī́dyagni** and **sthā́raçman** (RV., each once).

1300. Possessive compounds having a numeral as prior member are very common, and for the most part follow the same rule of accent which is followed by compounds with other adjectives: excepted are those beginning with **dvi** and **tri**, which accent in general the final member.

a. Examples with other numerals than **dvi** and **tri** are: **ékacakra, ékaçīrṣan, ékapad, cáturaṅga, cátuṣpakṣa, páñcāṅguri, páñcāudana, ṣáḍaçva, ṣáṭpad, saptájihva, saptámātṛ, aṣṭā́pad, aṣṭáputra, návapad, návadvāra, dáçaçākha, dáçaçīrṣan, dvā́daçāra, triṅçádara, çatáparvan, çatádant, sahásranāman, sahásramūla.**

b. Exceptions in regard to accent are but few, and have the tone on the final syllable, whatever may be that belonging originally to the final member; they are mostly stems in final **a**, used by substitution for others in **an, i,** or a consonant: thus, **caturakṣá** etc. (**akṣán** or **ákṣi**: **431**), **ṣaḍahá** etc. (**áhan** or **áhar**: **430a**), **daçavṛṣá** etc. (**vṛ́ṣan**), **ekarātrá** etc. (**rā́tri** or **rā́trī**), **ekarcá** etc. (**ṛ́c**); but also a few others, as **ṣaḍyogá, aṣṭāyogá, çatārghá, sahasrārghá, ekapará** (?).

c. The compounds with **dvi** and **tri** for the most part have the accent of their final member: thus, for example, **dvijánman, dvidhā́ra, dvibándhu, dvivartaní, dvipád; tritántu, trinā́bhi, triçóka, trivárūtha, tricakrá, triçīrṣán, tripád.** A number of words, however, follow the general analogy, and accent the numeral: thus, for example, **dvípakṣa, dvíçavas, dvyā̀sya, tríṣandhi, tryàra, tryā̀çir,** and sometimes **dvípad** and **trípad** in AV. As in the other numeral compounds, a substituted stem in **a** is apt to take the accent on the final: thus, **dvivṛṣá** and **trivṛṣá, dvirājá, dvirātrá, tryāyuṣá, tridivá**; and a few of other character with **tri** follow the same rule: thus, **trikaçá, trinākā́, tribandhú, tryudhán, tribarhís,** etc.

d. The neuter, or also the feminine, of numeral compounds is often used substantively, with a collective or abstract value, and the accent is then regularly on the final syllable: see below, **1312**.

1301. Possessive compounds having as prior member a noun which has a quasi-adjective value in qualifying the final member are very frequent, and show certain specialities of usage.

a. Least peculiar is a noun of material as prior member (hardly to be reckoned as possessive dependents, because the relation of material is not regularly expressed by a case: **295**): thus, **híraṇyahasta** *gold-handed*, **híraṇyasraj** *with golden garlands*, **áyaḥsthūṇa** *having brazen supports*, **rajatánābhi** *of silver navel.*

1302. Especially common is the use of a noun as prior member to qualify the other appositionally, or by way of equivalence (the occasional occurrence of determinatives of this character has been noticed above, **1280 d**). These may conveniently be called appositional possessives. Their accent is that of the prior member, like the ordinary possessive descriptives.

a. Examples are: **áçvaparṇa** *horse-winged*, or *having horses as wings* (said of a chariot), **bhū́migṛha** *having the earth as house*, **índrasakhi** *having Indra for friend*, **agníhotṛ** *having Agni as priest*, **gandharvápatnī** *having a Gandharva for spouse*, **çūráputra** *having hero-sons*, **jarā́mṛtyu** *having old age as mode of death, living till old age*, **agnívāsas** *fire-clad*, **tadanta** *ending with that*, **cāracakṣus** *using spies for eyes*, **viṣṇuçarmanāman** *named Vishnuçarman;* and, with pronoun instead of noun, **tvā́dūta** *having thee as messenger*, **tádapas** *having this for work*. Exceptions in regard to accent occur here, as in the more regular descriptive formation: thus, **agnijihvá, vṛṣaṇaçvá, dhūmaçikhá, pavīnasá, asāunāma, tatkúla,** etc.

b. Not infrequently, a substantively used adjective is the final member in such a compound: thus, **índrajyeṣṭha** *having Indra as chief*, **mánaḥṣaṣṭha** *having the mind as sixth*, **sómaçreṣṭha** *of which soma is best*, **ekapará** *of which the ace is highest* (?), **ásthibhūyas** *having bone as the larger part, chiefly of bone*, **abhirūpabhūyiṣṭha** *chiefly composed of worthy persons*, **daçāvara** *having ten as the lowest number*, **cintāpara** *having meditation as highest object* or *occupation, devoted to meditation*, **niḥçvāsaparama** *much addicted to sighing.*

c. Certain words are of especial frequency in the compounds here described, and have in part won a peculiar application. Thus:

d. With **ādi** *beginning* or **ādika** or **ādya** *first* are made compounds signifying the person or thing specified along with others, such a person or thing *et cetera*. For example, **devā indrādayaḥ** *the gods having Indra as first*, i. e. *the gods Indra etc.*, **marīcyādīn munīn** *Marīci and the other* *sages*, **svāyambhuvādyāḥ saptāi 'te manavaḥ** *those seven Manus, Svāyambhuva etc.*, **agniṣṭomādikān** *the sacrifices Agnishtoma and so on.* Or the qualified noun is omitted, as in **annapānendhanādīni** *food, drink, fuel, etc.*, **dānadharmādikaṁ caratu bhavān** *let your honor practise liberality, religious rites, and the like.* The particles **evam** and **iti** are also sometimes used by substitution as prior members: thus, **evamādi vacanam** *words to this and the like effect;* **ato 'ham bravīmi kartavyaḥ saṁcayo nityam ityādi** *hence I say "accumulation is ever to be made" etc.*

e. Used in much the same way, but less often, is **prabhṛti** *beginning:* thus, **viçvāvasuprabhṛtibhir gandharvāiḥ** *with the Gandharvas Viçvāvasu etc.*; especially adverbially, in measurements of space and time, as **tatprabhṛti** or **tataḥprabhṛti** *thenceforward.*

f. Words meaning *foregoer*, *predecessor*, and the like — namely, **pūrva, pūrvaka, puraḥsara, puraskṛta, purogama** — are often employed in a similar manner, and especially adverbially, but for the most part to denote accompaniment, rather than antecedence, of that which is designated by the prior member of the compound: e. g. **smitapūrvam** *with a smile*, **anāmayapraçnapūrvakam** *with inquiries after health*, **pitāmahapurogama** *accompanied by the Great Father.*

g. The noun **mātrā** *measure* stands as final of a compound which is used adjectively or in the substantive neuter to signify a limit that is not exceeded, and obtains thus the virtual value of *mere, only:* thus, **jalamātreṇa vartayan** *living by water only* (lit. *by that which has water for its measure* or *limit*), **garbhacyutimātreṇa** *by merely issuing from the womb*, **prāṇayātrikamātraḥ syāt** *let him be one possessing what does not exceed the preservation of life;* **uktamātre tu vacane** *but the words being merely uttered.*

h. The noun **artha** *object, purpose* is used at the end of a compound, in the adverbial accusative neuter, to signify *for the sake of* or the like: thus, **yajñasiddhyartham** *in order to the accomplishment of the sacrifice* (lit. *in a manner having the accomplishment of the sacrifice as its object*), **damayantyartham** *for Damayantī's sake* (*with Damayantī as object*).

i. Other examples are **ābhā, kalpa,** in the sense of *like, approaching:* thus, **hemābha** *gold-like*, **mṛtakalpa** *nearly dead*, **pratipannakalpa** *almost accomplished;* — **vidhā,** in the sense of *kind, sort:* thus, **tvadvidha** *of thy sort*, **púruṣavidha** *of human kind;* — **prāya,** in the sense of *mostly, often*, and the like: thus, **duḥkhaprāya** *full of pain*, **tṛṇaprāya** *abounding in grass*, **nirgamanaprāya** *often going out;* — **antara** (in substantive neuter), in the sense of *other:* thus, **deçāntara** *another region* (lit. *that which has a difference of region*), **janmāntarāṇi** *other existences*, **çākhāntare** *in another text.*

1303. In appositional possessive compounds, the second member, if it designates a part of the body, sometimes logically signifies that part to which what is designated by the prior member belongs, that on or in which it is.

a. Thus, **ghṛtápṛṣṭha** *butter-backed*, **mádhujihva** *honey-tongued*, **niṣkágrīva** and **maṇigrīva** *necklace-necked*, **pā́trahasta** *vessel-handed*, **vájrabāhu** *lightning-armed*, **ásṛṅmukha** *blood-faced*, **kīlā́lodhan** *mead-uddered*, **vā́jajaṭhara** *sacrifice-bellied*, **vāṣpakaṇṭha** *with tears in the throat*, **çraddhā́manas** *with faith in the heart*; with irregular accent, **dhūmākṣī́** f. *smoke-eyed*, **açrumukhī́** f. *tear-faced*; and **khā́dihasta** *ring-handed* (**khādí**). In the later language, such compounds are not infrequent with words meaning *hand*: thus, **çastrapāṇi** *having a sword in the hand*, **laguḍahasta** *carrying a staff*.

1304. Of possessive compounds having an adverbial element as prior member, the most numerous by far are those made with the inseparable prefixes. Their accent is various. Thus:

a. In compounds with the negative prefix **a** or **an** (in which the latter logically negatives the imported idea of possession), the accent is prevailingly on the final syllable, without regard to the original accent of the final member. For example: **anantá** *having no end*, **abalá** *not possessing strength*, **arathá** *without chariot*, **açraddhá** *faithless*, **amaṇí** *without ornament*, **açatrú** *without a foe*, **avarmán** *not cuirassed*, **adánt** *toothless*, **apád** *footless*, **atejás** *without brightness*, **anārambhaṇá** *not to be gotten hold of*, **apratimāná** *incomparable*, **aducchuná** *bringing no harm*, **apakṣapucchá** *without sides or tail*.

b. But a number of examples (few in proportion to those already instanced) have the prefix accented (like the simple descriptives: **1288 a**): thus, **ákṣiti** *indestructible*, **águ** *kineless*, **ágopā** *without shepherd*, **ájīvana** *lifeless*, **ánāpi** *without friends*, **áçiçvī** f. *without young*, **ámṛtyu** *deathless*, **ábrahman** *without priest*, **ávyacas** *without extension*, **áhavis** *without oblation*, and a few others; AV. has **áprajas**, but ÇB. **aprajás**. A very few have the accent on the penult: namely, **açéṣas**, **ajā́ni**, and **avī́ra** (with retraction, from **vīrá**), **apútra** (do., from **putrá**); and AV. has **abhrā́tṛ**, but RV. **abhrātṝ́**.

c. In compounds with the prefixes of praise and dispraise, **su** and **dus**, the accent is in the great majority of cases that of the final member: thus, **sukálpa** *of easy make*, **subhága** *well portioned*, **sunákṣatra** *of propitious star*, **suputrá** *having excellent sons*, **sugopā́** *well-shepherded*, **sukīrtí** *of good fame*, **sugándhi** *fragrant*, **subāhú** *well-armed*, **suyáṁtu** *of easy control*, **sukrátu** *of good capacity*, **suhā́rd** *good-hearted*, **susráj** *well-garlanded*, **suvármaṇ** *well-cuirassed*, **suvā́sas** *well-clad*, **suprā́ṇīti** *well guiding*; **durbhága** *ill-portioned*, **durdṛ́çīka** *of evil aspect*, **durdhára** *hard to restrain*, **durgándhi** *ill-savored*, **durādhī́** *of evil designs*, **durdhártu** *hard to restrain*, **duṣṭárītu** *hard to excel*, **duratyétu** *hard to cross*, **durdhúr** *ill-yoked*, **durṇā́man** *ill-named*, **durvā́sas** *ill-clad*.

d. There are, however, a not inconsiderable number of instances in which the accent of these compounds is upon the final syllable: thus, **suçiprá** *well-lipped*, **svapatyá** *of good progeny*, **susaṁkāçá** *of good aspect*, **svaṅgurí** *well-fingered*, **sviṣú** *having good arrows*, **supīvás** *well fatted*;

and compounds with derivatives in **ana**, as **suvijñāná** *of easy discernment*, **sūpasarpaṇá** *of easy approach*, **duçcyavaná** *hard to shake;* and AV. has **suphalá** and **subandhú** against RV. **suphála** and **subándhu**. Like **avíra, suvíra** shows retraction of accent. Only **dúrāçir** has the tone on the prefix.

e. On the whole, the distinction by accent of possessive from determinative is less clearly shown in the words made with **su** and **dus** than in any other body of compounds.

f. The associative prefix **sa** or (less often) **sahá** is treated like an adjective element, and itself takes the accent in a possessive compound: thus, **sákratu** *of joint will*, **sánāman** *of like name*, **sárūpa** *of similar form*, **sáyoni** *having a common origin*, **sávācas** *of assenting words*, **sátoka** *having progeny along*, *with one's progeny*, **sábrāhmaṇa** *together with the Brahmans*, **sámūla** *with the root*, **sā́ntardeça** *with the intermediate directions;* **sahágopa** *with the shepherd*, **sahávatsa** *accompanied by one's young*, **sahápatnī** *having her husband with her*, **sahápūruṣa** *along with our men*.

g. In RV. (save in a doubtful case or two), only **saha** in such compounds gives the meaning of *having with one*, *accompanied by;* and, since **saha** governs the instrumental, the words beginning with it might be of the prepositional class (below, **1310**). But in AV. both **sa** and **saha** have this value (as illustrated by examples given above); and in the later language, the combinations with **sa** are much the more numerous.

h. There are a few exceptions, in which the accent is that of the final member: thus, **sajóṣa, sajóṣas, sadṛ́ça, sapráthas, sabā́dhas, samanyú** and AV. shows the accent on the final syllable in **sāñgá** (ÇB. **sā́ñga**) and the substantivized (**1312**) **savidyutá**.

i. Possessive compounds with the exclamatory prefixes **ka** etc. are too few in the older language to furnish ground for any rule as to accent: **kábandha** is perhaps an example of such.

1305. Possessive compounds in which a verbal prefix is used as prior member with adjective value, qualifying a noun as final member, are found even in the oldest language, and are rather more common later (compare the descriptive compounds, above, **1289**; and the prepositional, below, **1310**). They usually have the accent of the prefix.

a. Most common are those made with **pra, vi,** and **sam**: thus, for example, **prámahas** *having exceeding might*, **práçravas** *widely famed;* **vígrīva** *of wry neck*, **vyàñga** *having limbs away* or *gone*, *limbless*, **víjāni** *wifeless*, **víparva** and **víparus** *jointless*, **vyàdhvan** *of wide ways*, **vímanas** both *of wide mind* and *mindless*, **vívācas** *of discordant speech;* **sámpatnī** *having one's husband along*, **sámmanas** *of accordant mind*, **sáṁsahasra** *accompanied by a thousand*, **sámokas** *of joint abode*. Examples of others are: **átyūrmi** *surging over*, **ádhivastra** *having a garment on*, **ádhyardha** *with a half over*, **ádhyakṣa** *overseer*, **ápodaka** *without water*, **abhírūpa**

of adapted character, **ávatoka** *that has aborted*, **ā́manas** *of favorable mind*, **údojas** *of exalted power*, **nímanyu** *of assuaged fury*, **nírmāya** *free from guile*, **nírhasta** *handless*.

b. In a comparatively small number of cases, the accent is otherwise, and generally on the final: thus, **avakeçá, upamanyú, viçaphá, viçikhá** (AV. **víçikha**), **vikarṇá, sammātṛ́**, etc.; in an instance or two, that of the final member: thus, **samçíçvarī** *having a common young*.

1306. Possessive compounds with an ordinary adverb as prior member are also found in every period of the language. They usually have the accent which belongs to the adverb as independent word.

a. Examples are: **ántyūti** *bringing near help*, **avódeva** *calling down the gods*, **itáūti** *helping on this side*, **ihácitta** *with mind directed hither*, **dakṣiṇatáskaparda** *wearing the braid on the right side*, **nā́nādharman** *of various character*, **purudhápratīka** *of manifold aspect*, **viçvátomukha** *with faces on all sides*, **sadyáūti** *of immediate aid*, **víṣurūpa** *of various form*, **smádūdhan** *with udder*, **adhástāllakṣman** *with mark below*, **ekatomukha** *with face on one side*, **táthāvidha** *of such sort*.

b. An instance or two of irregular accent are met with: thus, **purorathá** *whose chariot is foremost*, **evaṁkratú** *so-minded*.

1307. a. It was pointed out in the preceding chapter (**1222h**) that the indifferent suffix **ka** is often added to a pure possessive compound, to help the conversion of the compounded stem into an adjective; especially, where the final of the stem is less usual or manageable in adjective inflection.

b. Also, the compound possessive stem occasionally takes further a possessive-making suffix: thus, **yaçobhagín, suçiprin, varavarṇin, dīrghasūtrin, puṇyavāgbuddhikarmin, sutásomavant, tādṛgrūpavant, trayodaçadvīpavant, nārakapālakuṇḍalavant, amṛtabuddhimant.**

c. The frequent changes which are undergone by the final of a stem occurring at the end of a compound are noticed further on (**1315**).

1308. The possessive compounds are not always used in the later language with the simple value of qualifying adjective; often they have a pregnant sense, and become the equivalents of dependent clauses; or the *having* which is implied in them obtains virtually the value of our *having* as sign of past time.

a. Thus, for example, **prāptayāuvana** *possessing attained adolescence*, i. e. *having arrived at adolescence*; **anadhigataçāstra** *with unstudied books*, i. e. *who has neglected study*; **kṛtaprayatna** *possessing performed effort*, i. e. *on whom effort is expended*; **aṅgulīyakadarçanāvasāna** *having the sight of the ring as termination*, i. e. *destined to end on sight of the ring*; **uddhṛtaviṣādaçalyaḥ** *having an extracted despair-arrow*, i. e. *when I shall have extracted the barb of despair*; **çrutavistāraḥ kriyatām** *let him be made with heard details*, i. e. *let him be informed of the details*; **dṛṣṭavīryo me rāmaḥ** *Rāma has seen my prowess*, **bhagnabhāṇḍo dvijo yathā** *like* *the Brahman that broke the pots*, **ukhānṛtam ṛṣiṁ yathā** *like a sage that has spoken falsely.*

B. Compounds with Governed Final Member.

1309. Participial Compounds. This group of compounds, in which the prior member is a present participle and the final member its object, is a small one (toward thirty examples), and exclusively Vedic — indeed, almost limited to the oldest Vedic (of the Rig-Veda). The accent is on the final syllable of the participle, whatever may have been the latter's accent as an independent word.

a. Examples are: **vidádvasu** *winning good things*, **kṣayádvīra** *governing* (**kṣáyant**) *heroes*, **taráddveṣas** *overcoming* (**tárant**) *foes*, **ābharádvasu** *bringing good things*, **codayánmati** *inciting* (**codáyant**) *devotion*, **mandayátsakha** *rejoicing friends*, **dhārayátkavi** *sustaining sages*, **maṅhayádrayi** *bestowing wealth.*

b. In **sādádyoni** *sitting in the lap* (**sādat** quite anomalously for **sīdat** or **sadat**), and **spṛhayádvarṇa** *emulous of color*, the case-relation of the final member is other than accusative. In **patayán mandayátsakham** (RV. i. 4. 7), **patayát**, with accent changed accordingly, represents **patayátsakham**, the final member being understood from the following word. **Vidádaçva** is to be inferred from its derivative **vāídadaçvi**. Of this formation appear to be **jamádagni**, **pratádvasu** (**prathád**?), and **trasádasyu** (for **trasáddasyu**?). It was noticed above (**1299 c**) that **yuyujānásapti** is capable of being understood as a unique compound of like character, with a perfect instead of present participle; **sā́dhadiṣṭi**, on account of its accent, is probably possessive.

1310. Prepositional Compounds. By this name may be conveniently called those combinations in which the prior member is a particle having true prepositional value, and the final member is a noun governed by it. Such combinations, though few in number as compared with other classes of compounds, are not rare, either in the earlier language or in the later. Their accent is so various that no rule can be set up respecting it.

a. Examples are: **átyavi** *passing through the wool*, **atirātrá** *overnight*, **atimātrá** *exceeding measure;* **ádhiratha** *lying on the chariot*, **adhigavá** *belonging to the cow;* **adhaspadá** *under the feet*, **adhoakṣá** *below the axle;* **ánupatha** *following the road*, **anupūrvá** *following the one preceding, one after another*, **anuṣatyá** *in accordance with truth*, **anukū́la** *down stream*, etc.; **ántaspatha** (with anomalously changed accent of **antár**), *within the way*, **antardāvá** *within the flame (?)*, **antarhastá** *in the hand;* **ántigṛha** *near the house;* **apiprāṇa** *accompanying the breath* (**prāṇá**), **ápivrata** *concerned with the ceremony*, **apiçarvará** *bordering on night*, **apikarṇá** *next the ear;* **abhijñú** *reaching to the knee*, **abhívīra** and **abhísatvan** *overcoming heroes;* **ā́pathi** *on the road*, **ā́deva** *going to the gods*, **ājarasá**

reaching old age, **ādvādaçá** *up to twelve*; **upakakṣá** *reaching to the armpits*, **upottamá** *next to last, penultimate*; **upáribudhna** *above the bottom*, **upárimartya** *rising above mortals*; **tirojaná** *beyond people*; **niḥsālá** *out of the house*; **paripád** *(about the feet) snare*, **parihastá** *about the hand, bracelet*; **parókṣa** *out of sight*, **parómātra** *beyond measure*, **parogavyūtí** *beyond the fields*, **paraḥsahasrá** (**páraḥsahasra**, ÇB.) *above a thousand*; **purokṣá** *in front of the eyes*; **pratidosá** *toward evening*, **pratilomá** *against the grain*, **pratikūla** *up stream*, **pratyákṣa** *before the eyes*; **bahiḥparidhí** *outside the enclosure*; **vípathi** *outside the road*; **samakṣá** *close to the eyes, in sight*.

b. Compounds of this character are in the later language especially common with **adhi**: thus, **adhyātma** *relating to the soul* or *self*, **adhiyajña** *relating to the sacrifice*, etc.

c. A suffixal **a** is sometimes added to a final consonant, as in **upānasá** *on the wagon*, **āvyuṣá** *until daybreak*. In a few instances, the suffix **ya** is taken (see above, **1212 m**); and in one word the suffix **in**: thus, **paripanthín** *besetting the path*.

d. The prepositional compounds are especially liable to adverbial use: see below, **1313 b**.

Adjective Compounds as Nouns and as Adverbs.

1311. Compound adjectives, like simple ones, are freely used substantively as abstracts and collectives, especially in the neuter, less often in the feminine; and they are also much used adverbially, especially in the accusative neuter.

a. The matter is entitled to special notice only because certain forms of combination have become of special frequency in these uses, and because the Hindu grammarians have made out of them distinct classes of compounds, with separate names. There is nothing in the older language which by its own merits would call for particular remark under this head.

1312. The substantively used compounds having a numeral as prior member, along with, in part, the adjective compounds themselves, are treated by the Hindus as a separate class, called **dvigu**.

a. The name is a sample of the class, and means *of two cows*, said to be used in the sense of *worth two cows*; as also **pañcagu** *bought for five cows*, **dvināu** *worth two ships*, **páñcakapāla** *made in five cups*, and so on.

b. Vedic examples of numeral abstracts and collectives are: **dvirājá** *[combat] of two kings*, **triyugá** *three ages*, **triyojaná** *space of three leagues*, **tridivá** *the triple heaven*, **pañcayojaná** *space of five leagues*, **ṣaḍahá** *six days' time*, **daçāñgulá** *ten fingers' breadth*; and, with suffix **ya**, **sahasrāhṇyá** *thousand days' journey*. Others, not numeral, but essentially of the same character, are, for example: **anamitrá** *freedom from enemies*, **nikilbiṣá** *freedom from guilt*, **savidyutá** *thunderstorm*, **víhṛdaya** *heartlessness*, and

sáhṛdaya *heartiness*, **sudivá** *prosperity by day*, **sumṛgá** and **suçakuná** *prosperity with beasts and birds*. Feminines of like use are not quotable from RV. or AV.; later occur such as **triçatī** *three hundred* (481), **trilokī** *the three worlds*, **pañcamūlī** *aggregate of five roots*.

c. As the examples show, the accent of words thus used is various; but it is more prevailingly on the final syllable than in the adjective compounds in their ordinary use.

1313. Those adverbially used accusatives of secondary adjective compounds which have an indeclinable or particle as prior member are reckoned by the Hindu grammarians as a separate class of compounds, and called by the name **avyayībhāva**.

a. This term is a derivative from the compound verb (1094) made up of **avyaya** *uninflected* and √**bhū**, and means *conversion to an indeclinable*.

b. The prepositional compounds (1310) are especially frequent in this use: thus, for example, **anuṣvadhám** *by one's own will*, **abhipūrvám** and **parovarám** *in succession*, **ādvādaçám** *up to twelve*, **pratidoṣám** *at evening*, **samakṣám** *in sight*. Instances given by the grammarians are: **adhihari** *upon Hari*, **uparājam** *with the king*, **upanadam** or **upanadi** *near the river*, **pratyagni** *toward the fire*, **pratiniçam** *every night*, **nirmakṣikam** *with freedom from flies*.

c. A large and important class is made up of words having a relative adverb, especially **yathā**, as prior member. Thus, for example, **yathāvaçám** *as one chooses* (**váça** *will*), **yathākṛtám** *as done [before], according to usage*, **yathānāmá** *by name*, **yathābhāgám** *according to several portion*, **yathāṅgám** and **yathāparú** *limb by limb*, **yatrakāmam** *whither one will*, **yāvanmātrám** *in some measure*, **yāvajjīvám** *as long as one lives*, **yāvatsábandhu** *according to the number of relations*.

d. These compounds are not common in the old language; RV. has with **yathā** only four of them, AV. only ten; and no such compound is used adjectively except **yācchreṣṭha** RV., **yāvacchreṣṭhá** AV. *as good as possible*. ÇB. has **yathākārín, yathācārín, yáthākāma, yáthākratu** as adjectives (followed in each case by a correlative **táthā**). The adjective use in the later language also is quite rare as compared with the adverbial.

e. Other cases than the accusative occasionally occur: thus, instrumental, as **yathāsaṁkhyena, yathāçaktyā, yathepsayā, yathāpratiguṇāis**; and ablative, as **yathāucityāt**.

f. A class of adverbs of frequent occurrence is made with **sa**: e. g. **sakopam** *angrily*, **sādaram** *respectfully*, **sasmitam** *with a smile*, **saviçeṣam** *especially*.

g. Other adverbial compounds of equivalent character occur earlier, and are common later: for example, **ṛtekarmám** *without work*, **nānārathám** *on different chariots*, **ubhayadyús** *two days in succession*, **citrapadakramam** *with wonderful progress*, **pradānapūrvam** *with accompaniment of a gift*; etc.

Anomalous Compounds.

1314. As in every language, compounds are now and then met with which are of anomalous character, as exhibiting combinations of elements not usually put together, or not after such a method, or for such a purpose. Some of these, especially of those occurring in the old language, may well be noticed here.

a. Compounds having a particle as final member: as, **apratí** *having no equal*, **tuviprati** *mightily opposing*, **áthatha** *refusing*, **vitatha** *false*, **yathātathá** *as it really is*, **súsaha** *prosperity in companionship*, **aniha** and **anamutra** *having no here* and *no yonder*, etc.

b. Agglomerations of two or more elements out of phrases: thus, **ahampūrvá** *eager to be first*, **ahamuttará** *contest for preëminence*, **mamasatyá** *contest for possession*, **itihāsá** *legend* (**iti hā** ''**sa** *thus, indeed, it was*), **naghamārá** and **naghāriṣá** *not, surely, dying* or *coming to harm*, **kuvítsa** *some unknown person*, **tadídartha** *having just that as aim*, **kūcidarthín** *having errands in every direction*, **kācitkará** *doing all sorts of things*, **kuhacidvíd** *wherever found*, **akutaçcidbhaya** *out of all danger*, **yadbhaviṣya** *What-is-to-be*, etc.

c. Agglomerations in which the prior member retains a syntactic form: as, **anyoṅya** and **paraspara** *one another*, **avaraspara** *inverted*.

d. Aggregations with the natural order inverted: e. g. **pitāmahá** and **tatāmahá** *grandfather*, **putrahata** *with his sons slain*, **jānvākná** and **-jānvakta** *with bended knee*, **dantajāta** *provided with teeth*, **somāpahṛtá** *deprived of soma*, **paṅktírādhas** *having groups of gifts*, **gojara** *old bull*, **agrajihvá**, **agranāsikā**, etc. *tip of the tongue*, *of the nose*, etc. Compare also **1291 c.**

e. Aggregations of particles were pointed out above (**1111 a**); also (**1122 e**) cases in which **ná** and **mā́** are used in composition.

f. In late Sanskrit (perhaps after the false analogy of combinations like **tad anu**, viewed as **tadanu**, with **tad** as stem instead of neuter accusative), a preposition is sometimes compounded as final member with the noun governed by it: e. g. **vṛkṣādhas** or **vṛkṣādhastāt** *under the tree* **dantāntaḥ** *between the teeth*, **bhavanopari** *on top of the house*, **satyavinā** *without truth.*

Stem-finals altered in Composition.

1315. Transfers to an **a**-form of declension from other less common finals, which are not rare in independent use, are especially common in the final members of compounds. Thus:

a. A stem in **an** often drops its final consonant (compare **429 a**, **437**): examples are **akṣa, adhva, arva, astha, aha, takṣa, brahma, mūrdha, rāja, loma, vṛṣa, çva, saktha, sāma.**

b. An i or ī is changed to **a**: examples are **aṅgula, añjala, açra, kukṣa, khāra, nada, nābha, bhūma, rātra, sakha.**

c. An **a** is added after a final consonant, and sometimes after an u-vowel or a diphthong (compare **399**): examples are **ṛca, tvaca; uda, pada, çarada; apa; dhura, pura; ahna, açmana, ūdhna, rājña; anasa, ayasa, āyuṣa, urasa, enasa, tamasa, manasa, yajuṣa, rajasa, rahasa, varcasa, vedasa, çreyasa, sarasa; bhruva, diva, gava, gāva, nāva.**

d. More sporadic and anomalous cases are such as: **apanna-da (-dant), pañca-ṣa (-ṣaṣ), ajāika-pa (-pad), çata-bhiṣā (-bhiṣaj), vipaç-ci (-cit), yathā-pura (-puras).**

Loose Construction with Compounds.

1316. In the looseness of unlimited and fortuitous combination, especially in the later language, it is by no means rare that a word in composition has an independent word in the sentence depending upon or qualifying it alone, rather than the compound of which it forms a part.

a. Examples are: **rāyáskāmo viçvápsnyasya** (RV.) *desirous of all-enjoyable wealth;* **aṅhór urucákriḥ** (RV.) *causing relief from distress;* **mahādhané árbhe** (RV.) *in great contest and in small;* **svānāṁ çrāiṣṭhyakāmaḥ** (AÇS.) *desiring superiority over his fellows;* **brāhmaṇāñ chrutaçīlavṛttasampannān ekena vā** (AGS.) *Brahmans endowed with learning, character, and behavior, or with one [of the three];* **cittapramāthinī bālā devānām api** (MBh.) *a girl disturbing the minds even of the gods;* **vasiṣṭhavacanād ṛṣyaçṛṅgasya co 'bhayoḥ** (R.) *at the words of both Vasishtha and Rishyaçringa,* **sītādravyāpaharaṇe çastrāṇām āuṣadhasya ca** (M.) *in case of stealing ploughing implements or weapons or medicament;* **jyotiṣām madhyacārī** (H.) *moving in the midst of the stars;* **dārupātraṁ ca mṛnmayam** (M.) *a wooden and an earthen vessel;* **syandane dattadṛṣṭiḥ** (Ç.) *with eye fixed on the chariot;* **tasminn ullambitamṛtaḥ** (KSS.) *dead and hanging upon it.*

APPENDIX.

A. The following text is given (as proposed above, 3) in order to illustrate by an example the variety of Sanskrit type in use. It is given twice over, and a transliteration into European letters follows. The text is a fable extracted from the first book of the Hitopadeça.

The Hunter, Deer, Boar, and Jackal.

आसीत्कल्याणकटकवास्तव्यो भैरवो नाम व्याधः । स चैकदा मांसलुब्धः सन्धनुरादाय विन्ध्याटवीमध्यं गतः । तत्र तेन मृग एको व्यापादितः । मृगमादाय गच्छता तेन घोराकृतिः सूकरो दृष्टः । ततस्तेन मृगं भूमौ निधाय सूकरः शरेण हतः । सूकरेणाप्यागत्य प्रलयघनघोरगर्जनं कृत्वा स व्याधो मुष्कदेशे हतश्छिन्नद्रुम इव पपात । यतः ।

जलमग्निं विषं शस्त्रं क्षुद्व्याधी पतनं गिरेः ।
निमित्तं किंचिदासाद्य देही प्राणैर्विमुच्यते ॥

अत्रान्तरे दीर्घरावो नाम जम्बुकः परिभ्रमन्नाहारार्थी तान्मृतान्मृगव्याधसूकरानपश्यत् । आलोक्याचिन्तयदसौ । अहो भाग्यम् । महद्भोज्यं समुपस्थितम् । अथवा ।

अचिन्तितानि दुःखानि यथैवायान्ति देहिनाम् ।
सुखान्यपि तथा मन्ये दैवमत्रातिरिच्यते ॥

भवतु । एषां मांसैर्मासत्रयं समधिकं भोजनं मे भविष्यति । ततः प्रथमबुभुक्षायां तावदिमानि स्वादूनि मांसानि विहाय कोदण्डाटनीलग्नं स्नायुबन्धं खादामीत्युक्त्वा तथाकरोत् । ततश्छिन्ने स्नायुबन्धे द्रुतमुत्पतितेन धनुषा हृदि भिन्नः स दीर्घरावः पञ्चत्वं गतः । अतोऽहं ब्रवीमि ।

कर्तव्यः संचयो नित्यं कर्तव्यो नातिसंचयः ।
अतिसंचयदोषेण धनुषा जम्बुको हतः ॥

आसीत्कल्याणकटकवास्तव्यो भैरवो नाम व्याधः। स चैकदा मांसलुब्धः सन्धनुरादाय विन्ध्याटवीमध्यं गतः। तत्र तेन मृग एको व्यापादितः। मृगमादाय गच्छता तेन घोराकृतिः सूकरो दृष्टः। ततस्तेन मृगं भूमौ निधाय सूकरः शरेण हतः। सूकरेणाप्यागत्य प्रलयघनघोरगर्जनं कृत्वा स व्याधो मुष्कदेशे हतश्छिन्नद्रुम इव पपात। यतः।

जलमग्निं विषं शस्त्रं क्षुद्व्याधी पतनं गिरेः।
निमित्तं किंचिदासाद्य देही प्राणैर्विमुच्यते॥

अत्रान्तरे दीर्घरावो नाम जम्बुकः परिभ्रमन्नाहारार्थी तान्मृतान्मृगव्याधसूकरानपश्यत्। आलोक्याचिन्तयदसौ। अहो भाग्यम्। महद्भोज्यं समुपस्थितम्। अथवा।

अचिन्तितानि दुःखानि यथैवायान्ति देहिनाम्।
सुखान्यपि तथा मन्ये दैवमत्रातिरिच्यते॥

भवतु। एषां मांसैर्मासत्रयं समधिकं भोजनं मे भविष्यति। ततः प्रथमबुभुक्षायां तावदिमानि स्वादूनि मांसानि विहाय कोदण्डाटनीलग्नं स्नायुबन्धं खादामीत्युक्त्वा तथाकरोत्। ततश्छिन्ने स्नायुबन्धे द्रुतमुत्पतितेन धनुषा हृदि भिन्नः स दीर्घरावः पञ्चत्वं गतः। अतोऽहं ब्रवीमि।

कर्तव्यः संचयो नित्यं कर्तव्यो नातिसंचयः।
अतिसंचयदोषेण धनुषा जम्बुको हतः॥

āsīt kalyāṇakaṭakavāstavyo bhāiravo nāma vyādhaḥ. sa cāi 'kadā māṅsalubdhaḥ san dhanur ādāya vindhyāṭavīmadhyaṁ gataḥ. tatra tena mṛga eko vyāpāditaḥ. mṛgam ādāya gachatā tena ghorākṛtiḥ sūkaro dṛṣṭaḥ. tatas tena mṛgam bhūmāu nidhāya sūkaraḥ çareṇa hataḥ. sūkareṇā 'py āgatya pralayaghanaghoragarjanaṁ kṛtvā sa vyādho muṣkadeçe hataç chinnadruma iva papāta. yataḥ:

jalam agniṁ viṣaṁ çastraṁ kṣudvyādhī patanaṁ gireḥ,
nimittaṁ kiṁcid āsādya dehī prāṇāir vimucyate.

atrāntare dīrgharāvo nāma jambukaḥ paribhramann āhārārthī tān mṛtān mṛgavyādhasūkarān apaçyat. ālokyā 'cintayad asāu: aho bhāgyam. mahad bhojyaṁ samupasthitam. athavā:

> **acintitāni duḥkhāni yathāi 'vā "yānti dehinām,**
> **sukhāny api tathā manye dāivam atrā 'tiricyate.**

bhavatu; eṣām māṅsāir māsatrayaṁ samadhikam bhojanam me bhaviṣyati. tataḥ prathamabubhukṣāyāṁ tāvad imāni svādūni māṅsāni vihāya kodaṇḍāṭanīlagnaṁ snāyubandhaṁ khādāmī 'ty uktvā tathā 'karot. tataç chinne snāyubandhe drutam utpatitena dhanuṣā hṛdi bhinnaḥ sa dīrgharāvaḥ pañcatvaṁ gataḥ. ato 'ham bravīmi:

> **kartavyaḥ saṁcayo nityaṁ kartavyo nā 'tisaṁcayaḥ;**
> **atisaṁcayadoṣeṇa dhanuṣā jambuko hataḥ.**

B. The following text is given in order to illustrate by a sufficient example the usual method of marking accent, as described above (**87**). In the manuscripts, the accent-signs are almost invariably added in red ink. The text is a hymn extracted from the tenth or last book of the Rig-Veda; it is regarded by the tradition as uttered by **Vāc** *voice* (i. e. *the Word* or *Logos*).

Hymn (X. 125) from the Rig-Veda.

अहं रुद्रेभिर्वसुभिश्चराम्यहमादित्यैरुत विश्वदेवैः ।
अहं मित्रावरुणोभा बिभर्म्यहमिन्द्राग्नी अहमश्विनोभा ॥ १ ॥
अहं सोममाहनसं बिभर्म्यहं त्वष्टारमुत पूषणं भगम् ।
अहं दधामि द्रविणं हविष्मते सुप्राव्ये यजमानाय सुन्वते ॥ २ ॥
अहं राष्ट्री संगमनी वसूनां चिकितुषी प्रथमा यज्ञियानाम् ।
तां मा देवा व्यदधुः पुरुत्रा भूरिस्थात्रां भूर्यावेशयन्तीम् ॥ ३ ॥
मया सो अन्नमत्ति यो विपश्यति यः प्राणिति य ईं शृणोत्युक्तम् ।
अमन्तवो मां त उप क्षियन्ति श्रुधि श्रुत श्रद्धिवं ते वदामि ॥ ४ ॥
अहमेव स्वयमिदं वदामि जुष्टं देवेभिरुत मानुषेभिः ।
यं कामये तंतमुग्रं कृणोमि तं ब्रह्माणं तमृषिं तं सुमेधाम् ॥ ५ ॥
अहं रुद्राय धनुरा तनोमि ब्रह्मद्विषे शरवे हन्तवा उ ।

अहं जनाय समदं कृणोम्यहं द्यावापृथिवी आ विवेश ॥ ६ ॥
अहं सुवे पितरमस्य मूर्धन्मम योनिरप्स्वन्तः समुद्रे ।
ततो वि तिष्ठे भुवनानु विश्वोतामूं द्यां वर्ष्मणोप स्पृशामि ॥ ७ ॥
अहमेव वात इव प्र वाम्यारभमाणा भुवनानि विश्वा ।
परो दिवा पर एना पृथिव्यैतावती महिना सं बभूव ॥ ८ ॥

ahám̐ rudrébhir vásubhiç carāmy ahám ādityāír utá viçvádevāiḥ, ahám mitrā́váruṇo 'bhā́ bibharmy ahám indrāgnī́ ahám açvíno 'bhā́. 1.
ahám̐ sómam āhanásam bibharmy ahám̐ tváṣṭāram utá pūṣáṇam bhágam, ahám̐ dadhāmi dráviṇam̐ haviṣmate suprāvyè yájamānāya sunvaté. 2.
ahám̐ rā́ṣṭrī saṁgámanī vásūnām̐ cikitúṣī prathamā́ yajñíyānām, tā́m mā devā́ vy àdadhuḥ purutrā́ bhū́risthātrām bhū́ry āveçáyantīm. 3.
máyā só ánnam atti yó vipáçyati yáḥ prā́ṇiti yá īm̐ çṛṇóty uktám, amantávo mā́m̐ tá úpa kṣiyanti çrudhí çruta çraddhivám̐ te vadāmi. 4.
ahám evá svayám idám̐ vadāmi júṣṭam̐ devébhir utá mā́nuṣebhiḥ, yám̐ kāmáye tám̐-tam ugrám̐ kṛṇomi tám brahmā́ṇam̐ tám ṛ́ṣim̐ tám̐ sumedhā́m. 5.
ahám̐ rudrā́ya dhánur ā́ tanomi brahmadvíṣe çárave hántavā́ u, ahám̐ jánāya samádam̐ kṛṇomy ahám̐ dyā́vāpṛthiví ā́ viveça. 6.
ahám̐ suve pitáram asya mūrdhán máma yónir apsv àntáḥ samudré, táto ví tiṣṭhe bhúvanā́ 'nu víçvo 'tā́ 'mū́m̐ dyā́m̐ varṣmáṇó 'pa spṛçāmi. 7.
ahám evá vā́ta iva prá vāmy ārábhamāṇā bhúvanāni víçvā, paró divā́ pará enā́ pṛthivyā́í 'tā́vatī mahinā́ sám babhūva. 8.

C. On the next page is given, in systematic arrangement, a synopsis of all the modes and tenses recognized as normally to be made from every root in its primary conjugation, for the two common roots bhū *be* and kṛ *make* (only the precative middle and periphrastic future middle are bracketed, as never really occurring). Added, in each case, are the most important of the verbal nouns and adjectives, the only ones which it is needful to give as part of every verb-system.

√bhū *be*.	Present-system.	Perfect-system.	Aorist-system.	Future-systems.	
Active:					
Indic.	**bhávāmi**	**babhū́va**		**bhaviṣyā́mi**	**bhavitā́smi**
Opt.	**bháveyam**		**bhūyā́sam**		
Impv.	**bhávāni**				
Pple.	**bhávant**	**babhūvā́ṅs**		**bhaviṣyánt**	
Augm.-Pret.	**ábhavam**		**ábhūvam**	**ábhaviṣyam**	
Middle:					
Indic.	**bháve**	**babhūvé**		**bhaviṣyé**	[**bhavitā́he**]
Opt.	**bháveya**		[**bhaviṣīyá**]		
Impv.	**bhávāi**				
Pple.	**bhávamāna**	**babhūvāná**		**bhaviṣyámāṇa**	
Augm.-Pret.	**ábhave**		**ábhaviṣi**		

Pass.pple **bhūtá**; — Infin. **bhávitum**; — Gerunds **bhūtvā́, -bhū́ya.**

√kṛ *make*.					
Active:					
Indic.	**karómi**	**cakā́ra**		**kariṣyā́mi**	**kartā́smi**
Opt.	**kuryā́m**		**kriyā́sam**		
Impv.	**karávāṇi**				
Pple.	**kurvánt**	**cakṛvā́ṅs**		**kariṣyánt**	
Augm.-Pret.	**ákaravam**		**ákārṣam**	**ákariṣyam**	
Middle:					
Indic.	**kurvé**	**cakré**		**kariṣyé**	[**kartā́he**]
Opt.	**kurvīyá**		[**kṛṣīyá**]		
Impv.	**karávāi**				
Pple.	**kurvāṇá**	**cakrāṇá**		**kariṣyámāṇa**	
Augm.-Pret.	**ákurvi**		**ákṛṣi**		

Pass.pple **kṛtá**; — Infin. **kártum**; — Gerunds **kṛtvā́, -kṛ́tya.**

SANSKRIT INDEX.

The references in both Indexes are to paragraphs. In this one, many abbreviations are used; but it is believed that they will be found self-explaining. For example, "pron." is pronunciation; "euph." points out anything relating to phonetic form or euphonic combination; "pres.", to present-system; "int." is intensive; "des." is desiderative; and so on. A prefixed hyphen denotes a suffix; one appended, a prefix.

a, pron. etc., 19—22; combination with following vowel, 126, 127; loss of initial after **e** and **o**, 135, 175a; resulting accent, 135a; not liable to **guṇa**, 235a; lightened to **i** or **u**, 249; lost in weakened syllable, 253.
a, as union-vowel in tense-inflection, 621c, 631.
-a, primy, 1148; scdry, 1208, 1209; **-a** in **-aka**, 1181; — **a**-stems, dcln, 326—34; from rdcl **ā**-st., 333, 354; in compsn, 1270, 1287a.
a- or **an-**, negative, 1121a—c; in compsn, 1283ff., 1288a, 1304a, b.
-aka, prmy, 1181; **aka**-stems sometimes govern accus., 271c; scdry, 1222j, k.
-aki, see 1221b.
√**akṣ**, pf., 788.
akṣara, 8.
akṣán, **ákṣi**, 343f, 431.
aghoṣa, 34b.
√**ac** or **añc**, pf., 788b; pple, 956b, 957c; stems ending with, 407—10.
-aj, 219a, 383k. 5.
√**añc**, see **ac**.
√**añj**, euph., 219a; pres., 694, 687; pf., 788; **tvā**-ger'd, 991d.
-aṇḍa, 1201a.
-at, 383k. 3 — and see **-ant**.
-ata, see 1176e.
-ati, see 1157g.
-atu, see 1161d.
-atnu, see 1196c.
-atra, see 1185e.
-atha, see 1163c.
-athu, see 1164.
√**ad**, impf., 621c; caus., 1042g.
-ad, 383k. 4.
adhi, loss of initial, 1087a.
adhika, in odd numbers, 477a, 478b.
√**an**, euph., 192b; pres., 631.
-an, 1160.
an-, see **a-**.
-ana, 1150; stems in compsn, 1271, 1296b.
anaḍváh, euph., 224b; dcln, 404.
-anā, 1150.
-ani, 1159.
-anī, 1150.
-anīya, 962, 965, 1215b.
anu, changed to **ānu** after **an-**, 1087b.
-anu, see 1162c.
anudātta, 81.
anudāttatara, 90c.
anunāsika, 36a, 73a.
anuvrata, with accus., 272.
anuṣṭúbh, euph., 151d.
anusvāra, pron. etc., 70—3; transliteration, 73c.
anehás, dcln, 419.
-ant or **-at**, of pples, 584, 1172; their dcln, 443ff.

-anta, 1209 d.
antaḥsthā, 31, 51 a.
antara, in compsn, 1302 i.
-anti, see 1221 c.
anyá, dcln, 523.
ap or **āp**, dcln, 151 e, 393.
api, loss of initial, 1087 a.
-abha, 1199.
abhinihita-circumflex, 84 e.
√**am**, pres., 634; aor., 862.
-am, infin. in, 970 a; gerund, 995.
-amā, see 1166 b.
-aye, infin. in, 970 f, 975 b.
-ara, see 1188 d.
arí, dcln, 343 g.
-aru, see 1192 a.
√**arth**, so-called, 104 b, 1056, 1067.
artha, in compsn, 1302 h.
aryamán, dcln, 426 a.
árvan, **árvant**, 455.
√**arh**, pres., 613; pf., 788; aor., 862; desid., 1029 b.
-ala, see 1189 b.
alpaprāṇa, 37 d.
√**av**, aor., 838, 908; pple, 954 e; inf., 968 e; **ya**-ger'd, 992 c.
ava, loss of initial, 1087 a.
-ava, see 1190 a.
avagraha, 16.
√**avadhīr**, so-called, 104 b.
avayáj, **avayā́**, 406.
avyayībhāva, 1111 d, 1313.
√**aç** *attain*, pf., 788; aor., 834 b, 837—9, 847; fut., 936 c; inf., 968 d.
√**aç** *eat*, pf., 803 a des., 1029 b, 1031; caus., 1042 n.
√**as** *be*, pres., 636, 621 e; pf., 800 m; in periphr. conjn, 1070—2, 1073 d; in ppial periphr. phrases, 1075 d; in cmpd conjn, 1093, 1094.
√**as** *throw*, pres., 761 e; aor., 847; pple, 956 e; inf., 968 c.
as final, euph. treatment of, 175; exceptional cases, 176.
-as, 1151; dcln of stems in, 411 ff.; **as**-stems in compsn, 1278, 1296 b, 1298 b.
-as, infin. in, 970 a, 971.
asán, **ásṛj**, 398, 432.
-asi, 1198.
ásṛj, euph., 219: and see **asán**.
-ase, infin. in, 970 c, 973 a.
asthán, **ásthi**, 343 i, 431.
-asna, see 1195 a.
-asnu, see 1194 d.
√**ah** *say*, pf., 801 a.
√**ah** *connect* (?), 788 a.
áhan, **áhar**, **áhas**, 430.

ā, pron. etc., 19, 22; combination of final, 126, 127; elision of initial, 135 d; **vṛddhi** of **a**, 236 ff.; lightened to **ī** or **i**, 250; to **a**, 250 c; in pres., 661—6, 761 f, g; in aor., 884; in pple, 954 c; in des., 1028 d.
ā́, with ablative, 293 c, 983 a.
-ā, 1149.
ā-stems, dcln, 347 ff.
-āka, see 1181 d.
-āku, see 1181 d.
-ātu, see 1161 d.
ātman, used reflexively, 514 a.
ātmane padam, 529.
ādi, **ādika**, **ādya**, in compsn, 1302 d.
-āna, in pples, 584, 1175; used instead of **māna**, 741 a, 752 e, 1043 f; **-āna** in other derivatives, 1175 a.
-ānī, see 1223 b.
-ānu, see 1162 c.
ānunāsikya, 36 a.
√**āp**, 1087 f; pf., 783 d; aor., 847, 862; des., 1030.
ābhā, in compsn, 1302 i.
ām, impv. 3d sing. in, 618.
āmreḍita, 1260 d.
-āyana, 1219.
-āyī, 1220.
-āyya, 966 c, 1051 f, 1218.
-āra, see 1188 d, 1226 b.
-āru, see 1192 a.
-āla, see 1227 a, 1245 l.
-ālu, see 1192 b, 1227 b.
√**ās**, pres., 619 c, 628; inf., 968 d; periph. pf., 1071 c; in ppial periph. phrases, 1075 c.
ā́s, **āsán**, **āsyà**, 398 b, 432.
ās final, euph. treatment of, 177.

i, pron. etc., 19, 20, 22; **i** and **y**, 55; combinations of final, 126, 129, 797 f; with preceding **a**-vowel, 127; from **ya**, 252, 784 c, 769, 922 b, 954 b; cases of loss before **y**, 233 a.
i, union-vowel, 254, 555 b; in pres., 630, 631, 634, 640; in pf., 796—8, 803; in aor., 876 b, 877; in fut., 934, 935, 943; in pple, 956; in infin., 968; in des., 1031.
i-stems, dcln, 335 ff.; from rdcl **ī**-, **ṣt.**, 354; in compsn, 1276, 1287 c; sometimes govern accus., 271 f.

√i *go*, pf., 783 b, 801 d; fut., 935 a; ya-ger'd, 992 a, c; int., 1002 e, 1021 b; caus., 1042 l; in ppial periphr. phrases, 994 e, 1075 a; periphr. conj., 1071 f; irreg. comb. with prefixes, 1087 c; in compd conjn, 1092 b.
√i (in, inv) *send*, 716 a.
-i, prmy, 1155; scdry, 1221.
-ika, prmy, 1186 c; scdry, 1222 j, l.
-ikā, fem. to -aka, 1181 c, 1222 i.
√ich, 608 b, 753 b.
-ij, 219 a, 383 k. 5.
-it, 383 k. 3; advbl, 1109 a.
-ita, 1176 a, b, d.
íti, uses of, 1102 a—c; peculiar construction with, 268 b; abbrev'd to ti, 1102 d.
-iti, see 1157 g.
-itu, see 1161 c.
-itnu, see 1196.
-itra, see 1185 e.
√idh or indh, euph., 160 c; aor., 836, 837, 840 b.
√in (or inv), 699 b, 709, 716 a, 749 b.
-in, 1183, 1230; in-stems, dcln, 438 ff.; in compsn, 1275, 1287 e; sometimes govern accus., 271 b; used participially, 960 b.
-ina, see 1177 b, 1209 c, 1223 f.
ínakṣa, 1029 c.
-ineya, see 1216 d.
√inv, see in.
-ibha, see 1199 a.
-ima, 1224 a.
-iman, see 1168 i—k.
iy in euph. comb'n from an i-vowel. 129 a, c, d, 352 b.
-iya, 1214.
íyakṣa, 1029 c.
íyant, dcln, 451.
ir-stems, dcln, 392.
ira, see 1188 e, 1226 b.
irajya, iradha, 1021 a.
√il, caus., 1042 b.
-ila, see 1189 b. 1227 a.
iva. euph., 1102.
-iva, see 1190 a.
-ivas, see 1173 b.
√iṣ *desire*, pres., 608 b, 753 b; inf., 968 d; desid., 1029 b.
√iṣ *send*, caus., 1042 b.
-iṣa, see 1197 b.
-iṣṭha, 467—70, 1184.
-iṣṇu, 1194.
-is, 1153; is-stems, dcln, 411 ff.
ī, pron. etc., 19, 20, 22; combinations of final, 126, 129, 797 f; with preceding a-vowel, 127; circumflexed, 128; uncombinable in dual etc., 138; ī as final of stem in verbal compsn, 1093, 1094.
ī, union-vowel, 254; in tense-inflection, 555 b, c; of pres., 632—4; of impf., 621, 631—4; of s-aor., 880 b, 888—91; of int., 1004 ff.; ī for i, 900 b, 935 a, 968 d, f.
ī-stems, dcln, 347 ff.
-ī, 1156; to i before added sfx, 471 b, 1203 d, 1237 c, 1239 b; in compsn, 1249 d.
-īka, see 1186 c.
√īkṣ, aor., 862; desid., 1029 b; periph. pf., 1071 c, 1073 a.
√īḍ, pres., 628, 630; pf., 783 d.
īta- for eta-forms in optative, 738 b, 771 d, 1032 a, 1043 c.
-īti, see 1157 g.
-ītu, see 1161 c.
-īna, prmy, see 1171 b; scdry, 1223 d.
-īman, see 1168 j.
īya, conj.-stem, 1021 b.
-īya, 1215.
-īyas, 467—70, 1184; stems in, dcln, 463 ff.
√īr, pres., 628; pf., 783 d, 801 d; pple, 957 b.
-īra, see 1188 e.
-īva, see 1190 a.
√īç, pres., 628, 630.
īçvara, with infin., 984, 987.
√īṣ, euph., 225 a.
-īṣa, see 1197.
√īh, euph., 240 b.

u, pron. etc., 19, 20, 22; u and v, 57; combinations of final, 126, 129; with preceding a-vowel, 127; from va, 252, 784, 769, 922 b, 954 b, 956 d; cases of loss before v, 233 a; final u gunated in scdry derivation, 1203 a.
u-stems, dcln, 335 ff.; from rdcl ū-st., 354; desid. u-stems govern accus., 271 a.
-u, 1178; -u in -uka, 1180 a.
-uka, 1180; stems sometimes govern accus., 271 g.
ukṣán, dcln, 426 b.
√uch, 608 b, 753 b.
√ujh, periphr. pf., 1071 c.

√uñch, pres., 758.
uṇādi-suffixes, 1138a.
-ut, 383k. 3.
-utra, see 1185e.
-utṛ, see 1182b.
-utha, see 1163d.
√ud or und, pres., 694a, 758a;
  pple, 957d; desid., 1029b.
úd, údaka, udán, 398b, 432.
udātta, 81.
-una, see 1177c.
-uni, see 1158e.
upadhmānīya, 69.
√ubj, aor., 862.
√ubh or umbh, pres., 694, 758a.
-ubha, see 1199a.
ubháya, dcln, 525c.
ur or us as 3d pl. ending, 169b.
ur-stems, dcln, 392.
-ura, see 1188f, 1226b.
-uri, 1191a.
-ula, see 1189b, 1227a.
uv in euph. comb'n from an u-vowel, 129a, c. d, 352b, 697a.
uçánas, uçánā, dcln, 355a, 416.
√uṣ, pres., 608b; ya-ger'd, 992b; periphr. pf., 1071f.
-uṣa, see 1197c.
uṣás, cuph., 168a; dcln, 415b.
-uṣi, see 1221c.
uṣṇíh, euph., 223a.
-us, 1154; us-stems, dcln, 411ff.
usṛ́, 371j.
us or ur as 3d pl. ending, 169b.

ū, pron. etc., 19, 20, 22; combinations of final, 126, 129, 797f; with preceding a-vowel, 127; circumflexed, 128; uncombinable in dual, 138a.
ū-stems, dcln, 347ff.
-ū, 1179.
-ūka, see 1180f.
-ūtṛ, see 1182b.
-ūtha, see 1163d.
ū́dhan, ū́dhar, ū́dhas, 430d.
ūna, in odd numbers, 477a, 478b.
-ūna, see 1177c.
-ūra, see 1188f.
ū́rj, euph., 219a.
√ū́rṇu, so-called, 104b, 713; pf., 801g, 1071e; ya-ger'd, 992c.
-ūṣa, see 1197c.
ūṣman, 31, 59.
√ūh remove, infln., 968c; ya-ger'd, 992c.

√ūh consider, euph., 240b, 745a; pres., 894d, 897b.

ṛ, pron. etc., 23—6; objectionable pronunciation and transliteration as ṛi, 24a; question of ṛ or ar in roots and stems, 104d, e, 237; combinations of final, 126, 129; with preceding a-vowel, 127; exceptions, 127a; impedes change of preceding s to ṣ, 181a; changes succeeding n to ṇ, 189ff.; guṇa and vṛddhi increments of, 235ff.; irregular changes, 241, 243; variable final ṛ of roots (so-called ṝ), 242.
ṛ-roots, root-nouns from, 383b, g.
ṛ-stems, dcln, 369ff.
ṛ, variable (so-called ṝ), roots in, 242, 245b; their passive. 770c; aor., 885, 900b; prec., 922a; fut., 935a; pple, 957b; root-infin., 971; gerund in ya, 992a.
√ṛ, euph., 242c; pres., 608a, 699a, 753b, 643b, 645, 716a; passive, 770c; pf., 783a; aor., 834a, 837b, 840b, 847, 853, 862; pple, 957b; int., 1002e; caus., 1042i; caus. aor., 1047.
-ṛ, see 1182b.
ṛi, ṛī, bad transliterations for ṛ, ṝ, 24a.
√ṛc or arc, pf., 788a; aor., 862, 894d, 897b; ya-ger'd, 992b
√ṛch, 608, 753b; pf., 788b.
-ṛj, 383k. 5.
√ṛñj or ṛj or arj stretch out, pres., 758a; pf., 788b; aor., 894d, 897b.
√ṛṇv, 716a.
-ṛt, 383k. 3.
ṛtvíj, euph., 219.
√ṛd, pple, 957d.
√ṛdh, pres., 694; pf., 788a; aor., 832, 837, 838, 840a, 847, 862; des., 1029b, 1030.
ṛbhukṣán, dcln, 434.
√ṛṣ, pf., 788b.
ṛhánt, dcln, 450e.

ṝ, pron. and occurrence, 23—6; objectionable pronunciation and transliteration as ṝī, 24a; as alleged final of roots, 104d, 242 (and see ṛ, variable); changes succeeding n to ṇ, 189ff.

ḷ, pron. and occurrence, 23—6; objectionable pronunciation and transliteration as **ḷi** or **ḷri,** 24 a; its **guṇa**-increment, 236.

ḷi, ḷri, bad transliterations for **ḷ,** 24 a.

ḹ, 23 a.

e, pron. etc., 27—9; combinations of final, 131—3, 135; with final **a**-vowel, 127; uncombinable in dual etc., 138 a, b, f; **guṇa** of **i** and **ī,** 235 ff.; from radical **ā,** 250 d; as alleged final of roots, 251, 761 f.

e, infin. in, 970 a, 971.

éka, dcln, 482 a, **ḥ**; used as article, 482 c; in making 9's 477 a, b.

ekaçruti, 90 c.

√edh, pf., 790 c; desid., 1029 b, 1031 b; periph. pf., 1071 c.

-ena, 1223 e.

-enya, 966 b, 1038, 1217.

-eya, 1216.

-eyya, 1216 e.

-era, see 1201 a, 1226 b.

-eru, see 1192 a.

-elima, 966 d, 1201 a.

eṣás, euph., 176 a.

āi, pron. etc., 27—9; combination with final **a**-vowel, 127; as final, 131—3; **vṛddhi** of **i** and **ī,** 235 ff.; as alleged final of roots, 251, 761 e; for union-vowel **ī** in tense-inflection, 555 c; for **e** in subj. endings, 561 a.

āi as gen.-abl. ending, 365 d.

o, pron. etc., 27—9; combination with final **a**-vowel, 127; as final, 131, 132, 134, 135; before suffix **ya,** 136 b; uncombinable, 138 c, f; for final **as,** 175, 176; **ar,** 179 a; **guṇa** of **u** and **ū,** 235 ff.; as alleged final of roots, 251, 761 g.

oṁ, euph., 137 b.

-otṛ, see 1182 b.

odana, euph., 137 b.

-ora, see 1201 a.

oṣṭha, euph., 137 b.

oṣṭhya, 49.

āu, pron. etc., 27—9; combination with final **a**-vowel, 127; as final, 131, 132, 134 b; **vṛddhi** of **u** and **ū,** 235 ff.

ḥ, pron. etc., 67—9; makes heavy syllable, 79; occurrence as final, 148, 170 a; for the labial and guttural spirants, 170 d; from final **s,** 145, 170 a, 172; from **r,** 144, 178; allows change of **s** to **ṣ,** 183.

ṅ or **ṁ,** pron. etc., 70—3; makes heavy syllable, 79; occurrence as final, 148; allows change of **s** to **ṣ,** 183; occurrence, 204, 212, 213 e.

k, pron. etc., 39, 40; relation to **c,** 42; to **ç,** 64; **s** to **ṣ** after, 180 ff.; added to final **ṅ,** 211; from **c,** by reversion, 214 ff.; as final, and in internal combination, 142, 217; from **ç,** do., 145, 218; from **ṣ,** 226 e; anomalously from **t,** 151 a; to **t,** 151 c.

-ka, prmy, 1186; scdry, 1222; **ka** in **-uka,** 1180 a; in **-aka,** 1181.

-kaṭa, see 1245 k.

kaṇṭhya *guttural,* 39.

√kan, pf., 786 e; aor., 899 d.

√kath, so-called, 1056.

√kam, aor., 868; pple, 955 a.

kampa, 78 d, 87 d, 90 b.

kámvant, euph., 212.

-kara, 1201 a.

karmadhāraya, 1263 a.

√kal, caus., 1042 g.

kalpa in compsn, 1302 i.

√kas, pple, 956 b.

√kā, int. (?), 1013 b.

kāma, with accus., 272; in compsn with infin.-stem, 968 g.

kāmya as denom.-sign, 1065.

kāra, in sound-names, 18.

√kāç, int., 1017.

√kās, periph. pf., 1071 f.

kíyant, dcln, 451.

√kir, 756.

√kīrt or **kṛt,** so-called, 1056.

√ku, pres., 633.

√kuc, caus., 1042 h.

√kup, pres., 761 a; aor., 840 b; pple, 956 b.

√kumār, so-called, 104 b.

kuvíd, accent of verb with, 595 e.

√kṛ *make,* pres., 714, 715, 855 a; pf. 797 c, 800 k; aor. 831, 834 a—40, 847, 894 d; int., 1002 g, h; prefixes **s,** 1087 d; in periph. conjn, 1070—3; in compd conjn, 1091—4; special constructions, 268 a.

√kṛ, kir *scatter*, 242b; pres., 756;
  aor., 885; prefixes s, 1087d.
√kṛ *commemorate*, int., 1002d,
  1019b.
√kṛt *cut*, pres., 758; aor., 847,
  852a; fut., 935b.
-kṛt, see 1105.
kṛt-suffixes, 1138a.
-kṛtvas, see 1105.
√kṛp, pres., 745b; aor., 834b;
  caus., 1042b.
kṛcá as pple, 958.
√kṛṣ, 102a; euph., 226f; pf. 790c;
  aor., 916a, 920a; fut., 935d,
  936d; inf., 968d.
√kḷp, 26; pf., 786a; ◦fut., 935b,
  936d.
-knī, see 1176d.
√knū, caus., 1042l.
√krand, pf., 794d; aor., 847, 861a,
  890b; int., 1002g, h, 1017.
√kram, pres., 745d; aor., 833, 847,
  899d, 904a; fut. 935b; pple,
  955'a; inf., 968d; tvā-ger'd, 991b;
  des., 1031b; caus., 1042g; in
  periphr. conj., 1070c.
√krī, caus., 1042l.
√krīḍ, caus., 1042n.
√krudh, aor., 847.
√kruç, aor., 916a, 920a.
króṣṭu, kroṣṭṛ, 343k, 374.
√klam, pres., 745d, 761a, 763;
  pple, 955a.
√klid, pple, 957d.
√kliç, aor., 916a.
kṣ, combinations of, 146, 221.
√kṣan, pple, 954d; inf., 968e.
√kṣam, pres., 763; fut., 935b;
  pple, 955a, 956b; inf.; 968d;
  caus., 1042g.
kṣám, dcln, 388.
√kṣar, aor., 890.
√kṣal, caus., 1042n.
√kṣā, pres., 761e; pple, 957a.
kṣāma as pple, 958.
√kṣi *possess*, pres., 755; caus.,
  1042d, l.
√kṣi *destroy*, pres., 761b; fut.,
  935a; pple, 957a; ya-ger'd, 922a;
  caus., 1042l.
√kṣud, pple, 957d.
√kṣudh, pres., 761a; aor., 847.
√kṣubh, pple, 956b.
kṣāipra-circumflex, 84a.
√kṣṇu, pres., 626.
√kṣvid, pple, 957d.

·kh, pron. etc., 39; relation to ṣ, 61b.
√khan or khā, 102a; pass., 772;
  pf., 794e; aor., 890a; pple, 955b;
  inf., 968e; ya-ger'd, 992a; caus.,
  1042g.
√khā, 102a.
√khid, pf., 790b; pple, 957d.
√khud, khun, int., 1002g, h.
√khyā, aor., 847, 894c; fut., 936c.

g, pron. etc., 39; relation to j, 42;
  from j by reversion, 214ff.
gata, in compsn, 1273c.
√gam, 102a; pres., 608b, 747,
  855a; aor., 833, 834b. 837—40,
  847, 881e, 887b; pf., 794e, 805a;
  fut., 943a; pple, 954d; int.,
  1002g, h, 1003; des., 1028e, 1031b;
  caus., 1042g; root-noun, 383h.
√gal, int., 1002d.
√gā *go*, 102a; pres., 660; aor., 830,
  836, 839, 884, 894c; desid., 1028d.
√gā *sing*, 251; pres., 761e; aor.,
  894d, 912; pple, 954c; inf., 968f;
  ya-ger'd, 992a; caus., 1042j, k.
√gāh or gah, pple, 956e; int.,
  1002d.
√gir, gil, 756; caus., 1042b.
√gu, int., 1002d.
guṇa, 27, 235ff.
√gup, aor., 863a; inf., 968c; ya-
  ger'd, 992c; des., 1040.
√gur, pres., 756; aor., 834a; pple,
  957b.
√guh, euph., 155b, d, 223b, 240c;
  pres., 745c; pf., 793i; aor., 847,
  852, 916a, 920a, f; inf., 968e;
  ya-ger'd, 992c; caus., 1042b.
√gṛ *sing*, euph., 242b; aor., 894d.
√gṛ *swallow*, euph., 242b; pres.,
  756; aor., 836; ˙inf., 968d; int.,
  1002d.
√gṛ (or jāgṛ) *wake*, 1020; aor., 867,
  871.
√gṛdh, pf., 786a; aor., 847.
gó, euph., 134a, 236b; dcln, 361c, f.
gdha, gdhi, 233f.
√grath or granth, pres., 730a;
  pf., 794h; caus., 1042h.
√grabh or grah, euph., 155b, 223g;
  pres., 723, 729, 731, 732, 904d,
  1066b; pf., 794c, 801i; aor.,
  834b, 847, 900b, 904a, b; fut.
  936e; pple, 956d, e; infin., 968f;
  pass., 998f; des., 1031b; caus.,
  1042b.
√gras, pple, 956b.

√glā, pres., 761e; aor., 912; pple, 957a; caus., 1042j.
glāú, dcln, 361a.

gh, pron. etc., 30; h derived from, 66; from h, by reversion, 214ff., 402.
√ghaṭ, caus., 1042g.
√ghas, euph., 167, 233f; jakṣ from, 640; pf., 794d; aor., 833, 847; pple, 954e.
ghoṣavant, 34.
√ghrā, pres., 671, 749a; tvā-ger'd, 991d; ya-ger'd, 992c; caus., 1042d.

ñ, pron. etc., 39; occurrence as final, 143, 386. 2, 3, 407a; duplication as final, 210; adds k before sibilant, 211.

c, pron. etc., 42—4; as final, 142; from t before a palatal, 202a, 203; n to ñ before it, 208b; internal combinations of, 217; reversion to k, 216ff.; in pres., 681; pf., 787; int., 1002i; des., 1028f.
√cakās or cakāç, so-called, 677.
√cakṣ, pres., 444a, 621a, 628, 675.
catúr, dcln, 482g, h.
√cam, pres., 745d; pple, 955a; caus., 1042g.
√car, euph., 242d; aor., 899d; pple, 957b; inf., 968c; tvā-ger'd, 991b, c; int., 1002d, 1003, 1017; des., 1031b; in ppial periphr. phrases, 1075b.
√carv, pple, 956a, 957b.
√cal, int., 1003; caus., 1042g.
√cāy, pres., 761e; tvā-ger'd, 991c; ya-ger'd, 992b; periphr. pf., 1071f.
√ci *gather*, reversion of c to k, 2161, 681, 787, 1028f; pres., 716b, 855a; aor., 889; tvā-ger'd, 991d; ya-ger'd, 992a; caus., 1042l.
√ci *note*, pres., 645; aor., 834a.
√cit, reversion of c to k, 2161, 681, 787, 1002i, 1028f; pf., 790b, 801e; aor., 840a, b; int., 1002i, 1024; des., 1040; caus., 1042b.
√ceṣṭ, pf., 790c.
√cyu, pf., 785a; aor., 840b, 866, 867, 868a, 870; inf., 968c; caus., 1042e.

ch, pron. etc., 42, 44; as final, 142; from ç after t or n, 203; after other mutes, 203a; in internal combination, 220; duplication between vowels, 227; çch for, 227a.
cha present-stems, 608.
√chad, pple, 957d.
√chand, aor., 863a, 890b; caus., 1042g.
√chā, pres., 753c; pple, 954c; tvā-ger'd, 991b; caus., 1042k.
√chid, pres., 694a; pf. 805b; aor., 832a, 834d, 847, 887a; pple, 957d.
√chur, caus., 1042b.
√chṛd, pple, 957d; tvā-ger'd, 991d.

j, pron. etc., 42—4; as final, 142; in internal combination, 219; n to ñ before it, 202b; from t before sonant palatal, 202a; reversion to g, 215ff.; in pf., 787; in des., 1028f.; before na of pple, 957c; anomalously changed to d, 151c.
√jakṣ, 102a; euph., 233f; pres., 640, 675; pple, 954e.
jágat, dcln, 450d.
jagdha etc., 233f.
√jan, 102a; pres., 631a, 645, 680. 761b, 772; pf., 794e; aor., 834b, 904d; pple, 955b; inf., 968e; des., 1031b.
jáni, dcln, 343f.
janús, dcln, 415c.
√jap, pple, 956b; int., 1002d, 1017.
√jambh or jabh, inf., 968e; int., 1017.
√jalp, pf., 790c.
√jas, aor., 871.
√jā, 102a.
√jāgṛ, so-called, 104b, 1020; pf., 1071e.
jātya-circumflex, 84b.
√ji *conquer*, reversion of j to g, 2161; in pf., 787; in des., 1028f; aor., 839, 889, 894b, 904b; fut., 935a; caus., 1042l; caus. aor., 1047, 861b; periph. pf., 1071f.
√ji *injure* — see jyā.
√jinv, 716a, 749b.
jihvāmūlīya, 39a, 69.
√jīv, aor., 861a; des., 1028h, 1031b; caus., 1042n.
√jur, pres., 756, 766.
√juṣ, aor., 834b, 836, 840b; in sajūs, 225a, 392b.
√jū, pres., 728; pf., 786c.

√jṛ *waste away*, euph., 2161, 242b; pres., 756, 766; pf., 793h, 794k; pple, 957b; caus., 1042e.

√jñā, pres., 730b, 731; pf., 790b; aor., 830, 838, 894c, 912; caus., 1042j; caus. aor., 1047, 861b; caus. des., 1030; caus. pple, 1051b.

√jyā or jī, pres., 761b; pf., 785a, 794b; aor., 912; pple, 954c.

√jri, aor., 897b.

√jval, aor., 899d; caus., 1042g.

jh, pron. and occurrence, 42; as final, 142; in internal combination, 220b.

ñ, pron. etc., 42; from n after a palatal, 201; before j, 202b; ç, 203; c, 208b.

ṭ, pron. etc., 45, 46; from a final palatal, 142; ç, 145, 218; ṣ, 145; h, 147; adds t before s, 199e; added to final ṇ before sibilant, 211; from j in internal combination, 219; ch, 220; kṣ, 221; h, 222; ṣ, 226b.

ṭh, pron. etc., 45, 46.

ḍ, pron. etc., 45; ordinary derivation, 46; ḷ used for, 5a, 54; from d with preceding sibilant, 198d, 199d.

ḍh, pron. etc., 45, 46; ḷh used for, 54; from dh with preceding sibilant, 199d; from h with following t or th or dh, 222b.

ḍhvam or dhvam, 226c, 881b, 901a, 924a.

ṇ, pron. etc., 45; ordinary derivation, 46; as final, 143; change of n to, 189—95; from n with preceding sibilant, 199b; doubled as final, 210; adds ṭ before a sibilant, 211.

t, pron. etc., 47, 48; from final radical s, 145; do. in internal combn, 167, 168; with preceding sonant aspirate, 160; assim. to following l, 162; added after ṭ before s, 199e; after n before s or ṣ, 207; to palatal before palatal, 202; before ç, 203; anomalously changed to k, 151a; to ṭ, 151b; from k and j, 151c.

-t, added after short final vowel of root, 345, 376b, 383f—h, 1143d, 1147d, 1196a, 1213a; irregular cases, 1147e.

-ta, of pple, 952—6, 1176; ta-stems in compsn, 1273, 1284; scdry, 1245e.

√taṅs or tas, pf., 794d; aor., 847.

√takṣ, pres., 628; pf., 790b; pple, 956a.

√taḍ, euph., 198c.

tatpuruṣa, 1263a.

taddhita-suffixes, 1138a.

√tan *stretch*, pass., 772; pf., 794f, 805a; aor., 833a, 834b, 847, 881e, 890a, 899d; pple, 954d; ya-ger'd, 992a; des., 1028e.

-tana, 1245g—i.

tanū as refl. pronoun, 514b.

√tap, pres., 761b; aor., 834d, 233e, 865a; fut., 935b.

√tam, pres., 763; aor., 847; pple, 955a; inf., 968e.

-tama, 471—3, 487f, g, 1242a, b.

-tamam and -tāmam, 1111e, 1119.

-taya, 1245a.

-taye, infln. in, 970e, 975.

-tar, see 1109a, and -tṛ.

-tara, 471—3, 1242a, b.

-taram and tarām, 1111e, 1119.

-tari, infln. in, 970i, 979.

-tavant, pple in, 959, 960.

-tave and tavāi, infln. in, 970b, 972.

-tavya, 962, 964, 1212i.

√tas, see taṅs.

-tas, 1152; advbl, 1098.

-tā, 1237.

-tāt, impv. forms in, 570, 571, 618, 654, 704, 723, 740, 752c, 760c, 839, 1011a, 1032a, 1043d.

-tāt, 383k, 1238; advbl, 1100b.

-tāti, 1238.

√tāy, pres., 761e; periphr. pf., 1071f.

tālavya, 44a.

-ti, 1157; ti-stems in compsn, 1274, 1287d; scdry, 519, 1157h; advbl, 1102a—d.

√tij, euph., 219a; des., 1040.

-titha, 1242e.

√tir, 756, 766.

√tu, pres., 633; pf., 786c; aor., 868a; int., 1002g.

-tu, 1161, 970b, 972.

√tuj, caus., 1042b.

√tud, pres., 758; pple, 957d.

-tum, infin. in, 968, 970b, 972, 987, 988.
√tur, pres., 756, 766; des., 1029a; caus., 1042b.
-tur, 1182g.
√tul, caus., 1042b.
√tuṣ, caus., 1042b.
√tṛ, euph., 242b; pres., 709, 715c, 756, 766; pf., 794k, 801f, 804; aor., 904d; pple, 957b; inf., 968d; ya-ger'd, 992a; int., 1002d, g, 1003, 1017; desid., 1029a.
-tṛ, 943, 1182; tṛ-stems, dcln, 369ff.; govern accus., 271d; verbal use of, 946; make periphr. fut., 942—7.
tṛca, euph., 233a.
tṛta, tṛtīya, euph., 243.
√tṛd, aor., 836b, 837a; pple, 957d.
√tṛp, pres., 710, 758; pf., 786a; fut., 936d; aor. 847, 852a.
√tṛṣ, pf., 786a; aor., 840b, 847.
√tṛh or tṛṅh, euph., 223b, 224b; pres., 694a, 695; aor., 847, 916a.
toçás, dcln, 415b.
-tos, infin. in, 970b, 972.
tta for dāta, 955f, 1087e.
tti for dāti, 1157c.
-tna, 1245g, h.
-tnu, 1196.
tman, dcln, 426b.
-tya, for -ya, 992; scdry, 1245b—d.
√tyaj, 1087f; euph., 219a; pf., 785a[; fut. 935b; pple, 956b.
-tyāi, infin. in, 970e, 975a.
-tra, 1185; or trā, advbl, 1099.
√trap, pf., 794h.
√tras, pf., 794h; aor., 899d.
√trā, 102a; pres., 628; aor., 887d, 893a, 895.
-trā, see -tra.
tri, dcln, 482e, f; in compsn, 1300c.
-tri, see 1185g.
triṣṭúbh, euph., 151d.
-trī, 376c, 1182.
-tru, see 1185g.
-tva, gerundival, 966a, 1209h; scdry, 1239.
-tvatā, 1239d.
-tvan, see 1169.
-tvana, 1240.
√tvar, caus., 1042g.
-tvara, see 1171.
-tvā, 990, 991, 993.
-tvānam, 993c.
-tvāya, 993b.
√tviṣ, pres., 621a; aor., 916a.

-tvī, 993b.
-tvīnam, 993c.
√tsar, aor., 890a, 899d.

th, pron. etc., 47, 48; with preceding sonant aspirate, 160.
-tha, 1163; ordinal, 487c, 1242d; or thā, advbl, 1101.
-tham, advbl, see 1101a.
-thā, see tha.
-thāt, advbl, 1101a.
-thu, 1164.

d, pron. etc., 47, 48; anomalously changed to ḍ, 151b; do. from h, 404.
dákṣiṇa, dcln, 525c.
√dagh, euph., 155b, 160c; aor., 833, 836b, 838, 847.
√dad, 672; pf., 794j.
√dadh, 672; euph., 155e, 160c.
dadhán, dádhi, 343i, 431.
dán, euph., 389b.
dánt, dcln, 396.
dantya, 47.
√dabh or dambh, euph., 155b; pf., 794h; aor., 833; des., 1030.
√dam, pres., 763; pple, 955a; tvā-ger'd, 991b.
-dam, advbl, see 1103b.
√day, pres., 761f; periph. pf., 1071f.
√daridrā, so-called, 104b, 1024a; pf., 1071e.
√dal, caus., 1042g.
√daç ór daṅç, pres., 746; pf., 794d; tvā-ger'd, 991d.
√das, aor., 847, 852b, 899d.
√dah, euph., 155b, d, 223a; aor., 890a, 897a, 444a; fut., 935d; int., 1002d; des., 1030.
√dā give, pres., 667—9, 672, 855a; pf., 803a; aor., 830, 834a, 836, 837, 839, 847, 884, 894c; pple, 955f, 1087e, 1157c; inf., 968f; tvā-ger'd, 991b; ya-ger'd, 992a; des., 1030, 1034b.
√dā divide, 251; pres., 753c, 761g; aor., 834a; pple, 954c, 955f, 957a, 1087e, 1157c; ya-ger'd, 992a.
√dā bind, pres., 753c, 761g; aor., 884; pple, 954c.
√dā protect, alleged, pf., 787.
-dā, advbl, 1103a, b.
-dānīm, advbl, 1103c.
√dāç, pres., 444, 639c; pf., 790b, 803a.

√dās, pres., 444.
-di, advbl, 1103e.
didyót etc., 336e.
√div, see dīv.
dív, dcln, 361d.
√diç, euph., 218a; aor., 916, 920a; int., 1017.
√dih, euph., 155b, 223a; aor., 916.
√dīkṣ, des., 1031b; caus., 1042n.
√dīdī, so-called, 676; pf., 786b.
√dīdhī, so-called, 104b, 676; pf., 786b; aor., 897b.
√dīp, aor., 861a.
√dīv *play*, euph., 240b; pres., 765; pple, 955c; inf., 968e.
√dīv or dev *lament*, pple, 957a; inf., 968e.
√du or dū, pres., 716b; pple, 957a.
ducchúnā, euph., 168b.
√dudh, 102a.
√duṣ, euph., 240c, 1155a; aor., 847; caus., 1042b.
dus-, 225a, 1121; in compsn, 1284a, b, 1288e, f, g, 1304c, d.
√duh, euph., 155b, d, f, 223a; pres., 621, 635; pf., 801h; aor., 916, 920a—f.
√dṛ *pierce*, euph., 242c; pf., 793h; pple, 957b; int., 1002d, 1003, 1023; caus., 1042e.
√dṛ *heed*, pres., 757, 773; aor., 834a, 881b.
√dṛp, aor., 847; fut., 935b, 936d.
√dṛç, euph., 218a; pf., 790c, 801e, 805b; aor., 832, 834b, 836, 840b, 847, 890a, 894a; fut., 936d; pass., 998f; root-noun, dcln, 386. 3.
dṛç, dṛça, dṛkṣa, with pron.-stems, 518.
√dṛh or dṛṅh, euph., 155b, 223b, d; pres., 758, 761b, 767; pf., 786a.
devanāgarī, 1.
doṣán, dós, 398a, 432.
dyú and dyó, dcln, 361d, e.
√dyut, pf., 785a; aor., 840a, b, 847, 863a, 890a; int., 1002g; caus., 1042b.
-dyus, see 1105b.
√drā *run*, pple, 957a; int., 1024a.
√drā *sleep*, aor., 912; pple, 954c, 957a; int., 1024a.
√dru, pf., 797c; aor., 868; int., 1018a; caus., 1042e.
√druh, euph., 155b, d, 223a, c; aor., 834d, 847, 920e, f.
dvandva, 1252a.
dvā́r, dcln, 388. 3.

dvi, cmpds with, 1300c.
dvigu, 1312.
√dviṣ, euph., 226d, f; pres., 621a; aor., 916, 920b.

dh, pron. etc., 47, 48; from t or th after sonant aspirate, 160; h from, 223g.
-dha, see -dhā.
√dham or dhmā, pres., 750; pass., 772; aor., 912; pple, 955b; ya-ger'd, 992a.
√dhā *put*, euph., 223g; pres., 667—9, 672, 855a; aor., 830, 834—7, 839, 847, 884; pple, 954c; inf., 968f; tvā-ger'd, 991b; des., 1028d, 1030, 1031a; in periphr. conj., 1070c.
√dhā *suck*, 251; pres., 761f; aor., 868; pple, 954c; inf., 968f; ya-ger'd, 992a.
-dhā or -dha, advbl, 1104.
√dhāv *rinse*, pple dhāutá, 954e.
√dhi (or dhinv), 716a.
dhi, final of compds, 1155g, 1276b.
√dhū or dhu, pres., 712, 728a, 755; pf., 790b; aor., 868a, 887c; int., 1002g, 1003, 1018a; caus., 1042m.
√dhūrv, aor., 887c; des., 1028h.
√dhṛ, pres., 757, 773; pf., 786a; aor., 834a, 867, 871; int., 1003.
√dhṛṣ, pf., 786a; aor., 847, 852b; pple, 956b.
√dhmā, see dham.
√dhyā, pres., 761e; aor., 912.
-dhyāi, infin. in, 970g, 976, 1050f.
√dhvaṅs or dhvas, euph., 168; pf., 790c; aor., 847; caus., 1042g.
√dhvan, pple, 955a, 956b; caus., 1042g.
√dhvṛ, pple, 955e.

n, pron. etc., 47, 48; as final, 143; for final rdcl m, 143a, 212a; change to ṇ, 189—95; to ñ after and before palatals, 201—3. 208b; combinations as root-final, 204; loss as stem-final, 204b; assim. to palatals and linguals, 205; to l, 206; before sibilants, 207; treated as ns, 208, 209; duplication of final, 210; instability as final, 256, 1203b; used as union-cons., 257, 313, 482h; question of final of pañcan etc., 484; final n in secndry dervn, 1203c.

ná, comparative, 1122 h.
na added to **tha** or **ta** of 2d pl., 549 a, forms so made, 613, 616 b, 618, 621 b, 654, 658, 669, 690, 704, 707, 723, 735 b, 740, 752 b, 760 c, 831 a, 839, 849 a.
-na, of pples, 952, 957, 1177; euph., 161 b; sdry, 1223 g, 1245 f; in compsn, 1273, 1284.
√nakṣ, 102 a.
√nad, caus., 1042 g.
√nand, euph., 192 a.
√nabh, euph., 192 a; caus., 1042 g.
√nam, pf., 786 a; aor., 890 a, 897 b, 911, 912; fut., 935 b; pple, 954 d; inf., 968 d; int., 1017; caus., 1042 g.
-nam, advbl, 1109 a.
√naç *be lost*, euph., 192 a; aor., 847, 854 b, 867; fut., 935 d, 936 a; des., 1028.
√naç *attain*, euph., 218 a; pf., 801 g; aor., 833, 834 b, 837 b; des., 1029 c.
√nas, aor., 837 b.
nás, dcln, 387, 397.
-nas, 1152.
√nah, euph., 223 g; pres., 761 c.
-nā, see 1177.
nāgarī, 1 a.
nāsikya, 230 b.
ní, euph., 192 f.
-ni, 1158.
√niṅs, euph., 183 a; pres., 628.
√nij, euph., 219 a; aor., 847; int., 1024.
nitya-circumflex, 84 b.
√nind, pf., 790 b; aor., 840 b.
nilay, quasi-root, 1087 c.
níç and **niçā**, 397.
nis, loss of initial of, 1087 a.
√nī, aor., 889, 896, 900 b; fut., 935 a; inf., 968 c; **tvā**-ger'd, 991 c; int., 1017, 1018 a; periphr. pf., 1071 f.
-nī, fem. ending, 1176 d, 1223 c.
nīḍá, euph., 198 d.
√nu or **nū**, pres., 626 a; aor., 868 a, 887 c; int., 1002 g, 1003.
-nu, 1162.
√nud, aor., 834 d, 904 c; pple, 956 b, 957 d; int., 1017.
nṛ́, dcln, 371.
√nṛt, euph., 192 a; aor., 833, 847, 852 b; inf., 968 d; **tvā**-ger'd, 991 c.
néd, accent of verb with, 595 e.
néma, dcln, 525 c.
nāú, dcln, 361 a.
p, pron. etc., 49, 50.
-p, caus.-sign, 1042 i—l; aor. from such caus., 1047.
-pa, 1201.
pakvá as pple, 958.
√pac, pres. 761 b.
√pat, pf., 794 f, h; aor., 847; int., 1002 g; des., 1030, 1031; caus., 1042 g.
páti, dcln, 343 d, e; in dpndt compsn, 1267 a; denom. conj. from, 1054 a.
páth, pathí, pánthan, dcln, 343 j, 395, 433.
√pad, pres., 761 c; aor., 834 b, d, 836, 837 b; pple, 957 d; int., 1002 g; des., 1030.
pád, dcln, 387, 389 b.
pada, 111 a; **pada**-endings and cases. 111 a, b.
√pan, pf., 794 f; int., 1002 g.
pánthan, see **páth**.
pára, dcln, 525 c.
parasmāi padam, 529.
párucchepa, euph., 168 b.
palāy, quasi-root, 1087 c.
palyaṅg, quasi-root, 1087 c.
palyay, quasi-root, 1087 c.
√paç, pres., 761 c.
paçcima, dcln, 525 c.
√pā *drink*, pres., 671, 749 a, 855 a; aor., 830, 838; pple, 954 c; **ya**-ger'd, 992 a; des., 1028 d; caus., 1042 k.
√pā *protect*, aor., 912; caus., 1042 m.
pāda, 79, 93 d.
pādapūraṇa, 1122 b.
piṇak, euph., 190 c.
√pinv, 699 b, 716 a, 749 b.
√piç, pres., 758; aor. 840 b; pple, 956 b.
√piṣ or **piṅṣ**, euph., 226 d, f; pres., 694 a, 920 a; aor., 190 c, 758 a.
√pis, euph., 181 d.
√pīḍ, euph., 198 d.
pīpī, conj.-stem, 676, 786 b.
púṁs, púmāṅs, euph., 183 a; dcln, 394.
puraḥsara, puraskṛta, purogama, in compsn, 1302 f.
purā́, pres. in past sense with, 778 a.
puru, in compsn, 1284 b, 1290.
√puṣ, aor., 847.
√pū, pres., 728; aor. (?), 868 a. 894 d; inf., 968 c; caus., 1042 e.
pū́rva, dcln, 525 c; in compsn, 1251 e. 1291 c, 1302 f.

pūṣán, dcln, 426 a.
√pṛ *fill*, euph., 242 c; pres., 731, 761 b, 766; pf., 793 h; pple, 955 d, 957 b; inf., 968 c.
√pṛ *pass*, pf., 793 h; aor., 896.
√pṛ *be busy*, pres., 757, 773.
√pṛc, pres., 694 a; aor., 834 c, 836 b, 837 b, 840 b, 890, 894 a; pple, 957 c.
√pṛṇ, 731, 753.
pṛ́t, pṛ́tanā, 397.
pṛ́ṣant, dcln, 450 c.
√pyā or pī, pres., 761 e; pf., 785, 794 b; aor., 912, 914 b; pple, 957 a; caus., 1042 k.
pragṛhya, 138.
pracaya or pracita accent, 90 a.
√prach, euph., 220; pres., 756 a; pf., 794 c; aor. 834 c, 890; pple, 954 b.
√prath, aor., 840 b, 863 a.
prabhṛti, in compsn, 1302 e.
praçliṣṭa-circumflex, 84 d.
√prā, aor., 830, 889.
prāya, in compsn, 1302 i.
√prī, pres., 731; aor. (?), 866, 868; caus., 1042 m.
√pruth, ya-ger'd, 992 b.
√pruṣ, euph., 226 d, 392 b; pres., 732, 1066 b.
plāy, quasi-root, 1087 c.
√plu, aor., 863 b, 866; ya-ger'd, 992 a; caus., 1042 a.
pluta, 78.
√psā, 102 a.

ph, pron. etc., 49, 50.
√phaṇ, pf., 794 h; int., 1002 g, 1003.
√phal, pf., 794 h.
phullá as pple, 958.

b, pron. etc., 49, 50; interchange with v, 50 a.
√baṅh, euph., 223 b.
√badh or vadh, aor., 904 a; des., 1029 a, 1040.
√bandh, euph., 155 b; pres., 723, 730 a; pf., 794 d; fut., 935 b; inf. 968 d.
bahuvrīhi, 1293 b.
√bādh, euph., 155 b; aor., 904 d; int., 1002 d, 1003; des., 1029 a, 1031, 1040.
√budh, euph., 155 b; aor., 834 b, d, 839, 840 b, 847.
√bṛh, euph., 223 b; pres., 758; int., 1011; caus., 1042 h.
bṛhánt, dcln, 450 a.
bbh, occurrence, 151 e.
√brū, pres., 632; peculiar construction, 268 a.

bh, pron. etc., 49, 50; anomalously changed to a guttural, 151 d; h from, 223 g.
√bhakṣ, 102 a.
√bhaj, euph., 219 a; pf., 794 h; aor., 834 c, 867, 890 a; fut., 935 b; inf., 968 d.
√bhañj, euph., 219 a; pres., 694; pple, 957 c; tvā-ger'd, 991 d.
bhávant, 456, 514 c.
√bhas, euph., 233 f; pres., 678.
√bhāṣ, inf., 968 d.
√bhikṣ, 102 a.
√bhid, aor., 832, 834 d, 836 a, 840 a, 847; pple, 957 d.
bhiṣáj, euph., 219 a; denom. conj. from, 1054 a.
√bhī, pres., 645, 679; pf., 786 b; aor., 831 a, 840 b, 866, 891, 897 b; caus., 1042 l, m; caus. aor., 1047; periphr. pf., 1071 f, 1073 a.
√bhīṣ, 1042 m; aor., 861 a, 1047.
√bhuj *bend*, euph., 219 a; pple, 957 c; tvā-ger'd, 991 d.
√bhuj *enjoy*, euph., 219 a; pres., 694 a; aor., 836 b, 847, 912.
√bhur, pres., 756; int., 1002 d.
bhúvas, euph., 176 c.
√bhū, pf., 789 a, 793 b, 800 d; aor., 829, 830, 836—9, 853, 924; inf., 968 e; in periphr. conjn, 1070—72; in ppial periphr. phrases, 1075 d; in compd conjn, 1091—4.
bhūta in compsn, 1273 c.
√bhṛ, pres., 645, 855 a; pf., 789 b, 797 c; aor., 890 a; int., 1002 g, h, 1003; periphr. pf., 1071 f.
bhos, 456; euph., 174 b.
√bhraṅç or bhraç, pres., 767; aor., 847; pple, 954 b; caus., 1042 h.
√bhrajj or bhṛjj, euph., 219 b.
√bhram, pres., 763; pf., 794 h; pple, 955 a; inf., 968 d; tvā-ger'd, 991 b; ya-ger'd, 992 c; caus., 1042 g.
√bhrāj, euph., 219 b; pf., 790 c, 794 h; aor., 833.

m, pron. etc., 49, 50; as final, 143; as final radcl, 143 a, 212, 256; in extrnl combn, 213; before **rāj**, 213 b.
-ma, prmy, 1166; scdry, 474, 487 a, d, 1224 b, 1242 c.
√maṅh or **mah**, pf., 786 a; caus., 1042 g.
maghávan, dcln, 428.
√majj, euph., 219 a; pf., 801 g; aor., 887 a; fut., 936 a; pple, 957 c; inf., 968 e; des., 1028 j.
-mat, advbl, 1235 e.
√math or **manth**, pres., 730 a, 731, 732, 1066 b, 746; aor., 899 d; **ya**-ger'd, 992 b; caus., 1042 g.
√mad or **mand**, 102 a; pres, 628, 645, 764; aor., 833, 834 d, 839, 840 b, 887 a, 897 b, 899 d, 904 d; pple, 956 b; caus., 1042 g.
√man, pf., 794 f; aor., 834 b, 840 b, 881 e, 887 a, b; fut., 935 b; pple, 954 d; des., 1028 e, 1029 a, 1040; special construction, 268 a, 994 e.
-man, 1168; **man-** and **ma-**stems, 1166 c; **man**-stems in compsn, 1277 b.
manas, in comp. with infin.-stem, 968 g.
-mane, infin. in, 970 d, 974.
-mant, 1235.
√mantr, so-called, 104 b, 1056, 1067, 1073 d.
mánthan, dcln, 434.
√mand, 102 a: see **mad.**
-maya, 161 a, 1225.
-mara, 1201 a.
√mah, see **maṅh.**
máh, mahī́, 400 a.
mahánt, dcln, 450 b.
mahā́, 355 a.
mahāprāṇa, 37 d.
√mā *measure*, pres., 660, 663; aor., 839 f; pple, 954 c; inf., 968 f; **tvā**-ger'd, 991 b; **ya**-ger'd, 992 a; des., 1030.
√mā *exchange*, pres., 761 f.
√mā *bellow*, pres., 660, 663, 672, 676 c; aor., 868 e.
mā́ṅs, māṅsá (and **mā́s**), 397.
mātrā, in compsn, 1302 g; euph., 161 a.
-māna, 584 b, 1174.
mā́s, euph., 168 a; dcln, 389 b, 397: and see **mā́ṅs.**
√mi *fix*, aor., 911; des., 1030.
-mi, 1167.
√mikṣ, 1033 a; caus., 1042 b.
mitrá, 1185 c.
-min, 1231.
√mil, fut., 936 b.
√mī or **mi** *damage*, pres., 192 c, 731, 761 b; aor., 911; des., 1030; caus., 1042 l.
√mih, euph., 223 b; pf., 790 b; aor., 916 a, 920 a.
√mīv, pple, 955 b.
√muc, pres., 758, 761 b, 855 a; aor., 832, 834 c, 837 b, 839, 847, 890 a; des., 1030.
√mud, aor., 837 b.
√muṣ, pres., 732, 1066 b; pple. 956 b; caus., 1042 b.
√muh, euph., 223 a, c; pres., 761 a; aor., 847; pple, 955 e.
√mūrch, 220 a; pres., 745 f; pple, 954 e.
mūrdhanya, 45.
√mṛ *die*, euph., 242 c; pres., 757, 773; aor., 834 a, 837 b.
√mṛ *crush*, pres., 731.
√mṛj, euph., 219 b; pres., 621 a, 627, 745 e; pf., 786 a, 793 i; aor., 900 a, 919, 920; fut., 935 b, 936 d; pple, 956 b, d; inf., 958 c; **tvā**-ger'd, 991 c; **ya**-ger'd, 992 b; int., 1002 g, 1003, 1017; des., 1028 j; caus., 1042 b.
√mṛḍ, euph., 198 d; caus., 1042 b.
√mṛṇ, 731, 753 a.
√mṛd, fut., 936 d.
√mṛdh, aor., 838, 847.
√mṛç, pf., 786 a; aor., 916, 920; pple, 956 b; int., 1002 g, 1003, 1017.
√mṛṣ, aor., 834 c, 840 a, 847.
-mna, 1224 c.
√mnā, 102 a; aor., 912.
√mruc, aor., 847.
√mlā, pres., 761 c; aor., 912; pple, 957 a; caus., 1042 j.
√mluc, int., 1002 g.
y, pron. etc., 51, 55, 56; relation to **i**-vowels, 55; nasal **y**, 71 c, 213 d; **y** as union-consonant, 258, 313 b, 844, 1112 e, 1151 d, 1230 e, 995 b; resolved to **i**, 55, 113 b, 129 c; cases of loss of **i** before, 233 a; **y** of sfx treated as **i**, 1203 a.
ya contracted to **i**, 252, 769, 784 b, 794 b.
ya as conj.-class-sign, 606, 759; as passive-sign, 606, 768, 998 a;

added to intens. stem, 1016; in caus. sign, 1055a; as denom. sign, 1055—67.
-ya (or yā) of gerund, 990, 992, 993; of gerundive, 962, 963, 1213.
-ya, prmy, 1187, 1213; ya-stems in compsn, 1272; scdry, 1210—12.
yakán, yákṛt, 398a, 432.
√yaj, euph., 219b, 784b; pres., 628; pf., 784b; aor., 834c, 839, 890a, 894d; inf., 968d; des., 1029c.
√yat, aor., 840b; pple, 956b.
yáthā, accent, 1101b; in compsn, 1313c—e.
√yam, pres., 608b, 631a, 747; pf., 790b; aor., 833, 836—9, 887a, 890a, 896, 897b, 911; fut., 935b; pple, 954d; inf., 968d; tvā-ger'd, 991b; caus., 1042g.
yama, 230a.
√yas, aor., 847; pple, 956b.
-yas for -īyas, 470a.
√yā, 102a; aor., 894c, 912, 914c.
-yā, 1213d.
-yin, see 1230e.
√yu unite, pres., 626a, 755; ya-ger'd, 992a.
√yu separate, pres., 608a, 645; aor., 838, 868a, 889, 894b; int., 1018a; caus., 1042e.
-yu, 1165; see 1178h—j.
√yuj, euph., 219a; pres., 758a; aor., 832, 834b, 836b, 837a, 839, 840b, 847, 887a; root-noun, 386.
√yudh, aor., 834d, 836b, 839, 887a.
√yup, int., 1017.
yúvan, dcln, 427.
yūṣá, yūṣán, 432.
yóṣan, dcln, 426b.

r, pron. etc., 51, 52; r and l, 53b; r and s as corresponding sonant and surd, 117b, 158a, 164; final, 144, 169; words ending in original r, 169a; combination as final rdcl, 165; as other, 178; avoidance of double, 179; s or r as final of certain forms, 169b; from s after a, 176c; s to ṣ after, 180ff.; but not before, 181a, b; changes succeeding n to ṇ, 189ff.; duplication of consonant after, 228; svarabhakti after, 230c.
r-endings in 3d pl., 613, 618, 629, 699b, 738a, 752b, 799, 813, 818a.

ra and rā as increments of ṛ, 241.
-ra, prmy, 1188; scdry, 474, 1226, 1242c.
√rakṣ, aor., 899d.
√raj or rañj, euph., 219a; pres., 746, 767; caus., 1042g.
√radh or randh, pf., 786a, 794h; aor., 847.
√ran, pf., 786a; aor., 899d.
√rabh, pf., 786a, 794h; aor., 834d, 897b; des., 1030.
√ram, aor., 911, 912; pple, 954d; inf., 968d; tvā-ger'd, 991b; caus., 1042g.
√rā give, pres., 660, 666, 672; aor., 839, 896.
√rā bark, pres., 761e.
√rāj, euph., 213b, 219b; pf., 794h.
√rādh, pf., 794h; aor., 836; des., 1030.
√ri or rī, caus., 1042l.
-ri, 1191.
√ric, pres., 761b; aor., 834c, 839, 847, 890.
√riç, aor., 916.
√riṣ, euph., 226f; aor., 847, 852a, 853, 870; caus., 1042b.
√rih, euph., 223b; int., 1017.
√rī, see ri.
√ru, pres., 626, 633, 755.
-ru, 1192.
√ruc, aor.. 834c, 837b, 840b, 847; desid., 1031b.
√ruj, euph., 219a; aor., 832; pple, 957c; tvā-ger'd, 991c.
√rud, pres., 631; aor., 847; tvā-ger'd, 991d.
√rudh, pres., 694a, 758a, 855a; pf., 801h; aor., 832, 834d, 847, 887a, 890a; inf., 963d; ya-ger'd, 992b.
√ruç, aor., 916; caus., 1042b.
rúçant, dcln, 450c.
√ruṣ, pple, 956b.
√ruh, euph., 223b, d; aor., 840b, 847, 853, 916, 920a, b; fut., 935d; inf., 968d; ya-ger'd, 992c; caus., 1042l.
repha, 18.
raí, dcln, 361b, f.
-rhi, advbl, 1103d.

l, pron. etc., 51, 53; l and r, 53b; l for r in certain verbal prefixes, 1087c; nasal l, 71b, c, 206, 213d; as final, 144; assim. to, 117g; of t, 162; of n, 206; of m, 213d;

asserted s to ṣ after, 180b; duplication of consonant after, 228a; svarabhakti after, 230d.
-la, prmy, 1189; scdry, 1227.
√lag, pple, 957c; tvā-ger'd, 991c; caus., 1042g.
√lajj, pres., 754.
√lap, pple, 956b; infin., 968c.
√labh, aor., 834d; fut., 935b; des., 1030.
√lal, caus., 1042g.
√likh, fut., 936b.
√lip, pres., 753, 758; aor., 834d; 847.
√liç, aor., 916.
√lih, euph., 223b; aor., 916, 920a.
√lī cling, aor., 911; pple, 957a; ya-ger'd, 992a; caus., 1042¹, m.
√lī totter, int., 1018a, 1022.
√lup, pres., 758, 761b; aor., 887a.
√lubh, pres., 761a.
√lū, pres., 728a; pple, 957a.

l, pron. etc., 5a, 54.

v, pron. etc., 51, 57, 58; relation to u-vowels, 57a; interchange with b, 50a; nasal v, 71c, 213d; resolved to u, 58a, 113b; cases of loss of u before, 233a; duplication of consonants after, 228a.
va, contracted to u, 252, 769, 784, 794b.
-va, prmy, 1190; scdry, 1228; advbl, 1102e, f.
√vakṣ, pple, 956b.
√vac, euph., 216¹; pres., 660; pf., 784, 789d; aor., 847, 853, 854a.
√vañc, euph., 216¹; pf., 786a.
-vat, advbl, 1107, 1233f; scdry, 383k. 1, 1245j.
√vad, 102a; pres., 738a; pf., 784; aor., 899d, 904d; pple, 956d; int., 1017; desid., 1031b.
√vadh, see badh.
√van, pf., 786a, 794f; aor., 839, 887b, 912, 914; pple, 955b; des., 1028g.
-van, prmy, 1169; scdry, 1234; van-stems in compsn, 1277, 1287b.
-vana, -vani, -vanu, 1170; -vana, 1245l.
-vane, infin. in, 970d, 974.
-vant, 517, 959, 1233; prmry, 1233g.
√vand, 102a.

√vap, pf., 784; fut., 935b; pple, 954b.
√vam, pres., 631a; pple, 955a; tvā-ger'd, 991b; caus., 1042g.
vam (from vṛ), 543a.
-vam, advbl, 1102b.
-vaya, 1228b.
-vara, 1171.
-varī, fem. to van, 1169, 1171, 1234a.
varga, 32.
√varṇ, so-called, 1056.
-vala, 1228b.
√vaç, pres., 638, 660; pf., 784, 786a.
√vas shine, euph., 167; pres., 608b, 753b; pf., 784; aor., 834b; pple, 956b, d.
√vas clothe, euph., 167; pres., 628, 631a, 638a; pf., 786a.
√vas dwell, euph., 167; pf., 784; aor., 840b, 883; fut., 935d; pple, 956b, d; inf., 968c; tvā-ger'd, 991c; in periphr. conj. 1070c; periphr. pf., 1071f.
-ves, 1173b: and see vāṅs.
√vah, euph., 137c, 223b, 224b; pf., 784; aor., 837b, 839, 840b, 890a; fut., 935d; pple, 954b; int., 1002g, 1017; at end of compds, 403.
√vā blow, aor., 912; pple, 957a.
√vā droop, pres., 761e.
√vā or vi weave, pres., 761f; pf., 784, 801b; fut., 935c; pple, 954e; inf., 968f; caus., 1042k.
√vāṅs (or -vas), of pples, 584c, 802—6, 1173; vāṅs-stems, dcln, 458ff.
vāghát, dcln, 444a.
√vāç, pf., 786a; aor., 861a.
ví, dcln, 343h.
-vi, 1193.
vikampana, 87d.
√vic, int., 1024.
√vij, euph., 219a; aor., 834c; fut., 935b, 936c; pple, 957c; int., 1017, 1024.
-vit, see 1193b.
√vid know, 102a; pres. 613, 618, 621a; pf., 790a, 803a; fut., 935b; inf., 968d; des., 1031b; periphr. pf., 1071f, 1073a; periphr. aor. √and pres., 1073b, c.
vid find, 102a; pres., 758; pf., 805b; aor., 847, 852a; pple, 957d.
vidhā, in compsn, 1302i.

-vin, 1232.
√vindh, pres., 758.
√vip, aor., 840b; caus., 1042b.
virāma, 11.
√viç, euph., 218a; pf., 803a, 805b; aor., 834b, 916, 920a.
víçva, dcln, 524; in compsn, 1251e, 1280c, 1298c.
√viṣ, euph., 225a, 226d, f; aor., 916; int., 1024.
visarga, visarjanīya, 67: and see h.
√vī, int., 1017, 1024a.
√vṛ cover, 102a; pres. (ūrṇu), 713; aor., 831a, 834a, 836b, 839, 840b, 900b; inf., 968d; int., 1002g.
√vṛ choose, 102a; euph., 102a, 242c; pf., 797c; aor., 837b, 840b: inf., 968d; caus., 1042e.
√vṛj, euph., 219a; pf., 786a, 803a; aor., 832, 834c, 836—9, 919, 920a; int., 1002g.
√vṛt, pres., 643c, 855a; pf., 786a; aor., 832, 834b, 836b, 839, 840a, 847, 904d; fut., 935b, 943a; inf., 968e; int., 1002g, 1003, 1017, 1023.
vṛtrá, 1185c.
vṛddhi, 27, 235ff.
√vṛdh, pf., 786a; aor., 847, 852a, b, 897b; fut., 943a; inf., 968e.
√vṛṣ, pf., 786a; aor., 847; inf., 968d.
vṛ́ṣan, dcln, 426b.
√vṛh, aor., 916, 920a.
voc, quasi-root, 854a.
-vya, 1228c.
√vyac, 1087f; pres., 682; pf., 785, 794b.
vyañjana, 31.
√vyath, pf., 785.
√vyadh, pres., 767; pf., 785, 794b; fut., 936b; pple, 954b; inf., 968f; caus., 1042g.
√vyay, pres., 761f.
√vyā or vī, pres., 761f; pf., 785, 794b, 801c; aor., 847; fut., 935c; pple, 954c; caus., 1042k.
√vraj, euph., 219b; aor., 899d.
√vraçc, euph., 221b; pple, 957c; tvā-ger'd, 991c.
√vlī, pres., 728b; pple, 957a; int., 1017; caus., 1042l.

ç, pron., etc., 59, 63, 64, 119; relation to ṣ, 63a; as final, 145;
in intrnl combn, 218; with preceding t or n, 203.
-ça, 1229.
√çaṅs, pf., 790c; ya-ger'd, 992c.
√çak, aor., 837a, 839, 847; pple; 956b; des., 1030, 1040.
çakán, çákṛt, 398, 432.
√çaṅk, aor., 904d.
√çad prevail, pf., 786.
√çad fall, pple, 957d.
√çap, aor., 233e; inf., 968c.
√çam labor, pres., 634, 763.
√çam be quiet, pres., 763; aor., 847; pple, 955a; caus., 1042g.
√çaç, pf., 794j.
√ças, aor., 839.
-ças, advbl, 1106.
√çā, pres., 660, 662, 753c, 761g; aor., 834a; pple, 954c; caus., 1042k.
√çās (or çiṣ), pres., 444, 639, 675; aor., 847, 852a, 854c; pple, 954e, 956b; inf., 968c; ya-ger'd, 992c; desid., 1031b; āçís from, 225a, 392b.
√çiñj, euph., 219a; pres., 628.
√çiṣ leave, euph., 226f; pres., 694a, 758a; aor., 847, 853.
√çiṣ, see çās.
√çī lie, pres., 628, 629; pf., 806a; fut., 935a; pple, 956c; ya-ger'd, 992c.
√çuc, pres., 631a; aor., 847; inf., 968d; tvā-ger'd, 991c; caus., 1042a.
√çudh, caus., 1042h.
√çubh, pres., 758; aor., 852a, b 840b; caus., 1042b.
√çuṣ, pres., 761a.
çúṣka as pple, 958.
√çū, see çvā.
√çūṣ, euph., 240b.
√çṛ crush, euph., 242b; pres., 731, pf., 793b; aor., 900a, 904b; pple, 955d, 957b; inf., 968d.
√ççand, int., 1002g.
√çnath, pres., 631a; aor., 867.
√çyā or çī, pres., 761e; pple, 954c 957a.
√çrath, pres., 732, 1066b, 758: pf., 794h; pple, 956d.
√çram, pres., 763; pf., 794h; aor., 847; pple, 955a; caus., 1042g.
√çrā, pres., 761e; pple, 954b; caus., 1042j; caus. aor., 861b, 1047.

√çri, aor., 831, 867, 868, 889a; inf., 968e; caus., 1042l.
√çriṣ, aor., 847.
√çrī, pple, 955d.
√çrīv, see srīv.
√çru, euph., 243; pres., 699b, 711; pf., 797c; aor., 831, 836, 838, 839, 853, 866, 867; desid., 1040; caus., 1042e.
√çruṣ, 102a.
√çliṣ, euph., 226d, f; pres., 761c; aor., 847, 916.
√çvañc, aor., 863a.
çván, dcln, 427.
√çvas, pres., 631; pple, 956b; caus., 1042g.
√çvā or çvi or çū, pf., 786c, 794b; aor., 847, 868, 897b; pple, 957a; inf., 968e.
√çvit, aor., 832, 890.

ṣ, pron. etc., 59, 61, 62, 120, 182; relation to ç, 63a; ordinary derivation, 46; exceptional occurrence, 182; as final, 145, 145b; s changed to, 180—8; recurrence avoided, 181c, 184e, 1028i; as root final, 182a, 184c, 225, 226; changes succeding n to ṇ, 189ff.; assim. of dental after, 197; from ç, 218.
-ṣaṇi, (or -sani), infin. in, 970h, 978, 1159c, 1160a.
ṣaṣ, euph., 146b, 199c.
-ṣe (or -se), infin. in, 970c, 973b.
√ṣṭhīv, euph., 240b; pres., 745g, 765; pf., 789c; pple, 955c; tvāger'd, 991d.
-ṣyāi (or -syāi), infin. in, 970g, 977.

s, pron. etc., 59, 60; s and r as corresponding surd and sonant, 117b, 158a, 164; s or r as final of certain forms, 169b; as final, 145, 169, 170a; combinations of final rdcl s, 145b, 166—8; of other, 170—7; exceptional cases, 171, 173; final as, 175, 176; ās, 177; s to ṣ, 180—8; exceptional cases, 181, 184e, 185c, d, 186a; t adds t before, 199e; final n adds (retains) s, 208, 209; s lost between mutes, 233c—f; in s- aor., 834, 881, 883; after a vowel, 233b; exceptional combination after such loss, 233f; s anomalously from final root-consonant,

406a; s before ām of gen. pl., 313a, 496c; in aor., 874ff.; in fut., 931ff.; in desid., 1027ff.
-s, advbl, 1105.
-sa, 1197.
sa-, 1121e; in compsn, 1288g 1304f—h, 1313f.
saṁvṛta a, 21.
sákhi, dcln, 343a—c.
sakthán, sákthi, 343l, 431.
√sagh, aor., 836b.
√sac, pres., 660; pf., 794f; aor., 840b; saçç from, 673, 675.
√saj or sañj, euph., 219a; pres., 746; pf., 794d, h, 801h; aor., 834c, 887a; inf., 968f; des., 1028i; caus., 1042h.
√sad, pres., 748; aor., 847, 852a, 853, 899d; fut., 935b, 936c; pple, 957d; inf., 968d.
√san or sā, pf., 804; aor., 847, 853, 899d; pple, 955b; int., 1002g; des., 1028g, i, 1032a.
-sani, infin. in, see -ṣaṇi.
saṁdhi, 109.
saṁdhyakṣara, 28a, 30.
sannatara, 90c.
√sabhāg, so-called, 104b, 1067.
samānākṣara, 30.
samprasāraṇa, 252a.
samrāj etc., 213b.
-sara, 1201a.
sarágh or saráḍ, 389b.
sárva, dcln, 524; in compsn, 1251e, 1298c.
√saçç, pres., 444, 673, 675.
sás, euph., 176a, b.
-sas, 1152.
√sah, euph., 186a, 223b, 224b; pres., 628; pf., 786a, 790b, 803a; aor., 837, 838, 887a, 897a, b, 899d; fut., 935d; pple, 955e; inf., 968d; des., 1030; at end of cmpds, 405.
sahá, in cmpsn, 1304f, g.
√sā or si bind, pres., 753c; aor., 830, 834a, 839, 868a, 894c; fut., 935a, 936b; pple, 954c; inf., 968f; ya-ger'd, 992a; caus., 1042k.
-sāt, advbl, 1108.
√sādh, aor., 861a.
-sāna, ppial words in, 897b, 1175.
√sāntv, so-called, 104b.
√si, see sā.
√sic, pres., 758; aor., 847; tvāger'd, 991d; caus., 1042h.

√**sidh** *repel*, fut., 935 b.
√**sīv**, pres., 761 c, 765; pple, 955 c; des., 1028 h, i.
√**su** *press out*, pres., 699 b; aor., 839, 840 b, 867; fut. 935 a; **ya**-ger'd, 992 a.
su-, 1121 h, i; in compsn, 1284 a, b, 1288, 1304 c, d.
-su, see 1178 f.
√**subh**, pres., 758.
√**sū** or **su**, pres., 626, 628, 755; pf., 789 a; aor., 868 a; fut., 935 a, 936 b, 939 b; inf. 968 d, e.
√**sūc**, aor., 861.
√**sūd**, aor., 871.
√**sṛ**, pf., 797 c, 806 a; aor., 847; caus., 1042 e.
√**sṛj**, euph., 216 l, 219 b, c; aor., 834 b, c, 840 b, 890; fut., 936 d.
√**sṛp**, euph., 151 d; pf., 790 c; aor., 834 d, 847; fut., 935 b, 936 d; inf., 968 e; int., 1002 g.
-se, infin. in, see **-ṣe**.
soṣman, 37 d.
sk, original of **ch**, 42.
√**skand**, aor., 833, 890 b; pple, 957 d; **ya**-ger'd, 992 b; int., 1002 g, h.
√**skabh** or **skambh**, pres., 730, 732, 1066 b; pf., 786 a, 790 b, 794 d.
√**sku**, pres., 626 a; int., 1017.
√**stan**, pres., 631 a, aor., 899 d.
√**stabh** or **stambh**, euph., 233 c; pres., 730, 732, 1066 b; pf., 794 d; pple, 956 b.
-stāt for **-tāt**, advbl, 1100 b.
√**stigh**, desid., 1031 b.
√**stu**, pres., 626, 633; pf., 797 c; aor., 866, 894 b, d; fut., 935 a; **ya**-ger'd, 992 a; desid., 1028 i; caus., 1042 e.
√**stṛ**, euph., 242 c; pf., 801 f, 806 a; aor., 831, 834 a, 885, 900 a; pple, 957 b; inf., 968 d; **ya**-ger'd, 992 a.
stṛ́, dcln, 371 k.
√**stṛh**, aor., 916.
√**styā**, pres., 761 c; pple, 957 a.
strī, dcln, 366, 367 c.
√**sthā**, euph., 233 c; pres., 671, 749 a; aor., 830, 834 a, 836, 837, 840 a, 847, 884, 894 c; pple, 954 c; inf., 968 f; caus. aor., 861 b, 1047; in ppial periphr. phrases, 1075 c.
-sna, 1195.
√**snā**, caus., 1042 j.
√**snih**, euph., 223 a, c.
√**snu**, pres., 626 a.
-snu, 1194.
sparça, 31, 32.
√**spaç**, aor., 864 c.
√**spṛ**, aor., 831, 836 b, 839.
√**spṛdh**, euph., 242 d; aor., 834 b, 840 b.
√**spṛç**, euph., 218 a; aor., 916, 920 a; fut., 936 d.
√**spṛh**, euph., 223 b, d; caus., 1042 d.
√**sphā**, pple, 954 c; caus., 1042 m.
√**sphuṭ**, fut., 936 b.
√**sphṛ**, pres., 756; **tvā**-ger'd, 991 d; caus., 1042 b.
sphoṭana, 230 e.
sma, in pronom'l dcln, 493, 496 a, 503.
sma, pres. in past sense with, 778 b, c.
√**smi**, **tvā**-ger'd, 991 d; caus., 1042 l; periphr. pf., 1071 f.
√**smṛ**, pass., 770 c; **tvā**-ger'd, 991 d; caus., 1042 e.
sya as denom. sign, 1064.
√**syand**, pf., 785 a; aor., 861 a, 890 b; fut., 943 a; pple, 957 d; **tvā**-ger'd, 991 d; int., 1002 g.
√**syam**, pf., 794 h.
syás, euph., 176 a.
-syāi, infin. in, see **-ṣyāi**.
sráj, euph., 219 a.
√**sras** or **sraṅs**, euph., 168; pf., 790 c; aor., 833, 847; **ya**-ger'd, 992 b.
√**sridh**, aor., 847, 852 b.
√**srīv** (or **çrīv**), euph., 240 b; pres., 765; caus., 1042 b.
√**sru**, pf., 797 c; aor., 868; caus., 1042 e.
sva, 513 b, 516 c; dcln, 525 c.
√**svaj**, euph., 219 a; pres., 746; pf., 794 h; aor., 863 a; **tvā**-ger'd, 991 c.
svátavas, euph., 168 a, 415 b.
√**svad**, pple, 954 f.
√**svan**, pf., 794 h; aor., 899 d; int., 1002 g.
√**svap**, pres., 631; pf., 785 b, 794 b; aor., 867; fut., 935 b; pple, 954 b; des., 1028 h; caus., 1042 g.
svayam, in compsn, 1284 b.
√**svar**, aor., 890 a, 899 d.
svàr, dcln, 388.
svara, 30, 81.
svarabhakti, 230 c—e.
svarita, 81.
svávas, euph., 168 a, 415 b
√**svid**, pple, 957 d.

h, pron. etc., 59, 65, 66, 119; from **dh** and **bh,** 223 g; as final, 147; compensating aspiration of initial, 147, 155 b; with following **t** or **th,** 160 a; with preceding final mute, 163; **m** before **h** and another cons., 213 g; reversion to **gh,** 214 ff., 222; in inflection, 402, 637; in pf., 787; in intens., 1002 i; in desid., 1028 f; internal combn, 222—4; anomalously changed to a sibilant, 150 f; to **d,** 404; duplication of a cons. after, 228 a; **nāsikya** added after, 230 b; loss before **hi,** 1011 a.
-ha, advbl, 1100 a, 1104 b.
√**had,** pple, 957 d.
√**han,** euph., 192 b, 216 l, 402, 637, 787; pres., 637, 673, 709; pf., 794 e, 805 a; aor., 899 d; fut., 935 b, 943 a; pass., 998 f; pple, 954 d; inf., 968 d; int., 1002 g, h, i, 1003; des., 1028 e, f; caus., 1042 m; root-noun, 383 h, 402.
hánta, accent of verb with, 598 a.
√**has,** **jakṣ** from, 640.
√**hā** *move,* pres., 660, 664; des., 1028 d; caus., 1042 d.
√**hā** *leave,* pres., 665, 761 b; aor., 830, 889, 912; fut., 936 c; pple, 957 a; inf., 968 f; caus. aor., 861 b, 1047.
√**hās,** 102 a, 912.
√**hi,** euph., 192 c, 216 l, 674, 787; pres., 699 b, 716 a; aor., 831, 839, 840 b, 847, 889 a, 894 d; des., 1028 f.
hí, 595 e, 1122 b.
-hi, advbl, 1100 c.
√**hiṅs,** euph., 183 a; pres., 687, 696; des., 1031 b.
√**hinv,** 716 a.
√**hīḍ,** euph., 240 b; pf., 786 b; caus., 1042 b.
√**hu,** pres., 645, 647 c, 652; periphr. pf. etc., 1071 f, 1073 c.
√**hū** or **hvā,** pres., 761 f, 755; pf., 794 b; aor., 834 a, 847, 887 c, 912; fut., 935 c; inf., 968 f; caus., 1042 k; periphr. pf., 1071 f.
√**hṛ** *seize,* aor., 834 a, 890 a; inf., 968 d; caus., 1042 e.
√**hṛd, hṛdaya,** 397.
√**hṛṣ,** aor., 847; pple, 956 b.
√**hnu,** pres., 626 a.
√**hras,** pple, 956 b.
√**hrī,** pres., 645; aor., 840 b; pple, 957 a; caus., 1042 l; periphr. pf., 1071 f.
√**hvā,** see **hū.**
√**hvṛ** or **hvar,** euph., 242 c; pres., 652; aor., 863 a, 890; pple, 955 e.

GENERAL INDEX.

a-aorist (simple aorist, 2), 824, 846—54: in the later language, 846; roots forming it in the older language, 847; inflection, 848; modes, 849—51; participles, 852; irregularities, 853, 854.

a-class (first, bhū-class) of verbs, 606, 734—50: formation of stem, 734; inflection, 735—43; roots of the class, 744; irregularities, 745—50.

á-class or accented a-class (sixth, tud-class) of verbs, 606, 751—8: formation of stem, 751; inflection, 752; roots of the class, 753, 754; irregularities, 755—8.

a-conjugation — see conjugations.

a- or ā-declension, transference of cons.-stems to, 399, 415a, 429a, 437, 441b; 1148i, 1149a, 1166c, 1209; 1315.

a-stems (tense-stems), uniform inflection of, 733a.

abbreviation of consonant-groups, 231—3.

ablative case, uses of, 289—93; ablative of comparison, 292b; with prepositions, 293, 1128; used adverbially, 1114; abl. infinitive, 983; abl. by attraction with infin., 983b; abl. use of adverbs in tas, 1098d; abl. as prior member of compound, 1250f.

absolute use of instrumental, 281g; of genitive, 300b; of locative, 303b–d; of gerund, 994e.

absolutive — see gerund.

abstract nouns, secondary derivation of, 1206, 1236—40.

accent, general, 80—97: its varieties, 80–6; accentuated texts, 87; modes of designating, 87, 88; illustration of RV. method, pp. 518–9; over-refinements of Hindu theory, 90; modern delivery of ancient accented texts, 91; no sentence accent, 92; accentless words, 93; words doubly accented, 94, 1255, 1267d; accent of protracted syllable, 78a; freedom of place of accent, 95; — changes of accent in vowel combination, 128, 130, 135a; — accent in declension, 314—20; of vocative, 92a, 314; change of accent in monosyllabic etc. declension, 316—9; in numeral, 482g, 483a—c; of fractionals, 488a; of case-forms used as adverbs, 1111g, 1112e, 1114d; different accent of action-nouns and agent-nouns, 1144a; of determinative and possessive compounds, 1295; — accent of personal endings, 552—4; in relation to strong and weak forms, 556; of personal verb-forms in the sentence, 92b, 591—8; of periphrastic formations, 945, 1073e; of compounded verb-forms, 1082—5; — accent in primary derivation, 1144; in secondary, 1205; in composition, 1251; — ordinary accentuation of Skt. words by Western scholars, 96.

accusative case, uses of, 269—77: with verbs, 270, 274; with nouns and adjectives, 271, 272; with prepositions, 273, 1129; with verbs of motion and address etc., 274; cognate, 275; adverbial, 276, 1111; double, 277; accus. infinitive, 981, 986—8; gerund, 995; accus. as prior member of compound, 1250a.

action-nouns and agent-nouns, chief classes of primary derivatives, 1145, 1146.

active voice, in verbs, 528, 529.
acute (**udātta**) accent, 81.
ad-class of verbs — see root-class.
adjective, its distinction from noun, 322; from pple, 967; formation of compound adj., 323—5, 1292 ff.; inflection of adj., 321—465; comparison, 466—74; adj. pronominally inflected, 522—6.
adjective compounds, secondary, 1247 g, 1292—1313; of other than possessive value, 1294, 1309, 1310; adj. copulative compounds, 1257.
adverbs, 1097—1122: adv. by derivation, 1097—1109; case-forms used as adv., 1110—17; adverbial compounds, 1111 d, 1313; verbal prefixes etc. as adv., 1118—20; inseparable prefixes, 1121; other miscellaneous adv., 1122; adv. used prepositionally, 1123 ff.; adv. copulative compounds, 1259; forms of comparison, 473 b.
agent-nouns — see action-nouns.
aggregative compounds — see copulative compounds.
alphabets used for writing Sanskrit, 1; older Indian, 2; the Devanāgarī alph., 1—17; varieties of writing and of type for, 3, pp. 516—7; characters and transliteration, 5; arrangement, 7; theory of use, 8, 9; native mode of writing, 9 a, b; modifications of this in Western practice, 9 c—e; vowel-writing, 10; consonant combinations, 12—15; other signs, 11, 16; numeral figures, 17; names of characters, 18; signs and transliteration of **anusvāra,** 73.
alphabet, spoken — see system of sounds.
alterant vowels, changing following **s** to **ṣ**, 180.
analysis of language into its elements, 98, 99; anal. of compound words, 1248.
antithetical construction, its influence on accent of verb, 596, 597.
anusvāra, its pronunciation etc., 70—2; signs and transliteration, 73, 16 b: see also **ṅ, ṁ.**
aorist tense, 532; its uses, 926—30; in prohibitive expression, 579; — aor. system, 535, 824—930: classification of forms of aor., 824; character and occurrence, 825—7; variety from same root, 827 b, c; simple aor., 824, 828: 1. root-aor., 829—41; passive aor. 3d. sing., 842—5; 2. **a**-aor., 846—54; 3. reduplicated or causative aor., 856—73; sibilant-aor., 874—920: 4. **s**-aor., 878—897; 5. **iṣ**-aor., 898—910; 6. **siṣ**-aor., 911—15; 7. **sa**-aor., 916—20; aor. optative or precative of later language, 921—5; aor. in secondary conjugation, 1019, 1035, 1046—8, 1068; periphrastic aor., 1073 b; —**s**-aor. stem in derivation, 1140 c.
appositional compounds, 1280 d; appos. possessive compounds, 1302.
ar or **ṛ** in root and stem forms, 104 e, 237.
article, indefinite, represented later by **eka,** 482 c.
aspirate mutes, phonetic character etc. of, 37, 38; their deaspiration, 114, 153—5; restoration of lost aspiration to, 141 a, 147, 155; not before impv. ending **dhi,** 155 f; derivation of **h** from, 66; sonant aspirate with following **t, th,** 160; non-aspirate for aspirate in reduplication, 590 a: — and see the different letters.
aspiration (**h**), its pronunciation etc., 59, 65, 66: — and see **h.**
asseverative particles, 1122 a, b.
assimilation in euphonic combination, 115—20; with or without change of articulate position, 116; surd and sonant, 117, 156—64; nasal, 117 g, 198 b, 199 c; **l,** 117 g, 206; dental to lingual and palatal, 118; other cases, 118—20.
augment, 585—7; **ā** as augment, 585 a; omission, 587; irreg. combination with initial vowel of root, 136 a; irregularly placed, 1087 c, f; uses of augmentless preterit persons, 563, 587; with **mā** prohibitive, 579.
avyayībhāva compounds, 1313.

bahuvrīhi compounds — see possessive compounds.
benedictive — see precative.
bhū-class of verbs — see **a**-class.

cardinal numerals, 475; their combinations, 476—81; inflection, 482

—5; construction, 486; derivatives, 487—9.
case-endings — see endings of declension.
case-forms, prolongation of final vowel of, 248 b; used as adverbs, 1110—17; change of accent in such, 1111 g, 1112 e, 1114 d; their prepositional uses, 1125 d; derivatives from case-forms, 1202 b; case-forms in composition, 1250.
cases, 266; their order of arrangement, 266 a; uses, 267—305: — and see the different cases.
causative conjugation, 540, 607, 775, 856 ff., 1041—52; relation to so-called tenth or **cur**-class, 607, 1041 b; to denominative, 1041 c, 1056; formation of stem, 1041, 1042; inflection, present-system, 775, 1043; other older forms, 1044; perfect, 1045; attached reduplicated aorist, 1046, 1047, 856 ff.; other aorist forms, 1048, 1049; future etc., 1050; verbal nouns and adjectives, 1051; derivative or tertiary conjugations from caus. stem, 1052; caus. from intens., 1025; from desid., 1039; declinable stems from caus. stem, 1140 b; double object with causatives, 277 a, 282 b.
cerebral mutes, 33, 45.
changeable or variable **ṛ** of roots — see variable.
circumflex (**svarita**) accent, 81—6, 90 b; independent, 81—4; its varieties, 84; enclitic, 85; their difference, 86; designation, 87—9; occurrence from vowel combinations, 128, 130, 135.
classes or series of mutes, 32 ff.
classes of verbs — see conjugation-classes.
clauses, simplicity of combination of, 1131 a; dependent clauses, mode in, 581, 950; accent of verb in, 595.
collective singular form of copulative compounds, 1253 c; in Veda, 1255 e, 1256 b.
combination of elements, 100, 101: euphonic rules for, 109—260; distinction of internal and external, 109—12; general arrangement of rules, 124; order of comb. of three successive vowels, 127 b.
comparison of adjectives etc., 466—74; primary, in **īyas** and **iṣṭha**, 467—70, 1184; secondary, in **tara** and **tama**, 471—3, 1242 a, b; in **ra** and **ma**, 474, 1242 c; inflection of comparatives in **yas**, 463—5; comp. of nouns, pronouns, prepositions, 473, 474, 520, 1119; of verbs, 473 c; double comparison, 473 d; particles of comp., 1101 b, 1102 e, 1107, 1122 g, h.
comparison or likeness, descriptive compounds of, 1291 a.
compensatory vowel-lengthening, 246.
composition of stems — see compound stems.
compound conjugation, 540 a, 1076—95: roots with verbal prefixes and like elements, 1076—89; accent of comp. forms, 1082—6; irregularities, 1087; roots with inseparable prefixes, 1089, 1121 b, g, i; with noun and adjective stems, 1090—5.
compound stems, formation of, 101, 1246—1316: difference of earlier and later language as to composition, 1246 a; classification of compounds, 1247; their analysis, 1248; rules of phonetic combination, 1249; case-forms as prior member, 1250; accent, 1251; copulative comp., 1252—61; determinative: dependent, 1262—78; descriptive, 1279—91; secondary adjective: possessive, 1292—1308; participial, 1309; prepositional, 1310; adjective comp. as nouns and as adverbs, 1311—3; anomalous comp., 1314; stem-finals altered in comp., 1315; loose construction with comp., 1316.
conditional tense, 532, 940, 941; its uses, 950; conditional uses of optative and subjunctive, 581 b, e, f.
conjugation, verbal inflection, 527—1095; general, 527—98: voice, 528—31; tenses and their uses, 592, 776—9, 821—3, 926—30, 948—50; modes and their uses, 533, 557—82, 921—5; tense-systems, 535; present-system, 535, 599—779; perfect-system, 780—823; aorist-systems, 824—930; future-systems, 931—50; number and person, 536; personal endings, 541—56; verbal adjectives and nouns, 537—9, 951—95; secondary conjugations, 540, 996—1068; peri-

phrastic and compound conjugation, 540 a, 1069—95; examples of conjugation in synopsis, p. 520.
conjugation-classes, on what founded, 601; their characters, 602—10.
conjugations, first or non-**a**- and second or **a**-conjugation, 601—8, 733; transfers from the former to the latter, 625 a, 631 a, 665 a, 670—4, 694 a, 716, 731, 896.
conjunctions, 1131—3.
consonants, pronunciation etc., 31—75: mutes, 32—50; semivowels, 51—8; spirants, 59—66; **visarga** and **anusvāra** etc., 67—73; quantity, 76; cons. allowed as finals, 122, 139—52; occurring at end of stems and endings, 139 a: — and see the different classes and letters.
consonant-groups, how written in **devanāgarī**, 9, 12—5; their extension and abbreviation, 121, 227—33.
consonantal stems, declension of, 377—465; their classification, 382.
contemptuous prefix, 506, 1121 e; do. suffix, 521, 1222 d.
copulative compounds, 1247 a—c, 1252—61; of nouns, 1253—6; adjectives, 1257; adverbs, 1259; numerals, 1261; copulatives in later language, 1253, 1254; in Rig-Veda, 1255; in Atharva-Veda, 1256; accent, 1258; possessives from copulatives, 1293 b.
cur-class of verbs, 607, 775, 1041 b, 1056: — and see causative conjugation.

dative case, uses of, 285—8; dat. infinitive, 982, 986; dat. used adverbially, 1113; dat. by attraction with infin., 982 a; dat. as prior member of compound, 1250 c.
deaspiration of aspirate mutes, 114, 153—5; consequent re-aspiration of initial, 141 a, 147, 155.
declension, in general, 261—320: gender, 263; number, 264, 265; case, 266; uses of the cases, 267—305; endings of decl., 306—10; variation of stem and insertions, 311—3; accent, 314—20; — decl. of nouns and adjectives, 321—465: classification, 321 b, c; I. **a**-stems, 326—34; II. **i**-and **u**-stems, 335—46; III. **ā**-, **ī**-, and **ū** (and diphthongal) stems, 347—68; IV. **ṛ**-stems, 369—76; V. consonant-stems, 377—465: A. root-stems etc., 383—410; B. derivative stems in **as, is, us,** 411—9; C. in **an,** 420—37; D. in **in,** 438—41; E. in **ant,** 442—57; F. in **vāṅs,** 458—62; G. in **yas,** 463—5; — decl. of numerals, 482—5; of pronouns, 491—521; of adjectives inflected pronominally, 522—6.
declinable stems, composition of, with verbs, 1090—5; derivation of — see derivation.
decompound compounds and their analysis, 1248.
decrement and increment of elements, 123, 234 ff.
demonstrative pronouns, 495—503.
denominative conjugation, 540 a, 1053—68: formation without sign, 1054; with sign **ya,** from stems of various final, 1055—64; their occurrence, 1057; meaning, 1058; relation of **aya**- and **āya**-stems, 1059 c; relation to causative, 1041 c, 1056, 1067; with signs **sya, kāmya, āpaya,** 1064, 1065; with **āya,** beside **nā**-class verbs etc., 732, 1066; from other stems, 1066 a, c; inflection, 1068; declinable stems from denom. stem, 1068 b, 1149 d, 1178 h, i, 1180 d.
dental series of mutes (**t, th, d, dh, n**), pronunciation etc., 33, 47, 48; peculiar quality of Skt. dentals, 47 a; dent. character of **ḷ**, 25; of **l**, 51, 53; of **s**, 60; assimilation of dent. to palatals and linguals, 118, 196—203, 205; dent. sibilant and nasal converted to lingual, 180—95; anomalous conversions to guttural and lingual, 151 a, b; of guttural, palatal, and labial to dental, 151 c, e: — and see the different letters.
dependent clause, accent of verb in, 595.
dependent compounds, 1247 d—f, 1263, 1264—78; noun, 1264; adjective, 1265; their varieties, 1266—78: with ordinary noun or adjective as final member, 1267, 1268; with root-stem, 1269; derivative in **a**, 1270; **ana,** 1271; **ya,** 1272; participle in **ta** or **na,** 1273; **ti,**

1274; **in,** 1275; **i,** 1276; **van, man,** etc., 1277, 1278; dep. comp. in possessive use, 1296.
derivation of adverbs, 1097—1109; of declinable stems, 1136—1245: in general, 1136—42; primary, 1143—1201; secondary, 1202—45.
derivative or secondary conjugation — see secondary.
descent, adjectives and nouns indicating, 1206 a.
descriptive compounds, 1247 d—f, 1263, 1279—91; of ordinary adjective with noun, 1280; of appositional noun with noun, 1280 d; with participle as final member, 1283, 1284; with gerundive, 1285; with root-stem, 1286; with other verbal derivatives, 1287; with inseparable prefix as prior member, 1288; with verbal prefix etc., 1289; with other adverbial words, 1290; special cases, 1291; descr. comp. in possessive use, 1297 ff.
desiderative conjugation, 540, 1026—40; meaning, 1026, 1040; used in future sense, 1040 a; formation of stem, 1027—9; abbreviated stems, 1030; use of union-vowel **i,** 1031; inflection, present-system, 1032; other forms, 1033—6; derivative or tertiary conjugations from desid. stem, 1039; desid. from causative stem, 1052 c; declinable stems from desid. stem, 1035, 1036, 1140 b, 1149 d, 1159 b, 1161 d, 1178 g; desid. root-stems, 392 d; future in desid. sense, 949; desid. in future sense, 1040 a.
determinative compounds, 1247 d—f, 1262—91; dependent, 1264—78; descriptive, 1279—91; in possessive adjective use, 1293 ff.
devatā-dvandva compounds, 1251 a, 1255.
diminutives, secondary derivation of, 1206 b, 1222 d, 1243.
diphthongs (**e, āi, o, āu**), mode of writing with consonants, 10 g, h; pronunciation etc., 27—30; protraction of, 78 c; euphonic combination as finals, 131—5: — and see the different letters.
diphthongal stems, declension of, 360, 361.
div- or **dīv-**class of verbs — see **ya-**class.
double stems, present, 815; aorist, 894 d, 897 b.
doubling of aspirate mutes, 154; of a final nasal, 210; of **ch,** 227; of first consonant of a group, 229; of a consonant after **r** (and **h, l, v**), 228.
dual number, its use, 265; its forms in declension, 308; in personal pronoun, 492 b.
dual finals **e, ī, ū** uncombinable, 138 a, g.
dvandva compounds — see copulative.
dvigu compounds, 1312.

eighth class of verbs — see **u-**class.
elision of initial **a,** 135; how marked, 16; its infrequency in Veda, 135 c; elision of initial **ā,** 135 d; of final **a** or **ā,** 137 b.
emphasis, accent of verb for, 598.
emphatic pronoun, 513.
enclitic or dependent circumflex, 85, 86.
endings, of inflection and derivation, 98—100; of declension, 306—10; of singular, 307; dual, 308; plural, 309; normal scheme, 310; end. of **a-**stems, 327—9; of **i-**and **u-**stems, 336—8; of radical **ā-, ī-,ū-**stems, 349; of derivative do., 363; of **ṛ-**stems, 371; of personal pronouns, 492, 493; of general pronominal declension, 496; — end. of conjugation, 523, 541—69; of 1st sing., 543; 2d, 544; 3d, 545; of 1st du., 546; 2d and 3d, 547; of 1st pl., 548; 2d, 549; 3d, 550; normal schemes, 553; accent, 552—4; end. of 2d and 3d sing. taking the place of root-final, 555 a; union-vowels, 555 b, c; end. of subjunctive combined with mode-sign, 560—2; of optative, 566; of precative, 568; **tāt** of imperative, 570; — end. of derivation — see suffixes.
euphonic combination of elements, 100, 101; rules respecting it, 109—226.
exclamatory pronoun, 507; exclam. prefix from interrogative pronoun, 506, 1121 e.
extension of cons.-groups, 227—30.
external and internal combination, distinction of, 109—12; cases of

external comb. in declension, 111 a, b; in derivation, 111 c, d, 1203 e.

feminine stems: to ā-stems, 332, 334 b; to i- and u-stems, 344—6; to ṛ-stems, 376 a; to cons.-stems, 378 a, 401 c, 435, 436, 449, 452 b, 459, 463 d; fem. in ī from ya-stems, 1210 c; fem. stems in composition, 1250 h.
fifth class of verbs — see nu-class.
finals, permitted, 122, 139—52; most usual, 149; only one final consonant allowed, 150; exceptions, 150 b, c; anomalous changes of final mutes, 151; final consonants of stems and endings, 139 a.
final clauses, modes used in, 581 c, d.
first class of verbs — see a-class.
first or non-a-conjugation of verbs, its characteristics, 604.
forms, stronger and weaker, of roots and stems, 104 e, 105, 106; — and see variation of stem.
fourth class of verbs — see ya-class.
fractional use of ordinals, 488.
frequentative conjugation — see intensive.
future passive participles — see gerundives.
future tenses, 532; their uses, 948, 949; fut. systems, 535, 931—50; s-future and conditional, 932—41; periphrastic future, 942—7; future use of pres., 777; of desid., 1040 a; desid. use of fut., 948 b; fut. participial phrases, 1075 d.

gender in declension, 262, 263.
general and special tenses, 599 a.
genitive case, uses of, 294—300: with adj., 296; with verb, 297, 298; with prepositions, 299 a, 1130; with adverbs, 299 b; gen. absolute, 300 b; loss of accent of gen. with vocative, 314 d, e; gen. infinitive, 984; gen. used adverbially, 300 a, 1115; as prior member of compound, 1250 e.
gerunds, 539, 989—95; their uses, 989, 994; ger. in tvā, 990, 991, 993; in ya or tya, 990, 992, 993; in tvāya and tvī, 993 b; in tvānam and tvīnam, 993 c; adverbial gerund in am, 995.
gerundives, or future passive participles, 961—6, 1212 i, 1213, 1216—8; ger. in ya, 962—3, 1213; in tavya, 962, 964, 1212 i; in anīya, 962, 965, 1215 b; in tva, 966 a, 1209 h; in enya, 966 b, 1217; in āyya, 966 c, 1218; in elima, 966 d, 1201 a; ger. in composition, 1285.
grave (anudātta) accent, 81.
guṇa-strengthening, character and occurrence of, 27, 235—43, and *passim*; in primary derivation, 1143 a; in secondary, 1203 a, 1204 g.
guttural series of mutes (k, kh, g, gh, ṅ), pronunciation etc., 33, 39—41, 180 a; asserted gutt. character of a, 20 a; of h, 65 a; palatals from original gutt., 41—3; ç and h do., 64, 66; reversion of palatals etc. to gutt. form, 43, 64, 142, 145, 147, 214—26: — and see the different letters.

heavy and light syllables, 79.
hiatus, avoidance of, 113, 125—38; not avoided in Veda, 113 b, 125 c, 129 e; its occurrence as result of euphonic processes, 132—4, 175 b, d, 177.
hu-class of verbs — see reduplicating class.

imperative mode, 533, 569, 572, 575, 578; scheme of its endings, 553 d; its 1st persons old subjunctive, 533, 574, 578; impv. form in tāt and its uses, 570, 571; with mā prohibitive, 579 c; Vedic 2d sing. in si, 624; impv. use of infinitives, 982 d.
imperfect, tense, 532, 599; its use, 779.
imperfect time, no real designation of 532 a.
increment and decrement of elements, 123, 234 ff.
indeclinables, 98 a, 1096—1135: adverbs, 1097—1122; prepositions, 1123—30; conjunctions, 1131—3; interjections, 1134, 1135; derivative stems from indeclinables, 1202 b, 1245; compounds with indecl. as final member, 1314 a, f.
indefinite pronouns, 513 c; indef. use of interrogative and relative pronouns, 507, 511.

infinitives, 538, 968—88; later, 968, 987; earlier, 969—79; uses, 980—8; relation to ordinary verbal nouns, 969, 970 l.
inseparable prefixes, 1121; in descriptive composition, 1283 ff., 1288; in possessive, 1304.
insertions between stem and ending in declension, 313.
instrumental case, uses of, 278—84; of separation, 283 a; with prepositions, 284, 1127; gerundial, 989; used adverbially, 1112; as prior member of compound, 1250 b.
intensive (or frequentative) conjugation, 540, 1000—25; character and occurrence, 1000, 1001; reduplication, 1002, 1003; inflection, present-system, 1004—17; derivative middle inflection, 1016, 1017; forms outside present-system, 1018, 1019, 1025; doubtful intens. formations, 1020—4; derivative or tertiary conjugations from intens. stem, 1025.
interjections, 1134, 1135; their final vowel uncombinable, 138 f.
internal and external combination, distinction of, 109—12.
internal change, question of derivation by, 1208 i.
interrogative particles, 1122 f.
interrogative pronoun, 504—7; its indefinite use, 507; exclamatory prefix from it, 506, 1121 j.
inverted compounds, 1291 c, 1314 d.
iṣ-aorist, 824, 898—910: formation of stem, 898—900; inflection, 901, 902; roots making it, 903; irregularities, 904; modes, 905—8; from secondary conjugations, 1019, 1035, 1048, 1068 a.

jihvāmūlīya-spirant, 69, 170 d.

karmadhāraya compounds — see descriptive compounds.
krī-class of verbs — see **nā**-class.

labial series of mutes (**p, ph, b, bh, m**), pronunciation etc., 33, 49, 50; lab. character of **u, ū**, 20; of **v**, 51, 57, 58; anomalous conversion of labial to guttural, 151 d; to dental, 151 e: — and see the different letters.
lengthening of vowels in formation and inflection, 244—6; of final vowel in composition, 247, 1087 b; in the sentence in Veda, 248.
light and heavy syllables, 79.
lightening of **a** or **ā** to an **i**- or **u**-vowel, 249 ff.
lingual series of mutes (**ṭ, ṭh, ḍ, ḍh, ṇ**), pronunciation etc., 33, 45, 46; non-originality and ordinary derivation, 46; ling. character of **ṛ**, 25; of **r**, 51, 52; ling. **l**, 5 a, 54; ling. character of **ṣ**, 61; assimilation of dentals to ling., 118, 196 ff.; lingualization of **s** and **n**, 180—95: — and see the different letters.
locative case, uses of, 301—5; loc. absolute, 303 b—d; of goal of motion or action, 301 e, 304; with prepositions, 305, 1126; used adverbially, 303 e, 1116; loc. infinitive, 985; loc. use of adverbs in **tra**, 1099; in **ha**, 1100 a; in **dā**, 1103 b; loc. as prior member of compound, 1250 d.
long and short quantity, 76—9.

manner, particles of, 1101, 1102, 1107, 1122 k.
manuscripts, native Sanskrit, mode of writing in, 9 a, b.
middle stem-form in declension, 311.
middle voice, 528—30; its use as passive, 531, 998 c, d.
mode in verbal inflection, 533; subjunctive, 557—63; optative, 564—8; imperative, 569—71; uses of the modes, 572—82.
multiplicative numeral adverbs, 489 a, 1104—6.
mutes, series of, their pronunciation etc., 32—50: classification, 32—8; guttural series, 39—41; palatal, 42—4; lingual, 45, 46; dental, 47, 48; labial, 49, 50; assimilation, 117 a, b; mutes permitted as finals, 141—3; anomalous conversions from one series to another, 151: — and see the different series.

nā-class (ninth, **krī**-class) of verbs, 603, 717—32: formation of stem, 717; inflection, 718—26; roots of the class, 727; irregularities, 728—32; accompanying denominative in **āya**, 732, 1066 b.

nasal assimilation, 117 c, f, g, 161, 198 b, 199 c.
nasal class (seventh, **rudh**-class) of verbs, 603, 683—96: formation of stem, 683; inflection, 684—92; roots of the class, 694; irregularities, 693—6.
nasal increment in strong forms, 255, 386.
nasal mutes (ṅ, ñ, ṇ, n, m), 34, 36; their occurence as finals, 143; duplication, 210; assimilation of preceding mute, 161, 198 b, 199 b; abbreviation of consonant-group after, 231; — nasal spirant or **anusvāra,** 70—3; — nasal semivowels, 71 c, 206, 213 c; — nasal vowels, 71, 72: — and see the different letters.
nasality, Hindu definition of, 36 a.
negative particles, 1122 c—e; neg. prefix, 1121 a—c.
neutral pron. of **a,** 21.
ninth class of verbs — see **nā**-class.
nominative case, uses of, 267, 268; peculiar construction with verbs, 268 a; with **iti,** 268 b; with vocative, 268 c; used adverbially, 1117; nom. use of infinitive, 987; nom. form as particle, 1117; in composition, 1250 f.
noun and adjective, distinction of, 322; inflection of nouns — see declension.
nu-class (fifth, **su**-class) of verbs, 603, 697—716: formation of stem, 697; inflection, 698—707; roots of the class, 708; irregularities, 710—3, 716.
number in declension, 264, 265; in conjugation, 536; number-forms in composition, 1250 g.
numerals, 475—89; simple cardinals, 475; their combinations for odd numbers, 476—81; inflection, 482—5; construction, 486; ordinals, 487, 488; other num. derivatives, 489, 1104—6, 1245; num. figures, 17; possessive compounds with num., 1300; num. or **dvigu** compounds, 1312.

omission, sign indicating, 16.
onomatopoetic words, 1091, 1135 b.
optative mode, 533, 564—8; its formation, 564, 565; scheme of endings combined with mode-sign, 566; precative, 567, 921—5; scheme of prec. endings, 568; uses of opt., 573—82; with **mā** prohibitive, 579 b; optative use of augmentless preterit forms, 587.
order of subjects in the grammar, 107; as best taken up by a student, 108, 112; of subjects in euph. combination, 124.
ordinal numeral adjectives, 487, 488.

pada-endings in declension, 111 a.
palatal series of mutes (**c, ch, j, jh, ñ**), pronunciation etc., 33, 42—4; derived from original gutturals, 42; reversion to guttural form, 43, 214 ff.; euphonic combinations, 118, 119, 214—20; treatment as finals, 142; assimilation of dentals to, 196—203; pal. character of **i, ī,** 20; of **y,** 51, 56; of **ç,** 63, 64; palatal for guttural in reduplication, 590 b: — and see the different letters.
participial compounds, 1247 g, 1309.
participles, 534, 537, 583, 584, 1172—7; of present-systems, 619 etc. etc.; of perfect, 802—7; of aorist, 840, 852, 872, 897, 909; of future, 939; passive part., 952—8, 1176, 1177; active, in **tavant, navant,** 959, 960; future passive, 961—6; of secondary conjugations, 1012, 1013, 1019, 1037, 1043 e, f, 1051, 1068; part. in possessive composition, 1299; — inflection of part. in **ant,** 443—9; in **vāṅs,** 458—62; — part.-phrases, periphrastic, 1074, 1075; — relation of part. and adjective, 967.
particles, 98 a; prolongation of final vowel of, 248 a; part. giving accent to verb, 595 c, e, 598 a.
passive conjugation, 531, 540, 998; present-system (**yá**-class), 606, 768—74; aorist 3d sing., 842—5, 1048; periphrastic perfect, 1072; participle in **ta** or **na,** 952—8, 1051 b, 1176, 1177; future participles, 961—6 (and see gerundives); pass. use of infinitive, 988; pass. from intransitives, 999 a; pass. of secondary conjugations, 1025, 1039, 1052 a; pass. constructions, 282 a, 999.
past use of present tense, 777, 778.
perfect tense, 532; scheme of its

endings, 553 c; uses, 821—3; — perf.-system, 535, 780—823: formation of stem, 781—94; reduplication, 782—91; strong and weak stem-forms, 792—4; endings and their combination with stem, 795—9; union-vowel **i**, 796—8; inflection, 800; irregularities, 801; participle, 802—7; its inflection, 458—62; modes, 808—16; pluperfect, 817—20; — periphrastic perf., 1070—73.

perfect time, expressed by so-called aorist, 532 a, 825, 928; by perfect, 822, 823; by participial phrases, 1075 d.

periphrastic conjugation, 540 a, 1069—75; periph. future, 532, 931, 942—7; its uses, 949; perfect, 1070—3, 1018, 1034, 1045; aorist and precative, 1073 b; present, 1073 c; periph. participial phrases, 1074, 1075.

person in verbal inflection, 536.

personal endings — see endings of conjugation.

personal pronouns, 491—4; nouns used as such, 514.

phrases, derivatives from, 1202 b; compounds from, 1314 b.

place, particles of, 1099, 1100, 1122 i.

pluperfect tense, 532, 817—20; plup. time, no designation of, 532 a; save by participial phrases, 1075 d.

position, length of syllable by, 79.

possessive adjectives, 1206 a, 1229 b, 1230—35; pronominal, 516.

possessive compounds, 324, 1247 g, 1293—1308; poss. dependents, 1296; poss. descriptives, 1297 ff.: with ordinary adjective as prior member, 1298; with participle, 1299; with numeral, 1300; with appositive noun, 1301—3; with adverb, 1304—6; added suffixes, 1212 c, 1307; pregnant use, 1308.

precative optative, 533 b; its formation, 567; scheme of endings, 568; prec. in later language, 921—5; use, 573 c.

prepositions, 1123—30; words used as such, 1123—5; cases construed with them, 1126—30; gerunds used as, 994 g; — prep. in composition with roots — see verbal prefixes.

prepositional compounds, 1247 g, 1310; with added suffix, 1212 m.

present tense, 532; its uses, 777, 778; — pres.-system, 535, 599—779: prominence as part of verb-system, 600; varieties of form and their classification, 601—9; various from same root, 609; conjugations and conjugation-classes, 602—10; first or non-**a**-conjugation: I. root-class, 611—41; II. reduplicating class, 642—82; III. nasal class, 683—96; IV. **nu-** and **u**-class, 697—716; V. **nā**-class, 717—32; second or **a**-conjugation, 733: VI. **a**-class, 734—50; VII. accented **á**-class, 751—8; VIII. **ya**-class, 759—67; IX. **yá**-class, or passive conjugation, 768—74; so-called **cur-** or tenth class, 775; uses of tenses, 776—9; of modes, 572—81; — pres. stems, derivatives from, 1140 c.

present use of perfect, 821 c, 823; of aorist, 930.

presumption, or conjecture, future of, 948.

primary and secondary personal endings, 542 ff.; confusion of them in use, 636 d, 933 a, 938; normal schemes, 553.

primary derivation, 1138—1201: relation to secondary, 1139; from what made, 1140, 1141; union-vowels, 1142; form of root, 1143; accent, 1144; meaning, 1145, 1146; prim. suffixes and the derivatives made with them, 1148—1201.

prohibitive expression, 574, 579, 580.

pronominal roots, 490; their character, in inflection and derivation, 1137 b, 1138; adverbs from them, 1097 ff.

pronouns, 490—521: personal, 491—4; demonstrative, 495—503; interrogative, 504—7; relative, 508—12; emphatic, indefinite, 513; nouns used pronominally, 514; pron. derivative adjectives, 515—21; adjectives declined pronominally, 522—6.

pronunciation — see system of sounds.

protracted (**pluta**) quantity, 78; protr. final vowel uncombinable, 138 e.

punctuation, signs of, in **devanāgarī**, 16 d.

quantity of consonants and vowels, 76—8; of syllables, 79.

r-endings of 3d pl., 550d.
radical stems — see root-stems.
reduplicated (or causative) aorist, 824, 856—73, 1046, 1047; formation of stem, 857—63; inflection, 864—7; use in primary conjugation, 868; in causative, 1046, 1047; modes, 869—71.
reduplicating class (third, hu-class) of verbs, 603, 642—82; reduplication and accent, 642—6; inflection, 647—57; roots of the class, 659; irregularities, 658, 660—82.
reduplication, occurrence of, 259; general rules for forming, 588—90; present red., 643, 660 ff.; perfect, 782—91; aorist, 857—63; intensive, 1002; desiderative, 1029; in derivation, 1143 e; anomalous, 1087 f.
relationship, nouns of, in ṛ, 369 ff., 1182 f.
relative clauses, peculiarities of, 512; modes used in, 581 a; accent of verb in, 595.
relative compounds, improper name for possessive, 1293 d.
relative pronoun, 508—12.
repeated words, 1260.
resolution, in Veda, of semivowels into vowels, and of vowels into two syllables, 55 a, 58 a, 84 c, 113 b, 125 c, 129 e, 309 f, 353 a, 470 b, 566 c, 761 g, 771 g.
reversion, so-called, of palatal mutes and sibilant, and of h, to guttural form, 43, 64, 66, 119, 142, 145, 147, 214 ff., 681, 787, 1028 f, 1176 a.
roots, 98—100; roots of the Skt. language, 102—5; roots and root-forms acc. to the native grammarians, 103, 104.
root-aorist, 824, 829—45: in later language, 829; in older, 830 ff.; modes, 835—9; participles, 840; passive aor. 3d sing., 842—5.
root-class (second, ad-class) of verbs, 603, 611—41; inflection, 612—23; roots of the class, 625; irregularities, 624, 626—41.
root-stems, their occurrence and use, 323, 383, 1137, 1147; as infinitives, 970 a, 971; in dependent composition, 1269; in descriptive, 1286; inflection of such stems in ā, ī, ū, 349—361; in consonants, 383—410; sometimes govern accus., 271 d; neut. pl. forms, 379 b.
rudh-class of verbs — see nasal class.

s-aorist, 824, 878—97: formation of stem, 878, 879; endings and combination with stem, 880, 881; question of loss of s in certain forms, 834, 881; inflection, 882; irregularities, 884—91; absence of ī in 2d and 3d sing. in older language, 888—90; modes, 892—6; participles, 897; — s-aor. stem in derivation, 1140 c.
s-future, 931—9: formation of stem, 932, 936; use of union-vowel i, 934, 935; occurrence, 937; modes, 938; participles, 939; its preterit, the conditional, 940, 941; uses, 948.
sa-aorist, 824, 916—20: roots allowed later to make it, 916; occurrence in older language, 919, 920; inflection, 917, 918.
second class of verbs — see root-class.
second or a-conjugation of verbs, its characteristics, 605, 733.
secondary adjective compounds, 1247 g, 1292—1310.
secondary conjugations, 540, 996—1068: passive, 998, 999; intensive, 1000—1025; desiderative 1026—40; causative, 1041—52; denominative, 1053—68; tertiary, or derivative from secondary, 1025, 1039, 1052.
secondary derivation, 1138, 1139, 1202—45; relation to primary, 1139; union-vowels, 1142; forms of stem, 1203, 1204; accent, 1205; meaning, 1206; sec. suffixes and the derivatives made with them, 1207—45; external combination in sec. derivation, 111 c, d, 1203 e.
secondary personal endings, 542 ff.; normal scheme, 553 b.
semivowels (y, r, l, v), pronunciation etc., 51—8; nasal semiv., 71 c, f, 206, 213 d; semiv. assimilation, 117 d—f: — and see the different letters.
sentence, rules of euphonic combination in, 101; their probable artificiality, 101 a.
series or classes of mutes, 32 ff.

seventh class of verbs — see nasal class.
sh-sounds (ṣ and ç), 61, 63.
short and long quantity, 76—9.
sibilants (ç, ṣ, s), pronunciation etc., 60—4: — and see the different letters.
sibilant or sigmatic aorist, 824, 874—920: formation and classification, 874—7; 4. **s**-aorist, 878—97; 5. **iṣ**-aorist, 898—910; 6. **siṣ**-aorist, 911—5; 7. **sa**-aorist, 916—20; its stem in derivation, 1140 c.
simple aorist, 824, 828—55: 1. root-aorist, 829—41; passive aor. 3d sing., 842—5; 2. **a**-aorist, 846—55.
siṣ-aorist, 824, 911—5: formation of stem, and inflection, 911; forms in older language, 912, 913; modes, 914; middle forms, 915.
sixth class of verbs — see **á**-class.
sonant and surd sounds, 34, 35; Hindu definition of their difference, 34 b; mutes, 34, 35; aspirates, 37, 38; question as to character of **h**, 65 a; of final mute, 141 b; euphonic assimilation of the two classes, 117, 156—78.
special and general tenses, 599 a.
spirants, 59 ff.: sibilants, 59—64; aspiration, 65; other breathings, 67—9.
stems, inflectible, 98—100, 106; their derivation — see derivation.
strengthening and weakening processes, 234—60.
strong and weak, or strong, middle, and weakest, forms of stems in declension, 311; of roots and stems in general, 104—6; confusions of strong and weak forms in decl., 462 c; in conj., 556 a; strong forms in 2d sing., 723; in 2d du., 704, 831 a, 839, 1007 b; in 3d du., 793 h, 839; in 1st pl., 621 b, 658, 676 a, 793 h, 831 a, 832; in 2d pl., 618, 621 b, 654, 658, 669, 690, 704, 707, 723, 831 a, 839; in 3d pl., 793 h, 831 a.
su-class of verbs — see **nu**-class.
subjunctive mode, 533; formation and endings, 557—62; its first persons used later as imperative, 533, 574, 578; subj. use of augmentless preterit forms, 563, 587; uses of subj. mode, 574—82.
suffixes, 98—100; forming adverbs, 1097—1109; do. declinable stems — see derivation.
superlative — see comparison.
surd and sonant sounds — see sonant.
syllables, quantity of, 79; distinguished as heavy and light, 79.
system of sounds, 19—75: vowels and diphthongs, 19—30; consonants, 31 ff.; mutes, 32—50; semivowels, 51—8; sibilants, 59—64; aspiration, 65, 66; **visarga** and other breathings, 68, 69; **anusvāra**, 70—3; unwritten sounds defined by Hindu grammarians, 74, 230; scheme of spoken alphabet, with notice of comparative frequency of the sounds, 75; quantity, 76—9; accent and its designation, 80—97.

tan-class of verbs — see **u**-class.
tatpuruṣa-compounds — see determinatives.
tense in verbal inflection, 532; tense-systems, 535; present-system, 599—779; perfect-system, 780—823; aorist-systems, 824—930; future-systems, 931—950.
tenth class of verbs — see causative conjugation, and **cur**-class.
tertiary, or derivative from secondary, conjugations, 1025, 1039, 1052, 1068 a.
third class of verbs — see reduplicating class.
time, particles of, 1103, 1122 j.
transliteration, general method of, 5; of sign of elision, 135 b; of combined final and initial vowels, 126 a; of **anusvāra**, 73 c; of accent, 83 a, 89.
tud-class of verbs — see **á**-class.

u-class (eighth, **tan**-class) of verbs, 603, 697—716; formation of stem, 697; inflection, 698—707; roots of the class, 709; irregular root **kṛ** or **kar**, 714, 715; other irregularities, 716.
uncombinable (**pragṛhya**) final vowels, 138.
uninflected words — see indeclinables.
union-vowels, 254, 555 b, c; **i** in present inflection, 630, 631, 640; in perfect, 796—8, 803; in aorist,

876b, 877; in s-future, 934, 935; in periphrastic future, 943; in desiderative, 1031; in passive participle, 956; in infinitive and gerund, 968, 991; in derivation, 1142; — ī in present inflection, 631—4; in 2d and 3d sing., 555b; in intensive, 1004 ff.; ī for i, 900b; āi for ī, 555c.

upadhmānīya-spirant, 69, 170d.

variable or changeable ṛ of roots, 242; treatment of, 245b; in passive, 770c; in s-aor., 885; in iṣ-aor., 900b; in prec., 922a; in s-fut., 935a; in pple, 955d, 957b; in infin., 968d; in **tvā**-gerund, 991b; in **ya**-gerund, 992a; in desid., 1028b.

variation of stem-form in declension, 311, 312; in ṛ-stems, 370b; in consonantal stems, 379, 385—8, 421, 443, 444, 458, 463; — in conjugation, 556; in present-stem, 604; in perfect, 792—4; in aorist, 831 ff., 879, 899; in intensive, 1004; in primary derivation, 1143; in secondary, 1203, 1204; in composition, 1249b, c.

verb — see conjugation.

verb-forms, accentuation of, in the sentence, 92b, 591—8; prolongation of final **a** or **i** of, 248c, d; comparison of, 473c, 474; comb. with insep. prefixes, 1121b, g, i.

verbal prefixes, 1076, 1077; kindred words, 1078, 1079, 1120; composition with roots, 1076—87, 137; euph. effect on root, 185, 192, 1086; accent, 1082—5; their more independent use, 1084, 1118; prepositional uses, 1125; forms of comparison, 473b, 1119; declinable stems from roots compounded with them, 1141, 1282; use in descriptive composition, 1281, 1289; in possessive, 1305; in prepositional, 1310.

visarga (or **visarjanīya**), 67—9; quantitative value, 79; occurrence, 144, 145, 170—2; alphabetic order, 7a, 172a: — and see **ḥ**.

vocative case, form of, 266a, 307k; Vedic, in **as**, 425g, 454b, 462a, 465a; accent (along with qualifying word), 92a, 314; verb accented after, 594a.

voice in verbal inflection, 528—31.

vowels, how written in **devanāgarī** with consonants, 10; sign of absence of, 11; their pronunciation etc., 19—29: **a**-, **i**-, **u**-vowels, 19—22; **ṛ**-, **ḷ**-vowels, 23—6; diphthongs, 27—9; quantity, 77, 78; accent, 80 ff.; nasal vowels, 71; rules of vowel-combination, 125—38; resulting accent, 128, 130, 135a; exceptional cases, 136—8.

vṛddhi-strengthening, character and occurrence of, 27, 235—43, and *passim;* in primary derivation, 1143a; in secondary, 1204.

w-sound, belonging to **v**, 57.

weak, or weakest, form of stem in declension, 311.

weakening and strengthening processes, 234—60.

writing in India, 2a; mode of, in Skt. manuscripts, 9a, b; its modifications in western practice, 9c—e.

ya-class (fourth, **div**-class) of verbs, 606, 759—67: formation of stem, 759; inflection, 760; roots of the class and their classification, 761, 762; irregularities, 763—7.

yá-class of verbs, or passive present-system, 606, 768—74; formation of stem, 768—70; inflection, 771; irregularities, 772—4; **yá**-formation from intensive stem, 1016 1017.